The Russian's World

Life and Language

Cover Art: The Sirin

The image of the Sirin **Сирин**, part woman, part bird, is first recorded in 12th-century Russia; a similar figure was probably among the nature gods of earliest Russia. The legend of the Sirin spread from India through the Caspian and Black Seas as the story of a bird-girl who hypnotized sailors with her Siren's song. The untended boats crashed, and the sailors became her prey. On land, men followed her until they dropped, and then they too were hers.

Vladimir Nabokov used the pen name *Sirin*.

THE RUSSIAN'S WORLD

LIFE AND LANGUAGE

3RD, CORRECTED EDITION

GENEVRA GERHART

Bloomington, Indiana, 2001

SLAVICA

To Russians I have known

ISBN: 0-89357-293-4

PUBLISHER	TED BUCHHOLZ
SENIOR ACQUISITIONS EDITOR	JIM HARMON
PROJECT EDITOR	DEANNA M. JOHNSON
ASSOCIATE PROJECT EDITOR	KRYSTYN FREIDLIN
PRODUCTION MANAGER	CYNTHIA YOUNG
ART DIRECTOR	SCOTT BAKER

Slavica Publishers
Indiana University
2611 E. 10th St.
Bloomington, IN 47408-2603
USA

[Tel.] 1-812-856-4186
[Toll-free] 1-877-SLAVICA
[Fax] 1-812-856-4187
[Email] slavica@indiana.edu
[www] http://www.slavica.com/

PREFACE
Предисло́вие

This book is an attempt at the impossible: to describe for non-Russians what Russian common knowledge might be. (The angel marches in where the fools fear to tread.) It is the Russian obvious—that is, *ob+via*, in the road, in the way: what you might trip over if you ignore it or don't see it. It is the information one Russian assumes another has when they are talking together. It is the background against which words take on meaning. If one knew all of common knowledge, then all humor would be comprehensible. The book was written because the Russian equivalent for Thomas, **Фома́**, might share origin in language but certainly doesn't share place in society. It was written because in translation the obvious often isn't; and sometimes it's hard to answer when you don't know what your friend has in mind.

The book was written for the traveler who might be happier or even healthier knowing what to expect; it was written for those in business who want to avoid pratfalls as much as they want to see possibilities; and it was written for those studying the language who are blessed with curiosity and (temporarily of course) tired of verb forms. The assumption is not that the readers know Russian, but that they do want to know about Russians and their language. (There are also not a few hints on what to expect for Russians new to America.)

This second edition is much more than a revision: six chapters are totally new and two more have large additions; of course, all of the first edition has been reviewed and brought up to date.

Most Russians will agree with most of what is written here. None will agree with everything— the borders of common knowledge are not easily drawn. Nor is this all there is. For example, the investigation of Russian sayings revealed a treasure too large to carry back to the ship: there are so many of them so regularly used that self-respecting Russian majors should really own a text that explains (*not* just lists) the most common 500 or so.

There are many words arranged in lists because that is the way I believe people think about them: knives are allied with forks and spoons, names with other names, pansies with petunias, all to form a pattern that gives the individual a background of relationships. Heaven knows the lists are not for memorizing (though with time you will find familiarity comforting). Most of the book is a description of the Russian's world from the Russian point of view. The chapter on conduct is also partly from my point of view: you perhaps will find the generalizations regrettable, while I find them unavoidable.

Most passages in Russian have been translated and will be found either in the course of the text or at the end of the chapter. Passages not translated are usually poetry that have become part of the language; many Russians know them by heart. (That remark is, indeed, a hint.)

Accent marks appear as a great convenience to you and a great pain in the neck to me; some common words occasionally don't have them. If you don't see one on the word you are attempting to read, look in the previous few lines for the same word. When the stress falls on a capital letter, it is not marked.

Capitalizations are those used in the source.

Headings in Russian are not always translations of the English, though they are meant to be appropriate headings.

ACKNOWLEDGMENTS
second edition

Collecting, assembling, and correcting this amorphous mass would not have been accomplished without the moral support of Professor Charles Gribble of the Ohio State University and Lee Shenkman of Harcourt Brace to both of whom I am very grateful. Some people spent hours supplying huge chunks of information; they include: Irina Latysheva of Riga on *Food*, Ksenia Bednyakoff and Tatiana Bevan of Seattle on *Plants and animals*. Some gave particular help with particular chapters: Dr. Sergey Potapov of Moscow checked over *Medicine*; Professor Stephen Kerr and Alexander Sidorkin at the University of Washington helped with *Education*, as did Julia Sergeyeva, Tatiana Oksenkrug and Nina Gaysinskaya of Moscow; Hans Sauter, Seattle, checked over plant names; and Irene Barinoff of Seattle was particularly helpful on *The Church*. Varya Grace Fish of Seattle and Sharon K. Deeny of St. Petersburg combed out *Conduct*, and Marina Turkevich Naumann plowed through thickets in *Holidays and the Church*; Nadezhda Sviridova of Moscow reviewed the entire first edition. Anatoli Samochernov and Sergey Drozdov were particularly helpful in supplying information for new chapters and corrections for old ones. An entire contingent of professors of English in Nizhniy Novgorod supplied information for and reviewed late versions of the manuscript: I especially want to thank Margarita S. Krasilnikova, who was ably abetted by Irina Labutova, Lyudmila Levina, Gennadiy V. Sosnin, Tatiana A. Aleshina, and Olga Yeremina. I have mercilessly used friends who were kind enough to answer a broad variety of questions: they include Lev Ostroumov, Professor Zaretkhan Saraliyeva, and Drs. Tatiana and Boris Tolchenov, all of Nizhniy Novgorod; Nataliya and Vladimir Bagramyants in Moscow; Lyudmila Leontieva in St. Petersburg; and Pavla Yakubovskaya and Nataliya and Gennadiy Tartakovskiy of Seattle. Reviewers: Sarah P. Burke, Trinity University; Charles McDowell, the University of Texas at Arlington; James D. Wells, Oklahoma State University; Laszlo Dienes, the University of Massachusetts; Rima Greenhill, Stanford University. Professor Yevgeniy Vereshchagin of the Russian Language Institute of the Russian Academy of Sciences, graciously as always, answered frantic last-minute questions. The book may appear in a timely manner because of the speed and patience of editor, Deanna Johnson, timely and accurate corrections by Tatiana Zolotareva, and Julia Tolmacheva's willingness to do a prodigious amount of typing, review, and indexing. She and Prof. James Snell of CUNY Brockport also made possible the use of a computer without which the first edition now seems outright impossible.

Errors and omissions may be ascribed to those people I have listed. Of course, it could be that I was looking out the window when someone brought up a point. And for reviewers, may I say: И на стару́ху быва́ет проруха, and На вся́кого мудреца́ дово́льно простоты́.*

Genevra Gerhart, Seattle, October 1994

*"Even people who are supposed to know, make mistakes."
*"Even wise men are dumb about some things."

TABLE OF CONTENTS

PREFACE   Предисло́вие   v

PART I AN INTRODUCTION TO EXPECTATIONS   1

1 CONDUCT   Поведе́ние   3

How the Russian is different   3
Physical conduct   Как себя вести́   8
Proprieties   Пра́вила прили́чия   11
Particular ceremonies   Торжества́/Семе́йные пра́здники   25
Translations   31

PART II THE RUSSIAN: ASPECTS OF THE INDIVIDUAL   33

2 THE HUMAN BEING   Челове́к   35

Anatomy   Анато́мия   36
Hair, eye, and skin color   Цвет воло́с, глаз и ко́жи   42
Aspects of the self   Ещё о себе́   43
Relatives   Ро́дственники   49
Translations   52

3 NAMES   Имена́, фами́лии   53

What's your name?   Как вас зову́т?   54
Forms names can take   Фо́рмы имён   54
A table of names   Табли́ца имён   55
Growing up with a name   Имя и во́зраст   62
Addressing the Russian   Обраще́ния по-ру́сски   62
Names before the Revolution   Имена́ до револю́ции   63
Names after the Revolution   Имена́ после револю́ции   65
Pronouncing names and patronymics   Произноше́ние имён и о́тчеств   66
Surnames and their nationalities   Фами́лии и национа́льность   66
Russian surnames   Ру́сские фами́лии   66
Names for pets   Кли́чки   68
Translations   70

4 Clothing   Одёжда   71

    Contemporary clothes   Совреме́нная оде́жда   72
    The Russian folk costume   Ру́сский наро́дный костю́м   81

Part III The Russian at Home   85

5 Housing   Жили́ще   87

    A self-contained apartment   Отде́льная кварти́ра   88
    The communal apartment   Коммуна́льная кварти́ра   96
    The peasant house   Крестья́нский дом   96
    Contemporary rural housing   Совреме́нное се́льское жили́ще   105
    Translations   107

6 Food   Ру́сская пи́ща   109

    Raw materials   Проду́кты   110
    Preserving food   Загото́вка проду́ктов   129
    Cooking   Приготовле́ние пи́щи   130
    Meals ———   131
    Russian dishes   Блю́да ру́сской ку́хни   132
    In between meals, and after them   Ра́зные сла́дости   140
    Drink   Напи́тки   141
    Where can we eat?   Где мо́жно пое́сть?   144
    Translations   145

7 Medicine   Медици́на   147

    Personnel   Ка́дры   148
    Institutions   Учрежде́ния   149
    The Social Security Ministry   Минсобес   153
    Pregnancy   Бере́менность   154
    Are you sick? What's the matter?   Ты больна́? Что с тобо́й?   155
    Treatments   Лече́бные сре́дства   156
    Dentistry   Стоматоло́гия   159
    Translations   159

8 Work and money   Рабо́та и де́ньги   161

    Choices   Вы́бор рабо́ты   162
    Labor unions   Профсою́зы   164
    Time for work   Рабо́чее вре́мя   164

Tools   Инструме́нты   164
Money   Де́ньги   167
Translations   170

PART IV THE RUSSIAN IN THE COMMUNITY   171

9 SHOPPING   По магази́нам   173

How to get things   Как доста́ть ну́жную вещь   174
Manufactured goods   Про́мтова́ры   175
Food stores   Продово́льственные магази́ны   178
Services   Услу́ги   180
Translations   181

10 COMMUNICATIONS   Связь   183

Private communication   Сре́дства свя́зи   183
Mass communications   Сре́дства ма́ссовой информа́ции   193
Translations   197

11 TRANSPORTATION   Тра́нспорт   199

Public transportation   Обще́ственный тра́нспорт   201
Automobiles   Автомоби́ли   203
Trains   Поезда́   210
Ships   Суда́   211
Airplanes   Самолёты   212
Traditional transportation   Традицио́нный тра́нспорт   213
Translations   216

12 EDUCATION   Образова́ние   219

Levels in education   Ступе́ни образова́ния   221
Curriculum   Уче́бный план   228
Grades   Отме́тки   231
Administration   Администра́ция   233
In and out of school   Внутри́ и вне шко́лы   237
Different types of schools   Ра́зные типы школ   241
Translations   243

PART V IN THE RUSSIAN'S WORLD   245

13 SPEECH   Речь   247

Speech and society   Речь и общество   247
Some special concerns of Russian speech   Некоторые особенности русской речи   252
"Sudden" words and "semiwords"   Восклицания   257
Terms of rejection and endearment   Бранные и ласковые обращения   258
Expletives   Возгласы   260
Translations   261

14 NATURE   Природа   263

Climate   Климат   263
The forests and the trees   Леса и деревья   264
Fields   Поля   265
The plant world   Растительный мир   266
Index of plants   Указатель растений   273
Domesticated animals   Домашние животные   281
Animals in nature   Животные в природе   286
Translations   299

15 NUMBERS   Числа   303

Numbers and names for them   Числа и их названия   304
Reading and writing numbers   Чтение и написание чисел   306
Declining numbers in spoken Russian   Склонение числительных в разговорном языке   307
Arithmetic operations   Арифметические действия   308
Common geometric figures   Обыкновенные геометрические фигуры   313
Reading mathematical expressions   Чтение математических выражений   313
Measures   Меры   315

16 HOLIDAYS AND THE CHURCH   Праздники и Церковь   325

Contemporary holidays   Современные праздники   325
Traditional popular or folk holidays   Народные праздники   329
The Easter Season   Пасхальный сезон   333
Church holidays   Церковные праздники   335
The Church   Церковь   338
Translations   344

17 PLAY   Отдых   347

Free time   Свобóдное врéмя   347
Leisure time   Досýг   350
Official sports   Прúзнанные вúды спóрта   355
Children's play   Дéтские úгры   362
Traditional amusements   Традициóнные развлечéния   366
Translations   367

APPENDICES   369

SUGGESTIONS FOR THOSE IN BUSINESS   371
ABBREVIATIONS   373
THE TABLE OF RANKS   375
READING CHEMICAL FORMULAS   376
THE MORSE CODE   378
THE BRAILLE ALPHABET   378
AN INDEX OF COMMON RUSSIAN BIRDS   378
SOME REFERENCES FROM THE BEGINNING TO THE END OF RUSSIAN   382
MAPS   384

INDEX   391
УКАЗАТЕЛЬ   401

Что ни го́род, то но́ров, что ни дере́вня, то обы́чай.

Every city has its character; every village, its customs.

All the meaning is in the context.

> *Ilya Kabakov,*
> *Russian artist*

Послу́шайте, ребя́та,
Что вам расска́жет дед.
Земля́ наша бога́та,
Поря́дка в ней лишь нет.

Aleksey Tolstoy, 1868

Part I

An Introduction to Expectations

1

Conduct

Поведе́ние

HOW THE RUSSIAN IS DIFFERENT

The bulk of this chapter deals with some particular mechanisms of conduct—gestures, polite and impolite phrases, and ceremonies such as parties, weddings, and funerals. But first some note needs to be taken of the object of conduct. Not all societies have the same goals; not all good or bad behavior has the same end.

How Russians see themselves

In St. Petersburg I asked my thoughtful Russian friend to describe the Russian character. Barely hesitating, she said:

He's fairly long-suffering **терпели́вый** and slow to start, (Ilya Muromets **Илья́ Му́ромец** sat on the stove for thirty-three years before he set out; Bismark is supposed to have said of the Russians: They take a long time to saddle up, but they ride fast. **Ру́сские до́лго запряга́ют, да бы́стро е́дут.**) He is brave in battle **сме́лый во́ин**—willing to take huge chances. He is kind **челове́к до́брый**—capable of sharing his last bit of food, or bringing someone in from the cold. When he must, he is capable of hard work **трудолюби́вый** since things don't grow easily here. He loves his children **чадолюби́вый**, he saves the best for them, and continues to help them long after they're grown. He's not particularly neat **чистопло́тный**; now that the police don't fuss, people litter. Russians are kind, responsive **отзы́вчивые**, they love beauty.

How we see the Russians

Compared to people in the United States, the Russians are less selfconscious, though this trait is easier to describe than it is to document. They are unassuming and somehow feel less necessity to impose their person, or to impress, in order to enhance their "selves." Extravagant or loud behavior to this end is undesirable as well as unbecoming—except for famous people with whom such conduct is almost expected. **Ты вы́ступил, как на сце́не.** (You acted as if you were on stage.) Therefore, being self-confident, self-assured, self-reliant **самоуве́ренность, самонадёянность** are, in Russian, negative traits. She is too sure of herself = **Она́ уве́рена в себе́. Он самонадёянный** intimates that the man is so sure of himself or self-reliant that he is almost a snob. What's bad about these traits is that the occupation with or attention to one's self does not allow for sensitivity to, or care for, other people. And that's bad. (New Yorkers in particular and Americans in general should avoid talking loudly in public as a matter of course: drawing attention to oneself is considered bad manners.)

By culture (if not by nature) Russians are their brothers' keepers. Maintenance of public order and custom is the job of all. Comments are made not necessarily on behalf of oneself **от себя́** but on behalf of the group **о́бщество**. Miscreant children must contend not only with their parents but also with any other proximate humanity in their parents' absence. If you fall in the street, someone will help you up. If you have a run in your stocking, strangers, thinking it a kindness, will let you know. If you don't wear a hat when the weather is cold, older strangers might remark to you on your dangerous laxity.

Sadly, this trait is beginning to weaken, and some alienation is occurring, especially in the cities. With the new world order, fewer are willing to help out, and neighbors are becoming less neighborly.

The American knows that money is blood, but the Russian is only beginning to understand that. Before, these worries were smaller; everyone had a job, the job was secure, pensions bordered on the adequate, the doctor cost nothing, rent was just a few rubles, and bread was subsidized. So, why worry? Go ahead and spend two weeks' wages on a party. Learning how to budget money was unnecessary.

На́ тебе, Бо́же (убо́же), что нам не го́же.
Here, God (*or* poor one), take what we don't want.[1]

Incomes were very similar: egalitarian and low. The great American motivators, greed and avarice, were frowned upon; the use of piggy-banks represented the inculcation of bourgeois—that is, low—morals. But conditions are changing now, especially among the young. Older parents are often shocked by their children's acceptance of the new order. Suddenly, making money is more important than becoming educated, or, sometimes, money is needed to get the education. The dark corollary to money's new esteem is that the businessperson is often in deservedly low repute: **У нас ещё че́стного би́знеса ма́ло.** (We still have little honest business.) And when the Russian sees Jews and dark-skinned people **чёрные** from the Caucasus or Central Asia as those most able to put a profit together, both the causes of tolerance and capitalism sink further.

The Russian is brought up to be more dependent than are we. Thus, family bonds are stronger—people live closer together and derive mutual support from the closeness. Children are expected, at least outwardly, to do what they are told. (They are allowed their childhood.) Babysitting is not a

---

Вме́сте те́сно, а врозь ску́чно.
Crowded when together, but lonesome when apart.

---

1. A derisive description of those so cheap that they'll only give away something they can't use themselves.

source of teenage revenue and therefore neither a first step to psychological nor economic independence. Instead, grandma babysits the small ones, and the offer of money for the service would be insulting. Older children wait until they are out of school or college to get a job, and even then they often live at home until they marry. Eventually, grandma herself will be cared for when that is necessary. (Russians in America are shocked at our readiness to make other arrangements.) Just as dependence is expected in family life, independence has been discouraged: **Не́сколько десятиле́тий наро́д держа́ли за скот безду́мный. Я по́мню, как меня, совсем ещё юнца́, впервы́е обраща́ли в животи́ну. Моё ро́бкое оправда́ние «я думал. . .» одёрнули—«за тебя нача́льство думает, живи́ как все».**[a]

Friends and the friendly manner that expresses friendship are taken more seriously than in the United States. Many people maintain friendships that go back to early school days. **Ста́рый друг лу́чше но́вых двух.** (One old friend is better than two new ones.) Friends freely extend compliments and offer often unsolicited advice. Friends matter more, not only fulfilling a psychological need, but often a physical need as well: when times are hard, people without the safety net of friends can be in dire straits. You will many times come across a very old Russian saying, **Не име́й сто рубле́й, а име́й сто друзе́й.** "Don't have 100 rubles, have 100 friends." Friends are people you can call in the middle of the night who will either come over or invite you to come to them. Russians are friends in need if they are friends at all. Difficulties arise because of differences in expectations: you are nice to a Russian; he perceives your action as an invitation to friendship; if you pass him in the hall the next day and only nod in greeting, he cannot understand what he sees as your sudden coolness.

Друзья́ познаю́тся в беде́.
Friends make themselves known when there's real trouble. (A friend in need is a friend indeed.)

This closeness of family and friends creates two personas for each Russian: the public one with a hard exterior shell that knows you must shove or you won't get any, and the rich, warm, private one that goes to extraordinary lengths for one of her own. Listen as your sweet friend barks on the telephone to an outsider.

Order might be a governmental convenience, but it is not a personal virtue. The occasional straight line that appears in Russian buildings is often of non-Russian origin. Table settings will have the necessary tools to eat with, but their arrangement often varies. (Of course, what really matters is the company at the table.) Gardens will have one cluster of flowers here and others there, in no particular order, with the chickens meandering through the lot. The Russian countryside is often very beautiful, but it is not neat.[2] (The compulsive American occasionally feels that *everything* needs straightening, repair, cleaning, or a coat of paint.) The American notion of punctuality is quite strict when the occasion is social. The Russian arrives on time for a job interview, but friends can be late and they expect you to understand that being late does not mean being rude.

---

2. Margaret Wettlin in *Fifty Russian Winters* aptly reports that in Russia, efficiency is not a virtue; appointments are guidelines, not anchors; and Russians are unpragmatic and noncompetitive.

> **Гром не гря́нет, мужи́к не перекре́стится.**
> The peasant doesn't cross himself until the thunder claps. (He doesn't take care of things ahead of time.)

One has the impression that Russian women are stronger than men. A friend in St. Petersburg suggests that this, too, is Stalin's fault. He didn't pay men enough to keep women from having to work outside the house, nor did he set up institutions to make their domestic obligations easier. She does all the housework, cooking, meal planning, shopping, standing in line. She is the minister of finances for the family, and she pays the bills, for which she also stands in line. She is responsible for bringing up the children, dealing with poor report cards, and so on. She is offended by a hole in a sock. Through it all she goes to considerable lengths to maintain her femininity, about which she has fewer doubts than her counterpart in the United States. He can afford to be more capricious, more tender, while she takes on the qualities of a warrior. Listen to the resentment in a woman's lament: **Я и ло́шадь, я и бык, я и ба́ба, и мужи́к!** (I'm the horse, I'm the ox, I'm the woman, and the man!) Perhaps (my friend continues) the new order will make it possible for men to be more responsible and for more women to spend time with their children. Now, men are capable of reading a book and waiting for dinner. (I should add that I had come to my conclusion about Russian women and strength long before I met Russians of the Soviet persuasion.)

Women do not fare well as part of language. **Ба́ба с во́зу—кобы́ле ле́гче.** (It would be easier for the mare if the woman got off the cart.) **У бабы во́лос до́лог, да ум ко́роток.** (The woman's got long hair and a short mind.) **Ба́бушка на́двое сказа́ла.** ("Grandma told it two ways," referring to anything unclear or open to wide interpretation.)

Russians are fatalists. They seem to accept, much more readily than do we, that chance and circumstance are immutable and that they personally can do little to ameliorate conditions or influence events. This attitude does not encourage any kind of activism. (Also see the section on superstition.)

> **Чему́ быть, того́ не минова́ть.**
> What will be, will be.

Feelings are allowed a greater range: tears rise more easily (especially among women); romance is even more attractive; spontaneity is not undesirable; depression happens.

Anti-Semitism is sometimes denied, often admitted, but usually there. It comes out sometimes quite unexpectedly, but it comes out. Judaism may be a religion, but Jewishness is treated and thought of as a nationality, and an unsavory one at that. "Why was he rejected?" **По пя́тому пу́нкту.** Because of item five (the nationality item in a standard questionnaire). There are two words for *Jew*: the decent word has Hebrew as its base **евре́й, евре́йка,** and the indecent word shares origins with *yid* **жид, жидо́вка. Есть евре́и, есть и жиды́.** Most recent Russian-Jewish émigrés to the United States are actually irreligious but are Jewish in the Russian sense and therefore subject to the fairly common anti-Semitic prejudice—a major reason for emigrating. (Try not to overconclude: it is also true that it was *only* the Jew who could emigrate in the first place, therefore many people had to acquire Judaism in order to leave. Then again, many left less from prejudice than from the desire for a better life. The picture of Truth depends on the artist.) At root is distrust: Jews are seen as willing to do anything to get what they want; the Jew is not Russian and therefore any attachment to the land, or allegiance to it, does not obtain (during World War II the Jews had the reputation for being unwilling to fight); the

Jew is seen as practical while the Russian is not; many Russians give the Jews blame for both the Revolution and communism. The list goes on, and on, and on. Take note: when in Russia or when talking to Russians, a Russian and a Jew are usually two different people. And consider the plight of the émigré to Israel: in Russia a Jew, in Israel a Russian.

While we're on the subject, it might be well to warn blacks **не́гры** that they will experience racism in the largest cities. The Soviets imported and supported African students in large numbers, but the populace complained that some males were from privileged families and felt no limitations on their conduct. Today one sees comparatively few. The discrimination will be much less subtle than that of the Jews, rather like the South before the civil rights movement. Wandering the streets alone at night is not recommended. Caucasians (Georgians, Azeri, Armenians) and central Asians trading in the streets of northern towns are frequently referred to as *blacks* **чёрные, чернота́, черномазые**; the descriptions are unfriendly and insulting, caused by differing trading practices. Orientals are less subject to hostility: racial or ethnic purity has not been a major theme in Russian life, and a very large percentage of Russians are of mixed parentage. Pushkin's grandfather was an Ethiopian who would have had to use the fountain for "coloreds" in America.

Rules, regulations, taxes, and graders are frequently something to be got around rather than taken seriously; stealing from the office or work is almost expected, and cheating the powers that be is not really cheating. See the additional commentary on this point on p. 32.

How Russians see us

Russians who have actually known or dealt with Americans (as teachers, students, guides, businesspeople) find them to be naive (peaceniks and fundamentalists in particular) and incredibly ill-informed if not outright unschooled.[3] The following question, itself interesting, was posed by a correspondent of *Moscow News* and answered by Vladimir Posner. **Моско́вские но́вости, № 34, 22.8.1993.**

Q. You have almost become our major expert on America. What do you have to say about the popular point of view that Americans are, of course, good guys, but they're primitive?

A. The American is less educated than the former Soviet citizen. There [in America], for example, it has never been prestigious to have a large library. They have a different concept of what compliments a person. A house, a car, money. (By the way, we [Russians] are taking giant steps in that direction.) But not knowledge. America is anti-intellectual. In this sense it is true that the average American has a narrower world view than does the average Russian. But they are not more stupid, I assure you. It's just that their intellect and energy are directed elsewhere. I could say that in America I don't have the opportunity to converse at the same level that I do here [in Russia].

The Russian finds the American cold and calculating in personal affairs (by considering a schedule an obligation, focusing on "the bottom line," reducing relationships to evaluating whether they are "worth my while"). The Russian counts personal relationships as being more important.

The Russians are used to finagling to get what they want and are often nonplussed by American directness. Russian women are surprised when male companions ignore such courtesies as holding doors open.

Do not try to show how friendly you are by flashing a toothy grin in all directions. They are sickened by what they see as insincerity.

---

3. **Им легко́ ве́шать лапшу́ на́ уши.** It's easy to hang noodles on their ears. **Их легко́ обвести́ вокру́г па́льца.** It's easy to wind them around your finger.

PHYSICAL CONDUCT
Как себя вести

Some of the most difficult things to relearn are those we perceive as automatic or natural when in fact they are another aspect of our language; we are not thinking, but we are interpreting. Not a few examples of this problem have to do with posture, gestures, and social distance.

Russian talking range is closer than in the United States. A greater proximity than ours during conversation is not necessarily an invasion of personal territory, an aggression, or a sexual invitation (though it can represent friendliness). Try to avoid automatically backing away when you feel that your personal distance has been invaded. People who shove at the store merely want to see what's for sale; you can shove back if you want to see. Closeness often means comfort and friendliness, however; females in particular often walk down the street arm in arm. "Hello" and "Goodbye" kisses are fairly common among Russian females and are often on the lips. (You can be insulting if you automatically turn your head away.) Two women will sit right alongside one another (legs touching) to talk. But this closeness does not

Together can be comforting

Close is OK

imply more than friendliness. Also, you will often see snapshots of males with their arms around each other. They may be happy, but they are probably not gay. (Homosexuality **гомосексуа́льность** is much less common and much less acceptable there than it is here. Some sections of the population do not even seem to know of the phenomenon—an ignorance that permits members of the same sex, both males and females, to hold hands.)

We have accepted the smile as a part of speech, but the Russian has not. We use a smile very often merely as part of a greeting while the Russian uses it to express real pleasure. Russians new to the United States are often sickened by this treacle, and Americans don't understand why the Russians are so glum.

Just as closeness has its customs, Russian custom has phrases and ceremonies that specifically deal with long-term separation. (The

В музе́е (Henri-Cartier Bresson/Magnum Photos)

closest we come is a French borrowing, *Bon Voyage*, that carries overtones of the super-rich on a super-liner with none of the poignancy of significant separation.) Instead of "Goodbye!" **До свида́ния!** you say something closer to "Farewell!" **Проща́й!**, which at its root asks for forgiveness. Have a good trip or *Bon voyage* = **Счастли́вого пути́!** and has an answer: "Be happy in staying (behind)" **Счастли́во остава́ться!** Perhaps most touching, however, is that before any long trip, when the baggage is all packed and everyone is about to go out the door, someone will say "Let's sit down" **Дава́й, ся́дем** or **Прися́дем на доро́жку.** Everyone sits down for maybe a minute and is silent. In the old days, silent prayers were said: that the trip be safe, and that the return home be happy and whole.

Russian stance or posture is similar to ours. Sitting posture sometimes gives a lumpish impression at the dinner table—almost hunched over the food. Any stiff posture is non-Russian, excepting military or other ceremonial requirements. Even in literature, straight-laced is un-Russian:

Мно́гих кри́тиков смуща́ло, что Замя́тин—худо́жник, чу́ждый вся́кой расточи́тельности, ску́по отме́ривавший свои́ лири́ческие замеча́ния,—как-то не по-ру́сски сде́ржан, подо́бран, застёгнут на все пу́говицы.

Марк Сло́ним, Писа́тель и его тво́рчество [b]

Correct position is more important than is correct posture. For example, never put your feet up on furniture not explicitly designed for them, just as you should not sit on a table or on the floor. Joining your hands at the back of your head is too relaxed (except when alone or at home). You should also keep your hands away from your face. Women should avoid sitting cross-legged in public: the position is seen as vaguely suggestive at worst and sloppy at best. For the same reason, men should avoid sitting with an ankle supported by the opposite knee. Any position that even suggests aiming one's rump at someone else is offensive: face the people in the theater row as you enter or exit; if you must bend over to serve someone who is seated, make sure your bottom is not aiming in someone else's direction, or excuse yourself if it is. While eating, keep both hands in view and out of your lap (as is the custom in many European countries).

Generally, almost any physical abnormality or disability is more of a calamity, and efforts will be made to keep it hidden. Even such a thing as left-handedness **он/она левша** will be trained to right-handedness. Prosthetic devices **протéзы** and wheelchairs **колáски** might exist, but ramps **пáндусы** and manageable doors seldom do.

Gestures
Жéсты

Russians do not seem to "talk with their hands" as we think some Europeans do, but they do seem regularly to use a wider variety of gestures than Americans.

The most common gesture, **махнýть рукóй**, is a quick downward flick of the lower arm, or sometimes just the wrist. It indicates disapproval, rejection, or hopelessness; the expression for this gesture has entered the language to mean to give up on, to reject.

The traditional enumerating gesture starts with the left palm up, right index finger bending the fingers of the left hand toward the palm; it begins with the little finger so that the counted hand finishes as a fist.

To express relief (Whew!), say **Пронеслó!** (but Russians do not wipe their forehead as an accompanying gesture).

To "thumb a ride" don't use your thumb—face the traffic with one arm in the air (and expect to pay for your ride). Until conditions change, residents of the largest cities consider this to be dangerous.

To indicate that someone is crazy, the extended forefinger goes to the side of the head as does ours; but where we make a circle with that finger, the Russian instead holds the finger in one place and rotates his hand.

To indicate that someone is foolish or stupid, put your extended thumb up to the side of your head and flap your extended fingers forward and downward.

To express dismay at your own stupidity, knock your fist against your forehead and say something like "Dumb" **балдá!**

To say "That will get you nowhere!" or "You'll never make it!" make the sign of the fig **фúга**: hand in a fist with the thumb tip thrust between the first and second fingers. The expressions are **Фúгу тебе. Кýкиш тебе. Шиш тебе.** By making **фúга** a euphemism for an obscene three-letter word, adults will use the phrase **комбинáция из трёх пáльцев** to describe the gesture and to say "To hell with you." Naturally, the phrase is vulgar as a result.

For the motion of crossing themselves, Russians use the thumb and first two fingers together and employ the same motion Catholics do except that they go to the right shoulder first and finish up with the left. The Russian motion is often very large, from the top of the forehead to the stomach, from the very near shoulder to the very far one. (Crossing oneself is done when appropriate in church, when one is frightened, and when one wants to ward off evil forces.)

The sign of approval is a fist with an extended thumb pointing upward. (But turning thumbs down is unknown.)

If you have no money, or want your money, or if its existence is in doubt, extend your hand slightly and rub together your thumb and first two fingers.

A sign of agreement with the speaker is seen especially among women and children: a slight nod of the head while also blinking both eyes at once.

In greeting, the handshake is more frequent than here, and men don't necessarily wait for women to extend a hand first. When (older) people have not met for a long time, they often will embrace and kiss three times on alternate cheeks as is the custom on Easter after the announcement that "Christ Is Risen!"

Thumbing one's nose is done, but it is a child's gesture, accomplished using both hands:

"Thumb your nose at him!" (Show him who's ahead!) **Утри́ ему́ нос!**

Avoid pointing with your index finger: use your whole hand or resort to explaining rather than pointing. Notice that polite Russians go to considerable trouble not to use their index finger. (Instead they use a whole hand, or, disconcertingly, a middle finger.)

To indicate that a deal is made and accepted either shake hands on it or extend a palm to be brushed by the other's in a downward motion.

To celebrate an unexpected, or a good, idea, click your fingers. Finger clicking also indicates inordinate speed: **Раз. . . и не́ту!**

To indicate prison cross the extended forefinger and middle finger of both hands.

To indicate either too much to drink or an invitation to drink (alcohol), flick a middle finger against side of neck. (This gesture is, at best, informal. Also, see the section on *Drink*.)

There are also "dirty" signs one should never make. To suggest copulation make a circle with the thumb and middle finger of one hand and bring down the extended forefinger of the other hand through the aforementioned circle. The same suggestion can be made by bringing a flat hand palm down on the other fist. Our "up yours" arm signal is also theirs but our "giving the finger" signal is not used. These suggestions are all the sole prerogatives of the male of the species, and badly brought-up males at that.

PROPRIETIES
Пра́вила прили́чия

Table manners
Поведе́ние за столо́м

Perhaps the first thing one notices about Russians and food is the hospitality with which it is presented. "We are happy (to offer) our

---

Се́меро одного́ не ждут.
Seven (people) don't wait for one. (We don't have to wait for a latecomer.)

---

wealth (food)." **Чем бога́ты, тем и ра́ды.** "Eat up what God has sent." **Отку́шайте, чем Бог посла́л.** "Eat, for your health." **Ку́шайте, на здоро́вье!** [4]

Having a party is a major diversion, and a lavish supply of food is normal if it can be arranged. (Hospitality is also an obligation: your hostess will have run herself ragged or paid more than she should have in an attempt to accumulate the necessaries described here.) A hostess gift **пода́рок** is the rule, so don't forget one (flowers, candy, food, drink).

When you arrive, the table already has its heavy load of appetizers with their assorted wines, vodkas, and brandies. Rare is the occasion when it is possible to drop in on a friend without being offered tea, at the very least—and tea without some sort of food "empty tea," literally, **пусто́й чай** is almost never served. In fact, any invitation to "tea" in the evening should be considered an offer of the equivalent of an entire meal.

The next thing you will notice is that the noise level is higher—toasts are offered, jokes are told, magic tricks are played, songs are sung, even poetry is recited. A real effort to entertain is made, and people expect to enjoy themselves. (Visiting Russians have, on occasion, found our dinner parties outright boring.) You will know you have been to a party by the time you go home from a Russian one.

The next thing you might notice is fewer standardized notions about table equipment, its placement, and use. The equipment will usually be there, but not necessarily in the order or positions we observe.

Specific suggestions:

1. Appetizers are served family style, so help yourself from the common serving dishes. (Wait until the hostess offers, since it is her job to see that you are well-fed. If you refuse something, your hostess will continue to offer. If you are hostess, remember that your company expects you to insist.) Avoid heaping your plate with many varieties at

---

4. But: **Незва́ный гость ху́же тата́рина.** The uninvited guest is worse than a Tartar. (We trust you know about Tartars.)

once. Remember that appetizers are only the beginning of the meal.

2. Keep both hands above the table all the time (as do other Europeans).

3. Do not bother to switch your fork back to the right hand after having used the knife for cutting.

4. Expect some looseness in manner and posture, and do not worry about details of table manners—Russians are usually worried that your table manners are different from theirs.

5. Small dishes of chopped green onion or parsley or whole cloves of garlic (in addition to sour cream) are sometimes served with soup; they are a garnish and may be added as you wish.

6. Butter **ма́сло** is served not as a cube but as the contents of a small bowl **маслёнка**. This explains why Russians newly arrived in the United States scrape the top of the cube instead of slicing from one end.

7. If you are eating dinner and a Russian arrives, it is rude and insulting not to extend an invitation to join you at the table. (Waiting in the living room will not do!)

8. If you come upon friends who are in the midst of eating, the polite and common expression is **Прия́тного аппети́та!** which corresponds exactly to *Bon appetit!* The same expression is used when leaving a table at which others are still eating.

9. In the course of a meal you may comment on how tasty something is: **Как вку́сно!** or the like. But at the end of a meal, do not comment on a meal *in toto* as if you were bestowing an accolade. But be sure to thank the hostess: **Большо́е спаси́бо, Мари́я Влади́мировна!** She will answer with **Пожа́луйста** or **На здоро́вье!**

10. If you are hosting and are offering food (or anything else for that matter), then keep in mind that "Thank you" **Спаси́бо** actually means "No, thank you" and that the intended Russian recipient expects the repetition of the offer (rather like the Chinese who must be offered something three times before they can decently accept).

11. Do not bother offering your services as a dishwasher or even busboy. Your efforts will be regarded as a comment on the disabilities of the house or host. They won't help at your house, either. (*Close* friends help, of course.)

A saying used to encourage taking advantage of an offer:
Даю́т—бери́. Бьют—беги́.
(If they are giving out something, take it; if they are beating you, run!)

Спаси́бо э́тому до́му, пойдём к друго́му.
Thanks be to this house, let's go to the next!

Drinking at the table
Засто́лье

At home, or without a special reason, drink of any kind is not a requirement at table. In Russia, one does not employ water, milk, wine to wash the food down; instead one chews longer. (Maybe this explains the soup requirement.)

Parties or celebrations, however, can be identified by the bottles reaching from one end of the table to another. (It is the host's job to make sure your glass is full.) They normally include a wide range of alcoholic drinks **спиртны́е напи́тки** such as white or red wines (mostly for the women), vodkas and cognac (mostly for the men), and nonalcoholic drinks

The party is at the table

безалкого́льные напи́тки such as mineral water, a fruit-flavored drink **морс**, or a lemon-flavored carbonated drink **лимона́д**. People are allowed their tastes: some drink nothing but vodka, some nothing but sweet wines, and some drink nothing but cognac. Ice is never used because it is thought to engender sore throats, and mixed drinks (in our sense) will only occur as an effort to please the American guest. (Deducible stricture: never serve ice in a drink to a Russian without asking.) Drinking is, in polite society, done only at mealtime. There is no cocktail hour: you go to the party and sit right down at the table.

The more serious the party, the more likely there is to be a toastmaster **тамада́** (a Georgian word from a Georgian tradition) whose job is to offer or arrange toasts and refills at the right time to the right people, with humor and good will. The drinking glass (for liquor) **рю́мка** at the party table is normally empty because filling glasses immediately precedes the toast **тост**, after which glasses are emptied *in toto* and at once. (Contrary to our custom, you may join in the drinking if the toast is made to you.) Sipping is not usual behavior. (Imagine, if you will,

gulping down a dry martini, or chug-a-lugging cognac.)

If the use of the toastmaster is one way to encourage drinking, other customs serve as ways to make up for lost drinking. The person late to a party must drink a penalty glass **вы́пить штрафну́ю (рю́мку)**. There are also ways to make you drink more, or chug-a-lug. **Пей до дна!** (Drink to the bottom!) sounds like **пе́йданна**, is shouted in unison, and can be heard at many parties.

A major use of the appetizer, especially salt herring, is as a chaser to liquor. Beer or the cranberry drink **морс** are also used this way.

If you, as an uninitiated foreigner, find you have drunk too much alcohol, have the good grace not to blame your discomfort on the Russians. No one is actually forced to drink. The nondrinker can be made to feel uncomfortable, however, so bring a bottle of juice just in case. Some, usually lower, layers of society are insulted if males will not join them in drink. If you have any reasonable doubt about your capacity, lie firmly about having an ailment and categorically refuse to drink—some people are indeed insulted if you don't join them.

Table philosophy is not deep, but it is fairly consistent: in answer to a toast one often hears **Дай Бог, не после́днюю!** (God grant this is not our last one!) as the glasses are raised. And then there is **Пить бу́дем, гуля́ть бу́дем (а пора́ придёт, помира́ть бу́дем)!** (We will drink, we will have a good time; and then the time will come and we will die!) This is a description of acceptable drinking. Unfortunately, the uncontrollable use of alcohol in any form is the Russian scourge. "He's an alcoholic." **Он совсе́м спи́лся.** "I'll become an alcoholic here." **Я сопью́сь здесь.**

Table songs
Засто́льный пе́сенный репертуа́р

Singing at the (party) table is a major joy in Russian life, so you may be able to impress your Russian friends by knowing at least some of the words to these songs. (The Russian song-book **пе́сенник** includes the words but not the melody.) The titles of the songs are underlined.

Ой, цветёт кали́на
В по́ле у ручья́,
Па́рня молодо́го
Полюби́ла я.
Па́рня полюби́ла
На свою́ беду́.
Припе́в: Не могу́ откры́ться,
Слов я не найду́

Из-за о́строва на стре́жень
На просто́р речно́й волны́,
Выплыва́ют расписны́е,
Острогру́дые челны́.
На пере́днем Сте́нька Ра́зин,
Обня́вшись, сиди́т с княжно́й,
Сва́дьбу но́вую справля́ет,
Сам весёлый и хмельно́й.

Мой костёр в тума́не све́тит
Искры га́снут на лету́.
Но́чью нас никто́ не встре́тит,
Мы прости́мся на мосту́.

Шуме́л камы́ш
Дере́вья гну́лись,
А но́чка тёмная была́.
Одна́ возлю́бленная па́ра
Всю ночь гуля́ла до утра́.
Под у́тро пта́шечки запе́ли,
Уж наступи́л проща́льный час.
Пора́ наста́ла расстава́ться
И слёзы хлы́нули из глаз.

Stock phrases
Станда́ртные выраже́ния

The following are only the most common expressions used in everyday speech in the given situations. For a much more thorough list plus examples and exercises, see **Ру́сский речево́й этике́т** by **А. А. Аки́шина, Н. И. Формано́вская, изд. Ру́сский язы́к, Москва́** (1975), from which the phrases and classifications listed below have been taken. (By adjusting number, case, or gender endings, basic but entire conversations can be contrived.)

Getting their attention

To address someone you don't know:

Прости́те   Pardon (me) . . .
Извини́те   Excuse (me) . . .
Бу́дьте добры́. . . Бу́дьте (так) любе́зны. . .
   Be so good (as to). . .
Скажи́те, пожа́луйста   Tell (me) please. . .

These are the most common expressions to get someone's attention when you have a question or a request:

Граждани́н, Гражда́нка!   Citizen! (This form is receding, but can still be heard. It is more likely in government offices, especially the courts.)
Господи́н, Госпожа́, Господа́!   Mister, Miss or Mrs., Ladies and gentlemen! (This form, a reversion to tsarist days, now holds sway.)
Това́рищ!   Comrade! can still be heard, but is usual only in the military: **Това́рищ**

капита́н! The non-Russian is best off avoiding *Comrade* altogether.

Же́нщина! Woman! **Мужчи́на!** Man! Used in desperation when nothing else sounds right. The problem is that now, nothing sounds right. (Someone from St. Petersburg jokingly suggested Lady! **Да́ма!** if she is wearing a hat, and Old Lady! **Ба́бка!** if she's wearing a bandana.)

Друзья́! Дороги́е друзья́! Friends! Dear Friends! (A familiar form of address to an audience.)

Молодо́й челове́к! Де́вушка! Young man! (Young) woman! (To address young people, especially anyone waiting on you, even those whose youth is not all that obvious.)

Тётя! Дя́дя! Aunt, Uncle. (Commonly used by children to address adults they don't know. You may call them **Ма́льчик! Де́вочка! Ребя́та!**)

To address someone you have met:

Use names. This often involves remembering first names plus patronymics. (See *Names.*) Family members can also be addressed by their relationship or a diminutive thereof: **Ма́ма! Па́почка! Сыно́чек! До́ченька!** and so forth.

(And here we must add that in the presence of a third person, the latter must *always* be referred to by name and *never* by "he" or "she." Americans commonly make this mistake, thereby engendering no end of hurt feelings. Let them know you at least recognize who they are by actually using their names.)

Answering the address:

Что? Да? А? (The most common answers—it is more polite to add the asker's name, if you know it.)

Пожа́луйста is a polite answer, most often to a question that begins with **Извини́те** and the like.

Слу́шаю! Слушаю вас! Я вас слу́шаю! are rather formal answers, or they are used when it seems you didn't hear the first response. (Common on the telephone.)

Вы ко мне (обраща́етесь)? Are you talking to me? **Вы меня́ (зовёте)?** Are you calling me? (This is used when the answerer isn't sure who is being addressed.)

The reaction to an arrival:

Вы ко мне? Вы не ко мне? У вас ко мне де́ло? Did you want to talk to me?

Вы меня́ ждёте? Вы не меня́ ждёте? Are you waiting for me?

Вы мне хоти́те что-то сказа́ть? Did you want to say something to me? (All these expressions are possible when the arriver has not yet started speaking.)

Reactions to a knock at the door:

Войди́те! Входи́те! Да-да! (All give permission to come in.)

Прошу́! Прошу вас! More formal: Please do!

Подожди́те, пожа́луйста! Подождите мину́тку! These ask you to wait a minute please, while the following say the same only less formally: **Мину́тку! Одну́ мину́тку! Мину́точку! Секу́нду! Одну́ секунду! Секу́ндочку!**

The greeting

Здра́вствуйте! Hello! (This is the most common greeting. Used when addressing more than one person, or when addressing someone with whom **Вы** forms are used.)

Здра́вствуй! Hello! (The next most common greeting, when addressing everyone else.)

До́брый день! Good day! (More formal, less frequent and only during the day.)

До́брое у́тро! С до́брым у́тром! Good morning! (Used only in the morning, most often right after waking up.)

До́брый ве́чер! Good evening! (Used upon meeting in the evening.)

Приве́т! Hi! (Informal use, most often among young people.)

Phrases that follow a greeting:

Рад(а) вас ви́деть! Happy to see you!

Как хорошо́, что встре́тил вас! How nice that we met! (Used when you are pleased with a meeting.)

Как живёте? Как дела́? Как иду́т дела? How are things? (These replace our "How are you?" and differ in that the Russian often gives a substantive or subjective answer such as *awful, the dog died* when we would say "Fine, thank you" on the day of our mother's funeral. Therefore, be prepared to wait through the answer if you ask the question.)

Как здоро́вье? Как вы себя́ чу́вствуете? (Both ask after the health of someone you suspect is, or may have been, ailing.)

Как живёшь? Как жизнь? Как успе́хи? Как дела́? Что но́вого? Что слы́шно? These expressions, often preceded by **ну**, are friendly, informal, and used with good friends.

Answers to the greeting inquiries if things are going well:

Хорошо́. Well or good.

Прекра́сно. Splendidly.

Замеча́тельно. Wonderfully.

Великоле́пно. Marvelously.

Всё в поря́дке. Things are in good order.

Непло́хо. Not bad. (In this situation the word **Норма́льно** is often used, informally. It does not mean "normally" or "as usual"; it means "good" or "well.")

Answers to greetings if you are equivocal about how things are:

Ничего́. OK.

Та́к себе. So-so.

Ни хорошо, ни пло́хо. Neither good nor bad.

(Да) Как вам сказа́ть. What should I say? (I don't really know what to say.)

Не зна́ю, что и сказать. I don't know what to say.

Как бу́дто, ничего. It seems OK/all right.

(Да) Вро́де, ничего. It seems OK/all right.

Ка́жется, ничего. It seems OK/all right.

Оке́й. OK. (Less common, but still heard.)

Answers to greetings if things are not all right:

(Да) Так себе́, Нева́жно. So-so.

Пло́хо. Badly.

Скве́рно. Awful.

Как са́жа бела́. Literally "As white as soot," is an answer to **Как дела?** and means "not good."

Expressions used when a meeting was not expected:

Кака́я неожи́данность! What a surprise!

Какая прия́тная неожиданность! What a pleasant surprise!

Прия́тная неожиданность! A pleasant surprise!

Давно́ мы с вами не ви́делись! I haven't seen you for so long! These are the most common expressions.

Вот это да! can be used informally when the meeting is both a surprise and a delight with emphasis on the latter. (The expression is also very common for any total approval.)

Ско́лько лет, сколько зим! How many summers and winters! "Long time, no see!"

Кака́я встре́ча! Какая прия́тная встреча! Прия́тная встреча! How nice to see you! (These are informal expressions where the element of surprise is more pointed.)

(Да вот уж ника́к) Не ожида́л вас встре́тить! I didn't expect to see you! **Не ду́мал встретить вас!** I didn't think I'd meet you (here)! **Как вы здесь оказа́лись? / Каки́ми судьба́ми?** How come you are here? **Как вы сюда́ попа́ли?** How did you get here? (These expressions are used when you don't expect that person to be in that place.)

Expressions used when the meeting or arrival was expected:

Хорошо, что вы пришли́. It's good that you came. **Я рад, что вы пришли.** I'm glad that you came. (Both are used after the greeting, and suggest specific approval.)

Ну вот и я! Here I am! (Informal use by the expected arriver.)

Ну вот и ты! Well, there you are!

Наконе́ц-то ты пришёл! Finally you got here! (Informal use by the awaiter.)

Making acquaintance

When there is no one to introduce you, you can say: **Дава́йте познако́мимся, Бу́дем знако́мы, Я хоте́л бы с ва́ми познако́-миться, Дава́йте знако́миться** all of which, in essence, say "Let's get acquainted." Then you give your name in the form appropriate to relative ages and the situation: **Меня́ зову́т Алексе́й**, or **Меня́ зову́т Игорь Петро́вич**, or **Моя́ фами́лия Скворцо́в**. And finally, you ask for their name: **Как вас зову́т?** (The "thou" form can only be used with children at this stage of the acquaintanceship, and should be so used: **Как тебя́ зову́т?**) An introducer says: **Познако́мьтесь!** or **Знако́мьтесь!** or more formally, **Разреши́те вас предста́вить!** and then might help out with names: **Это Ольга Петро́вна** and perhaps a profession. It is also common for the introducees to announce their own names to each other.

Answers to the introduction:

Очень прия́тно! How do you do? (literally, "very pleasant")

Очень прия́тно с ва́ми познако́миться, Рад (Прия́тно) познакомиться! (variants) How nice to meet you!

Мы уже знако́мы, Мы уже встреча́лись. We've already met.

Я вас зна́ю. I know you. (Upon parting, the newly met can say **Очень прия́тно было познако́миться!**)

Я вас где-то ви́дел. I've seen you somewhere.

Я о вас слы́шал. I've heard of you.

Вы меня́ не узнаёте? Don't you recognize me?

The invitation

Приглаша́ю вас. . . , Хочу пригласи́ть вас. . . I invite you to. . . These are the most frequent invitation forms. **Я хоте́л бы пригласи́ть вас. . .** I would like to invite you to. . . is the same only softer.

Приходи́те к нам в го́сти. Come to our house (literally, come and be a guest at our place). **Заходи́те** Drop in. Sometime. . . on your way. More of a real invitation than is ours.

Входи́те, Заходи́те, Проходи́те! Come on in. Used when someone is standing at the door.

Прошу́ прийти́. . . Please come. A formal request.

Идём, Пойдём Let's go. . . (somewhere).

Добро́ пожа́ловать! Welcome! Fairly formal, associated with older people.

Сади́тесь! Have a seat!

В нога́х пра́вды нет.
There's no truth in our feet. (. . . while on our feet.)

Не бо́йся гостя́ сидя́чего, а бо́йся гостя́ стоя́чего!
Don't worry about the guest that's seated, but beware the guest that remains standing!

Ми́лости про́сим! Welcome! (Usually part of a polite invitation to sit down and eat. Perhaps closer to our "Please do!")

The request

Common phrases followed by the infinitive:

Прошу́ вас Please (as in a request)

Сове́тую вам I advise you . . .

Предлага́ю вам I propose . . .

Use of the imperative form of the verb is a standard way to express a request, advice, or a proposition: **Сде́лайте . . . Напиши́те. . .**, **Принеси́те. . .** To be polite, precede the former with **Пожалуйста, Бу́дьте добры́, Бу́дьте любе́зны** (somewhat old-fashioned) **Я хочу вас попроси́ть . . . Я хотел бы вас попросить** Could I ask you to . . .

Acceptance or denial

The acceptance:

Хорошо́. Good. (The common answer to an invitation, followed by expressions of gratitude.)

Пожа́луйста. (A frequently used positive response to a polite request.)

Ла́дно. OK. (Informal agreement.)

Сейча́с. Right away.

Сде́лаю. . . Напишу́. I will (do whatever the verb indicates).

Дава́йте. Let's (as in our, "Yes, let's do" or "Shall we?").

Пойдёмте, Пошли́. Let's go.

С удово́льствием, С ра́достью, Охо́тно (All three accept with pleasure.)

The refusal:

Не могу́, Нет, я не могу́, Я ника́к не могу́. I can't. (The polite person will attach **Извините** to those expressions.)

The indeterminate answer:

Мо́жет быть. Maybe. (Avoid "maybe" if what you mean is "no.")

Возмо́жно. Possibly.

Вероя́тно. Probably.

Наве́рное, Наве́рно. Surely.

Не зна́ю. I don't know.

Agreement and disagreement

Коне́чно. Of course.

Разуме́ется. It stands to reason.

Безусло́вно. Absolutely.

Пра́вильно. That's right.

Соверше́нно пра́вильно. That's absolutely right.

Ве́рно. Right.

Действи́тельно. Indeed.

Вы пра́вы! You are right!.

Коне́чно нет. Of course not; **Совсе́м нет** Not at all; **Разуме́ется нет** Of course not; **Безусло́вно нет** Absolutely not; **Отню́дь нет** Of course not (but with an element of doubt).

Нет, не так. No, not really.

When asked their opinion, Russians often give it in cases when Americans would not. (A young Russian being interviewed for a job with a soft drink company was offered one of the firm's products. "No, thanks," said he, "I never drink that junk." **Никогда не пью эту га́дость.**) The problem can be obviated by not asking questions with answers you really don't want to hear.

The excuse

Извини́те. Excuse me. (The expression to use when apology is least needed.)

Прости́те. Pardon me. (For either a major or minor encroachment.)

Both expressions are often followed by an admission of the error:
Извини́те за опозда́ние. Sorry for being late.

The response

Пожа́луйста, Ничего́, Не сто́ит (In this sense, each means, "That's all right.")

Congratulations, good wishes

Поздравля́ть (To wish well, on any occasion, or to congratulate.)

Поздравля́ем с пра́здником! (We wish you) a happy holiday!

Поздравля́ю! Congratulations!

С Но́вым го́дом! Happy New Year! (**Поздравля́ю** is understood.)

С днём рожде́ния! Happy Birthday!

С пра́здником! Happy Holiday! (Any holiday)

Прими́те мои́ поздравле́ния. Accept my good wishes. (Very formal. For good wishes without a holiday, use **жела́ть**.)

От всей души́ жела́ю сча́стья, успе́хов, и здоро́вья. With all my heart I wish you happiness, success, and health.

Успе́хов вам! Hope you make it! (Literally, *successes to you*, **жела́ю**, is understood.)

Сча́стья! Hope you'll be happy!

Уда́чи! Good luck!

Счастли́вого пути́! Счастли́во добра́ться! Have a good trip! (Sometimes answered with **Счастливо остава́ться!**)

Бу́дьте здоро́вы! Bless you! (A wish of good health after a sneeze)

Gratitude

Спаси́бо. Thank you. **Большо́е спасибо.** Thank you very much.

Благодарю́ вас. Thank you. (Slightly more formal. Both expressions are followed by **за** and the accusative if you want to be more detailed about your gratitude.)

Пожа́луйста! Не́ за что! Не сто́ит! (All three serve as "You're welcome.")

Leave-taking

До свида́ния! Goodbye! (Most common.)

Счастли́во. Goodbye. (Less formal.)

Пока́. See you. (Least formal.)

Проща́йте Goodbye or farewell (Reserved for the possibility that you will not meet for a long time, if ever.)

Всего́ хоро́шего! Всего́ до́брого! I wish you well! (Can be used along with or instead of "Goodbye." Both are common for "Goodbye" on the telephone.)

The following expressions can be used instead of "Goodbye" or along with it when you are planning to meet again:

До встре́чи! Until we meet again! (Grammatically more formal but socially on the same level as our "See you!")

До ско́рой встре́чи! See you soon!

До за́втра! See you tomorrow!

До воскресе́нья! See you Sunday!

До ве́чера! See you tonight!

Споко́йной но́чи! До́брой но́чи! Good night! (Just before going to bed.)

Переда́йте приве́т му́жу!/жене́! Give (my) regards to your husband/wife!

Приве́т мужу/жене. Say hello to your husband/wife (for me).

Superstitions
Суеве́рия

Superstitions persist as a part of language, if not thought, and some of them have entered the world of good and bad manners. In most Russian households, it is rude to whistle indoors; earlier it was thought not only rude but a sin, because in so doing you were giving comfort to the Devil **Бе́са те́шишь.** Your whistling will bring misfortune. **Беду́ насви́стишь.** The person that whistles doesn't make any money. **Кто свисти́т, у того́ де́ньги не водя́тся.** Generally, superstition plays a large role in the language and in life; many Russians actually do believe many of "signs" in the following list. So your whistling in the house will be both bad luck and rude. Astrologers are currently having a heyday, and I have talked to an engineer who was convinced that he had talked to or seen a house spirit **домово́й.** See *Russian Folk Belief* by Linda Ivanits, M.T. Sharpe, New York, 1992.

The existence of luck is itself a superstition: He is lucky **Ему́ везёт**; she was lucky **Ей повезло́.** Often the superstition surfaces via the "bad sign" **плоха́я приме́та**, which includes

Московские новости,
9 мая 1993

Вы платите только за международный телефонный разговор.

the number 13 and the black cat: **Не повезёт,
если чёрный кот доро́гу перейдёт.** [5]

Good and bad signs
Хоро́шие и плохи́е приме́ты

1. A broken mirror indicates the death or
   loss of a loved one. **Разби́тое
   зе́ркало—к сме́рти или поте́ре
   бли́зких.** (But if you throw it away
   immediately, nothing will happen.)

2. If your cheeks are burning, someone is
   praising you. **Щёки горя́т—кто-то
   хва́лит.** If your ears are burning, someone is swearing about you. **Уши
   горя́т—кто-то руга́ет.**

3. It's bad luck to meet a woman with
   empty buckets. **Встре́тить же́нщину с
   пусты́ми вёдрами—плоха́я приме́та.**

---

5. This saying is the starting point for a famous song by Bulat
Okudzhava:
   Говоря́т, не повезёт, если чёрный кот доро́гу перейдёт,
   А пока́ наоборо́т, а пока наоборот —
   Только чёрному коту́ не везёт.

Это не в путь, лу́чше не ходи́. On the
other hand, meeting a man is a good sign,
as is meeting a woman with full pails. A
wish of bad luck for someone who has
displeased you: **Чтоб тебе́ пу́сто было!**

4. Money found on the ground is a good
   sign if it is face up **орёл**, and a bad sign
   if it is face down **ре́шка** (tsarist coins had
   an eagle **орёл** on one side and a sort of
   grille **решётка** on the other).

5. Spill salt and there will be a fight. **Соль
   рассы́пать—ссо́ра будет.**

6. The young woman who sits at the corner
   of the table will remain unmarried seven
   years. **Сиде́ть на углу́—семь лет
   за́муж не вы́йти.**

7. If you put your clothes on inside out you
   will be beaten. **Оде́ть наизна́нку—
   быть би́тым.**

8. If she sleeps in a new place then the bride
   will dream of her bridegroom. **Спишь на
   но́вом ме́сте—присни́сь жени́х неве́сте.**

9. It's bad luck to leave and then return
   before finishing a trip. **Плохая**

примета—вы́йти и́з дому и верну́ться обра́тно—пути́ не бу́дет.

10. It's bad luck to shake hands over the threshold. **Нельзя́ здоро́ваться че́рез поро́г.**

11. If someone is going on a long trip, do not clean up or sweep out the person's room immediately or you will sweep out good luck **уда́ча** with the dirt, or harm will come to the person who left.

12. It's good luck to trip on your left foot. **споткну́ться на ле́вую но́гу.**

13. If the weather is good on **Покро́в день** (**Пра́здник Покрова́ Богоро́дицы**) then the winter will be warm. If it snows, forty more days of snow are to follow. (Weather "signs" number in the thousands and are recorded by the bookful.)

14. If a knife drops a man will come **мужи́к придёт**; if a fork drops, a woman will come **же́нщина придёт.**

15. On examination day, don't make your bed, don't wear anything new, and don't cut your fingernails. **Не заправля́й посте́ль, не носи́ но́вого, не стриги́ ногте́й.**

16. Give, or place in a vase, only an odd number of flowers: an even number symbolizes death and is the proper number for graves.

Folk beliefs
Наро́дные пове́рия

The possessor of the evil eye **дурно́й глаз** had the ability to inflict damage, especially on anything that might be expected to grow (babies, animals and crops), merely by staring intently at it or its mother. "She gave me the evil eye." **Она́ сгла́зила меня́.** Its possession could afflict the innocent possessor: one man blinded himself so that his gaze could not hurt anyone.

To ward off the evil eye, knock on wood and say **Как бы не сгла́зить!** As in English, the gesture and the expression remain to preserve good fortune, especially when it's threatened.

The magician/witch/warlock **колду́н,**[6] **колду́нья** was associated with the "dark forces" **чёрные си́лы** and could use charms **ча́ры** (*pl. only*; whence **очарова́ть** to charm) that could work for good or ill. In magic's absence, one could ward off evil forces **нечи́стая си́ла, зла́я си́ла** (terms used to avoid using the Devil's name), by spitting three times over the left shoulder. This is a very common phenomenon to this day. The expression is most often used after describing a good fortune that might be precarious. Actual spitting isn't necessary: one just turns to the left and says **Тьфу, тьфу, тьфу!** To fool the devil, one wishes the opposite: "Neither fluff nor feather!" **Ни пу́ха, ни пера́!** was originally a good-luck wish for hunters but is now used for any undertaking. Among students, a wish for good luck on an examination is often countered with "Go to the Devil!" **(Иди́) к чёрту!** It would seem that the Devil can be attracted to—and spoil—any event of major personal import. Therefore mothers will put off buying baby equipment until the very last minute, for fear of something dreadful happening to the yet unborn. Our general warning about not counting chickens is, to a Russian, quite specific. (Also see *Folk Medicine*.)

Цыпля́т по о́сени счита́ют.
Don't count your chickens before they hatch.

Contemporary behavior requires covering our mouths when we yawn; formerly (usually older), women would make the sign of the cross in front of the yawn so that the devil wouldn't fly in—**крести́ли рот, чтобы в э́тот моме́нт не залете́л нечи́стый.**

6. Today, it is possible to see advertisements for people offering their services as "колду́н."

Sanitation and sex
О чём не говорят

In private homes, the toilet **унитáз** will be found all by itself in the toilet room **туалéт, убóрная**[7] equipped with toilet paper **туалéтная бумáга** or neatly torn newspaper sheets to serve the same purpose. Wash your hands afterwards in the bathroom **вáнная**, which contains a sink and a bathtub. (Russians are fairly persistent about hand-washing, especially before eating.) Public facilities **общéственный туалет** are a caution, sometimes requiring an iron will, because upkeep rarely meets the demand. (Hotels are the best bet, or you might want to express your gratitude to McDonald's.) This is especially true anywhere outside the center of major cities, where the Turkish toilet is not uncommon. (It is always wise to carry your own paper with you.) Hope on the horizon appears with a new institution, the cooperative restroom **кооперати́вный туалéт**, where a small fee can get you no line to stand in and a modicum of cleanliness. **Жéнский туалет** is the Women's room; the Men's room is **Мужскóй туалет**. Also **Жéнская убóрная / Мужская убóрная**. Flush the toilet! **Спусти́ вóду в туалéте!** People traveling by car should consider bushes, etc., as probably preferable to public facilities which may be available. Expressions are "to go to the bushes" **пойти́ в кýстики**, or "to make a green stop" **сдéлать зелёную стоя́нку**.

Considerable attempts are made to avoid a direct reference to the fact that one must use the facilities **удóбства**: I have to go somewhere. **Мне нáдо кóе-кудá. Мне надо к начáльнику стáнции, Мне надо к дя́де Вáне,** and so forth. For children, "No. 1" is **Мне нýжно по-мáленькому (си́кать** ог **пи́сать)**, and "No. 2" is **Мне нужно по-большóму (кáкать)**. The

"window of opportunity" on a long bus ride is a "sanitary stop" **санитáрная останóвка**.

If menstruation **мéсячные** (literally, "the monthlies"—the formal word is **менструáция)** needs to be taken care of one makes one's own sanitary napkins out of cotton **вáта**, though sanitary napkins **гигиени́ческие пакéты** are sometimes available. Tampons **тампóны** are now in many stores, sometimes with a smiling attendant who is there to explain their use.

Sex
Половы́е отношéния

If persistent reports are to be believed, little meaningful information on this subject is passed from one generation to the next, and very little is supplied by outside institutions. On the other hand, jokes about sex abound and are liberally retold. Respectable Russian movies not infrequently contain nudity, and even significant portions of the sex act have been shown. One has the impression that Russians are not prudes, but they are in denial, as the saying goes.

И хóчется и кóлется и мáма не вели́т.
One wants to, very much, but mother says not to.

Euphemism is a great help in conversation: "She is in a family way." **Онá в положéнии.** "She is expecting." **Онá ждёт ребёнка.** All the while she is pregnant **берéменная.** The word *prostitute* **прости́тка** is avoided by using **ночнáя бáбочка, ýличная жéнщина, пута́на.** However, big city prostitutes make so much money these days that attitudes about their acceptability may change.

Condoms **презервати́вы** are sometimes available at pharmacies or at kiosks in a packet **пакéтик.** Married women can be fitted with a diaphragm **диафрáгма/колпачóк** or IUD **спирáль/зóнтик,** but the common alternative

---

7. The word **туалет** is foreign and therefore softer, less explicit than **убóрная**. Those who spurn euphemism use the latter. Other words for the facility, if not the equipment, are: **вáтер клозéт, кабинéт задýмчивости, сорти́р (вульг.), санузéл, писсуáр, гальи́н (морское), два нуля́, ноль-ноль, два очкá, отхóжее мéсто, нýжник.** (Many of the preceding words are for your amusement; most refer to outhouses, or at least facilities without plumbing.)

is abortion. (The abortion rate suggests that birth control products are unavailable or are not properly used.)

The American can be shocked by the attitude towards abortion **або́рт**: the process is expected and is accepted as perfectly normal. Inquiry among friends reveals not one or two abortions, but five to seven as a common number, and thought to be a reasonable number at that.

Homosexuality **гомосексуа́льность** exists and is rising, though it is much less acceptable than in the West. Sixty-two male gays were convicted of homosexuality in 1992, yet in the same year a political party for homosexuals **Па́ртия сексуа́льных меньши́нств** was founded in Moscow. A male homosexual is **гомосексуали́ст, педера́ст** while **го́мик, пе́дик** or **голубо́й** are slang (one student sued another one for calling him gay "**голубо́й**"). A lesbian is **лезбия́нка,** or **лезба́** in vulgar slang.

AIDS **СПИД, Синдро́м приобрете́нного имму́нно-дефици́та** has arrived in Russia, but the numbers still seem low. (One hundred twenty-seven full-blown AIDS cases were reported in June 1993 by the Russian Federation. In November 1993 *Komsomol'skaya Pravda* reported that only 682 people were infected with HIV. The World Health Organization estimated about 50,000 cases of HIV infection in all of Eastern Europe and Central Asia.) Because AIDS has been transmitted at medical institutions in the past, wide use is now being made of single-use syringes **одноразовые шприцы** for any inoculations. The article in *Komsomol'skaya Pravda* also reported that more than one thousand laboratories will test for HIV infection anonymously.

Really dirty words
Мат

What follows are the basic root words that are awful, obscene, taboo, and mostly unprintable in Russian. (Actually, the 1912 edition of Dal's dictionary includes them. Contemporary Ozhegov does not.) *Never, ever* use these words. They are *not* cute or funny, *nor* will you

be if you say them. These words are variously stronger for a Russian in Russian than are the similar words we use, and, as a non-Russian, you have *no* feel for their strength or appropriateness. Everybody knows these words, but life sometimes requires information we don't intend to use. They are included here so that you don't inadvertently either embarass yourself by asking their meaning or insult someone by repeating a phrase you thought harmless.

Russian abounds with taboo words and expressions, most of which are based on six or seven root words that refer to what such words usually refer. The total assemblage of four-letter or taboo words in Russian is called **мат** (from the most common of such expressions, which includes the word *mother*): **Он руга́ется ма́том/Он матери́тся.** (He uses dirty words.) Even **мат** is too strong for some people, who will instead euphemistically say, **Он выража́ется трёхэта́жными слова́ми**—literally, "He uses three-storied words." Swearing or a swear word is **ру́гань, руга́тельство** and may or may not include the aforementioned taboo words: **Он его́ вы́ругал.** (He cussed him out.) **Брань, бра́нные слова́** are also terms for swear words, but the connotation is not so strong.) The major standard "mother" expression is **Ёб твою́ мать!** (I copulated with your mother) which is used in anger at oneself or others, in unpleasant surprise (thumbnail-and-hammer), and by those who find pleasure in obscenity (Pass the copulate-with-your-mother salt **Переда́й, ёб твою́ мать, соль,** for example.) Even stronger is a "mother" expression that is only used toward someone else: **Иди́ к ёбаной ма́тери!** Go to your copulated-with mother! The obscene element is the taboo verb with the imperfective infinitives **еть, ети,** or **еба́ть (ебу, ебёт),** past tense forms **ёб, ебла́, ебли́,** or **еба́л** and the perfective infinitives **вы́еть, вы́ебать.** Many expressions use various forms of these verbs and all are obscene. Just as our "darn" replaces "damn," so **ёлки-па́лки** or merely **ёлки** replace the aforementioned vulgar expressions (without their awful connotations).

Parts of the body supply some major obscenities. For many Russians, no honest alternatives are available for some of these anatomical words; the technical words are so technical as to be incomprehensible, and the words everybody knows—that is, those that follow—are too awful to be uttered. Euphemisms are resorted to, such as the male "member" мужскóй член. The most common obscene word for penis is хуй or its equally awful substitute хер, the name of the first letter of the real obscenity. Common constructions are: Хуй с ним To hell with him Идѝ на хуй / Иди на хер Go to hell! These words also combine with на to make adverbs: на хер = not at all (Нá хер ты мне нужнá) and with ни to make a noun, ни херá = nothing at all (Ни херá не знáю). The relatively inoffensive euphemism is хрен, which in normal parlance means *horseradish*. Хрен с ним might equate to our "To hell with him."

Obscene *testicles* become *eggs* яйца, perhaps a more active description than our term. This is the only major indecent word that has a decent meaning, too, which may explain why relatively few ancillary expressions use this root.

Vagina пиздá is the major female obscenity. It may also be used to denote a weak or effeminate man or can be a term of abuse and may refer to either a male or a female Он пизда вонючая.

For arse/ass or arse-/ass-hole we have жóпа. Go to Hell! Иди в жóпу! and many, many similar expressions. Dark-skinned Caucasians or central Asians are черножóпые. One of the delights of research is finding this paraphrase in Dal's: the common saying На безрыбье и рак рыба (When there's no fish, then a crayfish can be a fish) converts to На бесптичье и жопа соловéй (When there are no birds, then your ass can be a nightingale!). This word, as its English correspondent, is also commonly used to refer to the stupid or unthinking. There exists yet another, though less common, word for the posterior orifice срáка, the related obscene verb of which, "to defecate" срать (сру, срёт or see Даль), is more often used.

One obscene noun for feces говнó is very widely used, not as an expletive, but as a descriptive. There are many forms and variations of the word, not to mention sayings such

as the well-known Своё говнó не воняет (One's own feces don't stink). The word is so common, even though unacceptable, that it is the first of these that the foreigner is likely to hear (Khrushchev used it to describe his view of some modern art.) Another obscenity for the same thing is дерьмó and is also widely used as a descriptive for anything useless or messy.

When defecation is out of control and diarrhea has set in, the obscene verb is дристáть; the noun is дрист.

The English "to fart" has the same root and meaning as the Russian пердéть, держý, пердѝт with the perfective пёрнуть and noun as a term of abuse пердýн. Another obscenity for passing gas бздеть, бзжу, бздит means to do so noiselessly.

The unprintable word for *whore* or *bitch* блядь retains that meaning but is also frequently used as an expletive or simply as an interjection for the sheer joy the young seem to experience in saying something awful: Он, блядь, достáл папирóс, блядь, и закурѝл, блядь, and so on. (Other unacceptable words for *whore* are кýрва, шлюха. Whores work in whorehouses бордéль or бардáк, бордáк, which can also mean mess or disorder. These words are printable.)

The term for someone very stupid or no good is мудáк; it is obscene because its root refers to the male genitalia.

Euphemisms abound. The trick is usually to take an initial syllable and convert it to something less alarming though often rhyming: ядрёный instead of ёбаный; ёлки-пáлки, ёшкин кот, ёксель-мóксель for ёб твою мать; мутáнт instead of мудáк; иди нá фиг or иди на три бýквы instead of иди нá хуй. Many euphemisms involve the first letter, and most are the first letter, thus жóпа becomes жэ, говнó becomes гэ, блядь becomes бэ. An element of play is also involved when the object is to give the impression of using awful words without actually having done so: Ух ты мýха дрозофѝла, мать мутáций!

(A helpful informant supplied the following degrees of awfulness: very bad: хуй, хер, блядь, пиздá, ебáться; bad: жóпа, говнó, перде́ть, срать, сцать; and sometimes acceptable: хрен, иди на́ фиг, шлю́ха, я́йца.

Parents often use a kind of baby-talk when bodily functions are involved: to pee пи́сать, пи́саю (children themselves say си́кать, си́каю) and to defecate ка́кать, ка́каю, and so on, with the noun ка́ка, кака́шка. A baby's bottom is по́пка, and "peter" пи́ська. These words are more baby-talk than they are offensive.

And finally, peasant usage supplies the onomatopoetic сцать or ссать, посцу́ or поссу́. I'm going to take a leak = Я пойду́, посцу́. He wet his pants = Он обосца́л свои́ штаны́, Он обси́кался. In general, the avoidance of euphemism among peasants is quite noticeable. Many of the words we have described as dreadful are not so dreadful in the countryside—your using them would be dreadful.

PARTICULAR CEREMONIES
Торжества́/Семе́йные пра́здники

Birth
Рожде́ние

Future mothers do not go out and buy baby equipment until the very last minute for fear that doing so might bring harm to the small one. A birth certificate свиде́тельство о рожде́нии must be applied for at the local registry office загс, and then, after things have settled down a bit, friends begin to call and come bearing gifts.

The Soviet government discovered, through trial, that life has ceremonies and that people actually need them. Marital arrangements via post cards simply weren't enough. So the authorities eventually instituted a number of substitute ceremonies, usually incorporating some aspects of the former religious rites. Instead of baptism креще́ние, they had a "naming" ceremony имянарече́ние in which infants received their birth certificate and perhaps a medal from the local administration. Boys received blue ribbons; girls pink ones.

8. This verb is used in the saying Хоть сци в глаза́, всё Бо́жья роса́. Literally, "Pee in their eyes and they still say it's God's dew." In other words, no matter what you do or say, they still pay no attention. The choice of pronoun is arbitrary.

Christening креще́ние was very important and even necessary in a Russian's life due to a very strong and sincere belief that one would go to hell without it. Baptism also supplied the child with godparents кре́стные роди́тели who would take over in the parents' absence and who were responsible for the child's Christian upbringing; one chose godparents with care, because from the moment of baptism onwards, the child's parents and the godparents were considered related to the family with the titles кум, кума́.

The sacrament дар/та́инство of baptism starts with the rejection of the Devil and the acceptance of Christ. Before the actual Christening, the child or the godparents repeat the credo Ве́рую. Then the priest свяще́нник prays and anoints with holy unction еле́й/миро́, the alleluia Аллилу́йя is sung and the priest immerses the child three times, baptizing it in the name of the Father, the Son, and the Holy Ghost во и́мя Отца́, Сы́на и Свято́го Ду́ха; the baby is then carefully wrapped all in white. Again anointed, the baby is taken up by the godparents who, with the priest, circle the font купе́ль three times. Finally, a snip of hair is taken as a sign that the child is given wholly to God. The sacraments of baptism and chrismation миропома́зание (the so-called "Holy Enlightenment" Свято́е просвеще́ние) conclude with communion Причаще́ние. Baby must be very patient because the service takes about an hour.

Christening is all the rage these days, for babies and for their elders.

The wedding
Сва́дьба

How to get married:
　She says Как вы́йти за́муж.
　He says Как жени́ться.

Our future bride неве́ста and groom жени́х must apply пода́ть заявле́ние at the local civil registry office, загс (За́пись а́ктов гражда́нского состоя́ния) where they will set a date for the wedding. Formerly, the couple received coupons **талóны** that allowed them to buy wedding or household items in short supply **дефицúтные товáры** at stores not open to the public **закрúтые магазúны**. One coupon gave the bride the right to a hairdo **причёска** on her wedding day without waiting in line.

The wedding itself **бракосочетáние** will take place either at the registry office (**Онú вчерá расписáлись** = "They got married yesterday") or, often in cities these days, at a more elaborate Wedding Palace **Дворéц бракосочетáний**; church can follow the registry office.

Our couple **пáра** must make plans for their honeymoon **медóвый мéсяц**, send out invitations **приглашéния**, and organize a dinner or make reservations at a restaurant for the wedding feast or supper **свáдебный ýжин, вéчер**. Relatives **рóдственники** must meet one another. Wedding clothes and the requisite household equipment must also come together.

The following describes a more elaborate marriage, especially in a large city where nowadays the attempt is to restore some semblance of ceremony. A wedding car decorated with intertwined rings **кóльцами** picks up the wedding party, which includes the bride, groom, and two witnesses **свидéтели**. The bride is probably wearing a white dress if she has not previously been married (or a pastel will do), and a headdress **фатá** that often includes a veil and flowers. The groom wears a dark suit. They first go to a waiting room **зал ожидáния** to make sure that all is in order, and finally the music **свáдебный марш** starts (Mendelssohn is likely but not obligatory). The wedding party enters the wedding hall where the marriage ceremony will be performed by one to three officials from the registry office. Throughout the Russian Federation the substance of the ceremony has these basic elements: (1) a few words to the young people on the significance of the creation of a new family; (2) their mutual affirmation of their desire to enter into marriage; (3) the affixing of signatures; and (4) congratulations offered by the administrator. The latter then gives out the rings for each, which are worn on the right hand; they

are pronounced husband and wife (**объявляю вас мýжем и женóй**); they kiss; photographs are taken; the wedding march is heard; and the party exits, perhaps to an adjacent rented room for champagne, chocolate, and flowers, or perhaps to lay flowers at the grave of the Unknown Soldier or to some other monument or site. (The latter new tradition is not observed among the intelligentsia.) The wedding ceremony itself lasts only a few minutes.

The evening is filled with a wedding meal **свáдебный ýжин, вéчер,** which starts out with a supper beginning with many appetizers and bottles of liquor or champagne and which ends in a noisy fog. Somebody's uncle is often the master of ceremonies **тамадá**, and it is he who starts the toasts and suggests that perhaps the wine or liquor is bitter: "It's bitter!" **Гóрько!** is shouted by everyone, until the bride and groom kiss, to sweeten things up. Though three days off of work are granted the newlyweds, Russians do not have our obligation to leave town at the end of the ceremony—the drinking party can last several days.

Russians do elope **тáйно венчáются**, but the Russian expression connotes only a secret marriage, with no flight necessary. The verb **венчáться** has at its root *crown* **венéц** because crowns are held over the heads of the bride and groom in the Russian Orthodox wedding service **венчáние**. The wedding ceremony at church is in fact quite similar to the christening ceremony. (Take any opportunity to attend a Russian Orthodox Church wedding ceremony—or funeral, for that matter. Wear comfortable shoes; nobody except the infirm is allowed to sit. Women wear skirts in church.)

Some wedding conventions from earlier days remain in the language and, sometimes, in *fact*, since they frequently fill a contemporary need. Marriage brokers **сват, свáха** were used to arrange a marriage **сватовствó**. Their job was to check out the families' requirements, including the size of a dowry **придáное**. When agreement **сгóвор** was reached, an engagement **помóлвка** was announced and formally confirmed in a church ceremony **обручéние**.

Венцы́—Венча́ние

Weddings call for parades

(Soviet authorities tried to introduce the engagement announcement **помо́лвка** at work places.) Before the formal church wedding the girls would have a party **деви́чник** where they would sing sad songs because the bride always left her home to join his. The bride would put on a married woman's headdress **ки́чка** and skirt **понёва** and would lose her braid. (Married women's hair could not appear in public.) On the wedding night **бра́чная ночь** the sheets were checked to assure that the bride had indeed been a virgin **де́вственница**. Many other ceremonies and job titles were associated with weddings, but they have been mostly lost to the common language.

The glue that holds a marriage **брак** together is no more sticky there than here—roughly one-half of those who marry later get a divorce **разво́д**. The wedding anniversary is known as **годовщи́на сва́дьбы,** and if the couple makes it through twenty-five years, they have a silver wedding **сере́бряная сва́дьба**; fifty years makes it a gold **золота́я сва́дьба.**

Funeral and burial
По́хороны

Умер наш дя́дя, хоро́ним мы его.
Он нам в насле́дство не оста́вил
**   ничего.**
А тётка хохота́ла, когда она узна́ла,
Что он нам в насле́дство не оста́вил
**   ничего!**

(This literary treasure has been sung by children to the tune of Chopin's *Funeral March*, but is not universal.)

Die in Russia. The Russian way of dealing with death is easier on your beloveds, who will have no chance to avoid or deny your demise (as is our custom), and they will have the help of friends arranged by ritual.

First, a doctor must certify the death **врач констати́рует смерть,** and the local registry office **загс** must be notified because one can't buy a coffin **гроб** without a death certificate **спра́вка о сме́рти**. If the death occurred at home, all the mirrors and the chandelier in the house of the deceased are covered. (The various explanations for this custom are nebulous, but center on the idea that the soul has not yet departed and something untoward might happen if it sees itself in the mirror.) All clocks in the house are stopped. Then the deceased **поко́йный, поко́йник** is washed (people can be hired to do this from the **похоро́нное бюро́** but often you do it yourself), then dressed in his or her best clothes and laid out on the dining room table—facing the door (to prevent easy return). Then the relatives come to say good-bye **попроща́ться**. This is a three-day period. If death occurs in a hospital, it will have facilities **поко́йницкая, морг** for storing the body and a room where relatives can come and say good-bye.

Some customs are probably pre-Christian: death is not a good thing so that the dead one's clothes are considered affected, if not infected, by the evil force **зла́я си́ла** and are thrown out. Old women often make their own burial costume **руба́ха без застёжек**. Considerable effort is made to assure that the departed will not return. To that end, one relative does not go to the church service on the third day but stays behind to turn on its side the table that held the body, and to sweep and wash the floors of all the evil forces' leavings. A glass of water is left in the window sill for nine days so the soul can wash itself. If church services are not required, then a civil ceremony **гражда́нская панихи́да** is held, or, for a big party boss of Revolutionary days, a **тра́урный митинг**.

For the religious, a memorial service **панихи́да** is held immediately while a funeral **отпева́ние** and burial service **по́хороны** take place on the third day after death. A procession **ше́ствие** from the house to the church **вы́нос** has first a path of evergreen branches, then someone carrying a picture of the departed, then the coffin lid and finally the coffin itself. The departed **усо́пший, поко́йник, у́мерший** lies in the casket **гроб**, often with a handkerchief and perhaps a candle in hand and the words to a

Evergreen branches indicate
a recent funeral

prayer on a tape across the forehead. The religious service differs from the civil in that they usually also sing: **Аллилу́йя, 118ый Псало́м, Ве́чная па́мять.** After the ceremony, mourners file past the open casket while those nearest and dearest kiss the deceased goodbye. Then the body is carried out, again feet first.

Most people prefer burial **погребе́ние** to cremation **крема́ция** because belief in an after-life is common, especially among the religious **ве́рующие.** A century ago, the peasants buried their dead with vodka, salt, tobacco, and so on to make postmortem life easier. Relatives arrange for a grave **моги́ла,** a tombstone **па́мятник,**

Бог дал, Бог и взял.
God giveth, and God taketh away.

На кла́дбище в дере́вне.

and a payment for care. The problem is that room for burial is, in cities, inadequate, and cremation is often the final answer.

The funeral procession **шéствие** traditionally includes an open coffin **гроб** (no matter what Jessica Mitford thinks); spruce branches or wreaths **венки́** decorate the coffin. In cities in winter the coffin is in the center of a bus and the mourners sit around the edges. At the cemetery **кла́дбище** a band plays, when possible. At the grave, depending on circumstances, more words are spoken by a priest, a rabbi, a co-worker, a friend, or a relative, and that is the end of that. Contemporaries might say: Rest in peace **Мир пра́ху**, while the older church expression is Kingdom of Heaven **Ца́рство ему́ небéсное**. After the casket has been lowered into the ground, the person closest to the deceased throws a handful of dirt on the coffin and the rest of the mourners follow suit.

But we're not done yet. The last part of the funeral ritual is, in fact, a party **поми́нки** where friends and relatives gather at a dinner at the departed one's house, and everyone recalls **помина́ть** the good things about the deceased. The menu for this meal seems to vary somewhat, some insisting on "kisel," a sweet pie, or blini, others on buckwheat kasha, but everyone agrees that one must have kutya **кутья́**, which is whole-grain wheat (or rice) cooked with some honey. Some people set a place at the table for the dead one; sometimes a glass of vodka and a slice of bread for the deceased will be kept until the ninth day after death. Glasses are never clinked at this party, and no toasts are offered

---

Двум смертя́м не быва́ть, а одно́й не минова́ть.
You can only die once. (Two deaths don't occur, but you can't escape one.)

Все там бу́дем.
We'll all be there someday.

---

and no one is thanked. A memorial service **панихи́да** and a similar party **поми́нки** are also held on the ninth and on the fortieth days after death **сорочи́ны** or **сóрок дней** ("Сегóдня мы собира́емся на сóрок дней"), when it is thought that the soul ascends to heaven. Subsequently the death is subject to an annual remembrance **годовщи́на** both at church and at home.

The condolence
Соболéзнование

Я вам соболéзную.   I'm so sorry.

Я приношу́ вам свои́ соболéзнования. I'm so very sorry.

Прими́те моё глубóкое и́скреннее соболéзнование.   Please accept my deepest sympathy. (Formal, written.)

Разреши́те вы́разить вам моё и́скреннее соболéзнование.   Allow me to express my deepest sympathy. (Formal.)

Celebrations
Пра́зднования

Parties
Вечера́, Вечери́нки

The standard party **вéчер** is an evening around a table to eat a supper **у́жин** that differs from a regular supper in that the appetizers **заку́ски** are numerous—as is the quantity and variety of bottles. Guests will spend the evening **вéчер** in an atmosphere of naturalness and spontaneity **непринуждённость** that allows songs to be sung, jokes to be told, poetry to be recited, and so forth; **тусóвка** (from **тусова́ть**, to shuffle) is common youth slang for any get-together. (Also see the section on drinking.)

The Birthday
День рождéния

The usual Russian birthday party has the impressive advantage of being the obligation

С днём рожде́ния!
Happy Birthday!

of the celebrant: You give your own party—
no surprises—and it will be a dinner party
including champagne **шампа́нское** when
possible. The birthday "cake" will be a
dessert pie **пиро́г** or torte **торт**, often with
birthday wishes or the honored one's name on
it. Candles **све́чки** are sometimes used, but
they seem not so obligatory as are ours.
Birthday cards are mailed if attendance is not
possible, but they are not integral to the event
itself. Guests do bring gifts **пода́рки**, however,
from flowers and drink, on up.

Within the family, birthdays are celebrated
each year—somehow—as are all children's
birthdays. A more lavish celebration (with
company, that is) is more likely for adults on
particular birthdays, especially multiples of ten
and the fifty-fifth and sixtieth birthdays, which
might correspond to retirement **ухо́д на
пе́нсию**.

These anniversary birthdays **юбиле́йные
да́ты** are especially important for the bosses at
work, where there will be some sort of cake, a
communal gift **пода́рок**, flowers, everybody's
signature on a congratulatory letter **по-
здрави́тельный а́дрес**, and finally, a congratulatory speech from a co-worker.

The Graduation
Выпускно́й ве́чер

Upon exit from school the members of the
graduating class **выпускники́** and their parents
attend a program at school where the graduates
are given their diplomas **вруча́ют аттеста́ты
зре́лости**. Particular emphasis is placed on
those who did especially well: those who
received all A's are awarded a gold medal, and
those with all A's but two get a silver medal
(providing, of course, that their conduct was
exemplary). Afterwards, the parents go home,
and the young ones remain for a party (food and

dance) that has been set up for them by their
parents and teachers. Thereafter, in the wee
hours of the night they used to roam the streets
(of the large cities) singing, but now roaming
the streets is not recommended. (This is a senti-
mental time: the students have gone through
most of their school lives together, and the
bonds are strong.)

A school reunion **вечер встре́чи
выпускнико́в** is a popular event that often
includes a dance; all former pupils are invited,
sometimes over the radio. University reunions
are often held on Tatiana's day on 25 January.
(She is the matron saint of students.)

The Housewarming
Новосе́лье

To celebrate moving into a new apartment, the
housewarming **новосе́лье** is again the charge
of those doing the moving. Guests bring a gift,
but it need not be house-related. The event is
treated merely as a cause for celebration, rather
than as a particular ceremony (like that
observed by the peasants when they moved into
a new log house **изба́**). (On the other hand, if
you have a cat, it enters the house first—the
first one to enter the house is the first to die.)

TRANSLATIONS

a. For several decades, people were kept like
unthinking cattle. I remember how, when I was
still quite young, the first time they turned me
into a domestic animal. My timid explanation,
"I thought. . ." was turned into "the boss thinks
for you, (you have to) live like everyone else."
Моско́вские но́вости, 14 февраля́ 1993

b. It bothered many critics that Zamyatin was
an artist completely devoid of any superfluity,
stingily measuring out his lyrical comments,
somehow un-Russian in his restraint, and neat,
with all his buttons buttoned.
Mark Slonim, *The Writer and His Creation.*

A NOTE ON RUSSIAN CHEATING

On p. 7, I use only a single sentence to characterize the Russian tendency to go around rules. Robert Hunter is more thorough; in an email message to me he wrote:

From:	Robert Hunter (rhunter@eckert.acadcomp.monroecc.edu)
Date:	Tue, 7 May 1996 10:53:54 EDT
Subject:	What to do about plagiarism by emigres
To:	Multiple recipients of list SEELANGS

After retiring from public school teaching in the US I taught in Russia for a year and then established a year-long high school program for students from the cities of Novgorod, Borovichi, and Staraya Russa to come to upstate New York. While teaching in Novgorod (high school and university), I was appalled at the extent of all kinds of cheating. Openly sharing answers, shpargalki **шпаргáлки**, and plagiarism were the norm—except during the oral part of final examinations. To expect Russian students to come with an understanding and willingness to abide by the American norms regarding academic honesty is, I believe, naive. One of the major issues covered in the orientation of the Russian students coming to the US to study is the very different approach to and standards regarding cheating/plagiarism. Going over the meaning and implications of cheating/plagiarism at the beginning of the semester is, I contend, insufficient. I believe the Russian students should be given a chance , i.e., when caught cheating/plagiarizing, repeating the explanation, and permitting the student to redo the work according to US academic standards.

In explaining the meaning and implication of cheating/plagiarism in US academic institutions, I believe it is important to emphasize how this fits into the larger cultural picture. This is important because the Russian understanding of and respect for rules and law is different from the American. In Russia, rules and laws and impediments meant to be circumvented one way or another. Here is a recent example. A Russian businessman was learning about Rotary. At a Rotary meeting in the US, he said that he had only one question regarding the possibility of organizing a club in Russia—how important was adherence to rules? He then commented that, for cultural reasons, it would be very difficult for future Russian Rotarians not to attempt to circumvent the rules.

I believe we owe Russian students, be they exchange or emigre, care and consideration in learning our culture. After having been given fair explanation and warning, rigid adherence to standards should be the norm.

Part II

*The Russian:
Aspects of the Individual*

2

The Human Being

Челове́к

This chapter deals mostly with nomenclature: names for parts of the body, what people carry with them, and some terminology for their relations. One's essence is not to be found in the names one gives to one's parts, but language students can find some small amusement in discovering that, although Russians do not commonly identify some anatomical features that we do—for example, knuckles or cuticles—but they do distinguish, for instance, two shades of blue eyes. Perhaps, however, the significance of terminology is greater when it relates to members of the family: four different words distinguish mothers- and fathers-in-law, for instance. The ways in which both medals and identification cards are used can also say something about a people. These subjects are included here:

Anatomy
Hair, eye, and skin color
Personal cleanliness
Cosmetics
Jewelry
Medals
With them, they carry . . .
Identification cards
Age
The man and his family

ANATOMY
Анато́мия

It is sometimes difficult to make an exact translation from English to Russian in dealing with parts of the anatomy. English, for example, separates parts that Russian does not, as in arm/hand рука́ (*pl.* ру́ки), leg/foot нога́ (*pl.* но́ги), finger/toe па́лец (*pl.* па́льцы), and chest/ breast грудь. There are words to specify a hand (кисть) and foot (ступня́) when it is vital to make the distinction: «У меня́ боли́т ступня́» is "My foot hurts." But context is most often relied upon to supply that distinction: «У неё дли́нные но́ги» is "She has long legs," while «У неё больша́я нога́» is "She has big feet." Many of the words for parts of the body involve accent shifts in the plural or oblique cases. In all the drawings of parts of the body that follow, the key near the drawing gives the English translation and then the nominative plural form if there is any change in the stress or the stem or if the plural is not formed by merely adding ы or и to the stem.

Дай ему́ па́лец, он и всю ру́ку отку́сит.
Give him an inch and he'll take a mile.

Sometimes it is easier to recognize or remember terminology when we can see where it came from: freckles весну́шки derive from spring весна́, which is the time they are expected to appear; подборо́док is the place under one's beard борода́, namely, chin. The words cited here are the standard ones. In everyday speech Russians tend to use more slang words, and even the relatively casual student of Russian can expect to hear them. Often such words are the ones that properly apply to animals. Very common is мо́рда for mug, but literally, an animal's face (намо́рдник, 'muzzle'); физиомо́рдия is a comical rendition of физионо́мия + мо́рда. Snout ры́ло is an abusive term for face (from "to root around" рыть, as does a pig). Animal paws or feet are ла́пы: "Get your paws off me!" «Убери́ свои́ ла́пы!» Брю́хо is, properly, an animal's stomach or underside, but it also can be "belly," especially a large one, in referring to humans.

Сы́тое брю́хо к уче́нию глу́хо.
A full stomach is not open to learning.

Babies' parts are almost always in the diminutive form: нос-но́сик, те́ло-те́льце, лицо́-ли́чико, рука́-ру́чка, нога́-но́жка, голова́-голо́вка, глаза́-гла́зки, рот-ро́тик, мо́рда-морда́шка, and so on, ad infinitum.

The body
Те́ло

A third-grade reader that describes and identifies many of the parts of the body included here introduces the subject this way:

Ка́ждый челове́к до́лжен обяза́тельно знать строе́ние своего́ те́ла. В те́ле различа́ют го́лову, ше́ю, ту́ловище и две па́ры коне́чностей: ве́рхние коне́чности, и́ли ру́ки, и ни́жние коне́чности, и́ли но́ги.[1]

The head, face, and neck
Голова́, лицо́ и ше́я

    (1) crown (*no pl.; gen.* те́мени)
    (2) hair (оди́н во́лос one hair)
    (3) forehead (*pl.* лбы)
    (4) temple (*pl.* виски́)
    (5) cheekbone (*pl.* ску́лы)

---

1. Е. Е. Соловьёва и др. Родна́я речь III (Москва́, Учпедгиз, 1964), стр. 249. Родна́я речь is a graded series of readers used in schools where Russian is a native language.

(6) (outer) ear
(7) ear (*pl.* **у́ши**)
(8) earlobe
(9) cheek (*pl.* **щёки**)
(10) bridge of nose
(11) nose (*pl.* **носы́**)
(12) nostril (*pl.* **но́здри**)
(13) jaw
(14) lip (*pl.* **гу́бы**)
(15) chin (*pl.* **подборо́дки**)
(16) neck
(17) Adam's apple (*pl.* **кадыки́**; formal **Ада́мово я́блоко**)

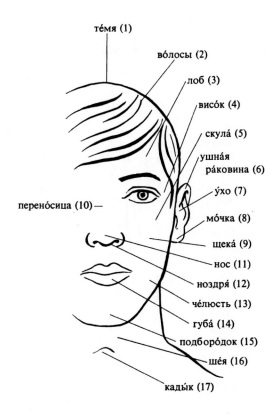

тёмя (1)
во́лосы (2)
лоб (3)
висо́к (4)
скула́ (5)
ушна́я ра́ковина (6)
у́хо (7)
перено́сица (10) —
мо́чка (8)
щека́ (9)
нос (11)
ноздря́ (12)
че́люсть (13)
губа́ (14)
подборо́док (15)
ше́я (16)
кады́к (17)

Also:

заты́лок   back of the head (*pl.* **заты́лки**)
бараба́нная перепо́нка   eardrum
морщи́на   wrinkle

я́мочка   dimple
двойно́й подборо́док   double chin
весну́шка   freckle
пе́рхоть   (*f., no pl.*) dandruff

Вы́ше головы́ не пры́гнешь.
You can't jump higher than your head.

The eye
Глаз

The eyes **глаза́** have many features that are commonly distinguished (the most common form cited first):

бро́ви   eyebrows (*sg.* **бровь**)
ве́ки   eyelids (*sg.* **ве́ко**)
ресни́цы   eyelashes (*sg.* **ресни́ца**)
белки́   whites of the eyes (*sg.* **бело́к**; *formal* **белко́вая оболо́чка**)
ра́дужная оболо́чка   iris (*informal* **ра́дужка**)
зрачки́   pupils (*sg.* **зрачо́к**)
глазно́е я́блоко   eyeball
рогови́ца   cornea (*formal* **рогова́я оболо́чка**)
хруста́лик   lens (**ли́нза** contact lens. **Она́ но́сит ли́нзы.**)
сетча́тка   retina (*formal* **се́тчатая оболо́чка**)
зри́тельный нерв   optic nerve

С глаз доло́й—из се́рдца вон.
Out of sight, out of mind.

Око за о́ко, зуб за зуб.
An eye for an eye; a tooth for a tooth. (**Око**, *pl.* **о́чи**, is an old, and now poetic, word for eye.)

The mouth
Рот (*pl.* рты)

(1) lip (*pl.* гу́бы)
(2) gum (*pl.* дёсны)
(3) palate
(4) uvula
(5) throat, pharynx (зева́ть to yawn)
(6) tonsil (*formal* минда́лина)
(7) teeth
(8) wisdom tooth
(9) molar
(10) canine tooth (*pl.* клыки́)
(11) incisor (*pl.* резцы́)
(12) tongue (*pl.* языки́)

The trunk
Ту́ловище

(1) shoulder (*pl.* пле́чи)
(2) armpit, general underarm area
(3) breast/chest (*f.*)
(4) nipple (*pl.* соски́)
(5) stomach (*pl.* животы́)
(6) waist/belt (*pl.* пояса́)
(7) waist
(8) navel (*pl.* пупки́; пупови́на is umbilical cord)
(9) groin
(10) back (*pl.* спи́ны)
(11) side (*pl.* бока́)
(12) hip (*pl.* бёдра)
(13) small of the back
(14) buttock (*informal,* "bottom" is по́пка)

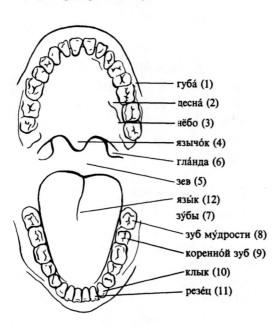

губа́ (1)
цесна́ (2)
нёбо (3)
язычо́к (4)
гла́нда (6)
зев (5)
язы́к (12)
зу́бы (7)
зуб му́дрости (8)
коренно́й зуб (9)
клык (10)
резе́ц (11)

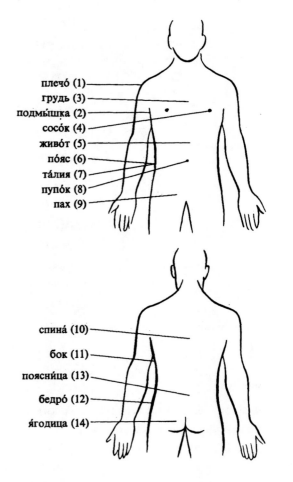

плечо́ (1)
грудь (3)
подмы́шка (2)
сосо́к (4)
живо́т (5)
по́яс (6)
та́лия (7)
пупо́к (8)
пах (9)

спина́ (10)
бок (11)
поясни́ца (13)
бедро́ (12)
я́годица (14)

Also:

слю́нные же́лезы   salivary glands
моло́чные зу́бы   baby teeth (*formal*) **зубо́к,
   зу́бик**   baby tooth (*pl.* **зу́бки**)
вставны́е зу́бы   false teeth
вставны́е че́люсти   dentures
мост   bridge
коро́нка   crown

The arm and hand
Рука́ (*pl.* ру́ки)

(1) elbow (*pl.* ло́кти)
(2) wrist (*pl.* запя́стье)
(3) hand (*specific*)
(4) thumb (*pl.* больши́е па́льцы)
(5) index finger
(6) middle finger
(7) ring finger
(8) little finger (*pl.* мизи́нцы)

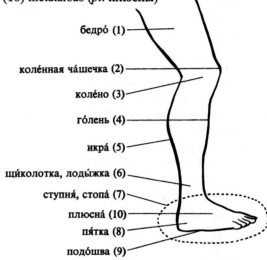

ло́коть (1)
запя́стье (2)
кисть (3)
большо́й па́лец (4)
указа́тельный па́лец (5)
сре́дний па́лец (6)
безымя́нный па́лец (7)
мизи́нец (8)

Also:

кула́к fist (*pl.* кулаки́)
ладо́нь palm

The finger and toe
Па́лец

The fingers or toes **па́льцы** seem to have fewer features distinguished than the English counterparts: fingernail **но́готь** (*pl.* но́гти) and moon **лу́нка** are distinguished. The cuticle does not have its own word in Russian but **ко́жица** (usually, thin skin, peel, or husk) can be used.

поду́шечка па́льца ball of the finger
заусе́ница, заусе́нец hangnail
отпеча́тки па́льцев fingerprints

The leg and foot
Нога́ (*pl.* но́ги)

(1) thigh (*pl.* бёдра)
(2) kneecap
(3) knee (*pl.* коле́ни)
(4) shin
(5) calf (*pl.* и́кры)
(6) ankle
(7) foot (specific, *pl.* ступни́)
(8) heel
(9) sole
(10) metatarsus (*pl.* плю́сны)

бедро́ (1)
коле́нная ча́шечка (2)
коле́но (3)
го́лень (4)
икра́ (5)
щи́колотка, лоды́жка (6)
ступня́, стопа́ (7)
плюсна́ (10)
пя́тка (8)
подо́шва (9)

Also:

подъём instep
большо́й па́лец (ноги́) big toe
ма́ленький па́лец (ноги́) little toe

The skin (and leather)
Ко́жа

Когда́ челове́ку жа́рко, то ко́жа покрыва́ется ма́ленькими ка́пельками по́та. Выделе́ние по́та име́ет для нас о́чень большо́е значе́ние. С по́том удаля́ются из те́ла вре́дные для нас вещества́. Пот выделя́ется из ко́жи че́рез ма́ленькие отве́рстия—по́ры. В жару́ пот испаря́ется и при э́том охлажда́ет ко́жу.[a]

The skeleton
Скелéт

(1) skull (*pl.* **черепá**)
(2) cheekbone (*pl.* **скýлы**)
(3) jawbone
(4) shoulder blade
(5) rib (*pl.* **рёбра; грудна́я кле́тка** for "rib cage")
(6) spine
(7) vertebra (*pl.* **позвонки́**)
(8) tail bone or coccyx
(9) pelvis
(10) clavicle
(11) breastbone or sternum
(12) upper arm bone
(13) lower arm bones (ulna and radius)
(14) wrist bone (*pl.* **запя́стья**)
(15) finger bones
(16) thighbone or femur (*pl.* **бёдра**)
(17) kneecap
(18) tibia (shinbone) and fibula
(19) toe bones

Also:

суста́в   joint
хрящ   cartilage and gristle
фала́нга   finger bone

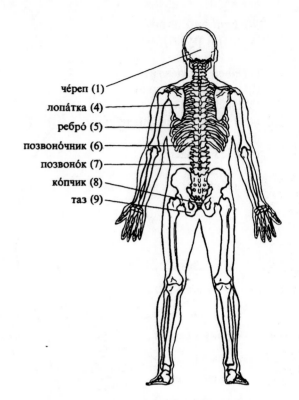

The respiratory organs
Óрганы дыха́ния

Following the air **во́здух** from the nose downward:

носогло́тка   nasal passage
гло́тка   pharynx (**глота́ть**, to swallow)
го́рло   throat
горта́нь   larynx
голосовы́е свя́зки   vocal chords
дыха́тельное го́рло   windpipe (*formal* **трахе́я**)
бро́нхи   bronchial tubes
лёгкие   lungs (*sg.* **лёгкое**)

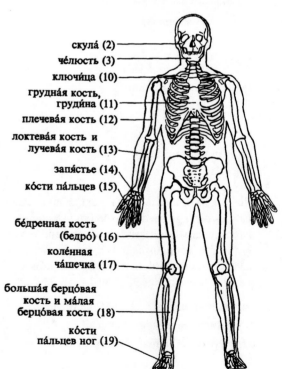

че́реп (1)
лопа́тка (4)
ребро́ (5)
позвоно́чник (6)
позвоно́к (7)
ко́пчик (8)
таз (9)

скула́ (2)
че́люсть (3)
ключи́ца (10)
грудна́я кость, груди́на (11)
плечева́я кость (12)
локтева́я кость и лучева́я кость (13)
запя́стье (14)
ко́сти па́льцев (15)
бе́дренная кость (бедро́) (16)
коле́нная ча́шечка (17)
больша́я берцо́вая кость и ма́лая берцо́вая кость (18)
ко́сти па́льцев ног (19)

Мы ды́шим во́здухом. Дыши́те и наблюда́йте за собо́й. То мы вдыха́ем во́здух (вдох), то выдыха́ем его (вы́дох).[b]

The digestive system
Пищевари́тельная систе́ма

(1) mouth (*pl.* **рты**)
(2) throat
(3) pharynx
(4) esophagus
(5) stomach (*pl.* **желу́дки**)
(6) liver
(7) gall bladder (*pl.* **жёлчные пузыри́**)
(8) pancreas (*pl.* **поджелу́дочные же́лезы**)
(9) small intestine
(10) large intestine
(11) caecum (a distinction not commonly made in English)
(12) appendix (*formal* **червеобра́зный отро́сток**)
(13) rectum
(14) anus

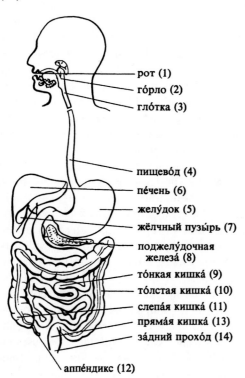

рот (1)
го́рло (2)
гло́тка (3)
пищево́д (4)
пе́чень (6)
желу́док (5)
жёлчный пузы́рь (7)
поджелу́дочная железа́ (8)
то́нкая кишка́ (9)
то́лстая кишка́ (10)
слепа́я кишка́ (11)
пряма́я кишка́ (13)
за́дний прохо́д (14)
аппе́ндикс (12)

Also:

пищевари́тельный кана́л   digestive tract
кише́чник   bowels, intestines
испражне́ния   feces (polite)
кал   feces (medical)

The brain and spinal cord
Мозг

One's gray matter **се́рое вещество́** is divided into the head part **головно́й мозг** and the spinal cord **спинно́й мозг**. Its plural, **мозги́**, is what you would like to have lots of. **У неё таки́е мозги́!** (She's really smart!) Other neurological terms include the nerve **нерв**, nervous system **не́рвная систе́ма**, and solar plexus **со́лнечное сплете́ние**, from **со́лнце** for *sun* and **сплести́** to *braid* or *plait*.

The urinary and reproductive organs
Мочевы́е и половы́е о́рганы

Some of these organs are shared by males and females, such as the kidney **по́чка**, ureter **мочето́чник**, bladder **мочево́й пузы́рь**, and urethra **мочеиспуска́тельный кана́л**.

Others are not. Male organs include the prostate gland **предста́тельная железа́**, penis **мужско́й половой член**, and testicle **яи́чко** (*pl.* **яи́чки**). Female reproductive organs are the ovary **яи́чник**, which produces an ovum **яйцо́**; fallopian tube **труба́ яи́чника**; womb **ма́тка**; and vagina **влага́лище**. Urine **моча́**, semen **се́мя**, and babies are the products.

The blood
Кровь

The Russian circulatory system **кровено́сная систе́ма** involves many words that are easily recognizable: **ао́рта**, **ве́на**, **арте́рия**, **капилля́ры**. Heart **се́рдце** and spleen **селезёнка** are harder to recognize as cognates, which they are. However, the jugular vein as a traditional object of savage attack has an interesting counterpart in **со́нная арте́рия**, the "sleep" artery (English, *carotid*). Pressure on this artery (which is right next to the jugular, by the way) is supposed to put one to sleep according to Russian popular science. (Don't try it; the sleep might be longer than you want: cardiac arrest.)

The muscles
Му́скулы или мы́шцы

Both words in the Russian heading above derive from the same root, *mouse*, as does the English word *muscle*.

Вы зна́ете, что снару́жи всё те́ло покры́то ко́жей. Прощу́пайте у себя́ ру́ки и но́ги. Под ко́жей вы нащу́паете что́-то мя́гкое. Это му́скулы. На конца́х му́скулов сухожи́лия.[c]

HAIR, EYE, AND SKIN COLOR
Цвет воло́с, глаз и ко́жи

The Russian terms one uses to describe the coloring of people can be confusing for English speakers. For hair color, black hair can be either **У него́ чёрные во́лосы** or **Он брюне́т** (although our word *brunet* refers to brown or dark brown hair). Brown hair is commonly either **кашта́новые во́лосы** (*chestnut*, **кашта́н**) or **шате́н**. **Она́ шате́нка** is a somewhat high-flown French and foreign term. In fact, all these words of French origin—**брюне́т, шате́н, блонди́н**—are somewhat citified, so that for brown hair, **тёмные во́лосы** is perhaps even more common. Red hair—**Она́ ры́жая. У неё ры́жие во́лосы**—is less common than in America, yet its rarity does not make it a treasure. Red hair is a liability for children, who are teased with, **Ры́жий, кра́сный, челове́к опа́сный** (опа́сный *dangerous*). **Что, я ры́жий?** means, "Why are you leaving me out? Why shouldn't I be included?" The term for light brown hair, **ру́сые во́лосы,** covers a rather wide

range from dark blond to light brown, including our "dishwater blond," both common and nondescript (from our point of view), but by no means undesirable to the Russians. Blond hair can be described in several ways: **Он блонди́н. У него́ светло-ру́сые во́лосы** is standard nomenclature for blond hair, as is **све́тлые во́лосы**. **Белоку́рые во́лосы** is a light blond, and the term is complimentary, while **белобры́сый** is a very light blond and uncomplimentary, often applied to small boys and similar pests. **Льняны́е во́лосы** (**лён** *cf. linen*) is "flaxen" hair, but the term is not quite so poetic and unusual in a land of flax. Gray and white hair are both **седы́е во́лосы**. When hair is turning from its usual color to gray or white, one can add **с седино́й** or **с про́седью** (**чёрные с седино́й, ру́сые с про́седью**).

Eyes, too, have a set of colors different from ours. Hazel eyes have no description, but Russians distinguish among brown eyes and blue eyes in ways we do not. The song title «**Очи чёрные**» means "black eyes," eyes so dark that one cannot distinguish the iris from the pupil. (**Око, о́чи** is a very old and now poetic word for *eye*. One now says, **У него́ чёрные глаза́**.) The more usual brown eyes are **ка́рие глаза́**. Blue eyes come in two shades: the common light blue eyes are **голубы́е глаза́**; much less common and held in very high regard are **си́ние глаза́**, eyes that are darker blue. Eyes can also be gray **се́рые глаза́** or green **зелёные глаза́**.

Facial complexion **цвет лица́** is thought to be at its best when it is light-colored (**У неё хоро́ший цвет лица́**) and pink-cheeked **с румя́нцем**. A dark complexion is **сму́глый цвет лица́**. Light skin color can also be **белоко́жий** or **светлоко́жий**, and dark skin is **тёмная ко́жа**. **Он бле́дный** means "He is pale."

The formal major racial distinctions are **европео́ид, монголо́ид, негро́ид**. Normal speech naturally uses other words. To distinguish a white person from others, one uses **он бе́лый**. A black can be **он негр** (**она́ негритя́нка**). The use of the Russian word for black **он чёрный** indicates a Caucasian—which it is better not to be these days. (Georgians and Azeris in particular are not thought to be totally straightforward in their business dealings.) Blacks (from Africa) are very commonly called **африка́нцы**. Because the racial minority is Oriental, it is they who have the largest number of somewhat derogatory words applied to them: **косогла́зый** (slant-eye); **азиа́т**, **жёлтый** (yellow); and others. If you see an Oriental and you wish to mention his or her race without being offensive, use **челове́к восто́чного ви́да/монго́льского ти́па**. American Indians are **он инде́ец, она индиа́нка**, and **они инде́йцы**. Our term "redskin" (which is both slang and derogatory) goes directly into Russian as **красноко́жий** and with the same connotation. For people from India, **он инди́ец, она индиа́нка**, and **они инди́йцы** are used. The words for a Hindu are **инду́с, инду́ска**, and **инду́сы**. (Be careful not to confuse either Western or Eastern Hemisphere Indians with **инде́йка** or **индю́шка**, a turkey!)

ASPECTS OF THE SELF
Ещё о себе́

Personal cleanliness
Ли́чная гигие́на

Personal dirt to Russians is a Bad Thing. The city-bred upper crust are close to fanatic about hand-washing after the bathroom or before meals. In the past, Russians did not sew themselves into their underwear as some early Americans are reputed to have done. Traditionally, bathing was accomplished once a week, typically on Saturday. But bodily cleanliness was one thing and keeping clothes and bedding clean was quite another. It was lack of laundering that accounted for the former prevalence of bedbugs, lice, and the like. The traditional avenue to cleanliness was the Russian sauna **ба́ня**.

Ба́ня в дере́вне. From the bathhouse into the river.

The traditional bathhouse
Традицио́нная ба́ня

The oldest and most common form of bathhouse **ба́ня** is a small, one-room log hut built some distance from the living quarters **изба́**, for fire protection, and close to a water supply. The major piece of equipment is a stove **пе́чькаменка** made principally of stones, in which the fire is built. A pile of stones is placed on top of this "stove," and once the stones are hot, some of them are used to heat water (for washing) in a trough. Then water is poured over the rest of the stones to produce the necessary steam. The traditional stove had no chimney **по-чёрному**; the stove opening was near the door, and the smoke went out the door. Naturally, one did not use the bathhouse until the fire had done its heating. The major furniture is a built-in bench **ла́вка** to sit on while washing and a shelf **поло́к** to sit or lie on while steaming: **Он сиде́л на полке́.**

The bathhouse in the country now has a chimney and the added convenience of a dressing room **предба́нник**. (But if you ever have the chance, take the offer of a bath **ба́ня** in the old-fashioned way **по-чёрному**. The smell of the smoke is marvelous.)

Bathing actually involves several processes, and getting clean is only one of the objects of the procedure. First one washes oneself for reasons of cleanliness, then one steams oneself for reasons of health. Steaming was and still is considered a major therapeutic device. (Steaming was so essential that the Russian stove was used as a steamer in those regions where fuel was at a premium or where it was too expensive to build a bathhouse separately.) In the course of steaming, the bathers thrash themselves or each other with a bundle of (usually birch) twigs **ве́ник** to bring the blood to the surface.

The use of a bathhouse seems to go back as far as Kievan Russia. Peasants too poor to build their own bathhouse either joined with others and built one or used the public bathhouse. One indicator of reasonable hospitality was an offer to heat the bathhouse for the traveler. No small amount of superstition was connected with the bathhouse. For one thing, it was supposed to be inhabited by an evil spirit **ба́нный, ба́нник** who would bewitch (or befoul) clothes if worn into the bathhouse. At one time, the reason for dousing oneself was to be cleansed of the evil that the **ба́нный** had somehow loosed. In some places, one could not go to church on the same day that the bathing occurred, for the same reason.

The contemporary bathhouse
Совреме́нная ба́ня

Happily, the Russian bath **ба́ня** is still in operation, somewhat modified in normal use but still preserving the elements basic to its original form.

Private bathhouses are now rather a privilege of those who live outside the big cities; the common bath is a public bath **обще́ственная ба́ня**. But do not confuse this bath **ба́ня** with the bathtub **ва́нна** found in a regular bathroom **ва́нная**. Before setting out for the bath, take your soap **мы́ло**, a towel **полоте́нце**, and the equivalent (in use) of a washrag **моча́лка**, which originally consisted of strands of linden fiber **моча́ло** that softened when wet; now **моча́лка** can also be a kind of sponge **гу́бка**. It is usually possible to rent or buy this equipment at the **ба́ня** itself, though most people bring their own.

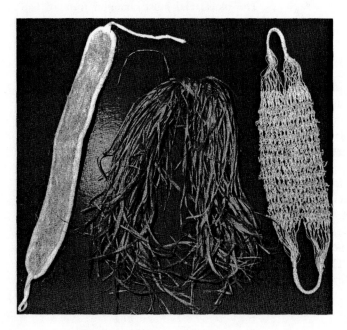

Моча́ло (в середи́не) и две моча́лки.
Washrags on bath day.

Upon entering, first check your coat, then proceed to the cashier's window **ка́сса** and pay for the services or facilities you will be using; you might want a pedicure, a hairdo, a massage, or a private bathroom **но́мер** in addition to—or instead of—the use of the public bath. The **ба́ня** itself has two separate divisions, **о́бщее мужско́е отделе́ние** and **общее же́нское отделе́ние**, both of which consist of three basic sections: (1) the dressing room **раздева́лка** where the woman in charge is a **ба́нщица** with whom you may leave your valuables (*m.* **ба́нщик**); (2) the main washing room **мы́льня, мы́льная** filled with rows of benches **скаме́йки**, on which there will be washtubs **тазы́** equipped with faucets **кра́ны** along one wall and a shower **душ** along another; and (3) a steam room, **пари́льня** when written on the door but **пари́лка** in normal speech. The steam room **пари́лка** has a large furnace stove for producing heat and steam, the latter obtained when bathers who desire it throw water on the heated stones in the stove. The steam room also has wooden benches or steps (**поло́к**, *sg.*) that you can mount. The higher you go, the hotter it becomes. In the steam room, Russians often use a bundle of birch twigs **ве́ник** to thrash one another. When you think you have cooked enough, proceed to the washroom. Fill a tub **таз** with water and start washing, head first, and with many changes of water. Do not hurry or your "Americanness" will show; this is a peaceful, relaxing time. Use the shower **душ** to rinse off and return to the dressing room (**раздева́льня**, formal, or **раздева́лка**, colloquial). On your way out you can relieve the enervated feeling by a drink at the buffet that usually accompanies a bathhouse. On your return home, your Russian friends will say, «**С лёгким па́ром!**» a wish of good health bestowed upon those who have just bathed or steamed in a **ба́ня**.

The public bath described here is currently used by two large groups of people: those who simply like the steam bath and those whose housing does not include a bathroom. Each group includes enough people to keep a large number of bathhouses operating even in major cities. Younger and less sophisticated Russians look upon the **ба́ня** as old-fashioned and even backward; it is your job to disabuse them.

Cosmetics
Косме́тика

In the major cities, at least, it is both chic and acceptable to use makeup **макия́ж** and, most noticeably, to dye or bleach hair: «**Она́ кра́сит во́лосы**»—"She dyes her hair." Auburn hair (within the range **кашта́новые во́лосы**) is currently very popular. Assorted coloring agents (lipstick, mascara) make good gifts.

Various creams **кре́мы** are often required in makeup **макия́ж** and skin care **ухо́д за ко́жей**. These are just a few:

крем под пу́дру   foundation cream
защи́тный крем   protective skin cream
пита́тельный крем   moisturizer
крем от зага́ра   suntan lotion
крем от весну́шек   freckle remover
крем для рук   hand lotion

Other basic equipment that might go in one's cosmetic case **космети́чка** includes:

каранда́ш для брове́й   eyebrow pencil
тушь *f.* mascara
щётка для ресни́ц, щёточка   eyelash brush
тень *f.* eye shadow
пу́дра   powder
пу́дреница   compact
пухо́вка   powder puff
губна́я пома́да   lipstick
румя́на   rouge
лосьо́н   makeup remover
туале́тная вода   toilet water
духи́   perfume
лак   fingernail polish
ацето́н/раствори́тель   fingernail polish remover
пи́лка   fingernail file

щи́пчики/пинце́т tweezers

фен fan for drying hair

Men require less:

крем для бритья́ shaving cream

пе́на для бритья́ shaving foam

бри́тва razor

ле́звие razor blade

одеколо́н, лосьо́н shaving lotion

Americans tend to shave and pluck with considerable fervor, taking second place only to the French, who seem willing to do anything for beauty's sake. Russian women do not consider all that plucking necessary. (Leg shaving is almost totally American.) And, although being overweight is not a national ideal (the young especially try to avoid the problem), throughout the population is a very strong feeling that someone who is thin is also therefore sickly. **Она попра́вилась у нас!** means "She put on weight (literally, got well) while she was here!" **Он похуде́л** means "He lost weight" (literally, *got worse!*).

Jewelry
Ювели́рные изде́лия

Russians are much freer about using jewelry these days; in cities they usually wear at least one of the following: a brooch **брошь, бро́шка**; a bracelet **браслет**; a necklace **ожере́лье**; a chain **цепо́чка**; or beads **бу́сы** (*sg.* **бу́синка**). (**Колье́** is a fancy necklace, especially one made of precious stones.) Generally, the Russian precious stones **драгоце́нные ка́мни** are our precious stones: diamond **бриллиа́нт**, pearls **же́мчуг** (*sg.* **жемчу́жина**), ruby **руби́н**, emerald **изумру́д**. However, a traditional and popular Russian ornament is cut and polished amber **янта́рь**, actually not a stone but a fossil resin, most of which comes from along the Baltic Sea coast. Green malachite **малахи́т** and lapis lazuli **ля́пис-лазу́рь** are also traditionally popular stones.

A note on rings: if the ring contains no major stone and is essentially a metal band, then the word is **кольцо́**. Technically speaking, if it has a stone, especially a prominent one, then it is a **пе́рстень**. (Therefore, our engagement rings are **пе́рстни**.) Russian wedding rings **обруча́льные ко́льца** are used by both men and women. They usually consist of a single gold band and are worn on the fourth finger of the right hand, not the left. (A widow wears her ring on the left hand.)

Earrings are among the most commonly seen jewelry. They come in two types: **се́рьги** (**одна́ серьга́**) are those earrings made for pierced ears; now, however, the other kind, for unpierced ears **кли́псы** (*sg.* **клипс**) are quite popular.

Medals
Ордена́, меда́ли

The distribution and wearing of medals is perhaps more Russian than Revolutionary: Chekhov's story **Анна на ше́е** refers, partly, to **Орден Свято́й Анны**. In Soviet times, both military and civilian medals were awarded: **Орден Ле́нина**, **Орден Кра́сной Звезды́**, **Орден Знак Почёта**, and many more. The original medal, **о́рден** (**меда́ль** is less prestigious), is usually not worn except for parades or similar occasions. Instead, one will often see the little colored bands, **ле́нты** or **ле́нточки**, in a jacket lapel or the like.

Not only people but entire factories and even cities and republics were awarded medals: **Москва́—го́род-геро́й**.

Almost everyone, but especially children, has a collection of **значки́** (*sg.* **значо́к**). These are small pins, sometimes merely decorative little enamels of animals, humans, or other designs. Most often they are commemorative of some person or event—political figures, perhaps, or the insignia of an art festival. Small school children **октября́та** used to wear one such pin with a picture of Lenin as a little boy with curls. These medals **значки́** are also a form of award; thus, a "Master of Sport," for instance, gets a значо́к Ма́стера Спо́рта. These pins are produced in such profusion and are sufficiently popular and inexpensive that they make a favorite item for souvenir collecting and exchanging both among Russians and tourists.

With them they carry . . .
При себе́ но́сят

A man's wallet бума́жник is the larger vest-pocket size and contains what you would expect. Coins моне́ты often go in pockets without benefit of a container. Other common necessities are, of course, a handkerchief носово́й плато́к, a comb расчёска, (a somewhat more common term than гребёнка or гре́бень), glasses очки́, a watch часы́, and a pen авторучка/ру́чка. Keys ключи́ are usually fewer and much larger than ours. Women's purses су́мки (*sg.* су́мка) carry those objects that men must plant on their person. Money is kept in a coin purse кошелёк. In addition to a comb, women usually carry a mirror зе́ркало, their lipstick губна́я пома́да, and powder пу́дра in a compact пу́дреница. In cities, almost all women and some men also used to carry a light net shopping bag (се́тка or аво́ська, from аво́сь, meaning "perhaps") so that they were ready "just in case" they came across something on their way around town that was worth buying. Now they carry a plastic bag just in case they can afford what is for sale. (A bag on wheels су́мка на колёсах is currently widely used.)

Identification cards
Докуме́нты

As in English, when someone asks "Who's that?" the answer will be either a name (Ива́н Ивано́в), a job title (дире́ктор шко́лы), or any outstanding relationship requiring description

(жена́ нача́льника, *the boss's wife*). But sometimes official documentation of identity is required; we need driver's licenses and credit cards—they need passports. (The loss of a passport used to be calamitous; it is now merely an awful pain in the neck.)

The passport па́спорт referred to here is also called the internal passport вну́тренний па́спорт, the one used within Russia. For foreign trips, the Russian must have an exterior passport заграни́чный па́спорт upon leaving the country.

The internal passport is issued to everyone sixteen or older living in cities. Young people in the country have theirs kept for them by the local rural authorities until they finish school. This document is a requirement for traveling anywhere within the country. In everyday use, the passport certifies identity for receiving money orders and parcels at the post office, withdrawing money from the bank under certain circumstances, registering at hotels or dormitories, getting a job, renting equipment, and so forth. The internal passport looks much like ours, except that it is red instead of blue. It includes more than the usual passport information and acts as a uniform general certifier: marital status семе́йное положе́ние includes wedding dates and names of spouses, names of children and their birth dates, dates of any divorces; there is a section on military obligation во́инская обя́занность (doctors and teachers, not just young men, can be called up for military service); and under the heading "residence" ме́сто жи́тельства, a permit прописка confirms legal residence in a particular place. The problematical part of the passport is question five: Национа́льность (Nationality), "Of what descent are you?" It requires the nationality эсто́нец, украи́нка, ру́сский, евре́й, таджи́к, и т.д. of both parents, and Russians must choose only one nationality to describe themselves if their parents are of different descent. This choice, once made, is not changeable, and it has been used against many groups as times and tides turn.

Perhaps the next most commonly held identifier is the trade-union card **профсою́зный биле́т, профбиле́т**, which verifies membership in the trade union attached to one's place of work. The trade-union card is no longer so necessary today, nor compulsory, but advantages sometimes accrue to those who belong.

Somewhere in the family archives is kept a birth certificate, colloquially called **ме́трика** and formally entitled **свиде́тельство о рожде́нии**. It is used as personal documentation up to age sixteen.

People in certain positions require special identification. Thus a student needs a dormitory pass **про́пуск в общежи́тие**, library pass **чита́тельский биле́т**, and so forth. Males subject to the draft must have their draft card **во́инский биле́т**. Many people carry a prepaid public transport pass **проездно́й биле́т** that allows them to use a bus, trolley, or subway without further payment. Travel is made cheaper this way and more convenient, reducing the need for a store of small change.

Job applications can be very revealing: even fictitious ones can be revelations. This one is from *Колле́ги* by Аксёнов.

Кто они́ таки́е?

В анке́тах они́ писа́ли: год рожде́ния—1932-й; происхожде́ние—из слу́жащих (Ка́рпов—из рабо́чих); парти́йность—член ВЛКСМ с 1947 го́да; уча́стие в во́йнах—не уча́ствовал; суди́мость—нет; име́ет ли ро́дственников за грани́цей—нет; и еще не́сколько «нет» до графы́ «семе́йное положе́ние» в кото́рой всё они́ писа́ли—хо́лост. Автобиогра́фии их умеща́лись на полови́не страни́чки, а расска́зывали они́ о себе́ так. . . .[d]

Age
Во́зраст

Age is mentioned here only because of distinctions commonly made in Russian that are not made in English. Technically speaking, our word *baby* should be **грудно́й ребёнок, малы́ш**, or **младе́нец** because **ребёнок** can be applied up to adolescence. A girl is **де́вочка** before puberty and **де́вушка** after puberty. As you can see, an obvious mistake in this distinction could be funny or insulting. If you wish to specify a girl at puberty, **де́вочка-подро́сток** is used. Older women **пожилы́е же́нщины** sometimes jokingly speak of each other as girls **де́вочки**, but even the aging saleswoman must be called **де́вушка** to get her attention because no better word is available. For getting the attention of young males use **молодо́й челове́к**. The word for a boy at puberty and beyond, **ю́ноша**, is more formal than **па́рень**, which is more common. A man's a man, before and after marriage, but a woman is a girl **де́вушка** before, and a woman **же́нщина** after. (**Стару́ха** and **стари́к** are so old that their age is insulting.)

Седина́ в бо́роду, бес в ребро́.
There's life in the old guy yet.

Со́рок лет—ба́бий век, сорок пять—ба́ба я́годка опя́ть.
There's life in the old girl yet.

These are by no means all the words that refer to people at different ages, but the others are diminutives, pejoratives, or words with much more specialized uses.

As you know, the grammatical plural of **ребёнок** is **ребя́та**, but **ребя́та** is more frequently used, meaning "the guys," "the gang," or "the kids." (And **девча́та** has been heard if they're a pack of little girls.) **Де́ти** is the plural of **ребёнок** in practice. Notice that no word exists for *child*, someone beyond the baby stage, except in the plural—**де́ти**; **детвора́** is a collective and colloquial singular for the small children.

RELATIVES
Ро́дственники

Family
Семья́

Two charts, "One man's family" and "One woman's family," give the many titles Russians

can use to identify those related by marriage. In the days of the extended family (in *War and Peace*, for example) the Russian used these many different words for a woman's relatives and for a man's relatives. Today's nuclear family tends not to make so many distinctions. Words in parentheses are no longer commonly used except among peasants, where the usage is not incorrect, merely old-fashioned. Though the

One man's family

(These are titles of those related to one man shown as ▼. X indicates marriage. Horizontal lines separate generations. Arrows indicate children from a marriage. Parentheses indicate outmoded usage.)

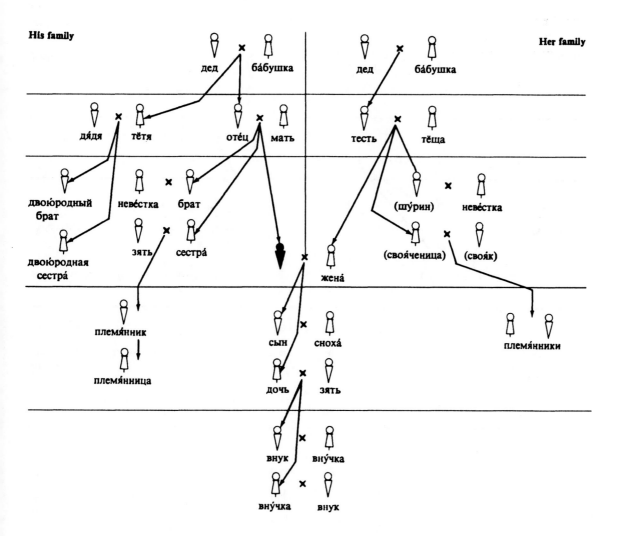

His family
Her family

дед   ба́бушка   дед   ба́бушка

дя́дя   тётя   оте́ц   мать   тесть   тёща

двою́родный брат   неве́стка   брат   (шу́рин)   неве́стка

двою́родная сестра́   зять   сестра́   (своя́ченица)   (своя́к)

жена́

племя́нник   сын   сноха́   племя́нники

племя́нница   дочь   зять

внук   вну́чка

вну́чка   внук

origin of **невéстка** is disputed, one explanation is **невéстка = не + вéдать** (not + to know).

The Russians are not much more aware of the titles their relatives might have than we are. The *Chart of Blood Relations* that follows was made to show the system that is used. Russian terminology seems to have a significant advantage over the English: no matter what the mod- ifier (**двою́родный** or **трою́родный**, for example), the noun modified at least indicates the generation in relation to the person spoken of. Thus, **брат** is in the same generation, **дя́дя** is in the preceding generation, and **племя́нник** is in the following generation. In English, many such relatives fade into degrees of cousinage that are lost to common comprehension.

One woman's family

(These are titles of those related to one woman shown as ♟. X indicates marriage. Horizontal lines separate generations. Arrows indicate children from a marriage. Parentheses indicate outmoded usage.)

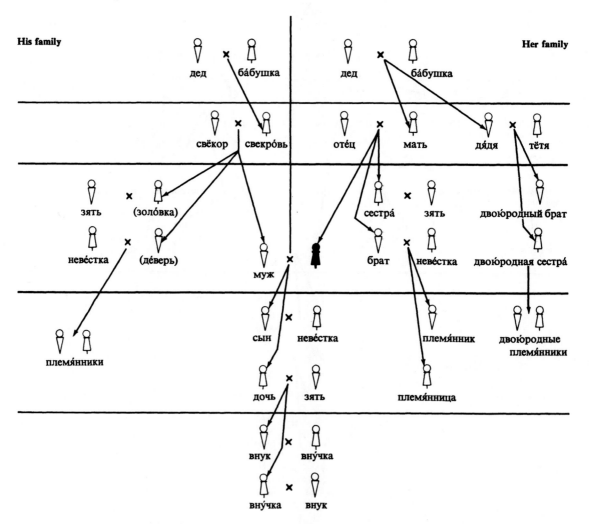

Chart of Blood Relations in Russian and English
(The arrows separate generations; dotted lines connect them.)

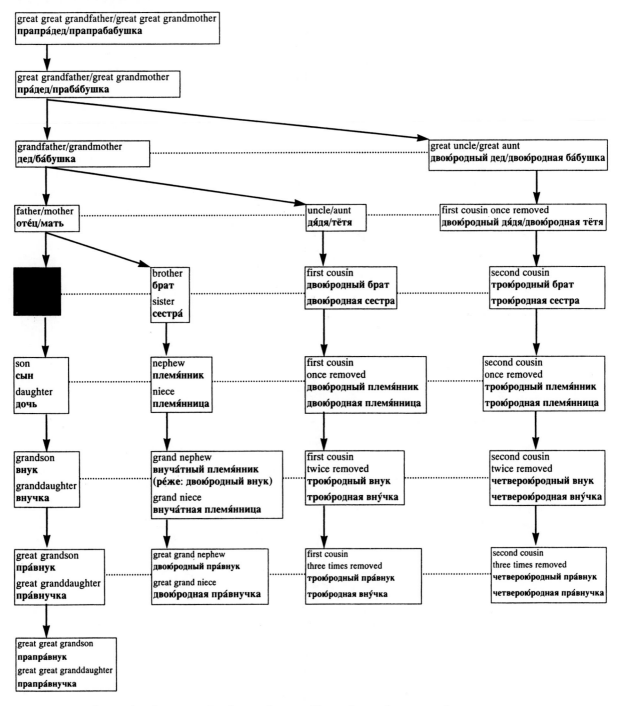

Relatives so distant that the connection is not clear are **Седьма́я вода́ на киселе́**.

TRANSLATIONS

a. When a person is hot, the skin becomes covered with small drops of sweat. Sweating is very important for us. Harmful substances are eliminated in sweat. Sweat is exuded from the skin through small openings—the pores. When the weather is hot, the sweat evaporates and cools the skin. **Соловьёва и др. Родна́я речь III, стр.** 261

b. We breathe air. Notice what you do when you breathe. First we breathe in air (inhale), and then we breathe it out (exhale). **Соловьёва и др. Родна́я речь III, стр.** 260

c. You know that the outside of your body is covered with skin. Feel your arms and legs. You will notice something soft underneath the skin. These are muscles. At the ends of muscles are tendons. **Соловьёва и др. Родна́я речь III, стр.** 253

d. Who are they?

They wrote in their questionnaires: year of birth—1932; family background—white-collar workers (Karpov, from a working class family); party membership—member of the Komsomols (VLKSM) since 1947; service in wartime—none; convictions—none; do you have relatives living abroad—no; and several more no's up to the column "family status," where they all wrote—single. Their autobiographies took up half a page, and this is how they described themselves. . . .

3

Names
Имена́, фами́лии

Every Russian has one given name. That can be news to those who read Russian novels in English and are bewildered by what seems to be an endless array of names. Name usages and forms in Russian are quite different from ours, so this chapter is intended both to guide and explain. Russian, of course, has a different selection of popular names: **Васи́лий** in Russian and Basil in English do not enjoy the same status in spite of their similar origin.

The first two columns from the *Table of Names* on pages 56–61 in this chapter can be used by students to choose their own Russian names for class. Until they have been chosen, students can be addressed by their last names, as is frequently the practice in Russia. The student should always address the teacher by first name and patronymic **и́мя и о́тчество**. Russians will tend to call us by our real (American) names: **Пит, Дик,** and **Джейн**. A foreign name, after all, has its charms.

Of course, you'll want to be able to correct "media" announcers who make a calling of mispronouncing much English and everything foreign, so you should acquire Morton Benson's *Dictionary of Russian Personal Names*, Second Edition, University of Pennsylvania Press, 1992. There you can find out where to stress Gorbachev and 25,000 other names. It's slightly less convenient, but much quieter, than having a Russian on hand. Here, the various aspects of naming are discussed in the following order:

What's your name?
Forms that names can take
A table of names
Growing up with a name
Choosing a name before the Revolution
Choosing a name after the Revolution
Pronouncing first names and patronymics
Surnames and their nationalities
Russian surnames
Names for pets

WHAT'S YOUR NAME?
Как вас зову́т?

This is the more familiar way of asking the question in Russian. Several answers to it are possible:

Са́ша

Алекса́ндр

Алекса́ндр Миха́йлович (Петро́в)

It is more formal to ask: **(Прости́те), как ваше и́мя и о́тчество? (Прости́те), как вас по и́мени и о́тчеству?** Somewhat old-fashioned and therefore ironic versions of asking for patronymics include: **Как вас велича́ют? Как вас по ба́тюшке? Как вас по отцу́?** If you are inquiring after a last name you say: **Как ва́ша фами́лия?**

People filling out forms are often asked for their **ФИО́**, which stands for **Фами́лия, Имя, О́тчество.**

FORMS NAMES CAN TAKE
Фо́рмы имён

The formal given name
По́лное ли́чное и́мя

The first column in the *Table of Names* lists the official name, the one listed on birth certificates, marriage licenses, or any official paper— for example, **Áнна, Ве́ра, Евге́ния, Алекса́ндр, Миха́ил.** This formal name is the only one used in combination with a patronymic **о́тчество.** A signature in Russian usually includes the first letter of this full-name form plus the surname: **В. Ивано́в.**

The patronymic
О́тчество

This name type, also listed in the first column, is formed from the father's given name to which are added the endings: **-ович, -евич, -ич (Ива́нович, Никола́евич, Ильи́ч)** for a

man, or **-овна, -евна, -инична, -ична (Ива́новна, Никола́евна, Ильи́нична, Са́ввична)** for a woman. (The **-ович, -овна** are added to names ending in a consonant, the **-евич, -евна** to names ending in **-й** or a soft consonant, and **-ич, -инична, -ична**[1] are added to some names ending in **-а** or **-я**.) If your given name is **Áнна** and your father's name is **Ива́н,** then you will be **Áнна Ива́новна.** If your name is **Миха́ил** and your father's name is **Никола́й,** then you will be called **Миха́ил Никола́евич.**

The patronymic is constantly used in spoken Russian because the use of the name and patronymic **и́мя и о́тчество** together is the only polite way to speak to someone who is not a close friend. The patronymic is usually not included in one's signature.

The patronymic alone used to be a term of address among the peasants and petty bourgeois. It usually referred to older people and was always both respectful and familiar. Thus, in Doctor Zhivago, we read:

—**Вам Его́ровна зна́ки де́лает,— шепну́л Ю́ра . . . На поро́ге стоя́ла Аграфе́на Его́ровна, ста́рая седа́я го́рничная.**[a]

Diminutives
Уменьши́тельные фо́рмы

The second column in the *Table of Names* gives the most common diminutive forms of the names in the first column; the less common are in parentheses. It is upon these diminutive forms that the endearing name forms (**ласка́тельные фо́рмы**) and the pejorative name forms (**пренебрежи́тельные фо́рмы**) are based. Thus, if the formal name is **Григо́рий,** the most common diminutive is **Гри́ша;** from the latter are formed the endearing **Гри́шенька** and **Гришу́ня,** and the pejorative **Гри́шка.** Notice that some formal names, especially the shorter ones, do not commonly

---

1. **-ична** is pronounced as **-ишна.**

have a diminutive. Instead, the endearing forms are taken from the original name, for example, **Глеб, Олéг, Вéра, Зóя**. Generally, the diminutives are used with members of one's family or good friends. Americans should not use the diminutives when speaking to a Russian unless told to do otherwise or when obvious circumstances require them (when addressing a child, for instance).

Endearing name forms
Ласкáтельные фóрмы

The third column lists only the most common endearing names. As an example of why not all such possible forms can be included, the following list gives some of the varieties of the word **пáпа**. Of course, not all these possibilities are equally popular—and a few are pejorative—but the list does give an idea of the possible range.

Пáпа

Папáша	Папýленька	Пáпушка
Пáпенька	Папýлечка	Папýшенька
Папáшечка	Папýльчик	Папáня
Папáшенька	Папýлька	Папáнька
Папáшка	Папýлик	Папáнечка
Папýся	Папýня	Папáненька
Папýсечка	Папýненька	Папáнюшка
Папýсенька	Папýнь	Папáнчик
Папýсик	Папýнька	Пап
Папýсь	Пáпка	Пáпище
Папýля	Пáпочка	Па

Russians themselves seem to enjoy making up name forms, so you should expect others.

Pejorative forms
Пренебрежи́тельные фóрмы

Pejorative name forms come in two major varieties, neither included here. The most common is used by (and toward) small children and consists of the diminutive of the name with **-ка** added to the stem: **Ваня, Ванька; Стéпа,** **Стёпка; Вера, Верка; Аня, Анька**; and so on. For a few names, however, this ending is endearing, so listen with care.

There are still other pejorative name types. For instance, **Алёха, Федю́ха,** and **Кирю́ха** carry the notion that those mentioned are big, and even stupid, clods. But as with almost all pejorative endings, the intended meaning depends almost entirely on the situation, and there are always dialectical variations to be considered as well. While these terms can be used as an endearment to a very close friend, do not use them toward someone you do not know well—they connote a lack of respect in that situation.

The table does not contain an abbreviated name form especially common between friends who are calling to one another or trying to get their attention. They will shorten the diminutive in the table's second column. For example, **Маш!** or **Марь!** for **Мари́я** or **Мáрья; Владь!** for **Влáдя; Тань!** for **Тáня;** or **пап!** for **пáпа**.

A TABLE OF NAMES
Табли́ца имён

Names that most educated Russians are likely to choose for their children are listed in the table. The choice is highly subjective, and, as names do go in and out of fashion, one is quite likely to come across others; however, most other names are relatively rare or carry the heavy burden of strong social or religious connotations. This is only a general guide, not a complete exposition of all possibilities. Many of the names cited here may be spelled in other ways. Usually the formal church spelling of the name (see the section *Choosing a Name before the Revolution*) is somewhat longer: **Дими́трий** and **Дми́трий, Илия́** and **Илья́, Иродиóн** and **Родиóн**. The table provides the spelling that is now most often used. The most popular names are underlined. Names and diminutives that are often associated with peasants are followed by an asterisk. Name forms in parentheses are less commonly used.

Табли́ца имён: мужски́е имена́

Full name, patronymic	Diminutive forms	Endearing forms
Пóлное ли́чное и́мя, óтчество	Уменьши́тельные фóрмы	Ласка́тельные фóрмы
Алекса́ндр Алекса́ндрович Алекса́ндровна	Cáшa, Шýpa, Cáня (А́лик)	Cáшенька, Cáшечка, Шýрочка, Cáнечка, Сашýня, Сашóк
Алексéй Алексéевич Алексéевна	Алёша, Лёша	Алёшенька, Лёшенька
Анатóлий Анатóльевич (-иевич)[1] Анатóльевна (-иевна)[1]	Тóля	Тóлик, Тóленька, Тóлечка, Тóлюшка
Андрей Андрéевич Андрéевна	Андрю́ша	Андрю́шенька, Андрéйка
Антóн[2]	Антóша (Тóша)	Антóшенька
Арка́дий Арка́дьевич (-иевич) Арка́дьевна (-иевна)	Арка́ша	Арка́шенька
Бори́с	Бóря (Бóба, Боб)	Бóренька, Бóречка
Вади́м	Ва́дик, Ва́дя	Ва́денька
Валенти́н	Ва́ля	Валёк, Ва́лечка, Ва́ленька
Валéрий Валéриевич (-ьевич) Валéриевна (-ьевна)	Валéра (Ва́ля, Лéра)	Валéрочка
Валерья́н	Валéра (Ва́ля, Лéра)	Валéрочка
Васи́лий Васи́льевич Васи́льевна	Ва́ся	Ва́сенька, Васёк
Вениами́н	Вéня	Вéнечка, Вéнюшка
Ви́ктор	Ви́тя	Ви́тенька, Витю́ша

---

1. **-иевич** is used but **-ьевич** is preferred.
2. Hereafter, except as noted, the patronymics of names ending in a hard consonant are formed by adding **-ович** or **-овна**.

Full name, patronymic	Diminutive forms	Endearing forms
Пóлное лѝчное ѝмя, óтчество	**Уменьшѝтельные фóрмы**	**Ласкáтельные фóрмы**
Витáлий Витáльевич (-иевич) Витáльевна (-иевна)	**Вѝтя**	Витáлик
Владѝмир	**Волóдя, Вóва**	Волóденька, Вóвочка, Волóдик
Владислáв	**Влáдик, Влáдя, Слáва**	Влáденька, Владю́ша
Всéволод	**Сéва**	Сéвочка
Вячеслáв	**Слáва, Слáвик**	Слáвочка
Геннáдий Геннáдиевич (-ьевич) Геннáдиевна (-ьевна)	**Гéна, Гéня, Гéша**	Гéнечка
Геóргий, Егóр* Геóргиевич Геóргиевна	**Жóра, Жорж, Гóша, Гóга (Гóра)**	Жóрочка, Егóрушка Гóшенька
Гéрман	**Гéра (Гéша)**	Гéрочка
Глеб	**Глеб**	Глéбушка
Григóрий Григóрьевич Григóрьевна	**Грѝша**	Грѝшенька, Гришу́ня, Гришу́та, Гришу́нька
Дмѝтрий Дмѝтриевич Дмѝтриевна	**Дѝма, Мѝтя**	Дѝмочка, Мѝтенька, Митю́ша
Евгéний Евгéньевич (-иевич) Евгéньевна (-иевна)	**Женя (Гéня)**	Жéнечка, Гéнечка
Ивáн	**Вáня** Ивáнушка	Ваню́ша, Вáнечка, Вáнюшка, Ваню́шечка,
Игорь Ѝгоревич Ѝгоревна	**Ѝгорь, Гóга, Гóша, (Гóра)**	Игорёк, Гóшенька Гóгочка, Игорю́шка
Илья́ Ильѝч Ильѝнична	**Илю́ша, Илью́ша**	Илью́шенька, Илю́шечка

Table of Names: Men's Names
Табли́ца имён: мужски́е имена́

Full name, patronymic	Diminutive forms	Endearing forms
По́лное ли́чное и́мя, о́тчество	**Уменьши́тельные фо́рмы**	**Ласка́тельные фо́рмы**
Климе́нт	**Клим**	**Кли́мочка**
Константи́н	**Ко́стя**	**Ко́стенька, Костю́ша, Костю́шка, Ко́тик**
Лев **Льво́вич** **Льво́вна**	**Лёва**	**Лёвушка**
Леони́д **Леони́дович** **Леони́довна**	**Лёня**	**Лёнечка**
Лео́нтий **Лео́нтьевич (-иевич)** **Лео́нтьевна (-иевна)**	**Лёня**	**Лёнечка**
Макси́м	**Макс**	**Макси́мочка**
Михаи́л **Миха́йлович** **Миха́йловна**	**Ми́ша**	**Ми́шенька, Мишу́тка**
Мстисла́в	**Сла́ва**	**Сла́вочка, Сла́вик**
Ники́та **Ники́тич** **Ники́тична**	**Ни́ка**	**Ники́тушка**
Никола́й **Никола́евич** **Никола́евна**	**Ко́ля**	**Ко́ленька, Никола́ша**
Оле́г	**Оле́г**	**Оле́жек, Оле́женька, Оле́жка**
Па́вел **Па́влович** **Па́вловна**	**Па́ша**	**Па́шенька, Па́влик, Павлу́ша, Павлу́шенька**
Пётр **Петро́вич** **Петро́вна**	**Пе́тя**	**Пе́тенька**
Родио́н	**Ро́дя**	**Ро́денька**

Full name, patronymic	Diminutive forms	Endearing forms
Пóлное лúчное úмя, óтчество	**Уменьшúтельные фóрмы**	**Ласкáтельные фóрмы**
Ромáн	Рóма	Рóмочка, Ромáша
Ростислáв	Слáва, Рóстя	Слáвочка, Рóстик, Слáвик
Семён	Сёма, Сéня	Сёмочка
<u>Сергéй</u>	Серёжа	Серёженька
Сергéевич		
Сергéевна		
Станислáв	Стáс (Слáва, Стась)	Стáсинька, Стáсик
Степáн	Стёпа	Стёпочка
Тимофéй	Тúма	Тúмочка
<u>Фёдор</u>	Фéдя	Фéденька, Федю́ша
Эдуáрд	Э́дик	Э́динька, Э́дичка
<u>Ю́рий</u>	Ю́ра	Ю́рочка
Ю́рьевич		
Ю́рьевна		
Я́ков	Я́ша	Я́шенька
Я́ковлевич		
Я́ковлевна		

Table of Names: Women's Names
Таблúца имён: жéнские именá

Full name Пóлное лúчное úмя	Diminutive forms Уменьшúтельные фóрмы	Endearing forms Ласкáтельные фóрмы
А́да, Аделаúда	А́да	А́дочка
<u>Алексáндра</u>	Сáша, Шу́ра, Сáня	Сáшенька, Сашу́ра, Шу́рочка
Алúна	А́ля (Лúна)	А́ленька
А́лла	А́лла	А́лочка, Алю́ша

Table of Names: Women's Names
Табли́ца имён: же́нские имена́

Full name По́лное ли́чное и́мя	Diminutive forms Уменьши́тельные фо́рмы	Endearing forms Ласка́тельные фо́рмы
Анаста́си́я, Наста́сья	На́стя, Та́ся, (А́ся)	Настю́ша, На́стенька, На́стька, Та́ська Та́сенька, На́стюшка, Тасю́ша, Та́сечка
А́нна	А́ня, Ню́ра (Ню́та, Ню́ша, Ню́ся)	А́нечка, Аню́та, Аню́точка А́ннушка, Ню́рочка
Антони́на	То́ня, То́ся	То́нечка
Бе́лла (Бе́ла, Бэ́ла)	Бе́ла (Бэ́ла)	Бе́лочка, Бэ́лочка
Валенти́на	Ва́ля (Ти́на)	Валю́ша, Ва́лечка, Валю́шенька
Вале́рия	Ва́ля, Ле́ра	Ле́рочка, Вале́рочка
Варва́ра	Ва́ря (Ва́ва)	Варю́ша, Ва́ренька, Варю́ха, Варю́шенька
Ве́ра	Ве́ра	Ве́рочка, Веру́ша, Веру́ня, Веру́шенька
Верони́ка	Ни́ка, Ве́ра, Ви́ка	Ни́кочка
Гали́на	Га́ля	Га́лечка, Га́лочка, Га́ленька
Да́рья	Да́ша	Да́шенька
Евге́ния	Же́ня	Же́нечка, Женю́ра
Евдоки́я (Авдо́тья*)	Ду́ся, Ду́ня*	Ду́сенька, Дуне́чка, Дуня́ша, Дуня́шенька
Екатери́на (Катери́на)	Ка́тя	Катю́ша, Ка́тенька, Катю́шенька
Еле́на (Алёна)	Ле́на (Лёля)	Ле́ночка
Елизаве́та (Лизаве́та)	Ли́за	Ли́зочка
Жа́нна	Жа́нна	Жа́ночка, Жану́ся
Зинаи́да	Зи́на	Зи́ночка, Зину́ля
Зо́я	Зо́я	Зо́енька, Зо́ечка
Изабе́лла, Изабэ́лла	Бе́лла (Бэ́ла, И́за)	Бе́лочка, Бэ́лочка
И́нна	И́нна	И́нночка, Ину́ся, Ину́ля
Ине́сса	И́на	И́ночка, Ину́ля, Ину́ся
Ираи́да	И́ра, И́да	И́рочка
Ири́на (Ари́на*)	И́ра	И́рочка, Ири́ша
Капитоли́на	Ка́па (Ли́на, То́ля)	Ка́почка
Ки́ра	Ки́ра	Ки́рочка

Full name По́лное ли́чное и́мя	Diminutive forms Уменьши́тельные фо́рмы	Endearing forms Ласка́тельные фо́рмы
Кла́вдия	Кла́ва (Кла́ня, Кла́ша)	Кла́вочка, Клавдю́ша
Кла́ра	Кла́ра	Кла́рочка
Ксе́ния (Акси́нья*)	Ксю́ша, Ксе́ния (А́ся)	Ксю́шенька, А́сенька
Лари́са	Ла́ра (Ло́ра)	Ла́рочка, Ла́ринька
Ли́дия	Ли́да (Ли́ля)	Ли́дочка
Ли́лия	Ли́ля	Ли́лечка
Любо́вь	Лю́ба	Любо́чка, Люба́ша
Людми́ла	Лю́ся, Ми́ла, Лю́да	Лю́сенька, Ми́лочка, Лю́дочка
Ма́йя	Ма́я	Ма́ечка
Маргари́та	Ри́та, Марго́	Ри́точка, Риту́ля
Мари́на	Мари́на (Ма́ра, Ри́на)	Мари́ночка, Мари́ша
Мари́я, Ма́рья	Ма́ша, Мару́ся, Ма́ня (Ма́ра, Му́ся, Му́ра)	Ма́шенька, Мару́сенька, Ма́нечка
Наде́жда	На́дя	На́денька, Надю́ша
Ната́лья (Ната́лия)	Ната́ша (На́та, Та́ша)	Ната́шенька
Не́лли, Нэ́лли	Не́ля, Нэ́ля	Не́лочка, Нэ́лочка, Не́лечка
Ни́на	Ни́на	Ни́ночка
Но́нна	Но́нна, Но́на	Но́нночка, Нону́ся
О́льга	О́ля (Лёля, Ля́ля)	О́ленька
Пелаге́я*	По́ля	По́лечка
Поли́на	По́ля	По́ленька, По́лечка
Праско́вья	Па́ша	Па́шенька
Раи́са	Ра́я	Ра́ечка, Раи́сочка
Ри́мма	Ри́мма	Ри́мочка, Риму́ля
Светла́на	Све́та (Ла́на)	Све́тик, Све́точка
Серафи́ма*	Си́ма	Си́мочка
Со́фья	Со́ня, Со́фа	Со́нечка
Тама́ра	Тама́ра (То́ма, Ма́ра)	Тама́рочка
Татья́на	Та́ня (Та́та)	Та́нечка, Таню́ша
Э́лла	Э́лла	Э́ллочка
Э́мма	Э́мма	Э́мочка
Ю́лия	Ю́ля	Ю́лечка, Ю́ленька

GROWING UP WITH A NAME
Имя и во́зраст

Probably the smallest babies are exposed to the largest and widest variety of names. Children might hear their full first name (from the table's first column) at birth and not again until they go to school. Russian mothers delight in using the most endearing name forms they know and then feel free to make up others if established ones are not enough. Pasternak illustrates this phenomenon:

> Она́ обожа́ла Ни́ку и из его́ и́мени Инноке́нтий наде́лала ку́чу немы́слимо-не́жных и дура́цких про́звищ, вро́де Ино́чек или Но́ченька.[b]

Small children hear their endearing name form (from the table's third column) so often that they might think it their official name. Chukovskiy, in *From Two to Five*, cites one such child:

> Слу́шай, ма́ма, а когда́ я роди́лся, отку́да ты узна́ла, что я Ю́рочка?[c]

The boy will hear **Ю́рочка** throughout his life, first from his mother and later, though less frequently, from his wife (who will usually call him **Ю́ра**). When he is old enough to socialize, his mother will introduce him to new friends as **Ю́ра** (from the second column). He will address those other children in like manner until he considers them good friends, at which point he and they will often switch to the usually derogatory name: To his friends and siblings he will be **Ю́рка**. The derogatory **-ка** endings are actually used in several ways: they can be used among children to say, "You're my pal"; among adult friends who might be saying something like, "You're crazy, but I like you anyway"; and by adults toward particularly offensive children. The neighborhood brat would probably be so referred to by almost everyone. Use of this form, however, does not meet with society's approval; it is considered crude. Therefore a teacher might avoid using it even though a pupil might well deserve it.

In class, Yuri's teacher will often refer to him by his last name alone, or sometimes as **Ю́рий** or **Ю́ра**. The younger he is, the more familiar the teacher will be. Out of class the teacher might call him **Ю́рий**, **Ю́ра**, or **Ю́рочка**, depending on the situation—**Ю́рий** or **Ю́ра** if emotion is not involved, and **Ю́рочка** if he has been hurt, for instance. He will always address his teacher and adults who are not in his family by their full name and patronymic.

At puberty many things change, not the least the boy's name. Now his friends call him **Ю́ра** or **Ю́рий** most of the time; **Ю́рочка** and **Ю́рка** remain for special rather than normal use. He comes into his own when he starts work; then he will normally be addressed by his full name and patronymic: **Ю́рий Ива́нович**. Only his relatives and good friends have the privilege of using the diminutive forms of his name.

Women's names are used in the same way as men's. Most women take their husband's surname when they marry, but to keep one's maiden name **де́вичья фами́лия** after marriage (as professional women often do in the United States) is fairly common. You should not think it unusual that a wife has a different surname from her husband. The least common alternative for a woman when she marries is to connect her surname to her husband's with a hyphen. This is done when there is thought to be some advantage in retaining both names.

ADDRESSING THE RUSSIAN
Обраще́ния по-ру́сски

The uses and kinds of name forms with the likely pronoun (**вы** or **ты**) are illustrated with our subjects **Никола́й Петро́вич Смирно́в** and **Любо́вь Леони́довна Смирно́ва**. (See: *You or thou?* on pp. 252–253.)

Това́рищ Смирно́в/Смирно́ва (Comrade Smirnov) used to be the thoroughly official and Soviet form of address, with **вы**.

Господи́н Смирнов (Mr. Smirnov), **Госпожа́ Смирно́ва** (Ms. Smirnov) was formerly only used in diplomatic circles toward or from foreigners of the non-Communist persuasion. (This was the common pre-Revolutionary form of address abandoned earlier because its root is "Lord" **Госпо́дь**.) Nowadays the title is coming into use again, but 70 years of "Comrade" makes any address form difficult. Nothing sounds right unless you are talking to someone you know, in which case a title is not necessary. Newspapers use **Господин**. In the store, calling the cashier **Госпожа** remains quite a ways from thinkable. **Граждани́н Смирнов/Гражда́нка Смирнова** (Citizen Smirnov) is also thoroughly official, confined mostly to courts; normally used with **вы**.

Никола́й Петро́вич/ Любо́вь Леони́довна is the common, polite form of address to anyone to whom one has been introduced. Respect is the basic ingredient, but that does not preclude friendship. Foreigners should remember that the first name and patronymic together are the only polite way to address an adult Russian to whom one has been introduced unless specific permission has been given for diminutive forms. Although this form is normally used with **вы**, if it is used when the first name only and **ты** is usual, it means either that some formality is required in the situation or that someone is mad at someone.

Никола́й/Любо́вь, the long form of the first name, is rarely used all by itself. To repeat: the use of the long form of the given name is unusual. Therefore, do not use it by itself. The Russian usage often indicates that a reprimand or at least a serious discussion will follow—usually with **ты**, sometimes with **вы**.

Ко́ля/Люба is most widely used toward people one knows well, to those of the same age or younger, in unofficial situations and when the parties are friends. Usually used with **ты**, though **вы** is frequent, the name and pronoun usages are not the same: first comes the name change, and then the transfer to "thou" as familiarity increases.

Ко́ленька/Любо́чка is a diminutive used toward loved ones when one is particularly well-disposed toward them or when wanting something. It is employed in a friendly or informal setting, and is used with **ты**. (Many other endearing forms are possible; this is merely the principal one.)

Ко́лька/Лю́бка is normal use between children; adult use is possible toward a naughty child, but such use is considered somewhat coarse—with **ты**.

Смирно́в/Смирно́ва is accepted as neutral among pupils and students at schools and colleges; among teachers and professors the use is familiar and informal—used with **ты** except between instructor and student, when **вы** is appropriate.

Петро́вич, Семёновна (the patronymic alone) is associated with peasant speech where the usage is both familiar and respectful. It can be used with either **ты** or **вы**. Lenin was **Наш Ильи́ч**.

Дя́дя Коля and **Тётя Лю́ба** are used by nieces and nephews and by the children of good friends. Adults use this form for a family retainer—a trusted, familiar worker who supplies some service. Relatives use **ты**, while the plumber gets either **вы** or **ты**.

(Refer to the booklet *Ру́сский речево́й этике́т* by **Н. И. Формано́вская**, Moscow, 1987 for more details and examples.)

NAMES BEFORE THE REVOLUTION
Имена́ до револю́ции

Before the Revolution, the choice of names that could be given a child was limited to a list of saints' names **свя́тцы** that had been approved by the Eastern Orthodox Church **Правосла́вная це́рковь**. Each saint had a day on the (Julian) calendar, and those who had been named after that saint celebrated this day more commonly than they did a birthday **день рожде́ния**. It was called a name day **имени́ны**. When the person celebrating the name day was male, then he was an **имени́нник**; if female, she was an **имени́нница**. For seventy years after the

Revolution one had a birthday **день рождения** and called it that, or had a birthday and called it a name day **именины**. The ambiguity still remains.

Most of the currently popular names are those that were acceptable to educated people before the Revolution. Other names were specifically avoided or were chosen because of strong associations. Therefore, some names were most often associated with the clergy.

Monks had names like:

Ага́пий	Гермоге́н	Никоди́м
Агафо́н	Зоси́ма	Ни́кон
Агафа́нгел	Иерони́м	Ти́хон
Амвро́сий	Илиодо́р	Феодо́сий
Варлаа́м	Не́стор	Филаре́т

Nuns were called:

Ага́пия	Глике́рия	Нимфодо́ра
Афана́сия	Диони́сия	Фео́ния
Вирине́я	Лео́нтия	Ювена́лия

Orthodox Russians (in essence, all Russians) also tended to avoid certain names, considering them Jewish in spite of the fact that many such names were in the list of saints **святцы**. Such names were:

Абра́м	Ди́на
Ада́м	Ли́я
Дави́д	Мариа́мна
Исаа́к	Рахи́ль
Ла́зарь	Ро́за
Мануи́л	Руфь
Моисе́й	Са́рра
Соломо́н	Эсфи́рь
Эммануи́л	

There were some names, as listed by Černyšev,[2] that were ordinarily only found in use among the peasants. (The spelling here follows that in the **святцы**. In everyday use many

of these names are slightly shorter, with occasional vowel and consonant changes, too.)

Some of the men's names:

Агафо́н	Карп	Пота́пий
Амвро́сий	Кири́лл	Пи́мен
Афана́сий	Ла́зарь	Про́хор
Гаврии́л	Лукиа́н	Созо́нт
Гера́сим	Мака́рий	Спиридо́н
Глеб	Макси́м	Стефа́н
Дании́л	Марк	Тара́сий
Диоми́д	Матфе́й	Тере́нтий
Евдоки́м	Митрофа́н	Тит
Евфи́мий	Наза́рий	Ти́хон
Заха́рий	Нау́м	Три́фон
Игна́тий	Ники́та	Трофи́м
Илия́	Нил	Фадде́й
Иа́ков	Они́сим	Фома́

Among the women's names were:

Ага́фия	Евдоки́я	Параске́ва
Агриппи́на	Ефроси́ния	Пелаги́я
Акили́на	Иули́тта	Стефани́да
Ани́сия	Ма́рфа	Фёкла
Васили́са	Матро́на	Феодо́ра
Да́рия	Мела́ния	Феодо́сия

Some names popular among the peasants also began to connote qualities commonly attributed by the upper classes to the peasantry, such as dirtiness, stupidity, and ineptitude. A few of these names were:

Агафо́н	Акули́на
Софро́н	Афроси́нья
Созо́нт	Мала́ния
Харито́н	Нени́ла
Фалале́й	Ули́та
Феду́л	Фёкла

One of the sayings **Даль** recorded was **И по рылу знать, что Созо́нтом звать**—"You can tell by his ugly mug that his name must be **Созо́нт**."

The peasants and petty bourgeois used a wider selection of names because they followed the custom of choosing a name for a child

2. V. Černyšev, "Les Prénoms Russes, Formation et Vitalité," *Revue des Etudes Slaves*, v. 4, fasc. 3 et 4 (Paris, 1934), p. 212.

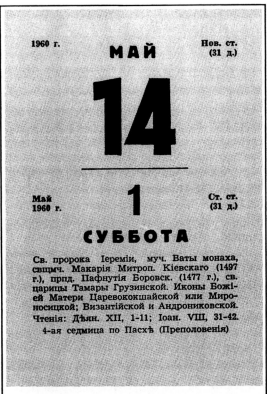

1960 г.

МАЙ

Нов. ст.
(31 д.)

14

Май
1960 г.

1

Ст. ст.
(31 д.)

СУББОТА

Св. пророка Іереміи, муч. Ваты монаха, свщмч. Макарія Митроп. Кіевскаго (1497 г.), прпд. Пафнутія Боровск. (1477 г.), св. царицы Тамары Грузинской. Иконы Божіей Матери Царевококшайской или Мироносицкой; Византійской и Андрониковской. Чтенія: Дѣян. XII, 1-11; Іоан. VIII, 31-42.

4-ая седмица по Пасхѣ (Преполовенія)

Святого пророка Иереми́и, му́ченика Ва́ты мона́ха, свяще́нному́ченика Мака́рия, Митрополи́та Ки́евского (1497 г.), преподо́бного Пафну́тия Бороко́вского (1477 г.), свято́й цари́цы Тама́ры Грузи́нской. Ико́ны Бо́жией Ма́тери Царевококша́йской и́ли Мироно́сицкой; Византи́йской или Андро́никовской. Чте́ния: Дея́ния XII, I-II; Иоа́нна VIII, 31-42.

Четвёртая седми́ца по Па́схе (Преполове́ния)[d]

child of good health, protection, and the like. Gogol humorously described how a half-hearted attempt to follow the tradition of using the church calendar produced the unfortunate name of **Ака́кий Ака́киевич**, the "hero" of his story "The Overcoat." The names **Мо́ккий, Со́ссий, Хоздаза́т, Трофи́ла, Ду́ла, Вараха́сий, Павсика́хий**, and **Вахти́сий** sound absolutely ridiculous to a Russian.

NAMES AFTER THE REVOLUTION
Имена́ по́сле револю́ции

The Revolution affected names almost as much as it did life. No longer were Russians confined to the use of church names.

One change was, happily, only temporary. In the 1920s it was not uncommon to name one's child after revolutionary events, leaders, and ideals. Thus, **Владле́н** is **Влади́мир + Ле́нин**; **Нине́ль** is **Ле́нин** spelled backwards; **Ким** is formed from the initials for **Коммунисти́ческий интернациона́л молодёжи**; and **Ор** is short for **Октя́брьская Револю́ция**. Women's names such as **Лени́на** and **Стали́на** appeared; **Дотна́ра** is **дочь трудово́го наро́да**. Most such names disappeared as quickly as they came. One no longer hears **Э́ра, Иде́я, По́эма, Робеспье́р**, or **Тру́да**. Nor would one dream nowadays of naming a child **Карм (Кра́сная А́рмия)** or **Ревди́т (революцио́нное дитя́)**. For a while, Western names were popular—**Кла́ра, Не́лли, Э́мма, Эми́лия, Альбе́рт, Арту́р, Леона́рд**— though these names are not common now. Very popular names now are those that go far back in history: **Влади́мир, Все́волод, И́горь**, and the like. Generally, names still carry the connotations that they did before the Revolution. **Акули́на** is still a peasant, and **Соломо́н** is still a Jew. As for birthdays and name days, those who remember their name days often celebrate them. More often, one has a birthday **день рожде́ния** but not infrequently refers to it as a **имени́ны**.

according to the day of birth. The church calendar would usually supply several names to choose from,[3] and superstition held that not to choose one of these names would deprive the

---

3. The 1864 list of the **Свя́тцы** published by the Academy of Sciences gave 825 male names and 202 female names. The majority of names in the **Святцы** remained either unused by or unknown to most people.

The passage that follows describes the importance of names for writers of romantic novels.

На после́днем сло́ге
(Сове́ты а́вторам же́нских рома́нов)

Положе́ние писа́тельницы я бы сравни́ла с положе́нием многоде́тной ма́тери. Ведь пре́жде чем её де́тища начну́т де́йствовать, их ну́жно оде́ть, обу́ть, накорми́ть, дать им жилпло́щадь и хоть каку́ю-нибудь обстано́вку. А кто э́то до́лжен сде́лать? Ну коне́чно мы, авторе́ссы. Геро́й роди́лся—на́до его́ назва́ть.... При́нципы подбо́ра имён, пра́вда, не но́вы. Положи́тельного геро́я мо́жно назва́ть Андре́ем, Алексе́ем, Па́влом, в кра́йнем слу́чае, Серге́ем. (Хотя́ в э́том после́днем слу́чае он обяза́тельно до́лжен поги́бнуть. Почему́-то Серге́и всегда́ ги́бнут.) Называ́ть положи́тельного геро́я Ива́ном, Петро́м, а тем бо́лее Кузьмо́й и́ли Про́хором не рекоменду́ется—чита́тельница мо́жет бро́сить чита́ть..... [e]

PRONOUNCING NAMES AND PATRONYMICS
Произноше́ние имён и о́тчеств

The first name and patronymic together (**Ива́н Ива́нович**) is rather long, yet is also used very frequently. As a result the patronymic is shortened somewhat in pronunciation (**Ива́н Ива́ныч**). The following table gives examples of this phenomenon taken from a classic reference on Russian pronunciation, **Р. И. Аване́сов**, *Ру́сское литерату́рное произноше́ние* (Москва́: Учпедги́з, 1954). This pronunciation is used in standard spoken Russian; emphasis, clarity, or a formal occasion can require the more distinct enunciation of each syllable. (In a hurried discussion, what are the full names of **Сан-Са́ныч, Сан-Се́йч?**)

SURNAMES AND THEIR NATIONALITIES
Фами́лии и национа́льность

The majority of Russian surnames end in **-ов/-ев** or **-ин** (**Ивано́в, Фоми́н**). Russian surnames also often end in **-ский**, but Russians themselves consider such names to be Polish (**Разумо́вский**), Belorussian (**Могиле́вский**), or Jewish (**Тарно́вский**); **-ский** endings are also associated with noble origin (**Милосла́вский**) or the church (**Благове́щенский**).

Typical Ukrainian surnames end in **-ко, -енко, -ак/-як, -чук** (**Гурко́, Шевче́нко, Вишня́к, Корнейчу́к**).

Armenian names often end in **-ян** (**Хачатуря́н**) and Georgian names in **-вили, -вали, -дзе, -яни, -ани**. (Stalin's real name was **Ио́сиф Виссарио́нович Джугашви́ли**.) Moslems, or former Moslems, tend to add Russian endings to their original names (**Ахмаду́лина**).

Typical Polish and Belorussian names end in **-ский** and **-ич** (**Якубо́вский, Ивано́вич**). The **-ич** ending is also strongly associated with Serbs or Croats (**Дра́ганич**).

Names ending in **-ьш, -ис, -ус, -ас** with an unfamiliar stem often turn out to be Latvian **Бе́рзиньш** or Lithuanian **Пожа́йслис**. Many German names are associated with the Baltic republics. Estonian and Finnish names are also typified by unrecognizable stems, but they sometimes can be identified by the use of many double consonants and vowels.

Of course, many different national groups live within the Russian Federation. If you want to ask for someone's nationality, you say: «**Како́й вы национа́льности?**»

RUSSIAN SURNAMES
Ру́сские фами́лии

Beginning Russian students are often delighted at the uses to which their newfound knowledge

Pronunciation of women's patronymics when used with first names:

From the name:	One writes:	One says:
Андре́й	Андре́евна	Андре́вна
Алексе́й	Алексе́евна	Алексе́вна
Серге́й	Серге́евна	Серге́вна
Никола́й	Никола́евна	Никола́вна
Ива́н	Ива́новна	Ива́нна
Алекса́ндр	Алекса́ндровна	Алекса́нна
Михаи́л	Миха́йловна	Миха́лна
Па́вел	Па́вловна	Па́лна
Васи́лий	Васи́льевна	Васи́льна
Влади́мир	Влади́мировна	Влади́мирна
Бори́с	Бори́совна	Бори́сна

Pronunciation of men's patronymics when used with first names:

From the name:	One writes:	One says:
Ива́н	Ива́нович	Ива́ныч
Михаи́л	Миха́йлович	Миха́лыч
Па́вел	Па́влович	Па́лыч
Алекса́ндр	Алеса́ндрович	Алекса́ныч
Андре́й	Андре́евич	Андре́ич
Серге́й	Серге́евич	Серге́ич
Алексе́й	Алесе́евич	Алексе́ич
Никола́й	Никола́евич	Никола́ич
Васи́лий	Васи́льевич	Васи́лич
Ю́рий	Ю́рьевич	Ю́рич
Дми́трий	Дми́триевич	Дми́трич

can be put. Consider the joy that accompanies the discovery that то́лстый and Толсто́й come from the same root. Count Leo Fat? And as vocabulary increases, so does the number of parallels that can be drawn; thus Хрущёв from хрущ (the May beetle, so destructive to agriculture); Грибое́дов from гриб + есть (mushroom-eater), and so forth. This joy is modified by the problems of declining Russian surnames; those that have the most common ending (-ов/ -ев or -ин) also have declensions that are part noun declensions and part adjectival declensions.

	Masculine	Feminine	Plural
N	Во́лков	Во́лкова	Во́лковы
G	Во́лкова	Во́лковой	Во́лковых
D	Во́лкову	Во́лковой	Во́лковым
A	Во́лкова	Во́лкову	Во́лковых
I	Во́лковым	Во́лковой	Во́лковыми
P	Во́лкове	Во́лковой	Во́лковых

Consider the Wolf family, for instance. The adjectival endings are underlined.

The relationship between the unending variety in the root meanings of surnames and their half-adjective and half-noun declensions goes back to the fifteenth century or so, when life was less complicated and it was usual to have both a Christian name **Ива́н** and a nickname so the devil wouldn't know which one you were: **Ива́н, Третья́к** (John, third child). When you had to be associated with your father, **Пётр**, they would make a short form adjective out of his name to modify the word "son": **Ива́н, Петро́в сын**. And finally, the century wore on, you became very old, and life became so complicated that the family had to have a name to pass down through generations. So they picked your nickname, and made it into a short form adjective. Since it had been around for so long, it became felt as a noun and stayed that way, denoting the family **Третьяко́в**.

These remarks have been an unforgivable reduction of **Б. К. Чича́гов, Из исто́рии ру́сских имён, о́тчеств и фами́лий** (**Москва́: Учпедги́з**, 1959), a fascinating book on Russian onomastics.

To answer a question you should be asking, the **-ович** or **-овна** endings that now form the current patronymics were originally confined to the very high nobility alone—princes and boyars. The saying remains: «**на́ши вичи́ едя́т калачи́**» (**кала́ч** a rich bun). The use or denial of these endings was used to flatter or to insult.

As time went on, the form spread downward to all classes.

The romance and design of Russian surnames has been described by B. O. Unbegaun in *Russian Surnames*, Clarendon Press, Oxford, 1972. It shows the many different ways of forming surnames, with many examples and a careful index. Accents are indicated. The book is so charmingly written that it's hard not to continue beyond one's original quest.

NAMES FOR PETS
Кли́чки

In English we associate certain names with certain animals. "Bossie" has to be a cow, "Dobbin" a horse, and "Rover" a dog. Russians, too, have a set of names particularly associated with certain animals. (In the following table of animal names an asterisk is placed after such traditional names.) Of course they also have a much larger set of names for pets or animals, and there is no real limit to the possibilities. For use in folk stories, the pig is **Хавро́нья Ива́новна**, the bear is **Михаи́л Ива́нович**, and the fox is **Лиса́ Патрике́евна**.

Notice that many of these names have to do with the color of the animal; this is especially true of horses and cows. The color of horses is **масть**: «**Ло́шадь како́й ма́сти?**» translates "What color is the horse?" There are many such

Animal	Живо́тное	Кли́чка
horse	ло́шадь	Гнедко́, Вороно́к, Рыжу́ха, Ры́жик
cow	коро́ва	Бурёнка,* Рыжу́ха, Беля́нка, Краса́вка, Бу́ська, Зо́рька, Ми́лка
pig	свинья́	Хавро́нья*
rooster	пету́х	Пе́тя* (Петушо́к)
chicken	ку́рица	Хохла́тка, Пестру́шка
bear	медве́дь	Миша,* Михаи́л Пота́пыч (Papa bear), Мишу́тка (Baby bear)
tomcat	кот	Ва́ська,* Пушо́к (Fluffy), Ба́рсик
cat	ко́шка	Ма́шка,* Му́рка,* Му́шка, Ми́лка

---

colors: вороная́ (масть) is black; бу́рая is black and brown; гнеда́я is bay (reddish brown); була́ный is very light brown; си́вая is gray; савра́сая is light bay with black mane and tail; пе́гая is spotted; and кау́рая is light brown. In the expression «Си́вка бу́рка, ве́щая кау́рка» from Конёк-горбуно́к by Ершо́в, the words си́вка, бу́рка, and кау́рка are horse names that are derived from horse colors, and ве́щий is "one able to prophesy."

If you want to give your dog a Russian name, here are some general notions of the meaning of common names for dogs with a note on genders to which they may apply.

Кли́чка	Пол	Значе́ние
Ша́рик*	м	шар (ball, balloon)
Кашта́нка	ж	кашта́н (chestnut)
Жу́чка*	ж	жук (beetle)
Ара́бка	ж	"Blackie"
Каб(ы)сдох	м	"Drop dead"
Ми́лка	ж	ми́лый (darling)
Полка́н*	м	пол + коня́ (centaur)
Бу́лька	ж	Boule de neige (snowball)
Буя́нка	ж	буя́н (ruffian)
Дружо́к*	м	друг (friend)
Зо́рька	ж	заря́ (dawn)
Ту́зик*	м	туз (ace)
Бу́ська	ж	бу́сы (beads)

There is also a fashion to call dogs by Western names:

Джон	Тéри
Ральф	Си́льва
Джек	Джу́ди
Ка́йзер	Джо́й

TRANSLATIONS

a. "Yegorovna is signaling to you," Yura whispered. . . . At the entrance [threshold] stood Agrafena Yegorovna, an old gray-haired housekeeper. **Бори́с Пастерна́к, До́ктор Жива́го**, Second Ed. (Ann Arbor: University of Michigan Press, 1958), p. 56.

b. She adored Nika. His [full] name was Innokentiy and from it she made a raft of ridiculously sweet and silly nicknames like Inochek and Nochenka. **Пастерна́к, До́ктор Жива́го, стр**. 18.

c. Say, [listen] mama. When I was born, how did you know I was Yurochka? **Корне́й Чуко́вский, От двух до пяти**, 17 изд. (**Москва́: Детги́з**, 1963), **стр**. 320.

d. Day of the prophet Saint Jeremy, the martyred monk Vata, the martyred Saint Makariy, Metropolitan of Kiev (1497), the Abbot Pafnutiy of Borovsk (1477), Saint Tamara, Queen of Georgia. Day of the icon of the Mother of God of Tsarevokokshaysk or the Mironositskaya [Myrrh-bearer] Mother of God; the Byzantine and Andronikov icons. Reading: Acts XII, 1-11; John VIII, 31-42.

Fourth week after Easter (Mid-Pentecost) [a church holiday midway between Easter and Pentecost].

e. On the Last Syllable. (Advice to writers of ladies' romantic novels)

I would compare the situation of the lady writer with that of mothers with many children. Before her children can begin to do something, they have to be dressed, fed, housed, and given some sort of environment. And who must do this? Why, we lady authors, of course. Our hero has been born—we must give him a name. . . . The principles of choosing a name are not new, of course. A positive hero can be called Andrey, Aleksey, Pavel, or in an extreme case, Sergey. (Although in the last case our hero must die. For some reason Sergeys always die.) To call a positive hero Ivan, Pyotr, or even worse, Kuz'ma or Prokhor, is not recommended—the reader might stop reading. . . . (The entire article, by A. Petrova, can be found in **Литературная газета**, 5 July 1967.)

4

Clothing

Одéжда

По одёжке встречáют, по умý провожáют.
The clothes matter when you meet; the mind matters when you keep company.

Before the Revolution there were essentially two main types of clothing a Russian might wear. The peasants—that is, the majority of Russians—wore what is described in the section on traditional peasant clothing. It was all homemade and some was handspun; stories of Russian folklore often show the spinning in process. And every village had people who made woven bast shoes and felt boots. Village stores supplied some materials and fixtures, but the great mass of Russian peasant clothing was a do-it-yourself affair that had little to do with the vagaries and refinements of upper-class clothing.

At the other end of the spectrum were the clothes worn by the upper classes, which, after Peter and then Catherine, were essentially the Western European clothing of the day. The relatively small middle classes of the nineteenth century wore some Western clothes but often combined them with clothes of peasant design.

Then came the Revolution, which brought some of its own designs to clothes. The attachment to the West was essentially broken, state money was spent on heavy industry (rather than on clothing), decimation came with World War II, and isolation followed that. When Stalin died, the door opened a crack and the flood of wonder and curiosity began, accompanied by the demand for a few of the refinements of living the Western world seemed to have. The flood is now two meters deep: the American wandering in downtown major cities in Russia wonders if the Russians are really borrowing the right things.

One of the linguistic problems brought about by the innovation and imitation is that some of the terminology for clothes has not really settled down yet. One person's **фуфáйка** used to be another's **кóфта**. Another problem is that though terminology, and even design, are often borrowed from the West, their application and use do not necessarily correspond to those of the Western source.

71

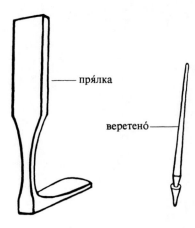

пря́лка

веретено́

The Russian distaff **пря́лка** and spindle **веретено́**

A grandmother who lives in the far north shows a contemporary young man how the spinning is done.

In this chapter, contemporary clothing is discussed first, including terminology for kinds of clothing and then sizes, materials, styles, and patterns; then the basic Russian folk costume for both men and women is considered briefly.

CONTEMPORARY CLOTHES
Совреме́нная оде́жда

Standard "outer" wear for men
Ве́рхняя оде́жда для мужчи́н

мужско́й костю́м a man's suit: **пиджа́к** a man's suit jacket, **брю́ки** trousers

тро́йка a three-piece suit including a vest **жиле́т**

ве́рхняя соро́чка a shirt

га́лстук a tie, **носки́** socks, **ту́фли** shoes

Standard underwear for men
Ни́жняя одежда для мужчи́н

ма́йка a sleeveless undershirt

трусы́ pants or shorts

ни́жняя руба́шка, соро́чка an undershirt with sleeves

кальсо́ны long underwear, long johns

эласти́чные трусы́ (literally, elastic pants) fulfill the function of athletic supporter as do **пла́вки** trunks.

Standard outer wear for women
Ве́рхняя оде́жда для же́нщин

же́нский костю́м a woman's suit: **жаке́т** a woman's jacket, **ю́бка** a skirt

блу́зка, джемпер или сви́тер a blouse or sweater

колго́тки panty hose

чулки́ hose

ту́фли shoes

The Russian dress **пла́тье** is equivalent to "dress," except that another word, **хала́т**, can be used for almost any dress (knee length or full) that usually opens down the front, especially if it is informal. (However, **хала́тность**

Однобо́ртный костю́м
A single-breasted suit
(Двубо́ртный костю́м)

Костю́м тро́йка
A three-piece suit

Повседне́вный костю́м
An everyday suit

is "negligence," where we see the connection with negligee, or "carelessness.") **Хала́т** can also be used for everything from a bathrobe to a surgical gown for both men and women. An item in traditional women's clothing, the sarafan **сарафа́н** now refers to anything that in America would be called a "jumper," namely, a sleeveless dress with straps over the shoulder that, in the daytime at least, requires a blouse or sweater under it.

Standard underwear for women
Же́нское бельё

бюстга́льтер, ли́фчик   a brassiere, or, for example, a bathing suit top (which can also be **верх**)

трусы́, тру́сики   underpants

по́яс   a belt, girdle; **по́яс с подвя́зками, по́яс с рези́нками** a garter belt; **гигиени́ческий по́яс** a sanitary belt

гра́ция a corset (Both girdles and corsets are less commonly resorted to in Russia than in the United States.)

комбина́ция (*coll.* **комбина́шка**) a slip (an item of clothing that has fallen into disuse)

Special purpose clothes
Ра́зные ви́ды оде́жды

For sleeping, women wear pajamas **пижа́ма** or a nightgown, **ночна́я соро́чка** or **руба́шка**. Men might wear a nightshirt with the same name or a pair of pajamas **пижа́ма**; they are also likely to wear their underwear for that purpose (or nothing at all, of course).

For swimming wear, a bathing suit is **купа́льный костю́м** or **купа́льник**, but if you wish to specify a man's swimming suit, then **купа́льные трусы́** or **пла́вки** can be used. (The latter is considerably briefer than ours.) A woman's two-piece suit is **разде́льный купа́льник, бики́ни.**

The general term for work clothes is **спецоде́жда** or **спецо́вка**. (Work shoes are **спецо́бувь**). Work clothes, of course, vary according to the job. Laborers commonly wear overalls **комбинезо́н**. Laboratory workers and doctors wear a **хала́т**. An apron is either **пере́дник** or **фа́ртук**; the latter is perhaps slightly more common. Leotards **трико́** are worn by ballet dancers and gymnasts and other exercisers.

Baby clothes
Бельё для новорождённых

Historically, Russians have been famous for swaddling babies (to swaddle **свива́ть**)—that is, tightly wrapping them so that only the head is left free to move. Nowadays, however, wrapping **пелена́ние** with the arms left free is recommended. Diapers and receiving blankets have the same title in Russian, **пелёнки**. A diaper is a small **пелёнка**, and when folded around the baby it has the title of **подгу́зник** (from **гу́зно**, a bird's rear end).

Aside from crawlers **ползунки́** the only other clothes unique to babywear are a short-sleeved undershirt **распашо́нка** and a bonnet

че́пчик. Otherwise, diminutives of common words are used: **руба́шечка, штани́шки, ко́фточка.**

Uniforms
Фо́рмы

Uniforms are no longer required in schools, though some standards still obtain: girls must wear skirts, and boys might be required to wear ties (but not Pioneer ties). Each school makes its own decision about such matters.

The illustrations indicate common terminology for military uniforms. Other clothing associated with the military includes:

мунди́р either specifically the jacket for a full dress parade uniform or the entire outfit as a whole

ки́тель a uniform jacket, single breasted, with no belt and a standing collar

шине́ль a uniform overcoat, usually somewhat longer than civilian overcoats

тельня́шка, те́льник a sailor's striped knit undershirt

руба́ха a sailor's middy

бескозы́рка a sailor's hat (**козырёк** brim)

бере́т a beret; worn by paratroopers **деса́нтные войска́**

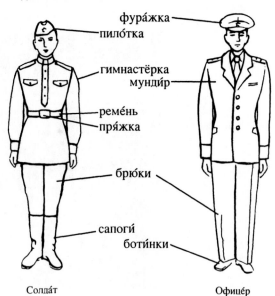

фура́жка
пило́тка
гимнастёрка
мунди́р
реме́нь
пря́жка
брю́ки
сапоги́
боти́нки

Солда́т   Офице́р

Kinds of coats
Ве́рхняя оде́жда

The usual word for the everyday overcoat is **пальто́: зи́мнее пальто́, ле́тнее пальто́, демисезо́нное пальто**. A short coat is **полу-пальто́**. For details on fur coats, see *Furs* in Chapter 14, page 299.

плащ   a raincoat (**непромока́емый плащ** a waterproof raincoat)

дождеви́к   (less commonly) a raincoat, often not as substantial as the **плащ**

наки́дка   a cape

дублёнка   a woman's sheepskin coat, fur inside

шу́ба   a fur coat; **полушу́бок** a short fur coat (a car coat)

мехово́е пальто́, меховое манто́   a fur coat, fur outside

штормо́вка   a parka

Kinds of jackets
Жаке́ты, ку́ртки. . .

As we have said, a man's suit jacket is **пиджа́к**, and a woman's suit jacket is **жаке́т**. A third kind of jacket, **ку́ртка**, is very frequently referred to and used by both men and women. It differs from the first two by its design: one should be able to button or zip it up all the way to the neck. Its major purpose is for sportswear (especially by women), though some uniform jackets that go up to the neck are also called **ку́ртка**. Another word for jacket is **тужу́рка**, which can either resemble a double-breasted suit jacket (when worn by the military) or any lightweight **ку́ртка**.

Телогре́йка, ва́тник, and **фуфа́йка** are short, warm work jackets that often have a cotton-padded lining sewn to the outer layer of cloth. (**Фуфа́йка** can also be a very heavy coarse-knit work sweater, or a cotton sweatshirt.)

The **блу́за** is a light, loose, often indoor jacket, worn by both men and women. (**Блу́за** can also refer to a sweater.)

Kinds of sweaters
Ко́фты, свитера́...

Russian usage for our *sweater* is not very clear. An old equivalent for sweater was **фуфа́йка**, but this is an obsolete usage. Some relief from the dilemma can be obtained by using the specific words for special kinds of sweaters or tops:

ко́фта   a woman's wool knit cardigan; rarely, a blouse

сви́тер   turtleneck or up to the neck, cotton knit or wool, long sleeves (*pl.* **свитера́, -о́в**)

пуло́вер   V-neck, usually knit wool, with sleeves, often a man's

дже́мпер   for men, a V-neck sweater with sleeves; also, a woman's knit top often of wool, usually with short sleeves, especially one that is worn in place of a blouse and is therefore relatively decorative

трикота́жный   (machine knit), **вя́заный** (hand knit), **жаке́т**   a heavier cardigan sweater, more often a woman's, often with a collar

трикота́жный, вя́заный жиле́т   a cardigan sweater, often a man's, without sleeves or collar

жиле́т   a sleeveless sweater

Kinds of shirts and blouses
Руба́шки, блу́зки. . .

руба́шка   almost any kind of shirt—day-wear, nightwear, and underwear (**бе́лая руба́шка, ночна́я рубашка, ни́жняя руба́шка**)—that is either knit or woven; primarily but not exclusively applied to men's shirts

соро́чка   used by some people interchangeably with **рубашка: ве́рхняя, ни́жняя соро́чка**; usually, however, an undershirt

соро́чка   a girl's or woman's undershirt, though usage is sometimes extended to refer to a slip

ма́йка   a sleeveless, knit undershirt

Goods are kept behind the counter

водола́зка a turtleneck knit top usually machine knit

блу́зка a woman's or girl's blouse, often fairly dressy

блу́за either a light, loose-fitting overshirt for men or women or, less commonly, a sweater, often one that opens down the front

футбо́лка a knit shirt, originally for playing soccer

те́нниска a man's short-sleeved knit sport shirt, sometimes worn for tennis, a popular game

ковбо́йка a cowboy shirt for men and boys, made of plaid, often with a button-down collar and buttoned pockets

Kinds of bottomwear
Брю́ки, штаны́ . . .

Almost any trousers are **брю́ки**, and almost any underpants are **трусы́** (for women, **тру́сики**). Another general word for pants is **штаны́**, but this term is much less formal. New business trousers might be **брю́ки**; old baggy pants are **штаны́** (though **штаны́** can also be underpants). **Панталóны** is a somewhat formal and foreign term, usually for women's and chil-

dren's underpants. **Рейту́зы** (German: *die Reithosen*, riding breeches) are usually heavy knit tights for women, children, and ice skaters, though they can also be knit pants as underwear. Tights, without feet, made of heavy material are **лоси́ны**. The terminology for pants in the shape of riding breeches has not yet congealed, so they are referred to in a number of ways: **брю́ки-галифе́, бри́джи, шарова́ры**. Shorts as outer wear are called **шо́рты**. American blue jeans **джи́нсы** are everywhere. Even a new word for light trousers **слéксы** has appeared in the stores.

Headwear
Головны́е убо́ры

In winter, at least, head covering is a vital necessity, and it is in winter (fur) hats that the Russian variety is most remarkable. The usual Western (business) hat is **шля́па** (women tend to call their hats **шля́пка**). What we call a fur hat, however, is **ша́пка**. The most common kind is **уша́нка** or **ша́пка-уша́нка**—the fur (or furlike) brims are normally turned up and tied on the top and turned down for protection only when it is very cold. This design for women is called **обма́нка**, because the ear flaps usually don't turn down; a flat-top flaring cylinder **куба́нка** made with astrakhan **кара́куль** is also popular. The other kinds of fur hats are almost endless, and, rest assured, they all have different names. Knit hats or berets **вя́заные шапки, бере́ты** are part of most wardrobes.

Other hats distinguished by any Russian are:

ке́пка, ке́пи a very common hat in Russia, shaped like a golf cap

фура́жка the hat worn by military officers and policemen in the United States

пило́тка an overseas cap

капюшо́н any hood

тюбете́йка a skullcap, common among central Asians, that is more highly decorated than the Jewish yarmulke **ермо́лка**

шлем, ка́ска   a helmet (the former is the more general word; the latter is mostly restricted to hard hats, an army helmet or a fire fighter's hat)

Scarves of various sorts are the most common (and in the winter, vital) kind of headwear for women. To some extent, shape tends to determine terminology. The square piece of material has the general title of **головно́й плато́к**. It may be light, merely to keep hair covered in the summer. A smaller decorative (and folded or made to be triangular) variety is the **косы́нка**. This is the one most like our bandana. A very large square of material is the **шаль**, worn on either or both head and shoulders, mostly for warmth in winter and decoration in summer.

Rectangular in shape is the **шарф**, worn mainly by women about the neck and head. What we think of as a winter scarf fits this category as does our stole. The smaller, more utilitarian scarf for men is the **кашне́**.

Socks and stockings
Носки́ и чулки́

Socks are **носки́**; **чулки́** refers to stockings or hose. Nylons **нейло́новые чулки́** are thought to be imports while **капро́новые чулки́** are similar but heavier and thought to be of domestic production; panty hose is **колго́тки**. ("I have a run in my stocking" can be **На чулке́ пое́хала петля́** or **У меня́ чуло́к пое́хал, У меня́ стре́лка на чулке́**.) **Го́льфы** are our knee-highs; these are worn mostly by children.

Портя́нки replace stockings for wear with the knee-high boots that don't lace **сапоги́** and with felt boots **ва́ленки**. **Портя́нка** is a rectangular piece of cloth about forty by ninety centimeters that is wrapped about the foot in place of stockings. This wrapping is used in the army (and elsewhere) and requires considerable know-how to put on. It has three advantages: (1) wear and tear is more evenly distributed than with stockings, (2) different sizes are not required, and (3) the wearer can rearrange the

wrapping if absorbed perspiration begins to freeze. This footwear is more rural than urban, except that it is standard in the army.

Footwear
Обувь

Shoes seem to present the same problem that hats do; the several varieties have different words to distinguish them, rather than fewer words requiring modifiers for distinction. The most common word for everyday shoes, both men's and women's, is **ту́фли**, especially if the shoes do not require laces. Oxford shoes are also called **полуботи́нки**. House slippers, especially those with a heel, are also **ту́фли** or **дома́шние ту́фли**. Slippers **шлёпанцы** consist of nothing but soles and toes.

Боти́нки are (usually men's) leather shoes that go up to the ankle. When women wear them, they are specifically for trudging in slush and snow. This word is also applied to the category of ski boots, skating shoes, and many kinds of footwear that go up to the ankle, no matter what their purpose. **Бу́тсы** for playing soccer are in this category. Boots that are not worn over another pair of shoes and that do not lace down the front are **сапоги́: рези́новые**

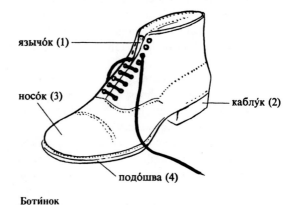

язычо́к (1)
носо́к (3)
каблу́к (2)
подо́шва (4)

Боти́нок

(1)   tongue
(2)   heel
(3)   toe
(4)   sole

Also:

сте́лька   innersole
шнурки́   shoelaces

Ва́ленки Summer storage of a winter necessity

сапоги, мехо́вы́е сапоги, зи́мние сапоги, сапо́жки.

Felt boots **ва́ленки** are the Russian contribution to the art of keeping warm on a low budget in very cold weather. Our familiarity with felt is poor preparation for the Russian object. How do you make boots out of hat material? By making the felt much thicker in the first place and stiffer in the second. Felt boots are traditional winter wear among the peasants. This background accounts for their rejection in the cities except among those whose work allows or requires their use. Children and grandmothers are not so accountable for style; warmth is more important. Children can often be seen wearing **ва́ленки** with rubber galoshes fitted over them.

Гало́ши or **кало́ши** are low-cut galoshes worn over other shoes; **бо́ты**, for men, and **бо́тики**, for women, are high cut. Rubber boots are called **рези́новые сапоги́**.

For lighter footwear, sandals are **санда́лии** or **сандале́ты**, while **босоно́жки** are sandals with heels, mostly for women. Tennis shoes with high uppers are **ке́ды** (Keds!) and are usually reserved for serious sport use while conventional tennis shoes or sneakers are **кроссо́вки. Та́почки** are everyday wear around the house. They have flat soles, cloth uppers, and are sufficiently simple that they are sometimes homemade. The words **та́почки**

and **бахи́лы** are also used for the very large slippers that go over tourists' shoes worn on some tours of historic buildings.

To tie your shoes Russian style, start out making the first knot as we do; then make a large loop of each lace and tie them together just as you tied the first knot.

Holders and fasteners
Засте́жки

по́яс, ремень belt

хля́стик belt loop

подтя́жки suspenders (less frequently, **по́мочи**)

пу́говица, пу́говка a button

   Брю́ки раньше застёгивались на пу́говки (to fasten **застёгивать**)

   Застегни́ руба́шку!

   Пу́говицы застёгиваются в пе́тли (петля́ loop or buttonhole)

пря́жка a buckle

   Пря́жки ча́ще всего́ употребля́ются на пояса́х, но иногда́ и на бо́тах, боти́нках и т.п.

мо́лния a zipper

   Он стал застёгивать мо́лнию на ку́ртке.

кно́пка snap, snapper

крючо́к и пе́телька a hook and eye

шнурки́ shoelaces

   Он ещё не уме́ет зашнуро́вывать ту́фли.

   Завяжи́ шнурки́! Tie your shoelaces!

   Развяжи́ шнурки́! Untie your shoelaces!

Sizes
Разме́ры

First, remember that when things are measured, they are measured in centimeters: **Где мой сантиме́тр?** "Where is my tape measure?" For most clothes (shirts, dresses, coats), take the bust or chest measurement and divide by two.

Thus, men's coats, women's dresses, and shirts all range in size from 44 to 56 (even numbers only). Other measurements are used for length or collar size, for instance, but they are secondary, and their range depends on what is being sold. Hose and stocking sizes are obtained by measuring the length of one's foot in centimeters (odd numbers only). Shoe sizes unfortunately come in a variety of scales. You may order your gloves straight from **ГУМ**; for some reason, glove sizes are the same all over the world. Hat sizes are obtained by measuring in centimeters the circumference of the head at the mid-forehead level. For adults the range is from 53 to 62.

Materials
Ткáни

Sometimes fashion magazines are especially interesting reading for foreigners. Here are some materials mentioned in one such magazine: **креп, джерси́, фланéль, тви́ды, буклé, шифóн, вельвéт, габарди́н, синтéтика, велю́р**, not to mention **брю́ки из эла́стика**. Those are mostly various weaves, of course, and the original materials from which they are woven carry suitably unrecognizable names:

хлопчатобума́жная ткань   (woven) cotton; to use the slang, say "**ха-бэ́**"

  хлóпок   raw cotton

  вáта   drugstore cotton

  бати́ст, штáпель, бязь, сати́н, си́тец cotton materials

шерсть   wool (**шерстянóй костю́м**)

шёлк   silk (**шёлковая руба́шка**), **крепдеши́н**

лён   linen (**льнянóе полотéнце**)

иску́сственный, вискóзный шёлк   rayon

капрóн, нейлóн   both nylon, but the former is coarser and cheaper (**капрóновые чулки́, нейлóновая блу́зка**)

Furs are very expensive—and, considering the climate, very desirable.

Styles
Сти́ли в одéжде

Some constants relate to clothing and style. One is the winter weather. It is hard to imagine that boots and very warm coats might disappear from the Russian wardrobe. Warm legwear is also necessary. And no Russian grandma worth her salt will let you out the door without a hat when the temperature drops below zero degrees centigrade.

Хорóшего человéка должнó быть мнóго!
There should be lots of a good person!

The Russian female figure tends to be full, and older Russian women dislike the manmade restraints (girdles) on that fullness. Urban young women, however, do not differ much from their Western peers in any of their stylistic extremes. For men, the white shirt, tie, and three-piece suit is business wear and therefore still relatively less common. A knit shirt, jacket, and pants is a more likely combination. (Except for older females, jeans make a good gift: standard brands only, please.)

Style is also affected by availability, and the cost is so high that popular styles are frequently hard to get (especially in the country). The cost of clothes in relation to income is also high. Entrepreneurs have lately been importing quantities of used clothing from other countries. Necessity forces the use of the service, but picking over other people's cast-offs is strongly resented. Ready-made clothes used to be government manufacture, a limiting factor on extremes in design. The affluent can have clothes made to order by a seamstress **портни́ха** or can even buy ready-made clothes from small manufacturers who are discovering the size and desires of the market, but most women know how to knit **вяза́ть** and sew **шить**.

Sewing and patterns
Шитьё и вы́кройки

Семь раз приме́рь, оди́н отре́жь.
Measure seven times, cut once.

ли́ния та́лии waistline

ли́ния бёдер hipline

перёд front

спина́, спи́нка back

вы́тачка dart

скла́дка pleat

подги́б, подши́вка hem

подо́л hemline

сгиб тка́ни a fold (of material)

вста́вка insert

сбо́рочки gathers

карма́н pocket

Sewing **шитьё** requires some equipment: a sewing machine **шве́йная маши́нка**, thread **ни́тки, нить**, a thimble **напёрсток**, a needle **иго́лка, игла́**, (the Russian needle has an ear rather than an eye: **ушко́ иглы́**), probably some straight pins **була́вки**, and maybe some safety pins **англи́йские була́вки**.

С ми́ру по ни́тке—го́лому руба́ха.
A thread from each of us will make a shirt for a poor (naked) man.

There are two kinds of patterns in Russia. The traditional **вы́кройка** usually refers to a small-scale design that the seamstress must enlarge to fit required proportions. The sewing section of a book on basic home economics (from which the pattern in the figure was taken) is divided in sections that show how to make various kinds of sleeves, collars, skirts, and so forth. Home economics classes include instruction on how to use this kind of pattern. The other kind of pattern, **патро́нка**, is a pattern as we know it, issued in various sizes and as large

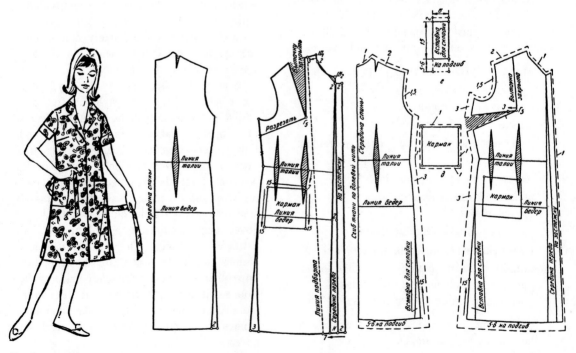

Хала́т для до́ма

as the piece of material that it is to shape. Sometimes **вы́кройка** is used for **патро́нка**.

THE RUSSIAN FOLK COSTUME
Ру́сский наро́дный костю́м

Russian literature and folk dance ensembles often refer to nineteenth-century peasant clothing, only the most basic aspects of which are described here.

Своя́ руба́ха бли́же к те́лу.
One's own shirt is closer to one's body.

The Russian men's shirt **руба́ха** opened at the neck, significantly left of center. If it had a small collar, it was called **косоворо́тка** (literally, sideways collar) and was somewhat more elegant than the shirt with no collar **голоше́йка** (literally, bare neck). For holidays, the shirt might have embroidered collars, sleeve ends,

A northern Russian girl wearing **руба́ха, сарафа́н**

Russian men's wear: **руба́ха, штаны́, ону́чи, ла́пти**

and a front panel. The Russian wore his shirt outside his pants with a belt over both of them. Men's pants **штаны́** were fairly narrow and were either tucked into the tops of boots or held in place below the knee by strings that also held **ону́чи** in place; they were relatively long and narrow pieces of cloth wound around the foot and lower leg in place of stockings. Ukrainian men wore baggy pants **шарова́ры**, the neck opening for the shirt was in the center, and the shirt was tucked into the pants. The Belorussian had narrow pants, his shirt was not tucked in, and the neck opening was down the center. Cossacks' clothes resembled Ukrainian rather than Russian clothes.

Russian women all wore a long-sleeved (shirt-) dress **руба́ха, руба́шка**. By itself this was decent wear for unmarried women, weather permitting. But marriage brought a further requirement: in the central and northern regions she had to wear a sarafan **сарафа́н** on top of the shirt-dress, and if she was from the south she had to wear a panelled skirt **пла́хта, понёва**

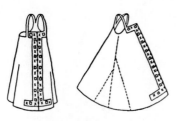

сарафа́н косокли́нный

сарафа́н кру́глый

A southern Russian woman wearing руба́ха, понёва, пере́дник

over the shirt-dress. A long apron **пере́дник** was sometimes worn over that combination.

Underwear **ни́жнее бельё** does not enter our discussion—they wore none. Defense against the cold came by adding another layer of outer clothing.

The most common footwear in the summer were **ла́пти** (*sg.* **ла́поть**), a cross between shoes and slippers woven from **лы́ко**, the fibers of the linden (lime or basswood) tree **ли́па**. Each village had its lapti-maker and, as already mentioned, they were comfortable, cheap, and readily available. For winter Russians wore felt boots **ва́ленки** that were also produced locally. When the weather was less cold, leather boots

руба́хи   понёвы

were used by those who could afford them; leather has the nasty habit of freezing and cracking in very cold weather.

Hats were of wool felt in summer, relatively high and conical; in winter they were of fur,

коко́кшники   ки́чка

Же́нские головны́е убо́ры конца́ XIX—нача́ла XX в.
Women's headwear at the end of the nineteenth century and beginning of the twentieth century

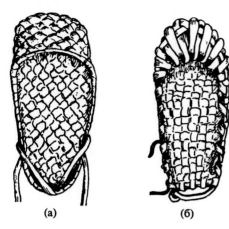

Ру́сские ла́пти: (а) моско́вского ти́па, (б) за́падного ти́па

sometimes with earflaps. His hat removed, a man's haircut resembled that obtained by putting a bowl over his head and cutting off what emerged. The Russian peasant usually let his beard grow, especially if he was older.

For lighter wear the Russian man had a cloth coat, caftan **кафта́н**, fitted at the waist and flaring at the bottom. In winter he wore a fur coat **шу́ба** with the fur inside. In very cold winter weather, especially for travel, he wore a very long coat **тулу́п**, usually consisting of nothing but a sheepskin, fur side in, over his usual coat.

For holidays, married women in the north had elaborate and large devices to cover their head and hair—a kind of hat plus drapery **коко́шник** that was often ornamented with shells, beads, and the like. Unmarried women could wear their hair in a single long braid down the back. They might also wear a crown-shaped headdress, which left the top of the head

uncovered. In any case, women's hair had to be restrained in some fashion, usually in braids: only on the day of her wedding could she let her hair down—long and loose tresses were considered unseemly. (They are still rare; women's hair today is usually either relatively short or else braided or tied up in some way.)

Hair and the married woman
Головно́й убо́р заму́жней же́нщины

Women's headgear was dominated by one single factor that was true for all the eastern Slavs. A married woman could not appear before her husband's relatives or before strangers without having all her hair covered. (Uncovered hair was "sinful," and is still considered so in the Russian church today.) One explanation for this custom is that it derived from a more ancient belief in which hair was ascribed some sort of magical power. Because early custom required that a wife come from other than one's own village, it would follow that all married women were strangers and therefore not to be trusted with their power running loose. You can assume that a woman pictured with any significant portion of her hair uncovered is not married. This custom probably accounts for the rather large number of bandanas still to be seen among the peasant women today when weather or working conditions would not seem to require them.

For those interested in greater detail and a discussion of smaller regional and class variations, see **То́карев, Этногра́фия наро́дов СССР** and **Алекса́ндров, Наро́ды европе́йской ча́сти СССР**.

Part III

The Russian at Home

5

Housing

Жили́ще

Моя ха́та с кра́ю.
My hut (or house) is out of the way; meaning, "I don't know anything about it (and I don't want to know)."

When Russians say they are going home, what do they expect to find when they get there? Russian housing is different from ours in several major aspects, of which size is most notable. In the Soviet era, things started out idealistically during the epoch of constructivism эпо́ха конструктиви́зма, during which everyone in a building дом комму́ны was to use one huge kitchen. Those buildings were eventually restructured at high cost and strange angles into apartments with one kitchen each. If you find yourself in a solid apartment building with high ceilings, and large rooms, then you may be in a Stalin House в ста́линском до́ме originally built for high military officers, party officialdom, the nomenclature, and, occasionally, scientists. Khrushchev attempted to alleviate the housing problem by the mass construction of very small apartments with no corridors, low ceilings, and all three bathroom fixtures in one room. These rabbit warrens are detested and given the name хрущёбы (from Khrushchev plus the word for slum трущо́ба). Despite these occasional spurts of housing construction, major state investment was in heavy industry, and the single major theme was to put as many people in as little space as possible. Marriage, divorce, and having children are still directly related to the amount of housing space available—an ad that says сдаётся у́гол means that a part (literally, a corner)[1] of a room is available for rent.

---

1. There is a paraphrase to the saying **Была́ бы ше́я, а хому́т найдётся**, "If there is a neck, a (horse's) collar will be found (to put on it)." It reads **Был бы у́гол, а жени́х найдётся!** "If there is (part of) a room, a groom will be found!"

Wanted: room to buy

Изба́ стро́ится

Most Russians, especially those that live in the city, think of a family of four as an upper limit in size, and the civil courts are filled with adjudications over who has how many or which parts of square meters of housing space. The amount of housing space is steadily growing, however, to the extent that young couples are beginning to expect a separate room for mother-in-law.

Although Russians in the past did not have much room, neither did they pay very much. Rent was rarely more than 5 percent of income. The space available is still small, but now the price is rising and those on a fixed income are having trouble. The homeless **бомж** ("without official place of residence" **без официа́льного ме́ста жи́тельства**, an acronym first used by the police), are becoming more numerous; some people are going back to building their own housing.

A third major difference is that many of the conveniences—indoor plumbing, hot water, or even running water—that we take for granted are not all that basic in the Russian Federation. City buildings and new major constructions have these services, but outside the cities, especially in smaller and older houses, they are frequently absent. Indeed, housing is one of the major fields in which the great disparity between city and country life is evident.

This chapter explains the various kinds of housing available to the Russian. A typical, new, self-contained apartment is discussed first because that is the most common type of new housing; types of rooms, along with their contents and equipment, are shown. Then the focus shifts to the older communal apartment, which also forms a significant fraction of available housing. Last, the classic features of the peasant "hut" are shown, along with changes in contemporary rural housing.

A SELF-CONTAINED APARTMENT
Отде́льная кварти́ра

Most Russians now live in a self-contained apartment that consists of at least one room—or more often two rooms (and sometimes more) plus a kitchen, bathroom facilities, and hallway. (The last three are not counted in describing the number of rooms or the number of square meters of housing space.) It differs from the communal apartment **коммуна́льная кварти́ра** described later, where the hallway, bathroom facilities, and kitchen are shared.

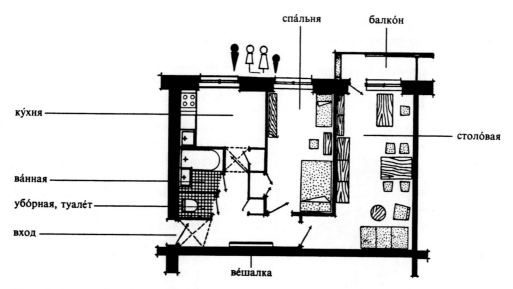

спа́льня

балко́н

ку́хня

столо́вая

ва́нная

убо́рная, туале́т

вход

ве́шалка

Кварти́ра для семьи́ из четырёх челове́к

The illustration shows a possible arrangement of furniture in a two-room apartment. The balcony is used for storing food and drying laundry. If a balcony intrudes rather than protrudes, its title is **ло́джия**. Notice that this apartment is supposed to be large enough for four people—in this case, a mother, father, grandmother, and small son.

In the entrance hall
В прихо́жей,
В пере́дней

Wipe your feet on the small rug **полови́к** before you enter. The front door is padded—for warmth with a little security thrown in. (Sometimes fearful residents install multiple doors, one of them often made of steel. Therefore doors are not knocked on—ring the bell instead.)

The entrance hall **прихо́жая** is small, with no coat closet; instead, a coat rack **ве́шалка** is used. The coat rack often has some arrangement of boards to protect the walls from wet raincoats (and vice versa). Hats are placed on a shelf **по́лка** above, and overshoes and street shoes often have a rack or shelf below. Other

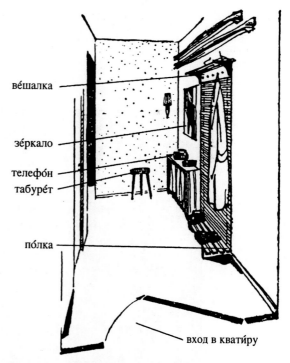

ве́шалка

зе́ркало

телефо́н
табуре́т

по́лка

вход в квати́ру

Прихо́жая в совреме́нной кварти́ре   The entrance hall in a contemporary apartment

furniture for an entrance hall might include a stool **табуре́т** and a mirror **зе́ркало**, which often also has a shelf under it.

A SELF-CONTAINED APARTMENT   **89**

Russians remove street shoes upon entering, though they may not require the same from you. Slippers **тапочки, шлёпанцы** may be supplied you. Though very hospitable, Russian women do not hang up men's coats—the service is felt to be too personal.

Столо́вая (или о́бщая) ко́мната. Note the child's bed behind the curtain. This drawing makes the room appear larger than it is in reality.

The main room
Столо́вая

In the dear dead days beyond recall, some people had houses with a number of rooms to which they assigned various purposes. Guests **го́сти** were received in the "guest" room **гости́ная** and meals were eaten from a table **стол** in another "table" room **столо́вая**. Now, one basic room fills both purposes so both names can be applied to it, though the latter is more common. (The term **о́бщая ко́мната** is also used.)

This room carries the major burden of living: it is a living room, dining room, bedroom, and study combined. Anything that resembles a sofa in the daytime doubles as a bed at night. Storage is an immense problem. Built-in closets **встро́енные шкафы́** or storage closets **кладо́вки** are rare. Instead people buy a "wall" **сте́нка** of coordinated cabinets. It's hard to find room for a playpen **мане́ж**.

Сте́нка   Added-on built-ins

The traditional heart of the room is the dining table **обе́денный стол**, which is moved to the middle of the room when company comes.

Decor
Интерье́р

Typifying the "Russianness" of Russian decor is difficult. No one style seems to predominate; indeed, the Russian ego does not seem to extend to household possessions. Older city apartments have a heaviness to them—reminiscent of Late Victorian in England—often with darker colors and hanging fringes here and there. The style of newer city apartments is closer to nondescript, with the effort to pack a modicum of furniture into very small rooms being the most impressive feature. Newer furniture design resembles Scandinavian models made by Sears Roebuck.

A common decorating device is the display of Persian-type rugs **ковры́** on the wall. A satirical article in the press described someone "sophisticated" as one who put the rugs on the floor rather than on the wall! The floors themselves always seem to be parquet, though linoleum **лино́леум** is well-represented, and small area rugs are used, if any at all. (Any notably thin or woven rug is called **пала́с**; any long narrow rug is a **доро́жка**.)

A constant item in Russian decor is the house plant. Every Russian dwelling from the country house to the city apartment almost invariably has some kind of house plant, from the lowly geranium **гера́нь** to a palm tree **па́льма**.

Windows
Окна

Winters are cold and Russians like it warm indoors, so double windows are traditional, often with the inside set of window frames removable for the summer. Both sets have a section in them, the **фо́рточка**, that can be

Фо́рточка

separately opened. A device **фраму́га** accomplishes the same purpose in some buildings. A house fan is a **вентиля́тор**.

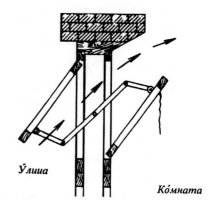

У́лица

Ко́мната

Фраму́га

Lighting fixtures
Прибо́ры для освеще́ния

A lamp is simply **ла́мпа**, a table lamp **насто́льная ла́мпа**; but a light bulb is **ла́мпочка**. Judging from the terminology for many light fixtures, illumination would seem to come from France:

свети́льник   any large lighting fixture

торше́р   a floor lamp

бра   a wall lamp

лю́стра   a chandelier

плафо́н   a ceiling light cover

выключа́тель   a switch

шнур   a cord

розе́тка   a (wall) socket

ви́лка   a plug

Включи́(те)/зажги́(те) свет!   Turn on the lights!

Он включи́л/зажёг ла́мпу.   He turned on the lamp.

Она́ вы́ключила/погаси́ла свет.   She turned off the lights.

Вы́ключите/погаси́те свет!   Turn off the lights!

Furniture
Ме́бель

Space is at a premium; a popular solution is a kind of built-in furniture with elements that can be variously combined to form a wall **сте́нка**. Sets of furniture are **набо́р ме́бели**.

серва́нт   a sideboard buffet

буфе́т   a tall, two-storied buffet

обе́денный стол   a dining room table

сту́лья   chairs

дива́н-крова́ть   a sofa bed, a hide-a-bed

кни́жный шкаф   a bookcase

пи́сьменный стол   a desk

стол или ту́мба для радиоприёмника или телеви́зора   a table or stand for a radio or television set

односпа́льная крова́ть, двуспа́льная крова́ть   single bed, double bed

комо́д   a chest of drawers

ту́мбочки   nightstands, bed-stands, small cabinets

платяно́й шкаф, гардеро́б   a wardrobe closet or cabinet

шифонье́р   a cabinet for linens

кре́сло   an armchair

Closets
Гардеро́бы, платяны́е шкафы́

New apartment buildings are using more built-in cabinets in the kitchens and closets in the bedrooms, but they are still very new and comparatively rare. Usually clothes are kept in a large movable wardrobe cabinet **гардеро́б**, **платяно́й шкаф** as they are in other parts of Europe. Clothing is hung on a coathanger **пле́чики, ве́шалка**. The latter is also the term for the wall rack that replaces a front closet.

The bedroom
Спа́льня

In two-room apartments, the second room is often a children's bedroom. Usually, though, a second room is not available unless the family has at least three to four people. If the second room is used by adults, then it will often also contain a desk **пи́сьменный стол**, a dressing table **трелья́ж**, or chest of drawers **комо́д**.

Beds
Крова́ти, посте́ли

The two words for bed are often used interchangeably: **крова́ть** refers essentially to the frame and legs of the bed, while **посте́ль** refers to what you might put on it—blankets, sheets, mattresses, and so forth. Other kinds of beds include:

односпа́льная, одина́рная крова́ть   a single bed

двуспа́льная, двойна́я крова́ть   a double bed

полутораспа́льная крова́ть a three-quarters bed

тахта́ a daybed

дива́н-крова́ть a sofa bed, or hide-a-bed

раскладу́шка a cot, a folding bed

кре́сло-крова́ть a combination armchair and bed

откидна́я крова́ть a wall bed, a Murphy bed

крова́тка a baby bed

ко́йка a hospital bed

двухэта́жная крова́ть a bunk bed

How to make a bed
Как убира́ть посте́ль

A lower sheet **простыня́** is affixed to the mattress **матра́с, матра́ц** as is ours. The Russian upper sheet **пододея́льник** is actually a sort of envelope for the blanket, which buttons onto the blanket **одея́ло** or comforter **стёганое одея́ло.** (A bedspread **покрыва́ло** might cover these.) This top arrangement is not tucked under the mattress. So, to make the bed, simply spread this enveloped blanket out evenly. (Our flat two-sheet system, however, is sometimes used.) The (square) pillow **поду́шка** has a pillowcase **на́волочка** and seems to average at least twice the size of our bed pillows.

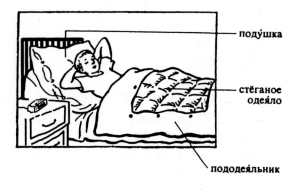

подушка

стёганое
одея́ло

пододея́льник

Bathroom facilities
Убо́рная, туале́т, ва́нна

Usually, bathroom facilities are divided between two rooms: the toilet **унита́з** is in one small room

убо́рная, туале́т, and the bathtub ва́нна and sink умыва́льник are in another ва́нная. (A kitchen sink is a ра́ковина.) Especially polite usage avoids the words убо́рная, туале́т; "conveniences" удо́бства can be used. Toilet paper туале́тная бума́га is now commonly available at stationery stores (and elsewhere), but home toilet paper still often consists of the daily newspaper, carefully torn into rectangles and put in a large envelope that hangs on the toilet room door. The bathtub-and-sink room often is also the storage room for any washing equipment, perhaps a washing machine стира́льная маши́на or a Russian washing tub коры́то, which has the shape of an abbreviated trough. Some citizens insist that washing machines are used even in households without running water, and still others report that most washing is done in the bathtub. Commercial laundries пра́чечные have a reputation for being inexpensive but hard on clothes. Commonly, people send bed linens, table linens, and towels to the laundry. Diapers and men's shirts are usually washed at home.

The kitchen
Ку́хня

The Russian kitchen is now much more likely to have some arrangement of built-in cabinets, shelves, and sinks; the ensemble is **ку́хонный гарниту́р,** and its presence makes storage and cooking a reasonable activity. Counter space is limited and often covered with oilcloth **клеёнка.** And notice in the following paragraph that the preferred method for washing dishes requires scrubbing with a brush under a stream of hot water. Standing water *per se* is thought of as unsanitary (to the chagrin of American travelers who can find no sink stoppers).

How to wash dishes
Как мыть посу́ду

Лу́чше всего́ мыть посу́ду и прибо́ры мы́лом и щёткой под струёй горя́чей воды́. Но, к сожале́нию, не во всех ещё дома́х име́ется водопрово́д с горя́чей водо́й и́ли водогре́й. Поэ́тому иногда́ мо́ют посу́ду в та́зиках. В любо́м слу́чае у ребя́т на́до выраба́тывать пра́вильные приёмы, кото́рые облегча́т и уско́рят весь проце́сс мытья́: спра́ва поста́вить гря́зную посу́ду, пе́ред рабо́тающим—таз с тёплой водо́й (с раство́ром горчи́цы и́ли со́ды), ря́дом, леве́е—второ́й таз с горя́чей водо́й для опола́скивания; сле́ва же ста́вить вы́мытую посу́ду. [a]

As the passage notes, soda or (dry) mustard **горчи́ца** is used as we use soap or detergent. The use of mustard as a cleaning agent is also commonly extended to floors and clothes. But soda or mustard is not used to the exclusion of soap **мы́ло**. The common word for cleaning substances in powdered form is **порошки́**. Dishes are washed with **порошки́ для мытья́ посу́ды**. Laundry soap (or detergent) is **хозя́йственный порошо́к**. In practice, brand names are often referred to, for example, **Я стира́ю в «Ло́тосе»** or **Я стира́ю в «Та́йде»** (**стира́ть** to launder).

Kitchen furniture and utensils
Ку́хонная ме́бель и посу́да

Stoves **пли́ты** in the cities are commonly heated by gas; those in newer apartments have an oven. When a stove is a stove in our sense of the word (two to four burners **конфо́рки, горе́лки** and an oven **духо́вка**), then it is a **плита́: га́зовая плита́, электри́ческая плита́**. The wood stove **дровяна́я плита́** (**дрова́** firewood) is of course limited to the countryside. Whether for reasons of economy, space, or availability, however, other devices are sometimes used—for example, a hot plate **электропли́тка**. (Other devices are also used where there is no gas or electricity supply. See *Contemporary rural housing* in this chapter.) Where space is at a premium, a smaller table-model oven **электро-духо́вка** might be used in conjunction with a hot plate; a **чу́до-пе́чка** is a specially constructed pan for baking on top of the stove using the heat from a regular burner.

The remaining furniture is not so complicated:

шкаф   a kitchen cabinet or cupboard

буфе́т   a tall piece of furniture, sometimes found in the kitchen, that holds table linens, silverware, and sometimes food

ра́ковина   a kitchen sink

холоди́льник   a refrigerator

Pots, pans, and containers include:

кастрю́ля   the usual cooking pot or pan

сковоро́дка, сковорода́   the former, a frying pan, not necessarily including a handle

сковоро́дник   a handle to grip pans that have none

котёл   large, heavy metal stewpot, a Dutch oven, or a kettle

гуся́тница   a roaster

кофе́йник   a coffeepot

ча́йник   a teapot or teakettle, **заварно́й ча́йник**   a teapot

лист (желе́зный)   a cookie sheet

про́тивень (желе́зный)   a large flat pan with low sides for making **пироги́**

фо́рма   a mold for **желе́, пу́динг**

коро́бка   a box or canister for storage

ба́нка   a glass jar (also a tin can)

подно́с   a tray

подста́вка   a holder or pad for resting hot pans

кры́шка   a lid

ми́ска   a bowl

For dealing with food in preparation:

мясору́бка   a meat grinder

кофемо́лка   a coffee grinder

овощере́зка   a vegetable slicer

соковыжима́лка   a juicer

ми́ксер   a mixer

тестомеси́лка   a dough kneader

ку́хонный комба́йн   the kitchen "combine," uses one motor to run the six preceding devices

сито и решето both sieves, often referred to together, with low round sides and a flat bottom; **решето** (*pl.* **решёта**) used for coarse sieving, **сито** for fine sieving

цедилка a strainer, especially for bouillon

дуршлаг a colander

ступка с пестиком a mortar and pestle

деревянный молоток a wooden hammer for pounding meat

сечка и корытце a special knife with a handle in the middle and a curved blade **сечка**, made for use with a wooden bowl (or trough) **корытце** for chopping vegetables, mainly cabbage

тёрка a grater

шумовка a shallow ladle with holes, for removing scum or retrieving **пельмени** (a sort of Russian ravioli) from boiling water

скалка a rolling pin, with or without handles

веничек a wire whisk

сбивалка a beater

разливная ложка, разливательная ложка, поварёшка a ladle

лопатка a spatula for cooking or serving

кухонные ножи и ложки kitchen knives and spoons, the former not usually differentiated except by size: **большой нож, нож, маленький нож, ножик**

For opening things:

штопор a corkscrew

консервный нож a can opener

ключ for prying off a lid

открывашка Can opener-and-church key

For cleaning up:

мочалка a washrag, sponge, or any scrubbing device; formerly strips of bark, now often dried vegetable sponge

ёршик a brush with bristles going in all directions

щётка a brush with a hard back, bristles on one side

сушилка usually a drying rack for dishes, but sometimes a plate-warmer; also, a clothes dryer

таз(ик) a dishpan in shape and *mostly* in use.

ведро a (garbage) pail. **Лучше в нас, чем в таз!** Better into us than into the garbage! (Throwing out food is sinful.)

Set the table
Накрой на стол!

The "Fannie Farmer" of the Soviet Union, **Книга о вкусной и здоровой пище**, recommends the following table equipment (in addition to a tablecloth **скатерть**) for serving six people. The meal that requires all this equipment is hardly an everyday affair, though.

солонка a salt shaker/cellar

перечница a pepper shaker

маслёнка a butter dish (a small bowl)

тарелки глубокие dinner soup bowls (that is, large, shallow, and rimmed)

тарелки мелкие dinner plates

тарелки закусочные hors d'oeuvres plates (resembling our salad plates)

тарелки пирожковые meat pie plates (resembling our butter plates)

тарелки десертные dessert plates (resembling our salad plates)

лоточек для сельди, селёдочница a long, narrow, oval dish (to suit the size of salt herring)

салатники salad bowls

миска суповая a soup tureen

соусник a gravy or sauce boat

блюдо круглое a round platter

блюдо овальное an oval platter

блюдо для хлеба a bread dish

бульонные чашки с блюдцами bouillon cups and saucers

судок для перца, горчицы и уксуса a condiment holder (usually for vinegar, mustard, salt, and pepper)

графи́н для воды́   a water pitcher (графи́н
  is in the shape of a decanter)

графи́н для фрукто́вого со́ка   a pitcher
  for fruit juice

графи́н для во́дки   a decanter for vodka

кувши́н   a pitcher

рю́мки для во́дки   vodka glasses, stemmed
  liqueur glasses in shape

рю́мки для вина́   small wine glasses

фуже́ры   large wine glasses

бока́лы для шампа́нского   champagne
  glasses

ножи́, ви́лки столо́вые и десе́ртные по 6
  dinner and dessert knives and forks, six each

   Not included by the Fannie Farmer are
spoons:

ча́йная ло́жка   a teaspoon

столо́вая ло́жка   a soup spoon

супова́я ло́жка   a soup ladle

десе́ртная ло́жка   a dessert spoon, not quite
  so large as a soup spoon

THE COMMUNAL APARTMENT
Коммуна́льная кварти́ра

Some older apartments are communal. One
apartment might include several individuals or
even families, all sharing the use of the kitchen,
hallway, and bathroom facilities, and the telephone if there is one. This is where the problem
of close quarters is really severe. The use of

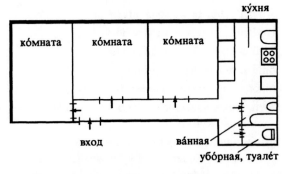

Коммуна́льная кварти́ра

common facilities must be scheduled, with a
clear definition of what belongs to whom, how it
should be maintained, and so forth. The problem
is not just the squabbles that arise over communal facilities but also the lack of privacy when a
family (two to four people) are living in one
room. Historically, the great mass of Russians
have lived at very close quarters with each other.

   The description of this type of apartment is
the same as for new apartments except that:

1. The individual rooms tend to be larger
    and have higher ceilings; both these fea-
    tures are highly desirable because contem-
    porary rooms are very small, and their low
    ceilings are oppressive. Kitchens are also
    larger, but the problems that arise when
    they must be shared far outweigh this
    advantage.

2. Since much of modern housing has the
    reputation of being jerry-built, the older
    buildings are often thought of as more
    solidly constructed and therefore less
    likely to require repair.

3. Decor tends to be older, larger, darker,
    and heavier.

THE PEASANT HOUSE
Крестья́нский дом

The Russian peasant hut изба́ had certain,
fairly regular features to it that our words
"hut" or "log cabin" do not convey. The peasant household described here is the forerunner
of the contemporary farmhouse; it is also the
peasant building of Russian fable, folklore, and
literature. After all, this is where most Russians
lived in the middle of the past century.

   Russian peasant housing offers a wealth of
fascinating material for the ethnographer, some
of which is worth exploration by language students, but only the major or most common
themes are discussed here. For more detail,
refer to publications of the ethnographic institute, Институ́т этногра́фии и́мени
Миклу́хо- Макла́я, Акаде́мия Нау́к.

Exterior
Вне́шний вид

Russians did not live in isolated farmhouses but in villages, with two kinds common to Old Russia: a **село́** was a village with a church and a few stores; it was therefore larger than a **дере́вня**, a village too small for a church. Villages were often located near a river or stream with the peasant houses lining one or both sides of a street that ran parallel to the stream. Either **дом** or **изба́** can be applied to a peasant house. **Дом** refers to the whole building and is especially used when the building is large (as in the north) or when the speaker wants to avoid connotations; **изба́** can refer either to the peasant house as a whole or to the main living room therein.

At first glance, anyone from the United States is likely to call the Russian **изба́** a log cabin, for indeed the central and northern Russian houses were made of logs chinked with moss **мох** or with hemp **конопля́** and built without a foundation in our sense of the word—for instance, tree stumps or stones were often used.

Use of tree stumps at foundation corners must have inspired the folk tales of the hut on chicken legs **избу́шка на ку́рьих но́жках** where the witch **Ба́ба-яга́** lived.

These are types of peasant houses that were common in various parts of Russia at the end of the nineteenth and beginning of the twentieth centuries: (1) northern regions, (2) central black-earth regions, (3) Perm oblast, (4) western regions, (5) southern black-earth regions, (6) the Kuban region. The two sided roofs are standard in most places except the south.

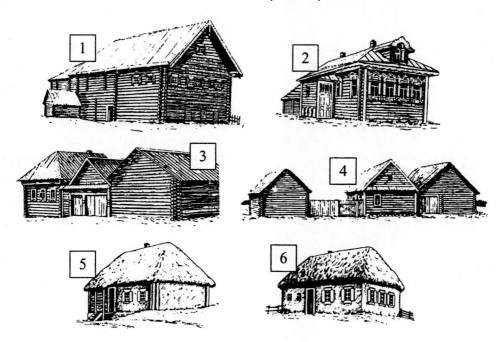

Roofs traditionally were made of straw **соло́менная кры́ша** or of planks **тесо́вая кры́ша** and were capped by a ridge beam. The front end of this beam, the end that extends toward the street, was often carved in the shape of a horse or rooster head, a remnant of the pre-Christian belief that such figures could bring good fortune or ward off misfortune.

A distinctive feature of Russian peasant houses was a **зава́линка**, a mound of earth held in by boards that was built around the outside of the house up to the level of the floor inside. Its purpose was to prevent cold winter air from circulating underneath the hut. The device has now disappeared, having been replaced by cement block foundations and an occasional bench for summer sitting.

In southern Russia and Ukraine, wood was scarce and peasant houses were made of combinations of brick and adobe made from clay and manure.

A contemporary window

Decor
Убра́нство до́ма

The southern houses **и́збы** (**изба́** is **ха́та** in Ukraine) were whitewashed and then decorated with brightly painted designs **ро́спись**. Further north any paint was confined to shutters. Instead, decoration consisted of fancy wood-carving **резьба́**, especially of beam ends, rims, and almost any shutters. The art of woodcarving was very highly developed in the northern regions of Russia, but, as the photograph demonstrates, contemporary central Russians are not slouches.

Size
Разме́ры

Variations in size also occurred from north to south. Southern buildings were usually smaller while those in the far north were huge two-storied affairs. (Farm animals could be kept from freezing by bringing them closer to the only supply of heat, in the same building as their owners.) For central Russia, the most common **изба́** had only one story, but its wood floor was constructed a few feet above ground level. The space below **подва́л**, **по́дпол** was used for storing vegetables, especially potatoes and other root vegetables.

The variations in size that seem large in the preceding figure are not due to real differences in housing, at least for people. The peasant household **крестья́нский двор** could include just a house and garden, perhaps a small fence and some outbuildings; this was common in the south. In central Russia, a house, a high gate, and farm outbuildings might be connected to each other by a fence, often in such a way as to enclose an area **двор**. The very large northern houses included the farm outbuildings **двор** and the peasant house **изба́**, all under one roof.

Design
Вну́тренняя планиро́вка

The most common farm building had three basic parts: (1) the heated hut **изба́**, one large room where all cooking, eating, and sleeping took place; (2) an unheated entrance room **се́ни** (*pl. only*) that might be used for sleeping in the summer or also some storage; and (3) either a barn area **двор** or a storage and summer sleeping room **клеть**. (In later use, toward the end of the nineteenth century, the **клеть** often became a **го́рница**, usually a heated room for receiving company and sleeping.) This three-part design (**изба́ + се́ни + клеть/двор**) was the most common. The very poor had to manage on just a one-room hut or a hut and an entrance room.

божни́ца   an icon shelf

воро́та   a gate or a large barn door (*pl. only*)

входна́я дверь   entrance

въезд   a ramp

голбе́ц   a structure alongside the stove, for lying on, containing an entrance to the lower floor, also called **лежа́нка**

голла́ндка   a stove for heating, covered with tiles **изразцы́**

го́рница   a second room, for sleeping or company

двор   the part of building used as a barn

крова́ть   a bed

крыльцо́   a porch

ла́вка   a built-in bench

печь   a Russian stove

пове́ть   a loft

пола́ти   a very large overhead shelf (*pl. only*)

посте́ль   a bed

посу́дник   a cupboard

рукомо́йник   a dispenser suspended over a large bucket, used for washing

се́ни   an entrance room (*pl. only*)

скамья́   a (movable) bench

чула́н   a storage room in a peasant hut (**кладова́я** is the usual word)

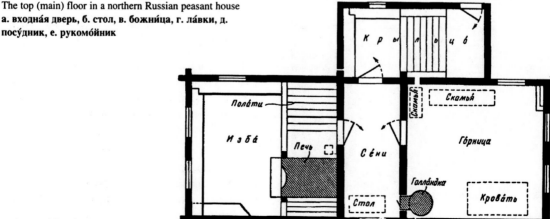

The top (main) floor in a northern Russian peasant house
а. входна́я дверь, б. стол, в. божни́ца, г. ла́вки, д. посу́дник, е. рукомо́йник

A central Russian peasant house

In the peasant hut
В крестья́нской избе́

Let us imagine what you would see if you went into a peasant house commonly found in north or central Russia. From the road you walk up a short path along the side of the house to a small covered porch **крыльцо́**. The first room you enter is the entrance room **се́ни**. From the **се́ни** you enter the living quarters **изба́**. (The threshold **поро́г** is at the entrance to the **изба́**, not at the entrance to the **се́ни**.) Take one step inside and you are facing the street. Either to the immediate right or left of you is a huge Russian stove **ру́сская печь** the size of a furnace; it takes up one-fifth to one-fourth the area of the room. (The whole room is not large, usually square, from sixteen to twenty-one feet a side.) Benches **ла́вки**, often built-in, line the remaining walls of

В избе́ се́верного ти́па. A Russian stove is to the left, the sleeping shelf **пола́ти** above.

the room. In the corner diagonal to the stove there is a table with perhaps an additional free-standing bench **скамья́** or some stools **табуре́тки,** or both. In the same corner (called the **пере́дний, кра́сный, Свято́й,** or **Бо́жий у́гол**) is an icon with a small oil lamp **лампа́дка** suspended in front of it and often also draped with a heavily embroidered "towel" **полоте́нце.** The wall opposite you (the front wall) usually has three small windows, and the side wall opposite the stove has another window or two. Above the windows along the walls are small shelves **по́лки.** Directly overhead is a very large shelf **пола́ти** (*pl. only*) usually extending from the stove to the opposite side wall, which is used for sleeping.

Which way did the Gingerbread Man **Колобо́к** go?

Надое́ло Колобку́ лежа́ть, он и покати́лся с окна́ на ла́вку, с ла́вки на пол, по по́лу да к дверя́м. Перепры́гнул че́рез поро́г в се́ни, из сене́й—на крыльцо́, с крыльца́—на двор, со двора́—за воро́та—да́льше да да́льше. [b]

Надое́ло Колобку́ лежа́ть, он и покати́лся с окна́ на зава́линку, с зава́линки на тра́вку, с тра́вки на доро́жку и покати́лся по доро́жке. [c]

Пере́дний у́гол

Ру́сская печь в ста́рой
крестья́нской избе́

The Russian Stove
Ру́сская печь

The Russian stove, a great mass of clay **гли́на** or brick **кирпи́ч**, was common to all the eastern Slavs as their answer to very cold winters. Its location, orientation, and decoration differed according to locale,[2] but every **изба́** had one. It was used any time any form of heat was required—for baking bread and cooking, for keeping both humans and farm animals warm, and in some areas even for taking a steam bath. In addition, it kept the **изба́** warm, grandma slept on it, and it dried both food and clothes. The earliest, then later the poorest, Russian **изба́** used a stove that operated without the benefit of a chimney pipe. This type was called **курна́я изба́, чёрная изба́**. Smoke went out either through the door or through a hole in the roof, which was closed once the smoking had stopped. By the end of the nineteenth century, the use of a stovepipe was more common. **Бе́лая изба́** was a house that had a chimney. The great size of the Russian stove made it a heat-holder and distributor. Food was cooked

and bread was baked deep inside the stove after the fire had died out and the embers and ashes were pushed over to one side. Therefore very long-handled devices were used to get the food in and out or to clean the oven. Some of the equipment used with a Russian stove included:

ухва́т a long rod, with one end a large U-shape to fit around the base of pots for taking them out of the stove

горшо́к

ухва́т

The long-handled **ухва́ты** are used for taking hot pots **горшки́** from deep inside the Russian stove

сковоро́дник a long rod with a hook and lever at one end for removing skillets from the oven

лопа́та a broad wooden shovel for loading and unloading loaves of bread

кочерга́ a poker (*gen. pl.* **кочерёг**)

метёлка a broom

2. In Ukraine, the stove was most often in a corner opposite, rather than next to, the entrance. South-central Russian stoves often faced the side wall rather than the front wall. Ukrainians whitewashed their stoves and often painted colorful designs **ро́спись** on them. Richer peasants often tiled the outside of their stoves.

квашёнка

миска   рукомо́йник   ко́вшик

кри́нка

ча́шечка
с пе́стиком

пло́шка   a flat bowl

чугу́н   a cast-iron (stew) pot

сковорода́   a large metal frying pan

ко́вшик   a short-handled ladle

кры́нка, кри́нка   a pitcher, usually without handles, especially for milk

кувши́н   a pitcher with handles for serving other liquids

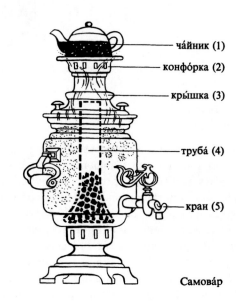

ча́йник (1)

конфо́рка (2)

кры́шка (3)

труба́ (4)

кран (5)

Самова́р

Cooking equipment
Ку́хонная у́тварь

Traditional cooking utensils were usually relatively large in size and few in number. People did not eat off individual plates. Rather, each person had an individual spoon and dipped into the common bowl **миска**. Members of the family took turns at dipping, with the eldest first; children who took food out of turn faced rebuke. A character in **Ра́ковый ко́рпус** by Solzhenitsyn explains that he does not know his interlocutor very well: «**А почему́ я до́лжен вам ве́рить? Мы с ва́ми из одно́й ми́ски щей не хлеба́ли**». ("Why should I trust you? We haven't eaten cabbage soup from the same bowl.")

A ceramic stewpot **горшо́к** was the basic container for cooking in a Russian stove. After the fire had been made early in the morning and the stove had warmed up, the embers were pushed to one side and the **горшо́к**, most often with a cereal **ка́ша** inside it, was put into the oven, using the long-handled **ухва́т**. The following are only the most common or most obvious cooking utensils:

Samovar
Самова́р

(1) teapot
(2) teapot holder
(3) lid
(4) central tube
(5) spigot

Also: **Заглу́шка** lid for the central tube

The Russian samovar **самова́р** (self-cooker) was a relative newcomer to the late eighteenth-century Russian household. But when it came, it stayed, for the samovar was an economical way to get hot water quickly. The samovar made hot water for tea, but the tea was never inside the samovar. A charcoal, kindling, or cone fire built in the central tube heated water that surrounded the tube in the body of the samovar. Naturally, smoke poured from the samovar chimney while the fire was being made, so that in the summer the samovar was started outside the house and in the winter its draft chimney (an extension of the central tube) was connected to a pipe in the Russian stove.

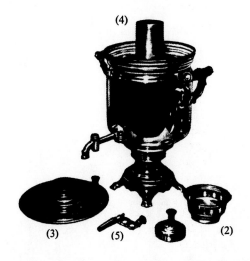

A very strong tea mixture was made in a small teapot that was then kept warm by resting on top of the samovar. A small amount of this strong tea was poured into a cup and then diluted with hot water from the samovar.

The kitchen
Ку́хня

The area between the stove and the wall it faced was for cooking. It had extra shelves for cooking utensils and maybe a small cupboard **посу́дник** for dishes. This area occasionally was separated from the rest of the room by a screen of some sort, but this was not usual.

The front "room"
Пере́дний у́гол

In the corner at a diagonal from the stove was the dining area. This was considered a place of honor: it was rude for a stranger to advance toward it without specific invitation. Here all the eating, the ceremonies, and the parties took place. An icon **ико́на, о́браз** was placed on a shelf **божни́ца** in this corner. Seating at the table was on benches or stools. (Chairs were a city invention and not a part of peasant furniture.)

Benches **ла́вки** were often attached to all the wall space not already occupied by the stove, and each one had a name that varied from place to place, though the actual use of the benches was less variable. The long bench **до́лгая ла́вка** on the side wall opposite the stove was often where the women did their spinning, mending, and weaving. The bench **ко́ник, ку́тник** from the doorway to the side wall was reserved for the man of the house. It was here that he repaired and cleaned his tools and equipment; therefore this was the part of the house reserved for dirty jobs.

Where do they sleep?
Где спят?

Nothing has been said about beds. At the beginning of World War II when the German soldiers first began to investigate peasant houses (in the western USSR) for their own use, they could not find the beds. The stove and table were obvious enough, but where did these people sleep? The answer was dramatically simple: on any flat surface. Grandmother or grandfather slept on the stove, the warmest and most desirable sleeping place. The children slept on the large shelf **пола́ти** just over the door. The baby slept in a cradle **лю́лька** hung from the ceiling, and the rest of the family used the benches and, if necessary, the floor.

Lighting
Освеще́ние

Lighting during the long winter months was a major problem: oil for lamps was too expensive to burn except in front of the icon, and kerosene lamps were a relatively modern invention; instead, long dry sticks **лучи́на** were used.

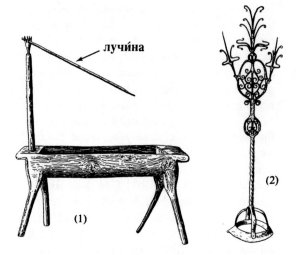

лучи́на

Приспособле́ния для держа́ния лучи́ны   Devices for holding sticks: (1) свети́льно с коры́том, (2) стари́нный свете́ц

These sticks were both cheap and readily available, but they were also dangerous and very short-lived: a new one had to be lit every fifteen minutes or so. In describing life in an average village in Leningradskaya Oblast in 1927 a correspondent asserted:

То́лько в не́которых дома́х жгут кероси́н. Про́чие освеща́ются лучи́ной и́ли за́светло ложа́тся спать. [d]

Plumbing
Водоснабже́ние

Water was obtained from a well коло́дец usually somewhere outside the house. Two types of well rigging are common in Russia. One is the wind-up kind with which we are familiar. Another very common device жура́вль uses a counterweight to help pull up the bucket of water. The long poles suspended at an angle often seen in pictures of Russian villages indicate the sites of wells.

From the well, peasants carried the water in buckets вёдра (sg. ведро́) that hung from both ends of a kind of yoke коромы́сло to a barrel чан located either in the entrance room or near

Не плюй в коло́дец, пригоди́тся воды́ напи́ться.
Don't spit in the well; you might want to drink from it.

A well   Коло́дец–жура́вль

the изба́ door. Inside, often near the Russian stove, was a рукомо́йник (literally, a handwasher), with some kind of dispenser hanging over a large bucket.

Sanitary facilities (toilets) varied with time and place. Some areas had none whatsoever. The following was written in 1926 regarding this problem about an area now known as Tverskaya Oblast, just north of Moscow:

Специа́льные убо́рные ста́ли то́лько о́чень неда́вно появля́ться в нове́йших постро́йках. Для э́того отгора́живается сте́нками оди́н из концо́в ма́ленького мо́стика на дворе́. В ста́рых постро́йках никаки́х осо́бых отхо́жих мест не бы́ло; и в э́тих це́лях испо́льзовался весь двор. [e]

In other areas, especially in the north, a special place (a hole in the floor) was provided somewhere in the **двор**, almost always near an outside wall to make cleaning easier. The accumulated soil was removed in the winter with pickaxes and baskets when, mercifully enough, everything was still frozen. Especially in the summertime, outhouses **нару́жные убо́рные** were also used.

The house "spirit"
Домово́й

Every house had to have a **домово́й** (and sometimes also a **домова́я**). Most people thought of this creature as having some real form or substance (unlike our amorphous ghost), but its actual description varied considerably according to locality. Generally it was thought of as relatively small, animal-like, and endowed with special powers. It would carry on conversations with mice or crickets who also were house dwellers. In any case, every house had to have one, and it had to be treated with care lest it leave. The following passage gives one local description of the **домово́й** and its invitation to

a newly built house. In this region a yard or barn spirit **дворово́й** was also part of the scene.

Любопы́тно при переселе́нии на но́вое ме́сто приглаше́ние домово́го и дворово́го. Хозя́ин стано́вится пе́ред воро́тами до́ма, кла́няется три ра́за в ра́зные сто́роны, повора́чиваясь че́рез ле́вое плечо́, и зовёт: «Ба́тюшка домово́й и ма́тушка домова́я, ба́тюшка дворово́й и ма́тушка дворова́я, со всем семе́йством, пойдёмте к нам на но́вое жили́ще, с на́ми жить.»

... Представле́ние о домово́м и дворово́м ещё живёт в широ́ких ма́ссах, и представля́ются они́ как бы двойника́ми хозя́ина. Они́ пока́зываются иногда́, но не к хоро́шему, и при э́том лицо́м похо́жи на хозя́ина. И. по хара́ктеру, и по скло́нностям они́ таки́е же, как и хозя́ин—е́сли тот небре́жно отно́сится к скоти́не, то и дворово́й начина́ет поша́ливать; но относи́ться к ним, во вся́ком слу́чае, ну́жно уважи́тельно, ина́че они́ мо́гут и уйти́. [f]

CONTEMPORARY RURAL HOUSING
Совреме́нное се́льское жили́ще

A house in the country these days may range from the traditional peasant house (in the 1920s poverty and lack of materials were so widespread that even then a few chimneyless **курны́е и́збы** were being built) to something

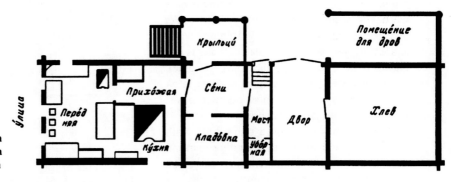

Ви́утренняя плани́ро́вка совреме́нного жили́ща
A contemporary floor plan

greatly resembling the city apartment discussed in the first section. Most contemporary rural housing is a cross between the two.

What remains
Что остаётся

In the single-family dwelling, the stove remains, though it might be a less romantic concrete block affair. It is sometimes situated in the center of the house, as one of its present purposes is to help divide the house into separate rooms. In fact, the major difference between the old and the new is the effort to create more privacy by dividing the housing area into separate rooms.

What has changed
Что изменилось

The environs of large cities are littered with rows of new dachas—the summer residences of those who have a garden plot **садовый участок**. Many are in the shape of a Dutch colonial—the second floor can be used for summer sleeping. Another startling sight in the country is the presence of large, multistoried solid(!) brick houses, called, interestingly enough, **коттéдж**. Such houses are being built by people with quantities of new money. Brick is always preferred because fire is the bane of Russian rural existence.

People with less money are building their own houses with logs. Because most private farming is still accomplished on a small lot, the area required for storage, equipment, and animals is much smaller than it used to be. Electricity now reaches most areas, but is usually limited to a light bulb hung from the ceiling. Running water and sewers are not usually available. Water is still drawn from a well, and the toilet **уборная**, **отхóжее мéсто** (*vulg.* **нужни́к**) is either in an outhouse or, especially in more northern areas, somewhere in the covered **двор**.

Furniture has taken on a citified air, with chairs, beds, and sofas the rule rather than the exception. Cooking equipment now embraces greater variety. Houses without electricity, or

with not enough of it, now commonly use the following devices for cooking (in addition to the Russian stove):

кероси́нка   the most common substitute for a hot plate, usually a one-burner kerosene stove with a cloth wick

керога́з   also a kerosene burner, but more economical to run

при́мус   a portable stove that burns vaporized oil

жидкий газ   liquid gas, used by many people; a large container **балло́н** lasts about a month

The kitchen, instead of the **рукомóйник**, might now have a **мóйка**, another word for kitchen sink (also called **ра́ковина**), used especially when running water is not available; thus it often includes a reservoir in a cabinet above to supply water, and a bucket in the cabinet below to catch the waste. The same device in a bathroom or bedroom is the **умыва́льник**. **Рукомóйник** now is a water dispenser, with a valve and lever at the bottom, that is placed either inside or outside the house. It is also frequently found on trains: if you can't figure out how to start the water on a train, push up on the stick protuding from the bottom of a container over the sink.

Рукомóйник: For water, push up on peg

TRANSLATIONS

a. It is best to wash dishes and silverware with soap and a brush under a stream of hot running water. But, unfortunately, not all houses have plumbing with hot water or a water heater yet. Therefore dishes are sometimes washed in dishpans. In any case the children should learn the right methods: they will simplify and speed up the entire washing process. The dirty dishes should be on the right, a dishpan of warm water (with a solution of mustard or soda) should be in front of the dishwasher, and next to it should be another dishpan with hot water for rinsing. The dishes that have been done should be placed on the left. **И.Н. Фёдорова и др., Домоводство (Москва: Просвещéние, 1967), стр.** 304 (a guide for teachers of home economics in grades V-VII).

b. The gingerbread man got tired of lying there, so he rolled from the window to the bench, from the bench to the floor, along the floor to the door. He jumped over the threshold to the entrance room, from the entrance room to the porch, from the porch to the yard, from the yard through the gate farther and farther. **О. Капи́ца, Ру́сские ска́зки про звере́й (Ленингра́д: Дéтгиз, 1951), стр.** 19.

c. The gingerbread man got tired of lying there. He rolled from the window to the "zavalinka," from the "zavalinka" to the grass, from the grass to the road, and on down the road. **А. Чу́хин, Малю́тка (Симферо́поль: Крымизда́т, 1964), стр.** 190.

d. Kerosene is used [burned] in just a few houses. The others are lit by burning sticks or [the people] go to bed early [before dark]. **И. Бугро́ва, "Деревéнские встрéчи," Ленингра́дская пра́вда, 1 января́** 1968, **стр.** 2.

e. Special bathrooms have begun to appear only very recently in the newest buildings. For this purpose they wall off one of the ends of the walkway in the "barn" [двор]. Old houses had no special lavatories; the entire "barn" [двор] was used for this purpose. **Вéрхне-Во́лжская этнологи́ческая энциклопéдия, Кресть-я́нские постро́йки Яросла́вско-Тверско́го кра́я (Ленингра́д: Госуда́рственная акадéмия исто́рии материа́льной культу́ры, 1926), стр.** 46.

f. Of interest to us is the invitation issued to the yard spirit and the house spirit when the peasants move to a new place. The owner stands in front of the courtyard gates, bows three times in different directions, turns his head over his left shoulder and calls: "Father house spirit, mother house spirit, father yard spirit and mother yard spirit, with the whole family, come with us to our new house, to live with us."

The concept of the house spirit and yard spirit is still quite alive among the peasants. They are often pictured as doubles of their masters. They appear every once in a while but for no good purpose, and their faces resemble that of their owner. And their character and tendencies are also like their owner's. If he is careless about the livestock, then the yard spirit will play pranks; but one must, in any case, treat these spirits with respect or they might go away. **Крестья́нские постро́йки Яросла́вско-Тверско́го кра́я, стр.** 47, 48.

6

Food

Русская пи́ща

Сы́тый голо́дного не разуме́ет.
The man who has eaten does not understand the man who hasn't.

We are encased in our own categories of what is edible, when, and how. These boxes are reinforced several times daily until we can barely contemplate cereal (mush) at dinner or salad at breakfast. Morning kippers turn an otherwise civilized Englishman into a queer duck. These set notions about food cause misery for travelers who forget to leave such baggage at home, where it applies. This chapter is the Russian such baggage.

The classic Russian pre-Revolution cookbook is known mostly by its author's last name, Molokhovets (**Еле́на Молохове́ц**, *A Gift to Young Housewives* **Пода́рок молоды́м хозя́йкам**). Large amounts of it have been translated in *Classic Russian Cooking* by Joyce Toomre (Bloomington: Indiana University Press, 1992); a long and splendid introduction sets the scene. If you like to read about Russian cooking we also recommend *The Art of Russian Cooking* by Anne Volokh with Mavus Manus (New York: Macmillan, 1983), a comprehensive book on Russian cuisine with recipes enhanced by literary references and personal reminiscences plus food titles in English and transliterated Russian. The standard post-war Soviet reference was the *Book of Tasty and Healthful Food* (**Кни́га о вку́сной и здоро́вой пи́ще**), a major reference for what follows.

First we consider the raw materials available, cooking, meals and their contents and times, the common dishes, what to drink, and where to eat out.

RAW MATERIALS
Продукты

Grain
Зерно

Grains, their cereals and flours, have been the historical mainstay of the Russian diet. Potatoes (and their related tomatoes) were a contribution from the New World. There is more than alliteration in the Russian version of "Cabbage soup and cereal is our food": **Щи да каша—пища наша.** A variety of grains still figure heavily in Russian cuisine.

Колос ржи.

Колос пшеницы.

Колос ячменя.

Просо.

Овёс.

Grasses that produce grain **хлебные злаки, хлеба** unify a field that includes the particular plants: wheat **пшеница**, rye **рожь**, millet **просо**, barley **ячмень**, rice **рис**, oats **овёс**, and corn **кукуруза**. Another grain, buckwheat **гречиха**, is not a grass. However, dried peas, beans, and lentils **бобовые** are also sometimes classified as grain **зерно**.

The whole grain from these plants is hulled, and then left whole or coarsely ground to become groats **крупа**, which when cooked become cereal **каша**. Poor consistency for cereal is the gooey gruel or mush **размазня** (also a weak-willed person); desirable consistency preserves the individuality of each grain.

The wheat plant **пшеница** yields a very finely ground farina **манная крупа, манка**, which when cooked becomes **манная каша** (cream of wheat), a staple for children at breakfast.

The buckwheat plant **гречиха** supplies buckwheat groats **гречневая крупа, гречка** in various grinds: whole **ядрица** and buckwheat bits that remain after the whole grains have been removed **продел**. Buckwheat cereal **гречневая каша** is one of the most popular cereals for use as a main dish.

Rice **рис** is associated with the south and its cuisine, especially in the variety of dishes called pilav **плов** which come from central Asia. Puffed rice **воздушный рис** is a children's snack, eaten dry.

Oat cereal **овсяная крупа** can be cooked and used as part of a main dish either whole **недроблёная** or coarse–ground **дроблёная**. Oats are cheaper and less highly regarded than are buckwheat or rice. A breakfast cereal comparable to our oatmeal uses the brand name "Hercules" **геркулес: геркулесовая каша, овсянка**. Oats are also the basis for a traditional Russian pretreated oat cereal **толокно** that is no longer popular but is thought to be good for the very young and the very old.

The millet plant **просо** provides millet cereal **пшено**, a fairly common main-dish cereal **пшённая каша/пшёнка** which tends to turn bitter if not parboiled and the water discarded before cooking. Millet has the advantage of being cheap.

The barley plant **ячмень** supplies two kinds of cereals, a fine grind **ячневая каша** and whole **перловая каша**. Both are cheap enough to feed the chickens.

Flour
Мука́

We associate Russians with rye **рожь**, but it is wheat **пшени́ца** that makes the Russian's world: winter wheats **ози́мые** and spring wheats **яровы́е**. Wheat flour comes to the consumer in three grades: the best is **крупча́тка** (**вы́сший сорт**), used for cakes or the finest cooking; then comes first grade **пе́рвый сорт**, which is acceptable for most uses; and finally second grade **второ́й сорт**. (All flour must be sieved, not just to reduce lumps, but to exclude what might be in the lumps.)

Rye flour **ржана́я мука́** is also used, but mostly by the bread-making industry; it is often not available to the consumer. Wheat and rye flours are the basis of the bread industry, but when they are in short supply it is not uncommon to add other things: ground peas, beans, or corn, for example.

Bread
Хлеб

Bread is the *sine qua non* of the Russian diet. Even cereal for breakfast can be accompanied by bread. Bread is part of the table setting at dinner, and is always served at supper. Bread is so close to existence itself that it used to be heavily subsidized and therefore so cheap that when grain was hard to get, many people fed the chickens with bread.

Bread has a crust **ко́рочка** and insides **мя́киш**, and some people prefer the heel **горбу́шка**. Everyone prefers fresh bread **све́жий хлеб**, but those who get to the store too late must resort to stale bread **чёрствый хлеб**. The four major kinds of dough are (1) "black" bread **чёрный хлеб**, which is mostly rye; (2) "gray" bread **се́рый хлеб**, which is part rye and part wheat flour; (3) white bread **бе́лый хлеб** from wheat flour; and (4) white bread dough with added fat and sometimes sugar and flavorings **сдо́ба**. Black and gray bread more often accompany first and second courses while white breads are more likely with tea (i.e., dessert) or for Russian (open-faced) sandwiches **бутербро́ды**. As elsewhere in Europe, darker breads are considered less formal, less elegant. A few common bread shapes are shown on the next page; the numbers following them correspond to the doughs from the preceding list.

A "karavay" **карава́й** is a very large circular loaf bought or made especially for presenting to guests or to newlyweds. This is the bread used in the ancient welcoming ceremony **поднести́ хлеб-соль** in which bread and salt are a symbol of welcome, **хлебосо́льство,** which means *hospitality*. Not quite so large, but also circular, is the common round loaf **кру́глый, столо́вый хлеб**. The Jewish chala **плетёнка, ха́ла** is also fairly common.

Rolls of various kinds also abound: a plain round roll **бу́лочка**; a long roll **городска́я, францу́зская булочка**; a long roll that is slightly sweet **са́йка**; and a roll in the shape of a padlock **кала́ч**.

What we would at first call a bagel **бу́блик** is actually very slightly sweet and is meant to be eaten fresh with tea (but never with smoked salmon). Smaller are "baranki" **бара́нки**, and smallest are little dry rings **су́шки**. All three ring-shaped "rolls" can appear with many varieties of flavorings; the latter two keep longer since they are expected to be dry.

None of the foregoing really prepares you for the marvelous richness of the Russian raised-dough cuisine. They seem to be able to do anything with yeast **дро́жжи**. In the old days people normally made their own bread, often using a sourdough starter **заква́ска** if it was black bread, and using a sponge dough **на опа́ре** if white. Now, so many kinds render complete descriptions impossible; for black bread, try Borodinskiy or Orlovskiy. Those who want to make their own rolls or tea breads can buy the dough **те́сто** and finish it off at home. Sweetened or flavored dough **сдо́бное тесто** is perhaps the most commonly used for making many kinds of sponge or coffee cakes **ке́ксы**, especially the Easter bread "kulich" **кули́ч**.

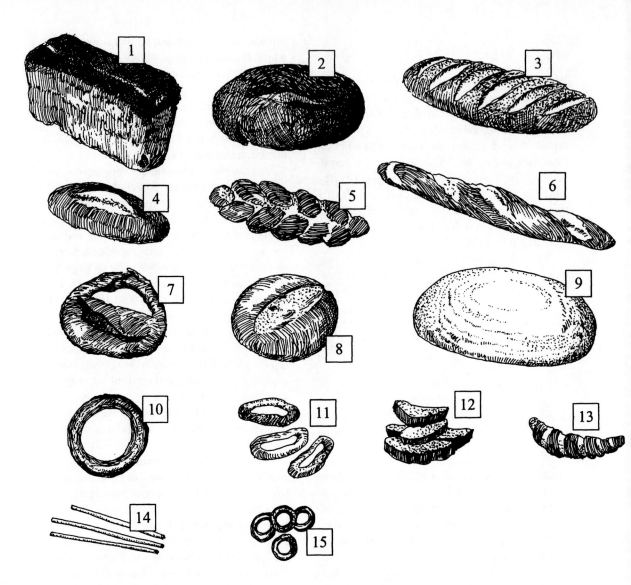

(1) буха́нка, (кирпи́чик) 1, 2, 3

(2) кру́глый, столо́вый, подо́вый хлеб 1, 2, 3

(3) бато́н 3

(4) городска́я бу́лка 3, 4

(5) ха́ла, плетёнка 3

(6) бато́н алта́йский 3

(7) кала́ч 3, 4

(8) (бу́лка) си́тник 3

(9) карава́й 2, 3, 4

(10) бу́блик 3, 4

(11) бара́нка 3, 4

(12) сухари́ 4

(13) рога́лик 3, 4

(14) соло́мка 3

(15) су́шки 3, 4

Russians don't make toast, though they do slice white bread and fry it in butter to make croutons **гре́нки**; or soak it in milk and eggs and then fry it in butter to make French toast **гренки** for breakfast (without syrup); or fry it in butter and serve it in larger pieces **гре́нки** with smoked salmon—when they have some.

Pasta
Макаро́нные изде́лия

Various kinds of pasta are widely used, both in soups and in main dishes. Our word *noodles* requires not only a shape but also egg, while all Russian macaroni products might have egg, depending on the grade. Noodle shapes are **лапша́**, a common soup ingredient; spaghetti shapes are **вермише́ль**; macaroni shapes are **макаро́ны**, including fanciful stars **звёздочки**, "ears" **у́шки**, crayfish shells **раку́шки**, and others.

Macaroni products are regularly eaten, but they are thought to be inelegant and are not used to impress company.

Milk and cheese
Молоко́ и сыр

Russians also are sour milk specialists, and great is your loss if you do not try some. Fresh unpasteurized milk **непастеризо́ванное молоко́** is available at peasant markets and stores, but Russians boil it unless they know the seller's habits. Pasteurized fresh milk **сыро́е молоко́** comes in bottles **в буты́лках** or in packages **в паке́тах** that include a date on the cap that is significant to the homemaker, who avoids buying milk more than a couple of days old. Milk also commonly comes in a large can **фля́га** for sale in stores, or barrels **бо́чки** for sale on the street in bulk distribution **разливно́е молоко́**. Both whole milk **це́льное молоко́** and skim milk **обезжи́ренное молоко́** are available, but the wonder comes with the many kinds of milk on its way to cheese. They are made as we do our buttermilk, yogurt, and sour cream—by the addition of various bacteria or yeasts. They are thought to be healthful and most are delicious. A modern variety, acidophilous milk **ацидофили́н**, kefir **кефи́р** (similar to our yogurt), and **простоква́ша** (similar to our buttermilk), are popular at breakfast. A particular pride of peasants, since they have the Russian stove so necessary for its making, is "heated" milk **топлёное молоко́**

made by leaving milk in the Russian stove for a very long time—until a brown skin forms on the top and some of the liquid has evaporated. This kind of milk plus a little sour cream mixed in is "varenets" **варене́ц**; this kind of milk when government-produced and without the skin is "ryazhenka" **ря́женка**. Our buttermilk **па́хта, па́хтанье** receives much less attention. Evaporated milk **концентри́рованное молоко́** is not so popular as sweetened condensed milk **сгущённое молоко́ с са́харом, сгущёнка**, which is used to sweeten coffee, make desserts, or substitute for fresh milk. Unopened cans of condensed milk are also put in water and boiled for several hours to make a thick light brown goo that children eat as is or spread on bread. Chocolate milk **шокола́дное молоко́** is also a children's favorite. Dried milk **сухо́е молоко́** may be available when other milk isn't, but its use is not common. Enriched milk **белко́вое молоко́** uses whey **сы́воротка** for the enrichment. Unfortunately, vitamins A and D are not

Ря́женка

added to milk, and as a result rickets **рахи́т** is not a rarity, especially in the north.

Among the Tartars, or where the horses are, kumiss **куми́с** is available—fermented mare's milk which may contain up to 4.5 percent alcohol and is thought to be especially good for the treatment of tuberculosis.

Cream **сли́вки** comes in two grades: regular **обыкнове́нные** at 20 percent butterfat, and heavy **жи́рные** at 35 percent butterfat. The latter, for making whipped cream **взби́тые сли́вки**, can be expensive. Cooking more often uses sour cream **смета́на**, which comes in three grades, the lowest of which has more fat than does ours. It is used for making many sauces and is also eaten straight, with perhaps some sugar or preserves. Sour cream is often sold in bulk **развесна́я смета́на**, and this is the best kind.

Despite the joy the various forms of milk might bring, even their role is probably overshadowed by a kind of curd cheese **тво́ро́г**, which is in the same family as our cottage cheese—but there the resemblance stops! It is often made at home, but stores have several grades according to the fat content; the foreign visitor to the Russian home is most likely to come across it as the main component of paskha **па́сха**, a Russian Easter dessert. Curd-cheese cakes **сы́рники**, and curd-cheese Danish **ватру́шки** are standard in the Russian diet. One form of this curd cheese is "little cheese" **тво́ро́жный сыро́к**, in which the curd cheese is used for a background for flavorings, popularly sugar, vanilla, and raisins, or is sometimes chocolate-coated: **глазиро́ванные сырки́**.

As much as sour milk (and curd cheese) is a specialty, its further development into cheese is less a Russian technique. Until fairly recently the Russian peasant considered cheese a smelly object (**Фу! Воня́ет.**[1]) and therefore *very* strong cheeses do not make a good hostess gift. Nevertheless, many good cheeses are made, and many are of foreign descent. (And many are currently hard to get.) Relatively mild and hard Dutch types are **голла́ндский, костром-ско́й, яросла́вский**, and **угли́чский**. Cheddar is **че́ддер**. Swiss types are **швейца́рский, алта́йский, сове́тский**, and **моско́вский**. Sharp, strong cheeses are **латви́йский, краснода́рский**. A soft Limburger type is **дорогобу́жский**, while "little tea cheese" **ча́йный сыро́к** is a similar soft cheese that has not been allowed to ripen. Some soft and strong cheeses are **заку́сочный, ру́сский камамбе́р**, and **рокфо́р**. Cheeses ripened in brine come mostly from the Caucasus and have suitably Caucasian names: **чана́х, сулугу́ни, грузи́нский**; this type includes brynza **бры́нза**, which is made from sheep's milk and is popular in Caucasian cooking. Green cheese **зелёный сыр** is made from skim milk that has been flavored and is often used grated over macaroni.

Bring your egg container!

---

1. Note that this is peasant—that is, unrefined—speech.

Meat **мясо** everywhere and not a thousand rubles to spend.

Process cheeses **пла́вленные сыры́** are common and include fancy cheeses **делика-те́сные сыры**, high-quality process cheeses to which any of a number of seasonings have been added.

Eggs
Яйца

The basic egg **яйцо́** is encased by a shell **скор-лупа́** and consists of a white **бело́к** (whence the Russian name for protein **белки́**), and a yolk **желто́к**.[2] Eggs are sold individually or by the "tens" **деся́тки**; the freshest are **диети́чес-кие**, which are no more than five days old; next are "fresh" **све́жие** or **столо́вые**, no more than thirty days old.

Meat
Мя́со

Meat used to be a sometime thing. In government meat stores **мясны́е магази́ны** the practice was to take what meat you could get and do with it what you could. The butcher **мясни́к** stood behind the counter with the meat in a pile

and you pointed to what you wanted; or perhaps the butcher would slice you a piece from a hanging carcass. If you asked for too much, the people in line behind you would complain that you were not leaving enough for them. The free market has brought the meat, but it is expensive.

Officially, cuts of meat are divided into three classes: the first class **пе́рвый сорт** has more meat and less bone, the second class **второ́й сорт** has more bone, and the third class is nought but skin and bones. Cleverly enough, it turns out that a large percentage of the carcass **ту́ша** is in the first class and therefore costs more; this is especially true of pork, 95 percent of which is first class. Within classes, prices are the same so that financial pressure encourages the buyer to think of meat as meat with little distinction bestowed on cuts and kinds. (It also happens that the butcher will ignore these distinctions altogether and will charge the first-class price for the whole thing. The meat business is not without its recompenses.)

Meat can also be acquired at the market **на ры́нке** from a private seller **ча́стник**. Advantages here are greater availability and the chance to specify the kind of meat you want. The disadvantage is the price, which is likely to be much greater than in the state stores—it is

---

2. Yellow, gold, **зо́лото**, yolk, **жёлтый**.... *Plus ça change, plus c'est la même chose.*

not difficult to spend a week's wages on a cut of meat for a party dinner.

And finally, fresh meat can also be obtained at the convenience food section **отде́л полуфабрика́тов** at grocery stores **продово́льственные магази́ны** or at "culinary" stores **магази́ны кулина́рии**, which are restaurant outlets that prepare ready-made precooked servings. It is fairly expensive but fast and welcome on Friday night when a weekend of meals faces the cook.

Beef
Говя́дина

Most contemporaries do not distinguish most cuts of meat, though some do recognize tenderloin **вы́резка** (**ланге́т** means slices of tenderloin) as being elegant and "rumpsteaks" **ромште́кс** and schnitzel **шни́цель** as being very good. Many others consider **вы́резка** to be any boneless meat **мя́коть**. Bone-in is better because it can cover two courses.

For historical and contemporary reasons, soups and stews are among the best Russian meat dishes; the shopper often asks for a part of the knuckle marrow bone **са́харная ко́сточка** as part of the order. (The round bone with nought but marrow is **мозгова́я кость**.) Stew meat is **поджа́рка**.

Veal
Теля́тина

Veal is expensive but thought to be good for the very young, the very old, and the ailing. Titles for the meat are the same as for beef.

Pork
Свини́на

Pork is popular, relatively obtainable, and common, especially in western and southwestern areas of the country. Many pork parts retain titles used for beef, including the hocks, shoulder, and shanks. The top rib area **коре́йка** is used for pork chops **котле́ты отбивны́е** and to make smoked pork **корейка копчёная**, while the bottom half **груди́нка** is used for soups and stews. The hind leg **о́корок** is ham **ветчина́** when salted and smoked, or **бужени́на** when fresh, boned, and roasted. Pork heads **свины́е го́ловы** are fairly cheap and commonly used to make head cheese **сту́день, холоде́ц**. The general word for *fat* **жир** includes pork fat **са́ло**, once a symbol of the good—that is, rich—life. **Ты са́ло с са́лом ешь.** "You're eating high off the hog." The more desirable outer fat layer is salted and becomes fatback **шпиг, шпик** while the internal fat is melted and becomes lard **сма́лец**. (Note: schmaltz.) For a long train trip the upper classes often pack a roast chicken, a boiled egg, and a white roll. The peasant brings a loaf of black bread, salt fatback, and a pickle. (Russians new to the United States sometimes use salt pork or bacon to spread on their bread.)

Lamb
Бара́нина

Lamb is popular and more readily available in the south and southeast, where the lambs are. All lamb meat on the top half of the animal, including the leg of lamb **бара́нья нога́**, is first class, the breast **груди́нка** and flank **паши́на** are second, while shank and hocks sink to third.

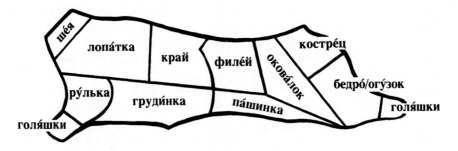

Sausage for sale

Variety meats
Мясны́е субпроду́кты

Insides of various sorts are not spurned (but neither are they considered meat); the accepted variety is greater than ours: brains **мозги́**, heart **се́рдце**, udder **вы́мя**, liver **печёнка**, tripe **рубе́ц**, and kidneys **по́чки**. A combination of liver, heart, and lungs is **ли́вер** (or *pluck* in British English, from which we can see that the person with pluck has guts). Tongue **язы́к** is a delicacy. Naturally, intestines **кишки́** are cleaned, dried, salted, and used to house sausage. Insides in general: **требуха́**. Otherwise, unused scraps—cheeks, lips, and so forth—are used to make the jellied meat appetizer **холоде́ц**, **сту́день**. Particularly good is **сту́день из уше́й** or **хвосто́в**. (Substandard slang for these poor parts is **си́ськи-пи́ськи-хвост**, which literally translated is "tits, peters, and tails." In one old story, a man goes to Astrakhan and inquires about the town: "What's the meat situation here?" Answer: "Oh, we have lots—three kinds, **си́ськи-пи́ськи-хвост!**")

Sausage
Колбаса́

Russia has a wealth of sausages, which, like other wealth, is not always in evidence. The simplest, least expensive, and most common kind is made at home as well as in the factory, the cooked sausage **варёная колбаса́**. The meat has been ground, soaked in brine for a short while, reground and combined with spices or fillers and then stuffed into casings and finally boiled or baked. This kind will keep for several days. The most common and least pretentious of this type is the tea sausage **ча́йная колбаса́**, closely resembling what we know as Polish sausage. Two other particularly good variations of this type are "doctor's" sausage **до́кторская** колбаса (less fat) and **люби́тельская кол-баса**. Hot dogs **соси́ски** and rather short, fat dinner franks **сарде́льки** are made this way. Cooked sausage is used both cold as an appetizer and heated as the meat in the main dish at any meal. The cooked and smoked sausage type **полукопчёная колбаса** is served as an appetizer; its best-known representative is hunter's sausage **охо́тничьи колба́ски**, which are very long and thin. They are cooked by adding them to a pan containing already-lit alcohol! The third type is cold-smoked for a long time **колбаса холо́дного копчения**; the method results in expensive but long-lasting sausage. This is party fare. Some of the best known are **сервела́т**, **сове́тская**, **краснода́рская**, **юбиле́йная**.

Fancy sausages **деликате́сные колба́сы** are those that use particularly fine ingredients, for example, tongue **языко́вая колбаса**, or look pretty when they are sliced—as do many of the "stuffed" sausages **фарширо́ванные колба́сы**. Some kinds should be very fresh if they are to be consumed without being heated: pluck sausage **ли́верная колбаса**, blood sausage **кровяна́я колбаса**, and head cheese **зельц**. The total extent and variety of sausages is almost incredible. Availability depends on location: goose sausage is made where there are geese, fish sausage where there are fish, camel sausage where there are camels, and even whale sausage where whales are processed. The grading system, when applicable, may be of some help: the best is high class **вы́сший сорт**, followed by first and second class **пе́рвый, второй сорт**.

Other meats

Canned meat **мясны́е консе́рвы** is used when the fresh is not available; it is the meat of choice for hikers. The common variety is stew meat **тушёнка**.

Salt meat **солони́на** is made where transportation is not available or other methods of preservation are not feasible. Salted meat is associated with peasanthood and is not held in high regard; the meat has been dry salted and is tough and sinewy—it is not our corned beef.

Rabbit meat **крольча́тина** used to be commonly available, as was the meat of animals raised for their fur, providing there was a factory nearby.

Poultry
Дома́шняя пти́ца

Chicken **ку́рица** is widely available whole (without feathers, sometimes with head and feet) at government meat stores or at the market. Ready-to-cook individual chicken servings, including ground chicken, are available at ready-to-cook counters **отде́лы полуфабрика́тов**. Goose, duck, and turkey are also available.

Wild meat
Дичь

Hunters make some contribution to both the public and private meat supply because a portion of their take must be given to the government. For example, of three bears taken, two go to the government, or the hunter's license is revoked. Of course, significant loss, or misdirection, of meat occurs due to "unavoidable" accident. This process is known as **браконье́рство**. Thusly obtained, wild fowl **дичь** are considered elegant food; they come with their feathers on and are sold at special "Gifts of Nature" stores **Дары́ приро́ды**. Varieties include snipe **бека́с**, snipe or woodcock **ва́льдшнеп**, wood grouse **глуха́рь**, gray partridge **куропа́тка**, quail **пе́репел**, hazel grouse **ря́бчик**, and black grouse **те́терев**. The most popular is wild duck **у́тка**—it's cheaper than chicken and its arrival at stores causes lines to form.

Vegetables
Овощи

In the United States, vegetables are one of the three basic piles on our traditional dinner plate.

Vegetables at the market

The Russian main dish **второе блюдо** usually has two basic piles: meat or substitute, plus something to go with it **гарнир** (not our garnish, therefore), which most often is potatoes or macaroni, but might also be peas or some other vegetable. Thus most vegetables are consumed in a soup, stew, or salad rather than being served separately. A short growing season limits the growth of some vegetables, and an inadequate transportation and distribution system compounds that limitation. Long winters require foods that can be readily stored or preserved; therefore, preservation itself promotes some food properties over others. Often the Russian finds the variety of vegetables at our markets to be overwhelming, yet also finds some of the vegetables pretty but tasteless. (Our cabbage can be watery and even bitter when sauerkraut is the desired result.) The Russian

will be unfamiliar with artichokes **артишоки**, asparagus **спаржа**, broccoli **брокколи**, and sweet potato **батат**. And we are equally unfamiliar with the Russian turnip **репа**, black radish **редька**, and sorrel **щавель**.

These days find much concern about the negative aspects of pesticides **пестициды** and chemicals **химикаты**. As a result, many homemakers peel their fruits and vegetables with fervor.

Potatoes **картофель** (usually the more familiar **картошка**) are the backbone of the vegetable trade: they keep well in the root cellar and supply significant calories and vitamins. Red potatoes are **розовая картошка**, and white are **белая картошка**. For main dishes, one looks for a potato that crumbles a bit **рассыпчатая картошка** as it cooks, while for soups and frying those that don't fall apart нерассыпчатая картошка are preferred. One of the joys of the beginning of summer is fresh new potatoes with fresh dill. For storage purposes, late potatoes поздняя картошка are the only kind to consider. No particular baking potato is sold; however, potatoes baked in the ashes are a frequent part of the edible fun at any campfire.

If potatoes are the first vegetable, then cabbage капуста is second, and a close rival, even if not comparable. Its major use is in sauerkraut квашеная капуста, which requires thin-leaved, heavy heads кочаны. Therefore, the cabbage should have undergone some frost because the slight freezing removes bitterness. White and red cabbage белая, красная капуста are the familiar kinds; unfamiliar are Savoy cabbage савойская капуста and brussel sprouts брюссельская капуста. Cauliflower цветная капуста is used, but never eaten raw.

Carrots морковь—especially blessed for their winter-keeping qualities—are a standard vegetable as are beets свёкла, a major constituent of borsch and much else. Young beet greens ботвинник are a welcome addition to cold beet soup свекольник, and are a regular constituent of cold greens soup ботвинья in the early summer.

Tomatoes помидоры, томаты are so popular that in major cities they can be bought almost the year round, though sometimes their price often reaches significant heights at the market, the only place they might be available. For fresh tomatoes the word помидор is more frequent, while томаты is for adjectival use and to describe tomatoes in cans.

The Russian turnip репа is an ancient staple, common and cheap: Проще пареной репы means "Simpler than a steamed turnip." The subspecies commonly used has no counterpart here: the Russian turnip is creamy yellow outside and inside, and the taste is milder than ours—it is often eaten raw. The related rutabaga (or the British English "swede") брюква is not so popular as the turnip, but it is a fairly frequent addition to soups and stews. (Watch out:

a turnip relative called турнепс *Brassica campestris* is used only for fodder.)

Squash has two major types. Winter squash тыква (which strongly resembles a green pumpkin) keeps well and has seeds семечки, which are popular in southern Russia for snacking. The major summer squash кабачок is light yellow, larger, and sweeter than our green and comparatively rare zucchini цукини. Small, white, bush-scallop squash патиссоны are frequently marinated and served as an appetizer.

Eggplant баклажан is mostly a southern vegetable though it is popular in cooking; see баклажанная икра. Parsnip пастернак is known to few.

Green vegetables are not a Russian forte, and it is in this regard that one feels most the limitations of a short summer. Spinach шпинат grows mostly in the south and central regions and is unfamiliar elsewhere. Instead, sorrel щавель (to make "green" soup зелёные щи) is popular in early spring as a relief from winter-stored vegetables. It is often gathered wild; nettles крапива are used the same way but are gathered only wild or bought on sale at the market. Lettuce (зелёный) салат finds its major use as a consumable decoration. Green salads exist, but they are not the quasi-requirement they are here. Of the other ubiquitous salad ingredients, the most significant is the cucumber огурец, which finds its greatest application as pickles солёные огурцы. The good ones are short, plump, and crisp. Он выглядит, как огурчик. "He's healthy." He looks like a cucumber.

A winter radish редька (very large, round, black-skinned, white-fleshed, and pungent) keeps very well, and when grated and served with oil and vinegar makes an excellent and common appetizer. What we would regard as radish редис, редиска is also popular.

The bean family generally does not receive much attention. In spite of the healthful qualities of its protein, it too often is regarded as a flatulence-inducing fruit and certainly not a fit food for state occasions. Peas **горóх** escape this slanderous consideration: green peas **зелёный горóшек**, often known in a canned version, are highly regarded, as are sugar peas (young pod and peas together) **сáхарный горóх**. Dried, usually yellow, peas **обыкновéнный горóх** have been removed from the pod but still have their skins on them; split peas **сéчка** are thought to be less healthful. Dried field, or "gray," peas **сéрый горóх** are food for people and animals; they have a fairly strong husk on them, and strongly resemble our garbanzos. (A single pea is called **однá горóшина**.) The more common bean **фасóль** *Phaseolus vulgaris* is, strangely enough, least well known in its green or string bean form **зелёная, сáхарная фасóль**. Rather, bean **фасóль**, refers to the small, dried, noisy kidney type. (The lima bean *Phaseolus lunatus* is a rarity in Russia that might be confused with horse or fava beans **бобы́**, also a rarity.) Lentils **чечевúца** share the beans' reputation and use. In the old days lentil soup was for poor people.

Corn **кукурýза** is relatively new in the Russian diet (but a constant in the Ukrainian diet). It usually appears canned, but corn on the cob has begun to appear on the streets; otherwise it's fodder. Popcorn **воздýшная кукурýза** is sometimes eaten as a snack and is beginning to appear on the streets as well. Cornflakes **кукурýзные хлóпья** are another childhood snack but not a breakfast food.

Rhubarb **ревéнь** (like cranberries) is a food plant both in Russia and here but is very uncommon elsewhere in the world.

Mushrooms
Грибы́

The mushroom **гриб** is a very popular food, but it is also a cause for recreation—hunting them is a major Russian pastime. Many cities have special mushroom trains that route the hunters to their hunting grounds very early in the morning. Some trade-union organizations arrange bus trips to favorite areas in late summer or

Грибы́ съедóбные:
Бéлые грибы́. Подосинóвики. Подберёзовики.
Опёнки. Груздú. Лисúчки.

early fall when mushrooms make their appearance. Mushroom hunters are equipped with a knife, a basket, and perhaps a picnic lunch. (The knife is to cut them off at their base, a practice our mycologists frown on because the identifying "death-cup" on Amanitas can escape notice this way. Conversely, the Russians are often horrified that we take the base and all because they are under the impression that we are pulling up an entire plant. Actually we are just picking the fruit of the fungi's mycelium.)

Nonhunters can buy wild mushrooms at the public market (a procedure we don't recommend because you have no way to check on the care taken in their selection). The commercially raised mushroom is a variety of the meadow mushroom **шампиньо́н** *Agaricus campestris*; this mushroom can sometimes be found at the store, but many wild varieties are thought to be better.

Some mushrooms are eaten "fresh," which means immediately, not raw—they are never eaten uncooked. Perhaps more often, mushrooms are either dried **сушёные**, marinated **мари́но́ванные**, or salted **солёные**, depending on the kind; boletes are usually dried, and gill mushrooms are more often salted. As food, mushrooms appear in everything but dessert.

The common Russian recognizes more mushrooms than does the mushroom-hunting hobbyist in the United States. Soloukhin complained in his book on mushrooms that Russians usually recognized *only* one quarter of the 250 varieties that commonly grew in the USSR. Russians are in almost total agreement about which mushrooms are best. The following classifications are commercial rankings, but they represent popular tastes. However, this accepted ranking often violently disagrees with Western estimations of what's good.

Any mushroom that is either not recognized by the speaker or which might be poisonous is called the "foul" or "filthy" one **пога́нка**. A few of the especially poisonous mushrooms have achieved the status of having their own names: "fly killer" **мухомо́р** can refer to any of the Amanitas, but usually to the pretty bright red one with white spots on the cap. The entire group of puff-balls **дождевики́** is usually ignored as are any of the *Coprinus* sp., **наво́зники** (**наво́з** is *manure*). Notice in the following list how low in estimation are the yellow chanterelles, a stupefying thought to our collectors.

The following are only the most commonly considered mushrooms, arranged in order of their desirability. Any self-respecting Russian knows at least a dozen more. English common names are supplied when they exist.

бе́лый гриб, борови́к *Boletus edulis*, King bolete. The undisputed, best mushroom, the French cepe and the German Steinpilz. It is sometimes eaten fresh though the flavor is said to improve with drying. (Learn this one, if no other!)

груздь *Lactarius resimus*. A first-class mushroom used salted only. A very desirable type despite the presoaking required to remove the bitterness.

ры́жик *Lactarius deliciosus*. Delicious milky-cap; first class either marinated, salted, or fried; can be eaten almost immediately after salting.

подберёзовик *Leccinum scabrum*. Rough-stemmed bolete. Second class; used mostly fresh or dried; can be marinated.

подоси́новик *Leccinum aurantiacum*. Orange-capped bolete; second class; prepared all ways.

маслёнок (*pl.* **масля́та, маслёнки**) A title applied to **по́здний маслёнок**, *Suillus luteus* and to **зерни́стый маслёнок**, *Suillus granulatus*, both of which are Slippery Jack in English. Second class; eaten all ways but best are young ones marinated. The slimy cap must be peeled off before use.

опёнок (*pl.* **опя́та, опёнки**) *Armillaria mellea*. Honey mushroom, second class; used fresh, marinated, and salted; caps only.

сыроёжка *Russula* sp. Any Russula without another common name; third class. So named because most can be eaten raw without harm (even though all mushrooms are commonly boiled before they are eaten). Often found in large quantities, which helps make up for their lack of class.

лиси́чка *Cantharellus cibarius*. Yellow chanterelle; third class; described in one Russian mushroom text as a "humble" mushroom (and by Russian friends as a mushroom to pick if there are no others).

мохови́к *Xerocomus subtomentosus* and *X. variegatus*. Third class; used fresh, dried, marinated, and salted.

сморчки́, строчки́ Both the true and false

morels; third class. The evident unwillingness to differentiate between the two types has led to the practice of preboiling before further preparing any of these, which are the only spring mushrooms of any significance.

Fruit
Фру́кты

To the Russian, the smell за́пах of a fruit (or berries or flowers) is what matters; looks come second. This criterion explains what might seem to us unusual Russian preferences, because we often rank good looks first, then perhaps texture, then taste, with little attention paid to smell. Consider yourself sensorially deprived if you've never come across some properly made morello cherry preserves.

Two words for fruit grace the Russian vocabulary: the inclusive fruit плод covers almost anything with seeds and also carries fruity figurative notions (fruits of labor плоды́ труда́); the exclusive fruit фрукт is fruit that grows on trees (including some foreign fruit that don't). Rhubarb is a vegetable, and melons are described here. Fruits described as rare may now be thought of as available, at least in major cities—merely prohibitively expensive. The following are the exclusive fruits фру́кты.

Fresh apricots абрико́сы are relatively rare as they require a warm climate (mostly central Asian) and do not transport easily. Russians come across them mostly as one of the possible dried fruits сухофру́кты from which a very liquid "compote" компо́т is made. Dried apricots with pits are урю́к, without pits курага́.

Quince айва́ is used to make preserves варе́нье.

A kind of prune алыча́, мирабе́ль *Prunus divaricata* has a small, yellow fruit used for making compote; spikes on the bush commend the plant for garden borders.

The pineapple анана́с, the orange апельси́н, and the banana бана́н all arrive from Africa and South America. Their expense makes them a great gift.

The sour cherry ви́шня *Prunus cerasus* is a major staple in the Russian fruit business; the best-known type is the Vladimir cherry (see Souloukhin sketch of the same name), but many other kinds are found, especially in Ukraine, which is the headquarters of the industry. Sour cherries are eaten fresh, made into compote and preserves, dried, and commonly used in the Ukrainian vareniki and pirozhki.

The pomegranate грана́т is available, for a price, year round at markets from Georgians. Served fresh to accompany meat or chicken, its juice is used frequently in Georgian dishes.

Grapefruit грейпфру́т grows in the Caucasus; some is sold up north, on occasion, for a price.

Pears гру́ши are an obligatory constituent of the dried fruit mix сухофру́кты; beyond that they are mostly a southern delight because the northern varieties are good only for compote.

The fig инжи́р comes mostly dried or candied. Canned figs are sold by weight from, not in, a can. Eaten fresh in the south and nowadays also up north.

Serviceberry ирга́ *Amelanchier rotundifolia* takes up a corner in many dacha gardens.

Cornelian cherry кизи́л *Cornus mas* appears in the Caucasus and the Crimea but only as preserves elsewhere.

Lemon лимо́н from Africa and the Caucasus is almost always available because the demand is high and it keeps well. Some homemakers buy them cheap in season and then preserve them in sugar. Tea with lemon is considered elegant.

Tangerines мандари́ны are to the Russians what Japanese oranges are to us: Christmas fruit. They are reportedly smaller and more aromatic than are ours.

Seabuckthorn облепи́ха *Hippophae rhamnoides* was originally a Siberian bush but now considers many a Russian yard to be home; its fruit and juice is famous for healthfulness. (Get sick and you'll have trouble turning down offers thereof.) Seabuckthorn "oil" from the

Seabuckthorn berries **облепи́ха** on a price list

Mountain ash berries **ряби́на**

berries is supposed to do wonders for the skin: look for it in skin cream.

Peaches **пе́рсики** grow in the south and therefore tend to be expensive.

Mountain ash berries **ряби́на** are picked after the first frost when they are sweeter. Preserves are made from them, and often they are used as a flavoring for vodka **ряби́новка** and brandy **ряби́на на коньяке́**. The taste is sharp and the fruit is thought of as a supplier of vitamins.

White, red, and black plums and prunes **сли́вы** are very popular fruit with the advantage of availability because plums grow in colder climates. They are eaten fresh, as preserves and jam, and are always included in the dried fruit mixture. Prunes **черносли́в** are the semidried fruit of the Hungarian (dark) plum.

Sloe or blackthorn **тёрн** grows on a very prickly sloe or blackthorn bush **терно́вник** *Prunus spinosa* in southern Russia and along the Volga. Used for preserves, syrup, and, when dried, even a coffee substitute.

Dates **фи́ники** appear dried **вя́леные** as do ours.

Persimmon **хурма́** is a southern fruit sold fresh, often by small-business people of southern extraction and low repute.

European bird cherry **черёмуха**, *Padus* or *Prunus racemosa*, is first admired for its early spring blossoms, but later some people dry the fruit, grind it up, and cook it in pies.

Sweet cherries **чере́шня** from *Prunus avium* do not boast the high regard they have here—Russians perceive them as having little aroma and therefore of little use except for compote.

Black chokeberry **черноплóдная ряби́на** *Aronia melanocarpa* is a small black fruit from a plant that originated in North America but was popularized by Michurin. The fruit is used for preserves, flavoring, and as a medicinal.

The apple **я́блоко** is the first fruit, the basic fruit without which the word fruit has little meaning. The first among them is the ancient and venerated "antonovka" **антóновка**. It is a very late apple, white and green in color, sour, and stores well. It is the apple of choice to make spiced apples **мочёные я́блоки**. Other common kinds of apples are **ани́с, бе́лый нали́в, кита́йка, шафра́н, уэ́лси, ме́льба**. See the recipe for spiced apples in the *Preserving food* section.

Russians who do crossword puzzles know that watermelons are berries. Watermelon **арбу́з** often appears in small sizes and has names like the "Ukrainian," "Moldavian," "Odessa," and the striped "Astrakhan," which is the sweetest. The large ones that resemble ours come from Central Asia and have names such as "Tashkent" or "Ashkhabad." Watermelons are often pickled.

Of the melons **ды́ни**, the most popular is the "Uzbek," while the "kolkhoz woman" **колхо́зница** is common, but details are usually familiar only where the melons grow. Melons are often air dried **вя́леные**.

Checking out a "kolkhoz woman" **колхо́зница**

Berries
Ягоды

Except for apples, plums, and perhaps sour cherries (all in the class of fruits), berries are closest to the historical Russian soul. Many are gathered wild in forest or field, free for the joy of gathering, a matter of the moment and treasured therefore. Four of them are cranberry and blueberry relatives in the *Vaccinium* genus. Common name equivalents are a snare and delusion—our commercial blueberry and cranberry are none of the following.

Lingonberry **брусни́ка** *Vaccinium vitis-idaea* is a northern bog plant, a small relative of our cranberry—which it resembles, but it is sweeter and meatier. Prepared spiced **мочёная**, as jam, and marinated (often served with meat).

Fresh grapes **виногра́д** of all kinds and colors come mostly from Bulgaria or Moldova and are available only in season. Grapes from the Caucasus or Central Asia are mainly consumed or processed locally.

Blueberry or bog huckleberry **голуби́ка** *Vaccinium uliginosum* also has the English English name of Alpine bilberry. These are rather large, dark blue berries, used fresh in preserves and jam but not so highly regarded as the lingonberry **брусни́ка** or blueberry **черни́ка**.

In the blackberry or bramble genus, **ежеви́ка** *Rubus caesius* is good for preserves or flavoring but is not highly esteemed, and is considered almost a weed.

Wood strawberry or European everbearing strawberry **земляни́ка** *Fragaria vesca* is probably the most desirable of all because of its smell **арома́т**. It is quite small, long, and somewhat darker red than our strawberry. It grows in the forest and is so delicate and yet treasured that the only way to get it is to gather it yourself or to get it from a friend who did. It is often made into preserves.

Two kinds of strawberry **клубни́ка** are common: the wild kind **ди́кая клубника**, *Fragaria viridis,* which has small roundish berries and grows in open fields, and the cultivated strawberry **садо́вая клубни́ка**, which is bigger but thought to be less aromatic; **викто́рия** is a popular strain thereof.

Small cranberry **клю́ква** *Vaccinium oxyccoccos* is a relative of our cranberry but smaller and perhaps even more sour; it keeps well enough to be available the year round. The best are gathered after the first frosts when the cold has converted some of their energy to sugar. "Kisel" is made of it, as is a cranberry drink **морс** often served at table as a chaser to vodka. Cranberry drink is especially good for colds.

European gooseberries **крыжо́вник** *Grossularia* or *Ribes sp.* have been in cultivation in Russia since the eleventh century—and are cultivated still. They come in various colors—black, white, and red—and are inexpensive and eaten fresh, as "kisel," compote, and even wine. Preserves made from gooseberries and walnuts are called the tsar's preserves: **ца́рское/импера́торское варе́нье.**

The European raspberry **мали́на** *Rubus idaeus* is popular as a liqueur flavoring and as preserves. Everybody knows that when you have a cold, tea with raspberry preserves is good for you. The raspberry is both cultivated and wild, but the wild naturally tastes better. It is very commonly dried and stored for use against the common cold.

Currants **сморо́дина** compete with wild strawberries for desirability; of the three kinds, all are esteemed: the red currant **кра́сная сморо́дина** *Ribes silvestre*; the thick-skinned black currant **чёрная сморо́дина** *Ribes nigrum*, and the less common white currant *Ribes album*. Liqueurs, juices, and "kisel" are made from them. Preserves are less successful because of the numerous seeds; instead they are often seived and then sugar is added without cooking; the mixture replaces preserves.

The very dark bilberry/whortleberry/blueberry **черни́ка** *Vaccinium myrtillus* is used in pies and preserves and is also dried for use in compote. It is also known for its medicinal qualities: a little is eaten to curb diarrhea; a lot is eaten to remedy the opposite condition, but many other ailments can instigate its use.

Nuts, seeds, and gum
Оре́хи, се́мечки, жва́чка

The range of Russian nuts is not wide: the hazel tree genus **лещи́на, оре́шник** *Corylus* sp. includes the common hazel **оре́шник обыкнове́нный** *C. avellana,* which supplies the nut **лесно́й оре́х.** The larger cultivated hazel **лещи́на кру́пная** supplies the similar but larger nut **фунду́к.** (Our hazel is the same genus, different species.) The English or Persian walnut **гре́цкий орех** *Juglans regia* is the most common and available nut, and the related pecan **пека́н,** a kind of hickory **ги́кори,** is very rare. "Cedar" nuts **кедро́вые орехи** are very popular, especially in Siberia; however, they do not come from cedar trees but from pine trees *Pinus cembra, P. sibirica*; our pine nuts come from other pines. The pistachio tree **фиста́шник** produces pistachio nuts **фиста́шки** familiar to southerners. Almonds **минда́ль,** occasionally available at the markets, are expensive and chic. Peanuts **ара́хис, земляно́й оре́х, кита́йский орех** are grown in southern areas.

Almost all the nuts grow in the south and therefore not all are easily available elsewhere; in their stead, for use as a snack, the Russians do quite well with seeds **се́мечки,** by which they usually mean sunflower seeds **подсо́лнечные семечки** but which also can mean pumpkin or squash seeds **ты́квенные се́мечки.** The latter are sold not only at markets but also in drugstores because they are supposed to defend against worms **глисты́.** At the market (i.e., among peasants) it is not uncommon to see someone toss a handful of seeds into the mouth and then, while carrying on a conversation, spit out the shells as the kernels are consumed.

Gum **жева́тельная рези́нка** ("chewing rubber" also known popularly as **жва́чка**) is a delight for Russian children though not for their elders, most of whom consider the practice of using it rude or at least bovine. (That was a hint.)

Seasonings for sale at the market

Seasonings and spices
Припра́вы и пря́ности

The Great Russian cuisine uses neither a wide variety of flavorings nor hot spices. But Russians do use what we think of as some strong seasonings. The following common seasonings (or condiments) **припра́вы** are listed in their Russian alphabetical order.

Mustard **горчи́ца** is so often used that, like salt and pepper, it is part of the table setting. Hungry restaurant patrons will spread mustard (or similar sauce-condiments) on their bread if the service is too slow for the hunger. Prepared mustard **гото́вая горчи́ца** can be bought, but some people like to make their own using mustard powder **суха́я горчи́ца** (also used to make

mustard plaster **горчи́чник**, a fairly common home remedy; as a meat tenderizer; as a preservative; and even as a household cleanser).

Onion **лук** is used there as here, in everything except dessert. Regular onions **ре́пчатый лук** and green onions **зелёный лук** are the common types; leeks **лук-поре́й** should not be confused with the green part of green onions **лук-перо́**. (Onion **лук** is a collective noun; individuals are **одна́ лу́ковица, одна́ голо́вка лу́ка**.)

Olives **масли́ны** are home-grown in the south and much resemble "our" Greek olives. Arabic countries lately have begun sending green olives.

Mint **мя́та** appears in mint tea **мя́тный чай**, a mint drink **мя́тный квас**, in cookies **мя́тные пря́ники**, and in candies.

Poppyseed **мак** used to be frequently encountered in the Russian south, in rolls, pastries, cookies, and even as a cereal. That ended when it was suspected that the seeds were used more often to grow poppies.

By *parsley* **петру́шка**, what is meant is Hamburg parsley, which has broad leaves and a large turnip-shaped root. The leaves and the root are used either uncooked in salads and fresh or dried as a very common soup and meat flavoring.

Celery root, celeriac **сельдере́й**, is almost as popular as parsley. The root is dried for use in soups, or fresh in salads. (The stems of this kind of celery are ignored.)

Dill **укро́п** (leaves, not seeds) is also used in almost everything but dessert and in all forms: fresh, dried, and salted. Summer soups and potatoes require it.

Vinegar **у́ксус** is also a standard in every kitchen. Regular store vinegar is a 9-percent acidity solution, but essence of vinegar **у́ксусная эссе́нция**, an 80-percent solution, is also popular.

Horseradish **хрен** is another indispensable flavoring, especially for appetizers. Horseradish is common in pickling because it helps to keep the cucumbers crunchy, and, like mustard, it is used to keep tomatoes fresh all the way to New Year's.

Garlic **чесно́к** is as popular as onion; it is grown in all gardens and is a favorite to flavor meats, marinades, and pickles. Southerners especially favor garlic—whole and uncooked(!) cloves of garlic **зу́бчики чеснока́** sometimes accompany soups and main dishes. Garlic sauce **чесно́чный со́ус** must accompany chicken tabaka, a Georgian dish popular in Russia.

A spice is **пря́ность** or **спе́ция**: the first word is the more common, the second is both foreign and therefore exotic, even chic. A special kind of spice cookie is **пря́ник**. Common spices **пря́ности** include the following:

вани́ль   vanilla; does not appear in (our) liquid form, but as "vanilla powder"

вани́льный порошо́к   dried vanilla bean ground with sugar, while "vanilla sugar" **вани́льный са́хар** is a mixture of vanillin (imitation vanilla) and sugar; both kinds are sold in premeasured one-use amounts. Vanillin is **ванили́н**. Real vanilla pods **стручки́ вани́ли** can be found, but they are very expensive and very rare.

гвозди́ка   cloves; used in marinades of all kinds, in some sweet breads and sometimes as a stew flavoring. Commonly used, but imported, cloves are often out of stock.

имби́рь   ginger; sometimes used in sweet doughs and spice cookies.

кори́ца   cinnamon; also appears in sweet doughs, cookies, and in hot punch for a cold night **глинтве́йн**. It, too, is subject to disappearance from the marketplace.

лавро́вый лист   bay leaf; used there as here; available and inexpensive

муска́тный оре́х   nutmeg; sold a few at a time, and whole; used in meat and fish dishes. Males who want to hide alcohol breath carry one in a pocket for use as needed.

пе́рец   pepper; a word used too broadly to stand alone in either language. Allspice **души́стый пе́рец** is used very frequently,

especially in marinades and pickling. Regular black or white pepper **чёрный, бе́лый пе́рец** is very commonly used, expensive and sometimes unavailable so that red pepper is a frequent substitute. Sweet pepper **сла́дкий пе́рец** is the vegetable or bell pepper that comes in red or green: **сла́дкий кра́сный пе́рец, сла́дкий зелёный пе́рец**. Red pepper **стручко́вый пе́рец, кра́сный пе́рец** *Capiscum sp.*, is mildly hot and more readily available because it is grown in southern areas of the country. Sold fresh or dried and whole for use in pickles, sauces, and soups, it is related to, but not so strong as, our chili and cayenne peppers. A well-known pepper-flavored vodka, **перцо́вка**, is associated with Ukraine, where the peppers grow.

тмин   caraway; sometimes used in sauerkraut, cheese, weiners, sausages, cookies, and bread doughs

шафра́н   saffron; is fairly rare and mostly used in doughs for its color

The following spices or seasonings are not common specifically to most Russian cooking, but are used in some areas of Russia or in major regional cooking of the former republics.

аджи́ка   a sauce of Georgian origin made from peppers, garlic, coriander leaves, dill and salt

ани́с   anise; used in medicines or as vodka flavoring

бадья́н, анис звёздчатый   star anise

базили́к   basil; common in Caucasus, Middle Asia

души́ца, майора́н   sweet marjoram

души́ца обыкнове́нная   oregano or wild marjoram

ка́персы   capers; common in southern cooking

кардамо́н   cardamom; used in doughs and hard to get

ки́нза, ки́ндза, кишне́ц посевно́й   coriander leaves; Chinese parsley; very common in the Caucasus, and available at major markets everywhere.

кориа́ндр coriander seeds

кунжу́т sesame (**сеза́м** is used with "open," but not in reference to seeds)

куркума́ turmeric

майора́н see **душица**

муска́тный цвет, маци́с mace

розмари́н rosemary

тимья́н, чабре́ц, богоро́дская тра́вка thyme

чабёр summer savory

шалфе́й sage

эстраго́н, кавка́зский тарху́н tarragon

PRESERVING FOOD
Загото́вка проду́ктов

Long cold winters produced traditions of food preservation that are still often used. Those who have the opportunity still use the root cellar **по́греб** for storing vegetables through the winter, especially potatoes, carrots, and beets. Other methods are also very widely used.

Salting **соле́ние** is the most common method, and it is applied most often to cabbage to make pickled cabbage or sauerkraut **ква́шеная капу́ста**. Many families even in cities buy huge, firm heads of late white cabbage, chop it, salt it, and flavor it with various combinations of carrots, cranberries, lingonberries, apples, bay leaf, red currant leaves, and caraway. The cabbage is allowed to ferment **ква́сить** then left at cool temperatures; thus stored, it will safely supply the vegetable foundations for many salads, soups, and main dishes. No vinegar is added, so the taste is much less astringent than what we popularly know as sauerkraut.

Cucumbers very commonly are pickled **солёные огурцы́**; the most desirable are those that use little salt **малосо́льные огурцы́** (and which therefore spoil easily).

Everyone makes pickles

Some mushrooms are preserved only by salting (**гру́зди, ры́жики, сырое́жки, беля́нки, волну́шки, гла́дыши, подгру́зди, свину́шки, черну́шки**) because they must be presoaked or preboiled to remove bitterness, or, according to some, poisons. (Just as we cook pork to eliminate trichinosis.) The soaking makes these mushrooms unfit for drying **суше́ние**, which is the only way to preserve most bolete and other quality mushrooms— **бе́лые, подоси́новики, подберёзовики**.

Commercially preserved products also are used very commonly—many kinds of fish are salted, especially herring **сельдь (селёдка)** or sprats **шпро́ты**, and air-dried **вя́леные (во́бла, лосо́сь)** or salted and smoked (**балы́к**). Of course, ham **ветчина́** is prepared this way. The dried spinal cord of sturgeon **вязи́га** used to be a very desirable constituent of savory pies. If you are served some, consider yourself honored.

Sausage-making is described under *Meat*.

Most Russians encounter fruit most frequently in the use of a dried fruit mix **сухофру́кты** that includes apricots, pears, peaches, plums, apples, and raisins in various combinations. This mixture is boiled and the result is "compote" **компо́т**, a frequent dessert drink.

Contemporary society makes wide use of commercially canned food **консе́рвы**, but canning itself is to us what pickling cabbage is to the Russians. However, we do share the practice of making jams, but with a difference. Jelly is not usual, but the kinds of jam are distinct and important: fruit "butter" **пови́дло** is ground

fruit plus sugar, cooked to a paste and often used as a filling; jam **джем** corresponds to its name; but preserves **варе́нье** maintain the shape of the original fruit in a heavy sugar syrup. It vaguely resembles our jam but is more liquid and is served all by itself as a dessert to accompany tea. One spoons it from its small saucer directly to the mouth without intervening bread.

Spiced apples
Мочёные я́блоки

Line the bottom of a clean barrel with a layer of black currant or sour cherry leaves. Thereupon, stem up, place several layers of clean apples. Cover them with another layer of leaves, then more apples, and so forth, until the barrel is almost full. The last layer is leaves. Cover with a weighted lid. Pour either a sweet or sour mixture over all, enough so that the lid is completely covered. Replenish as necessary. Leave in a cool place for thirty to forty days. (Sweet mixture: for each ten liters of water, use 400 grams of sugar or honey, three tablespoons of salt; bring to a boil, then cool. For a sour mixture, use 200 grams of rye flour and two tablespoons salt for each ten liters of water; boil and cool.)

COOKING
Приготовле́ние пи́щи

The cook *prepares* food rather than cooking it: "I'm making pirozhki." **Я гото́влю пирожки́.** If the situation is very informal, then you might hear the term **стря́пать**. "I don't like to cook." **Я не люблю́ стря́пать.** The last phrase is most likely to issue directly from the homemaker. The cook should not be called *cook* **куха́рка** unless regarded as a paid menial. Cook as **по́вар** is acceptable. **Шеф** is equivalent to *boss* but not a cook, unless combined with the word for cook, **шеф-по́вар**.

To illustrate some cooking terminology, what follows is a recipe **реце́пт** for "green shchi," a springtime soup. If you have a hard

На ку́хне

time finding the sorrel (which is easily grown), or the nettles, use spinach for both.

Зелёные щи

Шпина́т или крапи́ву перебра́ть, хорошо промы́ть, свари́ть в кипя́щей воде́ до мя́гкости, отки́нуть и протере́ть сквозь си́то. Щаве́ль перебрать и промыть, кру́пные ли́стики разре́зать.

Коре́нья и лук наре́зать ме́лкими ку́биками и поджа́рить в супово́й кастрю́ле с ма́слом, доба́вить к ним муку́ и продолжа́ть жаре́ние ещё 1-2 мину́ты. Зате́м положи́ть в кастрю́лю протёртый шпина́т, хорошо́ переме́шать, развести́ горя́чим бульо́ном и отва́ром, полу́ченным при ва́рке шпина́та, доба́вить лавро́вый лист, пе́рец и вари́ть 15-20 минут. За 5-10 мину́т до оконча́ния ва́рки положи́ть в кастрю́лю ли́стики щавеля́ и соль. К зелёным щам рекоменду́ется подава́ть смета́ну и сва́ренное вкруту́ю яйцо́.

На 500 г мя́са—500 г шпина́та, 200 г щавеля́, по 1 шт. коре́ньев и лу́ка, 1 ст. ло́жку муки́ и 2 ст. ло́жки ма́сла.

Green soup

Pick over the spinach or nettles, wash well, and cook in boiling water until soft; drain and rub through a sieve. Pick over and wash the sorrel; cut up the large leaves.

[Take] Root vegetables [including: parsely *root*, parsnip, celery *root*, carrots], chop fine and sauté in butter in the soup pan; add flour and fry 1–2 more minutes. Then put in the pan the sieved spinach, mix well, add the hot bouillon and the cooking liquid from the spinach, add bay leaf, pepper and cook 15–20 minutes. From 5–10 minutes before finishing cooking, add the sorrel leaves and salt. Green soup is often served with sour cream and hard-boiled egg.

For 500 grams of meat, use 500 grams of spinach, 200 grams of sorrel, one each of root vegetables and onions, one tablespoon flour, and 2 tablespoons butter/oil.

Cooking terminology is spread through the section on dishes, and is usually obvious. Less clear and a nuisance is that **жа́рить** means both *to fry* and *to roast*. So you mentally translate for the poor Russian who says he has been frying his coffee. Also, **пассерова́ть** is *to sauté*, and **панирова́ть** is *to bread* (roll in breadcrumbs).

Those wishing to do their own Russian cooking face an uphill battle: half the problem is an ignorance of processes and end products that deprives non-Russians of a goal and the other half is a materials shortage. Most Russian cooks find it hard to cook without these: **творо́г, квас, ква́шеная капу́ста, гре́чневая ка́ша, чёрная сморо́дина, брусни́ка, боровики́ и т.д.**

MEALS

No Russian word corresponds to our word *meal*, but Russians manage to eat without one (despite the logic of those who use the absence of a word to indicate the absence of the phenomenon). Specific meals have names enough; three meals a day is standard: breakfast **за́втрак**, dinner **обе́д**, and supper **у́жин**. Schoolchildren, and perhaps hospital residents, also have a morning snack **второй за́втрак** and perhaps an afternoon snack **по́лдник**. All meals include bread, without which a Russian refuses to function.

Breakfast **завтрак** normally contains (1) a hot drink, usually tea **чай** with quantities of sugar (in hotels and the like, often served in a glass **стака́н**, which is itself in a glass-holder **подстака́нник**); (2) something substantial: a meat or meat substitute such as hot dogs **соси́ски**, an egg **яйцо́**, cheese **сыр**, or sausage **колбаса́**; (3) a starch; for example, potatoes **карто́шка**, pancakes **блины́**, French toast гре́нки (without the syrup), or some kind of cereal ка́ша (especially for children). Milk or milk products, including kefir кефи́р or another kind of soured milk простоква́ша, "heated" milk топлёное молоко́, "cottage cheese" творо́г, or sour cream смета́на, are also especially popular at breakfast. These standard constituents allow for a wider choice than is our custom. Frequently, leftovers from the main dish of the day before are consumed at breakfast. And perfectly normal people enjoy salad (a Russian salad, not our green salad) or a stew for breakfast. Breakfast is a substantial meal, whatever its contents—school texts recommend a higher caloric content for breakfast than for the evening meal.

The *major* meal обед comes after the middle of the day, usually from about twelve to two o'clock. At this meal roughly half of the day's calories are accounted for; as an interruption to work or school, it is the dinner break обе́денный переры́в. *It is not lunch!* The usual dinner has three courses: a soup суп is the first course пе́рвое блю́до. The second course второ́е блю́до can have one, usually two, but possibly more constituents: a stew can stand alone, but if a piece of meat is on the menu, then what goes with it is called a garnish гарни́р. Our three-pile plate is not a Russian requirement. The third course тре́тье блю́до (or often the "sweet" сла́дкое) is dessert, which is either something sweet or a fruit, plus, usually, tea. (The word for *course,* блю́до, is often omitted: **Что вы хотите на пе́рвое?**)

По зако́ну Архиме́да
После вку́сного обе́да
Полага́ется поспа́ть.[a]

The evening meal, supper у́жин, is traditionally a light meal served fairly early in the evening: a heavy meal late in the evening is considered unhealthy, leading to indigestion and sleeplessness. A normal supper again has three parts: (1) an appetizer заку́ска or two, (2) a hot dish горя́чее (which might include soup if none was served earlier in the day), and (3)

dessert with tea. The word *tea,* чай, again means the drink, and also the meal or part of a meal at which tea is drunk, plus dessert. (Thus, if you are invited to tea in the afternoon, you may expect something more than an infusion of leaves with sugar in it.)

The supper у́жин is becoming more substantial these days because the new economy makes the cafeterias at work too expensive to maintain; workers now often bring a little food with them to work and eat the major meal as early in the evening as possible.

If dinner обе́д is celebratory пра́здничный обе́д, then the order we have described remains except that the whole thing is usually preceded by a wide selection of hors d'oeuvres заку́ски. If supper у́жин is a party meal, then the difference, again, is that the appetizer section of the meal is greatly enlarged: the table is laden with many dishes and dotted with bottles of hard liquor for the men and wine for the women.

Another basic type of party features the one-dish meal, which the hosts mention in the invitation. It is understood that that dish is, except perhaps for dessert, the only significant food that you will get. Typical of such one-dish invitations are: blini блины́, pelmeni пельме́ни, "pie" пиро́г, and shashlyk шашлы́к.

These indications have been necessarily general, but remember: breakfast is substantial; the major meal is in the *middle* of the day and always includes soup; supper is light; and bread goes with *all* meals.

RUSSIAN DISHES
Блю́да ру́сской ку́хни

These are not all the foods a Russian eats, only the most common (shchi), or those which occupy a special place in Russian food ideology (caviar). Keep in mind that (1) Russian food is very season-dependent; (2) fat жир in food is more often thought of as a plus rather than a minus; (3) attention is paid to making serving dishes look good at table; (4) composed (or casseroled) dishes (as compared to steaks or chops) are preferable because differences in cuts of meat are unfamiliar. (To paraphrase: do not order steak in a Russian restaurant—either the cook doesn't know what you expect or doesn't believe in rare meat.)

Foods are listed in the following sections according to the order in which they are served: appetizers, soups, main dishes, and desserts. (The custom of serving food in courses actually came to us from Russia, via France, of course.)

Where letters are used, they mean (a) a translation of the title of the dish; (b) a description of contents or cookery that might help; and (c) notes on use.

Appetizers
Заку́ски

One or two appetizers sometimes precede soup at the everyday dinner обед; as many as possible are served at the start of a party or celebration meal, the end of which might be hard to remember. Notice that this is when salads are served (and usually with a garnish of dill, parsley, celery, onion, or garlic).

сала́т из све́жих помидо́ров и огурцо́в (a) tomato and cucumber salad; (b) sliced, with sour cream or oil and vinegar dressing

салат из свёклы (a) beet salad; (b) julienned beets with oil and vinegar, or sour cream, or mayonnaise

салат с мя́сом, салат оливье́, зи́мний салат (a) Meat salad; (b) resembles our potato salad, plus cubed meat, carrots, pickles, and peas; (c) party dish

салат с ку́рицей, столи́чный салат same as the preceding, except with chicken

винегре́т из овоще́й (a) "vinaigrette"; mixed-vegetable salad; (b) beets, potatoes, carrots, apples, pickle, and so on, with oil and vinegar dressing or mayonnaise; (c) a very popular salad

сельдь с гарни́ром (a) herring with garnish; (b) salt herring that has been soaked, skinned, filleted, and cut into serving pieces; (c) the classic vodka-chaser

икра́ (a) caviar (black from sturgeon, red from Pacific salmon); (b) served with white toast, chopped hard-boiled eggs, lemon, and butter, or with blini, or as stuffing for hard-boiled egg halves; (c) if you don't like it, for Heaven's sake give it to someone who does

лососи́на, сёмга, кета́ с гарни́ром (a) лососи́на as an appetizer refers to salted Caspian salmon; сёмга is salted Atlantic salmon; кета salted Pacific salmon; (b) skinned, boned; sliced, and salted salmon with whatever garnish—heavily salted fish, кета, also require soaking; (c) elegance exceeded only by caviar

осетри́на, белу́га, севрю́га (a) poached sturgeon meats; (b) cooled, sliced, and arranged with a dressing

ры́ба под марина́дом (a) fish in a (Greek-style) sauce; (b) any fish cooked, cooled, and served with a sauce

колбаса́ (1) варёная, (2) полукопчёная, (3) копчёная (a) sausage (1) cooked, (2) lightly smoked, (3) smoked sausage; (b) skinned, sliced, and arranged

ветчина́, бужени́на, язы́к (a) ham, cold roast pork, or tongue; (b) Russian cold meats, served with horseradish, mustard, or mayonnaise

баклажа́нная икра́ (a) eggplant caviar; (b) eggplant, tomato, and onion, cooked with vegetable oil and vinegar; (c) popular, and an artful disguiser of eggplant

заливна́я осетри́на (a) sturgeon in aspic; (c) many aspic or jellied dishes are popular.

поросёнок заливно́й (a) suckling pig in aspic; (c) rare party fare—associated with Easter or New Year's dinner

сту́день говя́жий (a) beef in aspic (other kinds of meat are also common); (b) sliced or ground meat and seasonings in aspic, served with horseradish sauce; (c) very, very common. A less formal name is холоде́ц

битóчки в сметáне (a) small ground meat patties in sour cream sauce; (c) more frequently served as a main dish

форшмáк (a) "forshmak"; (b) ground cooked meat, salt herring, and potatoes bound with egg and served warm; (c) party dish

бутербрóд (a) sandwich, Danish style; (b) open-faced, that is; (c) often nothing more than a single slice of sausage (or whatever) on a single slice of bread and nothing in between

сыр (a) cheese; (c) usually served sliced

фарширóванные я́йца (a) stuffed eggs (not our deviled eggs); (b) stuffed with meat, onions, mushrooms, and so forth

Salad dressings
Сóусы и запрáвки для салáта

майонéз (a) mayonnaise; (b) sharper than ours

сметáна (a) sour cream; (b) plus a little sugar, salt, and pepper

расти́тельное мáсло с у́ксусом (a) Vegetable oil and vinegar

Soups
Пéрвые блю́да, бульóны и супы́

Soups are a required course at every dinner **обéд**, and on the farm they are sometimes served at breakfast and supper, too. Soups are a Russian forte and can be the best you'll ever taste.

мяснóй бульóн, кури́ный бульóн, рыбный бульóн, грибнóй бульóн (a) meat, chicken, fish, or mushroom bouillon; (b) a soup base, but often served on it own merits—clear bouillon is an elegant first course, while borsch is as common as . . .

щи из свéжей капу́сты, щи из ки́слой капу́сты (a) fresh cabbage soup, sauerkraut soup; (b) meat bouillon base plus cabbage, potatoes, and perhaps tomato, not to mention a bouquet garni, **корéнья**; (c) everyday as everyday can be (associated with northern Russia); served with sour cream

щи зелёные (a) sorrel, spinach soup, or both; (b) on a meat bouillon base; (c) one of the delights of spring (though sorrel can also be preserved)

борщ (a) borsch; (b) meat bouillon, beets, cabbage, onion, tomato, and so forth; (c) an everyday soup with many variations, served with sour cream—originated in the south and Ukraine

борщ холóдный (a) cold borsch; (b) beets, potatoes, cucumbers, onions, eggs, sour cream; (c) very popular in the summer

рассóльник (a) pickle soup; (b) usually a kidney base with pickles, celery, parsley, onion, potatoes, and barley

суп картóфельный со свéжими гриба́ми (a) mushroom and potato soup; (c) highly recommended

суп-лапша́ (a) noodle soup; (b) on a meat or chicken base with very little else

сбóрная мясна́я соля́нка (a) "solyanka" (from the word for village, **селó**); (b) meat bouillon, pickles, onions, tomato, capers, and olives (a friend insists that four olives per bowl is standard); (c) one of the very best—fish can also be a base, **ры́бная соля́нка**

харчó (a) "kharcho"; (b) lamb or beef, onion, garlic, tomato, rice, sour prunes, and coriander leaves; (c) a Caucasian soup now found in the deep north

уха́ (a) fish soup; (b) fish broth, fish, onions, potatoes; (c) a favorite way to use the little ones—should have at least three kinds of fish in it

окрóшка (a) "okroshka" (b) kvas base; boiled meat, cucumbers, onions, eggs, and sour cream; (c) a cold summer soup

ботви́нья с ры́бой (a) cold spinach or sorrel soup; (b) Kvas base; cucumbers, onion, horseradish, and poached fish

молóчная лапша́ (a) cream of noodle soup;

(b) noodles cooked in milk, butter, and a little sugar

супы́-пюре́   (a) pureed soups; (c) often thought of as food for babies or invalids

супы́ из я́год и фру́ктов   (a) berry and fruit soups; (c) most commonly found in the Baltic states where they are an example of the Scandinavian influence

Main dishes
Вторы́е блю́да

Except where noted, any of the following dishes can be the main course, all by itself. For example, it is quite possible to have nothing but boiled macaroni on your plate, or nothing but stuffed peppers. When pieces of meat, fish, or game are being served, they are accompanied by a "garnish" **гарни́р**, which is often potatoes or some other starch.

Fish
Ры́ба

In the United States, most people eat fish when they have to; the common Russian eats it any time it's available fresh, and sometimes when it's not. For kinds of fish and their desirability, see "Fish" in Chapter 14. Nowadays, frozen deep-sea fish are the most commonly available. Fish can be poached or boiled **отварна́я**, fried **жа́реная**, baked **запечённая**, or (rarely) steamed **парова́я**.

Meat
Мя́со

Any meat, whole or in pieces and cooked in an oven, can be **жарко́е**; thus, what you'll get may be a roast but is more likely to be braised meat or a stew. Our general *casserole* is the Russian's **запека́нка**.

азу́   (a) Tartar stew; (b) beef chopped small, stewed in a tomato and pickle sauce; (c) served with rice

говя́дина отварна́я под со́усом с хре́ном   (a) boiled beef with horseradish sauce

соси́ски; сарде́льки   (a) hot dogs, dinner franks; (b) surely with potatoes, cabbage, or canned peas; (c) a staple

ветчина́ с горо́шком   (a) ham and peas; (b) canned peas

ветчина́ жа́реная с помидо́рами   (a) fried ham slices and tomato halves

язы́к под бе́лым со́усом   (a) tongue with white sauce

говя́дина тушёная с лу́ком и карто́фелем   (a) stewed beef with onions and potatoes

гуля́ш из мя́са   (a) meat goulash; (b) browned and stewed meat in a tomato sauce with potatoes and onions; (c) no paprika!

соля́нка по-грузи́нски   (a) Georgian "solyanka"; (b) fine-sliced meat and onions, stir-fried; add tomato puree, chopped pickles, garlic, and wine, then braise

зра́зы из теля́тины   (a) stuffed veal rolls; (b) stuffing is onion and bread crumbs, braised; (c) from Poland

рагу́ из бара́нины   (a) mutton, lamb stew; (b) with potatoes, carrots, turnips, onion, and tomato puree

голубцы́ мясны́е   (a) stuffed cabbage rolls; (b) ground meat, onions, and rice, wrapped in cabbage leaves and stewed with sour cream and butter

говя́дина в сухаря́х (ромште́кс)   (a) chicken-fried steak; (b) the recipe says to use rib meat

беф-стро́ганов   (a) Russian beef stroganoff; (b) thin-sliced onions and good beef, stir-fried, with sour cream (properly done only in very good restaurants or perhaps at someone's house); (c) usually served with fried potatoes

зра́зы   (a) Polish meat patties; (b) meat wrapped around a filling then fried

зра́зы карто́фельные   (a) potato patties; (b) meat is the stuffing in potato patties, fried

бифште́кс   (a) steak; (b) served with fried potatoes, horseradish sauce; (c) "Rare" meat с кро́вью to a Russian is unacceptable, so in a restaurant choose what's done best—something else

говя́дина жа́реная (антреко́т) (a) rib steaks; (b) see preceding entry

лангет́ (ло́мтики вы́резки) с гарни́ром (a) tenderloin steak; (b) served with canned peas, or fried potatoes; (c) see preceding entries

колбаса́ жа́реная (a) fried sausage; (b) skinned first

котле́ты и биточки́ (a) ground meat patties, large **котле́ты** and small **биточки́**; (b) rolled in crumbs, then fried; (c) very common—served with a number of sauces

котле́ты отбивны́е и натура́льные (a) pork, lamb, or veal chops; (b) **отбивны́е** (here) is with a crumb coating; **натура́льные** is without the coating; (c) "cutlets" from ground meat are more common

печёнка в смета́не (a) liver in sour cream; (b) browned, then braised with sour cream

тефте́ли в тома́те (a) meat balls in tomato sauce; (b) browned, then braised

шашлы́к (a) shashlik; (b) lamb pieces on a stick, marinated, then broiled; (c) most commonly prepared and eaten at a picnic or in a special shashlik restaurant **шашлы́чная**, or from roadside stands

шни́цель (a) boneless pork or veal steaks; (b) dipped in egg, then bread crumbs, then fried

шни́цель ру́бленый, по-ве́нски, по-га́мбургски (a) thin ground-meat patties; (b) coated with crumbs, then fried

мясна́я запека́нка (a) meat casserole; (b) browned ground-meat and browned potatoes, bound with egg and baked; (c) a regular employ of leftovers

Sauces used for meat dishes
Со́усы к мя́су

кра́сный со́ус (a) red sauce; (b) what we call brown sauce

со́ус тома́тный (a) tomato sauce; (b) similar to preceding, but with more tomato

бе́лый со́ус (a) white sauce, or bechamel

со́ус с хре́ном (a) horseradish sauce

со́ус смета́нный (a) sour cream sauce

Domestic and wild fowl
Дома́шняя пти́ца и дичь

ку́ры или цыпля́та паровы́е (отварны́е) (a) boiled hen or chicken; (b) **паровы́е** in this sense means "tender enough to be steamed," so the directions said to boil

ку́рица под бе́лым со́усом (a) boiled chicken with white sauce

цыпля́та жа́реные (a) roast young chicken; (c) **жа́рить** means either to roast or to fry

котле́ты пожа́рские (a) chicken Pozharski; (b) ground chicken formed into patties and fried; (c) delicious

котле́ты по-ки́евски (a) chicken Kiev; (b) chicken breast stuffed with butter, coated, then fried; (c) it spurts when you slice into it

цыпля́та табака́ (a) Georgian chicken (b) split, flattened, then fried whole with lots of garlic; (c) delicious—finger food

Vegetables
Овощи

BOILED
Отварны́е

карто́фель отварно́й boiled potatoes

карто́фель молодо́й в смета́не young potatoes in sour cream

цветна́я капу́ста cauliflower

зелёный горо́шек в ма́сле green peas and butter

ты́ква отварна́я boiled winter squash

консерви́рованная кукуру́за с ма́слом canned corn and butter

FRIED VEGETABLES
Жа́реные о́вощи

карто́фель жа́реный   fried potatoes

карто́фельные котле́ты   fried mashed potato patties, often with mushroom sauce **с грибно́й подли́вкой**

котле́ты капу́стные   cabbage "cutlets"; chopped, boiled cabbage, bound with egg and semolina to make patties; fried

котлеты морко́вные   carrot cutlets prepared as preceding

шни́цель из капу́сты   cooked whole leaves folded as an envelope, dipped in egg, crumbed, and fried

кабачки́ жа́реные   thinly sliced summer squash, breaded then fried

лук ре́пчатый жареный   thinly sliced onions, fried

BAKED VEGETABLES
Запечённые о́вощи

запека́нка карто́фельная   potato casserole; two layers of mashed potatoes divided by onions then baked

карто́фельная запека́нка с мя́сом   same as preceding, but with ground meat between the two layers. A favorite device to use leftovers.

STEWED VEGETABLES
Тушёные овощи

карто́фель тушёный, со све́жими гриба́ми   potato and mushroom stew; browned potatoes, onions, and mushrooms that are stewed together

карто́фель тушёный, с копчёной груди́нкой   stewed potatoes and bacon

капу́ста тушёная   stewed cabbage, onions, and tomato puree

свёкла тушёная, в смета́не   stewed beets, with sour cream

рагу́ из овоще́й   stewed mixed vegetables

рагу́ из овощей с фасо́лью   stewed mixed vegetables with beans

баклажа́ны тушёные, в сметане   stewed eggplant slices

STUFFED VEGETABLES
Овощи фарширо́ванные

пе́рец фарширо́ванный   stuffed pepper

кабачки́ фарширо́ванные   stuffed zucchini (a large one)

голубцы́ овощны́е   cabbage leaves stuffed with vegetables

Mushrooms
Грибы́

After they have been cleaned, all fresh mushrooms are either parboiled or have boiling water poured on them before any other cooking takes place. At the table, they are usually served with a "garnish"—potatoes or the like.

грибы́ в смета́не   fried sliced mushrooms with sour cream

сморчки́ в сметане   fried morels with sour cream

грибы тушёные   stewed mushrooms

Cereals
Ка́ши

Keep in mind that these dishes can be the main dish **второ́е блю́до** all by themselves.

гре́чневая ка́ша с ма́слом   buckwheat and butter

гречневая каша из поджа́ренной крупы́   fried, then steamed buckwheat, with butter

гречневая каша с молоко́м   cold cooked buckwheat with milk

гречневая каша с гриба́ми и лу́ком   buckwheat with mushrooms and onion

пшённая каша с маслом   millet with butter

пшённая каша с ты́квой   millet with squash

каша из я́чневой или дроблёной овся́ной крупы   crushed barley or oat cereal

я́чневая каша со свины́м или бара́ньим са́лом   crushed barley with pork or lamb fat

моло́чные каши   milk cereals—all the usual grains can be cooked in milk to make the more substantial "milk" cereals

CEREAL CASSEROLES
Крупяны́е запека́нки

запека́нка пшённая, ри́совая, я́чневая или овся́ная   (a) casserole of millet, rice, barley, or oats; (b) cereal cooked in milk first, then baked with crumbs on top and bottom

крупе́ник из гре́чневой каши   (a) buckwheat casserole (b) buckwheat baked with cottage cheese, eggs and sour cream; (c) served hot as main dish or cold with soup

пу́динг ри́совый   (a) rice pudding; (c) more likely to be a dessert

плов с бара́ниной   (a) plov with lamb (plov is equivalent to pilaf); (b) rice served over lamb, with pomegranate

узбе́кский плов   (a) pilav with lamb; (b) rice cooked with browned lamb

Dishes using flour
Мучны́е изде́лия

клёцки   (a) dumplings; (b) using either flour or semolina; (c) served in bouillon, or as garnish for main dish

пельме́ни по-сиби́рски   (a) "pelmeni"; Russian ravioli; (b) small balls of ground meat encased in noodle dough, which are kept frozen, boiled on demand, and can be served in bouillon or with sour cream, butter, and vinegar; (c) homemade ones are esteemed, but they are so time-consuming that they are usually ready-made fast food

чебуре́ки   (a) chebureki; (b) cooked ground lamb, enveloped in noodle-dough then fried; (c) usually bought on the street

галу́шки   (a) galushki; (b) noodle-dough rolled, sliced, boiled, then fried; (c) served with sour cream—associated with Ukraine

макаро́ны, лапша́ и вермише́ль в ма́сле   (a) macaroni, noodles, or vermicelli in butter; (c) can be a main dish by itself

макаро́нник или лапше́вник   (a) macaroni or noodle casserole; (b) as preceding, but possibly with layers of meat or cottage cheese (that is, **творо́г**)

Egg dishes
Блю́да из яи́ц

Though perhaps more common at breakfast, eggs **яйца** can make a main dish, too (if they're not boiled).

всмя́тку   very soft boiled

в мешо́чек   not so soft boiled

вкруту́ю   hard boiled

(яи́чница-)глазу́нья   fried, sunny-side up

яи́чница   scrambled

омле́т   omelet

Milk product dishes
Моло́чные блю́да

We use the word *tvorog* rather than *cottage cheese* here, because the difference between the two is so large that they should not be thought of as interchangeable.

сы́рники; творо́жники   (a) "syrniki; tvorozhniki"; (b) tvorog, flour, sugar, and egg made into patties then fried

варе́ники с творого́м   (b) little ravioli filled with tvorog then fried or boiled; (**варе́ники с ви́шней** with cherries is also popular); (c) can be a main dish, for supper or tea

бли́нчики с творогом   (b) crepe envelopes filled with tvorog, fried; (c) served with tea, or as main dish

лени́вые варе́ники, галу́шки из творога́   (a) lazy man's "vareniki"; (b) tvorog, flour,

паук   spider
Паук плетёт паутину.[l]

оса́   wasp
Не тронь оси́ное гнездо́—беда́ бу́дет.[m]

пчела́   bee
Пчёлы живу́т в у́льях. Ма́тка - са́мая больша́я пчела́; она́ кладёт я́йца. Рабо́чая пчела́ собира́ет мёд, а тру́тень не произво́дит никако́й рабо́ты. Рой сле́дует за ма́ткой.[n]

сверчо́к   cricket
Сверчки́ ча́сто живу́т в дома́х за пе́чкой; ра́ньше счита́лось, что они́ разгова́ривают с домовы́м. Иногда́ они отождествля́ются с сами́м домовы́м.[o]

светля́к   firefly
Светляки́ появля́ются но́чью.[p]

стрекоза́   dragonfly
Чита́йте ба́сню Крыло́ва "Стрекоза́ и мураве́й."[q]

шмель   bumblebee
Шмели́ о́чень похо́жи на пчёл, но они́ бо́льше и мохна́тые.[r]

Harmful insects
Насеко́мые-вреди́тели

капу́стница   cabbage moth
Капу́стница (капу́стная ба́бочка) кладёт я́ички в стебельки́ капу́сты, а пото́м личи́нки их поеда́ют.[s]

клещ   tick
Лесно́й клещ передаёт энцефали́т.[t]

кома́р   mosquito
Че́шется. Кома́р укуси́л.[u]

кузне́чик   grasshopper
Зелёненький кузне́чик, коле́нками наза́д, Волну́ется, стреко́чет, чему́-то о́чень рад.[v]

ма́йский жук (и́ли) хрущ   May beetle
Ма́йский жук ест берёзу. Хрущ—вреди́тель се́льского хозя́йства.[w]

мокри́ца   sow bug or wood louse
Мокри́цы о́чень проти́вные; счита́ют, что они́ гря́зные.[x]

моль   moth
Про́тив мо́ли ну́жно употребля́ть нафтали́н.[y]

му́ха   fly
Обяза́тельно прочита́йте «Му́ху–цокоту́ху» Чуко́вского. Что́бы изба́виться от мух, употребля́ют и мухобо́йки, и ли́пкие ле́нты.[z]

саранча́   locust
Они́ набро́сились на стол как саранча́. (Всё очень бы́стро съе́ли.)[aa]

тарака́н   cockroach
Тарака́ны о́чень неприя́тные, и от них тру́дно изба́виться.[bb]

тля   aphid
(Сло́во «тля» употребля́ется гла́вным о́бразом в еди́нственном числе́.) Тля появи́лась. Там тля по́лзает.[cc]

уховёртка   earwig
Согла́сно суеве́рию, уховёртка проника́ет в у́хо и да́же в мозг.[dd]

Human infestation
Парази́ты челове́ка

блоха́   flea
Что ты ска́чешь, как блоха́?[ee]

вошь   louse
Вши пита́ются то́лько кро́вью челове́ка и млекопита́ющих. На челове́ка парази́ти́руют три ви́да вшей: головна́я, платяна́я и лобко́вая.[ff]

гни́да nit

Гни́да—это яи́чко вши. Они́ ме́лкие, бе́лые и не дви́гаются.[gg]

клоп bedbug

Клопо́в боя́тся ме́ньше, чем вшей, так как они́ обы́чно живу́т на веща́х, а не на те́ле.[hh]

From mollusks to amphibians
От моллю́сков до земново́дных

Of the mollusks **моллю́ски**, the most familiar are the snail **ули́тки** and slug **слизняки́**. The oyster **у́стрица** (and perhaps the mussel **ми́дия**), has been heard of but is far from familiar, while clams have not even reached that status. The squid **кальма́р** is associated with Oriental cookery and is also used in salads.

The most familiar of the crustaceans **ракообра́зные** is the crayfish **рак**, a popular accompaniment to beer. Crab **краб** is a highly regarded delicacy.

In the class of reptiles **пресмыка́ющиеся**, two kinds of native snakes **зме́и** are commonly distinguished: **уж** is the common garden snake, useful at least for eliminating garden pests; **гадю́ка** is poisonous and immediately distinguishable from the nonpoisonous snakes by a triangular-shaped head, noticeably separate from its body: **У гадю́ки ядови́тый зуб.** (**Клык** fang is not used in referring to snakes; only dogs and wolves have fangs: **Вы чита́ли «Бе́лый Клык» Дже́ка Ло́ндона?**) The lizard **я́щерица** and turtle **черепа́ха** are common and retain their reputations:

В слу́чае опа́сности я́щерицы спаса́ются, «теря́я» хвосты́.

Он ползёт, как черепа́ха. (Он о́чень ме́дленно идёт.)

The amphibians **земново́дные** include the frog **лягу́шка** (**голова́стик**, tadpole) and the toad **жа́ба**, a common animal that has retained its reputation, as well.

Согла́сно суеве́рию, у люде́й от жаб появля́ются борода́вки.[ii]

Fish
Рыба

—А кака́я у вас ры́ба?

—Ры́ба-то? Ры́ба вся́кая... И караси́ на плёсах есть, щу́ка, ну, пото́м эти... о́кунь, плотва́, лещ... Ещё линь. Зна́ешь линя́? Как поросёнок. То́-олстый! Я сам пе́рвый раз пойма́л—рот рази́нул. [jj]

Fish should supply a major source of protein in the Russian's diet; they are comparatively plentiful and relatively cheap so a Russian can distinguish many different kinds of fish. Currently good fish is hard to afford. **С ры́бой у нас пло́хо.**

The criterion for elegance is the fat content of the fish—the more fat, the better. Especially good fish are all the sturgeons and the salmon and also pike, sheatfish, eel, and burbot. Especially inexpensive fish are **ка́мбала (атланти́ческая), сельдь, сала́ка, ёрш.**

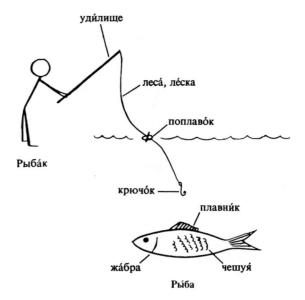

у́дочка = уди́лище + леса́ + крючо́к

уди́лище

леса́, ле́ска

поплаво́к

Рыба́к

крючо́к

плавни́к

жа́бра

чешуя́

Рыба

and egg, mixed and formed into snakes,
then snipped into sections and boiled; (c)
served with sour cream

творо́жная запека́нка   (a) baked tvorog;
(b) tvorog, semolina, sugar; baked on
crumbs and served with fruit syrup or sour
cream; (c) served with tea

творо́жный пу́динг с оре́хами
(b) steamed pudding made with tvorog,
eggs, raisins, and nuts; (c) served with tea

сла́дкая сырко́вая ма́сса   (a) sweet cheese;
(b) butter, tvorog, sour cream, sugar, and
flavorings; (c) served with tea

Dishes made with dough
Изде́лия из те́ста

Dough **те́сто** comes in various forms: yeast
dough **дрожжево́е тесто** uses yeast **дро́жжи**
and is sometimes used in its sourdough form **на
опа́ре**. Quick-rising or baking powder dough
ско́рое тесто, unleavened dough **пре́сное
тесто**, and a sort of puff pastry **слоёное тесто**
are also regularly used. Dough with added butter and sugar, nuts, or other good things has the
title **сдо́бное тесто, сдо́ба**. The dishes in this
section may be served at different parts of the
meal depending on composition and local custom.

пирожки́ (*sg.* **пирожо́к**)   (a) pirozhki; (b) a
filling of meat or any vegetables encased in
(usually yeast) dough, then fried or baked;
(c) served as an appetizer or to accompany a
clear bouillon on any occasion that allows
the time to make them—very popular and
often sold on the street corners

пиро́г   (a) pie (a very loose translation);
(b) two layers of (usually yeast) dough separated by a filling of meat, vegetables,
apples, or berries; (c) served as are pirozhki
with soup, especially bouillon; common
party fare

ватру́шка   (a) a danish that commonly
includes tvorog and sometimes other fillings; an open pirozhok

сла́дкий пиро́г   (a) a sweet pie; (b) two layers of dough with a jam or fruit filling

кулебя́ка   (a) found on our menus as "coulibiac" because of the French connection; (b)
layers of fish, rice, and mushrooms encased
in yeast dough then baked—taller and narrower than **пиро́г**; (c) very much a party
fare

беляши́, ватру́шки с мя́сом   (a) belyashi;
(b) a single layer of meat filling on yeast
dough, fried

ба́бка морко́вная   (a) yeast-dough carrot
cake; (c) served with tea

блины́ на опа́ре, блины ско́рые   (a) blini
from yeast dough; quick blini; (b) try them
with caviar and sour cream; (c) the first
might be a Sunday dinner; the latter, quick
kind might appear at breakfast

Пе́рвый блин ко́мом.
Expect your first (pancake) blin to be a
mess. "If at first you don't succeed . . ."

Pavla and her blini

ола́дьи (a) fritters; (b) fried yeast dough; (c) either at breakfast or dinner

бли́нчики (a) crepes; (b) which is to say, unleavened dough; (c) breakfast

бли́нчатый пиро́г (a) crepe pie; (b) layers of cooked crepes with one or several fillings, baked; (c) delicious

бли́нчатые пирожки́ (a) pirozhki made with crepes; (b) filling is wrapped in the crepes, then fried; (c) used when speed or using leftovers are the greatest consideration

Meat is by no means the only filling начи́нка for many of the preceding dishes; also likely are any edible insides ли́вер, fish, rice, mushrooms, cabbage, carrots, tvorog, green onions, eggs, apples, and dried apricots курага́. In the very old days, sturgeon spine marrow вязи́га was very elegant filling.

IN BETWEEN MEALS, AND AFTER THEM
Ра́зные сла́дости

Bakery goods
Сдо́бные изде́лия

Bread is a major staple in the diet and as such has been heavily subsidized; therefore, bread is practically never made at home. Other baking is done at home, however.

бу́лочки rolls

ша́нежки sweet rolls

кренделькѝ light sweet rolls in the shape of pretzels

руле́т с ма́ком poppyseed coffee cake (руле́т is *roll* as in *rolled up*)

сухари́ rusks, biscotti; sweet yeast dough flavored with cardamom, saffron, almonds; baked, then dried in slices

кули́ч kulich is a sweet bread cooked in a cylindrical shape at Easter and served with paskha па́сха at Easter; distinctive and delicious

ро́мовая ба́ба must be where baba au rhum came from

кре́ндель с миндалём sweet yeast-dough loaf in pretzel shape with almonds

Cookies (in the broadest sense)
Пече́нье

пече́нье дома́шнее vanilla sugar cookies

пече́нье песо́чное "sand" cookies

пече́нье сли́вочное cream cookies (common, bought cookies)

пря́ник from cookie size to very large, these are a soft, spice, cakish cookie often baked in a form with a design in it, the whole associated with Old Russia; different places specialize

минда́льное пече́нье almond cookies (almonds, sugar, egg whites, and almost no flour)

пече́нье бискви́тное vanilla cookies without the fat

коври́жка медо́вая honey-spice cookies

плю́шки the French "palmier" but made with yeast dough

по́нчики doughnut relative, sometimes with filling

пы́шки small, light, yeast-dough bun

ма́ковки на па́токе poppyseed and molasses bars (now a rarity since someone discovered where opium comes from)

пече́нье из ржано́й муки́ rye cookies

хво́рост deep-fried sweet-dough strips dusted with powdered sugar

ко́ржики shortbread

гале́ты a dry tasteless cracker associated with military rations

Pastries and pies
Пиро́жные, то́рты, ке́ксы

Though these are very general and don't indicate the kinds of dough used, a cake or any large pastry is a торт; a single-serving pastry is пирожное; coffee or sponge cake is **кекс**, and pie (any dough containing any filling) is **пиро́г**.

слоёное пирожное с я́блоками puff pastry and sliced apples

наполео́н; слоёное пирожное с кре́мом puff pastry and custard (or, often, whipped cream; the French mille-feuille)

песо́чное пирожное с миндалём cookie dough rings with almonds

бискви́тное пирожное с варе́ньем sponge cake with jam layers

экле́р; пиро́жное со взби́тыми сли́вками или заварны́м кре́мом eclairs filled with whipped cream or custard

корзи́ночки с я́годами pastry baskets with berries

руле́т бискви́тный rolled sponge cake with jam

бискви́т sponge cake rusks, biscotti

пиро́жное минда́льное layered almond pastry

торт песо́чный a sort of shortcake

кекс лимо́нный lemon coffee cake

кекс вани́льный vanilla coffee cake

тру́бочки заварны́е custard-filled puff-pastry cornucopias

Sweet dishes
Сла́дкие блю́да

безе́ meringue

кисе́ль kisel is a very popular dessert made of almost any fruit puree, sugar, and potato starch **крахма́л**.

компо́т compote from fresh or dried fruit is also very popular; the amount of water used varies greatly; sometimes served in a glass or cup as a liquid

желе́ и мусс gelatins and mousse

я́годный крем "cream" dishes add cream or sour cream to gelatin and flavoring mixture (here, berries)

сли́вки, взби́тые с са́харом essentially, whipped cream and sugar

смета́на, взбитая с сахаром whipped sour cream and sugar

сли́вочное моро́женое ice cream, with no doubt about the cream content

па́сха paskha; tvorog base to which is added large amounts of cream, butter, eggs, sugar, and seasonings; Easter dessert, along with kulich; arrives at table in pyramidal form; delicious and horribly fattening

Puddings and other sweet dishes
Пу́динги и други́е сла́дкие блю́да

ри́совый пудинг rice pudding; often served as a main dish, with preserves

возду́шный пиро́г из я́блок meringue with apples

гу́рьевская ка́ша semolina cooked in sweetened milk, then baked and served with fruit and almonds

печёные я́блоки с варе́ньем baked apples with jam

тру́бочки со сли́вками cream-filled and rolled crepes

я́блоки в те́сте apple rings dipped in sweet batter and fried

DRINK
Напи́тки

Nonalcoholic drinks
Безалкого́льные напитки

Coffee, tea, or milk?
Ко́фе, чай или молоко́?

Of the three, tea is still the major staple for breakfast and after dinner and supper. And it is still made much the same way: a strong infusion is first prepared and then hot water **кипя-то́к** is added later, either in the cup or in the teapot **ча́йник**. Russians like tea with an egregious amount of sugar, but milk is a regular component only in Siberia or the Far East.

Loose black tea **чёрный байховый чай** is standard and is grown in the south, though imported Indian and Ceylon types are preferred. Green tea **зелёный чай** is favored in central Asia, while pressed tea **плиточный чай** (either green or black) is popular in Siberia and points East. Brick tea **кирпичный чай** is something else again: green tea from the stems and coarse leaves that have been treated and pressed into large slabs. In central Asia, hunks of it are broken off and boiled with fat, flour, salt, butter, milk, mare's milk, rice, and so forth added.

Leftover tea is not wasted. Popular in rural communities is the use of the tea mushroom **чайный гриб**, which lives in a solution of tea and is fed tea with sugar from time to time. The tea changes to a pleasant, sourish thirst-quenching drink particularly popular in the summer; it is thought to be good for digestion.

Russian coffee **кофе** suffers either from high prices or low availability or sometimes both (therefore, do not expect its offer). Turkish and Baltic peoples pride themselves on their coffee. Theirs is, desirably, much stronger than the standard American variety. Coffee with condensed milk **кофе со сгущённым молоком** is most common in rural areas. Young urbanites learning Western wiles drink thick Turkish coffee from small cups; otherwise the standard desirability is instant coffee **растворимый кофе**. Roasted coffee beans are **кофе жареный в зёрнах**; grind with a coffee grinder **кофемолка**, and serve with milk. Coffee grounds are **кофейная гуща**.

Milk **молоко** is urged on children, especially at school, but it is certainly not the requirement it is here. To quote a Russian friend: "You Americans have a cult of milk!" Some of the best milk is supposed to come from Mozhaysk where the fat content might be as much as 6 percent. The word *cocktail* occurs most frequently in referring to a milk cocktail, **молочный коктейль**, a combination of milk and flavorings often served in night spots for young ones who aren't supposed to drink, and at juice **Соки, воды** stands.

Hot chocolate **какао** requires no urging, but it does require the cocoa beans that are not always available or affordable.

Water
Вода

Tap water **вода из крана** is used for washing but rarely for drinking, especially in the cities. (Those with foreign stomachs should follow suit.) Instead, Russians have a water cult, or rather culture, which takes full advantage of the many kinds and tastes of mineral water **минеральная вода** that have been developed, especially in the Caucasus: Borzhomi **Боржоми** and Narzan **Нарзан** are standard table waters and Essentuki No. 20, **Ессентуки № 20** is a standard medicinal water; hundreds more are available. Water, rather than flavored drinks, is used to relieve thirst **жажда**. ("I'm thirsty" **Хочу пить**.)

Carbonated water **газированная вода** with some sort of flavoring approaches our notion of a soft drink and is commonly sold on the street. The most popular, especially for children, is probably lemon-flavored carbonated water **лимонад**, but others are popular too: apple drink **яблочный напиток**, orange drink **апельсиновый напиток**, and so forth. Canned or bottled juices **соки** can be had, but they are expensive and are used at table for those who don't drink wine. Fruit syrup plus added water is **морс**, a drink often served at table; cranberry drink **клюквенный морс** is probably what you'll get if you request **морс**, and it is particularly recommended for colds.

"Kvas" **квас** is the summertime drink sold from great cisterns on the streets. It is dark, rather sour, somewhat bitter, and made from sugar, yeast, water, and toasted rye bread crumbs. The drink is very popular, refreshing, and about one percent alcohol, though Russians themselves do not think of it as an alcoholic drink. It is used as a base for summer soups, especially "okroshka" **окрошка**. It can also be had in bottles or made from a concentrate **концентрат** at home, not always successfully.

Kvas is a matter of the moment and normally unavailable in other seasons.

Alcoholic drinks
Алкого́льные напи́тки

Beer
Пи́во

Beer **пи́во** is drunk more often by males, more often in beer halls **пивны́е** (*low coll.* **пивну́шка**) or after a steam bath, mostly on draft **разливно́е пи́во** or from barrels or kegs **из бо́чек**, from large mugs **кружки́**, with dried salt fish **с во́блой**.

Wines
Ви́на

In their natural state (that is, unaffected by the ways of the West) Russians prefer their wines sweeter than we do—those opening a bottle of Russian champagne **шампа́нское** will have chosen a sweet **сла́дкое** or a semisweet **полусла́дкое** over a dry **сухо́е шампанское (вино́)**. Better wines are "brand name" wines **ма́рочные ви́на**, many of which have been laid down **вы́держаны** either in the barrel or in the bottle; "vin ordinaire" is **ордина́рное вино́**. Dry table wines **сухи́е столо́вые ви́на** can be found, and a few grape varieties should be familiar, such as **ри́слинг** and **каберне́**, while many more will not: **ркаците́ли** and **мцва́не** grapes make **Цинанда́ли** and **Гурджаа́ни** wines. The best producers are from the Crimea and the Caucasus—look for **Самтре́ст, Абра́у-Дюрсо́, Масса́ндра,** and **Арара́т** at tasting halls **дегустацио́нные за́лы** in the region.

Fortified (grape) wines **креплёные ви́на** are white and red port **бе́лый, кра́сный портвейн**, madeira **маде́ра**, sherry **хе́рес**, marsala **марса́ла**, barsac **барза́к**, and (go ahead, guess) **шато-икем**, cahors **каго́р**, muscats **муска́ты**, and tokays **тока́йские**. They are all sweet by our standards.

Strong (about 16 percent alcohol) fruit wines **кре́пкие пло́дово-я́годные ви́на** are made of almost any fermented fruit, berry, or combinations thereof—with, of course, added sugar. Among the most popular are **Бе́лое кре́пкое, Кра́сное кре́пкое, Ряби́новое, Сли́вовое, Абрико́совое, Земляни́чное. . .** and many others, the title depending on the fruit. This classification is the one most likely to be used by drunks.

Vodka
Во́дка

But, as a Russian friend said, why drink fortified wines when you can drink vodka? The best vodkas are **Столи́чная** and **Моско́вская осо́бая**, both at 40 percent alcohol. They are followed by other, slightly less refined or filtered kinds; their title includes alcoholic content. Vodka usually comes in half-liter bottles, but any bottle is thought to be the right amount for three (**сообрази́ть**) **на трои́х**. (The expression started when one could buy half a liter for 2.60 rubles, with 40 kopecks left for a little food to go with it—three people with a ruble each could get together and have a party.) Jokes without end are made about the search for the third person, who must be found because bottles were formerly capped such that they could not be recapped—and the entirety had to be consumed once the bottle was opened. Whoever puts a half-filled bottle on the table is either too cheap for words or is insulting the guests. (Russians newly arrived stateside sometimes do not understand how we can have liquor cabinets containing partially filled bottles!)

The New World Order has made vodka available everywhere. Its high price is the only saving grace.

Cognac, brandy
Конья́к

Brandy **конья́к** is the hard liquor of preference for those who can afford it—it's dry and the alcohol content is high. It is drunk as is vodka, at the table (throughout the meal), and not sipped. The labels on lesser cognacs feature stars to indicate the number of years they have aged, and better ones have letters that indicate even greater age. Armenian brandies are reputed to have a powerful bouquet; Georgian brandies are softer, with more finesse.

The infusion
Настойка

The infusion is made by taking a base of alcohol, usually vodka or brandy, and steeping flavorings in it: **зубро́вка** is vodka with a few stems of buffalo (**зубр**) grass; **перцо́вка** is vodka with peppers (**перец**); **ри́жский чёрный бальза́м** and hunter's vodka **охо́тничья** use a variety of flavorings. The infusion is usually fairly dry and strong and therefore favored by males (according to popular psychology). Both infusions and cordials are frequently made at home.

The cordial
Нали́вка

Cordials **нали́вки** are made by combining a fruit and sugar, waiting for them to coalesce, straining, and then adding alcohol of some sort. (May I recommend mountain ash berries and cognac, **ряби́на на коньяке́**?) The cordial is not so strong as the infusion and is always sweet and usually preferred by women. They are very common and often made at home.

Liqueurs
Ликёры

Liqueurs, which usually require distillation, are available, but they are mostly an introduction from the West since the Revolution. Their alcohol and sugar content is high enough that they are consumed during or after dessert. The base is often a fruit: **мали́новый ликёр**, **облепи́ховый ликёр**, **черносморо́диновый ликёр**.

Home brews
Напи́тки дома́шнего приготовле́ния

The word for honey, **мёд**, also is the root for mead, **медову́ха**, a beer made from honey and now produced to enhance the historicity of old cities (such as Novgorod).

In the bad old days, or perhaps still in some localities, a stronger, beer-like kvas was made: **бра́га**, **бра́жка** (fermentation, **броже́ние**). Today the word refers to any strongly alcoholic homemade brew. **Что э́то за бра́га?** means "What kind of firewater is this?"

Homemade vodka **самого́н** is prevalent, and indeed especially strong in Siberia, where the natives take pride in drinking almost straight alcohol (forewarned is forearmed). The recent curtailment of vodka production has made moonshine a favorite cottage industry, which has in turn reduced already inadequate sugar supplies.

> День прошёл—царя́ Салта́на
> Уложи́ли спать вполпья́на.
> Я там был; мёд, пи́во пил—
> И усы́ лишь обмочи́л.
>
> А. С. Пушкин[b]

WHERE CAN WE EAT?
Где мо́жно пое́сть?

Purveying food was not a major Soviet art. The best Russian food is made at home by a good Russian cook. The entire system of government-prepared food delivery bears the title "social food" **обще́ственное пита́ние**, irreverently reduced to **общепи́т** as the term for any institutional feeding establishment.

The top of the chain is the restaurant **рестора́н**, which used to have a long line **о́чередь** out in front, an occasional waiter **официа́нт**, a menu **меню́** that is often ignored, and with luck a place **ме́сто** to sit down (often with others not in your party). Mind you, Russians go to a restaurant less to eat than to have a good time: they are not in such a hurry, and good food is less important than good friends. In the evening many restaurants feature live—and often very loud—music to go with the dance floor. During the day, when a good time is not the point, most restaurants offer a set menu **ко́мплексный обе́д** at a set price that is less expensive and much faster than evening service.

New cooperative restaurants and cafes **кооперати́вные рестора́ны и кафе́** offer a higher standard of food served with much greater speed at very much higher rates.

The cafe **кафе́** might or might not include a full meal, and self-service **самообслу́жива-ние** can usually be expected. Here the choice of offerings is in some way limited and is some-times indicated in the title: **кафе-конди́тер-ская, моло́чное-кафе, кафе-моро́женое.** Others give no such information: **кафе Луна́, кафе Йвушка.** The title **кафе-гриль** is understood to be a cooperative. A pejorative for an unpretentious place to eat in the countryside is **харче́вня.**

The backbone and the workhorse of the feeding system, the cafeteria **столо́вая,** used to supply major meals at low prices to people either at their workplace or in their neighbor-hood. The selection was not large (one to three main dishes), but the meal was complete and inexpensive. Unfortunately, the network of cafeterias is beginning to wane because they are too expensive to maintain, so more people are having to bring their food to work with them.

Russian fast food exists! These are even smaller eating establishments limited to one dish plus what might be required to accompany it: tea, soft drinks, and so on. Many, though not all, are "standing cafes" (**стоя́чие кафе́**) where tables are small, elbow-high and where the cus-tomers do the standing—unpleasant but fast. Titles for such places depend on what they serve: a **бли́нная** serves blini, a **бутербро́дная** serves open-faced sandwiches, a **заку́сочная** serves appetizers (and used to serve vodka to go with it), a **пельме́нная** serves pelmeni, a **пирожко́вая** serves many kinds of little "pies," a **соси́сочная** serves sausages, a **ча́йная** serves tea and accompaniment, a **чебуре́чная** serves Caucasian meat pies, and a **шашлы́чная** serves shashlik.

The buffet **буфе́т** is a very small operation, maybe three or four tables and one or two peo-ple behind the counter to supply tea, coffee, a small variety of appetizers, perhaps some fruit, hard-boiled eggs, and maybe a fried egg in the morning. Foreigners will first see them down the hallway at their hotels.

Food is also available out on the city streets from movable carts **передвижны́е теле́жки,** where a large variety of finger foods, from doughnuts **по́нчики** to shashlik **шашлы́к,** can be had from time to time. And at a more sub-stantial booth **пала́тка, ларёк** one can buy juices, mineral water, and carbonated waters. Many Russians currently consider street food to be unsanitary, dangerous, or both. This new condition is another daily suggestion to urban Russians that their world is disintegrating.

TRANSLATIONS

a.   According to Archimedes' principle,
     After a tasty dinner,
     One should take a nap.

b.   A day went by and the Czar-Sultan
     Was put to bed half-drunk.
     I was there, drank honey and beer,
     And just got my whiskers wet.

                                    A. S. Pushkin

7

Medicine
Медици́на

Russian medicine has not been dealt with kindly in the Western press; truthfully, much has been done, but much remains to do. Currently, both patients and doctors are between the devil and the deep blue sea: one system of distribution is dying, a new one has not developed well enough to take its place, and the tide of human events overwhelms all but the strong and well situated. (In other words, no money, no medicine.) Patients are giving up on doctors and are treating themselves. The patients who are getting well are those who don't require a doctor to do so.

It has not been expected that one pays for one's illness; therefore hospital or sanatorium stays are long; so if what you really need is rest, you are in fine shape. But you can't get off work without a certificate of need signed by a doctor and stamped at a polyclinic.

The Russian doctor usually concludes that what patients don't know won't hurt them: patients are almost never told that a condition is terminal. Nor will the reasons for, or details of, the illness be explained. In sickness as in health, your thinking is thought to be best done for you.

The standard Russian patient is much more likely to self-treat than the typical U.S. patient because the wait for a G.P. can be several hours, because modern medicines are thought to be very strong, and because herbal or folk medicine can be more accessible. Counter-irritants are high on the list of used medicines: if it doesn't hurt, it probably isn't good for you.

Hospitals are free but understaffed; anyone recovering from an operation, for example, needs friends or family to help or to pay the nurse's aide extra in order to make sure the patient is taken care of. (This is especially true of the city hospital **городска́я больни́ца** compared to the "institutional" kind **ве́домственная больни́ца**.) Some westerners consider this bribery, whereas in Russia it might be considered reasonable payment. The doctor, however, is never bribed, though it is standard that a grateful patient will express gratitude for extraordinary services with a gift (cognac, candy, flowers). The doctor will be paid, of course, if this was a private arrangement to begin with. Such arrangements are legal now and becoming common, at least in major cities. Private clinics also exist, but getting equipment for them is not an easy task. The move from one social arrangement to another will probably include some private medical insurance **страхова́я медици́на**, which had not appeared on the scene by early 1994.

The medical world includes these topics:
Personnel
Institutions
Pregnancy
Ailments
Medicines
Dentists

PERSONNEL
Ка́дры

The doctor
Врач

The basic medical component is, of course, the doctor **врач**, who is addressed either as "Doctor" **До́ктор (Ивано́ва)** or, if introductions have been made, by first name and patronymic. The vast majority of Russian doctors are women, a shock for many U.S. males who must avail of their services. (Ha!, I might say.) As usual, though, the upper flights of doctordom are more frequently occupied by males.

Basic college-level medical training takes place at medical institutes that are entered immediately after secondary education. Medicine is a respected occupation, so several applicants take competitive entrance examinations for each available space. Any one of five areas of concentration is chosen: medicine **лече́бное де́ло**, pediatrics **педиатри́я**, hygiene and sanitation **гигие́на и санитари́я**, (all requiring six years of medical school plus one year of internship **интернату́ра, ордина́тура, пра́ктика**), dentistry or oral surgery **стоматоло́гия** (five years), and pharmacy **фармаколо́гия** (four and one-half years). Medical schools **мединститу́ты** offer from one to all five of these areas of study.

During the last year of medical school, and sometimes earlier, the students specialize. You are familiar with the alphabet, so the following medical specialties should be recognizable. First the type of doctor is listed, followed by the area of specialization (this allows a better display of the accent shift); the specialty is followed by some of the ailments such a doctor might treat:

кардио́лог, кардиоло́гия: боле́зни се́рдца—стенокарди́я, инфа́ркт миока́рда

онко́лог, онколо́гия: о́пухоли (злока́чественные — рак, есть и доброка́чественные о́пухоли)

эндокрино́лог, эндокриноло́гия: эндокри́нные болезни желёз вну́тренней секре́ции

дермато́лог, ко́жник, дерматоло́гия: боле́зни ко́жи

педиа́тр, де́тский врач, педиатри́я: де́тские болезни

психиа́тр, психиатри́я: психи́ческие заболева́ния

акуше́р–гинеко́лог, гинеколо́гия: же́нские болезни

уро́лог, уроло́гия: заболева́ния мочеполовой систе́мы, по́чек—нефри́т, цисти́т, простати́т

эпидемио́лог, эпидемиоло́гия: распростране́ние и пути́ переда́чи инфекционных боле́зней

офтальмо́лог, окули́ст, глазно́й врач, (глазни́к), офтальмоло́гия: болезни глаз: глауко́ма, катара́кта, конъюнктиви́т, дальнозо́ркость, близору́кость, поте́ря зре́ния

ортопе́д, ортопеди́я: деформа́ции косте́й, остеохондро́з (arthritis)

невропато́лог, невропатоло́гия: невро́зы, бессо́нница, головна́я боль, радикули́т

хиру́рг, хирурги́я: операти́вные вмеша́тельства

ревмато́лог, ревматоло́гия: болезни суста́вов и мышц рук, ног

(Everyday speech avoids the Latinisms when an alternative has been established.) A few specialties are less obvious: internist **терапе́вт, врач по вну́тренним боле́зням**, and the ear, nose, and throat practitioner **врач ухо-горло-нос**, can show off with a name like **ото-ларинго́лог**, who is supposed to have studied a lot of **отоларинголо́гия**. Other specialties are both less common and more recognizable: **геронто́лог, аллерго́лог, гастроэнтеро́лог, анестезио́лог (реанимато́лог), инфек-циони́ст**. The person who figures out what a **рентгено́лог** does deserves special mention.

Middle level medics
Сре́дний медици́нский персона́л

The following are medical assistants who have graduated from a medical (trade) school **медици́нское учи́лище** after two to four years of study and practice.

The best trained is the doctor's assistant **фе́льдшер**, who in the countryside might often be the major medical resource. In the city this specialty is common among ambulance atten-dants, those responsible for sports medicine, and also in polyclinics where they are in charge of the preparation room **кабине́т доврачебной по́мощи**.

The midwife **акуше́рка** (*masc.* **акуше́р**) is responsible for normal deliveries, only calling upon a doctor when something abnormal is suspected.

The standard nurse **медсестра́** (formerly **сестра́ милосе́рдия**, an indication of the reli-gious origins of nursing) is short for **медици́нская сестра́**, and generally corre-sponds to our registered nurses who do not have a bachelor's degree (the male nurse is **мед-бра́т**). The surgical nurse **хирурги́ческая сес-тра́** is a more demanding and more highly regarded nursing specialty.

The pharmacist is a **фармаце́вт**.

The nurse's aide **санита́рка**, familiarly called **ня́ня**, or **санита́р** for a male, is not expected to have any medical training. The job is poorly paid and held in low regard, so that they must often be paid extra by the patient or family; otherwise some of their work must be done by the patient's family. Some patient care

ухо́д за больны́ми is done these days by nurse's aides that are supplied by the church. They accept no payment, and are regarded as particularly sympathetic **серде́чные**. They weren't allowed in hospitals in earlier days because the authorities feared that they would proselytize—and they do.

Speaking familiarly, one might use **до́ктор-ша, фе́льдшерица** for females of the species; "medic" **ме́дик** or **меди́чка** can refer to either the doctor (especially one in training) or nurse; and the nurse gets "little sister" **сестри́чка**. (However, such words are better understood than used.)

INSTITUTIONS
Учрежде́ния

Russians assume that good medical care and equipment is found only in the largest cities; it was common knowledge in days gone by that much better medical care was provided by one's place of work, especially if it was a large producing factory or any powerful organiza-tion. These were the "institutional" **ве́дом-ственные** polyclinics or hospitals. A medical center **медсанча́сть** for factories with more than 4,000 workers or mining and chemical operations of more than 2,000 was responsible both for medical care and for the health aspects of the workplace. Now, that system is being combined with a direct and indirect pay system: for example, some institutions too small to maintain their own hospitals might rent a num-ber of hospital beds for their employees; and some medical procedures—for example, the mini-abortion—are only available for a fee.

The polyclinic
Поликли́ника

If the doctor is the major component of medical personnel, the polyclinic **поликли́ника** is the major unit of medical service. Each city has regional polyclinics **райо́нные поликли́ники** that are responsible for health-care delivery in

A sick list sheet **бюллетéнь**

their area. Each region is divided into sectors **учáстки**, each of which has its own sector doctor **участкóвый врач/терапéвт** who works in (and out) of the polyclinic. (Later we describe a visit to the polyclinic, but people who feel sick can request that the doctor come to the house, which she does!) Polyclinics have a number of sector doctors plus several specialists, for example: **гинекóлог, кардиóлог, урóлог**, not to mention a medical staff and equipment.

The polyclinic is essentially a confirmation, information, and referral service—examining patients, giving them medical excuses from work, treating the ambulatory treatable, and referring elsewhere those patients whose diagnoses are unclear or who require longer or more specialized care. The ailing patient **пациéнт** arrives at the polyclinic with medical chart **медицúнская кáрта** in hand,[1] goes to the reception room or office **регистратýра**, run by а **регистрáтор**; from here the medical record **медицúнская кáрта** is sent to the appropriate doctor. The patient gets a number **талóн**, the doctor's name, and the appointment time. The patient proceeds to a nurse's office **кабинéт доврачéбной пóмощи** for temperature, blood pressure, or other necessary measures. This same room is used for medical check-ups **медосмóтр** of people whose job requires them to be in good health: food workers, cooks, those

---

1. In some places the reception office keeps the medical charts. Letting the patient have the chart is a new phenomenon not observed everywhere.

who work with children, and the like. Then our patient waits; sometimes the appointment schedule is less than rigid—instead the patients form themselves into a line (q.v.) **жива́я о́чередь**, ask "Who's last?" **Кто после́дний?** and take their turn.

Our patient sees the doctor, and if she is indeed sick **больна́я**, she gets a sick-list sheet **больни́чный лист** that affirms inability to work **листо́к нетрудоспосо́бности**, which in turn gives the recipient the right not to work for a set period. This is also called **медици́нский бюлле́тень. Она́ на больни́чном, на бюллете́не.** Further, rather than, "Mr. Jones is sick today and cannot come to work," the sick-list sheet **больничный лист** is fairly detailed. One side requires the patient's name, age, address, workplace, a preliminary diagnosis, and the date. The form must include the medical system stamp in two places. The other side is filled out by the patient's boss, as well as the chairman of the trade union committee **председа́тель профко́ма**, who must determine the amount of reimbursement according to seniority **стаж**. (Currently, after eight years of work one gets full salary while sick.) Getting on the sick list with its right not to go to work is probably the major reason for seeing the doctor in the first place.

Wide use is made of treatments **процеду́ры** prescribed mainly to make the patient feel better. Thus massage is among the treatments at your local polyclinic. Water, both in and out and up and down **водолече́ние** is regarded as cleansing and healing. Some hospitals use electricity **То́ки Берна́ра** for lower back pain **радикули́т**. Others use magnetic waves.

But our doctor isn't sure why our patient is sick and so refers the patient to a specialist, either *in situ* or elsewhere: diagnostic centers **диагности́ческие це́нтры** with modern equipment can be found in major cities.

In addition to the standard clinics, each region also has children's clinics **де́тские поликли́ники** and dental clinics **стоматологи́ческие поликлиники.**

Most medical care is dispensed under the aegis of the Ministry of Health **Министе́рство здравоохране́ния (Минздра́в).**

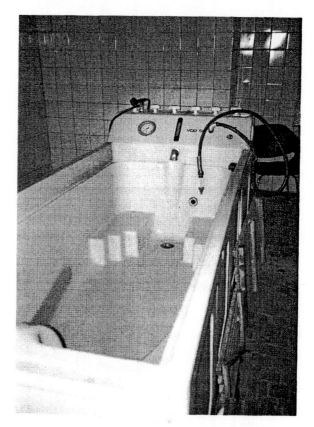

Ва́нна в больни́це

Physical therapy equipment is heavily used in Russian medicine

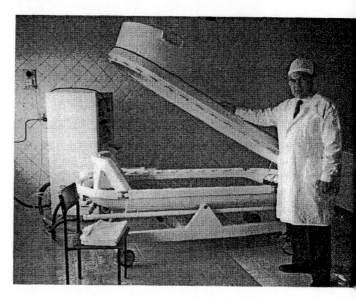

The Hospital
Больница

Hospitals **больницы** have a number of alternative appellations: **госпиталь** is, in fact, a military hospital; **стационар** is leftover war military terminology now used in the doctoring trade for any permanent—that is, not mobile—medical care facility, especially a hospital. (For example, a day-treatment hospital is **дневной стационар**). A hospital/clinic in the country, or one offering less elegant services is **лечебница**, an old-fashioned term from **лечить** to care for, to treat. **Он попал в лечебницу** means (probably) that he got sent to an alcoholic treatment center.

Hospitals specializing in one kind of ailment **однопрофильные больницы** are common, for

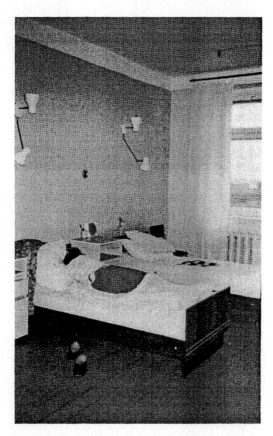

В больнице

example: **гинекологическая, инфекционная, онкологическая, наркологическая, психиатрическая, туберкулёзная**. Hospitals can be regional: **участковые, районные, городские, республиканские**; they can be supported by enterprises or ministries **ведомственные** instead of the local governments. If it is a teaching hospital, then it has medical-school staff **кафедра медфака** and is called a clinical hospital **клиническая больница**. Some medical schools have their own hospitals. A general hospital **многопрофильная больница** might have the following divisions **отделения**: **хирургическое, урологическое, глазное, ухо-горло-нос, стоматологическое, гинекологическое, травматологическое, кардиологическое**. A small hospital might have only the two most important divisions: medical **терапевтическое** and surgical **хирургическое**.

Instead of a registry, hospitals have an admissions office **приёмный покой**; patients **больные** stay in a ward **палата** of four to ten beds. The hospital is run by a head doctor **главный врач**, and the head nurse **главная медсестра** oversees the charge nurse **старшая сестра** who is assigned to each subdivision of the hospital. Titles on hospital doors are not without interest; as you walk down the hall, you'll see the doctors' room **ординаторская**, the nurses' room **сестринская**, X-ray **лаборатория рентгена**, physiotherapy **физиотерапия**, a treatment room **процедурная**, a recovery room **реанимация** or **реанимационная палата**, an intensive care unit **БИТ** (**Блок интенсивной терапии**), not to mention the enema room **клизменная**.

Some medical centers **центры** are large, national affairs, specialized in treating problems that are particularly intractable or complicated. They have both treatment and training facilities—for example, the center for treating congenital bone deformations **Центр по исправлению врождённых пороков суставов, позвоночника и т.д.**, and the center for ailments of the eye headed by academician Fedorov **Центр по болезням глаз Академика Фёдорова. Кардиологический центр, Онко-**

логи́ческий центр, Травматологи́ческий центр и т.д.

Russians go to the hospital sooner and stay longer than we do. Visitors are therefore less of an interruption and more welcome and expected. Conventional gifts include books, magazines, and healthy foods: курага́, оре́хи, мали́новое варе́нье и т.п.

Other medical services
Други́е медици́нские слу́жбы

Smaller medical institutions abound: a dispensary диспансе́р has clients who must be kept track of for medical reasons—for example, a tuberculosis dispensary (противо)тубер-кулёзный диспансе́р; a cancer dispensary онкологи́ческий диспансер; and a skin and venereal disease dispensary ко́жно-венероло-ги́ческий диспансер, which also treats impotence. The Russian medical community emphasizes both prevention and the treatment of early stages of the ailment.

An outpatient clinic амбулато́рия, usual in rural areas, offers more limited services than a polyclinic. This term can also refer to an outpatient clinic for a factory. A doctor's office здравпу́нкт is what smaller factories can get, while a nurse's office медпу́нкт might be available at a school.

Preventive medicine is actively practiced by the institution of the sanitary-epidemic station санэпидемста́нция.[2] These offices have a doctor in charge specifically trained to check on and assure good public health practices: pest control, food cleanliness, sanitation, working conditions, water purity, and the like. Doctors who come across dangerous communicable diseases must report the fact here. These are powerful little offices—they can shut down entire cities when necessary, not to mention individual restaurants and workplaces.

Emergency! Help!
На по́мощь!

Where you call or what you do depends on the emergency. Generally, you dial 03 and an ambulance ско́рая with a team брига́да that includes a doctor's assistant фе́льдшер and perhaps a male nurse медбра́т will arrive fairly soon. Or you can call your local polyclinic at the "Help at Home" number По́мощь на дому́. If you are about to have a baby, ask for the "Without delay" Неотло́жка. Or, emergency first-aid stations травмпу́нкты (separate facilities for adults and children) are capable of first aid пе́рвая по́мощь for accidents, burns, dog bites, and so forth.

THE SOCIAL SECURITY MINISTRY
Минсобес[3]

Subordinate to the Ministry of Social Security Минсобе́с, a special medical commission, ВТЭК (Враче́бно–трудова́я экспе́ртная коми́ссия), is responsible for ascertaining and certifying temporary or permanent disability инвали́дность. Once certified, one receives one's pension and doesn't darken the office door again.

Two kinds of sanatorium are used, both of which are available via one's work or trade union. One is the "night sanatorium" профи-лакто́рий where the worker goes for a better diet and rest when not at work. It is used by those who are recuperating and by those with high blood pressure, ulcers, and the like in an effort to get healthy but keep working.

The sanatorium stay путёвка is usually for twenty-four days, with an emphasis on rest and perhaps some physiotherapy, water therapy, or herbal therapy. The site is usually a pleasant, healthful seaside or lakeside, or maybe a spot known for its mineral waters. They are often

2. Санита́рно-эпидемиологи́ческая ста́нция

3. Министе́рство социа́льного обеспече́ния

specialized for the care and treatment of a particular ailment. The patient might be sent at the recommendation of the local doctor/G.P. **участко́вый терапе́вт** or through the workplace: sometimes free, sometimes with partial payment. Many such sanatoria are located in southern and salubrious areas outside the boundaries of the Russian Federation. They currently charge more than can be paid by the Russian market.

PREGNANCY
Бере́менность

1. Masha **Ма́ша** wants a baby but doesn't get one, so she goes to her local Women's Consult **Же́нская консульта́ция** where she receives advice that also doesn't work—so she is referred to the Marriage and Family Service **Брак и семья́**, which offers not only fertility specialists **специали́сты по беспло́дию** but also others **сексопато́логи** who can advise her on her sex life in general.

2. Masha does not want a baby. She goes to the Women's Consult where she learns about condoms **презервати́вы**. (Can you imagine the horror of immigrant Russians who find "preservatives" in their food?) Advisors are not always up on contraception **контраце́пция**,[4] and condoms are either expensive or non-existent, so one fine day she notices that her period **ме́сячные** does not come **менструа́ция не прихо́дит**. She requires an abortion **або́рт**. People don't talk too much, so she only knows a few home remedies for dissolving pregnancy: she can drink a solution of stewed tansy **отва́р пи́жмы**; she can try a sauna **ба́ня**; she can take a hot bath with mustard in it **горя́чая ва́нна с горчи́цей**; or she can illegally **подпо́льно** inject herself with sinestrol **синестро́л**. If she is willing to pay and if the fetus is less than a month old, she can get a "little" abortion **ми́ни-**

або́рт involving suction but no knives, scrapers, or the like.

3. Masha gets an abortion. This is not likely to be her first, or her last; four to seven is common. Her concern about the matter has almost nothing to do with moral issues—her concern is getting anaesthesia. Again, if she has the money and the information, she pays for the abortion **пла́тный або́рт**.

4. Masha is pregnant **бере́менная**, and wants to be! She signs up **встаёт на учёт** at her local Women's Consult and has her check-up **осмо́тр** once a month. She works up to the seventh month when she gets pregnancy leave with pay (**опла́чиваемый**) **декре́тный о́тпуск** (fifty-six days before to fifty-six[5] days after) and starts going to her Consult twice a month.

One fine day, feeling strange, she finally calls an ambulance **ско́рая по́мощь/неотло́жка** (**неотло́жная медици́нская по́мощь**) and is taken to the obstetrical hospital **роддо́м** (**роди́льный дом**) where first she goes to the preparation room **предродова́я**. The contractions **схва́тки** become stronger and, because she is dilated 3 centimeters **ше́йка откры́лась на 3 см**, they send her on to the obstetric room **родово́й зал** where her water **отошли́ во́ды** breaks. This room is presided over by a midwife **акуше́рка**. (The birth **ро́ды** is plural: **акуше́рка/врач/гинеко́лог принима́ет ро́ды**. "I had a hard time" is **У меня́ бы́ли тяжёлые ро́ды**.) After a lot of work, the baby **младе́нец** appears, the cord **пупови́на** is tied, and the process finally ends with the exodus of the placenta **плаце́нта**. If all goes well, Masha will stay in the hospital about a week. Her baby will be snugly wrapped **ту́го пелена́ть** but not swaddled **свива́ть** when it is brought to her for feeding **на кормле́ние**. If she can't supply enough milk, then other mothers will.[6] Fathers are not allowed in, though they can sometimes view the baby at certain hours.

---

4. The contraceptive device **противозача́точное сре́дство** does exist, however: the IUD **спира́ль** is used and the diaphragm **колпачо́к** has been heard of. For those with the means and access (that is, those with money in cities), birth control pills **табле́тки** are the device of choice.

5. Those with complications during birth can get seventy-two days off. Put that in your pipe and smoke it. Also see *Money* in Chapter 8.

6. It is from this process that we get the terms **моло́чный брат, моло́чная сестра́**: The same mother fed them.

This picture can change dramatically. If you pay for a private birth, suddenly anaesthesia is more available, and father can come visiting. However, it is still uncommon for the father to be present at the birth.

The medical institution involved for the next three years is the children's clinic **Детская консультация**. Each pediatrician **педиатр** is responsible for a certain area and has one or two visiting nurses **патронажная сестра**. One of these comes to visit Masha right away. She checks out the mother and baby, answers questions, and shows mother what to do. All babies are checked over by the pediatrician once a month. Most children's clinics are associated with a polyclinic in which case the child is watched over until he or she is fifteen years old.

If Masha's child has to go to a hospital, it's a children's hospital **детская больница**. Babies under two are required to have their mothers living in to look after them. After the age of two the baby would be well advised to have parents nearby.

If Masha cannot supply milk then she could turn to the local "milk kitchen" **молочная кухня**, which formerly had the obligation of supplying milk products for every child registered in the local children's clinic every day. These were especially indispensable when milk products were hard to find or required long lines.

ARE YOU SICK? WHAT'S THE MATTER?
Ты больна? Что с тобой?

Complaints
На что жалуетесь?

Я неважно себя чувствую.   I don't feel so good.

Я заболел, я заболела.   I got sick.

Я болен, я больна.   I'm sick.

Она долго болела.   She was sick for a long time.

Ей стало плохо.   She began to feel sick.

Я больной, я больная.   I'm a sick man/woman/person

Мне нездоровится.   I'm not well.

Мне плохо.   I don't feel good.

У меня болит голова.   I have a headache.

У меня температура.   I have a temperature.

У меня нет аппетита.   I have no appetite.

У меня пропал аппетит.   My appetite has gone.

У меня испортился сон.   My sleep is ruined.

Меня знобит.   I have the chills.

Меня тошнит.   I'm nauseated.

Many ailments **заболевания** are familiar: **пневмония (воспаление лёгких), невроз, гастрит, синусит (гайморит)**. Some are direct translations: high (blood) pressure is **высокое давление/гипертония**, low blood pressure is **низкое давление**; a stroke is **удар/инсульт**, a heart attack is **инфаркт**. However, some terms can be confusing: a (runny nose) cold **насморк** and influenza **грипп** are comprehensible enough, but a sore throat or tonsillitis is **ангина** yet has nothing to do with heart pains; and the diagnosis **диагноз** the doctor writes for a bad chest-cold or influenza is **ОРЗ (о-эр-зэ)**, for acute respiratory ailment **Острое респираторное заболевание** or perhaps **ОРВиЗ Острое респираторное вирусное заболевание**.

Children's diseases
Детские болезни

The common diseases specifically associated with children are chicken pox **ветрянка (ветряная оспа)**, whooping cough **коклюш**, scarlet fever **скарлатина**, mumps **свинка**, and measles **корь**. If one child in a family comes down with an infectious disease, then the other children in the family must also stay home. (Quarantine is **карантин**: **Он сидит на карантине**.) If one child in a class becomes infectious, then the whole class is kept from contact with other classes. Diptheria **диф-терит, дифтерия** is usually prevented via inoculation **прививка**, which includes vaccination **вакцинация** against whooping cough and tetanus **столбняк**. The rising incidence of diptheria may be due to parental fear—and therefore postponement—of the injection **укол**. (Such concern—that is, fear of dirty needles—might be a secondary effect of AIDS **СПИД**, or the diptheria vaccine might be ineffective.)

Infectious diseases
Инфекцио́нные/зара́зные заболева́ния

The Soviet government was well known for its ability to quarantine huge portions of the country when serious infectious diseases made an appearance. Smallpox **о́спа** is long gone all over the world, but outbreaks of other serious infectious diseases have occurred within living memory: typhus **сыпно́й тиф** is transmitted via body lice **вши (вошь)** and should not be confused with typhoid fever **брюшно́й тиф**, which comes from contaminated water, milk, or food handlers; cholera **холе́ра** is associated with the south and poor sanitation, as is dysentery **дизентери́я**; jaundice **желту́ха** there indicates a liver problem, here, hepatitis **гепати́т**; tetanus **столбня́к** is everywhere, so a DPT booster for the traveler wouldn't hurt; erysipelas **рожи́стое воспале́ние** can be encountered occasionally; and tuberculosis **туберкулёз** is alive and well and has certain hospitals, clinics and sanatoriums dedicated to its treatment.

TREATMENTS
Лече́бные сре́дства

The prescription
Реце́пт

"The doctor is writing a prescription" is **Врач выпи́сывает реце́пт**. Prescriptions are paid for by the recipient at the pharmacy **апте́ка**; if the medicines are not ready-made **гото́вые**, then the pharmacist **фармаце́вт, прови́зор** prepares them. The prices are high compared to income but adjustments are available—medicine is free for people with diabetes **диабе́т**, people with bad blood **гемотологи́ческие боле́зни**, those with cancer **онкологи́ческие боле́зни**, and people who no longer can take care of themselves. Medicine is half-price for people who are temporarily disabled. Mothers with several children can get medicines cheaper. The trouble with the system is lack of the desirable (usually imported) or necessary medicines. In order to get these, one must pay more, know somebody, or both.

Medicine
Лека́рство

When they are available, medicines **лека́рства** come in the usual forms: pills **табле́тки, ка́псулы (пилю́ля** is old-fashioned), liquid medicine **микстура** (cough syrup is **микстура от ка́шля**), gargle **полоска́ние**, ointment **мазь**, a medicine applied to a bandage or applicator **примо́чка**, massage goo **растира́ние**, and suppositories **(лека́рственные) све́чи**.[7]

Home medicines
Дома́шняя апте́чка

These are medicines that might be found around the apartment for common ailments:

Headache   **головна́я боль: анальги́н, барал-ги́н, максига́н**

Superficial cuts   **вне́шние поврежде́ния: йо́д, пе́рекись водоро́да, зелёнка (спирт + бриллиа́нтовая зе́лень), спирт, марганцо́вка ; антисепти́ческое сре́дство: бисепто́л**

Constipation   **запо́р: лист сенны** (i.e., *Cassia*), **табле́тки глаксе́мы**

---

7. **Makes you think: свеча́** is literally *candle*.

Diarrhea поно́с: фталазо́л, тетрацикли́н; сла́бый раство́р марганцо́вки

Stomach trouble гастри́т: желу́дочные ка́пли

High temperature температу́ра: све́чи цефеко́н, аспири́н; обтира́ние сла́бым раство́ром у́ксуса

Cough ка́шель: бронхолити́н, солута́н, пектуси́н; горчи́чники на́ спину и на грудь

Sore throat/tonsillitis ангина: стрептоци́д, полоска́ние го́рла—насто́й рома́шки /шалфе́я/эвкали́пта

Runny nose на́сморк: (ка́пли) нафтизи́н, сок ало́э

A cold просту́да: лук, чесно́к, ре́дька с мёдом

Heart pains бо́ли в се́рдце: валидо́л, корвало́л, нитроглицери́н

General infection сульфадиметокси́н

Toothache зубна́я боль: анальги́н, спирт снару́жи

Severe headache due to high blood pressure головна́я боль от высо́кого давле́ния: горчи́чник на заты́лок; па́рить но́ги в воде́ с горчи́цей

Low blood pressure ни́зкое давле́ние: чай, ко́фе, элеутероко́кк (!) (*Eleutherococcus senticosus*, a relative of *aralia*).

Glasses
Очки́

Glasses frames опра́ва (очко́в), at least good-looking ones, are hard to get and therefore prized. But the existence of squinting Russians has less to do with the lack of frames than with the Russian unwillingness to wear them. Interestingly, those who require prescriptions also know what their diopter is: ми́нус одна́ дио́птрия is equivalent to сла́бая близору́кость. Other vocabulary: bifocals бифока́льные очки́, contact lenses конта́ктные ли́нзы, crossed or wall-eyed косогла́зие, poor eyesight плохо́е зре́ние, blindness слепота́.

A nation of readers who don't like glasses

Unorthodox medicine
Нетрадицио́нная медици́на

Herbal medicine
Лече́ние тра́вами

Some unorthodox medicine, and here we mean herbal medicine, is orthodox in Russia. This orthodoxy has continued through all the revolutions up to the present day. Suspicion lingers that perhaps manufactured or modern medicines are too strong or likely to be dangerous. Reasons for this notion could be (1) valid, or (2) due to self-medication so that appropriate limits are not familiar (one tries what one can get), or (3) inaccurate prescriptions, either as written by the doctor or filled by the pharmacist. Herbs тра́вы are considered easier on the body, more natural. Of course, poison яд can be very natural too, but whatever the reason, perhaps a third of the pharмасу **апте́ка** is devoted to medicinal plants **лека́рственные расте́ния**. (q.v.) The medicinal use of herbs **фитотерапи́я** is becoming more popular—as one aspect of the "back to the old ways" movement, though others insist that this movement is an expression of dissatisfaction with medicine as it is currently practiced.

One example of a very popular natural medicine is "pantokrin" **пантокри́н**, a liquid extract obtained from the antlers of the noble and spotted deer, recommended for functional disorders of the nervous system, lowered sexual ability, and that general tired feeling. The *Large Soviet Encyclopedia* reported that pantokrin affects the circulatory system, the bowels, the womb, and skeletal muscles.

In the very old days (and sometimes today), the sick **больны́е** turned to a folk healer **зна́харь/зна́харка** who used a combination of herbs **тра́вы**, potions **зе́лье**, and incantations **за́говоры** based partly on folk wisdom on plant effectiveness and partly on the idea that ailments and injuries are caused by evil spirits who can be exorcised with the right set of charmed words. **Распу́тин владе́л зна́нием за́говора кро́ви.** "Rasputin knew how to charm blood (flow)." **Зна́харки загова́ривают зубну́ю боль** "The medicine women cast spells on toothache." These people were felt to be using a benevolent supernatural power. But a sorcerer **колду́н/колду́нья** was needed when the problem was so serious (impotence, barrenness, a very sick child) that someone with connections with the devil was required. Yet another kind of healer was the faith healer **цели́тель**, who used an ability to gather strength from God. **Цели́тели ле́чат наложе́нием рук.** "Faith healers work using a laying on of hands." **«Цели́тельница не́сколько лет подде́рживала Бре́жнева свое́й вну́тренней си́лой».**[a]

The communists thought herbs were fine, but the authorities were firmly against the assorted healers, folk or otherwise. A passage in a book on Russian folklore makes elaborate fun of an old healer **зна́харка** who is so foolish as to give cold water to a feverish person.

(The contemporary Russian belief is that cold water or ice will give you a sore throat.)

The problem is that the healer is still used. **«Знахарки загова́ривают ро́жистое воспале́ние, нары́вы, гры́жи.»**[b]

Many Russians put at least some store in supernatural healing methods and its practioners, and the phenomenon is growing. Television healers and hypnotists were very popular only a few years ago, and the extrasensory practitioner **экстрасе́нс** needs no defenders. You can expect to come across people who find cosmic rays to be healing, and homeopathy **гомеопа́тия** pharmacies are becoming as popular as folk medicines. Treatment, healing, and belief combine variously: consider the extrasensory masseur **массажи́ст-экстрасе́нс**.

Staying fit
В фо́рме

Everybody wants to be fit **быть в фо́рме**. All you need is a little language:

Stand up   **Вста́ньте**

Feet apart   **Но́ги в сто́роны**

Feet together   **Ноги вме́сте**

Hands out to the side   **Ру́ки в стороны**

Hands on hips   **Руки на по́яс**

Touch your toes   **Косну́ться па́льцев (ле́вой/пра́вой ноги́)**

Clap your hands over your head   **Хлопо́к над голово́й**

Walk in place   **Ходьба́ на ме́сте**

Squat   **Сде́лаем приседа́ния; присе́сть...встать**

Run in place   **Бег на ме́сте**

Bend your knees   **Согну́ть коле́ни**

Inhale   **Вдыха́йте (вдох, вдохну́ть)**

Exhale   **Выдыха́йте (вы́дох, вы́дохнуть)**

Stand on your toes   **Подня́ться на цы́почки (...опусти́ться)**

Jump in place   **Прыжки́ на ме́сте**

Return **Верну́ться в исхо́дное положе́ние; обра́тно**

Раз, два, Раз, два...
Раз, два, три, Раз, два, три...

DENTISTRY
Стоматоло́гия

Teeth might be called an unresolved problem; the efforts to fix them do not equate with the dimensions of needed repair. And preventive measures are not widespread: *flossing* does not translate. (One can reasonably estimate that every adult Russian is worth a minimum of $5,000 to an American dentist.)

The dentist can be **зубно́й врач** but is more likely to be **стомато́лог**, a somewhat more elegant name. A technician **зубно́й те́хник** has not had so broad a training and will deal with such things as making false teeth, crowns, and the like.

What's needed are better drills and other equipment; more novocaine; more defensive dentistry such as fluoride, flossing, and cleaning; and more dentists. The bad situation is made worse by patients who so fear the dentist that they severely postpone seeing one. This is not unusual, it is typical. A common problem: a purulent tooth and "no novocaine today."

Just getting an appointment is a further atrocity: you get up very, very early in the morning to stand in line at the dental polyclinic to get a ticket **тало́н** that allows you an appointment **тало́н к зубно́му врачу́**. The clinic opens at seven or eight in the morning and the nurse at the office **регистрату́ра** has maybe ten tickets for the day. If you are fifteenth in line you can forget about seeing the dentist that day. On the other hand, it is reported that those with a severe toothache **с о́строй бо́лью** can see the dentist immediately without waiting in line.

Dental clinics **стоматологи́ческие поликли́ники** have three divisions: the therapeutic **терапевти́ческое отделе́ние**, where teeth are filled; the surgical **хирурги́ческое отделе́ние**, where teeth are removed; and the orthopedic **ортопеди́ческое отделение**, where teeth are supplanted or added to **коро́нки, проте́зы**.

A toothbrush **зубна́я щётка** and toothpaste **зубная па́ста** are regularly used, but with time tartar **зубно́й ка́мень** builds up and encourages periodontitis **периодонти́т** and gingivitis **гингиви́т**. Eventually the tooth must be pulled **удаля́ть**. Often, teeth develop cavities **зубно́й ка́риес**, and the dentist must put in a filling **пло́мба**. Sometimes things get worse and a crown **коро́нка** is needed, or if a tooth goes, then we get a bridge **мост**; finally, we require false teeth **вставны́е зу́бы** (dentures **проте́зы**).

TRANSLATIONS

a.   A female faith healer used her internal strength to hold up Brezhnev for several years.

b.   Healers exorcise erysipelas, abscesses, hernias.

8

Work and Money

Работа и деньги

It is in under this heading that the size of the monkey wrench being hurled into Russian society becomes, finally, apparent. For many years now the great bulk of Russian society has received roughly the same reward for its work. The poor did not suffer and the high acheivers did not gain: one frequently hears the expression "How am I worse than other people?" **Чем я хуже других?**, which means something closer to "I've got my rights, I'm a citizen!" The only significant differentiator in society was occupational prestige, and prestige was not accompanied by egregious amounts of money. The doctor frequently made less money than his patients, the bus driver made more than the woman with graduate degrees who taught at the university. Officially, production workers (in construction or industry) made more money, via plan-fulfillment awards **премии**, than nonproduction workers (teachers, clerks, lawyers). Unofficially, many people used professional access to desirable and rare goods as a way of padding an otherwise light income. Sometimes professionals could receive gifts (gift, **подарок**; bribe, **взятка**) from grateful patients or pupils' families. Of course, people at the very top of the Party pinnacle, those who ran things **номенклатура**, did not wallow in the common poverty, but famous actors, for example, might.

There is something to be said for a society so ordered. One had to work to live—and not working was parasitic—but the workaholic and the "go-getter" did not have to be put up with. Fewer people worried about the impression they were making, noticeably fewer. The beggars were few, starvation nonexistent, and the choice of a profession was not based on money. But it did not work.

For contemporary Russians who may have forgotten:

> **У нас безработицы нет, но никто не работает.**
> **Никто не работает, но план выполняется.**
> **План выполняется, но ничего нет.**
> **Ничего нет, но всё есть.**
> **Всё есть, но все недовольны.**
> **Все недовольны, но все голосуют «за».**[a]

CHOICES
Выбор работы

The Communists formally divided working people **трудящиеся** into four groups (1) the workers **рабочие** were mostly the labor used in manufacturing—those who did the hardest and least respected physical labor (**Он из рабочих** means, in Brtitish English, "His family were working class"); (2) the peasants **крестьяне**, who were the farmers—they, too, had the reputation for more hard work and less respect; (3) the middle class **служащие**, which ranged from typists **машинистки** up through what was called the "working intelligentsia" **трудовая интеллигенция**, including doctors **врачи**, engineers **инженеры** and teachers **учителя**; (4) the creative intelligensia **творческая интеллигенция**, a thin layer at the top—artists, writers, and research scientists.

Not to work was not a choice, except perhaps, for the unclassified people **деклассированный элемент** in society whose place is taken today by the homeless **бомж (без официального места жительства)** and the bum or hobo **бич (бывший интеллигентный человек)** who can work, but chooses not to make the effort.

The more respected the job, the more desirable it was, even though a working-class person **рабочий** could make more money. Because we usually grow up into our parents' image of what is desirable, it was the parents who did the most planning, plotting, and prodding to ensure the education required for those jobs.

Work and education start in grade school where the subject is "The World of Work" **профориентация**, and boys go to shop and girls to cooking and sewing. Later, once a week they go to an actual work site, the **УПК (учебно-производственный комбинат, упэка)**, where boys might learn, for example, to repair cars, and girls might learn how to sell cheese. The most popular training is computer programming. Some schools manage to arrange the work training so that it bears some relation to school training. (The students in English schools get training as tourist guides, for example.) If the child goes through school with nought but 2's and 3's **двойки, тройки** then an uncomplicated job is available right away or more training as a lower-grade technician at a trade school, **ПТУ (профессионально-техническое училище)**. Students who do fairly well—mostly 4's **четвёрки**—go on to a technical school **техникум** for more highly trained technicians.

Going to college **институт, университет** is the ticket to a decent place to work, so it is toward this end that parents work hardest. (Not all parents: only those who themselves went to college are willing to make the investment of effort it takes to get a lesser student into a better institution. Workers and peasants are pleased to let the chips fall where they may.) As before, the very best students, gold medalists, can go almost anywhere they want, and ambitious parents send their children to the Moscow institutes of high repute. Formerly, though, parents of lesser students had to calculate where (1) it was easier to get in, (2) a course of study was not too demanding, (3) it was easy to find work later, and (4) better pay could be arranged. There were such things as **позво-но́чные студе́нты**, where admission had to do with a parental call **звоно́к**. If that didn't work then bribes **взя́тки** might be tried. This system still obtains to some extent, but is being seriously modified by new conditions: some schools are beginning to charge for their services, and the young want to make money. In the past it was assumed that youth would go to college if they could get in. Now, to the horror of their parents, they leave the academy for more lucrative opportunities. What matters now is "entrepreneurship" **хва́тка** (from **хвата́ть** to seize or grasp; **приватиза́ция = прихватиза́ция**). In the old days, one could reasonably be proud of a child who became an engineer. Now, a comic includes in his routine ". . . like a simple engineer. . . disgusting to see" . . . **как просто́й инжене́р. . . смотре́ть проти́вно!** And some formerly prestigious research institutes—**НИИ (Нау́чно-исследо-ва́тельский институт)**—are closing because the wages are too low for subsistence. One curse is, "May you live on one salary!" **Чтоб жить тебе на одну́ зарпла́ту!** Those whose regular salary is insufficient sometimes moonlight or do extra work off the books **халту́ра**, a word that has also come to mean poorly done work, hack work.

Women and work
Же́нщины и рабо́та

There, as elsewhere, is a one-way connection between one's sex and a job: downward. If it is harder physical work, if it is not productive labor (as in manufacturing or lumbering), and if it pays less, then it is much more likely to be women's work: the "cleaning lady" **убо́рщица**, the janitor **дво́рник**, the road worker **доро́жный рабо́чий**. With the New Day, more women are learning men's jobs.

Some lowly respected and poorly paid jobs **гардеро́бщица, дво́рник, убо́рщица** have the advantage of odd hours, which allows mothers more time to care for their children. And a preschool teacher **воспита́тельница** can always get her own children into the preschool without difficulty. It is also true that less demanding jobs can be seen as a requirement by those who must handle all the cooking, cleaning, shopping, and so on. "You pays your money and you takes your choice."

Getting a job
Устро́йство на рабо́ту

Formerly, your school **те́хникум, институ́т** would set you up in your first job in a system called distribution **распределе́ние**, which supplied workers where needed regardless of whether you wanted to go. Now you can find openings yourself, through advertisements on the radio, in the newspapers, or from signs at entrances to buildings. The best bet is of course relatives or friends with connections. The formal name for job requirements is **про́филь**. **Это не по моему́ про́филю** (I haven't had the training to do that) means "That's not *my* job!"

The documents necessary for getting a job include a passport **па́спорт**, a birth certificate **спра́вка о рожде́нии** for those younger than sixteen, a description of the last year at school/college **спра́вка о после́днем го́де заня́тий**, the work record **трудова́я кни́жка** for those formerly employed, a certification from one's residence **спра́вка с ме́ста жи́тельства**, and a school diploma or record **докуме́нт об образова́нии**.

A work record
Трудова́я кни́жка

Everyone with a (legal) job has a work record **трудова́я кни́жка**, which is kept in the personnel office **отде́л ка́дров** where one works. It includes a job title **занима́емая до́лжность, пост**, a record of training, any prizes or honors received, any dishonors, when the job began, when transfers were made, and to what other levels or institutions of employment they were assigned. In order not to lose seniority **стаж** necessary for a pension, the time between jobs should not exceed three months. If one is fired **уво́лен, уво́лена**, or laid off **сокращён, сокращена́**, the reason for the action also goes into the work record. In other words, your history follows you. (The implications give one pause.)

The personnel office **отде́л ка́дров**, with a chief **нача́льник** and inspectors **инспектора́**, also has another file **ли́чный листо́к по учёту ка́дров**, which includes one's vital statistics **анке́тные да́нные**.

Changing jobs
Сме́на ме́ста рабо́ты

Formally and formerly, a labor agreement **трудово́й догово́р** described the relations between the worker and the employment office. A transfer to other work **перево́д на другу́ю рабо́ту** can take place following changes in working conditions, wages **окла́д**, or privileges **льго́ты**. The labor contract can be dissolved **расто́ргнут** when a preset time limit expires, when one is called into the military, at the worker's request, at the administration's request, at the trade-union request, or in case of criminal or illegal behavior—which about covers the possibilities. Those who have trouble finding a new job can go to the employment office **центр по трудоустро́йству, би́ржа труда́**, which is supposed to propose alternatives or arrange training for some other job. "He has to be re-trained." **Ему́ на́до перепрофили́роваться.** This process began when unemployment **безрабо́тица** raised its ugly head.

Changing jobs is best done through recommendation, which is to say, through someone who knows and approves of you. Usually, one month's notice is given by workers leaving at their own request. Written recommendations **характери́стика** are technically supplied by the boss who is being left, but often the worker writes a boilerplate recommendation **по шабло́ну** and the boss merely signs it.

LABOR UNIONS
Профсою́зы

A very short while ago (up to 1991) this rose did not smell so sweet. Russian labor unions **профсою́зы** did some good things for the workers—arranging the distribution of scarce goods, for example, or being responsible for R-and-R trips. One could look upon them as the labor relations branch of the main office. Russian trade unions worked with the administration and were directly subordinate to them. Therefore, U.S. business groups were mistaken when they opposed trade-union representatives in joint enterprises. Trade unions were merely a branch of the administration. We are pleased to report that new and independent trade unions are beginning to form, and their structure is changing. The threat of a strike **забасто́вка** is both possible and real.

TIME FOR WORK
Рабо́чее вре́мя

The forty-hour week is standard for most people (though the application or devotion to work is typically less than the number of hours might indicate). Some professions that are considered hazardous or particularly taxing (coal miners or radiologists, for example) work fewer hours, have longer vacations, and retire earlier. The length of vacations varies considerably.

Women can retire at age fifty-five, when they can begin to get a pension. Men can retire at sixty. These are standard retirement times, but some people prefer to work longer and are allowed to. They receive both their pension and their regular pay.

TOOLS
Инструме́нты

A woodworker in the second grade needs the tools at the top of page 165.

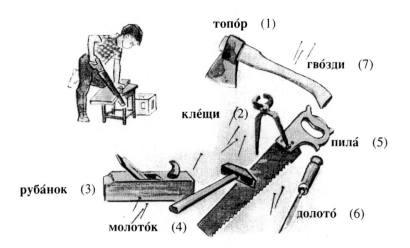

топо́р (1)

гво́зди (7)

кле́щи (2)

пила́ (5)

руба́нок (3)

долото́ (6)

молото́к (4)

(1) axe
(2) pincers
(3) plane
(4) hammer
(5) saw
(6) chisel
(7) nails

To attach a hinge **пе́тля** you will probably need a wood screw **шуру́п** or two, plus a screwdriver **отвёртка**. To drill a hole **отве́рстие** you will need either a small hand drill **дрель** or the larger brace **коловоро́т** and a number of bits **свёрла**. For finer chiseling or scooping out wood, use the chisel **стаме́ска** after the similar but coarser **долото́**. You might want to hold the wood in a vise **тиски́**. Finishing work might require a file **напи́льник** and sandpaper **нажда́чная бума́га, (шлифова́льная) шку́рка,** and perhaps a C-clamp **струбци́на** or two to hold it all. Metalworking requires a nut **га́йка**, a screw **винт**, a washer **ша́йба,** and gasket **прокла́дка**, as well as the aforementioned screwdriver and a wrench **га́ечный ключ**. Also you will need pliers **плоскогу́бцы, щипцы́** and a chisel for metal **зуби́ло**. To reach what you are fixing, use a stepladder **стремя́нка**.

Ло́мка стекла́:
а. рука́ми,
б. стеклоре́зом,
в. плоскогу́бцами

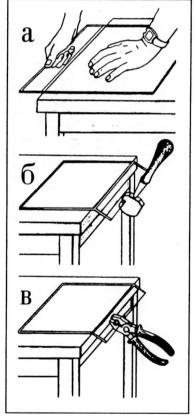

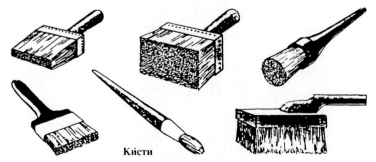

Ки́сти

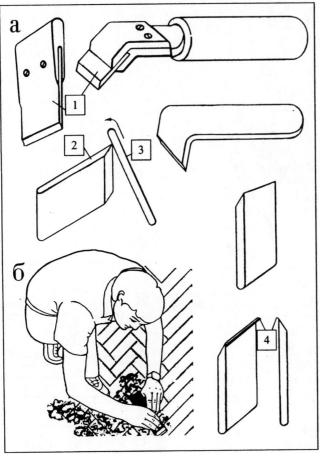

Циклева́ние парке́та: a. разнови́дности ци́клей, б. циклевание: 1. стальны́е пласти́нки, 2. запра́вка цикли, 3. штифт, 4. заусе́нец

1. Коса́, 2. Ви́лы, 3. Гра́бли, 4. Лопа́та, 5. Лёйка, 6. Серп

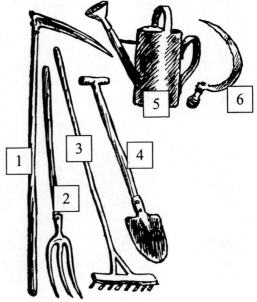

(The words in the captions to the figures above are not translated—you can do it.)

At the dacha or on the farm you will probably also require the illustrated tools, plus those in the following glossary list:

моты́га   a hoe

гра́бли   a rake

сово́к   any scoop-shaped tool from a small spade to a dustpan

сека́тор   clippers

вёдра   pails or buckets

носи́лки   a handbarrow

та́чки   a wheelbarrow

лом   a straight, long crowbar, for removing ice

ле́стница   a ladder

борона́   a harrow

комба́йн   a combine

жне́йка   a binder, harvesting machine

To fix the car:

монта́жка (монта́жный ключ)   a tire wrench

насо́с (качо́к)   a pump

домкра́т   a jack

MONEY
Де́ньги

Де́ньги лю́бят счёт.
Money loves to be counted.

Копе́йка рубль бережёт.
The penny takes care of the pound.

Russian coins **моне́ты** used to come in two varieties, silver coins **серебро́** and copper coins **медь**. As a group they are called "small stuff" **ме́лочь** or, in a certain position, "change" **сда́ча**. Either is good for starting machinery but not much else, these days.

Coins **Моне́ты:** 1, 5, 10, 20, 50, 100 **рубле́й**

Denominations of bills **купю́ры:** 10, 25, 50, 100, 200, 500, 1000, 5000, 10 000, 50 000 **рублей**

The loss of the kopeck **копе́йка** is the hardest for those who lived with it longest.

Old terminology for money, which you may come across in literature, includes:

алты́н   3 копе́йки

гри́венник   10 копе́ек

пятиалты́нный   15 копе́ек

двугри́венный   20 копе́ек

полти́нник   50 копе́ек

черво́нец   10 рубле́й

New (slang) terminology for money and not likely to appear in literature:

полти́нник   50 рублей

сто́льник   100 рублей

шту́ка, кусо́к, то́нна   1000 рублей

лимо́н   1000 000 рублей

(арбу́з   1000 000 000 рублей, unconfirmed)

ба́ксы   Should be recognizable

For years money was not presented to the population as something worth having: piggy banks were bourgeois, the penny-pincher was only cheap, one's possessions were not an extension of one's self, the bus driver made more money than the doctor, greed was a cardinal sin (rather than one of society's postulates), and everyone was covered. Thus, a friend can honestly report: "One cannot say that money, or people who have a lot of it, are the object of envy or imitation. It is true that, right now, there is a section of the population that is willing to do anything for money—usually something illegal. These people do not enjoy the positive regard of the rest of the population. Money is a necessary device, but if I had to choose between good money and a good job, I would take the job (on the assumption that my wages would at least support me)."

Не в де́ньгах сча́стье.
You'll not find happiness in money.

Де́ньги есть и де́нег нет.
Sometimes you have it, and sometimes you don't. (That is, having it doesn't matter.)

You sign for your pay which is in cash **нали́чные**

Wages
Зарпла́та

Wages **зарпла́та** (**за́работная пла́та**) a.k.a. **полу́чка** are normally issued at the cashier's office **ка́сса** at work twice a month, where the worker signs a receipt book **распи́сывается в ве́домости** and walks away, cash **нали́чные** in hand. It is possible to arrange for the money to be deposited in a bank account, but inflation encourages spending every cent in one's possesion. The first payment amount in the month is called an advance **ава́нс** and amounts to 40 percent of one's designated total. The second payment amount includes an accounting **подрасчёт** with all the deductions **вы́четы**: an income tax **подохо́дный нало́г** assessed on wages above a subsistence level; alimony **алиме́нты** (!) to assure payment for one's children or dependent parents not living with one; and a tax on the childless **безде́тный/**

ма́лосеме́йный нало́г. In addition, a land tax земе́льный нало́г is paid by those who own land; a tax is paid by those who have cars нало́г с владе́льцев тра́нспортных средств; and sometimes trade-union dues профсою́зные взно́сы are deducted rather than separately paid for.

Having children is encouraged: mothers can retain their seniority at work стаж for three years after the birth; a premium посо́бие по рожде́нию is paid at birth; and a monthly allowance посо́бие на ребёнка begins.

Wages can be paid on a piece-work basis сде́льная опла́та, can be organized to follow a stage in the work поэта́пно, акко́рдно, or can be paid on a daily basis повреме́нная опла́та. Some enterprises pay only once a month. If production has been unusually high, then sometimes a bonus трина́дцатая зарпла́та is distributed.

Banks
Ба́нки

The State Bank Госба́нк, Центра́льный банк, the Bank for Industrial Construction Промстройбанк, the Foreign Trade Bank Банк вне́шней торго́вли: these banks deal with state business and businesses. Individuals use a local branch отделе́ние of the Savings Bank Сберба́нк (Сберега́тельный банк) and others.

Aksyonov described Russia as a "prebank" economy, which, by comparison with our use of banks, is true; exclusively so if we are considering only checking or charging accounts and the like.

From reports, it would seem that most Russians do not use banks very much (even without inflation), but instead secrete their gains at home in a stocking в чулке́ or in a "money-pot" в кубы́шке: money-pot + stocking = mattress + cookie jar (?). Banks are used, though. One can store money вложи́ть де́ньги and get interest получи́ть проце́нты there. (Inflation makes current interest rates mind-boggling. It also makes saving a stupid thing to do.) One can make various deposits вкла́ды: a time deposit

сро́чный вклад gets more interest than an unlimited deposit вклад до востре́бования, and one kind of deposit вы́игрышный вклад (from lottery + deposit) was used in earlier days to encourage people to save. And some do have their pay sent directly to the bank via a transfer перево́д to a savings account сберега́тельная кни́жка at the local branch of the savings bank отделе́ние сбербанка.

Bank services also provide facilities for storing valuables—for example, bonds облига́ции and stocks а́кции.

Gambling
Аза́ртные и́гры

Gambling is a Russian thing to do—we have the *Queen of Spades*, after all, though the Soviets treated it and card-playing in general as immoral. Some games used for gambling are напёрсток, домино́, руле́тка; card games such as очко́, по́кер, сва́ра, девя́тка, and кинг were kept alive only in hiding during the Soviet period. Betting at the races на иппо-дро́ме was allowed, though the bets ста́вки в

РОСТОВСКИЙ
ИППОДРОМ

ОДИНАР
КАССА № 50

5

ОДИН РУБ.
СЕРИЯ ИП-5
19......г.

000607 ✳

A racing bet (that didn't win)

тотализа́тор were not large. The government has felt free to sponsor lotteries **лотере́и**, but smarter people saw through the web of deceit: **В аза́ртные и́гры с госуда́рством предпочита́ю не игра́ть!** "I prefer not to gamble with the government!"

And gambling machines **игровы́е автома́ты** can sometimes be seen where the public might gather. Games will have titles such as **домино́, лото́, бура́, тотализа́тор.** The card game **префера́нс** is a relative of bridge and is enjoyed by the more respectable elements of society.

TRANSLATIONS

a. We have no unemployment, but nobody works.

Nobody works, but the plan is fulfilled.

The plan is fulfilled, but there is nothing (to buy).

There is nothing (to buy), but everyone has things.

Everyone has things, but everyone complains.

Everyone complains, but everyone votes "yes."

Part IV

The Russian in the Community

9

Shopping

По магази́нам

Under communism, customer demand was defined by government planning, which did not agree with reality; buying low and selling high was speculation **спекуля́ция**, both criminal and a sin—not just smart as it is here. As a result, "getting" (**доста́ть**) things, not buying (**купи́ть**) them, was what mattered; people were not rich, but whatever they wanted seemed never for sale; scarcity was both haphazard and common. Some things were hoarded, some were bartered, and waiting in line became an art form. To some extent, this distribution system still obtains: some lines still remain, and one must still rely on the distribution system of goods at work, or use friends who might have access to special goods and services by using "pull" **по бла́ту**. Language has adapted to the circumstance: one says, "Make us some. . ." **Сде́лайте нам. . .** , but "using pull" **по бла́ту** is what is understood.

Currently, the market has taken over with a vengeance—if you have the money, lots of it, you can get almost anything, at least in major cities. Many lines have vanished since prices went so high, and the cost of many items seems to get higher every day. People look back, almost with nostalgia, on the old days when shortages brought on rationing **прода́жа по тало́нам**, because the rationing at least assured one's allotment. The people with money are the new business class, almost all of whom make several times as much money as the rest of the population. Especially at the market they are resented—many of them are thought of as Mafia—and if the dark skin of the Caucasus distinguishes them, then they are openly disliked at the very least.

HOW TO GET THINGS
Как доста́ть ну́жную вещь

If you have hard currency **валю́та** you are, currently, probably rich and can change your money, at varying rates, for huge quantities of rubles at the many "exchange points" **обме́нные пу́нкты** all over town. Late in 1993 one could still spend hard currency directly in many hard currency stores **валю́тные магази́ны**. It is currently illegal to do so.

If you are a typical Russian, you can look for a store that has what you want and then (1) wait in line to determine the cost of what you want and have it reserved for you; and then (2) go pay the cashier **касси́рша** for it and get a receipt **чек**; and then (3) return to the salesperson **прода́вщи́ца** with your receipt and trade that for your goods.

Another way to get things is through your work. Often the trade-union organization **профсою́з** makes deals with other organizations so that a variety of goods, often those in short supply **дефици́т**, can be offered in limited amounts to workers who sign up for them. This system is not so extensive as it has been, but it is still used in some places for some items.

And finally, if you are Russian, your family and friends are truly invaluable. When you come across an affordable treasure, it is common practice to overbuy and then split with grandma, a neighbor, or a family friend. They do the same for you.

The new economics has seriously reduced the necessity for a line; now one needs money more than patience, but the following description of behavior in a line still applies.

The line
Очередь

There are two kinds of lines **о́чередь**. One is a list **о́чередь по спи́ску**, which represents a long-time wait for a major item: an apartment **Меня́ поста́вили на о́чередь на кварти́ру в райисполко́ме**, a telephone **Я стою́ на очере-** ди в АТС, or furniture **Я в списке́ на ме́бель**, for example. The lines of people waiting for groceries and the like are called a "live" line **жива́я о́чередь**, and to say "I'm standing in line" is **Я стою́ в о́череди.**

You want something; you see a line of people waiting for it. What do you do? You do not merely go to the end of the line and stand there, sullenly cursing fate. Cope, instead, using accepted rules of line behavior.

First, you go to what appears to be the end of the line, and then you *must* ask "Who's the last (in line)?" **Кто после́дний?** or **Кто кра́йний?** The purpose is to find out whom you follow; the last in line may be resting on a nearby park bench and will be offended if you are taking no cognizance of precedence.

Second, if you are with someone, and if there are two or more lines for the same thing, make sure your companion stands in another line: one can never be sure which will move faster.

Third, in order to reduce total in-line time, establish your precedence in several lines at once. Thus, you can wait for cheese in one line, then say to the person in front of you "Will you be staying/standing?" which is taken as "Will you keep my place in line?" **Вы бу́дете стоя́ть?** "I have to go away for a while." **Мне ну́жно отойти́ ненадо́лго/на мину́тку**. Then go to whatever other (necessarily nearby) line leads to an object of your desire, and do the same thing while praying that your turn does not come up in both lines at once. This operation is standard practice and is not thought of as cheating. Sometimes people in line make friends on the spot and then exchange places in two lines at once.

Sometimes a line develops its own policeman **бригади́р о́череди**, who is one of the awaiters and who takes responsibility to organize the line, by issuing numbers, for example. In Russia, this is a helpful and selfless person—in America it would be a busybody.

Crashing lines is cheating and is not recommended: if you try, you will probably be informed loudly of your unsporting behavior: "He went ahead without waiting!" **Он без о́череди** прошёл/влез! or "Lady, you weren't waiting in line!" **Женщина! Вы тут не стояли!**

Other ways are used to minimize waiting. You have read that many stores have three sets of lines: one to order what you want **выписать товар**, another to pay a cashier for the specified amount, and a third to go back and pick up your package. Actually, the line that really matters is the first one; the tricks are to make sure the goods are reserved for you and to know exactly how much you must pay the cashier. This can be done by knowing what the price is ahead of time, which is not too hard if you buy things in premeasured, packaged amounts. For instance, you know that half a pound of butter costs xx rubles, so you go straight to the cashier, get a receipt **чек** for xx rubles, and the clerk will trade your receipt for the butter. The problem is that many things, such as meat, cheese, and so on are sold in bulk, and must be measured, so you must wait in line one. Not all stores have lines all the time: go to another store up the block if the first one is overloaded. Darting in and out of stores, especially in winter, can be trained for by playing (rugby) football.

Through it all, remember that a line forms a small community. You are all in this together—so you can comment to strangers, and even make friends, as you keep vigil. By contrast, we often stand alone, impatiently protecting our privacy and the right not to be disturbed or be delayed. Remember also that the presence of a line indicates the existence of something worth waiting for.

Signs of quality
Знаки качества

A "quality sign" **Знак качества** used to indicate a product with quality equivalent to international standards (that is, very high). It has disappeared. A trademark **торговая марка** can be used by a trade organization for a product made to standards that are specifically ordered by that store or organization. It usually indicates better quality.

Finally, everything sold by the government is supposed to have a tag **этикетка** or the same information stamped or printed on the item sold that includes much of the following information: name of the object, where it was made, date of production, size or weight, number of the applicable state production standard, quality level, any use restrictions, and price **цена**. Highest quality is **высший сорт**, then **первый сорт, второй сорт, и т.д.** People used to avoid buying things made at the end of the month when speedy plan-fulfillment efforts lowered quality.

The section
Отдел

Most stores are arranged into much smaller departments or sections **отделы**, which do not share bookkeeping responsibilities. So if you go to a bookstore and want to buy two books, one on botany and the other a novel, you must get a separate receipt **чек** from the cashier to give to each of the sales clerks in the "Botany" and "Novels" sections. The cashier **кассирша** will often ask you in which section the sale was made if you do not volunteer the information.

What might be called a saving grace is that the sections are usually clearly marked, but you have to know to look for them.

MANUFACTURED GOODS
Промтовары

What follows are kinds of store names used in the past when the connection between title and contents was the only consideration. The list should be useful for showing how the salable world is divided. Two processes have changed things: (1) with the private—that is, "commercial"—store **коммерческий магазин**, the actual name of the store more often bears no relation to contents; and (2) because privatization is new, practices have not settled down: fur coats, table-

Everything goes

cloths, or shoes might be on sale at a local bakery, or one can come upon a heap of watermelons in a bookstore. With time, the latter condition ought to disappear.

Goods **товáры** are, generally speaking, either manufactured goods **промтовáры** (**промы́шленные товáры**) or foods **продтовáры** (**продовóльственные товáры**). Privatization has encouraged a broad range of store titles, but many stores happily use their contents in their title:

Бельё   linens and underwear

Галантерéя   Essentially, the small-stuff store: from toothpaste, needles and threads, and shampoo to underwear and accessories including ties, wallets, purses, and belts. (Warning: **галантерея** is often translated in English dictionaries as "haberdashery," which turns out to be British English for "small stuff" rather than "Men's wear.") **Галантерея** is often coupled with knitwear

трикотáж, perfume **парфюмéрия**, or both in the title, as well as the contents.

Готóвое плáтье   ready-to-wear dresses

Головны́е убóры   headwear, hats

Дéтские товáры   toys, clothes and equipment for children

Зоомагазúн   small animals, pet food and equipment, not including cats and dogs themselves

Игрýшки   toys

Кнúги   books; for used, old, or rare books: **Букинистúческий магазúн**

Коврьí   rugs

Кýльттовары   radios, TV, games, phonographs, school supplies, records, photography, and so on; often allied with office supplies: **кáнцтовары** (**канцеля́рские товары**)

Малы́ш   for babies and young children

Мéбель   furniture

Мехá   furs

Нóты   "Notes"—that is, sheet music

Обувь   footwear, shoes; you are handed your shoes over the counter and try them on yourself.

Одéжда   clothes

Оптика   glasses

Охóтник   "The Hunter"; hunting equipment; often paired with fishing equipment, **Рыболóвные товары**

Подáрки   gifts

Прирóда   "Nature"—that is, garden supplies, small animal supplies, goldfish, and the like.

Свет   electrical supplies

Семенá   seeds

Спорт   sporting goods; also, "The Hiker", **Турúст**

Стройматериáлы   building supplies

Ткáни   materials (for sewing, though not including thread, and related items, which might be acquired at a "Haberdashery" store **Галантерéя**)

Тысяча мелочей "A Thousand Things," usually hardware

Хозтовары includes hardware **скобяные изделия** and a wide variety of housewares and building supplies

Художественные изделия art supplies

Часы clocks and watches

Цветы flowers

Ювелирные изделия jewelry

Other types of stores
Другие виды магазинов

The largest store type is the department store **универмаг (универсальный магазин)**; its most splendiferous representations are the "GUM" **ГУМ (Государственный универсальный магазин)** on Red Square in Moscow and **Гостиный Двор** on Nevskiy Prospekt in St. Petersburg. The department store **универмаг** has so many sections that the impression is of many small stores under one roof. The variety of goods for sale includes men's and women's ready-to-wear, shoes, "haberdashery," and goes up from there. The smaller the population served, the wider the variety is likely to be. Some department stores specialize, such as Children's World **Детский мир** in Moscow.

A large network of second-hand/antique stores **комиссионные магазины** in major cities allows goods to be left on consignment. The stores specialize: most sell used clothes and shoes, but others have sporting goods, antique furniture **антикварная мебель** or old art, crystal, and china, and so forth. (The telephone book lists what is where.)

"Commercial" stores **коммерческие магазины** are food or goods stores where the price can change daily, depending on the retailer's prices from the wholesaler. They are, therefore, what we think of as normal, not government, stores.

Each former republic used to have a "dollar" store—that is, a store accepting only Western hard currencies (and giving change in all of them variously). In the Russian Federation it was the Birch Tree **Берёзка**. Such amenities were replaced by the hard-currency store **валютный магазин**, which was designed for anyone with legal access to hard currency: they could spend it in these stores. Acceptable currency now is rubles.

The Markets
Рынки

The street fair
Ярмарка

The biggest, and surely most famous, fair, **Макарьевская ярмарка**, is and was the one in Nizhniy Novgorod, which was called Gorkiy during the Soviet regime. Every year in August and part of September, merchants and traders of all sorts and conditions met at this picturesque confluence of the Oka **Ока** and the Volga **Волга** to conduct their business. The Fair has been revivified in its traditional location. (Well, actually the fair began at the Makar'yev monastery, downstream from Nizhniy, which itself is a sight worth seeing.)

In large cities the fair **ярмарка** is less a fair than a place to sell things in addition to food. It consists of a group of tents strung up along a street, often with high foot traffic. In smaller cities a public square might be so used, and the atmosphere of a "fair" might be more apparent. Some of the sellers will be branches **филиалы** from regular stores, and signs will so identify them; some sell discounted merchandise **по сниженным ценам**; and some will be private sellers. Some fairs are open at regular intervals, especially the weekends. Almost anything can be for sale, but people expect that the prices will be lower than in a regular store.

The flea market
Барахолка, Толкучка

Junk, or well-used things **барахло**, is an inelegant but descriptive term. Such things are sold at a flea market **барахо́лка**, which is commonly near or part of a street market. The arrangement is informal, and it used to border on the illegal. Now it is a domestic fund-raiser for those on pensions, among others. People might take as little as a pair of shoes, display them, and hope that the price matches a buyer.

Another word, from "to push or shove" **толка́ть** is **толку́чка**, the same kind of market that might arise along any street anywhere.

Street sale of almost anything, almost anywhere people are, can be expected. Not too long ago the price differential allowed people to buy in a state store and sell on the street and still make a profit. Organization of sorts has arrived so that those who sell in the subway stations, for example, often must pay protection money to do so.

The pet market
Пти́чий ры́нок

Moscow has a special market near the Taganka Theater **Тага́нка**, that, although called the Bird Market **Пти́чий ры́нок**, is a jolly congregation of those who are selling pets of any kind, including cats and dogs. Pet supplies are also available here.

The black market
Чёрный ры́нок

The black markets used to be semi-formalized affairs: those interested in buying and selling books, for example, would meet regularly at the **Кузне́цкий мост** region of Moscow; people interested in other things would regularly meet elsewhere, and this pattern obtained in other cities. Now marketing is not necessarily a sub-rosa affair, but people with particular interests continue to have their special meeting places.

FOOD STORES
Продово́льственные магази́ны

Grocery stores **продма́ги** (**продово́льствен- ные магази́ны**) carry the central burden of

food staple sales: canned goods, flour, sugar, and so forth. Sometimes they include a bulk food department **бакале́йные изде́лия**, **бакале́я** that dispenses grains, macaroni, vegetable oil, and the like.

Most food is bought in stores that specialize, though they also often have sections that sell related foods. The following are the street signs for common stores:

Бу́лочная   bread and rolls

Хлеб   bread and sometimes rolls

Вино́   wine (though currently only "better" wines are available)

Вино-Фру́кты   wines, fruits

Гастроно́м   fancier food store, delicatessen, often including a section of semi-prepared foods **полуфабрика́ты**

Дие́та   foods required by people on special diets

Дары́ приро́ды   "Gifts of Nature": foods obtained in the wild (by hunters and gatherers); also sometimes called Mushrooms and Berries **Грибы́-я́годы**

Колба́сы   sausages; often sold with cheese **Сыр**

Колобо́к   "Gingerbread Man": special food for children

Конди́терский магазин   candy; often with a bakery **бу́лочная**

Бу́лочная-конди́терская   where fancy baked goods might be had

Консе́рвы   canned goods

Кулина́рия   prepared and partially prepared foods

Минера́льная вода́   mineral water

Молоко́   dairy products

Мя́со   meat

Овощи, Овощи-Фру́кты   vegetables, fruits

Ры́ба, Океа́н   fish

Со́ки-Во́ды   juices, bottled water (and occasionally beer **Пи́во**)

Таба́к   tobacco products

Чай-Ко́фе   tea, coffee

A few stores before the Revolution were so good that their old names have persisted to this day: a famous delicatessen, **Елисе́евский магази́н**, was renamed to **Гастроно́м № 1** but now has its original name back. In Moscow, it is right next door to a famous bakery, **Фили́пповская бу́лочная**, which also kept its name.

The Ministry of Agriculture **Минсельхо́з** (**Министе́рство Се́льского Хозя́йства**) is responsible for some agricultural cooperative stores **сельхозкоо́пы** selling fancy groceries for higher prices in larger cities.

The supermarket
Универса́м

The large scale self-service food store **универса́м**, short for **универса́льный магази́н самообслу́живания**, is in some places still viable. These are particularly welcome to the foreigner who can examine what's available without a crushing line behind. Expect that your bags will be subject to inspection upon exit, or that you will be asked to check large bags at the entrance. (Recently, most of these stores have been converted back to over-the-counter sales as a way to cut down on shoplifting.)

The market
Ры́нок, База́р

State stores are not the only place to look for food. The peasant market **ры́нок** (sometimes called **база́р**) allows the home grower to pad income, and not insignificantly. The market is a large enclosed space, with private sellers **ча́стники** in the center and government stores or their branches **филиа́лы** around the walls.

Грош им цена́ в база́рный день.
The price is low on market days. "The stuff is no good and will surely lose out with real competition."

Market goods were known for their higher quality and much higher prices, but now state stores and private prices are much closer to each other. Foreigners should make an effort to visit one—try a glass of "warmed" milk **топлёное молоко́**. Generally, Russians tend not to bargain, but Georgians and Azeri, for example, do, so Russians are becoming more adept at it. The following episode took place at the Danilovskiy market in Moscow:

Практи́чески любо́й из торго́вцев лю́бит и уме́ет торгова́ться и непреме́нно се́тует, что на ры́нок прихо́дит всё ме́ньше покупа́телей, владе́ющих э́тим иску́сством. При мне пришёл один тако́й челове́к.

Он реши́л купи́ть цветну́ю капу́сту. Ему́ назва́ли су́мму в 1500 рубле́й. Он предложи́л 500. Торгова́лись мину́т три́дцать. Покупа́телю, хорошо́ оде́тому пожило́му челове́ку, удало́сь сбить нача́льную це́ну до 800 рубле́й. Уходи́л он то́лько что не под аплодисме́нты прода́вцо́в, мно́гие из кото́рых ра́ди э́того зре́лища бро́сили свои́ рабо́чие места́.[a]

Unfortunately, the rest of the article made it clear that at least some of the Azeri fruit vendors were also vending opium.

Rationing
Тало́ны

Rationing of scarce items was still necessary as late as 1992. The public seemed not uncontent with rationing, as it assured everybody some of the scarcity. Coupons **тало́ны** are not currently in demand as the market tries to adjust to itself. People used to get rations at work: **Пайки́ по тало́нам на рабо́те получи́ли.**

Before rationing, other efforts were made to limit sales. The sign in a food store would read:

Но́рмы о́тпуска на одного́ покупа́теля продово́льственных това́ров: колба́сные изде́лия 2 кг, ма́сло живо́тное 8/10 кг, консе́рвы моло́чные 5 ба́нок, сыр полкило́.[b]

Another way to limit buying, especially by people from other regions, was not to sell things in short supply to those who could not produce a local passport.

SERVICES
Услу́ги

For the usual repair to the building—plumbing, electrical, and the like, one merely calls the Maintenance office, formerly **ЖЭК (Жили́щно-эксплуатацио́нная конто́ра)** and now called **РЭУ** (*pron.* **рэ́у—Ремо́нтно-эксплуата-цио́нное управле́ние**). (The latter organization does the same thing but takes in a much bigger area.) The service is part of the rent.

If a reason exists for arranging repair **ремо́нт** privately, then one may want to cultivate good relations with a plumber or gas installer **сле́сарь** (who can also fix the hot-water heater **га́зовая коло́нка** or the oven **га́зовая духо́вка**). If he does nothing but work on gas equipment, he is a **газовщи́к**; if he only does pipes, then a **водопрово́дчик**. An electrician is a **монтёр** or **эле́ктрик**, a carpenter is a **пло́тник**, a cabinet maker is a **столя́р**, and a painter or plasterer is a **маля́р**.

In extremis (which is to say, without friends), get a telephone book and look under (1) the listing for whatever is broken: (Watches, Repair of **Часо́в Ремо́нт**); or (2) under headings such as Services **Бытовы́е услу́ги, Дома́ бы́та**.

These are the services supplied by the "Sunrise" **Заря́** companies: Grandfather Frost will hand out gifts, and children can be wished a happy birthday; courses for the young homemaker on cutting and sewing, ikebana, machine and hand knitting, and macrame; beekeeping; the use and minor repair of sewing machines; photography; dusting and mopping floors, wiping glass and even insulating windows; care for sick adults and children; musicians' services; and "do-it-yourself" salons.

These are the services **бытовы́е услу́ги** supplied by the Combine for Equipping

---

БЫТОВЫЕ УСЛУГИ

Комбинатов бытовых услуг (КБУ) МГПО «Заря»
(Вручение подарков Дедом Морозом, поздравление детей с днём рождения; курсы кройки и шитья, икебана, машинного и ручного вязания, макраме, молодой хозяйки, пчеловодства, эксплуатации и мелкого ремонта швейных машин, фотографирования; натирка и мытье полов; протирка стекол, утепление окон; уборка квартир, уход за больными и детьми; услуги музыкантов; раскрой ткани; салоны «Сделай сам»)

Центральная диспетчерская
117331, ул. Марии Ульяновой, 9
138 01 33

Диспетчерские

КБУ № 1
Дмитровское ш., 25   **216 23 18**
КБУ № 2
Туристская, 2   **497 87 91**
КБУ № 3
Люблинская, 46   **350 14 64**
КБУ № 4
Фортунатовская, 33/44   **360 69 36**

Приемные пункты

Бабушкинский р-в КБУ № 1
ул. Малыгина, 20   **475 18 82**
Палехская, 11, к. 2   **183 28 47**
Снежная, 13   **180 94 73**
Бауманский р-в КБУ № 4
Потаповский п., 10   **923 74 58**
Волгоградский р-в КБУ № 4
3-я Институтская, 5, к. 2   **170 55 19**
Ташкентская, 17, к. 3   **174 52 92**
Гагаринский р-в КБУ № 2

Моско́вская телефо́нная кни́га

Комбината по оборудованию квартир Треста Мосжилремонт
(Циклевка и покрытие лаком полов, обивка дверей, установка карнизов, подвеска светильников, врезка замков и глазков, навеска ковров и полок, установка кондиционеров)
Центральная диспетчерская
109033, Гжельский п., 20   **278 12 21**
Приемные пункты
Бабушкинский р-н
ул. Малыгина, 20   **474 24 71**
Бауманский р-в
ул. Чернышевского, 31   **297 13 53**
Волгоградский р-в

Apartments: resurfacing and laquering floors, upholstering doors (for insulation), installing cornices, hanging light fixtures, cutting locks and eye-holes, hanging rugs and shelves, and installing air conditioners.

If small and crawling or scurrying creatures are making your life miserable, you call the local Public Health Authorities **Санэпидемстáнция**, but you probably will find little concern over cockroaches **таракáны** or bedbugs **клопы́**. The same authorities also deal with irregularities in waste disposal. Pest control is also a private business now.

For mending clothes, hats, furs, and so forth, look up Sewing **ПОШИВ** and then the item to be sewn: **одéжда, сорóчка, кóжаная галантерéя, мехá. . .**

If you want to rent anything from baby diapers to harps, consult the telephone book under **ПРОКАТ**.

For more personal services, you can go to the cleaners at the sign of the **Химчи́стка**, occasionally combined with a laundry **Прáчечная**. However, these services are often too time-consuming for the traveler; they also have a reputation of being rough on clothes. The sign that says "American laundry" **Америкáнская прáчечная** designates what we mean by "laundromat," but it also includes a mangle **гладúльная маши́на** for ironing flat things. For shoe repair, look for the **Ремóнт Обуви** sign—but not **Сапóжник**: that title is now lost because of the expression "He is drunk as a bootmaker" **Он пьёт, как сапóжник.** For a haircut **стри́жка** or hairdo, **зави́вка** make an appointment at your local **Парикмáхерская** or, for the more pretentious, **Салóн.** Again, you are best off with the recommendation of a friend. If you have serious beauty problems you can consult a cosmetic doctor **врач-косметóлог** (who works at a cosmetics office **косметúческий кабинéт**), or, if you merely want revivifying, try a medicinal mask **лечéбная мáска** or a face cleaning **чúстка лицá** at an institute of beauty **институт красоты́.** Private offices **чáстные мастерá** of cosmetologists **косметóлоги** do facials **макия́ж** or massages **массáж.**

Service with a smile?
А зачем улы́бка?

They take on your job, whatever it is, never smiling, sometimes not even looking at you, and, at best, scowl when they discover some unfulfilled requirement. Why do they do that? They do that because they reserve their smile for friends. We consider a smile a part of speaking and assign little meaning to it. They see us smile and either think that we might be laughing at them or that we are being disingenuous. Aksyonov's mother gave her approval to our way thusly: **Лучше формáльная любéзность, чем úскреннее хáмство.** [c]

TRANSLATIONS

a. Practically all of the sellers know how and like to bargain. They are sure to complain that fewer and fewer buyers understand the art. One such man arrived while I was there. He decided to buy a cauliflower. They named him the price of 1,500 rubles. He suggested 500 rubles. They bargained for about 30 minutes. The buyer, a well-dressed middle-aged man, managed to bring the original price down to 800 rubles. As he left the sellers were almost clapping for him—many had left their workplaces just to watch. (*Moscow News*, 11 Apr 93)

b. These are the limits for one buyer of food: 2 kilograms of sausage, 8/10 kg butter, 5 jars of canned milk, one-half kg of cheese.

c. "Better a formal kindness, than a sincere vulgarity."

10

Communications

Связь

Communication has, these days, mostly to do with facilities—and here the problem is telephone lines for a new economy. There is ample room for the foreign telephone companies who are currently marching into the void, and probably plenty of room for technician-installers and their trainers. The mail system works well where the possibility for enclosed valuables is nonexistent; and Russians are consistent and voluminous letter writers. But for us the real joy is with telegrams: they are inexpensive, fast, and reliable. Mass communications—radio, television, the presses—are still controlled to some extent by the government if political or economic questions are discussed; pornography displays, however, show what capitalism can do without a bridle. Here the greatest need is support for good programming, something other than old B-grade American flicks, or Mexican soap operas, for that matter.

Left over from the past is distrust of official news or information. A rumor repeated by a trusted friend will gain more credence than a pile of verifiable statistics presented by a knowledgeable saint.

First we deal with private communication: mail, telephones, telegrams, and the post office, then referring to telex, fax, and E-mail; the second stage is mass communications: radio, television, periodicals, and books.

PRIVATE COMMUNICATION
Сре́дства свя́зи

Mail
По́чта

Personal communications more often involve the mail: it is, these days, more affordable, and Russians have nothing against writing. However, it is assumed that any mail to or from other countries, especially the West, is subject to post-office thievery or simple molestation. (In the old days, the problem was government censorship or snooping. The effect on the mail was the same.) Therefore it is (and has been) standard procedure to ask travelers to take letters with them; Russians also expect to receive mail, especially packages, via friends of friends. Many letters commence with "I'm taking advantage of this opportunity . . ." «По́льзуюсь ока́зией . . . » which means

"I've come across someone who will take this letter. . . ." You have the solemn obligation to assure the delivery of any mail entrusted to you. If money or goodies are not involved, then the mails are usually reliable, if slow.

Addresses
Адреса́

The letter **письмо́** is folded into quarters and sent in a standard (16 x 11.5 cm) envelope **конве́рт**. (Large sizes cost more.) The order of the address is, naturally, the opposite of ours: postal zone (or country) first and addressee last.

1. The address   **Адрес**
   (a) 410855 **Москва**
   (b) **ул. Бухина**
   (c) д. 34 **корп. 2 кв. 328**
   (d) **Серовой Марии Сергеевне**

(a) **Куда́** = destination; postal zone (zip code) first, then city. Within Russia, the postal code appears in lower left corner of the envelope, not here

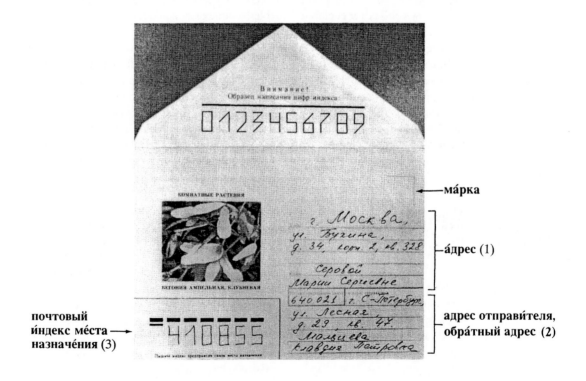

ма́рка

а́дрес (1)

адрес отправи́теля, обра́тный адрес (2)

почто́вый и́ндекс ме́ста назначе́ния (3)

(b) Street **у́лица** name or a feminine adjective understood to modify **у́лица**; also possible are boulevard **бульва́р**, prospect **проспе́кт**, lane **переу́лок**, highway **шоссе́**, cul de sac **тупи́к**, quay **на́бережная**

(c) **д.** is **дом**, the address number; a second number separated by a slash (д. 34/10) includes the address number on the cross street; **корп.** (or **к.**) is building number **ко́рпус**, fairly common in new huge developments; the **ко́рпус** can also be indicated by a letter, as in **пр. Гага́рина, д. 110Б**; **кв.** means **кварти́ра** apartment number.

(d) **Кому́** means *To whom*; always last name first, always in the dative case, and never separated by a comma

2. Sender's address **А́дрес отправи́теля**, or return address **Обра́тный а́дрес**, in the lower right-hand corner. Again, the zip code is first and the sender is last, usually in the nominative case

3. Zip code **Почто́вый и́ндекс** of the recipient, which must be written as shown on the back of the envelope

Those who rent a post office box **Абонеме́нтный я́щик** use the abbreviation **А/я. А/я № 227**. Those who want to mail a letter can use a mailbox **почто́вый я́щик**. A red one is for letters inside the city and the blue one is for elsewhere. In some places they are used either way.

Addresses to those living outside cities also start with the zip code and the largest destination first, for example:

643228 **Орло́вская о́бласть**
Одинцо́вский райо́н
Дер. Петушки́
д. 10
Ивано́ву Серге́ю Серге́евичу

райо́н – a subdivision of **о́бласть**
дере́вня – village

Kinds of letters
Пи́сьма

The undecorated postcard **почто́вая ка́рточка**, the picture postcard **откры́тка** and what we call greeting card **поздрави́тельная откры́тка** (that is, birthday or Christmas cards in envelopes), are usually on sale at the local post office and elsewhere. Mail can be either surface or air mail **АВИА**, and can go in three degrees of assurance: standard letter **просто́е письмо́**, registered letter **заказно́е письмо́**, and the insured (literally, *valuable*) letter **це́нное письмо́**. Oversize letters are sent at the insured rate. ("How much do you want to insure your letter for?" is **Во ско́лько вы оце́ниваете ваше письмо́?**) Russians often use registered mail to assure that the mail reaches its destination. By paying extra, one can get a signed receipt **квита́нция** from the addressee, and it's possible to prepay for direct delivery **с доста́вкой на́ дом**. The money order **де́нежный перево́д** is one way to send money if you are not in a hurry—the recipient must prove identity with a passport shown at the local post office, or the sender can prepay delivery **с доста́вкой на́ дом**. In a hurry, you can send a telegraph money order **телегра́фный перево́д**, also from the post office. COD—that is, cash on delivery—is **нало́женным платежо́м**. If you want a return receipt, ask for a letter, **с уведомле́нием**.

The letter
Письмо́

The personal letter differs from ours in punctuation and perhaps in effusiveness. The date is written Russian style, and the greeting is followed by an exclamation mark, not a comma, and need not start on the far left. The most likely greeting on a personal letter is Dear **Дорого́й/ая** or Darling **Ми́лый/ая**, plus a given name (or whatever else you want to call the person); or even warmer still (Beloved) **Родно́й/ая**, without a name following. Generally, what corresponds to our "Love" at the end of letters is "I kiss you" **Целу́ю**, but also likely are "I hug you" **Обнима́ю** or "I love you" **Люблю́**. Also usable for merely friendly letters are: "Yours" **Ваш/Ваша, Твой/Твоя́**, "Write!" **Жду отве́та**, "Goodbye" **До свида́ния**, and "See you soon" **До ско́рой встре́чи**. The date often comes near the signature, at the end of the letter.

In writing letters the words *you* **Вы** and *your* **Ваш** in all their forms are capitalized, but *Thou* **Ты** is not.

A pen pal is **друг по перепи́ске**.

The business letter **делово́е письмо́** follows our format with a logo centered at the top, including an address, telephone number, telex and fax number. Then a date follows on the right (day-month-year). Then, on the left, the name of the recipient in the dative case, is followed by an address. Directly under the address **Кас.** (for **Каса́ется**) replaces our "Re" (About) and under that goes the greeting: **Уважа́емый господи́н Серге́ев**, or much more formally, **Глубо́коуважа́емый господин Сергеев**. (If you have been introduced to the person, be sure to use the first name, plus patronymic.) The text of the letter is followed by the signature alone or by "Sincerely" **Искренне Ваш** or "Respectfully" **С уваже́нием** with the signature **по́дпись**.

A sample business letter:

Совме́стное Росси́йско–герма́нское предприя́тие «Рассве́т»
Росси́я, 197000

12 октября́ 1992

Санкт-Петербу́рг

Управля́ющему ба́нком

«АО Банк С.-Петербу́рг»

Головину́ Н. П.

Уважа́емый Никола́й Пантелеймо́нович!

Совме́стное Росси́йско—герма́нское предприя́тие «Рассве́т» выступа́ет с инициати́вой постро́йки в Вы́боргском р-не г. С.-Петербу́рга би́знес-це́нтра на осно́ве прое́кта, разрабо́танного фи́рмой "MSV Gmbh" (Berlin, Germany). Упомя́нутый ко́мплекс до́лжен включа́ть в себя́ зда́ния 2-х гости́ниц, вы́ставочный зал, помеще́ния для проведе́ния конфере́нций и семина́ров, рестора́н и 3 кафе́. Кро́ме того́, необходи́мой ча́стью би́знес-це́нтра должно́ явля́ться отделе́ние одного́ из крупне́йших ба́нков г. Санкт-Петербу́рга. Мы сочли́ бы за честь размеще́ние в да́нном ко́мплексе отделе́ния Ва́шего ба́нка.

Настоя́щим я убеди́тельно прошу́ Вас счесть возмо́жным проанализи́ровать прилага́емые материа́лы по да́нному прое́кту, а та́кже рассмотре́ть возмо́жность выделе́ния креди́та в су́мме . . . . . . .млн. руб. для проведе́ния строи́тельных рабо́т. Гара́нтом креди́та мо́гут явля́ться основны́е сре́дства на́шего предприя́тия. Те́хнико—экономи́ческое обоснова́ние прое́кта прилага́ется, при необходи́мости Вам бу́дет предоста́влена люба́я дополни́тельная информа́ция.

С уваже́нием,

С.А. Богда́нов

Генера́льный дире́ктор СП «Рассве́т»

Packages
Бандеро́ли, Посы́лки

Another category of mail is the small package **бандеро́ль,** which is anything weighing less than one kilogram. The post office wraps it for you. If you want to be assured that it arrived, you can send it as an "insured small package" **це́нная бандеро́ль** for which one can get a receipt **квита́нция**. If the weight is from one to eight kilograms, then it is a package **посы́лка** that must be in a sturdy container, which itself has its own special wrapping.

Any packages to be sent out of the country must be brought to an international or main post office (**междугоро́дный**) **почта́мт** before they are sealed or irretrievably wrapped. This makes mailing things to former Soviet republics **бли́жнее зарубе́жье** as difficult as to the rest of the world **да́льнее зарубежье**. A post office worker must certify that the package contains nothing disallowed. Do not wrap packages yourself ahead of time. You may have to supply a box, but the wrapping will be done for you.

The telephone
Телефо́н

насте́нный телефон   a wall telephone (mostly in communal apartments)

набра́ть но́мер   to dial

снять тру́бку   to answer the telephone

спа́ренный телефон   a party line: two households, two numbers

паралле́льный телефон   a shared line: one number, two households

Both the telephone itself and its installation are hard to come by **дефици́т**, often taking years: literally, some people die before their turn for a telephone comes up. A better rank in line **льго́тная о́чередь** is offered to World War II veterans and families with numerous children, but even quicker installation, without waiting in line **вне о́череди**, comes to (1) those who can

prove that they need one, (2) those in power, or (3) their friends, or (4) those with money (for business lines).

"What's your telephone number?" is **Како́й у вас но́мер телефо́на?** The answer can come in seven figures if it's in Moscow or St. Petersburg, or only four if the number of telephones in the area is very low. Report the numbers in pairs when possible: **Мой но́мер** 365-43-11 or 3-65-43-11. The extension number **доба́вочный** is written as **доб.** Emergency telephone numbers are at the very beginning of the telephone book, but as the latter is often lacking and similar numbers are likely for other cities, these are the Moscow emergency numbers as of 1993: 01 fire **пожа́р**; 02 police **мили́ция**; 03 emergency medical help **ско́рая медици́нская по́мощь**; 04 gas emergency **авари́йная слу́жба, Мосгаз** (for long dis-

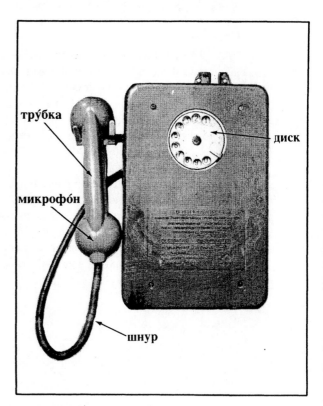

Телефо́н на у́лице

tance, call 07; for telephone number information, call 09; and to send a telegram, dial 06).

The telephone answering machine **телефон с автоответчиком, автоответчик** is coming into standard use; one's telephone can have a device **блок памяти** that will continue to dial a number until it answers, though it is not too common. Individuals are beginning to use caller I.D. capabilities **блок АОН (автоматический опознаватель номера)**. The caller's number appears and the answerer can decide whether to take the call.

The public telephone **телефон-автомат, таксофон** requires a token **жетон** for local calls, which requirement makes such pieces desirable (and therefore commercial) objects. ("I couldn't call—I didn't have a token" is **Я не мог позвонить. У меня не было жетона**.) Some telephones have not been converted and may require either a two-kopeck piece **двушка** or a fifteen-kopeck piece. The person seated near the public telephone sometimes makes it an occupation to supply change, for a price. The public telephone labeled **таксофон** officially gives you three minutes, so don't dawdle. Public telephones in major cities have fallen into some disrepair and others have been vandalized. Suspects are the Mafia, who thus make it difficult to summon aid. A telephone in a yellow box on the street is a direct line to the police **милиция**. Look for a public telephone inside a building where vandalism is more difficult.

The telephone call to friends does not necessarily involve language you don't ordinarily use except perhaps for Hello **Алло** (pronounced **альо**) and its equivalent **Слушаю (вас)**, literally, "I'm listening." It is slightly more formal. Least formal is Yes? **Да**? New language has more to do with getting your friend on the telephone in the first place.

Вы не туда попали. Wrong number.

Извините, я ошиблась (я ошибся) номером. I'm sorry, I dialed the wrong number.

Линия занята. Занято. The line is busy.

Передайте трубку Сергею, пожалуйста.
Попросите (позовите) Сергея к телефону, пожалуйста. May I speak to Sergey, please?

Передайте ему, что я перезвоню вечером. Tell him that I'll call in the evening.

When Russians want to spell something on the telephone and it's hard to hear, they use common first-name initials, thus the equivalent to Able, Baker, Charlie can be **Анна, Борис, Галя**, and so forth.

Long distance
Междугородняя

Long-distance direct dialing is available from most major city telephones via their local **ATC Автоматическая телефонная станция**. In Moscow, dial 8, wait for a dial tone **гудок**, then dial the city code **код города**, and then the number. Dial quickly—you only get five seconds between numbers. For long-distance information, dial 07, or look in the telephone book **Телефонная книга** (which is not likely to be available, but that's what friends are for). If someone offers a telephone number, don't lose it, and don't hope to find it elsewhere. Payment is arranged by buying a "token" **жетон**, which gives you the right to talk long distance to a certain city for a certain length of time; calling "on credit" **в кредит** results in a bill to the number dialed from.

Many towns do not have direct dialing available, so one can (1) order a call **заказывать разговор** through the long-distance operator or (2) go to a telephone center **переговорный пункт** to order a call.

Arranging a long-distance call
Заказ на переговоры

This is a typical sequence for Mrs. Petrova, who is arranging a call to Yalta from Nizhniy Novgorod. She first dials 07. Then . . .

телефони́стка: Междугоро́дняя, 20 слушает.

Петрова: (Алло!) Прими́те, пожалуйста, зака́з на разгово́р с Ялтой.

тел.: Говори́те номер. (Но́мер в Ялте?)

Пет.: 44-22-11

тел.: Кого позва́ть? (вы́звать)

Пет.: Ивано́ву

тел.: Если её нет, будете говори́ть?

Пет.: Да, кто подойдёт. (She could have specified a person.)

тел.: Номер в Нижнем Новгороде? (Ваш номер телефона?)

Пет.: 11-00-66

тел.: Служе́бный или дома́шний?

Пет.: Домашний

тел.: Заказ при́нят. Ожида́йте. (Жди́те)

Пет.: Спасибо.

Here our caller waits, from thirty minutes to three hours, for the phone to ring. One can start complaining after an hour.

Звоно́к!

Пет.: Алло!

тел.: Это 11-00-66? Ялту зака́зывали?

Пет.: Да, да. Заказывала.

тел.: Соединя́ю. Говори́те.

Пет.: Алло, здравствуйте. Будьте добры́ Ни́ну (позва́ть).

Иванов: Её сейчас нет до́ма.

Пет.: А когда можно перезвони́ть?

Ив. : Перезвони́те через час.

Пет.: Спасибо.

Now our caller hangs up кладёт тру́бку. In a few minutes, the operator calls her and tells her how much time she will be charged for. The bill will come in the mail.

The telegram
Телегра́мма

You can usually send your telegram from the local post office по́чта, but the main post office главный почтамт and the main telegraph office главный телегра́ф are separate entities.

Telegrams are very widely used because they are fast and do not require a telephone, though they can be ordered from a private telephone: you call the telegraph office, you give your telephone number, they hang up and call back. The four kinds are: the ordinary telegram (our night letter), проста́я, обы́чная телеграмма, which is delivered the next day; the good wishes telegram поздрави́тельная телеграмма, with a delivery date that can be specified, for a small price; the urgent telegram сро́чная телеграм-ма, which costs somewhat more, but is delivered in a few hours; and the verified telegram

```
      ТЕЛЕГРАММА

  X
МОСКВА 2/4827 22 7/9 1730=

СЕРИЯ Ж61 МОСКВА 123 УЛ КЛИМАШКИНА Д  5  КВ 47 БОГ В 0=

ДОРОГОЙ УЖИН РОВНО ВСЕМЬ ТЧК НЕ ОПАЗДЫВАЙ ВОСКЛ-
ННННН  1735 07.09 0039
```

Телегра́мма   Telegram as received

Telegram as ordered

заве́ренная телегра́мма, which can serve as legal certification for a document many miles away. Money orders by telegram де́нежные перево́ды телегра́фом can be used in a hurry.

Since words and punctuation are both counted by the piece in figuring the cost, telegrams tend to lack both punctuation and prepositions. Thus: **БУДУ ПЯТНИЦУ ПОЕЗД** 307 **ВАГОН** 9 **САША**[1]

Some post offices try to deliver such telegrams by telephone though the public prefers a real piece of paper.

The "good wishes" telegram has the advantage of making a bigger splash with its recipient than a mere card **откры́тка** might. The sender must not only compose a suitable message but also must choose between a variety of colored blanks to write it on. The following is a sample telegram of this sort as suggested by one post office in case its clients ran short of inspiration. Prepositions and punctuation are gone, additions and alterations are in parentheses. Capitalization is retained here as in a real letter.

Дорога́я Анна Петро́вна (Серде́чно) Поздравля́ем Вас днём рожде́ния (юбиле́я, Но́вым го́дом) Жела́ем кре́пкого здоро́вья успе́хов рабо́те (учёбе) сча́стья ли́чной жи́зни Ваши Си́доровы[a]

The post office
По́чта

The post office **по́чта** is the major dealer in the communications game because services include not only the mail **по́чта** but also the telephone, telegraph, and perhaps a branch savings bank **отделе́ние сберба́нка**. Not only are stamps sold, but also tables are provided for writing let-

1. Arriving Friday train 307 car 9 Sasha

ters. In a city, the main post office **почта́мт** offers the widest variety of services, including—if the title is International Post Office **Междугоро́дный почтамт**—packages to be sent abroad.

The usual post office **по́чта** handles the mails for its own zip code area **почто́вое отделе́ние**. As you enter the various services seem obvious enough, telegrams over here, telephones over there, but the meaning of the signs over the windows are less than clear; for example, **Прие́м**. . . has the meaning of "reception" at its base, but at the post office means "We take orders for . . ." so the translation is sometimes "Outgoing. . . ." Following is a collection of likely signs in the mail section:

Прие́м заказны́х пи́сем и бандеро́лей
Outgoing registered letters and small packages

Прие́м заказно́й корреспонде́нции из учрежде́ний Outgoing registered mail from institutions

Прие́м перево́дов, пе́нсий, це́нной корреспонде́нции, подпи́ска Outgoing money orders, pensions, insured correspondence, subscriptions

Вы́дача пе́нсий Pension payments

Прие́м подпи́ски на газе́ты и журна́лы Subscriptions to newspapers and magazines

Спра́вки Information (about post office regulations)

Прие́м и опла́та перево́дов Outgoing money orders, money order payment

Вы́дача корреспонде́нции до востре́бования Distribution of general delivery mail

Бюро́ пропуско́в Permissions office (government buildings where passage is restricted often have such offices)

Прие́м це́нной корреспонде́нции, ма́рки, откры́тки, конве́рты Outgoing insured mail, stamps, postcards, and envelopes

Вы́дача посы́лок distribution of (mailed) packages

The telegraph section will have these signs:

Прие́м телегра́мм Outgoing telegrams

Прие́м телеграмм по безнали́чному расчёту Outgoing telegrams paid for by organizations

Сро́чные телеграммы принима́ются вне о́череди Urgent outgoing telegrams, accepted immediately (but they cost more and must be delivered upon receipt at the post office)

The post office is sometimes accompanied by a savings bank **Сберба́нк** that might have a **контролёр**, **касси́р**, or **ка́сса**. Here, one can pay bills for housing and utilities.

The post office usually also has a telephone "station" **перегово́рный пункт**, where one can order a long distance telephone call **заказа́ть междугоро́дный телефо́нный разгово́р**. You pay ahead of time for the number of minutes you want and then wait (up to an hour); finally you hear: "Blagoveshchensk! Booth number 3!" **Благове́щенск! Каби́на но́мер 3!**—assuming that you were calling someone in Blagoveshchensk. Listen carefuiiy, however, because you might also be called up according to the number on your receipt **тало́н**.

Telex, fax, and E-mail
Те́лекс, факс, и электро́нная по́чта

Telex and fax are familiar to those in the business world, and usually only big business: Xerox **ксе́рокс** and photocopy **фотоко́пия** are also still limited to business use. E-mail **электро́нная по́чта** can be found in regular use at many scientific and educational institutions. (This device was used liberally during the 1991 putsch to let the whole world know what was going on. It could be argued that this form of communication will make a future iron curtain difficult to maintain as a spiritual entity.) Electronic mail is achieved via a modem **моде́м (мода́м)** and a computer **компью́тер**, (*coll.* **маши́на**). The latter is equipped with a screen **экра́н**, **монито́р** and a keyboard клавиату́ра (which has keys кла́виши) a mouse мышь, and perhaps an attached printer при́нтер which in turn might require a cartridge ка́ртридж for fonts фо́нты. The computer has disk drives дисково́ды A B C (а, бэ, цэ) for large and small floppy disks пятидюймо́вые и трёхдюймо́вые диске́ты; the hard drive is винче́стер (*coll.* винт). As you can see, the Russian is not a problem if you know the English. To make Russian appear on the screen, the Russian uses a руссифика́тор, of which there are many. E-mail across cultures more often uses English and the Internet. For a discussion of the techniques involved, subscribe to RUSTEX-L, and for browsing in Russia, do investigate the World Wide Web (WWW) server: Friends and Partners.

MASS COMMUNICATIONS
Сре́дства ма́ссовой информа́ции

Radio
Ра́дио

Two different systems supply radio services: one is the system we use, in which one tunes into a station кана́л broadcasting on long, medium, or short waves, FM or AM, and the like. This in Russian is a "radioreceiver" радиоприёмник. This is the device one must use to receive the BBC Би–би–си, Radio Liberty Ра́дио Свобо́да, or Voice of America Го́лос Аме́рики. The other system is a leftover from sterner days when it was in the state's interest to limit public access to radio waves. Instead, they offered what to us would be "cable radio," such that one could switch between several stations, but the equipment was still really a wired radio speaker радиото́чка, connected by a wire to a radio center радиоу́зел that had the responsibility of distributing acceptable programs. Now that both forms of radio are acceptable, the wired radio seems less nefarious, but because many people, especially the less sophisticated, have only the wired form, the possibilities for controlling information are still significant.

Stations, programs, and channels combine in ways differing from our use of the same words: радиовеща́тельная ста́нция is the formal expression for radio broadcasting station, with emphasis on the equipment; кана́л is the station, or the place on the dial to which one switches whether for radio or television; програ́мма is whatever sets of programs that station might carry.

There are two main stations кана́л, програ́мма: the first, пе́рвая програ́мма, is the major news and general interest station, now called Radio Russia Ра́дио Росси́и. It has news но́вости every hour and a major news analysis and review program that is repeated in the evening and the next day. The second station is "Lighthouse" Мая́к, which broadcasts a few minutes of news every half-hour, with a wide variety of all sorts of music in between. Other stations reflect regional or interest groups: Эхо Москвы́, Го́лос Ба́лтики (СПБ), и т. д.

The most basic receiving equipment is the single-wired radio speaker громкоговори́тель, дина́мик, радиото́чка. Your choices are "on or off" and "loud or soft." Next, but still wired, is the "three-programmer" трёхпрогра́ммник, which gives you two more stations. Finally comes the radio приёмник, which, if equipped properly, can make available all the programs on short waves на коро́тких волна́х, on medium waves на сре́дних волнах, and on long waves на дли́нных волна́х. Ультракоро́ткие во́лны УКВ corresponds to our frequency modulation FM. Other types of equipment are also available: радио́ла is a радиопрои́грыватель—that is, a radio and phonograph; a radio can be combined with a tape player, магнитофо́н, the tape ле́нта for which has been a fine gift for years.

Television, TV
Телеви́дение, ТВ

Television shares words for station, program, and the like, but brings new facilities to the equipment vocabulary: a television set is телеви́зор; the VCR is видеоплейер/видеомагнитофо́н, or more commonly, ви́дик or вида́к; its required tape is **кассе́та**. A TV-VCR combination is **видеодво́йка**. Of course, the camcorder is **видеока́мера** or more simply, **ка́мера**. (Our *camera* is **фотоаппара́т, аппара́т**.)

The best display of current television is the programming listing for Moscow published in many newspapers, though sometimes only once a week. Again, the major national station is the first "program" **Оста́нкино**, which is broadcast throughout the Russian Federation and in most of the former republics; the second channel ("program") is general interest and aimed at Russians; the third channel is the educational channel; and the fourth channel is the St. Petersburg channel. Other channels address the local markets. For those with the right equipment, the BBC and CNN are also available. In large cities a significant number of apartment houses are fed by cables that extend from the roof antennae downward. The arrangement is such that many people can receive a wide range of programming, not all of which is of the highest moral fiber.

When relatively free television coverage first became available, it was the object of fascination for millions. Now state news programs show what the state wants shown, soap operas are all the rage, cheap American films are common, and lurid pornography is readily accessible. Television is waiting for economics and politics to settle down.

Periodicals
Перио́дика

Communications **связь**, (literally, "the tying together") is one more aspect of life whose essence has changed with the New World. One no longer lies awake at night with worry about spending large amounts of life in a camp **ла́герь** for writing deemed offensive to the State. Though not free in our sense of the word, publishers **изда́тели**, editors **реда́кторы**, and journalists **журнали́сты** now have much greater range in which to express an opinion. They can also go out of business: paper is very expensive and subscription prices rise even faster than inflation, which amounts to fewer and fewer subscribers. **Комсомо́льская Пра́вда**, a very popular newspaper, had only 3.4 million subscribers in 1993, a loss of nearly 74 percent since 1992 (*The New York Times*, Jan. 26, 1993, p. A4). Other losses were not this great, but, as the figure shows, some periodicals will not survive without subsidy.

The Ministry of Communication **Мини́-сте́рство Свя́зи** (**Минсвязь**) handles the distribution of periodicals **перио́дика**, not only delivery **доста́вка** but also subscription **подпи́ска** and sales **прода́жа**. Subscriptions are taken at the post office **Прие́м подписки** or at the newsstands formerly called **Союзпеча́ть**, and at work. Subscription lines form at post offices in September through November for the following year. ("I subscribed to the *Literary Gazette*" is **Я подписа́лась на литерату́рку**.)

Both mail and periodicals are delivered by the mail carrier **почтальо́н** every day except Sunday, so that "daily" **ежедне́вно** means five to six times a week. Because some periodicals are hard to get and therefore subject to theft, some people rent post office boxes **абонеме́нтные я́щики** at their local post office.

The newspaper
Газе́та

ежедне́вная   daily (newspaper)
еженеде́льная   weekly
ежеме́сячная   monthly

Most of the old national **центра́льные** newspapers are still publishing (though few are saying the same thing): **Пра́вда, Изве́стия, Труд, Комсомо́льская Правда, Моско́вские но́вости, Семья́, Сове́тская Росси́я**, and **Литерату́рная газе́та**, for example. Many new ones have appeared: **Аргуме́нты и фа́кты, Досье́ ЛГ, Соверше́нно секре́тно, Незави́симая газета, Коммерса́нт**, and **Мегаполис–экспресс**.

In addition, every city of any size has its own local newspapers **ме́стные газеты**:

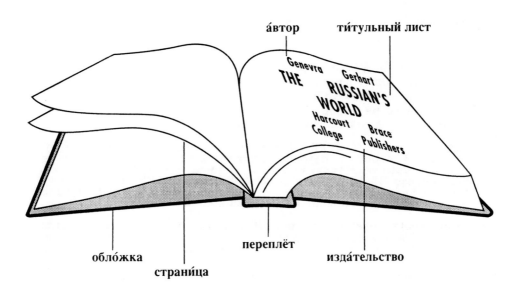

«Комсомольская правда»: для каждого своя!

Иван, дорогой читатель, мы доносим до очередной подписной кампании: на первое полугодие 1994 года. Никаких изменений сама процедура подписки не претерпела: талон, почтовое отделение, квитанция... Полные данные по подписке на нашу газету можно найти в каталоге «Известия» — он есть в почтовых отделениях.

Наши индексы:
50057 — «Комсомольская правда», включая субботний выпуск
50176 — «Комсомольская правда»—субботний выпуск
39800 — «Комсомольская правда», включая субботний выпуск [для читателей Москвы и Московской области].

Цена подписки без учета доставки для жителей России на полугодие:
50057 — 2202 рубля.
50176 — 600 рублей.
39800 — 1998 рублей.

Напоминаем, что подписка продлится два месяца — до 31 октября, но не стоит откладывать визит на почту до последнего дня, чтобы выстоять долгую очередь. Тем более что вы сможете выписать газету на оставшиеся до конца года месяцы — если еще не сделали этого — по старым ценам:
50057 — 150 рублей в месяц,
50176 — 48 рублей в месяц.
По всем вопросам звоните в редакцию — 257-70-09.

Subscription form: a newspaper helps out its readers, hoping for more of them.

Нижегоро́дские но́вости, Каза́нская пра́вда, and so forth, ad infinitum. Моско́вский Комсомо́лец has discovered the way to stay alive: its advertisement revenues keep it that way. Also, special-interest newspapers abound: Во́дный тра́нспорт, Кра́сная звезда́ (for the army), Медици́нская газе́та, and so forth.

Each publication has a five-digit number и́ндекс used for identification at subscription time. A catalogue of all available periodicals is kept at each post office.

Magazines
Журна́лы

Magazines are distributed the same way and also appeal to a broad range of human interests. Best known are the "fat" magazines то́лстые журна́лы where literature often sees the first light of day: Рома́н–газе́та, Москва́, Октя́брь, Нева́, Но́вый мир, Иностра́нная литерату́ра, Наш совреме́нник, Ю́ность, Звезда́, Молода́я гва́рдия. What interests us, of course, is not necessarily the names of these magazines, but rather that literature matters.

Books
Кни́ги

а́втор   ти́тульный лист

Genevra Gerhart
THE RUSSIAN'S WORLD
Harcourt College Brace Publishers

обло́жка   страни́ца   переплёт   изда́тельство

A handy squib at the back of books published in the Soviet era included the price цена́ and how many copies were printed тира́ж. (American publishers and writers will find the numbers unbelievably large.)

Another standard squib often at the beginning of the book describes the contents in addition to the price and publication numbers. (Current prices are now often listed as Цена́ догово́рная, which means any price agreed upon by the buyer and seller.)

Also at the *back* of Russian books is the table of contents Содержа́ние. An index указа́тель is, unfortunately, uncommon.

Russians are readers чита́тели, so books and their writers писа́тели are matters of moment, or were. Though the freedom to write is much greater now, writers suddenly have no walls to rail against—except perhaps publishers who must find paper enough for the printing and money enough for the paper. Books that sell now at high prices are pornography or business hints.

The use of libraries библиоте́ки has been everywhere encouraged, though the librarian библиоте́карь is used as a sieve through which all books must pass—that is, open shelves are not customary. Libraries come in all shapes and sizes from children's де́тские библиоте́ки, шко́льные библиоте́ки on up. One must first register at the library записа́ться в библиоте́ку, which requires only a passport (an internal passport is вну́тренний па́спорт). If the library has what you want, then it can be checked out with a library card формуля́р, which is actually a small booklet with your name (ФИО, фами́лия, и́мя, о́тчество), age во́зраст, and address а́дрес. Ten days is a usual time limit срок, and fines штра́фы are high if you lose a book. Libraries come in all sizes; the largest is the State Library in Moscow Госуда́рственная Библиоте́ка. Large university and technical libraries require a reader's card чита́тельский биле́т for access to reading rooms and to sections of books. (There was a time when only very reliable historians, for example, could get access to early editions of *Pravda* and *Izvestiya*.) The youngest user can start at age five at a local library by bringing a parent's passport. Many libraries have a reading room чита́льный зал, чита́льня where one can read books too much in demand to

ИВ № 4699

Василий Михайлович Песков

ВСЕ ЭТО БЫЛО...

Редакторы Л. Антипина, И. Аксенова
Художественный редактор Б. Федотов
Художник Ю. Боярский
Технический редактор З. Ахметова
Корректоры В. Назарова, Т. Крысанова

Сдано в набор 23.01.86. Подписано в печать 13.06.86. А07741. Формат 84×108¹/₃₂. Бумага типографская № 1. Гарнитура «Литературная». Печать высокая. Условн. печ. л. 17,64+1,68 вкл. Усл. кр.-отт. 19,74. Уч.-изд. л. 20,4. Тираж 150 000 экз. (50 001 — 150 000 экз.). Цена в переплете 95 коп. (100 000 экз.), цена в мягкой обложке 90 коп. (50 000 экз.). Заказ 2542.

Типография ордена Трудового Красного Знамени издательства ЦК ВЛКСМ «Молодая гвардия». Адрес издательства и типографии: 103030. Москва, К-30, Сущевская, 21.

release, in a location much more conducive to study than many living quarters.

Through a special network of stores, "Books by mail" **Кни́га – по́чтой**, it is possible to order a book COD **нало́женным платежо́м**. If the book is somehow elegant or otherwise desirable, however, it will not be available by this means.

One can also subscribe **подписа́ться** to a series of books **се́рия книг** or a collection of one author's works **собра́ние сочине́ний,** either at the post office or through one's work or at a bookstore. The problem in the past was to get access to the supply of books either through one's work or from friends. Now the supply is everywhere, but the money for it isn't.

To answer the demand, a few small book cooperatives have started publishing. The editing is poor, and the books are expensive and concentrate on murder mysteries **детекти́вы** or pornography **порногра́фия**.

Due to the persistent lack of good books **сто́йкий дефици́т на хоро́шие кни́ги**—or their expense—larger cities have developed the book "trade"; that is, you can trade **обменя́ть, вы́менять** one of your books for one you want, on the assumption that both are in shortage **дефици́т**. This trade can take place either at special counters **отде́лы** in bookstores **кни́жные магази́ны**, or at the public book market **кни́жный ры́нок** that meets weekly at places and times that are common knowledge in the locale. Of course, books in short supply can also be obtained at the market if you bring enough money with you.

TRANSLATIONS

a.   Dear Anna Petrovna (Warmly) wish you Happy Birthday (Anniversary, New Year's) wish you good health success in work (studies) happiness at home Yours Sidorovs

11

Transportation
Тра́нспорт

The vastness of their land has not been a deterrent to Russians. History, politics, and economics have encouraged and coerced them away from the family hearth. They are a traveling people, and huge distances do not seem to be an insurmountable obstacle. To the peasant it seems natural to go several hundred miles to a large city for major shopping. Contrast this with the stereotype of the English, who seem quite content to spend their entire lives in a small town. (Perhaps such opposite habits account for the wide variety of very strong English accents compared to the relative uniformity of Russian speech.)

Most transportation is accomplished via public means, but private transportation in the form of an automobile is no longer a luxury—though tending to the maintenance, not to mention the security, of a car can overwhelm all but the intrepid or relatively well-off. Traffic jams in downtown Moscow are normal rather than unusual. In the old days, a few large black cars would whisk through the streets and people would grumble about their leaders. Now many big black cars whisk through the streets and they grumble about the Mafia.

A section on traditional ways of getting around has been included for two reasons: (1) you will (if you have not already) come across many references in literature to various kinds of sleighs, carts, and carriages, not to mention the unique system the Russian has for hitching a horse to the vehicle it is pulling; and (2) though the section on traditional transportation describes practices that were common before industrialization, almost all the devices shown here are still being made and used in Russia, if only in the countryside. The pictures are contemporary.

Most of the chapter is devoted to contemporary means of transportation, including discussions of public urban transportation, the automobile, and other means for long-distance travel—trains, ships, and airplanes. The much briefer section on traditional means of transportation follows.

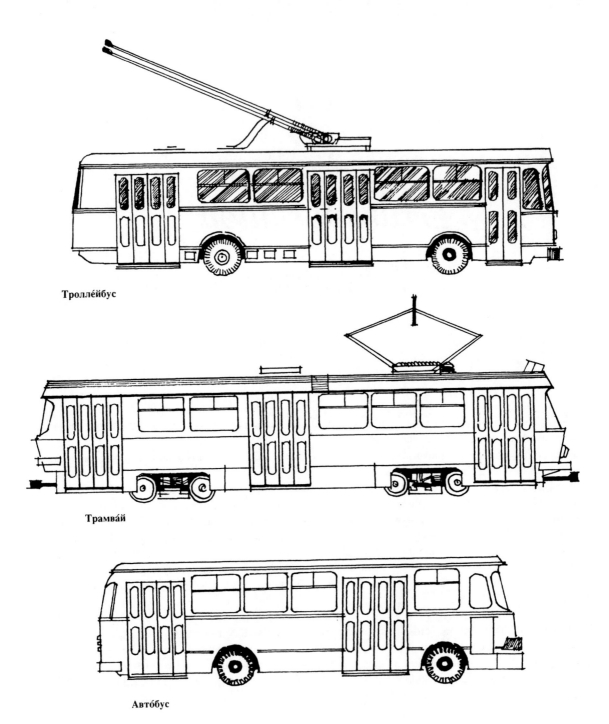

Троллéйбус

Трамвáй

Автóбус

PUBLIC TRANSPORTATION
Общественный транспорт

In Moscow it is quite common, during the daytime especially, to barely miss one bus, trolley, or trackless trolley and yet be able to see the next one coming a block away. This amount of public transportation seems very large to us, but it is still inadequate during rush-hour traffic **в часы пик**. The following is a paragraph from an article by **Гр. Горин** in **Литературная газета**, 15 **октября** 1969 г., making fun of the pushing and shoving required in boarding and riding:

А которые говорят, что в городе кругом давки да очереди, так те—не гуманисты. Я, например, многолюдье люблю... Я в пустой трамвай и не сяду. Что в пустом-то ехать? Уж лучше в такси. Там хоть с шофёром поговоришь за свои же деньги. А вот по утрам я на транспорте ездить люблю... Там тебя сожмут, стиснут, сдавят... Всё, думаешь, конец!... Ан, нет! Выкинут тебя на остановке, расправишь ты грудь, чувствуешь—жив! И такая радость на тебя находит, такое воодушевление... Чувствуешь, что горы своротить можешь! ...Садишься на трамвай и едешь в другую сторону.[a]

Like everywhere, of course, the further you are from major population centers, the harder it is to get from one place to another. Roads are frequently in poor condition, buses are obviously infrequent, and the train station can be miles away. Much greater use is made of trains, both suburban and interurban, than is our custom. However, they used to be relatively cheap but now are rather expensive.

Язык до Киева доведёт.
You can find your way to Kiev by asking.

Feel free to ask those who look as if they know their way around how to get to your destination, where schedules are, and so on. Have the place you are going written out in case your Russian fails you, and then simply ask. Following are some phrases you must have:

Как доехать до _____? How does one get to _____?

Какая следующая остановка? What's the next stop?

Вы сейчас выходите? Are you getting out now?

Разрешите пройти. May I get by, please?

The streetcar, trackless trolley, bus
Трамвай, троллейбус, автобус

Tickets **талоны** for the streetcar, trolley, and bus can be bought from the bus driver in ten-ticket lots, but it is much easier to buy a pass **проездной билет** for a day, a week, a month, or even longer, which gives you the right to get on any conveyance without further ado. For subway rides, one can buy individual tokens **жетоны**.

Maps showing central routes and stops are published for tourists. (Natives use more detailed maps, but these are not always available.) Routes **маршруты** are identified by numbers, but, more important, the stop **остановка** has a name—often the name of a cross street or a landmark—and also a sign indicating which vehicles stop there and how frequently they stop. Take into consideration that these stops are considerably farther apart (three to four Russian blocks) than you expect. Some conveyances have only a driver **водитель, шофёр** while some also have a conductor **кондуктор** (most are women). In the latter case you pay the conductor and keep the receipt, which may be checked by an inspector **контролёр**. When there is no conductor, which is the case most of the time, there will be a place on the side wall to punch **ком-**

Two "composted" bus tickets

пости́ровать the ticket. Often buses and trolleys are quite crowded, so reaching the device is impossible. The accepted thing is to pass a ticket forward and ask that it be punched for you «Пробе́йте, пожа́луйста» ("Punch it, please"); or «Переда́йте, пожа́луйста» "Pass it on, please." With time and luck on your side, the punched ticket will be returned to you. (Though it is not accepted behavior, students especially tend to think of riding without paying as a minor sport: «Он прое́хал за́йцем»—"He didn't pay for a ticket.")

Жето́н на метро́

The driver sometimes announces the names of the stops, but the likelihood that you will be able both to hear and understand is small enough that you should always be prepared to ask somebody for directions. You will find people very willing to help.

The subway[1]
Метро́

Entrance to the subway **метро́** is gained by placing a token **жето́н** in the turnstile **турнике́т** at the entrance. Getting around on the subway is less complicated than the above-ground methods because the system itself is simpler, and maps are easily obtainable. The major thing to remember is the name of the stop where you want to get off because each stop is listed on the direction signs as you walk through the marble halls. (The Moscow subway is as much a monument as it is a means of transportation.) The traveler should always have the name of the subway stop as part of a notebook address.

Taxis, minibuses
Такси́, маршру́тки

Taxis are a great convenience if you have the dollars to pay for them; otherwise you come after those who do. Identifiable by a black and white checkerboard pattern on the front doors, they can be hailed once found (if unoccupied). The taxi stand **стоя́нка такси́** exists, but it is not at all uncommon to see a line of people waiting there. Currently, and, one hopes, temporarily, taxis are considered a dangerous means of transportation by most of the population. They are also sometimes nowhere to be found. The best advice is to avoid being in such a rush that you are dependent on finding a taxi.

There is still another way to get around in the largest cities: **маршру́тное такси́ (маршру́тка)** uses minibuses **микроавто́бусы** to

1.   In referring to American subways and the English underground, Russians often use the word **подзе́мка** instead of **метро́**. Even **сабве́й** is sometimes applied to the American subway!

pick up people from a subway station or bus stop and then deliver them along their micro-routes. The fee is higher than for regular buses but much lower than for taxis.

AUTOMOBILES
Автомоби́ли

The formal term is **легково́й автомоби́ль**, but the word in standard speech is **маши́на**. They are expensive to buy and to maintain, but more and more people consider them worth it. Other means of locomotion include:

мотоци́кл   a motorcycle, especially popular in the countryside

мотоци́кл с коля́ской   a motorcycle with a sidecar

мотоколя́ска   a motorized wheelchair

мопе́д (педа́льный мотоци́кл)   a Moped

мотро́ллер   a motor scooter

So many people have cars these days that some are actually driving to work. Sensible owners leave the machine in a parking lot **стоя́нка** during the winter. Cars are hard to start at 20° C. below, anyway.

To drive a car is **води́ть маши́ну**. "I've been driving for ten years" is **Я уже́ де́сять лет вожу́ маши́ну**. A driver's licence is a **води́тельские права́**. Various makes **ма́рки** of cars, in ascending order, follow:

Запоро́жец   a very small car, resembling a Fiat, made in Ukraine; discontinued

Москви́ч   the most common private passenger car

Жигули́, Ла́да   a car produced at the Fiat factory at Togliatti **Толья́тти**

Во́лга   a bigger, roomier model, often used as a taxi

Ча́йка   a seven-passenger car that is elegant but newer than the **ЗИЛ**

ЗИЛ   a large model and the ultimate in respectability and elegance

All of them also have model numbers that might be familiar to small children and professional drivers: **Во́лга** 24, 99; **Москви́ч** 407, 412, 414.

Especially in the countryside, road conditions during the spring and fall require vehicles that can manage essentially without roads. This niche is filled by the **га́зик** (built by **Го́рьковский автомоби́льный заво́д**), which strongly resembles what we call a jeep.

Parts of the automobile
Ча́сти автомоби́ля

Outside the automobile
Автомоби́ль снару́жи

крыло́   fender

капо́т   hood

ба́мпер, бу́фер   bumper

облицо́вка   grill

фа́ра   headlight

указа́тель поворо́та   turn signal

две́рца   door

окно́, стекло́   window

ветрово́е стекло́   windshield

стеклоочисти́тель   windshield wiper (*informal* **дво́рник**)

фо́рточка   wing window

крыша   roof

колесо́   wheel

ши́на, автопокры́шка   tire

о́бод   rim (of wheel) (*pl.* **обо́дья**)

ка́мера   inner tube

номерно́й зна́к   license plate

но́мер (автомоби́ля)   license plate number

Inside the automobile
Внутри́ автомоби́ля

дви́гатель   engine

по́ршень   piston

кла́пан   valve

цили́ндр   cylinder

блок цили́ндров   cylinder block

голо́вка цили́ндров   cylinder head

карбюра́тор   carburetor

аккумуля́тор, батаре́я   battery

распредели́тель   distributor

переда́ча   transmission

карда́нный вал   drive shaft

ось   axle

дифференциа́л   differential

радиа́тор   radiator

вентиля́тор   fan

реме́нь вентиля́тора   fan belt

глуши́тель   muffler

выхлопна́я труба́   exhaust (pipe)

амортиза́тор   shock absorber

бензоба́к   gas tank

бензи́н   gasoline

ма́сло   oil

то́рмоз   brake

тормозно́й бараба́н   brake drum

тормозна́я жи́дкость   brake fluid

запа́льная свеча́   spark plug

On the dashboard
На щитке́

замо́к зажига́ния   ignition

спидо́метр   speedometer

указа́тель давле́ния ма́сла   oil gauge

термо́метр систе́мы охлажде́ния   temperature gauge

переключа́тель све́та   headlight switch

включа́тель стеклоочисти́теля   windshield wiper switch

кно́пка возду́шной засло́нки карбюра́тора   choke

контро́льная ла́мпочка генера́тора   generator indicator light

переключа́тель освеще́ния каби́ны   inside light switch

вещево́й я́щик   glove compartment (*coll.* бардачо́к—mess or whorehouse)

указа́тель у́ровня бензи́на   gas indicator

Below the dashboard or on the floor
Под щитко́м и́ли на полу́

ручно́й то́рмоз   emergency or hand brake

акселера́тор   accelerator

руль   steering wheel

рулева́я коло́нка   steering column

кно́пка, кольцо́ (звуково́го) сигна́ла   horn

рыча́г переме́ны скоросте́й, переключа́тель скоросте́й   gearshift

педа́ль сцепле́ния   clutch

педа́ль (гидравли́ческого) то́рмоза   foot brake

сиде́нье   seat

бага́жник   trunk (**бага́жник на кры́ше**: roof rack)

Spare parts **запасны́е ча́сти** are expensive and repair prices are so high that one must still disattach the windshield wipers whenever they are not in use.

Trucks
Грузовы́е автомоби́ли

In everyday speech a truck is a **грузови́к**; in official language it is a **грузово́й автомоби́ль**. Trucks are distinguished (usually among specialists) by the factories that make them and a model number: **ГАЗ-56, ЗИЛ-157 (Заво́д и́мени Лихачёва), УАЗ (Улья́новский автомоби́льный заво́д)**. The same is true for buses. Truck parts include a cab **каби́на** and load carrier **ку́зов**. Trucks and buses have their license number painted in very large figures across the back of the vehicle. (Four numbers plus three letters means the vehicle is owned by an institution; with letters on both sides of the number, it's privately owned.) The several kinds of trucks, trailers, and tractors include those on the next page.

Пика́п

фурго́н   a van

пика́п   anything from a station wagon (!) to a minibus **микроавто́бус**

самосва́л   a dump truck

автопо́езд   a combination truck

прице́п   a trailer

тяга́ч   a tractor used on highways with trailers

тяга́ч с полуприце́пом   a tractor-trailer, a tractor with a semi-trailer

тра́ктор   a tractor, used mostly for pulling farm equipment

колёсный тра́ктор   tractor with wheels

гу́сеничный тра́ктор   a caterpillar tractor

Teamsters follow an interesting practice. For the safety gained in numbers, trucks transporting goods often form a caravan **эшело́н**. These can be a challenge to the lone driver, especially when roads are mainly two-way, two-lane affairs.

For drivers
Для води́телей

Different countries have varying driving styles—regardless of the rules and regulations that are imposed from above. (If you are planning to drive in Russia, you should find out which apply at the time you are going. The rules change from time to time.) Driving "style" in this discussion refers to the manner and degree to which the people choose to obey or, to some extent, disobey those rules and regulations. In Paris, for example, driving is a sport and bluffing is a major play. In Moscow, however, driving is less formal than a sport and is more a game. The cars are toys, while pedestrians and other cars are not necessarily obstacles—timid drivers should not drive. Making a mistake and hitting something is a very serious affair, however, and the laws and their penalties are very much harsher than are ours. If police officers see you make an illegal turn, for example, they will fine you on the spot. You will be released if you pay. (This system obviously invites abuses.)

Russian pedestrians seem to follow two principles: (1) "every man for himself," and (2) go across if you can get across. As a driver you must expect pedestrians not to pay attention to details like momentum, not to mention traffic lights **светофо́ры**.

In cities, drivers at night sometimes use only parking lights, turning on the regular headlights only as a final warning in place of a horn signal, which is illegal except in emergencies.

Roads are not well marked. At a junction you must often choose the largest, widest paved road as the most likely place to continue. Nor are they well maintained; choose a vehicle with strong springs.

For pedestrians
Для пешехо́дов

You must assume that cars always have the right of way. This may seem an exaggeration, but it is not. You should act as if it were true, especially when you are alone on a street corner waiting to cross or when you are the front runner in a group. As a pedestrian **пешехо́д** you do have some advantages: downtown sidewalks are often very crowded, and you do get some protection in numbers. Another advantage built into the system is the underpass **перехо́д** for pedestrian use. (**Перехо́д** is also equivalent to our "Cross here" signs.) Sometimes these are so located as to be obvious, even unavoidable, but often they are built as part of subway entrances and exits so that their existence is far less obvious. As a general rule, on a busy downtown street, do not try crossing unless you see other people going the same way you want to go.

Gas stations
Бензоколо́нка, запра́вочная ста́нция

Gas is obtained from a gas pump **бензоколо́нка** located at a gas "station" **запра́вочная ста́нция, запра́вка**. These terms are used interchangeably because gasoline (and perhaps oil) is all that is available. Repair facilities **ста́нции техни́ческого обслу́живания** exist, but they are much less frequent than are the gas stations, and Russian car owners tend to avoid them by doing the repairs themselves or consulting knowledgeable friends. Getting gasoline **бензи́н**

is not an easy affair; the wait in line for gas can take hours and seem interminable. The gas stations themselves are infrequent enough to force planning on the most improvident driver. (Those who are willing to pay much more for their gasoline can get it from private distributors without waiting.) A much lower octane gas is used by Russian cars, so tourists with Western cars are given special coupons that allow them the privilege of buying higher octane gas at certain gas stations. You pay for your gas first, then pump it yourself.

Газу́й!   Step on it!

Запра́вьте маши́ну бензи́ном!   Fill'er up! (An expression you can only use toward a person hired for the purpose of getting the gas for you. Service stations don't have attendants.)

Мне на́до запра́виться.   I need to get some gas.

Hitchhiking
«Голосова́ние», автосто́п

Hitching a ride is a common practice, especially outside cities where public transportation is inadequate (though it used to be practiced widely within cities). The process merely requires standing at the side of the road with an arm raised above the head, whence the name **голосова́ть**, "to vote." **«Нахо́дка»** by **В. Тендряко́в** contains the following passage: **«Трофи́м проголосова́л и прое́хал по большаку́ до поворо́та на Копно́вку, а там—руко́й пода́ть.»** ("Trofim caught a ride and went along the main road as far as the turn to Kopnovka. From there it was just a short distance.")

Hitchhiking is not reserved for the young and the poor; it is used by anyone in need of a ride. The driver expects payment. In cities, agree on a price ahead of time if you feel confident enough to use this form of transportation at all. (It is currently considered dangerous in major cities.)

Пешехо́дный перехо́д. The pedestrian underpass, indicated by the sign on the right-hand side of this pole, can save your life.

Gas stations are not always obvious.

Road signs[b]
Доро́жные зна́ки

The Russians use the same system for traffic signs as is used in Western Europe, so that little or no literacy in any language is required to be able to "read" them. Of considerable help in distinguishing these signs are the different shapes and colors used for different categories of signs. These are by no means all possible types of signs, but one may extrapolate the rest from these.

Warning signs **Предупрежда́ющие зна́ки** are triangular with an orange red border, white background, and black figures. They indicate conditions the driver should watch for—slippery roads and the like.

Right-of-way signs **Зна́ки приорите́та** come in all shapes.

Prohibiting signs **Запреща́ющие зна́ки** are round, and most of them use the same colors as the warning signs. As their title states, these signs describe what one cannot do. The most critical is the "Do not enter" sign, III.1.

(I) ДОРОЖНЫЕ ЗНАКИ
ПРЕДУПРЕЖДАЮЩИЕ ЗНАКИ

 Железнодорожный переезд со шлагбаумом (1)

 Железнодорожный переезд без шлагбаума (2)

 Пересечение с трамвайной линией (3)

 Пересечение равнозначных дорог (4)

 Пересечение с круговым движением (5)

 Светофорное регулирование (6)

 Разводной мост (7)

 Выезд на набережную (8)

 Опасные повороты (9)

 Крутой спуск (10)

 Крутой подъем (11)

 Скользкая дорога (12)

 Неровная дорога (13)

 Выброс гравия (14)

 Сужение дороги (15)

 Двустороннее движение (16)

 Пешеходный переход (17)

 Дети (18)

 Пересечение с велосипедной дорожкой (19)

 Дорожные работы (20)

 Перегон скота (21)

 Дикие животные (22)

 Падение камней (23)

 Боковой ветер (24)

 Низколетящие самолеты (25)

 Тоннель (26)

 Прочие опасности (27)

(II) ЗНАКИ ПРИОРИТЕТА

 Главная дорога (1)

 Пересечение со второстепенной дорогой (2)

 Уступите дорогу (3)

 Преимущество перед встречным движением (4)

 Движение без остановки запрещено (5)

Преимущество встречного движения (6)

Notice also that a prohibition is often indicated by a diagonal slash through the sign; thus, III.9 means "No parking."

Limiting signs **Предпи́сывающие зна́ки** have blue backgrounds and white figures. They describe the only way something can be done: IV.1 directs that you can go only straight ahead and the next that you can turn only right.

Informational signs **Указа́тельные зна́ки** are square with a blue background; they let you know what you can do or what facilities are available: V.1 indicates a bus or trolley stop,

and V.2 indicates a tram stop. (Both are useful signs for the ambulatory traveler.) The underground crossing sign V.6 is particularly useful.

Services signs **Зна́ки се́рвиса** are what they say they are, except perhaps for VI.6, the State police of Russia. One drives slowly by their roadside stations, which carry this sign. And one pulls over, if so instructed.

The remaining signs are included for their usefulness.

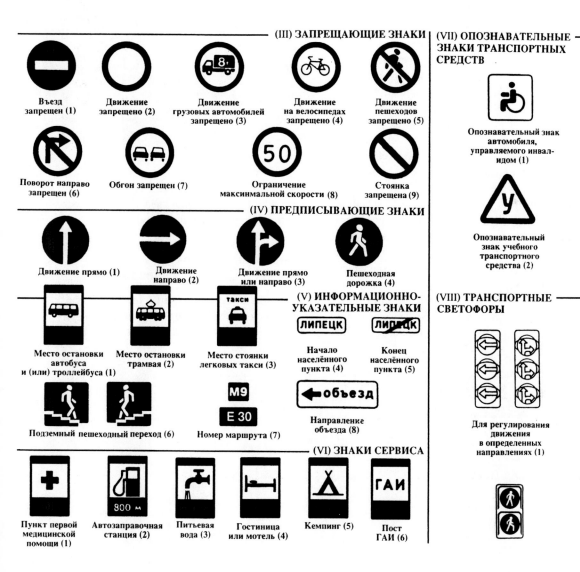

TRAINS
Поезда́

The train **по́езд** is the most common method for long-distance travel **по́езд да́льнего сле́дования**. Buses make such trips, but they are less often resorted to because of poor road conditions, especially in the spring and fall. Suburban trains **при́городные поезда́** are also widely used.

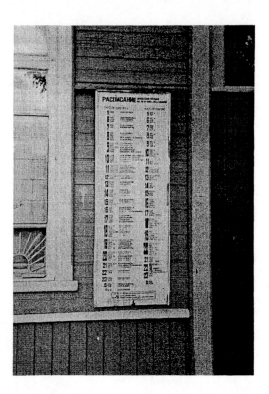

Suburban trains
При́городные поезда́

Major cities usually are the center of a network of suburban trains **при́городные поезда́** (called **электри́чка** in everyday life). They leave from a terminal **вокза́л** in a city, stopping at stations **ста́нции** on their way. Access is relatively simple. Usually, only one class of tickets is available, the so-called hard class **жёсткие (сиде́нья)**, in reference to the wooden seats. Tickets **биле́ты** are obtained either from a cashier **в ка́ссе** or from a slot machine **автома́т**, where care must be taken to put in the right amount of money for the length of trip you are taking. A schedule **расписа́ние** is posted—though they are sometimes out of date—and the only other worry is to ascertain which one of the tracks **пути́** the train leaves from. (In Russian one worries about which platform, **платфо́рма** or **перро́н**, to stand on. **«От како́й платфо́рмы отхо́дит по́езд?» «С како́го пути́ отхо́дит по́езд?»**) Tickets are not taken at the gate or door; in fact they are often not checked at all on local trains. But you had better have your ticket with you when the ticket checker **контролёр** does come around.

Long-distance trains
Поезда́ да́льнего сле́дования

More forethought is required for longer trips. Tickets can often be bought not only at the terminal but also at downtown central ticket

СЖД	АСУ "ЭКСПРЕСС"	ПРОЕЗДНОЙ ДОКУМЕНТ		Ц	52811

Can you tell who went where on which train on which car and how much it cost?

offices in advance. The two basic kinds of passenger space on a Russian train are coach and compartment, with dining facilities available for both. It is possible to check one's baggage **багаж** in the baggage car, but no thinking person would consider doing so.

Kinds of railroad cars
Разные вагóны

The least expensive way to go is seated **сидя́чие места́** in a coach car **в óбщем вагóне**. But distances are great and trains are not speedy, so a place to lie down can be very important. Here the barrack-like **плацка́ртный вагон** offers a reserved space to lie down, and one can rent bed linens and blankets. Next up the scale are the compartment cars **купéйные вагóны** that house four people who also rent bedding from the conductor **проводни́ца**. At the top are the sleeping cars **спа́льный вагон** (also called **СВ, эс-вэ**) whose compartments house only two or three people; they are not available on all trains. To the delight of some and dismay of others, the Russians make no attempt to separate the sexes in any train. (Males obligingly offer to leave so that the females can change; or some females simply plan on sleeping in their day clothes.)

Eating on trains
Пита́ние в пóезде

For eating while traveling, you may take advantage of the dining car **вагóн-рестора́н** or a sort of snack bar **буфéт** offering candy, sandwiches, wines, and so forth. Tea also is generally made available from a hot-water heater **тита́н** attended by the **проводни́ца**. You will find that most people eat what they have brought along with them for the trip. (You should carry at least a small amount of food with you on any longer trip.) When their own provisions give out, they buy food (meat pies, cucumbers, berries, and so on) at the train stops along the way. As a result, when a long-distance train stops for only a short while at a station, a crush of people develops—first trying to get off to be the first in line to buy food, and then scrambling to return to the train before it leaves the station.

You should also expect trains to be relatively slow, though usually on time.

On long-distance trains you might notice a wooden barrier **щиты́** or tree plantings **лесны́е поса́дки** that parallel the railroad tracks for many miles. Their purpose is to keep wind-driven winter snow from banking on the tracks.

SHIPS
Суда́

A respectable Russian geography book will explain the engineering feats being accomplished in and around the water now. Inland, the canals that unite various river systems, often with locks **шлю́зы**, are among the marvels that used to consume quantities of ink in the press.

Equal amounts of ink were spent in describing the dams **плоти́ны** that are significant in making rivers navigable, not to mention the hydroelectric power they provide: **Бра́тская ГЭС (Гидроэлектроста́нция), Вóлжская ГЭС, Цимля́нская ГЭС, Гóрьковская ГЭС.**

The river fleet
Речнóй флот

The rivers freeze over during the winter, but during the summer they form an avenue for vacations. A major boat passenger terminal is a **речнóй вокза́л**.

Мнóгие туристи́ческие маршру́ты начина́ются от Москвы́—от речнóго вокза́ла Хи́мки. Нóвые речны́е вокза́лы в Ни́жнем Нóвгороде, Каза́ни, Улья́новске и Осетрóве. Мéжду Москвóй и А́страханью пла́вает трёхпалубный ди́зель–электрохóд «Лéнин»—фла́гман речнóго флóта, котóрый рассчи́тан на перевóзку 439 **пасажи́ров.**[c]

Kinds of ships
Виды судов

Perhaps the most common word for ship is **пароход**, which refers to a ship with a steam engine; **теплоход**, technically a ship with an internal-combustion engine, is used almost interchangeably. Less frequent by far is the **электроход**, a ship powered by electricity. Of considerable popularity on inland waterways is the hydrofoil **ракета**: «Ракета—это теплоход (или судно) на подводных крыльях.» The names for kinds of ships are often acronyms:

линкор (линейный корабль) battleship

авианосец airplane carrier

миноносец torpedo boat

эсминец (эскадренный миноносец) destroyer

катер cutter, a yacht

подлодка (подводная лодка) submarine

крейсер cruiser (**Крейсер «Аврора»**)

паром ferry

плот raft

Other terms for ship include: **судно** (*pl.*, **суда**) a businesslike but very common term often applied but not limited to ships that operate on the open sea; **грузовое судно**, a freighter; and **корабль**, a somewhat more highflown, even poetic, term often applied to large naval vessels.

«Иван Франко»—один из серии пассажирских лайнеров торгового флота. На нём более 300 кают для 750 пассажиров. Скорость хода лайнера—20 узлов.[d]

Other ships are frequently mentioned in the press: **танкер** and **пассажирский лайнер** are obvious; an icebreaker **ледокол** is required to keep the northern passage (north of Siberia) open as long as possible; **буксир** is a tugboat (or **толкач**, when it pushes instead of pulls).

Boats
Лодки

Those who live near or work on the water, of course, also require boats **лодки**. Among the smaller craft are the rowboat **гребная лодка**, sailboat **парусная лодка**, and motorboat **моторная лодка**.

Boats using oars **вёсла** (*sg.* **весло**) include a rubber raft **резиновая (надувная) лодка**, a kayak **байдарка**, and a canoe **каноэ**. **Чёлн** was originally a small dugout (not necessarily in the shape of a canoe) used mostly for hunting and fishing; **ял**, **ялик** is a wide, large rowboat with one to three pairs of oars; a lifeboat **спасательная лодка** would be a kind of **ял**. **Шлюпка** is a small boat that can be rowed or sailed, but the common pleasure sailboat is a **яхта**. Those who sail in the winter (on ice) use an iceboat **буер**. **Моторная лодка** can be any small boat with a motor attached, but **катер** is in the shape of our typical motorboat.

AIRPLANES
Самолёты

Civil aviation was controlled by **Аэрофлот**. That agency flew airplanes **самолёты**, also obsoletely referred to as **аэропланы**, and poetically described as **воздушные корабли**. (A jet airplane is a **реактивный самолёт**; a helicopter is a **вертолёт**.) Airplanes land and take off from a landing field **аэродром** and are stored in **ангары**, both of which would be located at an airport **аэропорт**. They are flown by **лётчики**, and passengers **пассажиры** are attended by a **стюардесса**, **бортпроводница**. Press reports indicate that air travel between former republics can be unnerving, mostly because of passengers who ignore carry-on limits. Salespeople carry their goods with them. Airport facilities and services have yet to reach the level of adequate.

Airplanes are named after their principal designer, the most famous of whom is **Туполев**.

хвостова́я часть (1)

носова́я часть (2)

реакти́вный дви́гатель (3)

(1) tail
(2) nose
(3) jet engine
(4) landing gear
(5) fuselage
(6) wing

шасси́ (4)

крыло́ (6)

фюзеля́ж (5)

Also: возду́шный винт (propeller)

TRADITIONAL TRANSPORTATION
Традицио́нный тра́нспорт

Hitching a horse
Упря́жка ло́шади

The horse was formerly responsible for almost all transportation. It was so important to the Russian that the number of horses a person owned was an indication of wealth. The Russian's way of hitching the horse was distinctive. The horse collar **хому́т** does not look markedly different from ours, but it was connected to the **дуга́** (that arched piece of wood rising over the horse's shoulders found in any picture of a Russian horse pulling something), which linked the collar, **хому́т** to the shafts **огло́бли**. But the arch **дуга́** was also decorative in that it was often gaily painted and trimmed with bells **колоко́льчики**. The collar, arch, and shafts were all connected by a loop **гуж** attached to the collar, and it is this loop that has supplied the name for horse- (or animal-) drawn vehicles, **гужево́й тра́нспорт**.

Взя́лся за гуж, не говори́, что не дюж.
Don't start something unless you intend to finish it (**дюж** equates to **си́льный**).[2]

At the other end, the **огло́бли** were connected directly to the axle **ось** so that, in effect, the shafts both pulled and steered. Another way

2. Literally, "You took hold of [that loop], don't complain that it's not strong enough."

The horse collar **хому́т** has a leather strap **гу́ж** on both sides, which connects both the arch **дуга́** and the shafts **огло́бли**.

of hitching horses, **дышлова́я упря́жка**, is now commonly used when two horses side by side are needed. This method, of Ukrainian rather than Russian origin, involves a single shaft **ды́шло** that goes between the two horses. No arch is used.

The most common arrangement of horses **упря́жка** was one horse to a wagon or sleigh, but the most popular was the troika **тро́йка**, three horses side by side. The direction the wagon was to take was determined by the center horse **коренни́к**, because it carried the **хому́т–дуга́–огло́бли**. The outside horses **пристяжны́е**, connected by straps, only helped pull. These outside horses had to work under conditions that we would consider inhumane. Almost any picture of a troika in action will show them with their heads turned to the side. This occurred because, in addition to the two reins **во́жжи** attached to the center horse, a single rein on each side connected the other horses' bits on the outside; the driver pulled on these outside reins, forcing the two horses to turn their heads as they ran. This was done because the Russians thought the horses looked elegant running that way. (They still think so.)

Wagons and sleighs
Пово́зки и са́ни

Horses pulled several kinds of devices. When poor road conditions prevailed, either on moun-

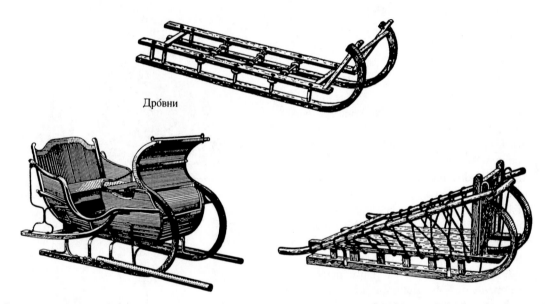

Дро́вни

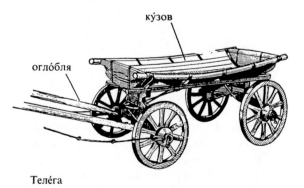

Са́ни легковы́е одноко́нные
This is a contemporary sleigh very similar to the most common sleigh for travel вы́ездны́е са́ни *that was used both in and between cities.*

Ро́звальни *is a traditional type of sleigh still widely used.*

ку́зов

огло́бля

Теле́га

Дро́жки

tainous paths or during the spring and fall "roadlessness" **бездоро́жье**, the horses themselves might carry the load: **вью́чный тра́нспорт, вью́чная ло́шадь. Волоку́ша,** the simplest device to be pulled, consisted merely of **огло́бли,** to which a load was attached toward the bottom end with the ends of the shafts dragging along the ground. (This arrangement is similar to the travois used by American Plains Indians.)

Sleighs **са́ни** supplied transportation for much of the year. The simplest kind of sleigh, the **дро́вни,** consisted of nothing but a long, narrow skeleton platform on runners **поло́зья** and served principally for hauling wood, a major winter occupation for the Russian peasant. Another traditional peasant type of sleigh, the **ро́звальни,** is still in use today and is considered the most convenient. The side rails **гря́дки** of this sleigh are much closer to each other at the front end than they are at the back. They serve not only to help form the top rim but also to keep the sleigh from turning over when cornering—a fast turn is especially subject to spills. Many Russian sleighs have similar rails for just that purpose. A child's sled is now **са́нки; сала́зки** is old-fashioned.

The general term for a vehicle for carrying either goods or people is **пово́зка. Теле́га** refers especially to peasant carts to accomplish this purpose. The two-wheeled cart **двуко́лка** was used as a last resort when the spring and fall "roadlessness" set in.

The many varieties of light, four-wheel carriages **экипа́жи,** principally for carrying two to four people, include the **таранта́с, проле́тка,** and **дро́жки.** The **каре́та** was a type of carriage **экипа́ж** completely enclosed and essentially reserved, for economic reasons, for those both highborn and rich. **Киби́тка** was any covered **пово́зка,** strongly resembling our covered wagon, though often much smaller and consisting of leather or cloth stretched over a frame.

The drivers
Ку́чер, изво́зчик, ямщи́к

The people whose lives were principally

involved in driving these vehicles had various titles: **ку́чер, изво́зчик, ямщи́к.** The **ку́чер** was hired for his services as a driver, while the **изво́зчик** was hired both for his services and for those of his vehicle. The **ямщи́к** was one who drove on a regular route **тракт** between two places that were part of a nationwide stage system. This **ямщи́к** was the driver who has been immortalized in countless songs and poems. Here are four verses of a very famous poem, «**Зи́мняя доро́га**» by **Пу́шкин:**

> **Сквозь волни́стые тума́ны**
> **Пробира́ется луна́,**
> **На печа́льные поля́ны**
> **Льёт печа́льный свет она́.**
>
> **По доро́ге зи́мней, ску́чной**
> **Тро́йка бо́рзая бежи́т,**
> **Колоко́льчик однозву́чный**
> **Утоми́тельно греми́т.**
>
> **Что-то слы́шится родно́е**
> **В до́лгих пе́снях ямщика́**
> **То разгу́лье удало́е,**
> **То серде́чная тоска́. . .**
>
> **Ни огня́, ни чёрной ха́ты,**
> **Глушь и снег. . . Навстре́чу мне**
> **То́лько вёрсты полоса́ты**
> **Попада́ются одне́.**[e]

Riding on water
Речно́й тра́нспорт

The early (before 1850) Russian small boat **ло́дка** was a dugout **долблёная ло́дка** formed from a single log. Later, when whole logs were less accessible, the boats were made from boards and more variety in shape appeared: **плоскодо́нка** was a flat-bottom boat. Traditionally, these small boats were pointed at both ends.

Russia's immense spaces required the full use of all routes of transportation, including the major rivers for shipping. Peter the Great saw the problem and started the building of canals to unite major riverways flowing north and south, but it was not until after he died that a connection was achieved between the Neva **Нева́** in the north and the Volga **Во́лга** in the south. Before the advent of the steamboat, sails **паруса́** supplied some of the power, but the Volga boatmen are more familiar to us as the Russian contribution to river transport. Men who could find no other work became "boatmen" **бурлаки́**, those who pulled the barges **ба́ржи** and ships **суда́** upstream from towpaths along the shore. These men inspired a very famous painting by Repin entitled **Бурлаки́**; they also supplied the world with the "Song of the Volga Boatmen":

Эй, у́хнем! Эй, у́хнем!
Ещё ра́зик, ещё раз!
Разовьём мы березу́,
Разовьём мы кудряву́,
Ай да, да, ай да,
Ай да, да, ай да,
Разовьём мы кудряву.[f]

Volga "boatmen" **бурлаки́** were not romantic figures, nor were they on boats.

TRANSLATIONS

a. Those who say that the city is nothing but shoving and long lines are just not humanitarians. I, for instance, love crowds. . . . I won't get on an empty trolley. Why ride in an empty trolley? Might as well take a taxi. There you can at least talk to the chauffeur for your money. I love to ride public transportation in the mornings. . . . There you can get squashed, squeezed, crushed. . . . "It's all over, that's the end," you think. But no! They throw you out at your stop, you straighten up, and you feel . . . you're still alive! Such a joy comes over you, such enthusiasm. . . . You feel you can move mountains!. . . You get on the trolley and go in the opposite direction.

b. **I. Warning signs**
1 Railroad crossing with barrier; 2 Railroad crossing without barrier; 3 Tramline/Streetcar crossing; 4 Intersection; 5 Traffic circle; 6 Traffic light; 7 Drawbridge; 8 Shore ahead; 9 Dangerous turn; 10 Steep incline; 11 Steep hill; 12 Slippery road; 13 Uneven road; 14 Gravel on road; 15 Road narrows; 16 Two-way traffic; 17 Pedestrian crossing; 18 Children at play; 19 Bicycle path crossing; 20 Road work; 21 Cattle crossing; 22 Wild animals; 23 Loose rocks; 24 Side wind; 25 Low flying aircraft; 26 Tunnel; 27 Other danger

II. Right-of-way signs
1 Arterial; 2 Secondary road crossing; 3 Yield; 4 Oncoming traffic must cede right-of-way; 5 Stop; 6 Oncoming traffic has right-of-way

III. Prohibiting signs
1 No entrance (one-way street); 2 No traffic; 3 No truck traffic; 4 No bicycle traffic; 5 No pedestrian traffic; 6 No right turn; 7 No passing; 8 Speed limit; 9 No parking

IV. Limiting signs
1 No turns; 2 Traffic to right only; 3 Traffic straight ahead or to right only; 4 Pedestrian path only

V. Informational signs
1 Bus or trolley stop; 2 Streetcar/tram stop; 3 Taxi stand; 4 You are entering . . . (slow down); 5 You are leaving . . . ; 6 Underground (street)

crossing; 7 Highway route numbers; 8 Detour

VI.   Service signs
1 First aid station; 2 Gas; 3 Potable water; 4 Hotel or motel; 5 Campgrounds; 6 State police Госуда́рственная авто-инспе́кция

VII.   Recognition signs
1 Handicapped driver; 2 Student driver

VIII.   Stoplights
1 Stoplights regulating the direction of traffic; 2 Pedestrian crossing light

c.   Many tourist itineraries begin at Moscow—from the Khimki River Terminal. There are new river terminals in Gorkiy, Kazan, Ulyanovsk, and Osetrov. The three-decker, diesel electric ship *Lenin* sails between Moscow and Astrakhan. It is the flagship of the river fleet and is designed for 439 passengers.

d.   The *Ivan Franko* is one in a series of passenger liners in the USSR commercial fleet. It has more than 300 cabins for 750 passengers. The speed of the liner is 20 knots.

e.   The moon breaks
Through the billowing fog,
Pouring [its] sad light
On the sad fields.
Along the tedious winter road
A swift troika runs,
Its monotonous sleighbell
Rings on wearisomely.
Something sounds of home
In the driver's long songs,
Now [songs of] abandon,
And revelry . . .
Then heartfelt melancholy.
Neither a light nor dark hut,
Silence and snow in front of me [facing me] . . .
Only striped roadmarkers
Appear one after another.

f.   Yo, heave ho! Yo, heave ho!
Once again, once again!
We will uncurl the birch tree,
We will uncurl the curly one . . .

12

Education

Образова́ние

За одного́ би́того двух неби́тых даю́т.
An experienced person is worth two inexperienced ones.[1]

Мно́го бу́дешь знать, ско́ро соста́ришься.
If you know too much, you'll get old quicker.

For the Soviet government mass education was a major priority and a major accomplishment. Schools and universities were not only free, but college students also received stipends. The pressure for education came not only from the government, which wanted and needed qualified workers, but also from the Russians themselves. Back-to-school day, the first of September, was (and remains) almost a national holiday. This support for education is rooted in the traditional respect accorded scholars and learning by the upper classes (as in Western Europe).

But recently, the acceptance of capitalism has vitiated the rewards of education somewhat—young people want to get out into the real world and make some real money, a prospect not formerly open to them. Parents who value education look on in sadness as their children seem eager to study accounting, computers, and English, yet less willing to engage in the arts and sciences, never mind a life in poverty. (Is this a society in which the parents are the idealists?)

The regard for education, at least in the upper classes, predates the Revolution. The Academy of Sciences, for instance, was founded by Peter the Great in 1724. Before the Revolution, Russia had the

---

1. Education and experience are here combined: teaching methods involved heavy use of the stick.

full range of schools, from primary schools to technical institutes and universities; it was, after all, possible for a Lomonosov (1711–1765), born of a peasant family in a fishing village in the far north, to become one of the great scholars of history. He was, however, a genius; and though Russia has had room for genius, it was not a fruitful breeding ground for the more commonplace competence. The framework of educational institutions existed but was not filled out with the muscle of the masses, partially because money and sometimes nobility were required for advanced education, and partially because education was not part of the lower-class mystique. The following quotations demonstrate several things at once: (1) the 1897 census revealed considerable illiteracy, (2) the Soviets chose figures that put the Old Regime in the darkest possible light (but that could be expected), and (3) one must pay great attention to modifiers in Soviet statistics if one assumes they are accurate in the first place.

По да́нным пе́реписи 1897 г., в Росси́и бы́ло гра́мотных мужчи́н 29,3%, же́нщин 13,1%; в э́то же вре́мя гра́мотных мужчи́н-рабо́чих было 59,9%, же́нщин-рабо́тниц 34,9%.[a]

По да́нным пе́реписи 1897 г., да́же в Европе́йской ча́сти на 1000 челове́к приходи́лось гра́мотных: мужчи́н—227, же́нщин—117.[b]

Before the Revolution, many groups had set up two- to four-year courses in the rudiments of learning, including the local government school **зе́мская шко́ла** and the church parish school **церко́вно-приходска́я шко́ла**. The real problem came with secondary education. That began at about the age of ten in a gymnasium (**класси́ческая**) **гимна́зия**, where classes concentrated on a classical (both Latin and Greek) education, or in a technical school **реа́льное учи́лище**. Nobility was not required for most of these schools but money usually was. And because most peasants needed the labor their children could provide, they were rarely sent to school even when it was otherwise possible to do so.

After the Revolution, efforts to bring literacy to the masses led to the establishment in 1920 of literacy schools **шко́лы ликбе́за** (**ликвида́ция безгра́мотности**), which flourished by the end of the decade. The principal aim of these schools was to teach reading and writing, mostly to adults. At the same time, workers' schools **рабфа́ки** (**рабо́чие факульте́ты**) were formed to prepare peasants and workers for university-level work.

By 1930 the government was able to declare that a primary education was obligatory for all (**Всео́буч—всео́бщее обяза́тельное нача́льное обуче́ние**), and by 1949 all children in the Russian Federation were to have seven years of education.

Постановле́нием ЦК ВКП(б) от 25 ию́ля 1930 г. с 1930/31 уче́бного го́да вводи́лось всео́бщее нача́льное обуче́ние, в города́х же и рабо́чих посёлках бы́ло введено́ всео́бщее семиле́тнее обуче́ние (повсеме́стно обяза́тельное семиле́тнее обуче́ние введено́ в РСФСР в 1949 г.)[c]

The Soviet educational system could be typified as a straitjacket. But it did accomplish its goal of producing a literate and technically able population (however apolitical). And its uniformity of organization and application plus a very detailed yet broad curriculum ensured that even in difficult circumstances almost all children would be exposed to at least some chemistry, physics, mathematics, and foreign language.

The new Russian educational system is certainly less restrictive than it used to be—uniforms are gone, as are the tenets of Marxism-Leninism and the total control of federal education authorities.

Also gone is reasonable support as government salaries fail to adapt to inflation. Colleges respond either formally by charging tuition or informally by requiring bribes, while researchers frantically seek funds to do what earlier they had been both paid and honored. School teachers are less willing to tutor potential repeaters. Those who teach at technical schools find a better life outside the Academy, so that branch of schooling is losing the battle.

Various aspects of education are discussed in the following order:

Levels in education
Curriculum
Grades
Administration
In and out of school
Different types of schools

LEVELS IN EDUCATION
Ступéни образовáния

The table correlates grade levels of Russian students, in relation to one another and also to their counterparts in the United States. Notice that now eleven grades are standard and that school-

ing begins at age six. (This change is not uniform—some schools prefer the former ten grades so they start at age seven.) The table lays out the usual but full range of possibilities; only primary and secondary schooling through the ninth grade is required of everyone.

Levels in education
Ступéни образовáния

USA			Russia			
School title	Grade	Age	Grade Level	Type of school	Those attending are called	When done they get
		28			**докторáнт**	**дóкторская стéпень стéпень дóктора**
		27				
		26				
		25				
		24	**аспирантýра**[4]	**вуз** [2]	**аспирáнт**	**кандидáтская стéпень**
Graduate School		23				
		22				
		21	**выпускни́к**[8]			

Levels in education (continued)
Ступе́ни образова́ния

USA				Russia			
School title	Grade	Age	Grade Level	Type of school	Those attending are called	When done they get	
College		20	четвероку́рсник	вуз	студент[5]	дипло́м	
		19	третьеку́рсник		студентка		
		18	второку́рсник	те́хникум			
	12	17	первоку́рсник	учи́лище	уча́щийся[7]		
High School	11	16	11 ⎤ по́лная	ПТУ[9]	уча́щаяся	аттеста́т зре́лости	
	10	15	10 ⎦ сре́дняя шко́ла	одиннадцатиле́тка[1]			
	9	14	9 ⎤	девятиле́тка[3]		свиде́тельство об	
	8	13	8 ⎥ непо́лная			образова́нии	
Junior High	7	12	7 ⎥ сре́дняя шко́ла				
	6	11	6 ⎦				
Grade	5	10	5 ⎦		учени́к, учени́ца		
School	4	9	4 ⎤		шко́льник, школьница		
	3	8	3 ⎥	шко́ла			
	2	7	2 ⎥ нача́льная шко́ла				
	1	6	1 ⎦				
Nursery		5					
School		4	де́тский сад		дошко́льник[6]		
or Day care		3					
center		2					
		1	де́тские я́сли				
		6 mo					

1. **Оди́ннадцатиле́тняя шко́ла** (formally, **Сре́дняя общеобразова́тельная шко́ла**). It is the basic eleven-year school. Now it is the most likely and direct way to college (that is **вуз**).

2. An acronym for **вы́сшее уче́бное заведе́ние**, an "institution of higher learning." University-level training is provided either at the university **университе́т** or at an institute **институ́т**. When speaking English, Russians often confuse our "high" school with their **вуз**.

3. The "nine-year school"; currently the level of education required for everyone.

4. Graduate student training. Though often delayed two years after graduation from college as shown, it can also begin right after finishing undergraduate work.

5. **Студе́нт** is a university-level student; **шко́льник, учени́к** are high school level and below: «**Он в пе́рвом кла́ссе**» ("He is in the first grade"); «**Он на пе́рвом ку́рсе**» ("He is a freshman [in college]").

6. A preschool-age child.

7. Most often used to refer to vocational or trade-school students.

8. Either a graduate of or a last-year student in **вуз** (**вы́пустить** to release, to get out).

9. **Профессиона́льно - техни́ческое учи́лище**. See text.

Nursery
Дéтские я́сли

If a mother has no one at home to look after her small child while she works, she enrolls the child in a nursery **детские я́сли** for ages six months to three years. The service used to be inexpensive though hard to find, but is now only affordable to those who work for the institution sponsoring the service **вéдомственные я́сли**. It fulfills the physical need for a babysitter, and the training emphasizes good habits and group relations. However, parents often try to avoid enrolling their children in nurseries because they fear exposure to germs and they believe that such young children need home care and attention. Still, space is not adequate, and demand is high and, now, very expensive.

Kindergarten
Дéтский сад

Some real effort at education begins here—letters and numbers, even simple "combinations," often as much as we accomplish in our first grade. The fee depends on whether you work for a sponsoring institution or on your income.

The children usually stay all day until a parent can pick them up after work. A teacher at this level is a **воспитáтельница,** and officialese for a pupil is **воспитáнник. Дошкóльник** is any preschool-age child. Kindergarten and nursery facilities are often combined and are expensive to all but those who belong to the sponsoring institution—that is, a factory, a ministry, and so on.

Grade school and high school
Шкóла

Real school now begins at age six for most pupils. (Some schools have returned to starting at seven; it's their choice these days.) From this point on, schooling is free. Parents are expected to buy books and supplies, however. Attendance is obligatory for nine years (or until the end of the school year in which the child reaches sixteen), normally nine grades, and may be continued for two more years at the same school or at another (most likely a trade school).

Several "schools" are shown in the table: **начáльная шкóла, (непóлная) срéдняя шкóла,** and **пóлная срéдняя шкóла.** They are an administrative convenience to indicate the

This document confirms completion of required education.

level of schooling. Students usually attend the same school building for the mandatory nine years **нача́льная и непо́лная сре́дняя шко́ла**; those who continue for two more years **по́лная сре́дняя шко́ла** also remain in the same school building. (Some schools in the country go only to the nine-year level, so continuing students must transfer elsewhere.) The major difference between the primary school **нача́льная шко́ла** and the upper grades is that the primary grades have the same teacher all day (except for physical education, music, and foreign languages, when possible or necessary), while the upper grades have subject specialists. The upper grades also have longer hours (see the curriculum table in the next section).

At the end of nine grades the pupil **учени́к, шко́льник** has several choices, including: quitting altogether; finding work while continuing secondary education at a night or correspondence school; or entering directly into a vocational school, sometimes obtaining the high school diploma **аттеста́т зре́лости** there. Or, the student can continue an essentially academic education for two more years in the **по́лная сре́дняя шко́ла**. The latter is the most likely and the most direct route to a higher education at the college level **вуз**. The vocational schools are worth some comment before discussing this direct route to higher education.

Vocational schools
Сре́дние специа́льные уче́бные заведе́ния, ССУЗ

The operative words are **сре́дние** and **специа́льные**, the former indicating that one of the schools' purposes is to continue academic

Приложение к аттестату
о среднем (полном) общем образовании

ТАБЕЛЬ
итоговых оценок успеваемости
(без аттестата о среднем (полном) общем образовании недействителен)

Баграмянц Каринэ Владимировне

за время обучения в средней общеобразовательной школе №20 с углублённым изучением английского языка Краснопресненского р-на обнаружила следующие знания:

Наименование предметов	Оценка
русский язык	5(отлично)
литература	5(отлично)
поэзия XX века	5(отлично)
алгебра	5(отлично)
геометрия	5(отлично)
история Отечества	5(отлично)
всеобщая история	5(отлично)
основы современной цивилизации	5(отлично)
география	5(отлично)
общая история	5(отлично)
общая биология	5(отлично)
физика	5(отлично)
астрономия	5(отлично)
химия	4(хорошо)
английский язык	5(отлично)
физическая культура	освобождена
обеспечение жизнедеятельности	5(отлично)
мировая художественная культура	5(отлично)
английская литература	5(отлично)
курс гидов-переводчиков	5(отлично)
машинопись на английском языке	5(отлично)

Сдал   квалификационные экзамены по профессии

Присвоен квалификационный разряд (класс, категория)

Кроме того, успешно выполнил ____ программу по факультативным курсам

Участвовал   в 19 ___ году в

и занял ____ место.
Награжден

Директор
… июня 1993 г.
город Москва

Grades are included in the high school graduation diploma.

A tekhnikum advertises.

The length of the course varies widely from a few months to several years, depending on the subject. Technically, one can go from any of the **те́хникум**, **учи́лище**, **профессиона́льно–техни́ческое учи́лище** schools into a **вуз**, but in practice the large majority of students (most often called **уча́щиеся**) in these schools go straight into a job.

Evening and correspondence schools are very widely used, especially by those who for some reason never finished the regular school. The **те́хникум** and **учи́лище** often have evening and second-shift divisions **вече́рние и сме́нные отделе́ния**; also available are the special correspondence schools or divisions of schools **зао́чные сре́дние специа́льные уче́бные заведе́ния**. The latter tend to have much greater contact with their pupils in the course of study than do ours. Very wide use of evening **вече́рнее отделе́ние** and correspondence **зао́чное отделе́ние** courses is also made at the university level, with about half the students getting their degrees **дипло́м** this way. Naturally, the studies take longer to complete, but one day off a week and an extra month of vacation are granted to correspondence and night-school students. The students themselves, however, consider this a much less desirable way to get their college education.

instruction through the equivalent of the tenth and eleventh grades (that is, until the high-school diploma has been earned), the latter stressing additional training in a particular kind of work. These schools have either of two titles: **те́хникум** applies to more highly skilled technical or clerical training such as electronic technology, some engineering, food processing, finance, and the like; **учи́лище** often provides somewhat lower-level training in nursing, medical technology, and so forth. (However, **учи́лище** is also used for a few particularly distinguished or university-level institutions.)

Courses in these schools vary from two to four years, usually depending on whether the student has already finished the eleven-year program.

A third kind of vocational school is perhaps better called a trade school **ПТУ** (**пэ–тэ–у́**, **профессиона́льно–техни́ческое учи́лище**), where emphasis is almost entirely on learning a trade such as carpentry, plumbing, and so forth. Most of the student's time is spent as an apprentice, and wages are paid accordingly.

Private commercial courses abound. This one specifically invites community college teachers.

Higher education
Высшее образование

The direct route to a higher education is the completion of all eleven grades of school that constitute secondary education **по́лная сре́дняя шко́ла**. The student is then about seventeen years old and has obtained the **аттеста́т зре́лости**. At this point, the student is technically eligible to enter a higher educational institution **вуз (вы́сшее уче́бное заведе́ние)**. This can be either a university **университе́т**, which offers a broad spectrum of subjects in the sciences and the humanities, or an institute **институ́т**, which specializes in two or three aspects of a single subject. Medicine, engineering, agriculture, and the like are more often studied at institutes than at universities, where emphasis is more on the humanities and on the pure rather than applied sciences. (Our general word "college," meaning any place of higher education other than a trade school, in Russian is **институ́т**: "Are you planning to go to college?" is «**Ты собира́ешься поступа́ть в институ́т?**»)

A high-school diploma does not guarantee access to higher education. Another obstacle remains. The real hurdle for the student now is to pass the competitive entrance examinations, for the number of would-be students greatly exceeds the number of openings in the universities and institutes. (Private tutors are frequently hired to help pass this hurdle.) Though universities are generally held in greater esteem than the institutes, some of the latter (often those in a science) are even harder to get into than the universities.

Once in the university (or institute), the course of study usually lasts about five years (though medicine takes six). In the late 1980s, university administrations were given more leeway to dismiss poorly performing students, but generally it is considered to be the instructor's responsibility to keep students there and working "at level."

Having finished college work and received a (first) degree **дипло́м**, the graduate

ВУЗ БЕСПЛАТНО ТОЛЬКО РАЗ

● Н. ХОМЧЕНКО: В прошлом году в институт не прошла по конкурсу, сейчас готовлюсь ко второй попытке, но как вспомню процедуру получения медицинской справки...

ОТВЕТ: Сосредоточивайтесь на подготовке к вступительным экзаменам. Медицинская справка исключена из набора документов. К заявлению о приеме вы приложите документы, удостоверяющие вашу личность, гражданство, аттестат (причем подлинник — при зачислении) и необходимое количество фотографий. Новый порядок приема в государственные вузы РФ отличают и другие новшества. В частности, бесплатное образование в государственных учебных заведениях можно получить только один раз. Увеличились льготы для медалистов: вузы вправе устанавливать для них особые условия приема, уменьшая количество испытаний. Кроме того, вузы сами разрабатывают правила приема, определяя количество и перечень вступительных испытаний, а также набор студентов из СНГ. Независимо от расширения вузовской самостоятельности сохраняются категории абитуриентов, имеющих право внеконкурсного зачисления: дети-сироты, военнослужащие, инвалиды I и II групп, а также чернобыльцы.

Some new entrance requirements

дипло́мник, выпускни́к used to be assigned a place to work though it was rarely where the graduate wanted to go. Now, finding work is a do-it-yourself affair though employment offices offer some help if your friends and family lack influence.

The student stipend
Студéнческая стипéндия

Most full-time students at the college level are paid to go to school (inadequately, due to inflation), but the amounts they receive depend on four criteria: (1) the field chosen—for example, historians are not so valuable as physicists; (2) year of study—that is, fifth-year students get more than first-year students; (3) academic progress **успевáемость**—in other words, good students get more money; (4) attendance **посещáемость**—a student **стáроста кýрса, староста грýппы** is elected and has duties that include checking attendance at lectures or classes. Some special larger stipends **имéнные стипéндии** carry the name of a well-known person and are granted to those who are academically talented. The higher stipends (mostly for science or technical majors) are used to encourage students to enroll in certain fields. Some universities have moved to a system under which the best students are admitted with stipends, those in the middle are admitted without financial support, and the weakest may attend if they pay substantial tuition. (Some enterprising colleges and universities have also sought to capitalize on the current popularity of things Western by changing the names of their degrees to **бакалáвр, магúстр**.)

Graduate work
Аспирантýра

Graduate work usually does not begin until after the hopeful student has worked for a few years. Then the student applies and takes yet another examination. Graduate work in Russia enjoys a different status than here: fewer are chosen for the honor, and, perhaps as a concomitant, the honor is vastly greater. Graduate work is not only more honorable but also used to be relatively well paid; it is not automatically associated with penury.

All graduate degrees must have the approval of the Higher Qualification Commission **Вы́сшая Аттестациóнная Комúссия (ВАК)** of the Ministry of Higher and Secondary Specialized Education. Both graduate degrees, the candidate degree and the doctor's degree, require the writing and public defense of a thesis **диссертáция**.

The candidate degree
Кандидáтская стéпень

This first graduate degree is also called **стéпень кандидáта наýк**. (Only graduate degrees are called *degree* **стéпень**.) The one doing the work is **аспирáнт**, whose graduate study is **аспирантýра**.

Graduate students **аспирáнты** earning their first degree normally spend three years doing so. In the course of the first one and one-half to two years, they must pass three tests, which together are called **кандидáтский мúнимум**. One test is in a foreign language, another in philosophy, including general philosophy, and a third test is in one's specialty for which there is no course work. These tests are not looked upon as a major barrier by students, and once they have been completed, thesis work is begun.

Though the candidate degree **кандидáтская стéпень** is the lesser of the two higher degrees, it probably comes close to our Ph.D. degree. (As an example, the student is expected to have published several articles *before* obtaining the degree.) The recipient is given the title **звáние кандидáта наýк (кандидáт педагогúческих наýк, кандидáт медицúнских наýк и т.д.)**. These degrees are sometimes abbreviated in print: **к.м.н—кандидат математúческих наýк, к.ф.н—кандидат философúческих наук.**

The doctorate
Дóкторская стéпень

This degree is very prestigious; it often, though not necessarily, takes many years to achieve and is awarded only to those who have done really significant work in their field.

(Recently, however, the demand for more staff with higher credentials has encouraged a plethora of new programs leading to the doctorate.)

For the **докторская степень** no course work is required for the applicant **докторант**. The degree must be applied for, however, and the dissertation **докторская диссертация** must be a major contribution to one's field. Up to one year is given with full pay **творческий отпуск** for writing the doctoral thesis, and the "student" **докторант** normally must advise and supervise candidate degree applicants working under his or her direction. The recipient of this degree has the title **доктор наук**. Eventually this person can be appointed professor **профессор**, a teaching rank at a university and, when supervision of candidate's degrees is necessary, an honorific at a research institution.

Russian Academy of Sciences
Российская Академия наук, РАН

The highest position of scholarship is occupied by the academician **академик**, one among some 245 (active) members of the Academy of Sciences. This institution is very prestigious and powerful, and its members are not only honored and influential but also (used to be) financially secure. The two levels of membership in the academy are the active member **действительный член** and the corresponding member **член-корреспондент**, the latter with less prestige, power, and remuneration than the former. Among its functions, the academy has many research institutes under its direction (many of which grant graduate degrees), it advises the government on the direction research should take, and it maintains contacts with foreign scholars via meetings, conferences, and through some seventy publications. The Russian (and, in general, European) regard for the scholar has no parallel in the United States. Our National Academy of Sciences is prestigious, perhaps, but only in their own small circle.

It should be noted that the Academy of Sciences includes not just the pure and applied sciences (as does ours) but also history, law, economics, literature, and linguistics.

CURRICULUM
Учебный план

In grade schools and high schools
В средних школах

The following curriculum chart is a suggested standard for Moscow for 1992–1993. It has two parts: (1) the basic curriculum standard for all the schools (the lion's share of the chart), and (2) the remaining class hours per week that the school can best allocate for itself depending on need, inspiration, and availability; it does give some room for individual schools to cope as they can. Some schools' curricula differ by design: for instance, a special school, **спецшкола**, gives more and earlier emphasis to a particular subject. Special schools might concentrate on, for example, mathematics and physics, ballet, or music; more commonly, the specialization is in a foreign language. The demand for these schools is higher than their availability so that their social position is similar to that of an American private school.

The Russian curriculum is a radical change for those of us who are used to curriculum deviation not only among school systems, but among individual teachers. The curriculum described here is much the same for the whole country.

A new law on education gives more leeway to all involved. Teachers, parents, and schoolchildren now all have "rights" and "obligations." Even home education is permitted providing the object of instruction can pass grade tests **переводные экзамены**. While there is less definition and control now from federal authorities, regional and city leaders have, in many cases, stepped in to set curricular standards.

A recommended core curriculum for Moscow schools, 1992–93
Учительская газета, №37—40, 20 окт. 1992

Class hours per week for each subject at each grade level

		I				II					III			
		Нача́льная школа				Сре́дняя школа					Ста́ршие классы			
Grade level	1	2	3	4	5	6	7	8	9	10	11	Totals	Subject
Уче́бные предме́ты													
Ба́зисный компоне́нт уче́бного пла́на	20	22	22	22	26	28	30	30	32	28	26	286	Proposed class hours in core curriculum
Ру́сский язык и литерату́ра	7	8	8	8	8	7	7	6	6	5	4	74	Russian language and literature
Иностра́нный язык					3	3	3	3	3			15	Foreign language
Исто́рия и обществове́дение					2	2	2	2	3	4	5	20	History and social studies
Му́зыка	2	2	2	2	2	2						12	Music
Изобрази́тельное иску́сство	2	2	2	2	2	2						12	Drawing
Иску́сство							2					2	Art
Окружа́ющий мир	1	1	1	1								4	Environment
Геогра́фия						2	2	2	2	2		10	Geography
Матема́тика и осно́вы информа́тики	4	5	5	5	5	6	6	6	6	4	4	56	Mathematics
Фи́зика и астроно́мия							2	2	2	3	4	13	Physics and astronomy
Хи́мия								3	2	2	2	9	Chemistry
Биоло́гия							2	2	2	2	2	10	Biology
Введе́ние в эконо́мику									2			2	Intro. to economics
Трудово́е обуче́ние	2	2	2	2	2	2	2	2	2	2	2	22	Work training
Физи́ческая культу́ра и ОБЖ[1]	2	2	2	2	2	2	2	2	2	4	3	25	Physical culture and first aid
Шко́льный компоне́нт пла́на	6	6	6	6	4	4	4	4	2	8	10	60	School's component[2]
ИТОГО	26	28	28	28	30	32	34	34	34	36	36		Total class hours per week

1. Обеспече́ние жизнедея́тельности First aid / CPR

2. The number of class hours per week at the suggested disposal of the school.

Sample test
Примéрный экзáмен

In 1993 the high school diploma examination for Russian literature had an oral examination. A list of 56 possible questions or themes билéты was published. These are a few:

3. «Лелéющая дýшу гумáнность» поэ́зии А. С. Пýшкина. Лирúческий герóй. Прочитáть наизýсть и проанализúровать однó из стихотворéний (по выбору учáщегося).

13. Облóмов, облóмовцы, «облóмовщина» (по ромáну И. А. Гончарóва «Облóмов»).

32. «Вéчные» проблéмы и путú их решéния в произведéниях И. Бýнина, А. Куприна́, В. Королéнко (анáлиз одногó-двух произведéний любóго писáтеля).

40. Напрáвленность сатирúческих произведéний В. Маякóвского. Прочитáть наизýсть и проанализúровать однó из стихотворéний.

44. Тéма трагúческой судьбы́ человéка в тоталитáрном госудáрстве в произведéниях А. Платóнова, А. Солженúцына, В. Шалáмова, Ю. Домбрóвского (по одномý úли нескольким произведéниям любóго áвтора).[d]

Some further notion of what is expected of students can be had from the following excerpts from the 1992 mathematics examination, given to those who intended to major in various sciences as shown at Moscow State University that year. This examination is more difficult than the usual high school diploma tests because it represents the higher expectations of the better students in the country. These were cited as examples of what could be expected in a *Guide for Applicants to Moscow State University*.[2]

2. Спрáвочник для поступáющих в Москóвский университéт, ред. Н.В. Баринова (Москвá: Издáтельство Москóвского университéта, 1993), стр. 74-88.

1. Мехáнико–математúческий факультéт:

Мáстер делает за один час цéлое числó детáлей, бóльшее 5, а ученúк—на 2 детали мéньше. Один мастер выполня́ет закáз за целое число часóв, а два ученикá вмéсте —на 1 час быстрéе. Из какого колúчества деталей состоúт заказ?

2. Факультéт вычислúтельной матемáтики и кибернéтики:

Какое из двух чúсел $\sqrt{\frac{1990}{1991}}$ или $\sqrt[3]{\frac{1991}{1992}}$ больше?

3. Физúческий факультéт:

Найти первый член и разность арифметúческой прогрессии, если извéстно, что пятый и девя́тый члены дают в сумме 40, а сумма седьмого и тринадцатого членов равна 58.

4. Химúческий факультéт:

Даны́ три сплáва. Состáв первого сплава: 60% алюмúния и 40% хрóма. Состав вторóго сплава: 10% хрома и 90% титáна. Состав третьего сплава: 20% алюминия, 5% хрома и 30% титана. Из них нýжно приготóвить новый сплав, содержáщий 45% титана. Какие знáчения может принимáть процéнтное содержание хрома в этом новом сплаве?

5. Биологúческий факультéт:

Прямоугóльный треугóльник АВС имеет перúметр 54 см, причём длина катета АС больше чем 10 см. Окрýжность рáдиуса 6 см, центр которой лежит на катете ВС, касáется прямых АВ и АС. Найти плóщадь треугольника АВС.

6. Факультéт почвовéдения: Решить уравнéние:[e]
$$2(\cos 6x + \sin 2x \cdot \cos 4x) = \sin 6x + \sin 2x$$

In vocational schools
В срéдних специáльных учéбных заведéниях

For those attending a тéхникум or an учúлище, the goals of attendance determine the curriculum. Part (about half) of the time is spent completing the academic requirements for an eleven-year education, and the remaining time is spent, both in class and to a limited extent on the job, in training in the specific vocation. Those in the trade school **ПТУ (профессиона́льно–техни́ческое учи́лище)** spend almost all their time in on-the-job training. Only about 20 percent of their time is devoted to related academics and theory.

In college
В ву́зах

In Russia, students essentially specialize upon entrance, and their college courses are preselected for them. No confusion exists about whether to take History 101 or Anthro 104. They may take courses in addition to those that are part of their major field of study, but they do so on their own. Such courses are called *elective* **факультати́вные ку́рсы**.

The usual degree program takes five years to complete. Technically, the student may switch from, say, architecture to engineering, but it is seldom done because credits in one subject are not necessarily applicable to another.

Not only does specialty training start earlier, it is also more narrow in scope, especially in technical fields in which the number of specialties seems close to endless.

Research as part of one's undergraduate work is encouraged: beginning in the second year of study, students can join a student research organization, **Студе́нческое нау́чное о́бщество (СНО)** or **Студе́нческое констру́кторское бюро́ (СКБ)**. (The latter attempts to solve primarily technical problems that have arisen in industry.) These organizations meet regularly, research is conducted under the guidance of faculty members, and annual competitions are held. The best papers are published by the Academy of Sciences.

A research requirement in the major field is the writing of a diploma thesis **дипло́мная рабо́та** to show that the student has some understanding of a field and some control over

its tools of investigation. This project is considered very important, and students in technical and scientific subjects are often given their final semester to devote to their research and writing.

Also required of the student is study of a foreign language for two to three hours a week of the first two years; in the third year the student must pass an examination on the foreign language.

Finally, most university students must take a few courses in pedagogy and do some practice teaching. Upon graduating, the student is eligible to teach in secondary schools, though there is no great rush to do so. Students whose specialty is not taught on a secondary level need not take such courses (those in law or medicine, for instance).

GRADES
Отме́тки

In school
В шко́ле

The school system uses five grades for distinguishing its pupils: **пятёрка (5) отли́чно** is excellent, **четвёрка (4) хорошо́** is good, **тро́йка (3) удовлетвори́тельно** is satisfactory, **дво́йка (2) неудовлетвори́тельно («не́уд»)** is poor, and **едини́ца (1) о́чень пло́хо** is very poor. The last two grades are both failing, and, in fact, **едини́ца** is only very rarely used.

For grade-school children, how and when those grades are given out is important (and drastically different from our practice). Every schoolchild has a booklet, in this case called **дневни́к** (also the word for a diary), which shows the assignment and sometimes a grade for every subject on every day of the school year. The illustration shows a typical page with a week's assignments and grades.

The columns (from left to right) give the date, the subject, the assignment, the grade, and the teacher's initials. The relative infrequency of the initialed grades is typical. The children never know when they are to be called on. Once they are called on, their answers or lack of them supply their grades in the subject for that week (or whatever other period—some teachers obviously are more assiduous than others). Also notice, at the bottom of the page, that the signature of the homeroom teacher **кла́ссный руководи́тель** and the signature of the parent **по́дпись роди́телей** are required. Attendance figures on the bottom left-hand side show the number of lessons lost because of absence and also any tardiness **опозда́ние** for the week.

The (proper) use of this **дневни́к** should (and probably does) have some outstanding advantages: the student is kept well aware of academic performance, and, perforce, so are his or her homeroom teacher and parents, every week! The latter also have specific information on the homework required of the child and are thereby able to carry out their responsibilities in seeing that it is done. Pupils in grades ten and eleven are no longer required to maintain this gradebook. At the end of each quarter **че́тверть**, every child receives a grade in each subject.

Notice that a grade is given for conduct **поведе́ние**. A grade of (5) indicates exemplary conduct **приме́рное поведе́ние**.

The booklet **дневни́к** also has a section at the back for quarterly reports on how well the child fulfills obligations in keeping the classroom in order or contributions to group projects for the common good—socially useful work **Обще́ственно-поле́зный труд**.

A student can legally quit school at the end of the nine-year school training **девятиле́тка, непо́лная сре́дняя шко́ла** or at the end of the school year after reaching the age of sixteen. A pupil who fails at one year's work must take the course over and becomes a repeater **второго́дник**. This unhappy prospect is diminished when the pupil realizes the disaster, studies during the summer, and retakes and passes the necessary tests before the next school year begins.

Graduating high schoolers **выпускники́** with very good grades are awarded their medals on graduation night **выпускно́й ве́чер**; to get a gold medal **золота́я меда́ль**, all final grades in all subjects in the last two years of school must have been A's **пятёрки**, and all tests taken after the end of school **на аттеста́т зре́лости** must also be A's. (A gold medal gives the applicant **абитурие́нт** the privilege of taking only one entrance examination into college.) Those receiving a silver medal **сере́бряная меда́ль** may have a few B's **четвёрки**.

In college
В вузах

Once at the college level, grades are given in the various subjects from time to time—for essays, homework, laboratory work, and the like—so the student has some measure of performance. Term paper is **курсова́я (рабо́та)**; a test or quiz is **контро́льная**. However, the final grades for subjects are given only at the end of the semester and on the basis of final examinations **экза́мены**. It is quite possible to do passing work all along and then fail the final exam and the course.

Some college grades come in four levels: excellent **отли́чно**, good **хорошо́**, satisfactory **удовлетвори́тельно**, and poor **пло́хо**. The last one is a failing grade. Other courses at the university level use only two grades, credit **зачёт** and no credit **незачёт**. Grades are important to the students: poor grades can reduce your stipend or have you expelled. Cheating is not uncommon: to copy is **спи́сывать**; a cribsheet **шпарга́лка**. The attitude toward cheating is somewhat different, as it is regarded more as a game than as a sin. Therefore, one can describe one's exploits to one's friends, provided of course that one was not discovered. The authorities try to get around the problem by wide use of the oral exam, which in turn has the drawback of giving total power to the interrogator.

The diploma **дипло́м** is usually given after five years of college courses. Extraordinary students get a diploma "with distinction" **дипло́м с отли́чием**, but most diplomas simply testify to the student's having taken and passed a course of study with a certain major. However, in addition to a diploma, the student also gets a kind of transcript (here called **вы́писка**), which, though not so detailed as ours, still gives an idea of the major courses the student took and performance in each. These are typically carried around and shown to potential employers in place of transcripts sent separately from the college.

ADMINISTRATION
Администра́ция

The people that work in education do so under closer supervision than we are used to, so that extremes either in teaching method or goal tend to be eliminated. At the secondary level, therefore, especially imaginative teachers have less scope than ours, but poor teaching gets quicker and surer correction. At the college level, there is less confusion about course content but some dissatisfaction with restrictions on methods and goals of research. Throughout, one works for the betterment of the group **коллекти́в**.

At school
В шко́ле

The teacher
Учи́тель

Teachers **учи́тель**, **учи́тельница** come in two major categories: those who teach in elementary school **нача́льная шко́ла** (grades one to four) and those who teach in the upper grades **сре́дняя шко́ла**. The primary teacher is in charge of the same group of children all day, every day, in every subject (sometimes excepting music, drawing, and physical education). The teacher's contact-hour (or lesson) load is, therefore, twenty-four hours a week (four lessons a day, six days a week).

ДИПЛОМ

С ОТЛИЧИЕМ

ЛВ № 306034

Настоящий диплом выдан *Толмачевой*
Юлии Юрьевне
в том, что она в 19 83 году поступила а
в *Ленинградский ордена Ленина и ордена*
Трудового Красного Знамени
государственный университет им. А.А. Жданова
и в 19 88 году окончил а, полный курс
названного
университета
по специальности *"Прикладная*
математика"

Решением Государственной экзаменационной
комиссии от 10 " июня 19 88 г.
Толмачевой Ю.Ю.
присвоена квалификация *математика,*
преподавателя

г. *Ленинград* „ 1 " июля 1988 г.

Регистрационный № 551

Московская типография Гознака. 1983.

ВЫПИСКА

из зачетной ведомости

(без диплома не действительна)

ТОЛМАЧЕВА
Юлия Юрьевна
за время пребывания на математико-механическом
факультете Ленинградского ордена Ленина и ордена
Трудового Красного Знамени государственного
университета имени А. А. Жданова
с 19 83 г. по 19 88 г. сдал а
следующие дисциплины:

1. История КПСС	ОТЛИЧНО
2. Политическая экономия	ОТЛИЧНО
3. Марксистско-ленинская философия	ОТЛИЧНО
4. Научный коммунизм	ОТЛИЧНО
5. Критика современной буржуазной философии, социологии и идеологии антикоммунизма	зачтено
6. Основы научного атеизма	зачтено
7. Советское право	зачтено
8. Физическое воспитание	ОТЛИЧНО
9. Гражданская оборона	ОТЛИЧНО
10. Иностранный язык (англ.	ОТЛИЧНО
11. Алгебра	

---

12. Геометрия	ОТЛИЧНО
13. Элементы математической логики и теории множеств	зачтено
14. Математический анализ	хорошо
15. Дифференциальные уравнения	ОТЛИЧНО
16. Теория вероятностей	ОТЛИЧНО
17. Приложения теории вероятностей	ОТЛИЧНО
18. Уравнения математической физики	ОТЛИЧНО
19. Функциональный анализ	ОТЛИЧНО
20. Математическая статистика	–
21. Методы вычислений	ОТЛИЧНО
22. Вычислительный практикум	зачтено
23. Специальный вычислительный практикум	зачтено
24. Программирование	зачтено
25. Экстремальные задачи	зачтено
26. Автоматизированные системы управления	ОТЛИЧНО
27. Математическое обеспечение ЭВМ	ОТЛИЧНО
28. Машинный язык	зачтено
29. Теория управления	зачтено
30. Теоретическая механика	ОТЛИЧНО
31. Теоретическая кибернетика	ОТЛИЧНО
32. Физика	ОТЛИЧНО
33. Курсовые работы	ОТЛИЧНО
34. Специальные семинары	зачтено

35. Специальный курс	ОТЛИЧНО
36. Специальный курс	ОТЛИЧНО
37. Специальный курс	ОТЛИЧНО
38. Специальный курс	хорошо
39. История математики	зачтено
40. Производственная практика	ОТЛИЧНО
41. Методика преподавания высшей математики с элементами педагогики	зачтено
42. Психология	зачтено
43. Педагогическая практика	ОТЛИЧНО
44. Основы экологии	зачтено
45.	

Защитил а дипломную работу на тему:
"Детермированный метод анализа
регулярных языков с исправлением
ошибок"

с оценкой ОТЛИЧНО и сдал а
государственный экзамен с оценкой ОТЛИЧНО
по научному коммунизму марксизму-ленинизму

This student graduated with highest honors **с отли́чием** so she has a red diploma rather than a blue one.

Training for the job is a three- to four-year program at a primary teachers' school **педагоги́ческое учи́лище**. But secondary school teachers are trained as subject specialists, most of them at a teachers' college **пединститу́т (педагоги́ческий институ́т)**. Training there takes four to five years and includes one or two major subjects of specialization. Sometimes these secondary-school teachers come straight from the universities, where everyone with an appropriate major is required to take a course in how to teach the chosen subject. The secondary-school teachers have a minimum of eighteen class hours a week, but most earn more money by teaching more.

Contrary to American habit, teachers are free to go once scheduled classes are over. (In other words, they are not required to stay at school until thirty minutes after the final bell rings.) However, other obligations include visiting pupils' homes (the rule, not the exception), attending numerous teacher and parent-teacher meetings, and leading an interest group **кружо́к** during the after-school hours.

The social status that Russian teachers enjoy is hard to establish, though evidence (often consisting only of innuendo) would suggest that they fare somewhat better than do teachers in the United States. Certainly parents pay more attention to them. These days the salaries are so low that many schools are held together by retirees (women over fifty-five) who want the income and have the interest.

Teachers, as well as professors, belong to a trade union, **Профсою́з рабо́тников просвеще́ния** or **Профсою́з рабо́тников вы́сшей шко́лы и нау́чных учрежде́ний**. This has not been an American trade union, but current academic salaries are low enough that the Russian manifestation has actually considered the option of a strike. The newspaper **Учи́тельская газе́та** is for teachers with problems presented by students, parents, or administrators. Other new newspapers, such as **Пе́рвое сентября́**, offer ideas for diversifying curriculums, methods, and educational philosophy.

The institution of substitute teaching is not used in Russia. Other teachers (or even the principal) cover for the absent one, or classes are doubled up.

The homeroom teacher
Кла́ссный руководи́тель

The homeroom teacher **кла́ссный руководи́тель** is charged with many of the same duties as are ours—the pupil's progress, conduct, health, and so forth—plus parent relations. Once a week the homeroom teacher leads a "class hour" **кла́ссный час** during which they discuss school monitoring, duties, grades, and class parties or trips. And the teacher maintains a "class journal" **кла́ссный журна́л**, which is a permanent school record of pupils' quarterly grades, and attendance. But there is one very major difference: the Russian **кла́ссный руководи́тель**, though a subject teacher for the class, also fulfills the duties of homeroom teacher not just for one semester but for the entire secondary-school period. This system encourages strong ties between class members themselves and between students and at least one member of the establishment who functions as a counselor.

The vice-principal
За́вуч

A school has at least two vice-principals, each with differing responsibilities. (The title itself, **за́вуч**, is an abbreviation of the phrase **заве́дующий уче́бной ча́стью**, which is no longer used. The title now is officially **замести́тель дире́ктора**, but remains **за́вуч** in normal conversation.) One vice-principal, **за́вуч (замести́тель дире́ктора) по уче́бной ча́сти**, is mainly responsible for assuring that the curriculum is being followed; another, the **за́вуч по нача́льним кла́ссам**, looks after the primary grades; and another, the **за́вуч по внекла́ссной рабо́те**, organizes extracurricular activities.

Special schools often have a vice-principal in charge of the school's specialty, for example, **за́вуч по англи́йскому языку́**. Vice-principals also teach, but their class load is less than that of a regular teacher (not more than twelve class hours a week). A similar title **завхо́з (заве́дующий хозя́йственной ча́стью)** is used for the bookkeeper who is personally responsible for school supplies.

Other specialists are increasingly appearing in schools. Many have a psychologist **психо́лог** to deal with testing and pupils' emotional difficulties. Some schools now have something like a social worker **обще́ственный учи́тель** to handle parental problems, truancy, and other concomitants of social breakdown.

The principal
Дире́ктор

The head of the school is the **дире́ктор**, who, often as not, is a woman.[3] The school principal has a somewhat different role to play than does ours. For one thing, the principal usually is responsible for some teaching, though not more than twelve hours a week. For another, she is also expected to be a "master teacher," able to do what she talks about. She also tends to keep a much tighter rein on what goes on in the school, regularly sitting in on classes, taking notes on the conduct of the class, the efficacy of the course, and reporting to the authorities (**ГорУНО́, Городско́е управле́ние наро́дного образова́ния** or just **департа́мент образова́ния**). Though a **дире́ктор** may criticize and reprimand, her opinions are still subject to the collective wisdom of the teachers among whom she works, usually expressed in a teachers' council **учи́тельский сове́т, педсове́т**.

The principal is also responsible for visitors to the school and for the care and treatment of recalcitrant children (or even parents). In rural areas, she has some status as a sort of village elder, so that she is often perforce involved in assorted community problems in addition to her own as principal.

School council
Сове́т шко́лы

A new "collective" authority is the school council **Сове́т шко́лы,** a group of teachers and parents who try to resolve school-related issues, and who are responsible for setting the school regulations **Уста́в шко́лы** for their particular school. (Involvement is worldwide!)

Others at school
Други́е в шко́ле

The equivalent of our custodian or janitor is **убо́рщица, техни́чка,** whose duties are the upkeep of the school. She is also sometimes in charge of the cloakroom when such an attendant is considered necessary. To aid her, the children themselves are called upon regularly to perform some small maintenance and cleanup work. They must help tape the (double) windows at the onslaught of winter, for instance; at lunch, the pupils take turns in arranging the distribution of food, china, and cutlery; and occasional cleanup projects are organized. For all these efforts, the children are given a grade each quarter for the previously mentioned socially useful work **обще́ственно-поле́зный труд.** (Also see *Classroom organization.*)

Some schools also have a nurse **медсестра́** on duty and a doctor on call.

At the college level
В вузах

The president or rector **ре́ктор** is in charge of a university or institute, and the **проре́ктор** is the vice-president. To aid and advise them, there is an academic council **учёный сове́т** or **сове́т институ́та** consisting of all the deans and some professors plus representatives of the

---

3. As a result of the devastation of World War II, known as the Great Patriotic War **Вели́кая Оте́чественная война́,** when so many were killed, especially men, it was discovered that women could do work formerly relegated to men.

Ministry of Higher Education **Министéрство Вы́сшего Образовáния** and the trade union **профсою́з**.

The **вуз** is divided into departments **факультéты**[4] which are headed by a dean, **декáн**. Typical departments are **истори́ческий факультéт (истфáк), хими́ческий факультéт (химфáк), филологи́ческий факультéт (филфáк)**. (Moscow University has fourteen such departments.) The department is also equipped with an academic council of its own. Each department is further divided into two or more subspecialties **кáфедра** (*sg.*) with a chief, **завкáфедрой (завéдующий кáфедрой)**, usually a professor in rank.

Academic ranks
Академи́ческие дóлжности и звáния

On the top of the ladder is the professor **профéссор**,[5] who usually has a doctor's degree **дóкторская стéпень** and its title **дóктор наýк**. Next is the **доцéнт**, who normally has the **кандидáтская стéпень** and the title **кандидáт наýк**. (**Наýка**, the word for science, is used as freely in Russian as philosophy is in English.) The more important teaching problems, such as major lectures to larger classes, are assigned to teachers from these two ranks. An intermediate level is **стáрший преподавáтель**. The lowest level of the regular faculty belongs to the **ассистéнт**, who has lesser teaching responsibilities, laboratory courses, quiz sections, occasional substitution for a senior faculty member, and so forth. The title *instructor* **преподавáтель** is used for those who do not have their candidate degree but who teach quiz sections or ancillary courses—foreign languages, for instance; the rank is not usually considered to be a step on the academic ladder.

4. Russian universities are not divided into colleges as in the United States. **Факультéт** is translated here as "department," a close approximation.

5. The Academician **акадéмик** is an award and a title bestowed for outstanding research. It is not a teaching rank, but its status is higher than that of a professor.

Universities and institutes are expected to do research as well as teach; therefore, most also have research ranks, **млáдший наýчный сотрýдник**, and **стáрший наýчный сотрýдник**. A research institute, **НИИ (Научно-исследовáтельский институ́т)**, has research ranks: **лаборáнт, млáдший и стáрший наýчный сотрýдник, ведýщий наýчный сотрудник**. For vocational schools, the chief in charge is the **дирéктор**, but the teaching staff does not go beyond the **преподавáтель** level.

IN AND OUT OF SCHOOL
Внутри́ и вне шкóлы

The school building
Шкóльное здáние

The school building itself naturally varies from small (three hundred to five hundred pupils in rural communities) to large (eight hundred to one thousand pupils in a large city school). Standard titles for rooms in a school include:

класс, клáссная кóмната, кабинéт   a classroom

компью́терный класс   the classroom with computers

коридóр   a hall

учи́тельская   the teachers' room

столóвая   the lunchroom, if whole meals are served, **буфéт** if snacks alone are served

медпýнкт   the nurse's room or office

кабинéт дирéктора   the principal's office

физкультýрный зал, спорти́вный зал   the gymnasium

раздевáлка   the cloakroom, invariably near the entrance to the school

áктовый зал   the room for assemblies, school parties, and other functions

The names for some of these types of rooms change at the university level. A class is most often held in a tiered lecture room **аудито́рия**; assemblies, meetings, or ceremonial affairs take place in an auditorium **а́ктовый зал**. At the entrance to the building one sometimes must show a pass **про́пуск** and then check one's coat at the cloakroom **гардеро́б** (a more elegant term than **раздева́лка**), receiving in exchange for the coat a chit **номеро́к, би́рка**. The administrative division most affecting the student is the department **факульте́т**, and the name both for this administration and for the offices it occupies is **декана́т**.

Classroom furnishings
Ме́бель в кла́ссе

The classroom has school desks (**па́рта**, *sg.*), which traditionally seat two pupils side by side. Some desks are equipped with hooks for hold-ing the briefcase **портфе́ль** each child carries. Small children carry satchels (**ра́нец**, *sg.*) on their backs. The teacher's desk **пи́сьменный стол** is in the front of the room. The blackboard **доска́** works only with Russian chalk **мел** and requires a rag **тря́пка** for erasing. The Russian obsession with potted plants also extends to the classroom.

Classroom organization
Поря́док в кла́ссе

Pupils are organized in several ways for several purposes. The class duty officers for the day **дежу́рный, дежу́рная** keep the room clean and in good order, open and close windows, keep the rags used for erasing the blackboard both clean and wet, and perform other such functions. (The janitor's only concerns are the halls and primary school rooms.) Other obliga-tions of pupils include taking charge of the

На уро́ке

The first day of school. Dress-up clothes are in order.

lunch table: setting the table, serving the food, and making sure the cutlery and plates are removed when all is done. This job дежу́рство is arranged by rotation among the class members. Two are on duty at any time.

School atmosphere
Атмосфе́ра в шко́ле

The atmosphere in a Russian classroom naturally depends directly on the personality of the teacher, which, given the nature of the human condition, varies. Conduct is more restricted in the sense that some rules are observed that we think of as formal. The pupils rise when the teacher enters the room and seat themselves only when so instructed. They rise when they are called upon to answer a question and generally do not speak at all without permission. They are (overtly at least) respectful to their teacher, as a matter of course greeting the teacher in a chance meeting in the hall, for instance. Classroom posture does not include slouching, and hands are raised with the elbow still in contact with the desk. (Some new types of schools offer a more relaxed atmosphere that would feel more familiar to a Western pupil: ва́льдорфская, Монтессо́ри, шко́лы развива́ющего обуче́ния, школа диало́г культу́р, и т. д.) On the other hand, the teacher's attitude toward the children, especially outside the classroom, is not one of severity and repression but rather that of a benevolent dictator. As mentioned, the homeroom teacher system used in the secondary schools tends to build a close association between at least one teacher and a group of students, creating a bond that often lasts well beyond school years. Class size is usually about thirty-five to forty pupils, sometimes more, rarely less.

School collective
Шко́льный коллекти́в

So what, you may ask, has happened to the Party? It is sufficiently out of fashion that nothing is done in its name or for its sake. Some fondly remember the Good Old Days of clean, safe streets and affordable food. Currently, however, those who luxuriate in the freedom to express an opinion without going to jail are holding sway, even as their summer gardens turn into life-saving vegetable plots. The "Little Octobrists" are gone, as are the Pioneers and the Komsomols. What remains is a concern for the school group in addition to the new-found individual. Beneficent activities formerly associated with the Party (such as school trips) continue, but without the "drum roll" **без зво́на бараба́на**. (Of course, this setup won't work, either, if they continue not to pay the teachers.)

Law and order
Зако́н и поря́док

Law and order is not usually maintained by threat of bodily punishment, which is officially outlawed. Other, often more powerful devices are used.

One such device is the use of the group: antisocial behavior and poor grades are equivalent to letting the team down. The "team" here can mean any of a number of groups, including the family. Part of this group syndrome is the great dislike a tattletale **я́беда** often arouses. (The taunt is "**я́беда-беда́!**") The pupils support each other, and they consider telling on someone sinful. The problem is two-sided: the philosophy of mutual support and helpfulness in problems or projects concerning goals the teacher finds desirable is described as «**Оди́н за всех, все за одного́**»—naturally, all-for-one and one-for-all is a Good Thing; the other side is when the children hang together against the establishment—that is, the teacher. This is called **кругова́я пору́ка**—that is, collusion, and is obviously the bane of the teacher's existence.

The teacher is far from alone in efforts at maintaining law and order and keeping the academic backsliders from falling over the edge. After using the class groups first to aid positively, next perhaps to ridicule, then the teacher can use school honor (or ridicule) to make a point. The teacher can also report to the parents and enlist their cooperation. Most recalcitrants are taken care of by one of these means. In an extreme case, the student can be expelled from school. (Severe discipline problems are sometimes handled at boarding schools.) The academic nonachiever must be sent back to take a course over again **второго́дничество**. In maintaining academic achievement, however, the teacher is also held responsible. With too many repeaters, the teacher is regarded as not doing the job well.

The "PTA" meeting
Роди́тельское собра́ние

At least once a quarter is an evening meeting of teachers and parents. Any discipline or academic problems are discussed, and parents are expected to help resolve these problems. School or class projects and academic successes are also discussed. Parents are particularly involved in planning and arranging the graduation party **выпускно́й ве́чер**. Attendance at these meetings is barely short of obligatory.

Also, each class has a parents' committee **роди́тельский комите́т**, active parents who help arrange trips, invite famous writers to school, and the like. For the entire school is the parent group **шко́льный комите́т**, composed of parents from each grade level. It is they who help arrange the graduation party, and members of their group often assist homeroom teachers who expect trouble from parents they must call on.

Homework
Дома́шние зада́ния

One tenet of Russian pedagogy would seem to be that the busy child is doubly blessed; time spent for good in studying or practicing is time unavailable for unproductive mischief. In the first grade the pupil is not expected to exert strenuously, but the second grader requires about an hour every day on homework, and the ninth grader is expected to put in a minimum of three to four hours. High schoolers expect four and five hours a day as a minimum. (Note the terminology: зада́ча is a particular problem or task; зада́ние is an assignment, in school or otherwise.)

Extracurricular activities
Внекла́ссные заня́тия

The school also has much to do with activities not directly related to academic schoolwork. Homeroom teachers are often expected to take occasional small expeditions (for example, to a museum) with the classes in their charge; teachers are also expected to lead an interest group кружо́к. The vice-principal in charge of extracurricular activities is responsible for setting up these groups кружки́ that meet regularly to explore the joys of chess, puppetry, biology, chemistry, dancing, singing, and so on.

Time spent at school
Вре́мя в шко́ле

The most common type of secondary school сре́дняя шко́ла begins at about half past eight in the morning and ends at about two in the afternoon. The younger pupils at the primary level нача́льная шко́ла get out about noon. Class "hours" last forty-five minutes, with a ten-minute break переры́в between classes. One or two of these breaks are lengthened to twenty minutes to allow the pupils time enough to have a brief lunch or a snack за́втрак. (Food is not free, though it is subsidized for some pupils.) The children usually go home after school to eat their major meal of the day, but they can get it at school if they want.

Some schools have arrangements for children of primary school age to stay at school all day while their parents work. Their homework and play is supervised and they are fed dinner обе́д and later a snack по́лдник if necessary. The children are cared for, but still living at home. The title is "prolonged day" group гру́ппа продлённого дня or продлёнка.

School starts in the fall on the first of September and ends on about May 24th, when the last bell после́дний звоно́к sounds for the graduating eleventh graders. It is a day of copious tears for the graduates and quantities of flowers for the teachers. Graduation night выпускно́й ве́чер is a month later and the interim is filled with examinations, beginning with the seventh grade and especially for the ninth graders who will get their grade-school certificates and the eleventh graders who expect to get their diplomas.

DIFFERENT TYPES OF SCHOOLS
Ра́зные ти́пы школ

Boarding school
Шко́ла-интерна́т

Another type of school is the шко́ла-интерна́т, where pupils reside. Often special schools (described in the next section) are of this type. But many boarding schools have a regular curriculum. These schools are required, for instance, to care for orphans; they also have children who for some reason cannot be adequately cared for at home, through parental illness or neglect; and they frequently take children who have become a discipline problem. These schools should not be thought of as solely devoted to children with problems, however. Many children are in boarding schools simply because of the enormous convenience—not such a crass notion if one considers the extent of the housing problem. Contacts with home and the outside world are maintained as much as possible: many children spend their Sundays at home, and frequent trips to museums, factories, or soccer games are made to remind the children of the world around them. The boarding school employs not only teachers **учи́-тельницы** but also "upbringers" **воспи-та́тели**, who concern themselves with the physical and moral progress of the children in their care.

Special schools
Спецшко́лы

These schools emphasize developing special abilities, correcting or coping with special inabilities, or dealing with special situations. Some are schools for "difficult" children **для тру́дных подро́стков** and some for the retarded **для у́мственно отста́лых дете́й**. When at all possible, the regular curriculum is followed, except in those fields dealt with specifically in the specializations.

The Russian language student in the United States has probably heard of the language schools, for instance. These schools introduce a foreign language in the second grade (for three lessons a week) and then continue it all the way through school. In later grades, sometimes geography and literature, or perhaps technical translation, are taught in the foreign language. Moscow alone has more than one hundred such schools. English—the Queen's, rather than American English—is the most popular language, replacing French (of the nineteenth century) as the language of style. These schools are popular with parents not only because the quality of instruction is thought to be high but also because of the restrictions on who may attend: no child with hearing difficulties is accepted, and a child who seems to have less than average general ability is often not accepted. Often acceptance requires either "pull" or a substitute. Special schools are not devoted solely to foreign languages; special mathematics or physics schools, for example, are also fairly common.

Almost in a class by themselves are a relatively few but famous special talent schools. Those students who display considerable abilities in the arts are sent to schools that train musicians, ballet dancers, and artists. They are often boarding schools. A (largely experimental) school in **Академгородо́к** near **Новосиби́рск** has been established for those who show considerable abilities in the sciences, especially mathematics and physics.

And two types of schools are for training future army and navy officers: **Суво́ровское учи́лище** for the army (named after **Алекса́ндр Васи́льевич Суво́ров**, 1730–1800, who commanded Russian troops against the Turks at Rymnik and Izmail and against the French in the Italian and Swiss campaigns), and **Нахи́мовское учи́лище** for the navy (named for **Па́вел Степа́нович Нахи́мов**, 1802–1855, an admiral especially famous for his defense against the Turks in the Crimean War). These, too, are boarding schools. Preference is given to the orphaned children of army and navy personnel, but otherwise entrance is by competitive examination. As usual, the curriculum is the same as for the rest of the country, but also includes some military and naval studies.

New schools
Но́вые шко́лы

The great bulk of schooling has been described; they are the converted schools of yore. Before them were other schools, which are now returning to the business, literally, because they charge tuition. One is the "gymnasium" **гимна́зия**, which is associated with the former upper classes. The curriculum includes Latin or Greek, esthetics, and the like, and covers grades one through eleven. Also new is the lyceum **лице́й**, which is confined to the tenth and eleventh grades and which always has a specialty **с укло́ном**, perhaps the liberal arts, mathematics, law, or pedagogy. Some new schools specifically include religious teachings, and some have specific ethnic foci (Armenian, Georgian). Others attempt links to Western curricula (Accelerated Christian Education, International Baccalaureate), and there are an increasing number of alternative public schools. Most of these schools are also notable for their relatively smaller class size, of twenty to twenty-five pupils.

These schools have monetary problems above and beyond those associated with tuition fees: creating something from nothing is much more difficult than converting an existing framework.

TRANSLATIONS

a. According to the census of 1897, 29.3% of the men were literate and 13.1% of the women were literate in Russia; at the same time 59.9% of the men workers [as opposed to peasants] were literate, and 34.9% of women workers were literate. (**Александров, Народы, стр.** 475.)

b. According to the census of 1897, even in the European part of the country, for every 1000 people, 227 men were literate and 117 women were literate. (**Народное образование в РСФСР** (1917–1967 **гг.**) (**Москва**: **Просвещéние,** 1967), **стр.** 2.

c. A decree of the Central Committee of the Communist Party of July 25, 1930, established universal primary education beginning with the 1930–1931 school year; a seven-year universal education was established in cities and towns. (Obligatory universal seven-year education was established in the Russian Federation in 1949.) **Наро́дное образова́ние в РСФСР** (1917–1967 **гг.**), **стр.** 6.

d. 3. "A humanity that embraces the soul"— the poetry of A. S. Pushkin. The lyric hero.
   13. Oblomov, oblomovites, oblomovism (in Goncharov's Oblomov).
   32. "Eternal" problems and ways to solve them in the works of Bunin, Kuprin, Korolenko. (Analysis of one or two works of any of the writers.)
   40. The goal or aim of Mayakovskiy's satirical works. Recite one poem from memory and analyze it.

44. The theme of the tragic fate of man in a totalitarian state in the works of Platonov, Solzhenitsyn, Shalamov, Dombrovskiy (in one or several works of any of the writers).

e. 1. Department of Mechanics and Mathematics:
A journeyman can make more than 5 units (parts) in an hour while an apprentice can make 2 units less. A journeyman completes an order within a whole number of hours, but two apprentices together can do (the same job) one hour faster. How many units were ordered?
   2. Department of Computational Mathematics and Cybernetics:
Which of the (displayed) numbers is greater?
   3. Department of Physics:
Find the first term and the difference in an arithmetic progression if it is known that the fifth and ninth terms add up to forty, and the seventh and thirteenth terms add up to 58.
   4. The Chemistry Department:
There are three alloys: the composition of the first is 60% aluminum and 40% chrome. The second is 10% chrome and 90% titanium. The third is 20% aluminum, 5% chrome and 30% titanium. From them one must make an alloy that is 45% titanium. What percentage of chrome can there be in the new alloy?
   5. Department of Biology:
A right angle ABC has a perimeter 54 cm long. Side AC is more than 10 cm long. A circle with a radius of 6 cm whose center is on the line BC touches sides AB and AC. What is the area of the triangle? (Hint: the right angle must be labeled C to get the answer in the answer book.)
   6. Department of Soils:
Solve the equation (shown).

Answers: **1.** 24 **2.** $\sqrt[3]{\frac{1991}{1992}}$ **3.** a = 2, d = 3 **4.** [25; 40] **в проце́нтах.** **5.** 121,5 cm^2 **6.** $-\pi/8 + к\pi/2, \pi/16 + к\pi/4, к \in Z$

V

In the Russian's World

13

Speech

Речь

This chapter deals with some major and minor aspects of speech and language that are not usually discussed in language texts. It is important to be able to recognize northern and southern Russian accents or "illiterate" speech (if such is possible) and to know some of the common expletives. Russian "pig Latin" is included just for fun. The following major topics are discussed here:

Speech and society
Some special concerns of Russian speech
"Sudden" words and "semiwords"
Terms of rejection and endearment
Expletives

SPEECH AND SOCIETY
Речь и общество

Styles of speech
Стили речи

With time and considerable practice you will begin to notice the different language styles. Try reading many newspapers, and then read many children's stories, for example. Don't bother to look up all the words you don't know, but notice how many words and phrases are repeated again and again. Observe how some characters in modern writing tend to use phrases you learned in school and how others seem to have no relevance to your school texts. Notations in dictionaries that indicate style or obsolescence are helpful; for example: **книжн.(ое слово)**, literary or pedantic; **прост.(оречие)**, informal or slang; **устар.(евшее)**, obsolete; **обл.(астное)**, regional; **бран.(ное)**, abusive or swear word; **разг.(оворное)**, informal; **стар.(инное)**, archaic.

For guides to various levels of speech or styles in writing, many books are available with **культу́ра ре́чи** or **стили́стика** in the title. One very good, relatively short text by L. A. Kiselyova and others, *A Practical Handbook of Russian Style* (Moscow: Progress Publishers, no date), deals especially with styles in Russian for speakers of English and includes a key to the exercises. And **Корне́й Чуко́вский, Живо́й как жизнь** (Москва́: Изд. «Де́тская литерату́ра,» 1966) gives a clever and delightful presentation of one man's view of Russian, and how it has changed in his lifetime, including the trends he thinks are unfortunate, which are unavoidable, and which are to be relished.

For those interested in contemporary colloquial Russian usages, especially recommended are Russian sources, including publications of the Pushkin Russian Language Institute in Moscow **Институ́т ру́сского языка́ и́мени Пу́шкина**. Teachers of Russian would profit from the center's magazine, **Ру́сский язы́к за рубежо́м**, which often contains articles describing current styles and levels, which greetings are used and when, how to phrase requests, and so forth. Both Moscow and St. Petersburg Universities have published a number of very good texts for developing conversational Russian (with titles such as **Посо́бие по разви́тию ре́чи**). Their only drawback is that they are frequently out of print. Such publications are useful because usages change, and the spoken language reflects those changes more quickly than the written language. Russians in the United States speak the language that was in use when they left.

To enumerate the world of Russian slang **жарго́н** is a larger task than space allows here. (Though neither is a slang dictionary, there are two excellent sources for contemporary usage, including slang: one is Stephen Marder's *A Supplementary Russian-English Dictionary*, Slavica, 1992, which includes words and expressions the Oxford Russian Dictionary did not; and the other is *Vocabulary of Soviet Society and Culture* by Irina Corten, Duke University Press,

1992, which stresses background for contemporary expressions.) Slang in another language can often be identified by the appearance of an unusual or unfamiliar word or expression in place of the expected. Here are some examples from **Живо́й как жизнь**, by **Чуко́вский**:

хорошо́!—блеск! си́ла! мирово́! мирове́цки!

напи́ться допьяна́—накиря́ться

пойдём обе́дать—пошли́ руба́ть

мне э́то неинтере́сно—а мне до ла́мпочки

спать—кима́рить, заземли́ться

расска́зывать анекдо́ты—трави́ть анекдо́ты

The foreigner is better off making a rule not to use either slang or expressions labeled **просторе́чие** in the dictionary. **Просторе́чие** seems to cover a nebulous area of speech that ranges from slang to colloquial.[1] The reason for this ban is simply that the foreigner is rarely aware of the appropriateness, strength, and limitations of these expressions. The label **просторе́чие** does not really separate the unacceptable from the merely informal. The reason for this prohibition is perhaps clearer in English. Imagine that you are talking, in English, to a Russian teacher of English who regularly refers to his pupils as "кидз." A normal colloquialism? Yes, but even if you are not a schoolteacher, this "кидз" sounds very strange. Even with a strong accent, "children" would have been better.

Speech and education
Речь и образова́ние

Пусть ко мне в ко́мнату войдёт незнако́мец, и я по его́ ре́чи в пе́рвые же де́сять мину́т определю́ духо́вную его́ биогра́фию и уви́жу, начи́танный ли он челове́к,

---

1. For purposes of this discussion, "slang" is defined as nonstandard and unacceptable usage; "colloquial" here refers to a perfectly acceptable but conversational use of language.

враща́ется ли он в культу́рной среде́ и́ли он забулды́га, водя́щий компа́нию с неве́ждами.[a]

Distinguishing educated speech is an easy enough task for the native speaker. In English one double negative or an incorrect third person singular verb is all that is necessary to make an initial assumption about the speaker. "He don't do nothing" is a fine example. Leaving the *g* off the *-ing* makes it worse. The less educated Russian makes mistakes, too.

If you have been studying Russian using a system that stresses hearing and speaking, you have been learning the accepted educated forms. It follows, therefore, that consistent or frequent lapses (by the native speaker) from those patterns or forms often indicates uneducated (or careless) speech. Misplaced stress is one such lapse.

Incorrect	Correct
зво́нит	звони́т[2]
ква́ртал	кварта́л
мага́зин	магази́н
мо́лодежь	молодёжь
по́ртфель	портфе́ль
хозяева́	хозя́ева

Even for the beginning student of Russian, many of these words have been repeated correctly so often that the incorrect stress sounds wrong. Russian stress references tend to be conservative so that advanced students of Russian will notice that a few words carry a stress among contemporary educated Russians that stress dictionaries disallow. For example, buttonhole or loop пе́тля is often heard as петля́, salmon, ло́сось, as лосо́сь; and the dictionary gives "Whoops!" as "Оп-пля́!" but people say "Оп-пля!"

Grammatical forms are also a problem, even for the native speaker. Here are some of the more common mistakes:

Incorrect	Correct
бежа́т	бегу́т
да́дено	дано́
мно́го дело́в	мно́го дел
е́хай	поезжа́й
пеке́т	печёт
ско́лько вре́мя [3]	кото́рый час
ско́лько разо́в	ско́лько раз
место́в нет	мест нет
моё фами́лие	моя́ фами́лия
хуже́е	ху́же
чего́ ты де́лаешь?	что ты де́лаешь?

Overcompensations and the attempt at snobbery
Языково́й сноби́зм

Misguided people in all countries try to impress with their erudition, refinement, and sensibility. Too often they bend over so far backward that they fall flat on their faces. How might a Russian be snobbish in speech? Perhaps by pronouncing a foreign word as one imagines it to be pronounced in its language of origin: for instance, the Russian might say Викто́р Юго́ instead of the accepted Викто́р Гюго́. Or may try replacing е with э in any foreign word: милиционэ́р instead of милиционе́р; музэ́й instead of музе́й. (Contemporary young Russians would describe such speech as речь ста́рого интеллиге́нта. They themselves amaze us with their anglicisms.) Beyond this grayish area of poor taste is the wasteland of bad grammar and incorrect usage. Я ку́шаю is used by the pretentious ignoramus. Ку́шать is a verb suggesting considerable refinement: dining, rather than eating: Ба́рин ку́шает, а коро́ва ест. Its use in the first person singular arrogates a delicatesse that is so out of place when referring to oneself that it is wrong. On the other hand, the imperative Ку́шайте is polite and more formal than е́шьте. Using

2.   This pair brought up some discussion—the "incorrect" form is southern and is actually wrong, even if many people have to stop and think about which is correct.

3.   But Ско́лько вре́мя? is now becoming an acceptable expression for "What time is it?" Ско́лько вре́мени? is a standard expression for either "What time is it?" or "How long?"

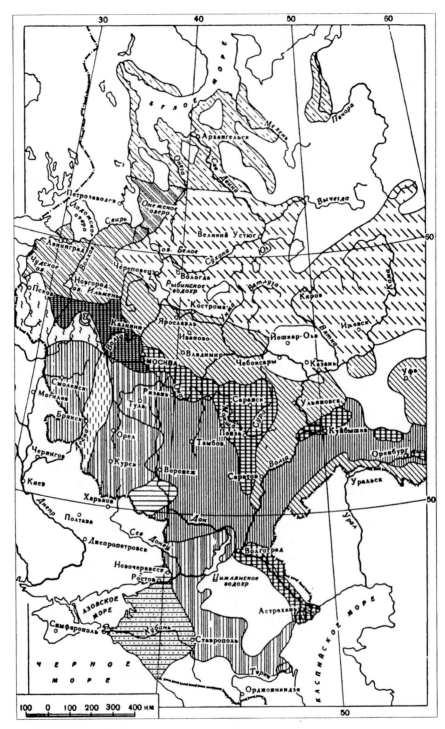

Russian dialects: northern are slanted lines, southern are perpendicular lines, and central dialects are cross-hatched areas.

words of foreign origin, often with the stress moved to the last syllable (reminiscent of French), is also a sign of affectation. By analogy, perhaps, with **докуме́нт**, **аргуме́нт**, **инструме́нт**, the would-be person of culture will say **фундаме́нт** (which is incorrect) instead of **фунда́мент** (the correct form).

Regional accents
Ме́стные го́воры

The English have quite a rigid system for establishing social status: one either speaks upperclass (Oxford) English or one has a regional and lower-class accent. In the United States we might detect generally where a person is from and whether that person has pretensions to education. However, in our conclusions about speech and social status we can be far less secure than the English. The Russian is in about the same predicament as we. In Russia, conformity to the standard (**литерату́рный язы́к**) phraseology, stress, and grammar is more important than ridding oneself of a local accent. This is true, of course, only if the accent is slight **о́канье** or **а́канье**, which is described later. The other characteristics of northern and southern accents are thought of as peculiar to peasant/lower-class/uneducated speech. Mr. Gorbachev is from southern Russia, and his frequent lapses in stress supplied a mountain of source material for comedians and opponents (**на́чать**, **при́нять**, **изобре́тение и т. д.**). Upon hearing a northern accent, the Russian will perhaps smile and mentally note where the speaker is from, but the speaker usually will not be looked down upon until the rules of acceptable grammar, stress, or usage are regularly breached.

The three major accent areas in spoken Russian are the northern, southern, and central.[4] The major distinguishing feature of the northern Russian accent is **о́канье**, the clear enunciation of all o's as **o**: **вода́**, **хорошо́**, **золото́й**. This is the feature you are most likely to hear and recognize. (Recordings by **Ура́льский наро́дный хор** supply examples.)

However, less vital and sometimes less common features of the northern accent include:

1. Pronunciation of unstressed **e** as **ё** at the end of a word or in front of hard consonants: **жена́**, **жёна́**; **село́**, **сёло́**; **весло́**, **вёсло́**; **пла́тье**, **пла́тьё**.

2. Pronunciation of the old **ять** as **и** (as in Ukrainian): **хлеб**, **хлиб**; **пе́сня**, **пи́сня**; **ме́сто**, **ми́сто**.

3. When stressed, pronunciation of **я** as **e**: **зять**, **зеть**; **взять**, **взеть**; **грязь**, **грезь**.

4. The yod (**й**) between vowels sometimes disappears: **быва́ет**, **быва́т**; **ду́мает**, **ду́мат**.

5. Pronunciation of the genitive singular masculine and neuter adjectival endings as **во** rather than **го**: **до́брого**, **до́брово**; **си́него**, **си́н(ё)во**; **того́**, **тово́**.

The major feature of the southern Russian accent is **а́канье** or **я́канье**, the pronunciation of unstressed **o** as **a** or **ъ**: either **харашо́** or **хърашо́** is heard. The **o** is heard only when stressed: **мой дом**, **о́кна**. Other southern peculiarities are that sometimes:

1. Unstressed **e** sounds like **и** or **я**: **река́**, **рика́/ряка́**; **несу́**, **нису́/нясу́**; **перо́**, **пиро́/пяро́**.

2. The **г** becomes a pharyngeal fricative as in Ukrainian. You can hear this sound when a Russian says **Го́споди!** since standard biblical pronunciation came from the south.

3. Third person singular and plural verb forms are pronounced as if there were a soft sign on the end: **нисеть**, **пайдеть**, **бируть**.

4. These classifications and examples of accent areas are cited in **А. М. Фи́нкель и Н. М. Баже́нов, Курс совреме́нного ру́сского языка́, 2-е изд. (Ки́ев: Изда́тельство «Радзя́нска шко́ла», 1965), стр. 17–19.**

4. Adjectival genitive singular masculine endings are pronounced as **го** rather than **во**.

5. Pronunciation of accusative-genitive cases of personal and reflexive pronouns use **e** in place of the **я**: **тебя́, т(и)бе́; меня́, м(и)не́; себя́, с(и)бе́.**

The central Russian (Moscow) accent found itself in the relatively small wasteland between the northern and southern accents and took the democratic way out. Its vowels are pronounced in the southern way and its consonants in the northern way, except for the southern replacement of **e** for **я** in pronouns.

Despite these differences in the northern and southern accents in Russian, what is truly amazing and quite satisfying for the student of Russian is the relative uniformity of the language for speakers from one end of the huge country to the other. The differences described are really quite small and rarely impair understanding; rather, they indicate that the speaker does not know or care to hide the regional accent.

SOME SPECIAL CONCERNS OF RUSSIAN SPEECH
Не́которые осо́бенности ру́сской ре́чи

You or thou?
Вы или ты?

Although it would seem that trying to speak Russian imposes decisions about choices of personal pronouns, **вы** or **ты** (*you* or *thou*), in fact it's easy—use **вы** until something else is offered. (Just because someone can call you "thou" does not mean that you can do the same to them. Rank and age make a big difference. Wait until the Russian makes a suggestion.) Of course, the problem of choosing **ты** or **вы** arises only in the singular because the plural *you* must be **вы** no matter how near and dear the referents might be. Part of the difficulty in describing the use of **ты** is determining what constitutes formality and

closeness. That depends very much on the individuals involved and the practices observed in the (speech) community from which each came. For instance, northern Russians are reputed to be somewhat more reserved in using it than are southern Russians. In the nineteenth century all the peasants of one village commonly used **ты** with one another. Indeed, according to one authority, the use of **вы** to refer to only one person was a borrowing from the French (*tu/vous*), unknown in Russia until about 1700.

Among Russians, the use of **вы** is polite and is used towards (1) someone you do not know well; (2) those in any official or formal situation; (3) those whom one respects; (4) those in a superior position, or those of your generation or older (assuming that you are grown up).

Ты can be used (1) when politeness is not a specifically required factor; (2) in unofficial situations; (3) in friendly and familiar relations with the person spoken to; (4) addressing someone inferior in rank and younger in age; (5) talking to God. The foreigner should use **вы** toward all but children and infants unless specifically given leave to use **ты**. No student should ever use **ты** with an instructor.

From the foregoing you should conclude that switching from **вы** to **ты** and back again takes place fairly often: a formal situation can change **ты** to **вы** and anger can change **ты** to **вы** (a spouse who's decided *not* to let well enough alone), and vice versa (a boss trying to impress a subordinate about something). In the following quote the speaker switches from the formal address in front of others to the familiar: **Здра́вствуйте, я не опозда́ла? Бори́с Серге́евич, вы ещё не на́чали? . . . Послу́шай,**

Борь, я хочу вы́ступить, но лучше в конце́, ла́дно? ("Hello, I'm not late, am I? You haven't begun yet, have you Boris Sergeyevich?... Listen, Boris, I want to give my talk, but I'd rather do it at the end, all right?")

Ты и Вы
Пусто́е *вы* серде́чным *ты*
Она, обмо́лвясь, замени́ла,
И все счастли́вые мечты́
В душе́ влюблённой возбуди́ла.
Пред ней заду́мчиво стою́;
Свести́ оче́й с неё нет си́лы;
И говорю́ ей: как *вы* ми́лы!
И мы́слю: как *тебя* люблю́![b]

Пу́шкин

Я, ве́рно, был упря́мей всех,
Не слу́шал клеветы́
И не счита́л по па́льцам тех,
Кто звал тебя́ на «ты». ...[c]

Си́монов

The use of thou **ты** with name forms is described in Chapter 3, under "Addressing the Russian."

Switching Over
Перехо́д на ты

Thou **Ты** is all a child will hear until about age fourteen or about the (Russian) eighth grade when some teachers, especially those of the opposite sex and teachers new to the class, will begin to use *you* **вы**.

What the "thou" form does not emphasize is respect. Because some people require some of that, they can get huffy when they think the thou form has been misapplied to them: **Что ты мне ты́каешь? Я с тобой свине́й не пасла́!** "How come you are using 'thou' with me? We didn't herd pigs together!" The overuse of *thou* is associated with the peasants, while the intelligentsia sometimes hold onto **вы** through long and dear friendships. Also, older people tend to be slower to accept *thou* and younger people, among themselves at least, make the transition sooner. The use of **ты** is rather like walking around in your underwear—with some people and situations, it simply isn't right. It is perfectly reasonable and common that one of a pair might say, "You call me **вы**, and I'll call you **ты**." This device is frequently resorted to when an age or rank difference is notable. (See the silhouette.)

Once adults have agreed on a mutual "thou," then the event can be confirmed with a short ceremony, usually accomplished at a dinner party, called "drinking to brotherhood" **вы́пить на бру́дершафт**. Glasses are filled (and not with water), the arms holding the glasses are intertwined, and the glasses are emptied from that position. They kiss, and it's "thou" forevermore. (The ceremony is not a requirement, but has its advantages.)

Highly recommended for those reading Russian literature in the original is Paul Friedrich, "Structural Implications of Russian Pronominal Usage," *Sociolinguistics*, ed. William Bright, Janua linguarum, Series maior 20 (The Hague: Mouton, 1966), pp. 215–259. Despite the verbiage, many examples and much background information are included. For those who expect to work (not just tread on) the soil of Academe, the discussion at the end supplies fine examples of academic one-upmanship and a few delightful anecdotes.

The Russian "Lisp"
Карта́вость

Two sounds seem to be especially difficult for a few (native) Russian speakers to make, the *r* and the hard *l*. The standard mispronunciation of either or both of these sounds is a kind of lisp called **карта́вость**[5] (**карта́вить**, to lisp this way): «**Он карта́вит на эр и́ли на эл.**» This particular lisp consists of a uvular *r* as in French or German, pronouncing the hard *l* as *u*, or both. Thus a Russian can sound French when saying **кукуру́за**; and **сала́т** becomes **сауа́т**. This lapse in pronunciation is frequent enough to suggest cultural as well as physical reasons for its persistence. In the past, when French (and

---

5. Speech defects caused by a physical deformation such as a cleft palate are referred to as **косноязы́чие**.

earlier, German) was the language of culture itself, the French *r* was something to be cultivated, not made fun of. There is even another verb to denote the use of the uvular (French) *r*—грасси́ровать: Она́ говори́ла, коке́тливо грасси́руя.

Nowadays, this **карта́вость** is not encouraged,[6] and indeed it seems to be much less frequent among younger Russians.

Using diminutives
Употребле́ние уменьши́тельных форм

Conversational Russian makes a very wide use of diminutive forms. Most of the time, these forms are used to indicate the speaker's attitude toward the subject. Regarding anything as cute, charming, small, lovable, or the like, the speaker will use a diminutive: for example, **ёж, ёжик**; **стол, сто́лик**.

The speaker who wants something will often lace at least part of a request with diminutives, thereby either expressing the smallness of the request or describing how nice the person might be who is to fulfill it: «чайку́, пожа́луйста» is vastly more pleasant than «ча́ю, пожа́луйста»; and **немно́жко** sounds like less but probably amounts to the same as **немно́го**.

Diminutives are also frequently found in use by or in reference to women and their belongings: **шля́па, шля́пка**; **ко́фта, ко́фточка**. And women almost invariably refer to their children with a more lavish use of diminutives.

Па́па	Ма́ма
Андрю́ша	Андрю́шенька
Пе́тя	Пе́тенька
Же́ня	Же́нечка

These are some of the frequent but optional uses of diminutives. On occasion, however, their use is obligatory. In discussing babies, their attributes, parts, and possessions, diminutives are always used. A red-haired baby is **ры́женький**, never **ры́жий**, a red-haired adult. For babies: **штаны́—штани́шки**; **руба́шка—руба́шечка**; **рука́—ру́чка**; **нога́—но́жка**. And babies are **краси́венькие, хоро́шенькие, гря́зненькие, чи́стенькие**, and so forth.

These distinctions are not found in English, so you must make a special effort first to recognize diminutives and later to use them. A warning especially applicable to reading: not all the words that look like diminutives are diminutives. **Воро́нка** is not a small crow or raven but a funnel; a Christmas tree must be **ёлка** while **ель** is a spruce tree. **Рука́** is a hand, but **ру́чка** can be, besides a small hand, a handle or a pen. Also, **ла́мпа** is a lamp, but **ла́мпочка** is a light bulb; **кры́ша** is a roof, but **кры́шка** is a lid.

The excessive use of diminutives can indicate rather low social status, limited education, or simply poor taste.[7]

Russians and their alphabet
Ру́сская а́збука, ру́сский алфави́т

In the beginning of Russian writing, in the ninth and tenth centuries, there were two alphabets as shown. Two Macedonian-Bulgarian brothers and monks, Cyrill and Methodius, since sainted, were assigned the task of designing the scriptures (Cyrill) and translating them (Methodius). The origin of Glagolitic **глаго́лица**, evidently the earlier alphabet, depends upon who is telling the story: St. Cyril himself may have been responsible; Cyrillic **кири́ллица** looks Greek to us because it *was* Greek, with the addition of a few necessary sound representations that the Greeks didn't have. This Greek version won out over the other (it was obviously much simpler) and was itself simplified by a reform of Peter the Great in 1710: some letters vanished (**юс ма́лый, юс большо́й, пси, кси, оме́га,**

---

6. It is often attributed to Jews, for instance. Lenin's enemies used this lisp in their arguments to suggest that he was at least part Jewish.

7. For more details on the formation and use of diminutives, see B. V. Bratus, "The Formation and Expressive Use of Diminutives," *Studies in the Modern Russian Language*, no. 6, ed. Dennis Ward (New York: Cambridge University Press, 1969).

НАЗВАНИЯ БУКВ	КИРИЛЛИЦА	ГЛАГОЛИЦА
АЗ	А а	
БУКИ	Б б	
ВЕДИ	В в	
ГЛАГОЛЬ	Г г	
ДОБРО	Д д	
ЕСТЬ	Є єєє Ю ю	
ЖИВЕТЕ	Ж ж	
ЗЕЛО	Ѕ ѕ ѕ ѕ	
ЗЕМЛЯ	З з	
ИЖЕ	Н н и	
И	І (ï) ï (ћ)	
КАКО	К к	
ЛЮДИ	Л л	

НАЗВАНИЯ БУКВ	КИРИЛЛИЦА	ГЛАГОЛИЦА
МЫСЛЕТЕ	М м	
НАШ	N n	
ОН	О о	
ПОКОЙ	П п	
РЦЫ	Р р	
СЛОВО	С с	
ТВЕРДО	Т т	
УК	ОУ оу оу	
ФЕРЬТ	Ф ф	
ХЕР	Х х х	
ОТ	Ѡ ѡ ѡ	
ЦЫ	Ц ц	
ЧЕРВЬ	Ү ү ч (çч)	
ША	Ш ш	

НАЗВАНИЯ БУКВ	КИРИЛЛИЦА	ГЛАГОЛИЦА
ШТА	Щ щ	
ЕР	Ъ	
ЕРЫ	Ъı ъı (ъı) ън	
ЕРЬ	Ь ь	
ЯТЬ	Ѣ ѣ	
Ю	Ю ю	
И + А = Я	Iа iа	
МАЛЫЙ ЮС	Ѧ ѧ Iѧ	
БОЛЬШОЙ ЮС	Ѫ ж (Ѫ)	
	Ѭ ѭ	
КСИ	Ѯ ѯ	
ПСИ	Ѱ ѱ	
ФИТА	Ѳ ѳ	
ИЖИЦА	Ѵ ѵ ѵ	

A sample of old orthography written by a late 19th-century musicologist

йжица, зело́), and others were changed. This alphabet was in use up to 1918, when it too was simplified to the one now in use, by the removal of **ять, фита, i,** and by dropping the use of the hard sign at the end of a word.

Essentially every English-speaking child learns the ABC's—that is, how to pronounce the letters of the alphabet and in proper sequence. The Russians seem to have a problem with their alphabet. Neither the pronunciation of the letters in the alphabet nor the order in which they appear are of great concern. If you ask a Russian to recite the alphabet, you are most likely to hear a jumble of sounds that amount to what the letters sound like rather than a formal recital of the names of the letters. And toward the end of the alphabet, order is also usually lost.

Evidence of this phenomenon appears in the common pronunciation of letter abbreviations. Some letters can be pronounced two ways: for instance, **эр** or **рэ**; **эс** or **сэ**; **эф** or **фэ**; **ка** or **кэ**. Although both dictionaries and school texts have tables showing the proper pronunciation of the letters of the alphabet, even they disagree!

This version appears in a first-grade text and is probably the most common:

Аа	Бб	Вв	Гг	Дд	Ее	Ёё
а	бэ	вэ	гэ	дэ	е	ё

Жж	Зз	Ии	Йй	Кк	Лл	Мм
жэ	зэ	и	(и кра́ткое)	ка	эль	эм

Нн	Оо	Пп	Рр	Сс	Тт	Уу
эн	о	пэ	эр	эс	тэ	у

Фф	Хх	Цц	Чч	Шш	Щщ	Ъъ
эф	ха	це	че	ша	ща	твёрдый знак

Ыы	Ьь	Ээ	Юю	Яя
ы	мягкий знак	э	ю	я

Nevertheless, the student of Russian should learn both the order and the pronunciation of Russian letters. Russian vocabulary learning is such that those who know the order of the letters will find their words fastest.

The Russian pronunciation of Latin and Greek letters, so commonly used in mathematics, are in Chapter 15. And the occasional use of letters in chemical formulas is described in the Appendix, as are the Morse code and the Braille alphabet in Russian.

Russian "pig Latin"
Фуфа́йский язы́к

Russian unfortunately does not have a single child's language that corresponds in its universality to our pig Latin. Instead there are a variety, if not a welter, of similar possibilities. One, for instance, is to take the last syllable of a word and put it at the beginning: **сюда́, дасю́**. Other varieties introduce nonsense syllables: **я хочу́ пить, я́хонцы хочу́хонцы пи́тьхонцы**. The form cited in the heading, **фуфа́йский язы́к**, places **фа** or **фу** before each syllable. Thus, **ничего́** becomes **фани́-фаче́-фаго́** or **фуни́-фуче́-фуго́**. Other syllables—**по, ка**, and so on—are used in the same way. So, yes the phenomenon of children's languages exists, but not an equivalent of pig Latin.

"SUDDEN" WORDS AND "SEMIWORDS"
Восклица́ния

Interjections
Междоме́тия

Expressions used almost unconsciously or involuntarily for agreement, warning, pain, and the like are called **междоме́тия**. They are used constantly in daily speech but are not often granted the status of *word,* and some are not even capable of standard transcription. Careful attention should be paid to them, however, because misinterpreting some of the most common ones is so easy.

The following list gives a few of the common expressions of this sort. The Russian equivalents of the American *uh-huh* (assent) and *huh-uh* (dissent) require a somewhat fuller explanation. In the United States, when we say,

"uh-huh," we mean "yes" or are at least admitting agreement with whoever is talking. Russians make the same sound, but it is merely a supportive sound to indicate that they are listening. It does not necessarily indicate agreement with what is being said (although it *can*), nor even that the Russian has understood what has been said (although it can mean *that*, too). Because both Russians and Americans use this expression almost unconsciously, it is very easy to misinterpret it. The Russian sound is often written as **Угу́** or **Ага́** but is pronounced as **аха́** (with the mouth open more broadly than in English). A Russian understanding you and wishing to express agreement might say **так, так**, often drawing out the vowel: **та-а-ак**. The Russian expression **ни-ни́** is equivalent to "**ника́к нельзя́**" (total denial), and **не-е-е** is often a request meaning, "Thanks, don't bother. . . . I'd rather not."

Other interjections that you might come across include:

Уф! Phew! (I'm tired.)

Ай! **Ай-ай**! **Ой**! **Ой-ой**! Ouch! (It hurts.)

Уа́! Wa! (baby's cry)

Фу! **Фу-фу́**! Pee-you! (It stinks! **Фу**! is also used for mild disappointment.)

Тс-с-с! **Ш-ш-ш**! Sh! (not voiced), **Ша**! (loudly and voiced) Be quiet/Shut up! (strong and low, i.e., vulgar)

Цыц! Sh! (peremptory command to a small child)

Тс-с-с! Psst! (Listen to this.)

Чхи! **Ап-чхи́**! Ah-choo!

О́п-пля́! Whoops! Oops! Alley-oop! (Up you go!) (can also be used for dogs doing tricks, as can **Гоп**!)

Ой! Oh! (surprise, combined with fright)

Ах! Oh! (surprise, delight, or fright)

Ну! **Да ну́**! Well! (surprise and some disbelief)

Ну! Come on! etc. (the word of a thousand uses: as prod, dismay, delight)

Ox! Oh! (dismay, sadness, pain)

Эй! Hey! (You, there!)

М-м-м, Э-э-э, М-м-гм Uh-h, ah-h . . . (hesitation, when rendered in print, though the actual sound, made with the mouth shut, is not much different from ours)

М-м-да. Well, yes. (doubtful agreement)

Аý! Halloo! (A signal for "Where are you?" commonly used among Russians, who are out together hunting mushrooms or gathering berries, in order not to lose one another. It is also used in answer to any loud call.)

Как аýкнется, так и откли́кнется. People will respond in the same way they are addressed.[8]

Ай-ай! Ой-ой! Oh, oh! (disappointment or dismay)

Ай-ай-ай! (pronounced "**айяяй**") Tsk-tsk! (Shame on you!) (The English clicking sound "tsk-tsk" in Russian is used to call small animals.)

Тьфу! (Strong disgust or disappointment: our equivalent might be anything from "Nuts!" to "Damn it!" The Russian sound resembles spitting, and is easily achieved by starting out with your tongue between your teeth.)

Бр-р! Br-r! (It's cold!)

Чу! "Listen!" or "Look!" (old fashioned)

Чур! Originally, a warning of a limit in a child's game; now, a general warning: "Watch out!"

Чур меня́! Don't touch me! Stay away! I don't want to play. (Originally, an instruction to the Devil, to stay away; later, it became part of child's play.)

Айда́! Used mostly among country children for "C'mon!" or "Let's go!"

---

8. In other words, people will treat you the same way you treat them.

«У-упс»,—поду́мал я уже на америка́нский лад (на свой лад, я поду́мал бы «о-опс»).

В. Аксёнов[d]

Warnings and alarms
Предостереже́ния и трево́га

If you will come to serious harm by continuing to do what you are doing, the Russian will yell "**Береги́сь!**" or "**Стоп!**" (**Стоп** is also commonly used as part of the set of traffic signals.) Wishing to turn your attention to a possible danger, the Russian says "**Смотри́ по́д ноги/что де́лаешь!**" or, more formally, "**Осторо́жно!**" Among children, the whispered shout "**Ата́с!**" is a warning of approaching authority (teachers, grown-ups, and others).

When you have already come to grief, the cry is **Помоги́те!** or **Спаси́те!** with especially long stress on the **и**. To summon the aid of others (either as an observer or as a victim), "**На по́мощь!**" or "**На подмо́гу!**" can be used.

If you need police assistance, yell "**Карау́л!**" This call is also a request for personal aid, so that it can mean "Help!" in addition to "Police!" For fire, the scream is "**Пожа́р!**"

TERMS OF REJECTION AND ENDEARMENT
Бра́нные и ла́сковые обраще́ния

Technically, the list of names people call one another is almost endless and most can be found in dictionaries. The foreigner cannot spend forever in a dictionary, however, nor will the dictionary reveal the strength or commonness of a word. Compiled here is a very select list of the most commonly used terms of rejection and endearment. Modern literature can supply dozens more. Any of these words can be used alone, but they are also often modified for added strength. "**Скоти́на безро́гая!**" ("Hornless cattle!") is somehow worse than merely "Скоти́на!" And "Ду́шенька моя́!" seems just a little stronger than "Ду́шенька!"

Name-calling
Бра́нные обраще́ния

The strength or seriousness of name-calling is often quite dependent on situation. As in *The Virginian*, if one smiles when saying it, the intent can be just the opposite of the literal meaning of the words used: **парши́вый поросёнок**, translated, means "mangy little pig," but it is used often as a term of endearment, especially toward small children.

Most of the words listed below, however, are usually used in their pejorative sense and were chosen for their frequency of use. They are divided into two sets, the general and the specialized. The general words might be compared to calling someone a "dirty bum" in American English, even when the name-caller is quite well aware that the object of derision is in fact neither dirty nor a bum. Though they are used in a general sense, they usually refer to a specific vice or fault. Words referring specifically to men (m.) or women (f.) and especially mild or strong words are noted.

General pejorative terms include the following:

балда́ stupidity (from the thick end or stump of a stick)

болва́н (m.) stupidity or laziness (from an idol, a roughly hewn log, or a stone)

гад (m.), **га́дина** vileness (**гадю́ка** the common poisonous snake of Russia; **га́дость** something revolting, disgusting—very strong)

дуби́на stupidity (a large oak stick).

дура́к, ду́рень (m.), **ду́ра** (f.) stupidity (m.: weak; f.: fairly strong)

зара́за pestilence personified

идио́т (m.), **идио́тка** (f.) stupidity

мерза́вец (m.), **мерза́вка** (f.) vileness (**ме́рзость** something revolting, sickening, disgusting—strong)

наха́л (m.), **наха́лка** (f.) brazenness

негодя́й (m.), **негодя́йка** (f.) worthlessness and nastiness (**никуда́ не годи́тся**) good for nothing)

осёл (m.) stupidity or stubbornness (an ass)

па́костник (m.), **па́костница** (f.) defilement or contamination, often with deception involved (**па́кость** something dirty/revolting—strong)

парази́т (m.), **парази́тка** (f.) parasitism

паску́да vileness (**паску́дить** equates to де́лать га́дости—very strong and crude)

подле́ц (m.) **подлю́га, по́длая** (f.) dishonesty or lowness (from bottom, base; **под** hearth; **подо́шва** sole)

подо́нок (m.) scum or slime (very strong)

свинья́ crudeness or vileness (from swine, hog)

сво́лочь general lowness (strong)

скоти́на crudeness or stupidity (from cattle—strong)

сте́рва lowness (from carrion—strong)

су́ка promiscuousness (bitch—strong)

су́кин сын (m.) general lowness (son of a bitch—strong)

хам (m.), **ха́мка** (f.) rudeness (from the biblical character Ham)

холе́ра general nastiness (from cholera)

хулига́н (m.), **хулига́нка** (f.) rascality exceeding mischievousness (from hooligan)

Among the words for specific offensiveness:

ба́ба a peasant wife or woman (mild when applied to women who are not peasants; stronger when applied to men with traits of weakness, indecision)

безде́льник (m.), **безде́льница** (f.) a shiftless, lazy person (**без де́ла**)

ве́дьма (f.) a mean, bad-tempered woman; a witch

дармое́д (m.), **дармое́дка** (f.) a freeloader (**да́ром ест**) мошéнник (m.), мошéнница (f.)   a swindler, cheater (from мошнá purse)

недонóсок (m.)   a prematurely born person; therefore, one thought to be weak and poorly put together, mentally and physically

потаскýха (f.)   a whore

проходúмец (m.), проходúмка (f., rarely used)   a person capable of doing almost anything dishonest, especially by wile

разгильдя́й (m.), разгильдя́йка (f.)   someone who pays no attention to appearance or business affairs; a slob

растя́па   a careless, awkward, and stupid individual

стáрая каргá (f.)   a mean old woman; a witch

стáрый хрен (m.)   an "old man," implying impotence

холýй (m.)   a slovenly and subservient man

шалопáй (m.)   a purposeless and uninterested person, often applied to a teenager

шлю́ха (f.)   a streetwalker or prostitute (strong)

Terms of endearment
Лáсковые обращéния

It is perhaps a sad comment on humanity that it is much easier to think of commonly used bad names for people than good ones. Here are some good ones, with the major forms in which they appear, their meaning, and special notes on frequency and strength:

голýбчик   from гóлубь, pigeon (very common)

голýбушка

голубóк

дорогóй (-ая)   dear (mild and very common)

дорогýша   (bordering on the saccharine)

дорогýля

душá (моя́)   soul (old-fashioned)

золотóй (-ая) ты мой (моя́)   gold

ты моё зóлото

зóлотце моё

красáвец, красáвица   beautiful

лáпочка, лáпонька   little paw, "sweetheart," (fairly common)

любóвь моя́   love

любúмый (-ая)

мúлый (-ая) моя́   darling (very frequent)

мúлочка

мúленький (-ая)

ненагля́дный (-ая) мой   I-can't-get-enough-of-looking-at-you (very strong and less frequent)

роднóй (-ая) мой   birth, family, kin, or country (common)

сéрдце моё   heart

сердéчко моё

сóлнышко моё   My sunshine! (especially endearing, considering the climate; very common)

EXPLETIVES
Вóзгласы

The use of expletives here and there makes an interesting contrast. For us, "God!" is "taking the name of the Lord in vain," while for the Russian "Бóже!" and "Гóсподи!" call upon God without any hint of poor taste and without offense to anyone. The following are other expletives used in Russia, regardless of any religious convictions:

Бóже мой!   Good heavens! (common and used in surprise, dismay, and disbelief; Бóже is a remnant of the vocative case for Бог God)

Гóсподи!   Good Lord! (an equivalent in intent and prevalence to "Бóже мой," also in the vocative case)

Рáди Бóга!   For heaven's sakes! (often part of a plea: "Рáди Бóга, не ходú тудá опя́ть!" "For heaven's sake, don't go there again!")

Не дай Бог!   Упасú Бог! Бóже упасú!   Heaven forbid!

Слáва Бóгу!   Thank heaven!

Other such locutions sometimes fill several pages in a Russian dictionary (under **бог**). These are the most common, however. (Notice that the Soviets were careful not to capitalize God.)

Though God is called upon frequently and almost with impunity, the Devil cannot be referred to so easily. The problem for the foreigner is to know when using "the Devil" expressions is all right—they are sufficiently strong that most people are offended by their use. The prohibition against the Devil is particularly rooted in the superstition that calling upon him is likely to make him appear, and this explains the many substitutes for devil **чёрт**: **шут, пёс, нелёгкая, нечистая (сила), бес, леший**. On the other hand, these expressions are not so offensive as "Not bloody likely!" was for Liza in *Pygmalion*. The degree of offense taken by the use of these words is highly dependent on who uses them and under what conditions. They are stronger when specifically directed against other people; thus, **Иди к чёрту!** can equal "Go to hell!" while **Чёрт возьми!** can mean merely "Darn it!" **Чёрт! К чёрту! Чёрт побери (подери, возьми)!** and (the strongest) **К чёртовой матери!** are the most commonly used expressions, but many others are in circulation. Soldiers doubtless use these expressions for any mild offense. They are sufficiently strong that they are not recommended for use by foreigners.

The list of usable (inoffensive) words to express anger, disgust, and the like does not seem to offer a large variety, but the following are strong enough to be worthwhile, yet safe enough to use.

Фу! Фу-фу́! Фу́-ты! Фу́-ты, ну́-ты! (relatively mild dismay or disgust, very common)

Тьфу! (strong rejection, disgust, dismay)

Ёлки-па́лки! (fairly strong surprise and dismay)

Ерунда́! (Каки́е) глу́пости! Вздор! Бред! Nonsense! That's silly! Hogwash! Balderdash!

Пустяки́! It's nothing. It's trivial. (dismissal of importance, also, therefore, used as an answer to "thank you")

Unprintable words **Непеча́тные слова** are so awful that they are described under conduct, rather than mere speech.

TRANSLATIONS

a. A stranger need only come into the room and in the first ten minutes I can tell his cultural biography; I can tell whether he is well read and whether he moves in cultivated society or whether he is a drunk who keeps company with numbskulls. **К. Чуко́вский, Живо́й как жизнь, стр.** 38.

b.   Thou and You
She made a slip: by replacing an empty "you" with a warm "thou" she awakened all the happy dreams in an enamored soul. I stand in front of her lost in thought; I haven't the strength to take my eyes off her; And I say: how kind of you! And I think: Oh, how I love thee!   Pushkin

c. It's true, I was more stubborn than all the rest, I did not listen to the slanders, and I did not count on my fingers all those who called you "thou.". . . Simonov

d. "Oops," I thought, in the American way. My way, I would have thought, "Oh-ohps." V. Aksenov[9]

9. (We highly recommend *In Search of Melancholy Baby В поисках грустного беби* by V. Aksenov for his descriptions of Russian reactions to life in America.)

14

Nature

Природа

Мы не можем ждать милостей от природы; взять их у неё — наша задача.[1]

Мичурин[a]

Less than a lifetime ago, most Russians had to deal directly with nature—the land, the seasons, the plants and animals—not only to stay alive, but to make a living as well. As Russia tries to revamp its economic system, the proximity of this collective memory may be enough to keep hunger and cold from killing the enterprise. People still remember how to plant potatoes, salt the cabbage, pickle the cucumbers, raise ducks and geese, and even how to build log houses.

The land is huge. The rolling flatlands seem to go on forever, but it is not our Midwest transplanted. There is something vaguely wild about it, or at least unkempt. The mere fact that it is on another continent changes the mix of what willingly grows, and the physical separation from our ancestors has allowed another set of ways to use nature. And Russia is much farther North—New York is at the same latitude as the southern border of the Black Sea. (They think "Black Sea" when we think "Caribbean.")

CLIMATE
Климат

It is colder there: it's much closer to the North Pole **се́верный по́люс** and no broad seas or oceans ameliorate or contain the great masses of cold air that spread to the south and west in the winter **зима́**. The "cold pole" of the world is in Yakutsk (Eastern Siberia) with a January average temperature of –40C° (which, oddly enough, is also –40F°). But Moscow and Minneapolis share similar winter temperatures. Those who reject the use of fur coats (or raising animals for their fur) freeze sooner. When I mentioned that there were such people in the United States, a Russian friend suggested they come to Russia and wait for the bus in January.

---

1. A politically correct statement in the earlier days.

The latitude makes the winter not just colder, but also longer.

Зимнее у́тро

Моро́з и со́лнце, день чуде́сный!
Ещё ты дре́млешь, друг преле́стный—
Пора́, краса́вица, просни́сь:
Откро́й со́мкнуты не́гой взо́ры
Навстре́чу се́верной Авро́ры,
Звездо́ю се́вера яви́сь! . . .

Пу́шкин

Зимний ве́чер

Бу́ря мглою не́бо кро́ет,
Ви́хри сне́жные крутя́;
То, как зверь, она́ заво́ет,
То запла́чет, как дитя́; . . .

Пу́шкин

Spring весна́ finally does come, the ice on the rivers breaks up "Лёд тро́нулся!" with a great grinding noise, and suddenly—for the seasons времена́ го́да are very marked—birds come in flocks, some greening appears, and the country roads доро́ги become impassable бездоро́жье—mud is everywhere.

Люблю́ грозу́ в нача́ле ма́я,
Когда́ весе́нний, первый гром,
Как бы резвя́ся и игра́я,
Грохо́чет в не́бе голубо́м. . . .

Тю́тчев

Summer ле́то is short. Leaves, flowers, berries, and fruits appear in quick succession, and then as quickly disappear until next year. Mushrooms flash onto the scene with late summer and early fall rains, and suddenly the most urban of Russians is out in the woods, a basket in one hand and a knife in the other. With good luck there will be a long Indian summer ба́бье ле́то.

Ох, ле́то кра́сное! люби́л бы я тебя́,
Когда́ б не зной, да пыль, да комары́,
да му́хи. . . .

Пу́шкин

Autumn о́сень brings the harvest урожа́й, and is marked by flocks of birds on their flight south; animals retreat to their winter cover and small children look forward not only to ice hockey, skating, and skiing, but also to making small ice mountains ледяны́е го́рки and sliding down them. It was Pushkin's favorite season:

Осень

Уны́лая пора́! оче́й очарова́нье!
Прия́тна мне твоя́ проща́льная краса́—
Люблю́ я пы́шное приро́ды увяда́нье,
В багре́ц и в зо́лото оде́тые леса́,
В их се́нях ве́тра шум и све́жее дыха́нье,
И мглой волни́стою покры́ты небеса́,
И ре́дкий со́лнца луч, и первые моро́зы,
И отдалённые седо́й зимы́ угро́зы.

Пу́шкин

THE FORESTS AND THE TREES
Леса́ и дере́вья

In the farthest North is the tundra ту́ндра, where what life can subsist, with the cold above and the permafrost ве́чная мерзлота́ below, is small and mean as the conditions it is offered. Some grasses зла́ки, fast-blooming wildflowers тра́вы, and dwarf shrubs ка́рликовые куста́рники provide some grazing for reindeer or refuge and food for small animals who themselves are food for the passing polar fox песе́ц.

The taiga тайга́ is the northern evergreen forests вечнозелёный лес of coniferous trees хво́йный лес, including pine сосна́; spruce ель; juniper можжеве́льник; and cedar кедр; plus the deciduous conifer, the larch ли́ственница. Fir пи́хта is associated with Siberia. The area covered by these forests is tremendous, encompassing almost all of Siberia and the Far East that is not tundra ту́ндра. This wealth of forest is beginning to be exploited by foreigners with money but no other stake in the environment окружа́ющая среда́. The government has made some attempts to protect it, one of

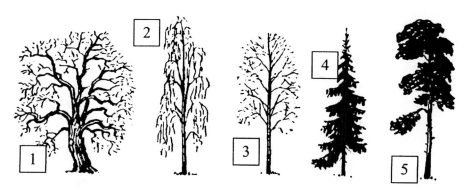

Second graders are asked to identify these trees. Possible answers: **1 дуб, 2 берёза, 3 тополь осина? 4 ель, 5 сосна.**

which is the list of endangered species, the Red Book **Красная книга**.

Central Russia is the mixed forest **смешанный лес** that combines the conifers and the broadleaf forest **лиственный лес**, which is mostly birch **берёза** but also can include willow **ива**, poplar **тополь**, aspen **осина**, alder **ольха**, oak **дуб**, linden **липа**, mountain ash **рябина**, European bird-cherry **черёмуха**, and the ash **ясень**.

The south is associated with the chestnut **каштан**, the black locust **белая акация**, the elm **вяз**, the cypress **кипарис**, and the pyramid poplar **пирамидальный тополь**. But waving fields of grain characterize the south more than any forest.

Russians have a set of words that describe where certain trees grow: the spruce **ель** grows in **ельник**, the pine **сосна** in **сосняк**, the birch **берёза** in **березняк**. Similarly, young trees are what grow in **молодняк**, a campfire is **костёр**, and a burnt-over area is **кострище**, while a cut-over area is **вырубка**, and a road cut through the forest is **просека** (**просекать**, to cut through).

FIELDS
Поля

The field **поле** has given its name to wildflowers **полевые цветы**, of which Russians are great collectors. Our relative lack of interest causes questioning concern among Russians. Signs are sometimes posted: Rare flowers, don't pick or pull up **Редкие цветы, не собирать, не рвать**. And sometimes: Don't chase butterflies **Не ловить бабочек! Ловля бабочек запрещена!** A major factor influencing this collection is that the Russian did not have to worry about impinging on someone else's property to get them: the land belonged to everyone.

Russian agriculture **сельское хозяйство** (from **село**, village) has had, you might say, a tough row to hoe. Over all was the **АПК, Агропромышленный комплекс,** those institutions responsible for the total production, supply, and distribution of agricultural products. In the dim dark days we can still recall the kolkhoz **колхоз** (**коллективное хозяйство**), a union of farm workers who shared the income from their production while the much larger sovkhoz **совхоз** (**советское хозяйство**), was organized as a factory and paid the workers a salary. Neither was successful by contemporary standards (from overregulation, lack of supplies, transportation, and incentive).

Much better results (that is, more food) were obtained from the plots of land around the farmers' houses **приусадебные участки**, which yielded produce the farmer could use or sell as he wished. Many people would have been hungry sooner without them. To enlarge on this production, the government has established the distribution (often requiring money, position, or both) of land **садо́вый уча́сток**, which is the owner's to keep and use or sell. (It is said that perestroika gave smart people cooperatives **кооперати́вы**, dumb people garden plots **садо́вые уча́стки**, and the rest the newspaper **Аргуме́нты и фа́кты**. The age of the joke shows: in late 1994, academics required a garden plot to help keep body and soul together.)

The word for farm, **фе́рма,** used to be more limited than our *farm*. The Russian word specifically denoted the place where (farm) animals are raised. An animal farm is **животно-во́дческая фе́рма**. Now, **фе́рма** is most often a small private farm in our sense, and those who work on it are **фе́рмеры**.

Individual farmers have been given more leeway with the family contract **семе́йный подря́д**: the farmer is given land but is under contract to supply a certain amount of its produce, with excess production to be disposed of at the farmer's discretion. The redistribution of land from kolkhoz and sovkhoz is progressing with difficulty because people do not want to give up what they already know and have. Collectivization in the 1930s was brutal. Privatization **приватиза́ция** is not easy.

THE PLANT WORLD
Расти́тельный мир

"Among some fifty college students whom I once happened to ask (in planned illustration of the incredible ignorance concerning natural objects that characterizes young Americans of today) the name of the tree, an American elm, that they could see through the classroom windows, none was able to identify it: some hesitantly suggested it might be an oak, others were silent; one, a girl, said she guessed it was just a shade tree."

V. Nabokov, *Eugene Onegin*, vol. 3, p. 9, Bollingden Foundation, New York, 1964.

Russian plants, as considered by the American speaker, suffer from miscomprehension for many of the same reasons that Russian animals do: the natural world has mattered more to the Russian so that more and different distinctions are commonly made; translations in dictionaries are more likely to suit British rather than American usage (knapweed?); some occupy quite different places in schemes of necessity or desirability. Our tumbleweed (*Amaranthus sp., Salsola kali*) is not their **перекати́-по́ле** (*Gypsophila paniculata*) in spite of its name. We know it as baby's breath.

The plant
Расте́ние

By specialists and grade-school texts, the plant kingdom **расти́тельное ца́рство** is further divided into the phylum **тип**, class **класс**, order **поря́док**,[2] family **семе́йство**, genus **род**, species **вид**, and subspecies **подви́д**. *Origin of the species* is **Происхожде́ние ви́дов**. The lower plants **ни́зшие расте́ния** include bacteria **бакте́рии**, algae or seaweed **во́доросли**, (literally, "water growers"), molds **пле́сени**, fungi **грибы́**, and lichens **лиша́йники**. The higher plants **вы́сшие расте́ния**, those with roots, stems, and leaves, include true moss **мох**, the horsetail **хвощ**, the fern **па́поротник**, and the flowering plants (which follow).

The plant **расте́ние** (to grow, **расти́**) has many of the subdivisions as do ours: tree **де́рево** (*pl.* **дере́вья**), a conifer **хво́йное де́рево**, a broadleaf tree **ли́ственное де́рево**, and evergreen tree **вечнозелёное де́рево**. But a bush **куст** is often used to denote a particular bush while **куста́рник** is used either for a bush or for a less specific collection of them. The bush **куст**, **куста́рник**, can also be used for any plant that branches from its base, for example the wild strawberry **земляни́чный куст**. Any higher plant that is not a tree or a bush can be **трава́**, **травяни́стое расте́ние**, especially if wild. (Garden plant, **садо́вое расте́ние**; annual plant, **одноле́тнее расте́ние**; biennial,

2. In classifying animals, *order* is **отря́д**.

Sign says "Don't walk on . . ." Do you see any grass?

двухлéтнее растение; perennial, многолéт-нее растение.)

Grass is where comparability really falls apart. *Botanical grass* is злак, *cereal grass* is хлéбные злáки. Any small plant is травá, with no room left over to translate what's in your back yard except lawn газóн, which is a French and foreign concept: a sharply delimited area containing small plants трава usually associated with a monument and meant not to be stepped on. A golf course uses лужáйка, a word more often applied to a clearing in the forest.

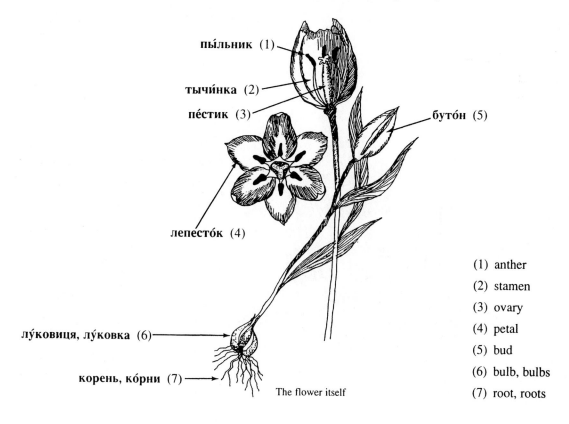

пы́льник (1)

тычи́нка (2)

пéстик (3)

бутóн (5)

лепестóк (4)

лу́ковиця, лу́ковка (6)

корень, кóрни (7)

The flower itself

(1) anther
(2) stamen
(3) ovary
(4) petal
(5) bud
(6) bulb, bulbs
(7) root, roots

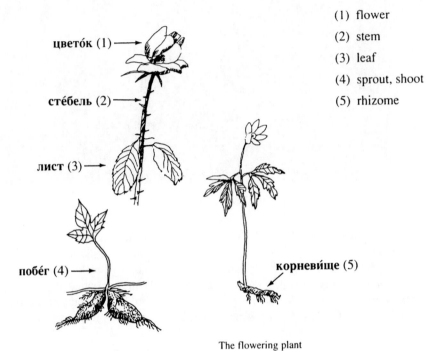

цвето́к (1) →

сте́бель (2) →

лист (3) →

побе́г (4) →

корневи́ще (5)

(1) flower

(2) stem

(3) leaf

(4) sprout, shoot

(5) rhizome

The flowering plant

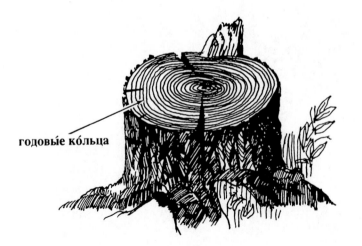

годовы́е ко́льца

пень

The Tree (*next page*)

(1) crown, top of tree

(2) large branch

(3) hollow

(4) trunk

(5) bark

(6) needles

(7) catkins

(8) small branch

(9) leaves

(10) cones

(11) leaf bud

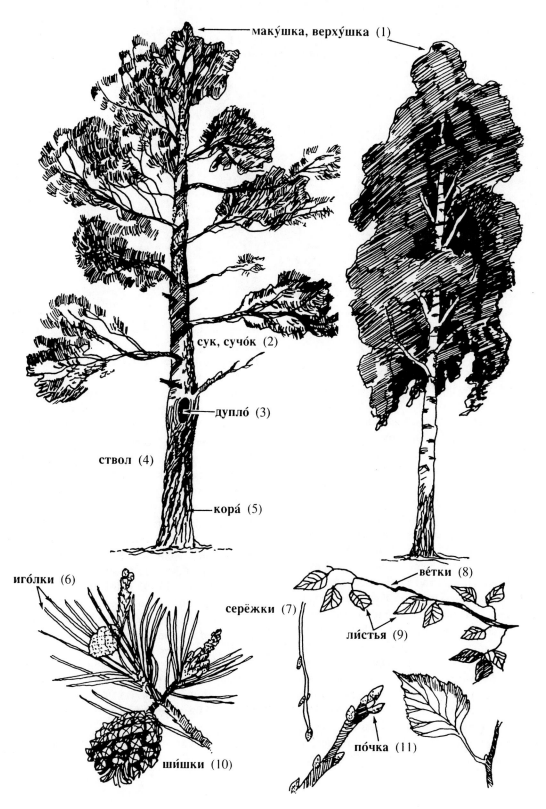

макушка, верхушка (1)

сук, сучок (2)

дупло (3)

ствол (4)

кора (5)

иголки (6)

серёжки (7)

ветки (8)

листья (9)

почка (11)

шишки (10)

Клу́мба

The garden
Сад

Nature's plants grow where they can, but man's must try where they are set: in a garden **сад** (**сад**, *set*, and *sit* share parentage). Garden varieties include: the botanical garden **ботани́ческий сад**, which often turns out to be a delight for the monumented-out tourist, and the flower garden **цвету́щий сад**; yet **цветни́к** is any delimited area for flowers alone, often as part of a "clump," **клу́мба**, a phenomenon that can appear in front of any institution.

The winter garden is **зи́мний сад**. Summer garden **ле́тний сад** is a word combination inseparable from St. Petersburg. The orchard is **фрукто́вый сад**. Flowers and exotica also grow in a conservatory **оранжере́я**, seedlings **расса́да** are often started in a hothouse **тепли́ца**, and watermelons are grown on melon plantations **на бахча́х**.

A friend who has a plot **садо́вый уча́сток** not far from Moscow grows the following flowers: **и́рис, люпи́н, ро́за, при́мула, кале́ндула, ба́рхатцы, хризанте́ма, разби́тое се́рдце, флокс, ли́лия, пио́н, а́стра, асти́льба, георги́н, дельфи́ниум, сире́нь** and others (see items with asterisk in the Plant Index).

We repeat (see the *Fruit* section in Chapter 6) that a major reason for growing flowers is not just for the sight of them, but also for their smell.[3]

Home-grown vegetables do not grow in a garden **сад** but in a garden **огоро́д** (whose root originally referred to a fenced-in area; the Russian word for city, **го́род** and the English word *garden* share this same root). The Russian vegetable garden is further divided into raised rows **гря́дки**, which can themselves become the word for garden: *to weed the garden* is **поло́ть гря́дки**. A second-grade reader includes the following vegetables in the school garden **огоро́д**: dill **укро́п**, pumpkin **ты́ква**, zucchini and summer squash **кабачки́**, tomatoes **помидо́ры**, potatoes **карто́фель/карто́шка**, beets **свёкла**, radishes **реди́с**, black radish **ре́дька**, turnip **ре́па**, peas **горо́х**, green beans **фасо́ль**, sunflower **подсо́лнечник**, carrots **морко́вь**, lettuce **сала́т**, and cucumbers **огурцы́**. A second-grade reader reports:

Наш тре́тий класс доложи́л о своём о́пыте с проре́живанием морко́ви, кото́рая взошла́. Мы вы́дернули мно́го морко́вок.

3. "In the use of the olfactory apparatus Americans are culturally underdeveloped." Edward T. Hall, *The Hidden Dimension*, Anchor Books, Doubleday, New York, 1969, p 45.

Между растениями мы оставляли расстояние в 10-12 сантиметров. Часть морковок мы не проредили, и морковь здесь уродилась мелкая. Морковки теснили друг друга, отнимали друг у друга пищу, влагу и свет. От этого все они дали тонкие корни. Этот опыт учил нас тому, что морковь надо прореживать, чтобы получить корни крупные, сочные. Сорняки тоже теснят морковь и отнимают у неё пищу, влагу и свет, поэтому сорняки нужно выпалывать.[b]

A palm tree at school

Weeds
Сорняки

Weeds **сорняки** concern Russians more in their capacity as agriculturists than as home gardeners because many people live in apartments with no land to work anyway; those who do have some land have relatively small plots, and grass as a part of domestic gardening is unknown.

According to a third-grade reader, the worst weed **сорняк** of all is quackgrass **пырей** (Это злейший из злейших сорняков). Other major invaders of grain fields are the morning glory **вьюнок**, the bachelor button **василёк**, wild oats **овсюг**, and shepherd's purse **пастушья сумка**. Other unwanted invaders include ragweed **амброзия** (an import from the New World), orache **лебеда**, burdock **лопух**, **репейник**, chickweed **мокрица**, dandelion **одуванчик**, sow thistle **осот**, plaintain **подорожник**, winter cress **сурепка**, horsetail **хвощ**, beggar ticks **череда**, and thistle **чертополох**. Weeds matter enough to have a collective noun for tall weeds **бурьян**; "overgrown with weeds" is **поросло бурьяном**.

House plants
Комнатные растения

Indoor plants are popular everywhere, even in institutions. Large rooms can hold large plants: expect a palm tree **пальма**, a rubber tree

фикус, or even a hydrangea **гортензия**. At home, the geranium **герань** is the epitome of ordinariness, but I have also seen an orange tree with oranges on it in a private house in a very small town in central Russia.

These are some of the most common house plants:

амариллис amaryllis

аспарагус ornamental asparagus

бабьи сплетни, традесканция wandering Jew

бегония begonia

ванька-мокрый impatiens

герань geranium or pelargonium

глоксиния gloxinia

гортензия hydrangea

ка́ктус cactus

кита́йская ро́за Chinese rose

кро́кус crocus

мимо́за mimosa

монсте́ра (pronounced **монстэ́ра**) philodendron

олеа́ндр oleander

па́льма palm

пеларго́ния our store-bought geraniums, but a fancier name

плющ ivy

при́мула primrose

столе́тник aloe

(узумба́рская) фиа́лка African violet (Yes, the same one.)

фи́кус rubber plant (tree)

фу́ксия fuchsia

цикламе́н cyclamen

ча́йная ро́за tea rose

Medicinal plants
Лека́рственные расте́ния

One is struck, upon entering a pharmacy, to see an entire section of the store devoted to medicinal herbs. They are widely used, at least to some extent, by most Russians. According to a Soviet medical encyclopedia (for home use) about 1,700 plants that grew in the USSR had some medicinal significance, although only 170 were regularly so used. One advantage herbs may have is their availability, as they are regularly gathered, and they do not require a prescription to obtain. *Herbs*, that is, any low plant, is **тра́вы**; a doctor who specializes in herbal medicine is **тра́вник**, or **гомеопа́т**. The ailments that are treated seem to be essentially all those we are heir to, except perhaps a broken leg (but then valerian would be needed). Books are filled with lists of medicinal herbs—these are just a few of the most common (and every Russian you meet will cite five more!):

ало́э aloe—a freshly cut leaf applied directly to a superficial wound is supposed to reduce the likelihood of infection and stop the flow of blood; extract of aloe is used for intestinal disturbances; drops are good for a runny nose

валериа́на valerian, roots—tranquilizer, very common

женьше́нь ginseng, roots—a general tonic and a restorer of sexual competence

зверобо́й St. John's wort—broth has antiseptic action for digestive disturbances; gargle for sore throat; add to your tea

кукуру́зное ры́льце corn stigmas (the long hairs just under the husk)—a digestive aid (encourages the flow of bile) and a sedative

ла́ндыш lily of the valley, above-ground parts—tranquilizer, diuretic, and heart medicine

ли́па broth made from linden blossoms for fever and sore throat

мали́на raspberry—tea made from dried berries, for fever; very common remedy

мать-и-ма́чеха coltsfoot, buds and leaves—lung medicine, coughs, also surface lesions

мя́та пе́речная peppermint—broth made from the leaves to stimulate the appetite

облепи́ха seabuckthorn—berries a good source of vitamin C, and oil of seabuckthorn is used for stomach ulcer

подоро́жник plantain—broth is made for gastritis; fresh leaf is used for healing superficial wounds

рома́шка daisy—tea is made of the blossoms for tranquilizing effects internally and antiseptic effects externally

ряби́на чернопло́дная *Aronia melanocarpa*—fruits (also used as food); as vitamins; for high blood pressure and arteriosclerosis

сморо́дина currant—broth made from berries for fever

толокня́нка kinnikinick—leaves, bladder medicine

ты́ква pumpkin, seeds—for intestinal worms (про́тив глисто́в)

черёмуха European bird cherry—broth made from the fruit to deter diarrhea

черни́ка small-leaved huckleberry—leaves used for diabetics, fruit for diarrhea

чесно́к garlic, cloves, and greens—arteriosclerosis, high blood pressure, flu, intestinal worms

шалфе́й salvia, leaves, flowers—general remedy, anti-inflammatory

шипо́вник cinnamon rose—broth made from the berries for vitamin C, general tonic; oil of cinnamon rose is used to prevent infection

эвкали́пт *Eucalyptus clobulus*—leaves; antiseptic, especially for throat

The following passage is from a third-grade reader:

Зелёная аптека

Акаде́мик Н. Ци́цин

Пойди́те в лес и́ли на по́ле, и вы попадёте в зелёную апте́ку. Вот у ва́ших ног стебелёк невзра́чного сорняка́—пасту́шьей су́мки. Семена́ э́того расте́ния созрева́ют в треуго́льных коро́бочках, похо́жих на су́мку. Но ма́ло кто зна́ет, что в э́той су́мке сорняка́ соде́ржится це́нное лека́рство: оно остана́вливает кровотече́ние.

На пустыря́х растёт ядови́тая белена́, из ли́стьев кото́рой приготовля́ют лека́рство, успока́ивающее боль....

Из корне́й валерья́ны изготовля́ют лека́рство—валерья́новые ка́пли. Из цвето́в и ли́стьев ла́ндыша де́лают ка́пли, кото́рые принима́ют при боле́знях се́рдца.

А вот и лесны́е я́годы. Они́ то́же облада́ют целе́бной си́лой: сушёная мали́на—потого́нное сре́дство, а кисе́ль из сушёной черни́ки закрепля́ет желу́док.[c]

INDEX OF PLANTS
Указа́тель расте́ний

Familiar plants
Знако́мые расте́ния

These are plant names that might be familiar to you and most gardening Russians; most are plants in cultivation that need no further description.

абрико́с, аквиле́гия, акони́т, али́ссум, ало́э, амара́нт, ани́с, а́стра, бальзами́н, барбари́с, бего́ния, валериа́на, вербе́на, гелиотро́п, гера́нь, гиаци́нт, гладио́лус, дельфи́ниум, жасми́н, и́рис, ка́лла, ка́нна, кедр, кориа́ндр, лавр, маттио́ла, ли́лия, лобе́лия, ло́тос, люпи́н, мимо́за, нарци́сс, насту́рция, кале́ндула, па́льма, пеларго́ния, пету́ния, при́мула, пио́н, пире́трум, реди́с, ро́за, рудбе́кия, сала́т, са́львия, сельдере́й, спа́ржа, таба́к, тюльпа́н, фи́кус, флокс, фу́ксия, цикламе́н, цинера́рия, ци́ния, шпина́т, эдельве́йс

«Я посади́л в саду́ о́коло со́тни тюльпа́нов, ли́лий, нарци́ссов, гиаци́нтов, жонки́льи, и́рис. . .» (Из письма́ А. П. Че́хова Ал. П. Че́хову 21 октября́ 1893 г.)

Most, not all, of the following plants grow wild in central European Russia. Plants best known for their use as food are discussed in Chapter 6 (in the sections *Vegetables, Fruit, Berries, Seasonings, Nuts, Mushrooms*). Their Russian names are followed by the scientific name including both the genus and species when applicable, but by only the genus name when the common Russian name does not distinguish species. An English equivalent common name follows, but the reader should be aware that common names are by no means reliable identifiers and the British and U.S. sources often differ on common names. (I used whatever common name I could find.) Usages, images, and associations complete the assemblage. Those plants preceded by asterisks are cultivated garden plants, some of which also grow wild. The criterion for inclusion is whether most Russians might recognize or know about the plant. Obviously some people will know of more, and some fewer. (Those living in the country will distinguish more plants. I found it painful to eliminate a listing merely because the city-bred did not recognize it. But I did.)

ака́ция бе́лая *Robinia pseudoacacia*. Black locust. Southern decorative tree famous for pleasant smell. Notice that we see it as black and they see it as white. (We look at the trunk, they look at the flowers.)

ака́ция жёлтая *Caragana arborescens*. Siberian pea-shrub, pea tree. Grows everywhere, decorative. Children make whistles **свисту́льки** from the pods.

алыча́ *Prunus divaricata*. See *Fruit*.

ало́э, столе́тник *Aloe arborescens*. Aloe. Succulent house plant, medicinal, decorative.

амбро́зия *Ambrosia artemisiifolia*. Common ragweed. A New World weed with an interesting name. Known only as a weed (**зло́стный каранти́нный сорня́к**) and an instigator of allergies. *Hay fever* is **сенна́я лихора́дка**.

ани́с *Anisum vulgare*. Southern plant known as a cough medicine flavoring: **Ка́пли да́тского короля́**. Also used in cooking.

анча́р *Antiaris toxicaria*. A poisonous plant from Java made known to all Russians via Pushkin's poem of the same name.

*аню́тины гла́зки *Viola sp.* Pansy. Very common and treasured garden flower.

*а́стра *Aster sp.* Very popular late season flower, the most common one to bring to teacher on the first of September.

багу́льник *Ledum palustre*. Evergreen bush in Ericaceae family, a close relative of our Labrador tea.

*ба́рхатцы (*sg.* **ба́рхатец**) (African) marigold

барбари́с *Berberis vulgaris*. Barberry. Decorative bush with sour little berries used dried to make a seasoning for meat dishes.

Белена

белена́ *Hyoscyamus niger*. Henbane. Poisonous, and famous as such. (Our source of scopolamine.) The everyday expression for "Are you out of your mind?" is **Ты что, белены́ объе́лся?**

берёза *Betula sp.* Birch. The most common deciduous tree, represents Russianness to Russians themselves. It's used for medicinal purposes (the leaves are dried, then boiled), birch juice **берёзовый сок** is often diluted and commonly drunk, its bark **берёста** was traditionally used for making containers, its bundled twigs **ве́ник** make brooms or sauna thrashers. Every woody purpose except construction.

берёзка See **вьюно́к**.

бересклёт *Euonymus europaeus*. Spindle tree. As its name implies, used for its wood. The genus is large and varied. One of the bushes is famous for being poisonous.

*бессме́ртник, цмин *Xeranthemum annuum*. Common immortelle. A daisy-like flower, often part of bouquets especially in the winter or at cemeteries because it keeps its good looks even when it dries out. Also medicinal.

боя́рышник *Crataegus sp./sanguinea* Hawthorne. Decorative bush or small tree, widely cultivated in gardens and parks, some types medicinal. Edible berries used as flavoring.

брусни́ка *Vaccinium vitis-idaea*. Lingonberry. See *Berries*.

бузина́ *Sambucus sp.* European elder. Red elder is an adaptable decorative small tree, and its wood is used for making toys. Black elder is good for teas and medicines.

бук *Fagus sp.* Beech. Southern tree.

Валериана

валериа́на *Valeriana exaltata.* Valerian. The most famous tranquilizer, made from the roots.

василёк *Centaurea cyanus.* Bachelor button. One of the most famous flowers, incorporated into song, and also a weed in grain fields. Other names: cornflower, knapweed.

ве́рба See **и́ва**

ве́реск *Calluna vulgaris.* (Wild) heather. Small bush with sweet smell. Marshak translated Burns: **Ве́ресковый мёд**

ветла́ See **и́ва**

ви́шня *Prunus cerasus.* Cherry. See *Fruit.*

воро́ний глаз *Paris quadrifolia.* In the lily family. Resembles our trillium, but with four petals and one black berry. Poisonous, and known as such.

вьюно́к, берёзка *Convolvulus arvensis.* Wild morning glory. Weed, but used for medicinal purposes. Also called **граммофо́нчики**.

вяз *Ulmus laevis, U. effusa.* Elm. Used widely in furniture making. More common in south. Also called **ильм, берест**

*гвозди́ка *Dianthus sp.* Carnation. Garden flower all over central Russia. Also the flower of the Revolution. Also see *Spices.*

*георги́н Dahlia.

*гера́нь *Geranium pratense.* Geranium. This is the wild kind with small flowers. What we call geraniums are also called **герань** and are house plants of the commonest kind.

голуби́ка *Vaccinium uliginosum.* Blueberry. See *Berries.*

горо́шек *Adonis sp.* Wild pea.

*горте́нзия Hydrangea

горчи́ца *Sinapis arvensis.* Wild mustard, a plentiful weed.

грана́т *Punica granatum.* Pomegranate. Southern fruit tree with red fruit that have medicinal applications. See *Fruit.*

гречи́ха Buckwheat plant. See *Grains.*

гуси́ный лук *Gagea lutea.* Geese and sometimes people eat this small, onion-like plant.

до́нник *Melilotus officinalis.* Yellow sweet clover. Mostly medicinal but also good for beekeepers and fodder.

*души́стый горо́шек Sweet pea.

дуб *Quercus sp.* Oak. Very important commercial tree; slow-growing and large. Peter the Great is supposed to have planted some that lived until the mid-1980s on **Ка́менный о́стров** in St. Petersburg. Acorns **жёлуди** are collected to make starch, alcohol, and pig food; ground and roasted, people make oak coffee **желудёвый ко́фе**.

ежеви́ка *Rubus caesius.* See *Berries.*

ель *Picea sp.* Spruce. Very important commercial soft wood, but best known as the source of the Christmas/New Year's tree **ёлка**.

женьше́нь *Panax ginseng.* A well-known general tonic and also an aphrodisiac, grown only in the Far East and known only as medicine.

жи́молость *Lonicera xylosteum.* One of the honeysuckles. Another name for the plant tells you that the fruit is poisonous: **во́лчьи я́годы**

за́ячья капу́ста   *Sedum purpureum*. Common term for all the sedums, some of which are edible. Small plant, red flowers, meaty leaves.

зверобо́й   *Hypericum sp*. St. John's wort. Used to make cough medicine and to heal wounds, for dyeing, and flavoring liquor and tea.

земляни́ка   *Fragaria vesca*. Wild Strawberry. See *Berries*.

*золото́й шар   *Rudbeckia lanciniata*. Popular, very tall with bright golden flowers.

зубро́вка   *Hierochloe odorata*. Buffalo grass. Vodka flavoring.

и́ва, ветла́, белоло́з   *Salix sp*. Willows. The willow is to the Ukrainian what the birch is to the Russian, though they grow throughout Russia. **Ве́рба** is the pussy willow. Thus, on Palm Sunday **Ве́рбное воскресе́нье** Russians take pussy willows to church to be blessed. (When there's no palm, a pussy-willow is a palm.)

Ива́н-да-Ма́рья   *Melampyrum nemorosum*. A yellow and purple field flower.

Ива́н-ча́й   *Chamaenerion/Epilobium angustifolium*. Fireweed. Famous for growing on cut-over land, "poor-man's" tea can be made from its leaves.

ирга́   *Amelanchier sp*. Shadbush, serviceberry. Raised for its fruit.

*и́рис, каса́тик   *Iris sp., pseudacorus* and others. Iris. Very common, decorative and wild.

кали́на   *Viburnum opulus*. European cranberry bush. Grows along rivers, has medicinal red berries.

камы́ш   *Scirpus lacustris*. Cattail.

кашта́н   *Castanea sativa/vulgaris*. Chestnut tree, southern, decorative, with edible fruit. As opposed to the inedible fruited horse chestnut **ко́нский кашта́н**.

кедр   *Cedrus sp*. Cedar. Cones, nuts, and associated with Siberia.

кизи́л,   *Cornus mas*. Cornelian cherry

ки́нза, киндза́, кишне́ц посевно́й, кориа́ндр   *Coriandrum sativum*. Coriander, the leaves of which are a common seasoning in Caucasian cooking.

кипари́с   *Cupressus sempervirens*. Cypress. Very southern, decorative tree.

кле́вер   *Trifolium sp*. Clover. Good for cattle and honey. (*Informal* **ка́шка**).

*клема́тис   see **ломоно́с**

клён   *Acer sp*. Maple. **Клён ты мой опа́вший**...Yesenin.

клубни́ка   The cultivated strawberry—of less moment than the wild one. See *Berries*.

клю́ква   *Vaccinium oxycoccos*. Small cranberry. See *Berries*

ковы́ль   *Stipa sp*. A wild grass of the steppes that sounds when the wind blows.

Колоко́льчик

*колоко́льчик   *Campanula sp*. Bluebells. A field weed and a familiar meadow flower.

> **Колоко́льчики мои́,**
> **Цве́тики степны́е!**
> **Что гляди́те на меня,**
> **Тёмно-голубы́е?** . . .
>
> А. К. Толсто́й

конопля́ *Cannabis sativa.* Hemp (the old-fashioned name). Used to make rope, low quality material, and for stuffing in the chinks of the log house.

кориа́ндр Name used for seeds of coriander **кинза.**

костяни́ка *Rubus saxatilis.* A kind of red blackberry with a single large seed. Used to make jam and juice **морс.**

коша́чьи ла́пки *Antennaria dioica.* Everlasting or Pussytoes. Small silver-leaved plant that acts as background to a cat's paw flower.

крапи́ва *Urtica dioica.* Stinging nettle. It stings **жжётся**, but in early spring it used to be gathered for use in soup as the first greenery of the season.

кра́сное де́рево Mahogany. See also **тис.** Both have red wood used in furniture making.

Крушина

круши́на *Frangula alnus* or *Rhamnus frangula.* European or Alder Buckthorn. Bush, the dried bark of which is used as laxative.

крыжо́вник *Grossularia reclinata.* Gooseberry. Anciently wild, now common, cultivated, and relatively inexpensive for jams and the like.

кувши́нка *Nymphaea candida.* White water lily. The more common of the two, an image of beauty.

куку́шкины слёзки *Orchis maculata.* A pleasant wildflower often found near water. The story is that the cuckoo leaves her eggs in other birds' nests and then cries for her lost children. These are her tears. Protected.

купа́льница *Trollius europaeus.* Resembles a huge buttercup. Very yellow. Protected.

лавр *Laurus nobilis.* Bay laurel. Source of bay leaves, laurel wreaths, and large hedges in southern areas.

Ландыш

ла́ндыш *Convallaria majalis.* Lily of the valley. Very familiar and beloved and poisonous. One report is that the USSR required about 200 tons of fresh blossoms a year for perfume and medicinal purposes. A common heart medecine is **ла́ндышевые ка́пли.** Protected.

лебеда́ *Atriplex patula.* Orache. A widely occurring weed.

*левко́й, ночна́я фиа́лка, маттио́ла *Matthiola fragrans.* Stock. This is the wild version. Plant is known commonly as a very pleasant-smelling cultivated flower.

лён *Linum usitatissimum.* Flax. The source for linen and linseed oil. Tall reedy plants with small blue flowers.

ли́па *Tilia cordata.* Linden, basswood. Grows everywhere. Very useful and used tree. **Ли́повый мёд** is linden honey.

ли́ственница *Larix Sukaczewii.* Larch. Deciduous conifer commonly planted in cities; loses needles.

ломоно́с *Clematis* *клема́тис (Really included here only because of Mr. Lomonosov.)

лопу́х *Arctium sp.* Burdock. Huge-leaved weed. Children play with the seeds which scrunch together and then attach to anything. The plant name is also assigned to a country boob: «Он тако́й лопу́х!»

ло́тос *Nelumbo nucifera.* Lotus. Actually grows at the mouth of the Volga and in the Far East, but better known as a source of Egyptian or Indian legends.

*льви́ный зев *Antirrhinum majus.* Snapdragon. Popular in garden.

лю́тик *Ranunculus sp.* Buttercup. Common field flower, gathered.

люце́рна *Medicago sativa.* Alfalfa. Known only as fodder.

*мак *Papaver sp.* Poppy. Red flower with dark center grown in southern fields for the seeds, which are eaten, and for opium. Also garden flower. See *Seasonings.*

мали́на *Rubus idaeus.* European red raspberry. See *Berries.*

*ма́льва *Malva sp.* Hollyhocks. Cultivated plant associated with Ukraine. Related weed is *Malva neglecta* просви́рник

*маргари́тка *Bellis perennis.* Daisy. Common garden flower.

масли́на *Olea europaea.* Olive tree. Very southern. See *Seasonings.*

*маттио́ла See **левко́й**

мать-и-ма́чеха *Tussilago farfara.* Coltsfoot. ("Mother-and-stepmother") The peasants explain that one leaf surface is smooth and cold—the stepmother—while the other leaf surface is fuzzy and warm—the mother. Early spring flower, medicinal, and weed in some places.

меду́ни́ца *Pulmonaria obscura/officinalis.* Small blue and pink flowers provide medicine and honey.

мимо́за *Mimosa sp.* Mimosa only grows in hothouses. This is the flower to give on Women's Day, March 8. The name is often incorrectly applied to the true acacia.

минда́ль *Amygdalus communis.* Almond. Southern tree famous for nuts, and a description of eyes (**миндалеви́дные глаза́**)

можжеве́льник *Juniperus communis.* Juniper. The bush that smells pleasantly of gin. Used to prepare barrels for pickles.

молоча́й *Euphorbia sp.* Spurge. As the Russian name suggests, this plant exudes milky juice where injured. Many weeds.

моро́шка *Rubus chamaemorus.* Cloudberry. Northern yellow swamp berries, medicinal.

муска́тный оре́х Nutmeg. See *Spices.*

мя́та *Mentha arvensis.* Mint. Used in mint cookies, to make tea. See *Seasonings.*

наперсти́нка *Digitalis grandiflora.* Foxglove relative. Strongly resembles a small yellow foxglove, medicinal.

*нарци́сс Daffodil, narcissus.

недотро́га *Impatiens noli tangere.* Touch-me-not. When the seeds are ripe, the plant is capable of throwing them if touched. Children like to play with it.

незабу́дка *Myosotis palustris.* Forget-me-not genus. Common small blue flower in forests near water.

*ноготки́, кале́ндула Calendula. Common garden flower. Wide medicinal application, especially for female problems.

Мать-и-ма́чеха

облепи́ха *Hippophae rhamnoides.* Seabuckthorn, Oleaster *sp.* Bush with yellow flower from whose berries jam and juice are made. Medicinal.

овёс *Avena sativa.* Oats. Food for all the animals. See *Grains.*

одува́нчик *Taraxacum officinale.* Common dandelion. **Можно сдуть семена-парашю́тики.** Children also weave wreaths **венки́** from them in the spring. And parents make early spring salads of them. Medicinal.

ольха́ *Alnus sp.* Alder. Common. Alder catkins is **ольхо́вые серёжки.**

оре́х гре́цкий *Juglans regia.* English walnut. Grows in south. Preserves made from the green nuts. See *Nuts.*

оре́шник, лещи́на *Corylus avellana.* Hazelnut. See *Nuts.*

оси́на *Populus tremula.* A kind of aspen. "He's shaking like a leaf" **Он трясётся/дрожи́т, как оси́новый лист.**

осо́ка *Carex sp.* Sedge. Known as a grass-like plant that grows near the water.

па́льма *Palmae.* Some grow in the south and the rest are indoor hall decoration.

па́поротник Fern. Everywhere in the forest.

пасту́шья су́мка *Capsella bursa-pastoris.* Shepherd's purse. Very common weed in the grain fields. Also medicinal.

*первоцве́т, при́мула *Primula sp.* The "first flower." The first is its wild title, and the second is its garden name.

пи́жма, ди́кая ряби́нка *Tanacetum vulgare.* Common tansy. Resembles a daisy, is supposed to kill flies and is used medicinally.

пи́хта *Abies sp.* Fir tree. The Russian Christmas tree is a spruce **ель.**

плау́н *Lycopodium sp.* Club moss.

подоро́жник *Plantago major.* Common plantain. A weed, but Russians know it better as wound healer.

подсне́жник *Galanthus sp.* Flowers very early, decorative.

подсо́лнечник *Helianthus annuus.* Sunflower comes in two varieties: one is the major source of vegetable oil, and the other supplies a favorite snack.

полы́нь *Artemisia absinthium.* Absinthe wormwood. Most remarkable characteristic is its strong fresh smell. Used therefor. **Го́рький, как полы́нь.**

*при́мула Primrose. See **первоцве́т.**

пусты́рник *Leonurus villosus/cardiaca.* Motherwort. Medicinal properties apply to high blood pressure, and heart ailments.

пуши́ца *Eriophorum vaginatum.* Cotton-grass. Swamp plant or sedge with a white puff on top. An indicator of swampy land.

пыре́й *Agropyron repens.* Quack-grass. Grassy weed that takes over. (**Пыре́й— это жуть!**)

*разби́тое се́рдце *Dicentra sp.* Bleeding heart

раки́та, и́ва хру́пкая *Salix fragilis.* One of the willows.

раки́тник *Cytisus sp.* Broom.

ре́дька *Raphanus sativus var. major.* Black radish. Large and strong. Grate and add carrot and oil or sour cream to make appetizer. Also medicinal. (Its juice, extracted with sugar or honey, makes children's cough medicine.)

*резеда́ *Reseda odorata.* Mignonette. Very pleasant smell but undistinguished flowers.

репе́йник, репе́й Same as **лопу́х.** Can refer to the fruit alone. A weed with seeds that stick to anything. **Он приста́л, как репей** is "A man who bored others to death by insisting on returning to one problem."

рого́з *Typha latifolia/angustifolia.* Swamp plant, grows all over. Used for weaving, packing, and stuffing.

рома́шка *Matricaria inodora.* Daisy, or rather, one form thereof. A number of plants vie for the title. Other species in the same genus are widely used for bleaching hair and medicinal purposes.

ряби́на *Sorbus aucuparia.* European mountain ash. (U.S. source reports the berries to

Ромашка

be inedible but the Russians haven't read that book.) Berries are collected after the first frosts when they are sweeter. Used to make preserves, infusions. Tree is also planted as a decorative. Medicinal. See *Fruit*.

самшит *Buxus sp.* Box (tree). Very hard-wooded tree, grown for wood and decoration only in the south. Tree is famous for its pleasant-smelling wood and pink flowers.

*сирень *Syringa vulgaris*. Lilac. Very popular, widely used.

слива *Prunus domestica*. Prune/plum. Most widely available and used fruit in both wild and cultivated forms. See *Fruit*.

смородина *Ribes sp.* Currant. See *Berries*. **Загадка: Что это такое? Она чёрная? Нет, она красная. А почему она белая? Да потому что зелёная!** (i.e., not ripe)

сон-трава, прострел раскрытый *Pulsatilla patens*. Decorative.

спаржа *Asparagus officinalis*. Asparagus. Cultivated kind eaten when available; the wild kind has medicinal applications.

сурепка, сурепица *Barbarea vulgaris*. Winter cress. Small yellow flowers aid in honey production; raised for fodder but otherwise considered a weed in fields.

*табак Nicotiana.

таволга *Spiraea sp.* Decorative bush.

тёрн, слива колючая *Prunus spinosa*. Sloe plum. Collected after first frost and made into compote, jam.

тимофеевка *Phleum pratense*. Timothy. Good forage, widely cultivated.

тис, тисс, красное дерево *Taxus baccata*. Common yew. (**Красное дерево** also refers to mahogany.)

толокнянка *Arctostaphylos uva-ursi*. Kinnikinick. Leaves widely used in the treatment of bladder ailments. A northern ground cover.

тополь *Populus sp.* Poplar. Many kinds, grown all over. They make "snow" in June with their cottonwood seeds **тополиный пух**.

тростник *Phragmites communis*. Common reed. Swamp grass.

туя *Thuja plicata*. Western red cedar. An import from North America now common in the south.

тысячелистник *Achillea millefolium*. Yarrow. Medicinal

*тюльпан Tulip. Common, both wild and cultivated.

*фиалка *Viola sp.* Violet. The wild plant is associated with forest floors where there is some water.

фикус *Ficus elastica*. Indoor fig. Fig.

хвощ *Equisetum arvense*. Horsetails. A common weed with many medicinal applications. Also used as pan cleaner.

*хмель *Humulus lupulus*. Hops. Meadow and garden vine.

хрен *Armoracia rusticana*. Horseradish. Common seasoning and garden plant that quickly can turn to a weed if not controlled.

череда *Bidens tripartita*. European beggar-ticks(!) A weed commonly used medicinally to help clear skin.

черемша *Allium ursinum*. Wild onion often used as seasoning.

черёмуха *Padus/Prunus racemosa*. European bird-cherry. Beautifully blooming tree. Fruit dried and used medicinally. **Черёмуховые**

холода́ is very cold weather in the late spring when it would not be expected.

чере́шня *Prunus avium.* Cherry tree, as we know cherries. See *Fruit.*

черноплóдная ряби́на, черноплóдная арóния *Aronia melanocarpa.* Black chokeberry. A large deciduous bush with small black fruit; originated in North America but popularized considerably by Michurin. Fruit used for flavoring, also as medicinal.

чертополóх *Carduus nutans/crispus.* Thistle. Common weed.

шалфéй *Salvia pratensis.* Sage. Medicinal.

шипóвник *Rosa cinnamomea.* Cinnamon rose. Widely used as decorative; also, fruits used for syrup and rose hip tea. Remarkable source of vitamin C.

Шиповник

эдельвéйс *Leontopodium ochroleucum.* Edelweiss. The symbol of alpine meadows.

я́сень *Fraxinus excelsior.* Ash. Common tree.

DOMESTICATED ANIMALS
Дома́шние живóтные

Animals have been important to Russian existence and therefore have a greater role in the language; the Russian is quicker than we to specify the kind—not just "little bird." Then too, since Russia is a continent away, animals tend not to correspond. And we tend to forget that British English is a foreign language, one often used in our Russian-English dictionaries. The British say "elk," and we say "moose."

What do you think a "capercaillie" is? Every Russian knows.

Pets
Кóмнатные живóтные

The word *pet* is untranslatable; **дома́шние живóтные** are those animals raised for pleasure or profit and therefore include cats, dogs, cows, sheep, rabbits, and so on. **Кóмнатные живóтные** are those animals that can consider the inside of a house to be home. (A doghouse is **конура́, собáчья бýдка.**) Cats, birds, and hedgehogs can live inside. Pet stores **зоомагази́ны** sell birds, hedgehogs, turtles, guinea pigs, goldfish, and white mice, and pet food, but they do not sell cats or dogs. Major cities have markets that specialize in pets; in Moscow it's the bird market **пти́чий база́р** not far from the Taganka theater.

Дог

Боксёр

Пекинéс

Борзá́я

Пýдель

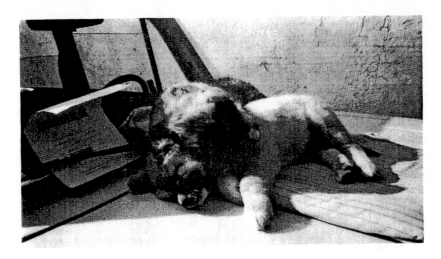

For sale at the market: their papers are under the windshield wipers.

Dogs
Собáки

People who go to the trouble of maintaining dogs in the city also often go to the added expense of making it a purebred **порóдистая собáка** with a pedigree **с родослóвной** of which they can be proud. The dog of "mixed parentage" **дворня́жка, дворня́га** is the norm in the country. Dogs are thought of as being less tame: a Russian is much more careful about patting a strange dog than we are, and many dogs are fitted with muzzles **намóрдники** and must be on a leash **на поводкé**. In the large cities the small size of the apartments is a good reason that dogs are less frequently a part of family life. Instead, birds are popular as pets, especially the **чиж, щегóл** (see *Birds*) and the parrot **попугáй**, the parakeet **попугáйчик**, and the canary **канарéйка**.

By far the best known breed of dog **порóда собáк** is the German shepherd **немéцкая овчáрка** or just **овчáрка** (**овцá** is *sheep*). In this country they are thought of as police dogs or guide dogs for the blind, but for Russians they are guard dogs. Other Russian shepherd breeds, such as **кавкáзская, южнорýсская овчáрка**, strongly resemble the English sheepdog; of course, **шотлáндская овчáрка** is a **кóлли**.

The two major breeds of Russian origin are, **борзáя** and **лáйка**; only the first (borzoi[4] or Russian wolfhound) is familiar in the United States. The borzoi is a very large, graceful dog originally developed to run down wolves for the hunting nobility. The other major Russian breed, **лáйка**, is not so elegant in appearance, nor so large, but much more useful. It is a hunting dog developed in the north for chasing and treeing game, howling or barking (**лáйка, лáять,** to bark) until the hunter comes. Of the four kinds of **лáйка** only one, the all-white Samoyed, is known commonly outside of Russia. More common is (**рýсская**) **лáйка**, which resembles the Samoyed in shape though its fur is less fluffy and its coloring varies, usually black and white with various gradations in between. (**Лáйка** can also be any dog's name, especially a noisy one.)

The nobility also hunted using a class of medium-sized dogs, **легáвые,** for stalking and pointing game birds. This group includes **пóйнтер** and **сéттер.** (**Легáвые** also became a pejorative slang word for the police.) Russian breeds in the hound family **гóнчие собáки** are the **рýсская гóнчая** and the **рýсская пéгая гóнчая**; they most resemble a large beagle, but their fur is less smooth.

4. The English transliteration probably refers to **борзóй пёс.**

Common Russian breeds include many that are familiar to us: **пу́дель, боксёр, сенберна́р, спание́ль, бульдо́г, фокстерье́р, тойтерье́р, ньюфа́ундленд, бассе́т, бультерье́р, эрдельтерье́р, доберма́н-пи́нчер. Та́кса** is a variety of dachshund; **ище́йка** (**иска́ть**, to search for) is a bloodhound or any dog used for hunting down people; and, of all things, **дог** is a Great Dane.

Cats
Ко́шки

The range of cats is not so broad; the long-haired varieties are **сиби́рские, перси́дские коты́;** Siamese cats **сиа́мские коты́** are infrequent. This does not mean that cats themselves are a rarity. Their small space requirements commend them for life in the city, and their habit of keeping the mouse population under control commends them for life in the country. Those one sees in the streets are a shaggy lot.

Animal husbandry
Животново́дство

Animal husbandry has never been the major concern of the Russian farmer—crops were the problem. This does not mean that the farmer had no animals, for even the poorest probably had at least one goat. Of all the animals, however, the most important was a horse **ло́шадь**. It was only with the horse that the farmer could plow the land and get crops to market.

Cows were the next most valuable animal, kept for their milk and manure. A peasant household would also keep two to three sheep **о́вцы**, rarely more, for their wool and their meat. Goats **ко́зы** were also common, raised both for their hair[5] and for their milk. Among the poorer peasants the goat took the place of a cow.

---

5.   A famous Russian scarf, **оренбу́ргский плато́к**, made from the finer hair **пух** of a special longhaired goat, was very light, very large, and very expensive (and still is).

In most areas of Russia, the village hired a shepherd **пасту́х** whose job was to tend cattle for the summer. This job was the least prestigious in the entire village; only orphans or the poorest boys without prospects would take it on as an occupation. The whole village paid him a salary for the summer, either in kind or in money, and village families would take turns feeding and housing him. The process is described in «**Матрёнин двор**» by **Солжени́цын**:

> Ещё суета́ больша́я выпада́ла Матрёне, когда́ подходи́ла её о́чередь корми́ть ко́зьих пастухо́в: одного́—здорове́нного, немоглухо́го, и второ́го—мальчи́шку с постоя́нной слюня́вой цига́ркой в зуба́х. О́чередь э́та была́ в полтора́ ме́сяца раз, но вгоня́ла Матрёну в большо́й расхо́д. Она́ шла в сельпо́, покупа́ла ры́бные консе́рвы, расста́рывалась и са́хару и ма́сла, чего́ не е́ла сама́. Ока́зывается, хозя́йки выкла́дывались друг пе́ред дру́гом, стара́ясь накорми́ть пастухо́в полу́чше.[d]

The cattle also had their church calendar days. On April 23, St. George's Day **Его́рьев день**, when the cattle were sent out to pasture for the first time that year, they were specially blessed by the village priest. **Вла́сий** was also considered a protector of cattle; and on July 20, **Ильи́н день**, some animals were sacrificed, blessed, cooked, and eaten to give thanks to St. Ilya for preserving the cattle.

The animals were not especially well fed. Hay was not sown for them; instead, one of the regular summer jobs was to mow the grasses in the meadows and along the roadside to provide animal feed. Slaughtering was mostly done in the late fall so that the animals did not have to be fed over the winter, and the Russian winter was a convenient freezer.

Pigs **сви́ньи** were also common farm animals; the Ukrainians raised them for their fat, while the Russians raised them for their meat.

Domestic animals (nomenclature)
Дома́шние живо́тные

Russian [1]	Meat	Young	Male	Notes	English
ло́шадь (лоша́дка)	кони́на[2]	жеребёнок, жеребя́та	жеребе́ц	кобы́ла—mare ме́рин—gelding	horse
коро́ва (коро́вушка)	говя́дина	(бычо́к)	бык	вол—ox, steer	cow
	теля́тина	телёнок, теля́та			calf
овца́ (ове́чка)	бара́нина	ягнёнок, ягня́та	бара́н (бара́шек)		sheep
коза́ (ко́зочка)	козля́тина	козлёнок, козля́та	козёл[5] (ко́злик)		goat
свинья́	свини́на	поросёнок, порося́та	каба́н	бо́ров — barrow	pig
ку́рица	ку́рица, ку́ра	цыплёнок, цыпля́та	пету́х (петушо́к)	(pl. ку́ры)	chicken
гусь	гуся́тина	гусёнок, гуся́та	гуса́к	(female гусы́ня)	goose
у́тка	у́тка	утёнок, утя́та	се́лезень		duck
индю́шка, инде́йка	инде́йка	индюшо́нок, индюша́та	индю́к		turkey
кро́лик	крольча́тина	крольчо́нок, крольча́та		(female крольчи́ха)	rabbit
соба́ка[3]	соба́чина[4]	щено́к, щеня́та	кобе́ль	су́ка — bitch	dog
ко́шка	коша́тина[4]	котёнок, котя́та	кот (ко́тик)		cat

1. The general term for the type of animal is given; it sometimes also refers to the female of the species. Common diminutives are in parentheses.

2. The name for horse meat come from the now poetic (and sometimes military) word for *horse* конь (конёк): "Тата́ры едя́т кони́ну" means "Tartars eat horse meat."

3. Пёс is frequently encountered. It is old-fashioned and familiar, much as hound is used in English when not applied to a specific breed or type of dog.

4. Dogs and cats are not eaten, but their meat is a term of opprobrium for real meat.

5. Also the name for someone both stupid and stubborn.

Chickens ку́ры, geese гу́си, and ducks у́тки, in that order, were raised almost everywhere; turkeys индю́шки could be found in the south. Chickens and geese also had their church calendar days, but for them the date was the end, not a beginning. Chickens were traditionally slaughtered on November 1, день Кузьмы́ и Демья́на, while geese came to the same end on September 15, день Ники́ты гуся́тника.

Beekeeping пчелово́дство was also quite common, hives being maintained in hollowed-out logs especially set up for the purpose. (hive:

What do the animals say?
Как «говоря́т» живо́тные?

Как говори́т живо́тное	Звук	Значе́ние
ло́шадь ржёт	и-го-го́	a horse neighs
коро́ва мычи́т	му, му	a cow moos
овца́ бле́ет	бэ-бэ, бе-бе	a sheep bleats
свинья́ хрю́кает	хрю, хрю	a pig oinks
соба́ка ла́ет	гав-гав, ав-ав	a dog barks
щено́к, ма́ленькая соба́ка тя́вкает	тяв-тяв	a pup or small dog yips
ко́шка мяу́кает	мя́у	a cat mews
ко́шка мурлы́кает	мур, мур	a cat purrs
ку́рица куда́хчет (куда́хтать)	куд-куд-куда́х, куда́х-куда́х	a chicken clucks
пету́х кукаре́кает	кукареку́	a rooster crows
у́тка кря́кает	кря-кря	a duck quacks
гусь гого́чет (гогота́ть)	га-га-га́ [1]	a goose honks
воробе́й чири́кает [2]	чик-чири́к	a sparrow chirps
куку́шка куку́ет (кукова́ть)	ку-ку́, ку-ку́	a cuckoo cuckoos
лягу́шка ква́кает	ква-ква	a frog croaks
пчёлы, му́хи жужжа́т	ж-ж-ж	bees and flies buzz

1. Гу́си, гуси, га-га-га: есть хоти́те? Да-да-да!

2. Не все пти́цы чири́кают: наприме́р, жа́воронки и соловьи́ пою́т (sing), иногда́ и́волга звени́т (rings), воро́на ка́ркает и го́лубь вору́ет. Не́которые ма́ленькие пти́цы щебе́чут (twitter).

---

sg. у́лей, *pl.* у́льи) Honey, along with berries and mushrooms, was also often the object of searches in the wilds.

Talking to animals
«Обраще́ния» к живо́тным

The sound made to start a horse involves puckering your lips and sucking in air or clicking your tongue. Another alternative is to shout "**Ho-o-o**" (in Russian). Saying «**пру**» or «**тпру**» loudly, as if trying to pronounce all the letters at once, will stop the horse. ("Giddy-up" and "whoa," unfortunately, will not work.)

To call a cat, the sound to make is «**кс-кс**», «**кис-кис**», or «**кы́ська**», all with a high-pitched voice. To make it go away, the usual sound is an unvoiced «**кш, кш**» or «**кыш, кыш**». An equivalent for "scat" is «**брысь**» though the Russian word is somewhat more formal than ours.

Chickens and ducks are called by saying «**цып, цып, цып**» while ducks alone get «**у́ти, у́ти**» all in a high-pitched voice, and geese can be called with «**те́ги, те́ги**» or «**те́га, те́га.**» «**Тря, тря**» will summon sheep or goats, though perhaps more frequently sheep are called by «**бара́шки**» or «**бя́ша!, бя́ша!**» Cows are called by name, «**Краса́вка!**»; «**тпрусь!**» will call in the calves.

Contemporary animal husbandry is still not a Russian forte, but it is evolving. See *Fields*.

ANIMALS IN NATURE
Живо́тные в приро́де

Worms
Че́рви

The general worm is **червя́к**, **червь**: «Ма́льчики иска́ли черве́й для ры́бной ло́вли.» Larva, grub, or maggot is **личи́нка**; therefore, **гу́сеница—личи́нка ба́бочки.**

Глисты́ are any intestinal worms: «Не ешь сыро́е мя́со—полу́чишь глисты́» "Don't eat raw meat or you'll get worms." Common parasitic worms are the tapeworm **солитёр**, the roundworm **аскари́да**, and the pinworm **остри́ца**.

Leeches
Пия́вки

Children look for leeches in still-water ditches or ponds to sell them to drugstores. For medicinal purposes they are still sometimes used when bloodletting is thought to be an appropriate treatment—for example, in thrombophlebitis, some types of hypertension, miocardial infarction, and so on.

В СССР пия́вок медици́нских ло́вят преиму́щественно в Краснода́рском кра́е, Молда́вской, Украи́нской, Грузи́нской и Армя́нской ССР, а та́кже разво́дят в лаборато́рных усло́виях.[e]

Insects and the like
Насеко́мые и им подо́бные

The lists that follow name insects that every Russian schoolchild recognizes; almost all of these names appear in beginning school readers. Two very useful words in Russian denote almost any insect too small or insignificant for more accurate identification—**бука́шка** and **козя́вка**. Anything even vaguely resembling a beetle can be **жук** or **пау́к** (е́сли во́семь ног).

And any very small animal with many legs is **сороконо́жка** or **многоно́жка** (sometimes applied to a caterpillar **гу́сеница**).

Historically, if not currently, those insects that relate so well to people have been the bane of the Russian's existence. This is true of the flea **блоха́**, louse **вошь**, bedbug **клоп**, and cockroach **тарака́н**, especially the latter two.

Moths and butterflies are divided into different categories in Russian. **Мотылёк** is a kind of small moth known for flying in swarms at night; **моль** is a small moth, the larvae of which eat clothes or infest granaries. All the rest to a Russian are **ба́бочки.**

Useful or harmless insects
Поле́зные и́ли безвре́дные насеко́мые

ба́бочка   butterfly or moth
Мно́гие коллекциони́руют ба́бочек.
В жи́зни ба́бочки есть четы́ре эта́па: (1) яйцо́, (2) гу́сеница, (3) ку́колка, (4) ба́бочка.[f]

бо́жья коро́вка   ladybug
Бо́жья коро́вка, улети́ на не́бо. Там твои́ де́тки ку́шают котле́тки. (Улети́ на не́бо, принеси́ нам хле́ба.)[g]

жук   beetle

Жук—это любо́е насеко́мое с твёрдыми кры́льями.[h]

мотылёк   moth
То́ же, что и ба́бочка, но ча́сто появля́ется на у́лицах но́чью. Мотылёк порха́ет.[i]

мошка́   gnat (**мошкара́** swarm of gnats)
Мошкара́ появля́ется гла́вным о́бразом ве́чером при захо́де со́лнца.[j]

мураве́й   ant
Мураве́й рабо́тает день и ночь, он си́мвол трудолю́бия. Муравьи́ живу́т в мураве́йнике.[k]

паук spider
Паук плетёт паутину.[l]

оса wasp
Не тронь осиное гнездо—беда будет.[m]

пчела bee
Пчёлы живут в ульях. Матка - самая большая пчела; она кладёт яйца. Рабочая пчела собирает мёд, а трутень не производит никакой работы. Рой следует за маткой.[n]

сверчок cricket
Сверчки часто живут в домах за печкой; раньше считалось, что они разговаривают с домовым. Иногда они отождествляются с самим домовым.[o]

светляк firefly
Светляки появляются ночью.[p]

стрекоза dragonfly
Читайте басню Крылова "Стрекоза и муравей." [q]

шмель bumblebee
Шмели очень похожи на пчёл, но они больше и мохнатые.[r]

Harmful insects
Насекомые-вредители

капустница cabbage moth
Капустница (капустная бабочка) кладёт яички в стебельки капусты, а потом личинки их поедают.[s]

клещ tick
Лесной клещ передаёт энцефалит.[t]

комар mosquito
Чешется. Комар укусил.[u]

кузнечик grasshopper
Зелёненький кузнечик, коленками назад, Волнуется, стрекочет, чему-то очень рад.[v]

майский жук (или) хрущ May beetle
Майский жук ест берёзу. Хрущ—вредитель сельского хозяйства.[w]

мокрица sow bug or wood louse
Мокрицы очень противные; считают, что они грязные.[x]

моль moth
Против моли нужно употреблять нафталин.[y]

муха fly
Обязательно прочитайте «Муху–цокотуху» Чуковского. Чтобы избавиться от мух, употребляют и мухобойки, и липкие ленты.[z]

саранча locust
Они набросились на стол как саранча. (Всё очень быстро съели.)[aa]

таракан cockroach
Тараканы очень неприятные, и от них трудно избавиться.[bb]

тля aphid
(Слово «тля» употребляется главным образом в единственном числе.) Тля появилась. Там тля ползает.[cc]

уховёртка earwig
Согласно суеверию, уховёртка проникает в ухо и даже в мозг.[dd]

Human infestation
Паразиты человека

блоха flea
Что ты скачешь, как блоха?[ee]

вошь louse
Вши питаются только кровью человека и млекопитающих. На человека паразитируют три вида вшей: головная, платяная и лобковая.[ff]

гни́да nit

Гни́да—это яи́чко вши. Они́ ме́лкие, бе́лые и не дви́гаются.[gg]

клоп bedbug

Клопо́в боя́тся ме́ньше, чем вшей, так как они́ обы́чно живу́т на веща́х, а не на те́ле.[hh]

From mollusks to amphibians
От моллю́сков до земново́дных

Of the mollusks **моллю́ски**, the most familiar are the snail **ули́тки** and slug **слизняки́**. The oyster **у́стрица** (and perhaps the mussel **ми́дия**), has been heard of but is far from familiar, while clams have not even reached that status. The squid **кальма́р** is associated with Oriental cookery and is also used in salads.

The most familiar of the crustaceans **ракообра́зные** is the crayfish **рак**, a popular accompaniment to beer. Crab **краб** is a highly regarded delicacy.

In the class of reptiles **пресмыка́ющиеся**, two kinds of native snakes **зме́и** are commonly distinguished: **уж** is the common garden snake, useful at least for eliminating garden pests; **гадю́ка** is poisonous and immediately distinguishable from the nonpoisonous snakes by a triangular-shaped head, noticeably separate from its body: **У гадю́ки ядови́тый зуб.** (**Клык** fang is not used in referring to snakes; only dogs and wolves have fangs: **Вы чита́ли «Бе́лый Клык» Дже́ка Ло́ндона?**) The lizard **я́щерица** and turtle **черепа́ха** are common and retain their reputations:

В слу́чае опа́сности я́щерицы спаса́ются, «теря́я» хвосты́.

Он ползёт, как черепа́ха. (Он о́чень ме́дленно идёт.)

The amphibians **земново́дные** include the frog **лягу́шка** (**голова́стик**, tadpole) and the toad **жа́ба**, a common animal that has retained its reputation, as well.

Согла́сно суеве́рию, у люде́й от жаб появля́ются борода́вки.[ii]

Fish
Ры́ба

—А кака́я у вас ры́ба?

—Ры́ба-то? Ры́ба вся́кая... И караси́ на плёсах есть, щу́ка, ну, пото́м эти... о́кунь, плотва́, лещ... Ещё линь. Зна́ешь линя́? Как поросёнок. То́-олстый! Я сам пе́рвый раз пойма́л—рот рази́нул.[jj]

Fish should supply a major source of protein in the Russian's diet; they are comparatively plentiful and relatively cheap so a Russian can distinguish many different kinds of fish. Currently good fish is hard to afford. **С ры́бой у нас пло́хо.**

The criterion for elegance is the fat content of the fish—the more fat, the better. Especially good fish are all the sturgeons and the salmon and also pike, sheatfish, eel, and burbot. Especially inexpensive fish are **ка́мбала (атланти́ческая), сельдь, сала́ка, ёрш.**

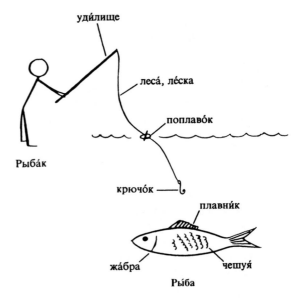

у́дочка = уди́лище + леса́ + крючо́к

уди́лище

леса́, ле́ска

поплаво́к

Рыба́к

крючо́к

плавни́к

жа́бра

чешуя́

Ры́ба

The preserving of fish is both a science and an art, with such varieties as canned "bullheads in tomato sauce," smoked salmon (or sturgeon), and many kinds of salted, dried, and pickled fish. Of course, fish are also sold fresh, frozen, and live, especially **карп, кара́сь, саза́н, сте́рлядь, форе́ль, щу́ка, лещ.**

The traditional Russian fish were freshwater fish. They are the ones you are most likely to encounter in Russian literature, and in the discussions that follow they are marked with an asterisk (*). Fishermen may be interested in the *Russian-English Glossary of Names of Aquatic Organisms and Other Biological and Related Terms*, circular no. 65, compiled by W. E. Ricker (Nanaimo, B.C.: Fisheries Research Board of Canada, 1962).

Sturgeon family
Семе́йство осетро́вых

Sturgeon is an elegant, expensive, and very traditional fish because of its rich meat and even richer roe (caviar). The sturgeon are called "red" fish **кра́сная ры́ба** even though the meat is white, for the same reason the main square in Moscow is called "Red" Square—the word was formerly equivalent to "good" and "beautiful." Except for **сте́рлядь**, most sturgeon is sold frozen or smoked.

осётр* Russian sturgeon, *Acipenser guldenstadti* (commonly weighs 30 to 40 pounds)

севрю́га stellate sturgeon, *Acipenser stellatus* (weighs between 14 and 64 pounds and is especially highly valued for its meat)

белу́га beluga, *Huso huso* (the largest sturgeon, commonly 70 to 140 pounds, though some grow to be huge)

сте́рлядь* sterlet, *Acipenser ruthenus* (the smallest sturgeon, usually from 6 to 12 pounds, but its meat is supposed to be the best of all)

Други́е осетро́вые ры́бы: шип, калу́га.

Really fresh fish. These sterlet are still wiggling.

Caviar
Икра́

Caviar comes from two major sources: salmon from the Far Eastern rivers supply red caviar **кра́сная и́ли кето́вая икра́**, and black caviar **чёрная икра́** is supplied by the sturgeon family.

Red caviar is generally considered to be only slightly less desirable of the two. The smaller and lighter colored roe (from **горбу́ша**, the humpback salmon) are thought to be the best.

Black caviar **чёрная икра́**, however, dominates the scene; the larger-sized and lighter-colored roe are preferred. One way of describing caviar is to name the fish that supplied it: **Белу́жья зерни́стая икра́ счита́ется са́мой лу́чшей, за ней идёт осетро́вая икра́, на тре́тьем ме́сте севрю́жья икра́.**

Black caviar is prepared in two main ways. In the first, **зерни́стая икра́**, the individual eggs are clearly distinct from one another. Caviar prepared this way can be bought fresh (presumably the best), but it does not keep well. More commonly, it is pasteurized in little glass jars. It is in this form that most in the United States come across caviar. **Па́юсная икра́**, the second kind of preparation, is pressed caviar, in which the individual eggs are not distinct and the resultant mass vaguely resembles a thick gray blackberry jam. Pressed caviar keeps longer than **зерни́стая икра́**: «**Наилу́чшая па́юсная икра́—севрю́жья.**»

Salmon family
Семе́йство лососёвых

The Russian salmon family is both elegant and large, including not only Atlantic and Pacific salmon, but also some trout, inconnu, and whitefish that have white meat (**сиг, о́муль, не́льма, белоры́бица**) and are often therefore referred to as **бе́лая ры́ба**, not to be confused, however, with the white-meated **кра́сная ры́ба** of the sturgeon family. Salmon is currently available canned, smoked, or salted.

The fish that we usually think of as salmon (and therefore not including trout, whitefish, and so forth) comes in two major categories: Atlantic salmon and Pacific salmon. All salmon can be referred to as **ло́со́сь**, but that word perhaps more often identifies the Atlantic salmon, the specific word for which is **сёмга**. It is often smoked or air-dried.

For very large-scale commercial fishing, however, the Pacific (Far Eastern) salmon takes first place by far. Of the six fish in this family, three are of major economic importance in Russia. First comes the humpback or pink salmon **горбу́ша**, then the chum or dog salmon **кета́**, and finally the sockeye or red salmon **не́рка**. The chum salmon **кета́** has given its name to red salmon caviar **кето́вая икра́** and to Pacific salmon in general: **Кета́ идёт** means "The salmon are running." (*King salmon* is **чавыча́**; *silver salmon* is **ки́жуч**.) The species name for Pacific salmon are Russian.

Of the smaller fish in the salmon family, **форе́ль** is any of the salmon trout and is often raised in ponds. The char **голе́ц** is less well known but of major economic importance to the Arctic fishing industry.

Perch family
Семе́йство окунёвых

Famous for their spiny fins, these fish can also be distinguished by dark horizontal stripes. In this family, only pike perch **суда́к** is commonly and joyfully eaten. The other two are most frequently come upon by the amateur who is more interested in going fishing than in catching anything.

о́кунь* perch, *Perca fluviatilis* (small, rarely on sale, but commonly caught and made into fish soup)

ёрш* ruff, *Acerina cernua* (very small, bony, and famous both for its belligerence and bony spines: "**Он всегда́ ерши́тся**" means "He always has his back up.")

суда́к* pike perch, *Lucioperca lucioperca* (highly regarded, averaging from two to five pounds, and often especially raised in reservoirs)

Cod family
Семе́йство треско́вых

The cod family, mostly saltwater fish, is of great economic significance, especially in North Russia.

треска́ cod (caught in the northern seas, it is relatively bony but of significant economic interest; the liver is canned separately and sold as a delicacy)

нали́м* burbot (predatory, long, narrow, and without scales; considered to be very good; the only freshwater fish in this category)

нава́га *Eleginus sp.* (very small, bony, but especially tasty and caught in the northern seas: **беломо́рская нава́га**)

пи́кша haddock (very much like **треска́**, but somewhat smaller)

хек European hake, *Merluccinus sp.*, or Pacific hake, **тихоокеа́нский хек** (both fished commercially in large numbers and commonly sold frozen in the markets)

минта́й Alaskan pollack, *Theragra chalcogramma*, Pacific bottomfish voted least expensive and most likely cat food

Carp family
Семе́йство ка́рповых

Carp is very common, usually cheap, and quite bony. Some kinds (**карп, лещ**) are very commonly raised in ponds or reservoirs because they adapt quickly and grow very fast. Many of them are sold live.

карп carp (at their best at three to four pounds; often specially raised in ponds)

саза́н* (the same fish as **карп**, except they are wild and expected to be much bigger)

песка́рь* gudgeon (very small, only weighing a few grams, and caught for fun and fish soup)

лещ bream, *Abramis brama* (usually from six to fourteen inches long; the largest are the best)

кара́сь* crucian carp, *Carassius carassius* (small, often sold live, fished for fun, or raised where no other fish will grow)

во́бла Caspian roach, *Rutilus rutilus caspicus* (relatively cheap and common: **вя́леная во́бла** is the air-dried Caspian roach; "**Она́ худа́я (и́ли суха́я) как во́бла**" means "She's as thin (or dry) as a Caspian roach."

плотва́ roach, *Rutilus rutilus*

тара́нь Azov roach, *Rutilus rutilus heckeli*

Other well-known fish
Други́е изве́стные ры́бы

бычо́к goby, sculpin, bullhead, or Gobiidae (Like our tuna fish in that they are cheap and always sold canned: **бычки́ в тома́те** are bullheads in tomato sauce.)

кефа́ль gray mullet (small, caught in the Black Sea and the Mediterranean, commonly canned: **кефа́ль в тома́те**, dried or smoked, and also eaten fresh; prized for its high fat content)

ка́мбала flounder, sole, or any flatfish (taken commercially in large numbers and frozen; not very highly regarded, principally because of its "fishy" taste)

морско́й о́кунь redfish or ocean perch (usually sold frozen; smaller ones weighing up to four pounds are considered the best)

па́лтус halibut, a major fishery in the North Pacific

ску́мбрия, макре́ль mackerel (small, relatively fatty, often smoked or canned)

нототе́ния *Nototheniidae* (newcomer to markets and an example of how far commercial fishermen are willing to go: the fish is found in deep waters of the Antarctic)

селёдка (salt) herring (this fish used to be a major staple in the Russian diet; indeed it is hard to imagine drinking vodka without it—it could also be bought fresh; formal term is **сельдь**)

салáка Baltic herring (popular, and sold salted, smoked, and fresh)

шпрот, кúлька sprat (usually sold smoked and considered to be very elegant)

сом* sheatfish or Danube catfish (easily distinguished from other fish by its "whiskers" **ýсики** and lack of scales; very large, up to five meters long, though only the smaller ones are considered the best eating and often are sold live)

ýгорь eel (large, with a high fat content, and therefore often smoked and considered a delicacy)

щýка* pike (relatively large, predatory, and a freshwater variety, it is often considered at its best when stuffed; for its traditional place in Russian lore, read the fairy tale «По щýчьему велéнью.»)

Curing fish
Солéние и копчéние рыбы

Ice and rapid transportation have made fresh (or frozen) fish available in addition to what can be caught in the local pond or river. But Russians preserve fish in many ways for later consumption, usually as hors d'oeuvres **закýски**.

The first step in curing fish is always to salt it, applying either salt in solution or dry salt for varying lengths of time depending on the kind of fish and its further treatment. To make salt fish **солёная рыба**, the process could stop at this stage. The fish must then be soaked and cooked before being eaten. Pickled fish **маринóванная рыба** is simply wet-salted fish with vinegar and spices. Especially fatty fishes require more than salting: smoking or drying under certain conditions is used to preserve what the salting cannot.

Вяленая рыба is fish that has been salted, washed, drained, and then hung on special frames and dried either by air or a combination of air and sun for seven to thirty days: **В вяленом виде готóвятся вóбла, сазáн, шемая, рыбéц, тарáнь**. **Балы́к** is the boneless, thick top part of sturgeon (either **осётр** or **севрю́га**) and whitefish (**белорыбица, нéльма**, or **óмуль**) prepared this way. As a delicacy, **балы́к** is outranked only by caviar.

Рыба горя́чего копчéния is fish that has been salted, washed, and then smoked for three to four hours at 80° to 140° C. Often used for carp, sturgeon, salmon, eel, and many others, this method produces a delicious result; but fish so prepared does not keep well and must be eaten within a few days. Fish that has been salted, washed, drained, and then cold-smoked (at 28° to 32° C) for two to four days is **рыба холóдного копчéния**. This method is used when fish must keep for a long time. Almost all fish can be preserved this way.

Finally, **сушёная рыба** denotes dried fish, with or without a foretreatment of salt. This method can be used for a low fat-content fish and requires that the fish be cooked before it is eaten.

Birds
Пти́цы

Óсень
Лáсточки пропáли
а вчерá зарёй
всё грачú летáли
да как сеть мелькáли
вон над той горóй.
С вéчера всё спúтся,
на дворé темнó,
лист сухóй валúтся,
нóчью вéтер злúтся
да стучúт в окнó . . .
Лýчше б снег да вью́гу
встрéтить грýдью рад!
Слóвно как с испýгу
раскричáвшись, к ю́гу
журавлú летя́т.

А. Фет

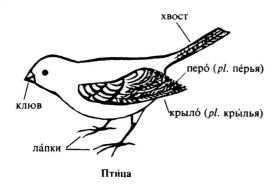

хвост

перо (*pl.* пе́рья)

крыло́ (*pl.* кры́лья)

клюв

ла́пки

Пти́ца

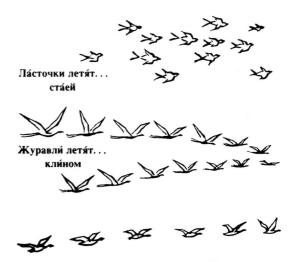

Ла́сточки летя́т. . .
  ста́ей

Журавли́ летя́т. . .
  кли́ном

Гу́си летя́т. . .
  верени́цей

К кру́пной ди́чи отно́сят куропа́тку, ря́бчика, те́терева, глухаря́, фаза́на, ди́кого гуся́ и у́тку; к ме́лкой—пе́репела, бека́са, ду́пеля, ва́льдшнепа. kk

Birds are a fine place to consider different world views. For example, to us the starling **скворе́ц** is such a pest that thousands of dollars have been spent on its elimination. The Russian orchardist might be unhappy that starlings like cherries, but the bird is still highly regarded both for its capacity for insects and also simply because it is always around. The word for birdhouse is "starling house" **скворе́чник, скворе́чня**. Some time in March, Russian children run home to mother with the delighted cry, «**Скворцы́ прилете́ли! Скворцы́ прилете́ли!**» (It seems

Соро́ка

Воробе́й

Снеги́рь

Сини́ца

Воро́на

Зи́мние пти́цы

Грач

Жа́воронок

Куку́шка

Жура́вль

Те́терев

Тетёрка

that many birds are harbingers of spring, especially rooks, starlings, and larks.) Conversely, Russians do not share our affection for hummingbirds **коли́бри**. They have none.

The following are birds particularly noticeable in Russian life and literature. All, in addition to the starling, are familiar to Russian preschoolers. A section on birds in the Appendix gives scientific names, sizes, color descriptions, and comments on most birds that any eight-year-old Russian knows.

снеги́рь   bullfinch (small, gray and red in color, and well liked for its prettiness and the fact that it arrives and stays throughout the winter when most other birds have left; it spends its summers deep in northern forests far from the common view)

воробе́й   sparrow (very common and renowned for its quarrelsomeness, thievery, and the fact that it doesn't fly south for the winter)

солове́й   eastern nightingale (noted for a gay, proud song in contrast to that of the sad western nightingale familiar to West Europeans; its gray feathers are as plain as its song is brilliant)

This is the way Professor Kaygorodov reports the nightingale's song:

Проф. Д. Н. Кайгоро́дову удало́сь все стро́фы пе́ния соловья́ изобрази́ть на челове́ческом языке́. Это вы́глядит приме́рно так:

(1) **Фи-тчурр, фи-тчурр, вад-вад-вад-вад-ции!**
(2) **Тю-лит, тю-лит, тю-лит.**
(3) **Клю-клю-клю-клю.**
(4) **Юу-лит, юу-лит.**
(5) **Ци-фи, ци-фи, ци-фи.**
(6) **Пью, пью, пью, пью.**
(7) **Ци-фи, ци-фи, чочочочочочо-вит!**
(8) **Цици-вит, тю-вит, тю-вит.**
(9) **Юу-лит, юу-лит, чочочочо-тррр-ц!**
(10) **Пи-пи-пи-пи, клю-клю-клю-клю.**
(11) **Чричи-чу; чричи-чу, чричи-чу.**

(12) Ци-вит (тихо), клюи (громко), клюи (очень громко).

Ф. Ф. Остапо́в, Певчие пти́цы на́шей ро́дины (Москва́: Акаде́мия нау́к СССР, 1960), стр. 140.

сини́ца titmouse (related to the chickadee and known as a sociable busybody; it seeks populated places for food in the winter)

Лу́чше сини́ца в рука́х, чем жура́вль в не́бе.
Better a titmouse in hand, than a crane in the sky.

соро́ка magpie (medium-sized, black and white, a very long tail, and almost always pictured with its bill open—not for food, but to complain; it is famous both for an unpleasant squawk and for a tendency to take anything: **соро́ка-воро́вка** thieving magpie)

воро́на crow (mostly gray with black patches and thought of as a not very bright pest: **Воро́на—рази́ня** means "A crow is a gawk." It is distinguished from the **соро́ка** by the mnemonic: **Все соро́ки белобо́кие, все воро́ны чернобо́кие.** A sore thumb is **бе́лая воро́на**.)

грач rook (all black, and generally seen in great flocks whose appearance denotes the arrival of spring; a famous painting is «Грачи́ прилете́ли» by **Савра́сов**)

жа́воронок skylark (the preeminent harbinger of spring)

куку́шка cuckoo (noted for its nasty habit of depositing its eggs in the nests of other birds; when the egg hatches, the newborn cuckoo pushes any other egg out of the nest and the mother-hostess has the joy of raising the stranger)

жура́вль crane (often kept as a pet, relatively easily tamed, and well loved as evidenced by the number of stories about it; the children's name for it is **жу́рка**)

Вот они́, жу́рки! Ух, как бли́зко! Что за пти́цы удиви́тельные! А но́ги-то но́ги— бу́дто дли́нные па́лки!
. . . Оди́н жу́рка разбежа́лся. [II]

Соловьёва, Щепето́ва и Карпи́нская, Родна́я речь: кни́га для чте́ния во II кла́ссе нача́льной шко́лы (Москва́: Учпедги́з, 1964), стр. 32.

глуха́рь wood grouse, capercaillie (very large, black, quite popular, and noted for its deafness during its mating call when ear passages are blocked off [**глухо́й**, deaf]; the hunter runs up close while the call lasts and then freezes until the next call is under way)

те́терев black grouse (the male is black, somewhat smaller than a chicken, and readily distinguishable by its rather large tail in the shape of an upside-down lyre; the female **тете́рка** is brown, with a plain tail; both find refuge from the winter's cold in snowbanks)

Mammals
Млекопита́ющие

We compress the discussion to eleven mammals **млекопита́ющие** that seem to have the most associations in Russian life and are familiar to Russian preschoolers. A more extensive listing of mammals familiar to third and fourth graders follows.

To us, the hamster **хомя́к**, *Cricetus cricetus*, is a cute children's pet or a laboratory animal. The Russian hamster, on the contrary, is a scourge of grain farming and the object of efforts at eradication. Because the hamster likes ripened grain, it eats as much as it can and then carries off the rest in cheek pouches to a hole in the ground. These grain depositories have been raided by starving peasants in times of famine.

Another major pest in grain fields is the suslik **су́слик**, *Citellus suslicus*, a ground squirrel that prefers unripened grain. It lives in large colonies and is famous for sitting on its hind feet and whistling loudly when alarmed. This animal

Су́слик

it is hunted for its fur. Properly, *rabbit* should be used only when applied to **кро́лик**, the domesticated rabbit of Russia, which is eaten and which also supplies fur.

Ёж

devastates by biting off green stems and sucking the juice (whence its name, **су́слик**): «Хомяки́, су́слики, полёвки, мы́ши—враги́ урожа́я. С ни́ми ведётся беспоща́дная борьба́» means "Hamsters, susliks, field voles, and mice are enemies of the harvest. They are being fought without mercy."

Related to the shrew and mole is the hedgehog **ёж**,[6] *Erinaceus europaeus*. The hedgehog is close to beloved to a Russian; it is thought of as cute, charming, and even useful. Sometimes hedgehogs are kept as pets and are traditional residents of basements where their duties are to eliminate mice, small snakes, and the like. Their nocturnal habits tend to keep them out of sight.

Бе́лка

Барсу́к

The squirrel **бе́лка**, *Sciurus vulgaris*, there as here, is thought of as a "little forest friend." The common squirrel is grayish red in summer and reddish gray in winter, and it always has tufted ears. Especially in Siberia, the squirrel is the object of commercial hunters' expeditions.

Two hare are relatively common and well known: (1) **за́яц-беля́к**, or simply **беля́к**, (*Lepus timidus*), turns white for the winter; and (2) **за́яц-руса́к**, or **руса́к**, (*Lepus europaeus*), keeps the same color, a light brown, all year. Hare is eaten only in very dire necessity, though

The European badger **барсу́к**, *Meles meles*, is omnivorous and is noted for digging up plants, often invading gardens and removing whole plants for winter storage. Its numbers are not large enough to constitute a real threat, however. The badger is featured in a short story by Konstantin Paustovskiy, «Барсу́чий нос,» and Leonid Leonov's first novel is **Барсуки́**.

6. In Europe, the hedgehog and the porcupine are two quite different animals, though they are both unpleasant to the touch. The porcupine **дикобра́з** lives only in more remote southern areas of the former USSR. Hedgehogs have spiny fur, not quills.

The common fox лиси́ца or лиса́, *Vulpes vulpes*, is red with a white-tipped tail, but varieties of this species extend from almost all-black to all-white. The чернобу́рая лиси́ца is dark brown or black, which is rare and therefore much more valuable. Кресто́вка and сиводу́шка are more like the red fox but have a significant amount of brown or black in their fur. Three kinds of silver fox are bred artificially and raised in captivity: серебри́сто-чёрная, пла́тиновая, and белосне́жная лиси́ца. Stories about the clever fox abound in folk tales, not to mention Krylov's fables. Лиси́ца is the usual word for fox, while лиса́ is somewhat more poetic (and also the term for fox fur).

The wolf волк, *Canis lupus*, is in the foreground, not the background, of the Russian language. A predator of farm animals and formerly a threat to human life (especially in the hungry winter months), it is a standard figure in Russian stories and sayings. The wolf's number has dwindled now, but its reputation remains undimmed.

Во́лка но́ги ко́рмят.
The wolf gets his food by using his legs.

The deer family, including the moose and reindeer, frequently collides in the dictionary. The problem is that the moose лось, *Alces alces*, is often translated as *elk* because *elk* is British English for *moose*. The moose, partly because of its size, is thought of as a benevolent king of the forest (лесно́й царь—лось), and, as it is well protected by game laws, it is actually a fairly common sight in the taiga. The other major problem for translators is the *reindeer* versus *deer* confusion. A reindeer (a very close relative of our caribou) is се́верный оле́нь, *Rangifer tarandus*, and should not be translated as *northern deer*. The reindeer is domesticated and widely used for hides, food, and services in the far north.

Perhaps the most "Russian" animal is the (brown) bear (бу́рый) медве́дь, *Ursus arctos*. It is a close relative of the grizzly and the Alaskan brown bear: Медве́дь—хозя́ин ле́са. The bear is perhaps thought of as fearsome because of its size, but it is certainly not as feared as the wolf. The Russian thinks of the bear as honest, simple, but not without dignity. The children's story name for it is Ми́ша.

Following are other mammals familiar to most Russians and found outside a zoo, pen, or laboratory. The asterisk indicates those animals that supply fur.

байба́к   see суро́к

барс   snow leopard or ounce, *Uncia uncia* or *Felis uncia* (spotted, with a large fluffy tail; rare in reality but a symbol of size and strength in the cat family. The name Ба́рсик for a cat is equivalent to our "Tiger")

бе́лый медве́дь*   polar bear, *Ursus maritimus*

бобр* (technical), бобёр (colloquial) Beaver, *Castor fiber* (highly regarded for its industry and also thought of as good, even kind: Он добёр, как бобёр)

бурунду́к   chipmunk, *Eutamis sibiricus*

вы́дра*   otter, *Lutra lutra* (prized for its fur; the animal has given its name to any ugly and mean woman)

вы́хухоль*   desman, *Desmana moschata* (large, shrewlike, prized for its fur; it lives near water)

горноста́й*   ermine, *Mustela erminea* (white with a black-tipped tail in the winter: У царя́ была́ горноста́евая ма́нтия)

ди́кая ко́шка   wildcat (of several varieties, not ususally distinguished)

ено́т   *Nyctereutes procyonoides* (of the canine family; its full name is енотови́дная соба́ка or уссури́йский ено́т, not to be confused with our ено́т-полоску́н below, which it resembles; native to the Far East, but more than successfully transplanted to central Russia.)

ено́т-полоску́н   raccoon, *Procyon lotor* (полоска́ть, to rinse!) native to North America but acclimatized in some areas of Russia

землеро́йка shrew, literally *earth-digger*; *Sorex araneus* (without the unpleasant connotations of the English counterpart)

зубр bison, *Bison bonasus* (freely roamed the European plains in the past but now confined to preserves, such as **Белове́жская пу́ща**)

бизо́н American plains buffalo, *Bison bison*

каба́н boar, wild pig, *Sus scrofa* (or uncastrated male pig)

кала́н see **морска́я вы́дра**

коза́ (лесна́я, ди́кая) see **косу́ля**

колоно́к* (Siberian) kolinsky, *Mustela sibirica* (in the weasel family; hunted for its cheaper fur)

корса́к* fox, *Vulpes korsac* (small and found in the Asian steppes)

косу́ля roe deer, *Capreolus capreolus* (very small and therefore also called **ди́кая (и́ли) лесна́я коза́**)

ко́тик see **морско́й ко́тик**

крот mole, *Talpa europaea* (noted for its blindness: «**Он слепо́й, как крот.**»)

кры́са rat (notorious as here: «**Ух, кры́са!**» means "The dirty rat!")

куни́ца* marten, *Martes sp.* (prized for its fur; in the weasel family and of the same genus as the sable: «**Осо́бенно це́нится мех лесно́й куни́цы**» means "The fur of the European pine marten is especially [highly] valued")

ла́ска weasel, *Mustela nivalis* (smallest of the weasel family and famous for taking prey by pouncing and biting the back of the prey's neck)

летя́га flying squirrel, *Pteromys volans*

морска́я вы́дра* sea otter, *Enhydra lutris* (historically famous for luring the Russians to Alaska for its fur; also called **кала́н, камча́тский бобр**)

морско́й ко́тик* northern fur seal, *Callorhinus ursinus* (prized for fur; also responsible for bringing the Russians to Alaska)

мышь mouse (characterized much as it is here; **лету́чая мышь** is a bat)

не́рпа* seal, family: *Phocidae* (several varieties of true seals, the best known of which is **байка́льская не́рпа**, a seal that lives more than 1,000 miles from salt water)

но́рка* mink, *Mustela lutreola* (well known for its fur)

ну́трия* coypu (imported from South America and acclimatized for fur)

оле́нь deer

благоро́дный, настоя́щий олень red deer, *Cervus elaphus* **мара́л, изю́бр** (subspecies of red deer, raised and hunted for their antlers, which supply a common tonic, **пантокри́н**)

онда́тра* muskrat, *Ondatra zibethica* (native to North America but imported and acclimatized for fur)

песе́ц* polar fox, *Vulpes lagopus* (resembles a cross between a dog and a fox; prized for fur: **бе́лый песе́ц, голубо́й песе́ц**

росома́ха* wolverine, *Gulo gulo* (largest of the weasel family; predatory; because of its reputation as unkempt and dirty, it has given its name to women with disheveled hair)

рысь lynx, *Felis lynx* (fierce and fearless; «**У ры́си ки́сточки на уша́х.**» means "The lynx have tufts on their ears")

се́рна chamois or mountain goat, *Rupricapra rupricapra* (famous for beauty, grace, speed, and nervousness: «**Она́ пугли́вая, как се́рна**» means "She is very easily frightened")

со́боль* sable, *Martes zibellina* (of the weasel family and noted for highly prized fur: «**На боя́рах бы́ли собо́льи шу́бы**» means "The boyars wore sable coats")

суро́к woodchuck, marmot, *Marmota bobac* (famous for whistling: «**Суро́к свисти́т в степи́**» translates "The woodchuck is whistling on the steppes"; and hibernating: «**Он спит как суро́к**» means "He sleeps like a log") тигр   tiger, *Panthera tigris*

тюлéнь*   any seal (a general term; reputed to be pleasant but lazy and slow)

хорь, хорёк   (European) polecat or fitch, *Mustela putorius* (of the weasel family; thought of as ugly and mean: «Ах ты, хорёк вонючий»; not to be confused with the skunk скунс, вонючка, a native of North and Central America)

шакáл   jackal, *Canis aureus* (a symbol of nastiness, meanness)

Death in the animal kingdom is treated with euphemisms: Horses and cows "fall" корóва пáла. Падёж скотá. Fish go to sleep Рыба заснýла. And in general, animals "breathe their last": издóхнуть/дóхнуть (прост.) сдóхнуть/сдыхáть. One person named his dog "Drop-dead" Кабысдóх.

Russian furs
Рýсские мехá

Furs may be politically dubious in the United States, but in Russia their owners are warm. Those who don't have a coat try to have a fur hat. Many animals are raised in captivity for their fur, but the very best skins still are from the wild animals of the northern taiga тайгá, where weather forces a warmer coat. Fur bearers from the Western Hemisphere, including our raccoon енóт (-полоскýн), the muskrat ондáтра, and the coypu нýтрия, have been imported and acclimatized. Also note the fur-bearers in the preceding list, those with an asterisk.

The major supplier of furs is in fact the plain old sheep овцá whose life is spent making sheepskin овчинá, which, in turn is the raw material for the тулýп (an extra long coat of sheepskin, fur side in) and the шýба (not so long and somewhat more elegant). Technically, шýба is a fur coat with the fur inside, and the correct way to denote what we call a "fur coat" is меховóе пальтó (a mink coat is пальтó из нóрки, нóрковое мантó). However, popular usage often includes шýба to mean any fur coat. If the sheepskin is sheared, then it will be мутóн, and if it is also dyed it becomes цигéйка (formerly goatskin so treated). Каракýль comes from baby karakul lambs not more than three days old: каракульчá comes from the same animal, but it is obtained before the animal has had time to be born. This is a very elegant fur and one of the largest branches of the fur industry. Considerably less elegant, perhaps, is calf fur опóек and pony fur жеребóк.

TRANSLATIONS

a.   We can't wait for kindnesses from Nature. Our task is to take them from her.

Michurin

b.   Our third-grade class reported on its experiment on thinning carrot plants (that had come up). We pulled up many carrot plants. In between the plants we left a distance of 10 to 12 centimeters. We did not thin one section of the carrot plants, and the carrots here were small. The little carrots crowded out each other, took each other's food, moisture and light. And therefore they all had slender roots. This experiment taught us that carrots have to be thinned in order to get large juicy roots. Weeds also crowd carrots and take food, moisture and light from them, and therefore weeds must be dug up (weeded out).

c.   The Green Pharmacy

by Academician N. Tsitsin

If you go into a forest or a field, you will find yourself in a green pharmacy. There at your feet is a small shoot of an insignificant weed—shepherd's purse. The seeds of this plant ripen in triangular little boxes that look like a purse. Not many people know that in this weed-purse is a valuable medicine: it stops the flow of blood.

Poisonous henbane grows on waste land. Its leaves are used to make a medicine that lessens pain. . . .

Valerian drops are made from the roots of valerian. . . . The flowers and leaves of lily of the valley are used to make drops that are taken by those who have heart trouble.

And there are forest berries. They also possess a healing effect: dried raspberries help to induce sweat, and *kisel'* made from dried blackberries is good for the digestion.

d.   Matryona had another big chore when her turn came to feed the goatherds: one of them was a solidly built deaf-mute and the other was a kid with a wet, homemade cigarette eternally on his lip. Her turn came once every month and a half, but Matryona had to pay dearly for it. She went to the country store, bought canned fish, and paid out money for sugar and butter, which she herself was not used to eating. It turned out that the women would try to outdo each other in feeding the herders.

e.   In the USSR medicinal leeches are caught mostly in Krasnodarskiy Kray, in the Moldavian, Ukrainian, Georgian, and Azerbaijan republics. They are also raised in laboratories. **А.Н. Бакула́ев и Ф.Н. Петро́в, Популя́рная медици́нская энциклопе́дия (Москва́: Изда́тельство «Сове́тская энцик-лопе́дия»,** 1966), **стр.** 679.

f.   Many people collect butterflies. There are four stages in the life of the butterfly: (1) egg, (2) caterpillar, (3) chrysalis, (4) butterfly.

g.   Ladybug "Ladybug, fly away to the sky. There your children are eating cutlets." [Earlier version: Fly away . . . bring us some bread.]

h.   The beetle is any insect with hard wings.

i.   Same as the butterfly, but it appears outside at night. Moths are flying around.

j.   Gnats appear mostly in the evening, at sundown.

k.   The ant works day and night; it is a symbol of industriousness. Ants live in anthills.

l.   Spiders spin webs.

m.   Don't touch a wasp nest or there'll be disaster.

n.   Bees live in hives. The queen is the largest bee; she lays eggs. The worker bee collects honey, and the drone doesn't do any work. The swarm follows the queen bee.

o.   Crickets often live in houses near the stove; earlier, it was thought that crickets talk to the house spirit. Sometimes they are identified as the house spirit itself.

p.   Fireflies come out at night.

q.   Read "The Dragonfly and the Ant" by Krylov.

r.   Bumblebees are like bees, only bigger and shaggier.

s.   Cabbage moths lay eggs in cabbage stems, and then their grubs eat the stems.

t.   The forest tick transmits encephalitis.

u.   "I itch. A mosquito bit [me]."

v.   [A ditty] Little green grasshopper, with his knees [bent] back; He's excited, chirring, for some reason very happy.

w.   The May beetle eats birch trees. The May beetle is destructive to agriculture.

x.   'Sow bugs are very repulsive; they are thought to be dirty.

y.   Naphthalene may be used against moths.

z.   Be sure to read "Mukha tsokotukha" by Chukovskiy. In order to get rid of flies, they use fly swatters and [fly] paper.

aa.   They attacked the table like locusts. (They ate up everything very quickly.)

bb.   Cockroaches are very unpleasant and are hard to get rid of.

cc.   (The word for aphid is used mostly in the singular.) Aphids have come out. Aphids are crawling there.

dd.   According to superstition, the earwig will burrow into [one's] ear and even into the brain.

ee.   "Why are you jumping like a flea?"

ff.   Lice live off the blood of man and mammals. Three kinds of lice are parasitic on man: head lice, clothes lice, and pubic lice.

gg. Nits are louse eggs. They are small, white, and they don't move.

hh. Bedbugs are feared less than lice, since they usually live in [furniture] rather than on the body.

ii. According to superstition, people get warts from toads.

jj. "What kind of fish are there here?"

"Fish? All kinds of fish. . . . There are crucian carp in the deeper pools, pike, and, well then, those perch, roach, bream, and then tench. Do you know tench? It's fat as a little pig. First time I caught one myself, my mouth fell open." **Юрий Казако́в**, «Ти́хое у́тро» На полуста́нке: расска́зы (Москва́: Сове́тский писа́тель, 1959), **стр.** 8.

kk. Among the larger game birds are the gray partridge, the hazel grouse, the black grouse, the wood grouse, the pheasant, the wild goose, and the duck; among the smaller game birds are the quail, snipe, great snipe, and the woodcock. **Е. и М. Нико́льские, Кни́га о культу́ре бы́та** (Москва́: Профизда́т, 1967), **стр.** 195.

ll. "There are the cranes! [Look] how near they are! What marvelous birds they are! And their legs—like long sticks!"

. . . One crane took off.

15

Numbers
Чи́сла

It is said that mathematics is a language. Perhaps, but our mental pictures of 30 pounds, 60 miles per hour, 4 yards, or 212°F. must be translated to scales used in Russian before they can have meaning for a Russian. For the native, punctuation and arrangement of numerals sometimes supplies significant context: (555) 555-5555 must be a telephone number to an American. In other cases, the numbers themselves may hold specific meaning: 36-26-36, for example. (Though this arrangement could be a telephone number in Russia. The Russian Miss World 1992 had the following measurements: **рост-182, обьём груди́-88, та́лии-60, бедёр-90.**)

Special locutions used in Russian express the same systems we use: latitude and longitude; 2 x 4 = 8. Those locutions are rarely mere translations of the words we use, but that is the stuff of language books like this.

Most of the discussion centers on the most basic arithmetic and geometric terminology and its practical applications, though a few sections are of interest to those in mathematics, engineering, or the sciences. The topics to be covered include:

Numbers and their names
Reading and writing numbers
Declining numbers in spoken Russian
Arithmetic operations
Common geometric figures
Reading mathematical expressions
Measures

NUMBERS AND NAMES FOR THEM
Числа и их названия

The numbers
Числа

For your convenience, a table of numbers shows units, tens, hundreds, thousands, and so on, up to the billions.

When Russians are counting they do not usually say «оди́н, два, три .....» but rather, «раз, два, три.....» («Оди́н раз» is understood.) On the other hand, a few fussy people do insist on observing a rule to the effect that in counting objects (to count=счита́ть), one starts with оди́н, but in counting actions (such as keeping time to music), one may start with раз. The Russian equivalent for "One, two, three, go!" is «Раз, два, три, вперёд!»

Числа[1]

Едини́цы	Деся́тки	Со́тни	Ты́сячи
0—нуль, ноль[2]	10—де́сять	100—сто	1000—ты́сяча
1—оди́н, одна́, одно́	11—оди́ннадцать	200—две́сти	2000—две ты́сячи
2—два, две	12—двена́дцать	300—три́ста	3000—три ты́сячи
3—три	13—трина́дцать	400—четы́реста	4000—четы́ре ты́сячи
4—четы́ре	14—четы́рнадцать	500—пятьсо́т	5000—пять ты́сяч
5—пять	15—пятна́дцать	600—шестьсо́т	6000—шесть ты́сяч
6—шесть	16—шестна́дцать	700—семьсо́т	7000—семь ты́сяч
7—семь	17—семна́дцать	800—восемьсо́т	8000—во́семь ты́сяч
8—во́семь	18—восемна́дцать	900—девятьсо́т	9000—де́вять ты́сяч
9—де́вять	19—девятна́дцать		
	20—два́дцать		
	30—три́дцать		
	40—со́рок		
	50—пятьдеся́т		
	60—шестьдеся́т		
	70—се́мьдесят		
	80—во́семьдесят		
	90—девяно́сто		

деся́тки ты́сяч 10 000–90 000

со́тни ты́сяч 100 000–900 000

миллио́ны 1 000 000–9 000 000

деся́тки миллио́нов 10 000 000–90 000 000

со́тни миллио́нов 100 000 000–900 000 000

миллиа́рды 1 000 000 000 - 9 000 000 000

---

1. For declensions of these numbers, and the formation of the ordinal numbers, consult your grammar book.
2. Though both pronunciations are common, «нуль» seems to predominate in the oblique cases.

Just for exercise:

Сосчита́йте по́ два до 20 (двадцати́). (2, 4, 6, 8, . . .)

Сосчита́йте по́ три до 30 (тридцати́). (3, 6, 9, 12, . . .)

Numerical nouns
Имена́ числи́тельные коли́чественные

Russian has a set of "numerical nouns" in addition to the cardinals (оди́н, два, три, . . .), the ordinals (пе́рвый, второ́й, тре́тий), and the collectives (дво́е, тро́е, че́тверо, . . .) that are usually treated in grammar books. They are frequently encountered in everyday conversation and are usually limited to the numbers one to ten:

1—едини́ца	6—шестёрка
2—дво́йка	7—семёрка
3—тро́йка	8—восьмёрка
4—четвёрка	9—девя́тка
5—пятёрка	10—деся́тка

These numerical nouns are principally used two ways: (1) to name an item in a sequence, or (2) to refer to objects containing the indicated number of units. The best example in English for the former is the use of an article or the words *number* or *figure* before a cardinal number: the 4 четвёрка, the figure 8 восьмёрка, the 2 of spades дво́йка пик. Often, context must tell what the number relates to: "He came on a No. 7 bus" (that is, route no. 7) is «Он прие́хал на семёрке»; or the number 5 (*ball*, for example), пятёрка. A very frequently heard application of the numerical noun is in the form of school (and most university) grades, where "a five" пятёрка is an A grade, "a four" четвёрка is a B, and so on: Он получи́л дво́йку по арифме́тике.

These numerical nouns are also used to refer to objects that contain the indicated number of units. Thus, тро́йка can be a team of three horses, a triumvirate, or a three-piece suit (jacket, vest, and pants). Пятёрка can be a five-ruble and деся́тка a ten-ruble bill, or дво́йка

can be a boat with two oars. This usage presents many problems for language students, however.[1] Тро́йка can be a team of three horses, but a team of two horses is па́ра. The five- and ten-ruble bills can be пятёрка and деся́тка, but a one-ruble bill cannot be едини́ца. (Едини́ца is commonly used both in the singular and plural to mean units or ones. See the description of an abacus.)

Words derived from or containing numbers
Сло́жные слова́ с числи́тельными в ко́рне

Nouns, adjectives, and adverbs formed from the genitive case of the number itself are both very common and easy to recognize:

двугла́вый орёл   a two-headed eagle

двухдне́вный срок   a two-day period

треуго́льник   a triangle

трёхколёсный велосипе́д   a tricycle

пятиле́тка   a five-year period (or plan)

Those formed from the collective numbers two, three, and four are just as easily recognizable:

двоежёнство   bigamy

троекра́тно   three times

четвероно́гий   four-footed

Other sets of words have numbers as their base: двойно́й means *double* or *twice as much* (в двойно́м разме́ре or в двухкра́тном разме́ре) and тройно́й means *triple* or *three times as much*. Четверно́й, пятерно́й, шестерно́й, семерно́й, восьмерно́й, девятерно́й, and десятерно́й are used in spoken Russian, and then only rarely.

Двойни́к and тройни́к are common, as in двойни́к (your double or someone who "looks just like you"), or тройни́к (a three-way plug or pipe). Четвери́к, пятери́к, шестери́к,

1. Imagine a similar problem in the restricted usages of English words with a root that signifies *two*: duo, duet, dual, deuce, double, twain, twice, and so on.

семери́к, восьмери́к, девятери́к, and деся-
тери́к can refer to measurements or objects
containing the indicated number of units; for
instance, **упряжка шестерико́м** is a team of
six horses. But these words are rarely used.

In mathematics and electronics one often
uses the binary system **двои́чная систе́ма
счисле́ния** and the quinary system **пятери́чная
систе́ма счисле́ния**; the decimal system is
десяти́чная систе́ма.

Children born at the same time of the same
mother are **близнецы́**, which naturally means
twins but can also apply to look-alikes. One can
be specific about the number of children using
the series **двойня́**, **тройня́**, or (in conversation)
двойня́шки, тройня́шки: «Она́ родила́
тро́йню» is "She had triplets." The concept of
quadruplets and quintuplets is often para-
phrased: **Она́ родила́ сра́зу четверы́х дете́й.**

READING AND WRITING NUMBERS
Чте́ние и написа́ние чи́сел

Writing whole numbers
Написа́ние це́лых чи́сел

Russians (as do other Europeans) write numbers differently from the way we do:

$$1, 2, 3, 4, 5, 6, 7, 8, 9$$

Notice that the *one* often has a hook on the
front of it; the *two*, *six*, and *nine* often are
rounded whereas ours are not; and the *seven*
almost always has a line drawn through it.

In writing large numbers, thousands are
sometimes separated by periods: 24.432
(**два́дцать четы́ре ты́сячи четы́реста
три́дцать два**); but almost more often the
thousands are not separated at all: 60000
(**шестьдеся́т ты́сяч**). In print, thousands are

most often separated by a space: 28 123
(**два́дцать во́семь ты́сяч сто два́дцать
три**).

Writing and reading decimals
Написа́ние и чте́ние десяти́чных дробе́й

The Russian system is the reverse of ours: they
indicate the decimal point with a comma **запя-
та́я**; they use the period **то́чка** as our comma.

По-англи́йски	По-ру́сски
0.32	0,32
4,256.01	4.256,01

These examples show how decimals are
read out loud:

0,0	ноль це́лых, ноль деся́тых
1,1	одна́ це́лая, одна́ деся́тая
2,2	две це́лых, две деся́тых
3,3	три це́лых, три деся́тых
20,01	два́дцать це́лых, одна́ со́тая
21,02	два́дцать одна́ це́лая, две со́тых
42,001	со́рок две це́лых, одна́ ты́сячная
546,438	пятьсо́т со́рок шесть це́лых, четы́реста три́дцать во́семь ты́сячных

Це́лая, це́лых is often omitted and
replaced by **и**; for example, 43,5 can be read
со́рок три и пять деся́тых. To do so is less
formal but quite common.

Russians do try, much harder than we, to
report tenths, hundredths, thousandths, and so
forth. But even they have their limits. When
faced with decimals carried out to many places,
they simply read the decimal point **запята́я**
and then continue the list of numbers, breaking
them up as they wish. Thus, 89,031824 can be
read **во́семьдесят де́вять запята́я ноль
три́дцать оди́н во́семьсот два́дцать
четы́ре**. The point at which one no longer
bothers counting decimal places is also a matter
of convenience and formality: 57,368 can be
read as **пятьдеся́т семь це́лых, три́ста
шестьдеся́т во́семь ты́сячных** or as **пять-**

десят семь запята́я три́ста шестьдеся́т
во́семь.

The adjectives used in reading decimals
(це́лая, це́лых, деся́тая, деся́тых, со́тая,
со́тых, ты́сячная, ты́сячных . . .) are thought
of as modifying до́ля едини́цы or часть and
are therefore feminine.

Reading simple fractions
Чте́ние просты́х дробе́й

With one exception, the denominator is in the
genitive plural.

$\frac{5}{8}$ пять восьмы́х

$\frac{18}{41}$ восемна́дцать со́рок пе́рвых

$\frac{135}{159}$ сто три́дцать пять сто пятьдеся́т
девя́тых

That exception occurs when the last digit in
the numerator is a *one* (excluding *eleven*); then
the denominator is in the nominative singular
feminine, because either the word до́ля or
часть is understood to be modified.

$\frac{1}{2}$ одна́ втора́я[2]

$\frac{1}{3}$ одна́ тре́тья[2]

$\frac{1}{4}$ одна́ четвёртая[2]

$\frac{1}{5}$ одна́ пя́тая

$\frac{1}{61}$ одна́ шестьдеся́т пе́рвая

$\frac{41}{23}$ со́рок одна́ два́дцать тре́тья

Notice, too, that either до́ля or часть is
understood to be the word modified, so both
one and *two* in the numerator appear in the feminine.

Mixed numbers
Сме́шанные чи́сла

Mixed numbers are sometimes read using
це́лая, це́лых, but more commonly и is used
instead, as shown in the next column.

---

2. The forms (одна́) полови́на, треть, and че́тверть are perhaps more often used in daily life, while одна́ втора́я, тре́тья,
and четвёртая are more common in arithmetic and mathematics.

$1\frac{2}{3}$ одна́ и две тре́тьих
одна́ це́лая две тре́тьих

$48\frac{3}{8}$ со́рок во́семь и три восьмы́х
со́рок во́семь це́лых три восьмы́х

DECLINING NUMBERS IN
SPOKEN RUSSIAN
Склоне́ние числи́тельных в
разгово́рном языке́

You have perhaps seen the tables in your
Russian grammar book giving the declensions
of numbers. Take as some consolation that
Russians have a hard time with such intricacy,
too—so much so that for practical purposes,
only two cases, the nominative and the genitive,
are commonly used. If you are talking to a
Russian and suddenly realize that you are supposed to decline a number but cannot remember
how, go ahead and use the nominative, especially if you are dealing with numbers specifically, as in mathematics or statistical reports.

The Russian has devised circumlocutions to
avoid declining numbers. For instance, the
preposition ме́жду requires the instrumental
case. But when asked to read «Найти́ ра́зность
ме́жду 341820 и 239619» ("Find the difference
between . . ."), the Russian will probably say,
«Найти́ ра́зность ме́жду чи́слами . . .»
("Find the difference between the numbers . . .")
and then read off the numbers in the nominative.
The words for equal(s) in Russian—равно́,
ра́вен, равна́, равны́, or равня́ется—take the
dative. Often the Russian ignores that fact altogether and uses the nominative instead, especially
if the numbers are long or involved. Or, often
other words are used that do not require the
dative. For instance, есть, бу́дет, э́то, and
полу́чится can all be interchanged with равно́
yet do not require the dative. Sometimes no verb
or substitute is used at all.

As a general guide, you may consider that
the smaller the number, the more likely it is to
be declined.

ARITHMETIC OPERATIONS
Арифмети́ческие де́йствия

Addition
Сложе́ние

Some basic terminology for the operation of addition follows. Notice in the example that the plus sign is placed higher than ours.

```
плюс ───────▶        14 ← слага́емое
(зна́к сложе́ния)    + 7 ← слага́емое
                      ──
                      21 ← су́мма
```

Of the many ways of saying "seven and fourteen is twenty-one," this version is both very common and the easiest for us to use: **Семь плюс четы́рнадцать бу́дет два́дцать оди́н.**
And in performing the following addition problem, the Russian will say to himself (**про себя́ говори́т**):

```
   57
 + 42
   96
  ───
  195
```

Семь плюс два—де́вять, плюс шесть— пятна́дцать. Пять пи́шем, оди́н в уме́.
Пять и оди́н—шесть, плюс четы́ре—де́сять, плюс де́вять—девятна́дцать.

These are a few typical problems in addition зада́чи на сложе́ние:[3]

1. **Одно́ слага́емое** 16427, **друго́е** 8697. **Найти́ их су́мму.**

2. **Пе́рвое слага́емое** 9688, **второ́е на** 397 **бо́льше пе́рвого, а тре́тье равно́ су́мме пе́рвых двух слага́емых? Чему́ равна́ су́мма трёх слага́емых?**

---

3. Each of the problems in the arithmetic section has been taken from Russian school arithmetic books.

3. **Су́мму двух чи́сел** 13708 **и** 6075 **увели́чить на** 10970.

4. **Вы́полнить сложе́ние и сде́лать прове́рку:** 30478 + 137 + 590

5. **На уча́стке посади́ли в пе́рвый день** 60 **дере́вьев, а во второ́й день** 80 **дере́вьев. Ско́лько дере́вьев посади́ли за два дня?**

6. **Найти́ неизве́стное слага́емое** x (икс): x + 625 = 1200

Отве́ты на зада́чи на сложе́ние: (1) 25124; (2) 39466; (3) 30753; (4) 31205; (5) 140 **дере́вьев;** (6) x = 575.

The Russian abacus
Счёты

The Russian abacus can be seen almost anywhere money is to be paid. Cashiers and bookkeepers use them, and children are taught how to add and subtract on them, principally so that they may learn the relationship of units, tens, hundreds, and so on. Elementary classrooms often have a large abacus on a rack at the front of the class. Many people have one at home as well.

The illustration shows the regular version of the Russian abacus. The set of four beads is used either for separating kopecks from rubles or for computing one-quarter units. Japanese and Chinese abacuses are differently arranged.

How to add on the Russian abacus
Сложе́ние на счётах

1. Add 23 and 45. (Always start out with all the beads on the right side.) To set up the first number, move two beads from the second rank (tens) to the left side. Move three beads (three units) from the first rank to the left side. The second number is done the same way: move four beads from the second rank (tens) to the left and five beads from the first rank to the left. As a result the abacus has six beads on the second rank

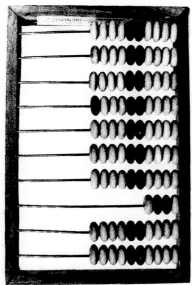

Счёты

704 832 на счётах

миллио́ны
со́тни ты́сяч
деся́тки ты́сяч
ты́сячи
со́тни
деся́тки
едини́цы

(tens) and eight beads (units) on the first rank. Therefore: 23 + 45 = 68.

2. Add 52,314 and 5,362. For the first number, move five beads to the left in the fifth rank, two beads in the fourth rank, three beads in the third rank, one bead in the second, and four beads in the first rank. For the second number, move five beads to the left in the fourth rank, three in the third rank, six in the second rank, and two in the first rank. Result: 52,314 + 5,362 = 57,676.

3. Add 156 and 278. Set up the number 156 on the left side, exactly as before. Now, for the second number move two beads (hundreds) to the left in the third rank. Because it is now impossible to move seven beads to the left in the second rank (tens), you must now move one more bead (hundred) to the left in the third rank and then three beads to the right in the second rank (100 – 70 = 30). For the units, because you cannot move eight beads to the left in the first rank, instead move one of the beads in the second rank to the left and then move two beads in the first rank to the right (10 – 8 = 2). The result: 156 + 278 = 434.

Subtraction
Вычита́ние

For subtraction, the minus sign is also placed higher than ours. The terminology applicable to the operation includes:

ми́нус ⟶ (знак вычита́ния)

$$\begin{array}{r} 35 \\ -4 \\ \hline 31 \end{array}$$ ← уменьша́емое ← вычита́емое ← ра́зность

This is a common way of saying "thirty-five minus four equals thirty-one": **Три́дцать пять ми́нус четы́ре бу́дет три́дцать оди́н.**

Про себя́ говоря́т:

$$\begin{array}{r} 698 \\ -489 \\ \hline 209 \end{array}$$

От восемна́дцати—де́вять, это бу́дет де́вять.
От восьми́—во́семь—ноль.
От шести́—четы́ре—два.

$$\begin{array}{r} 35 \\ -4 \\ \hline 31 \end{array}$$

От пяти—четы́ре—оди́н.
Три сно́сим, бу́дет три́дцать оди́н.

Зада́чи на вычита́ние:

1. Уменьша́емое 1080, вычита́емое 675. Найти́ ра́зность.

2. Ско́лько полу́чится, е́сли из 85 (восьми́десяти пяти́) вы́честь 25? 96 уме́ньшить на 24?

3. На ско́лько 76 бо́льше 36 (тридцати́ шести́)? 17 ме́ньше 80 (восьми́десяти)?

4. В библиоте́ке бы́ло 2000 книг. 500 книг вы́дали. Ско́лько книг оста́лось?

5. Река́ Ле́на длинне́е Днепра́ на 1979 км, Днепр коро́че Во́лги на 1403 км. Найти́ длину́ Во́лги и Днепра́, е́сли длина́ Ле́ны 4264 км.

Отве́ты на зада́чи на вычита́ние: (1) Ра́зность 405; (2) 60, 72; (3) на 40, на 63; (4) Оста́лось 1500 книг; (5) длина́ Во́лги 3688 км; длина́ Днепра́ 2285 км.

Multiplication
Умноже́ние

These terms are applicable to the notation system for multiplication:

$$\begin{array}{r} \times\ 12 \\ 5 \\ \hline 60 \end{array}$$

косо́й крест (знак умноже́ния)

то́чка (знак умноже́ния) 5 • 12 = 60

This is how to say "five times twelve is sixty." **Двена́дцать умно́жить на пять (бу́дет) шестьдеся́т.**

The verb **помно́жить** is used as well as **умно́жить**. A stress change occurs when multiplying (or dividing) "by two" **на́ два**, "by three" **на́ три**, and in the following cases, both ways: **на́ пять, на́ шесть, на́ семь, на́ сто.**

12 x 5 = 60   Двена́дцать помно́жить на́ пять (бу́дет, э́то) шестьдеся́т

9 x 3 = 27   Де́вять помно́женное на́ три—два́дцать семь.

6 x 2 = 12   Шесть умно́женное на́ два—двена́дцать.

2 x 2 x 4 x 3 x 6 = 288   Два умно́жить на два, на четы́ре, на́ три, на шесть бу́дет две́сти во́семьдесят во́семь.

The multiplication table
Табли́ца умноже́ния

Watch out for the stress changes in the numbers *five* through *nine* when they are multipliers. In reciting the multiplication table, **бу́дет** is almost always eliminated.

1 x 9 = 9   Оди́ножды де́вять (бу́дет, э́то) де́вять.

2 x 4 = 8   Два́жды четы́ре—во́семь.

3 x 6 = 18   Три́жды шесть—восемна́дцать.

4 x 5 = 20   Четы́режды пять—два́дцать.

5 x 3 = 15   Пя́тью три—пятна́дцать.

6 x 2 = 12   Шестью́ два—двена́дцать.

7 x 4 = 28   Се́мью четы́ре—два́дцать во́семь.

8 x 6 = 48   Во́семью (и́ли во́сьмью) шесть—со́рок во́семь.

9 x 8 = 72   Де́вятью во́семь—се́мьдесят два.

Про себя́ говоря́т:

$$\begin{array}{r} \times\ 755 \\ 36 \\ \hline 4530 \\ 2265 \\ \hline 27180 \end{array}$$

Пя́тью шесть—три́дцать. Ноль пи́шем, три в уме́. Пя́тью шесть—три́дцать, да три в уме́—три́дцать три, три пи́шем и три в уме́. Ше́стью семь—со́рок два, да три—со́рок пять. Три́жды пять—пятна́дцать, оди́н в уме́. Пятна́дцать да оди́н—шестна́дцать, оди́н в уме́. Ноль, во́семь, оди́н, оди́н в уме́, шесть, семь, два. Два́дцать семь ты́сяч сто восемьдесят.

Зада́чи на умноже́ние:

1. Число́ 284 увели́чить в 36 раз.

2. Записа́ть при по́мощи зна́ка де́йствия и зна́ка ра́венства: число́ 280, умно́женное на 6, даёт 1680.

3. Мно́жимое 94, мно́житель 27. Вы́числить произведе́ние.

4. Оди́н из сомно́жителей 18, друго́й 15. Найти́ произведе́ние.

5. Вы́полнить умноже́ние и сде́лать прове́рку: 85 x 28, 407 x 652

6. Самолёт лети́т со ско́ростью 326 км в час. Ско́лько киломе́тров пролети́т самолёт за 6 часо́в, е́сли бу́дет лете́ть с той же ско́ростью?

Отве́ты на зада́чи на умноже́ние: (1) 10224; (2) 280 x 6 = 1680; (3) 2538; (4) 270; (5) 2408, 265364; (6) 1956 км.

Division
Деле́ние

At first, the Russian system of stating long division problems seems quite different from ours.

In Russian		In English
		25
дели́мое 200|8 дели́тель	8⟌200
16 ⟌25 ча́стное	16
40	40
40	40
0	0

This is one way of saying "twenty-seven divided by nine equals three": Два́дцать семь раздели́ть на де́вять, бу́дет три.

This is a long division problem and its answer:

$$\begin{array}{r|l} 1434 & 22 \\ \underline{132} & 65 \\ 114 & \\ \underline{110} & \\ 4 & \end{array}$$

1434 ÷ 22 = 65 и 4 в оста́тке. (Ты́сяча четы́реста три́дцать четы́ре делённое на два́дцать два равно́ шести́десяти пяти́ и четырём в оста́тке.)

Про себя́ говоря́т:

Сто со́рок три (делённое) на два́дцать два бу́дет приме́рно шесть. (Двена́дцать, оди́н в уме, двена́дцать да один—трина́дцать. Оди́н, оди́н.) Сто четы́рнадцать (делённое) на два́дцать два, э́то бу́дет приме́рно пять. Сто де́сять и четы́ре. Полу́чится шестьдеся́т пять и четы́ре в оста́тке.

Зада́чи на деле́ние:

1. Дели́мое 240, дели́тель 12. Найти́ ча́стное.

2. Найти́ ча́стное от деле́ния 9600 на 10.

3. Ско́лько полу́чится, е́сли 720 раздели́ть на 8 ра́вных часте́й? 640 уме́ньшить в 8 раз? взять восьму́ю часть от 560?

4. Во ско́лько раз 480 бо́льше 8? Ско́лько раз 8 соде́ржится в 200?

5. Вы́полнить деле́ние и результа́т прове́рить умноже́нием: 3216÷48, 86904÷284.

6. По пла́ну заво́д до́лжен вы́пустить 3640 сельскохозя́йственных маши́н за 26 дней. Рабо́чие реши́ли вы́полнить план досро́чно и выпуска́ли в день на 42 маши́ны бо́льше, чем бы́ло наме́чено по пла́ну. На ско́лько дней ра́ньше сро́ка заво́д вы́полнил план?

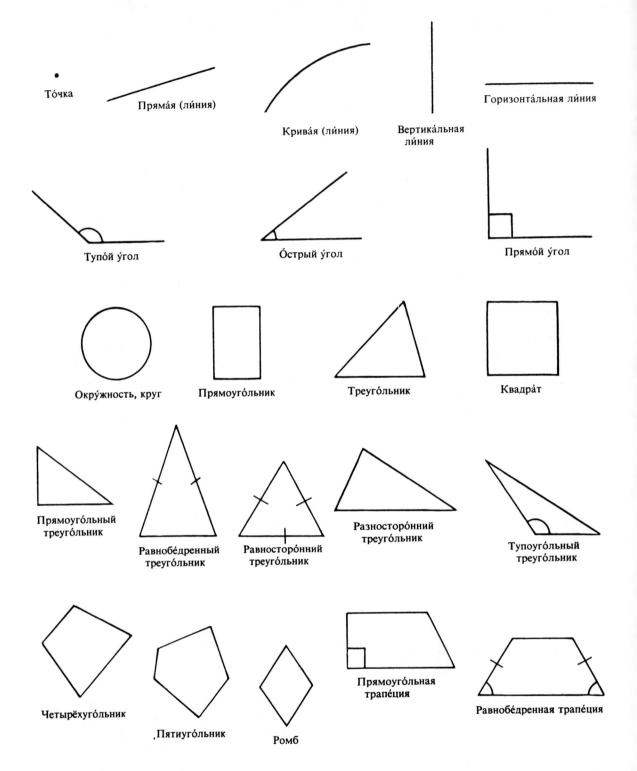

Тóчка

Прямáя (лúния)

Кривáя (лúния)

Вертикáльная лúния

Горизонтáльная лúния

Тупóй ýгол

Óстрый ýгол

Прямóй ýгол

Окрýжность, круг

Прямоугóльник

Треугóльник

Квадрáт

Прямоугóльный треугóльник

Равнобéдренный треугóльник

Равносторóнний треугóльник

Разносторóнний треугóльник

Тупоугóльный треугóльник

Четырёхугóльник

Пятиугóльник

Ромб

Прямоугóльная трапéция

Равнобéдренная трапéция

7. Из сле́дующих чи́сел: 56, 64, 78, 90, 96, 120, 140, 160 вы́писать те, кото́рые: де́лятся на во́семь без оста́тка и де́лятся на во́семь с оста́тком.

Отве́ты на зада́чи на деле́ние: (1) 20; (2) 960; (3) 90, 80, 70; (4) 60, 25; (5) 67, 306; (6) **На шесть дней ра́ньше**; (7) **без оста́тка**: 54, 64, 96, 120, 160; **с оста́тком**: 78, 90, 140.

COMMON GEOMETRIC FIGURES
Обыкнове́нные геометри́ческие фигу́ры

Many words in geometry resemble ours: **диа́метр, ра́диус, хо́рда, перпендикуля́р, центр, трапе́ция, э́ллипс, фо́рмула, гипотену́за, пери́метр, ромб, куб, пирами́да, параллелепи́пед, цили́ндр, ко́нус, при́зма**. But note that sphere is **шар**.

Зада́чи по геоме́трии:

1. **Начерти́те прямоуго́льник длино́й 7 см, ширино́й 4 см. Вы́числите су́мму длин сторо́н прямоуго́льника.**

2. **Найти́ пло́щадь по́лной пове́рхности ку́ба, ребро́ кото́рого ра́вно 25 см.**

3. **Два равнобе́дренных треуго́льника име́ют о́бщее основа́ние. Бокова́я сторона́ одного́ из них втро́е бо́льше боково́й стороны́ друго́го. Пери́метры треуго́льников равны́ 28 и 68 см. Найти́ сто́роны ка́ждого из треуго́льников.**

Отве́ты на зада́чи: (1) 22; (2) 3750 см ; (3) основа́ние—8 см, одна́ сторона́—10 см, друга́я сторона́—30 см.

READING MATHEMATICAL EXPRESSIONS
Чте́ние математи́ческих выраже́ний

The alphabets
Алфави́ты

The pronunciation of the Greek alphabet and a few more technical expressions and terms are included here because they are very difficult to find elsewhere, yet are important to the mathematician, physicist, or engineer who has occasion to talk to Russian colleagues. For chemists,

Pronunciation of the Latin alphabet

Бу́ква	Произноше́ние	Бу́ква	Произноше́ние
a	а	n	эн
b	бэ	o	о
c	цэ	p	пэ
d	дэ	q	ку, кю
e	е	r	эр
f	эф	s	эс
g	же	t	тэ
h	аш	u	у
i	и	v	вэ
j	йот	w	дубль вэ
k	ка	x	икс
l	эль	y	и́грек
m	эм	z	зет

Как и в англи́йском, неизве́стные выража́ются ча́ще всего́ и́ксом, и́греком и зе́том.

Гре́ческий алфави́т

Бу́ква	Назва́ние бу́квы	Бу́ква	Назва́ние бу́квы
α	а́льфа	ν	ню
β	бе́та[1]	ξ	кси
γ	га́мма	o	о́микрон
δ	де́льта[1]	π	пи
ε	э́псилон	ρ	ро
ζ	зе́та[1]	σ	си́гма
η	э́та	τ	та́у
θ	тэ́та	υ	и́псилон
ι	йо́та	φ	фи
κ	ка́ппа	χ	хи
λ	ла́мбда	ψ	пси
μ	мю	ω	оме́га

1. **Бе́та, де́льта**, and **зе́та** are ususally pronounced as «бэ́та», «дэ́льта», «зэ́та».

the Appendix includes the periodic table in Russian and instructions on how to read a few chemical formulas.

Equations and formulas used in mathematics look similar ours, but when the Russian reads them out loud, the sounds are quite different. In equations and formulas in Russian scientific works, you should assume that the letters that you are looking at are either Latin or Greek, but not Russian.

Squares, cubes, and roots
Стёпени и кóрни

Пи́шут	Говоря́т	
3^2	три	
4^2	четы́ре	квадра́т, в квадра́те, во второ́й стёпени
8^2	во́семь	

Пи́шут	Говоря́т
2^3	два
6^3	шесть — в ку́бе, в тре́тьей сте́пени
10^3	де́сять
5^4	пять в четвёртой стёпени
10^{10}	де́сять в деся́той стёпени
$a^н$	"а" в стёпени "эн," "а" в э́нной
$\sqrt{-1}$	ко́рень квадра́тный из ми́нус едини́цы
$\sqrt{2}$	ко́рень квадра́тный из двух
$\sqrt{-2}$	ко́рень квадра́тный из ми́нус двух
$\sqrt{49}$	ко́рень квадра́тный из сорока́ девяти́
$\sqrt[3]{27}$	ко́рень куби́ческий из двадцати́ семи́
$\sqrt[4]{81}$	ко́рень четвёртой стёпени из восьми́десяти одного́

Common formulas: how they are read
Основны́е фóрмулы: как их чита́ть

По-англи́йски	По-ру́сски	Произноше́ние
$C = 2\pi r$ Circumference of a circle	$L = 2\pi r$ Длина́ окру́жности	эль равно́ два пи эр
$A = 1/2 ab$ Area of a triangle	$S = ah/2$ Пло́щадь треуго́льника	эс равно́ полови́на (одна́ втора́я) а на аш (и́ли) эс равно́ полови́не (одно́й второ́й) а на аш
$A = \pi r^2$ Area of a circle	$S = \pi r^2$ Пло́щадь кру́га	эс равно́ пи эр квадра́т
$A = 4\pi r^2$ Area of a sphere	$S = 4\pi r^2$ Пло́щадь пове́рхности ша́ра	эс равно́ четы́ре пи эр квадра́т
$V = 4/3 \pi r^3$ Volume of a sphere	$V = 4/3 \pi r^3$ Обьём ша́ра	вэ равно́ четы́ре тре́тьих пи эр куб
$a^2 + b^2 = c^2$ Pythagorean Theorem	$a^2 + b^2 = c^2$ Теоре́ма Пифаго́ра	а квадра́т плюс бэ квадра́т равня́ется цэ квадра́т
$sin^2\,\theta + cos^2\,\theta \equiv 1$ Trigonometric identity	$sin^2\,\theta + cos^2\,\theta \equiv 1$ Тригонометри́ческое то́ждество	си́нус квадра́т тэ́та плюс ко́синус квадра́т тэ́та тожде́ственно равно́ едини́це
$tan\,\theta = sin\,\theta/cos\,\theta$ Definition of a tangent	$tg\,\theta = sin\,\theta/cos\,\theta$ Определе́ние та́нгенса	та́нгенс тэ́та (есть) си́нус тэ́та делённый на ко́синус тэ́та

Reading common formulas
Чтéние основны́х фóрмул

Some Latin letters are known to most schoolchildren in Russia because many of the common formulas use them rather than the Russian equivalent: L = length, S = surface (area), V = volume, d = density, P = weight (poids), p = pressure, h = height, F = force, and so forth. The table below gives some common formulas with their pronunciation and equivalent in English. Notice that the Greek "pi" is pronounced «пи,» and that tangent is abbreviated as "tg" rather than "tan," as in English.

The official wording of the Pythagorean Theorem is **Квадрáт гипотену́зы рáвен су́мме квадрáтов кáтетов.** But unofficially the children have reworded the expression, **«Пифагóровы штаны́ во все стóроны равны́.»**

Other terminology
Други́е тéрмины

The following signs and terms are commonly used in algebra, geometry, and mathematics in general.[4]

+2	положи́тельное числó
-2	отрицáтельное числó
|2|	абсолю́тная величинá
-a; +10; ab; (a + b)c; (a - b)/c	одночлéн
(a + b)c + ab	многочлéн
$6a^2b$	-6- коэффициéнт
$x^2 + 2 = 3x$	уравнéние
3x - 3y = 21 2x - 3y = 3	систéма уравнéний
x; y; z . . .	неизвéстные
=	равнó (рáвен, равнá, равны́)

4. Information used here is taken from the booklet **Готóвимся слу́шать лéкции; вы́пуск 1, ред. И. К. Гáпочка (Москвá: Университéт дру́жбы нарóдов и́мени Патри́са Луму́мбы,** 1963), стр. 33–35.

≡	тождéственно равнó
≠	не равнó
<	мéньше
>	бóльше
≤	мéньше и́ли равнó (но не бóльше)
≥	бóльше и́ли равнó (но не мéньше)
≪	значи́тельно (и́ли мнóго) мéньше
≫	значи́тельно (и́ли мнóго) бóльше
$\log_b$	логари́фм при основáнии b
lg	десяти́чный логари́фм (2 = lg 100)
ln	натурáльный логари́фм
(); []; { }	скóбки кру́глые, квадрáтные, фигу́рные
lim	предéл
→	стреми́тся к . . .
∞	бесконéчность
i	мни́мое числó ($\sqrt{-1}$)
Δ	прирашéние
d	дифференциáл
∫	интегрáл
⊥	перпендикуля́рно
∥	параллéльно
$\vec{d}$	вéктор d

MEASURES
Мéры

Length, area, and volume
Длинá, плóщадь и объём

A few people are aware that Russians (along with the rest of the world) use the metric system: The meter м (about 39.37 inches) is the basic unit for measuring length, height, distance, and

Выраже́ние	**Как оно́ чита́ется**
$ax^2 + bx + c = 0$ (квадра́тное уравне́ние)	а икс квадра́т плюс бэ икс плюс цэ равня́ется нулю́.
$x_{1,2} = \dfrac{-b \pm \sqrt{b^2 - 4ac}}{2a}$ (ко́рни квадра́тного уравне́ния)	Икс оди́н, два равня́ется ми́нус бэ плюс-ми́нус ко́рень квадра́тный из бэ в квадра́те ми́нус четы́ре а цэ (делённое) на два а.
$\lvert 2 - 4 \rvert = 2$	Мо́дуль два ми́нус четы́ре равня́ется двум. (То́же мо́жно: абсолю́тное значе́ние ра́зности два ми́нус четы́ре равня́ется двум.)
$a^2 - b^2 = (a + b)(a - b)$	а квадра́т ми́нус бэ квадра́т есть а плюс бэ (помно́женное) на а ми́нус бэ.
$\sqrt{x} = x^{1/2}$	Ко́рень квадра́тный из икс есть икс в сте́пени одна́ втора́я.
$\ln a = (\ln 10) \log a$	Логари́фм натура́льный а есть логари́фм натура́льный десяти́ на логари́фм а по основа́нию де́сять.
$10^{10} \gg 1$	Де́сять в деся́той сте́пени мно́го бо́льше едини́цы.
$\lim\limits_{x \to 0}\left(\dfrac{\sin x}{x}\right) = 1$	Преде́л отноше́ния си́нус икс к икс при икс, стремя́щемся к нулю́, ра́вен едини́це.
$e^{ix} \equiv \cos x + i \sin x$	е в сте́пени и икс тожде́ственно равно́ ко́синус икс плюс и си́нус икс.
$\dfrac{dx}{dt} \equiv \lim\limits_{\Delta t \to 0}\left(\dfrac{\Delta x}{\Delta t}\right)$	Произво́дная дэ икс по дэ тэ э́то есть преде́л отноше́ния прираще́ния де́льта икс к де́льта тэ при де́льта тэ, стремя́щемся к нулю́.
$\int e^x\, dx = e^x + c$	Интегра́л от е в сте́пени икс дэ икс равня́ется е в сте́пени икс плюс цэ.
$y = f(x)$	И́грек равня́ется эф от икс.
$a^4 - b^4 \neq (a + b)^2(a - b)^2$	а в четвёртой сте́пени ми́нус бэ в четвёртой сте́пени не равно́ а плюс бэ в квадра́те на а ми́нус бэ в квадра́те.
$\sphericalangle\, \theta < 90°$	У́гол тэ́та ме́ньше девяно́ста гра́дусов.
$[a(a^2 + b)(c - d)]^2 - 4d$	Откры́ть квадра́тную ско́бку, а умно́жить, откры́ть кру́глую ско́бку, а квадра́т плюс бэ, закры́ть кру́глую ско́бку, умно́жить, откры́ть кру́глую ско́бку, цэ ми́нус дэ закры́ть кру́глую ско́бку, закры́ть квадра́тную ско́бку, всё в квадра́те, ми́нус 4 дэ.

so on. Multiples of the meter, 0.001 meter (a millimeter, **мм**), 0.01 meter (a centimeter, **см**), 1000 meters (a kilometer, **км**), are very common units of measure. Measures of area **пло́щадь** use squared length measures: **кв.см, кв. м (гекта́р=га=100 кв.м)**. To get a better feeling for the size of these measures, get a meter stick and actually measure objects, especially yourself. Calculate how far away you are from the center of your city or from some familiar but relatively distant point. You should not have to stop and think when a Russian tells you that a certain village is only twenty kilometers away from another village (one kilometer = 0.6214 or 5/8 mile), or that a box is ten centimeters high, fifteen centimeters long, and five centimeters wide. So how tall are you?

Old units of measure
Ста́рые ме́ры

Other units of measure come up constantly in literature, and a few of them are still used by the older generation. Below is a listing of the most common ones and their equivalents in the metric system.

верста́ равна́ 500 (пятиста́м) саже́ням—1,067 км

саже́нь равна́ 3 (трём) арши́нам—2,134 м

арши́н ра́вен 16 (шестна́дцати) вершка́м—0,711 м

вершо́к ра́вен 4,4 см

фут $\frac{1}{7}$ (одна́ седьма́я) саже́ни—30,5 см

дюйм $\frac{1}{12}$ (одна́ двена́дцатая) фу́та—о́коло 25 мм

десяти́на равна́ 2,400 (двум ты́сячам четырёмстам) кв. саж. (квадра́тным саже́ням)—1,092 гекта́ра

бо́чка равна́ 40 (сорока́) вёдрам—о́коло 480 л

ведро́ равно́ 20 (двадцати́) буты́лкам—о́коло 12 л

буты́лка 0,6; 0,76 л

Housing space
Жилпло́щадь

In the United States, when you are asked to describe the size of a house, it is expected that you will reply with the number of rooms. Though this is a possible answer in Russian—«У меня́ двухко́мнатная кварти́ра»—the same question in Russia is often phrased, «Ско́лько у вас ме́тров?» (**Жилпло́щади** is understood.) **Жила́я пло́щадь** is the number of square meters of living space (housing), not including kitchens, bathrooms, or hallways. In 1990 only those families with an average of less than 9 square meters of living space per person could apply for a bigger apartment. (Different cities had differing requirements.)

How to ask about distance, area, and volume
Как спроси́ть о расстоя́нии, пло́щади и объёме

Since grammar books often omit a description of how to ask about length, height, and so on, some examples are included here.

Како́го он ро́ста? (рост, *growth or height*)

Он ро́стом метр 13 сантиметров.

(Его́ рост) оди́н метр 13 сантиметров.

Како́го разме́ра вам ну́жен ковёр? (разме́р, *size*)

Како́й величины́ нам ну́жен ковёр? (величина́, *magnitude*)

Ковёр разме́ром в 3 ме́тра ширино́й и 5 ме́тров длино́й.

Три ме́тра в ширину́ и пять ме́тров в длину́.

Три на пять (3 х 5).

Како́й высоты́ э́то де́рево? (высота́, *height*)

(Это де́рево) высото́й в 10 ме́тров.

Де́сять ме́тров в высоту́.

Де́сять ме́тров.

Како́й длины́ э́та ко́мната? (длина́, *length*)

(Эта ко́мната) 4 ме́тра в длину́.

Длино́й в 4 ме́тра.

Четы́ре ме́тра.

На како́м расстоя́нии от Земли́ нахо́дится са́мая бли́зкая звезда́? (расстоя́ние is *distance*)

На расстоя́нии четырёх световы́х лет.

Четы́ре световы́х го́да.

(В кни́жном сти́ле пи́шут: **Какова́ высота́ э́тих гор? Какова́ длина́ кла́сса?**)

Weight
Вес

The metric standard also applies to measures of weight: the gram is the basic unit; other measures of weight are merely multiples of the gram. A kilogram (1000 grams) is equivalent to about 2.2 pounds, a metric ton is 2204.6 lbs.

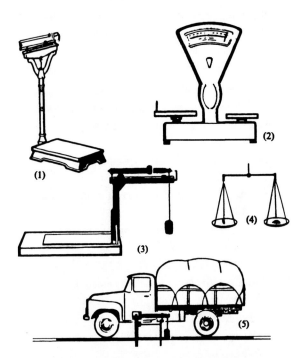

Ви́ды весо́в: (1) медици́нские весы́, (2) насто́льные торго́вые весы, (3) десяти́чные весы, (4) шко́льные весы́ (5) весы для взве́шивания автомаши́н

Following are the weights in the metric system.

Табли́ца мер ве́са (notice the use of commas and periods)

0,001 г	1 миллигра́мм (мг)	
0,01 г	1 сантигра́мм (сг)	
0,1 г	1 децигра́мм (дг)	
1 г	1 грамм (г)	
1.000 г	1 килогра́мм (кг)	= 2.205 lbs.
100 кг	1 це́нтнер (ц)	
1.000 кг	1 то́нна (т)	

Ме́ры ве́са до введе́ния метри́ческих мер: золотни́к—4,25 г; фунт ра́вен 96 золотника́м—409,5 г; пуд[5] ра́вен 40 фу́нтам—16,38 кг.

Weighty expressions are:

вес weight. **Сли́вы продаю́тся на вес.**

ве́сить to weigh, have a certain weight. **Я ве́шу 54 кило́. Письмо́ ве́сит 25 грамм.**[6]

взве́шивать, взве́сить to weigh something. **Она́ сейча́с взве́шивает паке́т.**

взве́шиваться, взве́ситься to weigh oneself. **Они́ взве́сились вчера́.**[7]

В метри́ческой систе́ме мер за едини́цу ве́са при́нят грамм (сокращённо г или Г). **Грамм—э́то вес одного́ куби́ческого сантиме́тра чи́стой воды́, взя́той при температу́ре 4°C.** (Четы́ре гра́дуса по Це́льсию.) **Килогра́мм** (кг или кГ) **- э́то вес 1 дм** (одного́ куби́ческого дециме́тра) **чи́стой воды́ при температу́ре 4°C.**

Вес одного́ куби́ческого сантиме́тра вещества́ в гра́ммах называ́ется уде́льным ве́сом э́того вещества́.

---

5. **Пуд** is still commonly used in reporting grain shipments and the like.

6. The official genitive plural of **грамм** is **гра́ммов** but in colloquial (acceptable spoken) Russian **грамм** is used.

7. A word of warning: **Он пове́сился** is "He hanged himself."

Time
Вре́мя

Time, at least, does not involve a different system from ours. If you are not already familiar with them, you will recognize the time units mentioned in the following list by the numbers.

Столе́тие равно́ 100 (ста) года́м.

Век ра́вен 100 (ста) года́м.

Год ра́вен 12 (двена́дцати) ме́сяцам.

В просто́м году́ 365 дней.

В високо́сном году́ 366 дней.

Ме́сяц ра́вен 30 (тридцати́) дням и́ли 31 (тридцати́ одному́) дню.

В феврале́ 28 и́ли 29 дней.

Су́тки равны́ 24 (двадцати́ четырём) часа́м.[8]

Час ра́вен 60 (шести́десяти) мину́там.

Мину́та равна́ 60 (шести́десяти) секу́ндам.

Daylight saving time is ле́тнее вре́мя, декре́тное вре́мя; standard time is зи́мнее вре́мя.

---

8. In an interesting article, "Twelve Names for Twelve Things" **Ру́сский язы́к за рубежо́м**, No. 4 (1969), **стр.** 79–86, L. S. Barkhudarov points out that the Russian су́тки, a twenty-four-hour period, is divided into four parts: у́тро, from sunrise to about eleven o'clock in the morning; день, from about ten or eleven o'clock in the morning to sunset (four to five o'clock); ве́чер, from sunset to ten or eleven at night; and ночь, from ten or eleven o'clock at night to sunrise. Thus, for example, the English phrase "two o'clock in the morning" should be «Два часа́ но́чи» in Russian.

У́тро ве́чера мудрене́е.
The morning is wiser than the evening.[9]

Clocks and watches
Часы́

All instruments that tell time are часы́, but if you want to be specific: wall clock, насте́нные часы́; pocket watch, карма́нные часы́; wristwatch, нару́чные часы́; sundial, со́лнечные часы́; and hourglass, песо́чные часы́. Some timepieces, however, are not built on the word часы́. Thus, хо́дики is similar to our cuckoo clock (but the bird is optional); an alarm clock is буди́льник (буди́ть, to awaken someone); and a stop watch is секундоме́р (ме́рить, *to measure*). All clocks and watches have a dial or face, цифербла́т; an hour hand, часова́я стре́лка (стрела́ arrow); and a minute hand, мину́тная стре́лка.

Часы́ говоря́т «тик-та́к, тик-та́к». Ти́кание—негро́мкий звук. Вы слы́шите, как ва́ши часы́ ти́кают?

Russian language texts usually attend to the problem of telling time in Russian. (Вы ду́маете, что трёхле́тний ма́льчик зна́ет, как определя́ть вре́мя?) In writing down the time, however, notice that hours are separated from minutes by a period rather than a colon (as in continental Europe): «Нача́ло сеа́нса в 18.30»; «По́езд при́был в 7.39 утра́.»

For railroads, post offices, theaters, or wherever any official time is cited, the twenty-four-hour time scale is used, so that one o'clock in the afternoon becomes thirteen o'clock **13 часо́в**, and so forth.

Time zones
Часовы́е пояса́

It is perhaps easier to appreciate the size of the country if you realize that it requires eleven

---

9. Our equivalent saying would be "Sleep on it."

time zones **часово́й по́яс** (*sg.*). Railroad and airplane schedules between cities within Russia are listed according to Moscow time in order to obviate the problems that can arise in a country with that many time zones.

Calendars
Календари́

Days are usually listed at the left rather than across the top, and the weeks start with Monday rather than Sunday.

Май

Пн.		6	13	20	27
Вт.		7	14	21	28
Ср.	1	8	15	22	29
Чт.	2	9	16	23	30
Пт.	3	10	17	24	31
Сб.	4	11	18	25
Вс.	5	12	19	26

Russians are fond of the tear-off calendar **отрывно́й календа́рь**, one page for each day, which is different from the desk calendar **перекидно́й календа́рь** at the office.

The Julian and Gregorian calendars
Ста́рый стиль и но́вый стиль

Julius Caesar, on the advice of an astronomer, set up the Julian calendar (also now called Old Style, O.S. **Ста́рый стиль, ст.ст.**) with a year's length of 365 days, 6 hours—slightly longer than the solar year of 365 days, 5 hours, 48 minutes, 46 seconds. As the centuries went by, the discrepancy between the counting method and natural appearances widened by about ten days. So in 1582 Pope Gregory XIII introduced the calendar now in general use, the Gregorian calendar (also called New Style, N.S. **Но́вый стиль, н.с./нов.ст.**). The Roman Catholic countries quickly accepted the change, but England (and the United States therefore) did not change over until 1752; the USSR changed over in February 1918. Much of the Eastern Orthodox Church continues to use the Old Style, Julian calendar.

Until February 28, 1700, the difference in calendars remained ten days and has increased

Now, tear-off calendars often include Names days.

by one day every one hundred years so that since 1900 the difference has been thirteen days. This explains why the Great October Revolution (October 25, O.S.) was celebrated on November 7 and why Orthodox Russians celebrate Christmas on January 7.

The date
Число, дата

In conversation, the usual word for *date* is число: «Како́е сего́дня число́?» When a document, letter, or something official is being referred to, then the word becomes да́та: «Да́та почто́вого ште́мпеля.»

Russians write the date in a different order: the day, the month, then the year. The month is usually written as a Roman or an Arabic numeral: 13.6.95 or 13/VI-95 or 13.VI.

«Трина́дцатое шесто́го девяно́сто пя́того» is what is said; and the complete expression is «Трина́дцатое число́ шесто́го ме́сяца, ты́сяча девятьсо́т девяносто пя́того го́да.»

A.D. and B.C. are expressed by на́шей э́ры (н.э.) and до на́шей э́ры (до н.э.).

Кали́гула у́мер в со́рок пе́рвом году́ на́шей э́ры. Архиме́д жил с двести во́семьдесят седьмо́го по двести двена́дцатый год до на́шей э́ры. (Или: Архиме́д жил в две́сти во́семьдесят се́дьмом—две́сти двена́дцатом года́х до на́шей э́ры.)

Centuries are almost always expressed in Roman numerals: Пу́шкин жил в нача́ле XIX ве́ка.

The seasons
Времена́ го́да

The year is divided into:

зи́мние ме́сяцы (зима́): дека́брь, янва́рь, февра́ль

весе́нние ме́сяцы (весна́): март, апре́ль, май

ле́тние ме́сяцы (ле́то): ию́нь, ию́ль, а́вгуст

осе́нние ме́сяцы (о́сень): сентя́брь, октя́брь, ноя́брь

Indian summer **ба́бье ле́то** (literally, a country-woman's summer) arrives toward the end of September and probably explains why Pushkin so loved the fall.

For the summer and winter solstices and the vernal and autumnal equinoxes, the dates and names are: 22 ию́ня — день ле́тнего солнцестоя́ния, 22 декабря́ — день зи́мнего солнцестоя́ния, 21 ма́рта — день весе́ннего равноде́нствия, 23 сентября́ — день осе́ннего равноде́нствия. Notice the similarity between solstice and **солнцестоя́ние**, equinox and **равноде́нствие**. The Russians, however, do not consider that the seasons officially start on these days.

Temperature
Температу́ра

Someday, we, too, will use the Celsius (centigrade) scale шкала́ Це́льсия rather than the Fahrenheit scale шкала́ Фаренге́йта. Until then we must learn what it means when a Russian says 10°. As you know, the centigrade scale sets the boiling point of water at 100° and freezing at 0°.

Це́льсий—термо́метр со шкало́й в 100 гра́дусов от то́чки та́яния льда до то́чки кипе́ния воды́. Замерза́ние воды́ происхо́дит при температу́ре 0° (ноль гра́дусов). Вода́ кипи́т при 100° (ста гра́дусах) по Це́льсию.

To convert degrees Fahrenheit to centigrade and vice versa, use the formulas:

$$F° = (C° \times 9/5) + 32$$
$$C° = (F° - 32) \times 5/9$$

These are a few equivalents:

Centigrade	Fahrenheit
–40°	–40°
–17.8°	0°
–10°	14°
0°	32°
5°	41°
15°	59°
21.1°	70°
28°	82.4°
35°	95°
37°	98.6°
38°	100.4°
40°	104°
41.1°	106°
100°	212°

Ways of stating temperature include:

10°	плюс де́сять гра́дусов
3°	три гра́дуса вы́ше нуля́
1°	оди́н гра́дус тепла́
0°	ноль гра́дусов
–2°	ми́нус два гра́дуса
–1°	оди́н гра́дус хо́лода (моро́за)
–20°	два́дцать гра́дусов ни́же нуля́

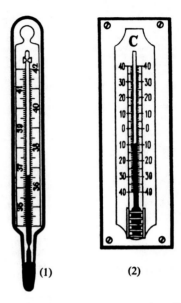

Ви́ды термо́метров: (1) медици́нский термо́метр, (2) нару́жный термо́метр

Weather
Пого́да

You have a feeling for how hot or cold a certain number of degrees is in English. About 80° is where hot begins, and 90° is very hot. How cold "cold" is depends on where you live. The following are two weather forecasts from **Изве́стия** for midwinter and midsummer.

Прогно́з пого́ды на 15 января́: В Москве́ и о́бласти 15 января́ ожида́ется холо́дная пого́да: температу́ра но́чью о́коло ми́нус 20°, на се́вере о́бласти до ми́нус 25°, днём ми́нус 16-17 гра́дусов. Небольша́я о́блачность, без оса́дков, ве́тер уме́ренный.

Прогно́з пого́ды на 11 ию́ля: в Москве́ и о́бласти 11 ию́ля ожида́ется переме́нная о́блачность, места́ми кратковре́менные дожди́ и гро́зы. Ве́тер за́падный, от сла́бого до уме́ренного, температу́ра о́коло 25 гра́дусов. Жа́рко (28-33 гра́дуса) бу́дет в респу́бликах Закавка́зья. Здесь места́ми пройду́т дожди́ и гро́зы.

Thermometers
Термо́метры/гра́дусники

The thermometer **термо́метр** is usually used in either more formal or technical situations; what is found around the house is a **гра́дусник**.

Обы́чные нару́жные термо́метры име́ют шкалу́ от -50° (ми́нус пяти́десяти гра́дусов) до +50° (плюс пяти́десяти гра́дусов).

An indoor thermometer **ко́мнатный термо́метр** registers from 0°C to 50°C. The accepted indoor temperature is about 20°C.

The well-equipped household, especially one with children, also has a medical thermometer **медици́нский термо́метр, гра́дусник**. The scale is from about 34°C to 42°C. The Russian medical thermometer is much less breakable and much bigger than ours. Russians take temperatures by putting the thermometer in an armpit and leaving it there for ten minutes. (If you put a Russian thermometer in your mouth, the Russians would *know* you were sick.) A normal temperature is 36.6°C. **(говоря́т: три́дцать шесть и шесть).**[10] A reading of 37.5° **(три́дцать семь и пять)** indicates that something is wrong, and if it goes up to 40°, the patient is very sick.

Temperature regulators on ovens **регуля́торы для духо́вок** are relatively new devices—the great majority of recipes do not mention heat, though they usually do indicate how long the item is to be cooked. (If you are following a Russian recipe at home and no indication of temperature is given, use 350°F and hope.) Newer ovens do have them, and the range is from 50° to 350°C.

Pressure
Давле́ние

The usual unit of pressure encountered in everyday life is grams or kilograms per square centimeter.

$$1\frac{\text{Г}}{\text{СМ}^2} \quad \text{и́ли} \quad 1\frac{\text{КГ}}{\text{СМ}^2}$$

Children in school learn the formula: $p = \frac{F}{S}$

$$\text{Давле́ние } (p) = \frac{\text{си́ла давле́ния } (F)}{\text{пло́щадь } (S)}$$

Tire pressure **давле́ние в ши́нах** is measured in grams per square centimeter (**в гра́ммах на оди́н квадра́тный сантиме́тр**).

Atmospheric pressure
Атмосфе́рное давле́ние

Баро́метр-анеро́ид

The illustration shows a Russian aneroid barometer, the common household kind. The words around the perimeter are also commonly found on the face of such a barometer: low pressure and storms on the left, to high pressure and dry on the right. Normal atmospheric pressure is about 760 mm of mercury at sea level (760 мм рту́тного столба́ на у́ровне мо́ря).

Speed
Ско́рость

The usual unit of speed is in kilometers per hour **в киломе́трах в час (км/час, км в час).** The speed limit **преде́льно допусти́мая**

ско́рость in cities is now up to sixty kilometers per hour on major arteries unless restrictions are posted. Outside cities the speed limit is ninety kilometers per hour unless restrictions are posted. (Remember, one kilometer is about five-eighths of a mile.)

Electricity
Электри́чество

Household voltage **напряже́ние** is usually 220 volts now. The usual voltage in the United States is 110 volts, except for major appliances, some of which operate on 220 volts. In Russia the frequency of the alternating current **частота́ переме́нного то́ка** is 50 cycles a second, 50 **герц**, while in the United States the frequency is 60 cycles per second. (It can be concluded from this that all equipment run by synchronous motors will be off by 50/60. Also, if you use electrical equipment designed for 110, especially in places wired for 220 voltage, which is most of Russia, then you will either have to replace a fuse or replace the equipment. Only a transformer can solve the problem.) Some of the newer appliances come supplied

with a transformer switch **переключа́тель на трансформа́торе** that makes the appliance usable at either voltage.

Электри́ческие ла́мпочки продаю́тся по ва́ттам.

Latitude and longitude
Широта́ и долгота́

Latitudes **широ́ты**, of course, are either northern or southern, and longitudes **долго́ты** are eastern or western. The following text should help you read latitude and longitude indications in Russian:

Координа́ты Москвы́—55°45' (пятьдеся́т пять гра́дусов со́рок пять мину́т) с.ш. (се́верной широты́) и 37°37' (три́дцать семь гра́дусов три́дцать семь мину́т) в.д. (восто́чной долготы́) по Гри́нвичскому меридиа́ну. О́стров Кергеле́н в Инди́йском океа́не нахо́дится на 50°ю.ш. (пятидеся́том гра́дусе ю́жной широты́). Гибралта́рский проли́в—на 5°з.д. (на пя́том гра́дусе за́падной долготы́).

In order to "get your bearings," you might need a Russian compass:

Ко́мпас

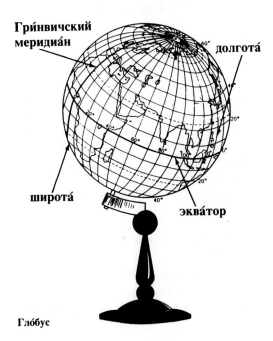

Гло́бус

На дне коро́бки ко́мпаса нанесены́ деле́ния, обознача́ющие гра́дусы—от 0° до 360°. Если освободи́ть стре́лку ко́мпаса, то коне́ц стре́лки, пока́зывающий на се́вер, бу́дет соотве́тствовать 0°—360°, юг—180°, восто́к—90° и за́пад—270°.

16

Holidays and the Church
Праздники и Церковь

The adoption of Christianity has shown how easily pagan rites and customs (Christmas trees, yule logs, and Easter eggs, for instance) could be incorporated into Christian celebrations. The Russian experience shows that it might be impossible to eradicate belief; the celebration of Christian holidays continues, expands, and returns to the inside of the church.

One of the joys of visiting Russia is to see the rejuvenation of the churches. One may walk in now without thereby making a statement of protest, but the seventy-year interregnum has not been without effect: the fraction of nonbelievers **неверующие** is high (one-half to three-quarters). The believers **верующие** themselves are not always familiar with the customs and prayers of their forebears. The description of religious holidays is included, partly because this aspect of life is likely to grow, and partly because much Russian literature in its Golden Age referred to these events. We start with contemporary holidays, then traditional popular holidays, church holidays, and finally, the church itself.

CONTEMPORARY HOLIDAYS
Современные праздники

Legal holidays, days off work
Праздничные дни, красные дни календаря

These were the days off work throughout the Russian Federation at the end of 1993. Other local holidays might also be observed, thus, 30 октября—**День памяти жертв коммунизма** ("Day for Remembering Those Who Were Sacrificed to Communism") might include a march to Lyubyanka Prison in Moscow, but no day off work.

1 января—**Новый год**   New Year's Day

7 января—**Рождество Христово** (25 декабря по ст. ст.[1])   Christmas

8 марта—**Международный женский день** (**Праздник Восьмого марта, Женский день**)   Women's Day

---

1.   **по старому стилю** Old Style or Julian calendar. See *Time* in Chapter 15.

325

1 мая—**День весны́** (formerly **День междунаро́дной солида́рности трудя́щихся**) May Day

9 ма́я—**День побе́ды над фаши́стской Герма́нией** (**Пра́здник Побе́ды, День Побе́ды**) Victory Day

12 ию́ня—**День приня́тия деклара́ции о госуда́рственном суверените́те Росси́йской Федера́ции** Russian Federation Day **День незави́симости** Independence Day, **День Росси́и** Russia Day

7 ноября́—**День октя́брьской револю́ции** October Revolution Day (was a day off in 1993)

The New Year
Но́вый год

Generally, the nonreligious festivities we associate with Christmas are part of the Russian New Year; this is the holiday for Grandfather Frost **Дед Моро́з**, our Santa Claus, the Snow Maiden **Снегу́рочка**, and the Christmas tree **ёлка**.

Grandfather Frost **Дед Моро́з, Де́душка Моро́з** reportedly brings gifts for children during the night of December 31. The children actually see him only at children's parties **у́тренники**. The popular portrayal features a taller and thinner personality than our Santa Claus. He also has more options on clothes, perhaps in red with white trimming, blue with white, or even white with white. (**Моро́з** was, originally in folk stories, the personification of winter cold and had nothing to do with Christmas. Of course, St. Nicholas had nothing to do with Christmas, either.) The idea of Grandfather Frost seems to be relatively new, surely less than 100 years old. It is as if, having the Christmas tree thrust upon them, the Russians looked around and discovered they also needed a counterpart to Santa Claus (and also to Black Peter of the Dutch legend; the latter transformation was perhaps the most startling, to **Снегу́рочка**).

The snow maiden **Снегу́рочка** occupies two places in popular legend. She is (and was originally) the subject of a folk story that told how an old, lonesome, and childless couple made the figure of a young girl out of snow. The girl came to life and became a wonderful companion to her makers, only to melt away when enticed outside to play with her friends in the warmer weather. As Saint Nicholas's (**Дед Моро́з**) helper, she more resembles a fairy, regularly accompanying him and helping to distribute gifts to small children.

The Christmas tree, introduced by Peter the Great, is now a New Year's tree, (**Нового́дняя**) **ёлка**, and universally a part of that day's celebration. Every home that can manage one does so, and the trees also appear in clubs, stores, and public squares. The decorations **украше́ния** resemble ours.

The New Year's children's party
Нового́дний у́тренник

У́тренник is a children's party (from the hour it is given, **у́тро** morning): **У нас бу́дет у́тренник**. The party at this time of year is also called **ёлка**, as it centers on having a tree, dancing around it, and so on: **Приходи́те к нам на ёлку**. The party might be given at school (before the New Year's school vacation, January 1–10), at a club, or at home. The requirements for a **нового́дний у́тренник** are all of the aforementioned: **Дед Моро́з, Снегу́рочка, ёлка**, not to mention the children.

The basic ceremonies involved in this party are not complicated, but they are quite regular: at one point, the children join hands and walk around the tree (**Де́ти во́дят хорово́д вокру́г ёлки**) singing songs. This one is common:

Ёлочка

В лесу́ роди́лась ёлочка,
В лесу́ она́ росла́.
Зимо́й и ле́том стро́йная,
Зелёная была́. . . .

Р. Кудашёва

Ёлка, Дед мороз, снегу́рочка и «ря́женые»

In schools and clubs, a program of some sort is arranged: some children might recite poetry, or a magician appears. At many of these parties you will see children around the tree, often dressed in costumes such as animals (rabbits, hedgehogs, wolves, hawks); characters (fairies, Grandfather Frost, the New Year, princesses, monsters, the evil warlock **Кощей Бессмертный**, who is skinny and old); or another nationality (Scottish, Norwegian, and so on). These costumes are a remnant of mummery **ряженье** (to be described), though the children might not be aware of that.

Sometime during the festivities, **Дед Мороз** and **Снегурочка** appear with a large bag of many small gifts for the children. When the party is given at home, there might not be room enough to dance around the tree; instead, the children have their own party at a table and **Дед Мороз**, though he might not have **Снегурочка** with him, must appear. He is often required to supply the entertainment (in addition to small gifts).

The New Year's party
Новогодний вечер

The New Year's party for adults is the brightest of the year, combining the atmosphere of our New Year's parties with the gluttonous tendencies we reserve for Thanksgiving—all with a Christmas tree in the background. The party often begins in the early evening. Unlike New Year's parties in the United States, the celebration centers on especially elaborate food (and drink). The guests arrive and immediately seat themselves at a table crammed with plates of hors d'oeuvres **закуски** and bottles of wine, champagne, and vodka. Some form of appetizer usually remains on the table throughout the meal, to be eaten with the many toasts offered during the course of the night. These hors d'oeuvres, however, are merely the beginning of the meal. They are followed by a main dish, perhaps a goose with apples or a roast chicken. The meal naturally concludes with a dessert and tea (or, especially in large cities, coffee). Several things have been happening in the course of the meal, however. The action at the table includes many toasts, and the table is also the center of the midnight ritual: slightly before midnight, the champagne is uncorked, the television is turned on, and at the stroke of midnight one hears the Kremlin bells **бой Кремлёвских курантов**; everybody rises, raises a glass in a toast to friends at the New Year, "**С Новым годом!**" then clinks glasses with the others at the table, finishes a first glass of champagne, and settles down at the table again. Someone in the party might go to the door and open it, to let the New Year in **впуск нового года**. The New Year's dinner commonly is subject to other interruptions; dancing and singing are often as basic to the party as is the food. The time for the beginning and the end of the party and the time for serving the various courses (except the first) are quite variable. It is not at all unusual for the party to last all night.

Gifts
Подарки

The emphasis at this time of year is on merry-making, not on gifts. Gifts are exchanged, but they are not so numerous or lavish as is our custom. The major problem at this time of year is not how to pay for gifts for the children but rather how to pay for refreshments for the New Year's party. Gifts are usually wrapped, but not in the ornate manner so obligatory in the United States. Any dinner guests always bring gifts of flowers, food, or drink to the host and hostess.

New Year's cards
Новогодние открытки

New Year's cards are regularly used but not to the same extent as are Christmas cards in the United States. Russians tend to confine their lists to friends living out of town. The usual greetings are «**С Новым годом!**» «**С Новым счастьем!**» or perhaps «**С праздником!**» or «**С Новогодним праздником!**» Telegrams to send these messages are also widely used.

Christmas (January 7)
Рождество́ (Христо́во)

Christmas is purely a religious holiday—our secular concomitants, Santa Claus and Christmas trees, remain with the New Year's celebration. It is a day off work, however, and many people do go to church.

Women's Day (March 8)
Пра́здник Восьмо́го ма́рта

American readers should be on guard—this holiday is not equivalent to Mother's Day. First, it is an official day off for everyone; second, it is a salute to all females, not just mothers. For this day, the boys in grade school will get a gift for a female teacher, and they will also offer best wishes or a small gift to the girls in their classes. On Army and Navy Day (**День А́рмии и Фло́та, 23 февраля́**), schoolgirls sometimes return the compliment. University students (males) might throw a party for their female classmates, and women who have been especially successful at their jobs are given awards at work. Special women in one's life get special treatment, wives from husbands and mothers from children. Though almost any gift is appropriate, flowers are especially popular: it is also a custom to send Women's Day postcards **по-здрави́тельные откры́тки** on this day; thus, women who work often get a card from their office, workshop, or ministry, as well as from friends both male and female. The standard greeting is «**Поздравля́ю с пра́здником Восьмо́го ма́рта.**» («**Я купи́л откры́тки к Восьмо́му ма́рта**» means "I bought some Women's Day cards.")

May Day
День весны́, Пе́рвое ма́я

Soviet Russians celebrated May Day as Labor Day, as do the French, for instance. (The Second Socialist International in 1889 designated May 1 as the holiday for radical labor.) That's over with, and what remains is a eupho-ria based on the arrival of spring and celebrated by the serious with a trip to the country to put the vegetable garden in order and by the young with a trip to a local park **гуля́нье в па́рке**.

Victory Day (May 9)
День Побе́ды

This day commemorates victory over Nazi Germany and is the time to visit the graves of those millions who died during World War II **Вели́кая Оте́чественная война́**. For some years after the war, this was a day for parades, but now consists of memorial meetings and a recounting of war stories. It must be noted that World War II still looms large in the Russian mind. (By comparison, we have forgotten.)

Russia Day (June 12)
День Росси́и

Independence Day, Russia Day (June 12) **День незави́симости, День Росси́и** will include perhaps a parade, and fireworks **салю́т**.

October Revolution Day (November 7) **День Октя́брьской револю́ции** was a holiday in 1993, though perhaps the last one; the parades are not military, though they could be political.

TRADITIONAL POPULAR OR FOLK HOLIDAYS
Наро́дные пра́здники

Dates in this section are Old Style. (See *Time* in Chapter 15.)

The Christmas holidays
Свя́тки

The pre-Soviet Christmas holiday season (December 24 to January 6) was especially gay, and not unlike our Christmas; Christian festivals everywhere cleverly incorporated folk beliefs and customs, most of which had to do with ensuring and celebrating a good harvest and were often therefore in some relation to the seasons: the winter and summer solstices, the coming of spring, and so on. The holiday began on Christmas Eve **сочéльник**, and continued until Epiphany **Крещéние**. The entire two-week period **свя́тки** was a time for parties, including the usual singing and dancing **хорово́ды и пля́ски**, and also special celebrations usually reserved for this time of year, **ря́женье, гада́ние, колядова́ние**.

The Christian feature of Christmas Eve **сочéльник** was church attendance. Handily, the festival of the god **коляда́ (бес Коляда́)** was celebrated with songs on December 24, strangely coincident with Christmas Eve **сочéльник**. The songs **коля́дки** were sung at **колядова́ние**, when children and young people would go from house to house, singing their wishes for wealth and a good harvest. The singers expected small gifts of food or money in return for their efforts. Here is one example of a **коля́дка**:

> Коляда́, коляда́,
> Отворя́й ворота́,
> Снéги на зéмлю па́дали,
> Перепа́дывали.
> Как пришло́ рождество́
> К господи́ну под окно́,
> Ты встава́й, господи́н,
> Разбужа́й госпожу́.
> Хлéбом-со́лью нас корми́,
> Путь-доро́жку укажи́.
> Как у на́шей-то ма́тки
> Теля́тки-то гла́дки,
> Ска́чут чéрез гря́дку,
> Копы́тцами щёлкают,
> Зéмлю не хвата́ют.
> Што у на́шей-то хозя́йки
> Усто́и—те то́лсты,
> Смета́ны—те гу́сты,
> Ма́сла—те жёлты...
> Мы берём не рупь, не полти́ну,
> Одну́ четверти́ну,
> Пиро́г да ша́ньгу,
> Зо́лоту дéньгу . . .[a]

Н. Колпако́ва, Кни́га о ру́сском фольклóре (Ленингра́д: Учпедги́з, 1948), стр. 30.

As the connection with Christ's birth became stronger (very late in some places), the ritual took on more Christian symbols: the singing group carried a large star (of Bethlehem) at the end of a stick, and **коля́дки** came to mean Christmas carols "in praise of Christ" **Христа́ сла́вить**. Typical of the evening (and still fasting; see the Fasts) meal was a dish called **кутья́**[2]; it consisted of steamed wheat (or other grain), raisins, honey, and nuts and was served as dessert.

The major feature of Christmas Day **Рождество́** was food. Among the peasants the day provided the most lavish meal of the year: if possible a suckling pig was served. (The lavishness was one of the remnants of a custom that was to assure a good harvest.)

The Christmas (that is, spruce) tree **Рождéственская ёлка**, became a part of the upper-class Christmas celebration fairly soon after Peter introduced it but was not common in the peasant hut until much later. As a matter of fact, it was not uncommon for the "noblesse" to "oblige" the common folk by allowing them to come in and see the Christmas tree. Gifts for children were put under the tree, but this was not a time for extensive gift-giving. A child might expect a small toy; adults received nothing.

Mummery
Ря́женье

A major feature of the Christmas holidays was mummery **ря́женье**, when people, especially children, would put on costumes and disguises, most often in animal shapes, and go from house to house, again receiving small gifts for their trouble. The Soviet motion picture *War and Peace* had one small scene showing such a

2. Also a requirement at post-funeral meals **поми́нки**.

group. This is how the book itself describes the event:

Наря́женные дворо́вые: медве́ди, ту́рки, тракти́рщики, ба́рыни, стра́шные и смешны́е, принеся́ с собо́ю хо́лод и весе́лье, снача́ла ро́бко жа́лись в пере́дней; пото́м, пря́чась оди́н за друго́го, вы́теснились в за́лу; и снача́ла засте́нчиво, а пото́м всё веселе́е и дружне́е начали́сь пе́сни, пля́ски, хорово́ды и свя́точные и́гры. Графи́ня, узна́в ли́ца и посме́иваясь на наря́женных, ушла́ в гости́ную. Граф Илья́ Андре́ич с сия́ющею улы́бкой сиде́л в за́ле, одобря́я игра́ющих. Молодёжь исче́зла куда́-то.[b]

Л.Н. Толсто́й, Война́ и мир, том II, часть 4, гл.10

This custom, though especially associated with the Christmas holidays (compare the Mummers' Parade in Philadelphia), also occurred during Carnival **ма́сленица**. The custom has not died out yet, but it probably is most often observed in the country rather than the city. The following passage describes the event as it was celebrated in a village in 1960:

В дни свя́ток и ма́сленицы ря́женые обхо́дят дома́ и на со́бранные проду́кты и де́ньги устра́ивают вечери́нку. Так, в дни свя́ток зимо́й 1960 г. в Кли́мове по дере́вне ходи́ли же́нщины, ря́женные «кула́шника-ми», медве́дем с поводырём, бе́гали ребяти́шки, подро́стки в костю́мах цыганя́т. [c]

Совреме́нный ру́сский фолькло́р, ред. Э. В. Помера́нцева (Москва́: Нау́ка, 1966), стр. 70–71.

Fortunetelling
Гада́ние

Fortunetelling **гада́ние** usually relates to the prediction of when and whom a girl might

marry. It was therefore mostly enjoyed by the unmarried girls of the village. All sorts of props were used: the number of grains of wheat a rooster consumed indicated how many months until the wedding took place; shoes thrown over the fence would indicate the direction from which the beloved would come; if one stared in a mirror in the right way, one could see the image of the future husband; and so on. In Tolstoy's *War and Peace* an old maid describes an incident that reportedly took place when one young lady awaited signs of her future husband in the bathhouse:

...в ба́не гада́ть, вот э́то стра́шно!—говори́ла за у́жином ста́рая де́вушка, жи́вшая у Мелюко́вых.

...вот как-то пошла́ одна́ ба́рышня,—сказа́ла ста́рая де́вушка,—взяла́ петуха́, два прибо́ра—как сле́дует се́ла. Посиде́ла, то́лько слы́шит, вдруг е́дет... с колоко́льцами, с бубенца́ми, подъе́хали са́ни; слы́шит, идёт. Вхо́дит совсе́м в о́бразе челове́ческом, как есть офице́р, пришёл и сел с ней за прибо́р.

—А! А!...—закрича́ла Ната́ша, с у́жасом выка́тывая глаза́.

—Да как же он, так и говори́т?

—Да, как челове́к, всё как должно́ быть, и стал, и стал угова́ривать, а ей бы на́до заня́ть его́ разгово́рами до петухо́в; а о́на заробе́ла; то́лько заробе́ла и закры́лась рука́ми. Он её и подхвати́л. Хорошо́, что тут де́вушки прибежа́ли...[d]

Л.Н. Толсто́й, Война́ и мир, том II, часть 4, гл. 11.

And this first stanza of the poem «Светла́на» by **Жуко́вский** is familiar to (and often memorized by) most Russians. Almost every line describes a future husband or the date of the wedding. Though **гада́ние** could be engaged in almost any evening during the

Christmas holidays, it was especially popular on New Year's night and on Epiphany Eve **Креще́нский ве́чер.**

> Раз в Креще́нский вечеро́к
> Де́вушки гада́ли:
> За воро́та башмачо́к,
> Сняв с ноги́, броса́ли;
> Слу́шали; корми́ли
> Счётным ку́рицу зерно́м;
> Я́рый воск топи́ли;
> В ча́шу с чи́стою водо́й
> Кла́ли пе́рстень золото́й,
> Се́рьги изумру́дны;
> Расстила́ли бе́лый плат
> И над ча́шей пе́ли в лад
> Пе́сенки подблю́дны.[e]

Epiphany
Креще́ние

The last day of the Christmas holidays **свя́тки** and one of the major church holidays is Epiphany or Twelfth Night **Креще́ние**, in celebration of Christ's baptism (**крести́ть**, to baptize). On that day (January 6), after the church ceremony, the priest led the flock to the local river (or lake) where a hole was broken in the ice. The priest blessed the water and then some of the especially hardy and faithful would take a dip.

> Свя́тки ока́нчивались на креще́ние. В э́тот день кре́стный ход шёл на Иорда́нь—к про́руби в реке́; по́сле «освяще́ния» воды́ не́которые купа́лись в про́руби.[f]

Алекса́ндров, Наро́ды европе́йской ча́сти СССР, стр. 414

January brings the coldest frosts, and the term **креще́нские моро́зы** remains to denote them.

The coming of spring
Жа́воронки

Traditionally, the skylarks **жа́воронки** arrived in March announcing spring. Special rolls were baked in their shape to celebrate their arrival. While the rolls named after the skylarks are still made, the reason for them is all but forgotten. The seasons were of considerable importance to agriculture, and in ancient times the children or young girls would go out in the fields on March 9, throw bread to the birds, and shout a call of welcome to spring.

Week-long Mardi Gras, Carnival
Ма́сленица

Carnival **ма́сленица** (from **ма́сло**, *butter*) was the week immediately preceding Lent **Вели́кий пост**. Though the date for **ма́сленица** was dependent on when Easter was celebrated, **ма́сленица** itself was strictly a pagan holiday, a salute to the sun and the warmth that made the grain grow high. It was a week of joy that gave special sanction to arsonists, gluttons, and wild drivers because its major features were bonfires, pancakes **блины́** in large quantities, and sleigh rides. (Compare Mardi Gras, Shrove Tuesday.)

Fire of some sort was almost always part of the celebration. In the north, children would gather combustibles into a great pile on a hilltop for a week. The pile was set on fire at night and so arranged that the flaming mass went crashing down the hillside. In other places, burning wheels of straw drenched in pitch were carried in a procession; and in still others, mere bonfires were sufficient.

Large quantities of food were consumed during this week, enough so that one way to describe living high off the hog is «не житьё, а ма́сленица.» (The restrictions of Lent that followed were severe enough to make up for this week of gluttony.) The food to be consumed were blini **блины́**, the round shape evoking the sun.

And always associated with **ма́сленица** were sleigh rides, with a troika if possible, but in any case using horses bedecked with gaily colored ribbons and sleigh bells **колоко́льчики**. Some said the sleigh was to ride in great semicircles to commemorate the path of the sun through the sky.

Fun and games continued for the whole week. By tradition this was the time of year that the Russian swings **каче́ли** were first used. In many places a snow city **сне́жный городо́к** was built, the young people divided into two groups, and a snow fight ensued that always ended in the fall of the snow city. (A famous painting by **Су́риков** is **Взя́тие сне́жного городка́** *The Conquest of Snow City*.) Dressing up in costumes **ря́женье** occurred during carnival **ма́сленица** almost as frequently as at Christmas. The general merriment intensified toward the end of the week **широ́кая ма́сленица**, and in some places on the night before the beginning of Lent, the stuffed effigy

of **ма́сленица**, often in the shape of a country woman, was burned in yet another fire and buried until the next year.

THE EASTER SEASON
Пасха́льный сезо́н

Palm Sunday
Ве́рбное воскресе́нье

The Sunday before Easter, Palm Sunday, is called Pussy Willow Sunday **Ве́рбное воскресе́нье**. Pussy willow branches are taken to church, blessed, and then taken home to be propped up behind the icon, located in the beautiful/red corner **кра́сный/пере́дний у́гол** of the main or living room of the house. On this day, Moscow used to have a Pussy Willow market **Ве́рбный база́р** in Red Square where tradesmen sold all kinds of toys and sweets and where the well-to-do came to show off their clothes, carriages, and girlfriends.

Ве́рбочки

Ма́льчики да де́вочки
Све́чечки да ве́рбочки
    Понесли́ домо́й.

Огонёчки тепля́тся,
Прохо́жие крестя́тся,
    И па́хнет весно́й.

Ветеро́к уда́ленький
До́ждик, дождик ма́ленький,
    Не заду́й огня́!

В Воскресе́нье Ве́рбное
Завтра вста́ну пе́рвая
    Для свято́го дня. [g]

Алекса́ндр Блок, 1906

The week between Palm Sunday and Easter is Holy Week **Страстна́я Неде́ля** and the days of the week are **Вели́кий Понеде́льник/ Вто́рник, Вели́кая Среда́, Страстно́й**

Каче́ли

Четве́рг, Страстна́я Пя́тница, Страстна́я Суббо́та. For Easter week, each day is "bright" све́тлый: Све́тлое Воскресе́нье, Све́тлый Понеде́льник. . . Све́тлая Суббо́та.

Easter
Па́сха

Russian Easter starts the night before, not including the cooking. The faithful arrive at church in the late evening bringing their traditional Easter dessert **па́сха**[3] and Easter sweet bread **кули́ч** and some Easter eggs to be blessed. Church attendance at this ceremony is, as elsewhere, at its highest, leaving many people outside the church, candle in hand. Near midnight the priest opens the doors to the church and leads a procession of deacons, altar boys, the choir, and any parishioners wishing to join. The procession is called a **кре́стный ход**, which in this case symbolizes the search for Jesus's body by Mary Magdalene and others (see Mark 16), and the subsequent discovery that Christ is risen. The procession circles the church three times, its members singing as they go. The church doors represent the sepulchre, and when they are opened the priest announces several times that Christ is risen: «**Христо́с воскре́с**!» The audience each time answers, "Truly He is risen!" «**Вои́стину воскре́с**!» Directly after this ceremony and for several days thereafter, a delightful ritual takes place, usually between friends though complete strangers also participate: one person goes to another and says: «**Христо́с воскре́с**!»; the other *must* answer, «**Вои́стину воскре́с**!» and then they kiss three times on alternate cheeks. (The verb is **христо́соваться**.) Directly after church that night, the first meal with eggs, butter, and meat is eaten; the fast is broken. Participation at this meal is called **ро́зговенье**

(to participate, **разговля́ться**). It can be a small family group eating a snack after the long church ceremony, or it might be a long night of eating and drinking without too much thought for the holiness of it all.

Easter eggs **кра́шеные я́йца** loom as large in Russian Easter as in ours, although no Easter bunny is given credit for bringing them. The eggs are usually dyed by boiling with onion skins. Some are taken to church and blessed—these are later either eaten or placed on the shelf with the icon; those not blessed can be used for games. **Ката́ть я́йца** is an egg-rolling contest in which eggs are laid in a line; each contestant can keep the eggs that are hit out of that line when she rolls her own egg. **Бить я́йца** is played by two people holding eggs who bang the pointed ends into one another; the one holding the unbroken egg wins.

Pentecost, Whitsunday, Trinity Sunday
Тро́ица

This feast overlies a pagan holiday, the main feature of which was spring greenery, especially birch **берёза**. Its adaptation to Christian rites involved bringing flowers and greenery to bedeck the church. For the religious, this holiday affirmed the trinity **Тро́ица** of God and also signaled the end of the Easter holiday cycle.

John the Baptist's Day
День Ива́на Купа́лы

День Ива́на Купа́лы, June 24, superseded the pre-Christian holiday of the summer solstice. John the Baptist (officially **Иоа́нн Крести́тель**) became connected with this festival because of his association with water. The day in mythology was associated with **Купа́ла** (or **Купа́ло**), a god that had to do with water (**купа́ться**, *to swim, bathe*). On this day one could expect either a dunking from a pail of water or perhaps a less ceremonious push into the river. The night before, **Ива́нова ночь**, had

---

3. Recipes and pictures of **па́сха, куличи́, блины́** are now available at your local bookstore. Variety of description is only normal; every cook has her own preferences. (Russian males have not been freed for cooking.)

some magical qualities: it was believed that the fern **па́поротник** blossomed on this night, and anyone who could pick the flower would find all the buried treasure in the surrounding countryside. Bonfires were lit and jumped over,[4] and this was also a time for fortunetelling.

The Harvest Celebration
Дожи́нки

Дожи́нки was a harvest celebration that occurred especially in grain-producing areas on the last day of the harvest. When the last stalks of grain had been gathered, the harvesters lay down on the ground and rolled around, so that the earth would give back some of the strength it had taken away. Then ribbons were tied around a handful of stalks, which was paraded around the village and finally put to rest in the **кра́сный у́гол** (see "The peasant house" in Chapter 5) of the person from whose field it came.

The old and the new
Ста́рое вме́сте с но́вым

Many features of the ancient holidays remain in some localities. In villages (far from the cities, that is), the pagan rites continue. Children get dressed in costumes **ря́женье**; they also go from door to door singing songs **коля́дки** that wish a happy New Year, or perhaps now a merry Christmas. The unmarried girls still engage in **гада́ние** for the fun of it. The "altar holidays" (**престо́льные пра́здники**, described in the next section) are still often celebrated, especially far from major cities.

In other ways, the traditional celebrations have been incorporated into new (local, rather than national) festivals. You are likely to hear about **Пра́здник ру́сской зимы́**, however, which incorporates the joys of **ма́сленица** into other entertainments—dances and con-

certs, for instance. Local festivals of dance, music, and sports are also often arranged, but these can no longer be called holidays in our sense of the word.

April Fool's Day **Пе́рвое апре́ля** is celebrated exactly as is ours, though without any particular association with fools: «**Пе́рвый апре́ль—никому́ не верь!**» ("On the first of April, don't believe anybody!")—this is practical jokes day.

CHURCH HOLIDAYS
Церко́вные пра́здники

The official church holidays are numerous and of varying importance. Easter **Па́сха**, the holiest of days, is in a class by itself and above all the others. Then there are the "twelve" holidays, **двунадеся́тые пра́здники** deemed of special significance by the church and to be observed by all. And finally, the "altar" holidays **престо́льные пра́здники** are those celebrated in each locality on the name day of the patron saint of the local church or monastery.

The "twelve" holidays
Двунадеся́тые пра́здники

The Russian Orthodox Church **Правосла́вная Це́рковь** (in Russia) requires observance of these especially important holidays.[5] Because the church has yet to recognize the Gregorian calendar, dates for these holidays follow the Julian calendar, also known as Old Style, which has been thirteen days later than the Gregorian calendar since 1900.[6] All dates here are Old Style. When several titles refer to the same holiday, the most commonly used is the first. Many place names, church names, and surnames are based on these holiday names.

---

4. From pictures of the event, this is probably the day **Снегу́рочка** came to her sad end.

5. Eight of them celebrate events of religious significance in Christ's life and four have to do with Mary.

6. The difference increases: see *Time* in Chapter 15.

Число́ по ст. ст.[1]	Назва́ния двунадеся́тых пра́здников	Перево́д на англи́йский
6 января́	Креще́ние (Госпо́дне), Богоявле́ние	Epiphany or Twelfth Day
2 февраля́	Сре́тение (Госпо́дне)	Presentation of Christ in the Temple[5]
25 ма́рта	Благове́щение (Пресвято́й Богоро́дицы)	Annunciation
_____ [2]	Ве́рбное воскресе́нье, Вход Госпо́день в Иерусали́м	Palm Sunday
_____ [3]	Вознесе́ние (Госпо́дне)	Ascension
_____ [4]	Тро́ица, День Свято́й Тро́ицы, Пятидеся́тница	(Trinity), Whitsunday, Pentecost
6 а́вгуста	Преображе́ние (Госпо́дне)	Transfiguration
15 а́вгуста	Успе́ние (Пресвято́й Богоро́дицы)	Assumption
8 сентября́	Рождество́ Пресвято́й Богоро́дицы	Birthday of Our Lady
14 сентября́	Воздви́жение (Креста́ Госпо́дня)	Elevation of the Holy Cross, Exaltation of the Cross
21 ноября́	Введе́ние во храм (Пресвято́й Богоро́дицы)	Presentation of the Virgin Mary
25 декабря́	Рождество́ (Христо́во)	Christmas

1. по ста́рому сти́лю Old Style. See *Time* in Chapter 15.

2. Always the Sunday before (Russian) Easter. Perhaps due to an absence of palms, this day is literally called Pussy Willow Sunday.

3. Always on Thursday, the fortieth day after (Russian) Easter.

4. Always on Sunday, ten days after (Russian) Ascension.

5. The Roman Catholic and Episcopal churches refer to this same day as the Feast of the Purification of the Virgin, or Candlemas. Still others are familiar with it under the title of Groundhog Day.

When is Easter?
Когда́ Па́сха?

Three of the "twelve" holidays depend on when Easter is celebrated. The date for Russian Orthodox Easter is not simply the thirteen-day difference between the two calendars. The popular formula sets Easter **Па́сха** as the first Sunday after the first full moon **полнолу́ние** following the vernal equinox **весе́ннее равноде́нствие**. The day so chosen must follow Jewish Passover (also called **Па́сха**), and if it does not, then Easter is celebrated the following Sunday. As a result, Russian Easter falls between March 22 and April 25 Old Style (between April 4 and May 8 New Style) and most often follows Western Easter by a couple of weeks.

The "altar" holidays
Престо́льные пра́здники

The altar holidays **престо́льные пра́здники** are celebrations occurring on the name day of the local church or monastery: **Тро́ицкая це́рковь** would have its celebration on Pentecost, **це́рковь Свято́го Михаи́ла** celebrated on one of the St. Michael's days, and so on. On this day the local inhabitants and those from neighboring villages would attend church services and then gather in the square, either near the church itself or on the edge of town. Here traders would have small booths selling foods, sweets, inexpensive decorations, and the like. Larger villages might have extensive fairgrounds with swings **каче́ли** and merry-go-rounds **карусе́ли**. Some fairs

я́рмарка (*sg.*) at monasteries became famous and would draw people from a great distance. Eating, drinking, singing, and dancing were naturally a part of these country holidays. Not so obviously, but very traditionally, the joys of rural holidays culminated in semiorganized brawls between the young males of two or more villages. An entire story, «Оби́да» by Солоу́хин, describes what happened to an unwilling contestant in one such fight. The first line of the story sets the scene:

Черку́тино бы́ло ра́ньше больши́м торго́вым село́м, куда́ на я́рмарку ли в петро́в день, на ма́сленицу ли съезжа́лись крестья́не из окре́стных дереве́нь.[h]

Other saints' days
Други́е церко́вные пра́здники

Less official "church" holidays were various saints' days that from one association or another were familiar to the peasants. Especially in the country, it was (and still is) common to refer, not to a date, but to a specific saint's day. In «Матрёнин двор» by Солжени́цын, Матрёна says,

По-быва́лошному кипе́ли с се́ном в меже́нь, с Петро́ва до Ильина́.[i]

Following are some of the more frequently noted days:

Петро́в день   June 29, До Петро́ва дня взора́ть пары́, the end of plowing (Ты мне ну́жен, как в петро́в день ва́режки![7])

Илья́н день   July 20, До Ильина́ заборони́ть, harrowing done

Его́ров день or **Ю́рьев день**   April 23 (Вот тебе, ба́бушка, и Ю́рьев день! is said of any unpleasant surprise; on this day peasants had been allowed to move to another landlord until **Алексе́й Миха́йлович**, Peter's father, declared that they must remain with the land.)

Спа́сов день   August 1, До Спа́са посе́ять

Покро́в день   October 1 (**Покро́в Пресвято́й Богоро́дицы**, Protection of the Holy Mother of God) Snow on this day means a cold winter.

Нико́лин день

Нико́ла ве́шний   May 9, "Altar" day; **Нико́льщина**   the accompanying week-long celebration

Нико́ла коча́нный   June 27, the day cabbage begins to form heads

Нико́ла зи́мний   December 6, roads are now passable

День Петра́ и Па́вла   June 29, protectors of fishermen

Татья́нин день   January 12 (25 January N.S.), patron saint of students

Ве́ра, Наде́жда, Любо́вь и мать их Софи́я   September 30 (N.S.); so many people celе́brate these name days that forgetting is impossible

The fasts
Посты́

To some extent, holidays can be defined by their opposites, the preceding fasts. The Russian Orthodox fast was notable in that those who observed it ate neither meat nor eggs, milk, cheese, or butter. Some people even refused white (refined) sugar because bone ash was used in the refining process; brown sugar **по́стный са́хар** was used instead. What remained to be eaten was fish, vegetables, and bread; vegetable oil was used for fat. Food was not the only deprivation called for during the fasts—marriages were not performed while they were in effect. (And because what one might do, if married, was also to be abstained from, "fasting" was also another form of birth control.)

7.   I need you like I need mittens in July!

There were four major fast periods in a year:

Вели́кий пост   the seven weeks before
Easter

**Фили́пповский (и́ли Рожде́ственский)
пост**   the six weeks before Christmas

Петро́в пост (петро́вки)   from May 31 to
June 29

Успе́нский пост   from August 1 to
August 15

Only Lent **Вели́кий пост** was regularly
observed by most people, but the very devout
could deprive themselves even further since
Wednesdays and Fridays were also days of fasting. Such devotion could considerably lower
the egg and meat bill: more than half the days
in the year were officially days of denial.

THE CHURCH
Це́рковь

The Church building
Храм

(1)
жéртвенник (2)
алта́рь (3)
престо́л (4)
Ца́рские Врата́ (5)
иконоста́с (6)
амво́н (7)
кли́рос (8)
подсве́чник (9)
храм (10)
притво́р (11)
све́чи, просфо́ры, запи́ски (12)
панихи́дный сто́лик, кану́н (13)
Распя́тие (14)
анало́й (15) «...И вспо́мнил я тебя пред
анало́ем, И звал тебя, как мо́лодость свою́.»
Блок, О доблестях... 1908
диа́конские врата́ (16)

Church floor plan

(1) The business end of the church is always
on the east side of the church
(2) Table of Oblation, where priest prepares
the sacraments **Дары́**
(3) Sanctuary, an area (not the altar table) during the services, reserved for celebrants, and
famed as an area where females may not tread
(4) Altar table: where the Gospels **Ева́нгелия**
are kept
(5) Royal doors, those that only the ordained
can use
(6) Iconostasis: an icon screen separating the
sanctuary from the nave
(7) A raised platform in front of iconostasis,
where priest delivers sermon
(8) A raised area on both sides of church which
may be used for choir, confession, reading
(9) Candleholder; often placed in front of
especially revered icons

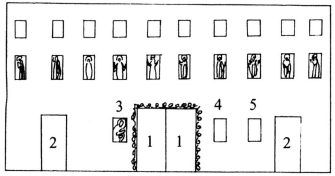

Iconostasis design

Icon

(10) Nave, or the central part of the church

(11) Narthex, the area near or just outside the entrance

(12) Candles, church breads sold here (or on opposite side); intercessory prayer lists **запи́ски** submitted here also

(13) Where memorial services **панихи́ды** are held, in front of the crucifix

(14) Crucifix and candleholder; the crucifix is the only statue allowed, if there is one at all

(15) A stand for holding icon whose feast day it is; also may hold icon of the church's patron saint, or other church vessels

(16) Deacons' doors

Iconostasis
Иконоста́с

Ца́рские Врата́ (1)
боковы́е две́ри, диа́конские врата́ (2)
Бо́жья Ма́терь (3)
Спаси́тель (4)
Ико́на це́ркви (5)

(1) Royal doors; the Last Supper **Та́йная ве́черя** is often pictured directly above

(2) Deacons' doors, often with Archangels Michael and Gabriel

(3) Icon of the Virgin, always on the left

(4) Icon of the Savior, always on the right

(5) Usually, this place holds the icon of the patron saint of that particular church

If the church is poor, the iconostasis can be minimized to the foregoing icons or icon tier **ме́стный я́рус**. Often, there are other tiers **я́русы**: the next up will either have the apostles—often with Christ enthroned in the center with John the Baptist on His left and the Virgin on His right—or the next tier will show significant feast days (see text); above them can be the prophets distinguishable by their scrolls; and above them the patriarchs of the church.

Icon
Образ, ико́на

The icon **о́браз** pictures a sacred person or event. Though people pray in front of them, the icons themselves are not worshipped; rather, they act as a kind of interface between the worshipper and God or the spiritual aspects of His representatives on earth. During the 18th and 19th centuries it was popular to cover all but the faces and hands of the icons with an often highly decorated metal panel **ри́за, окла́д**.

See Leonid Ouspensky and Vladimir Losskey, *The Meaning of Icons.*

Orthodox cross

Orthodox Cross
Православный крест

The smaller crossarm at the top is to contain the sign "Jesus of Nazareth, King of the Jews" **Иисýс Назорéй, Царь Иудéйский**. The slanted crossarm toward the bottom shows Christ's agony on the cross and indicates that the robber on His right went to heaven for having confessed to Christ, while the one on His left denied Him. Sometimes the Orthodox cross on the top of churches is shown with an Islamic crescent at its base: this indicates the victory of Christendom over the Tartars (who, it is said, had lopped off all the crosses and substituted crescents).

The Bells
Колокола́

Bell ringing **звон** must have been one of the major pleasures supplied by the Russian church. The bells sounded before the service to summon the people to church, at certain times during the church service, and at the end of the

service. They sounded as the body was carried out of the church after the funeral ceremony. After the Easter ceremonies were concluded, village boys were allowed to ring the bells one after another (**пасха́льный) перезво́н**. Before radios and telephones, the bell in the country church was used to summon help **наба́т** in case of fire or other disaster (a single loud bell rung repeatedly), and bells also formed an early warning system installed in fortress walls.

The bell ringer **звона́рь** was unlike his British cousin who only rang one or two bells by pulling on a rope so that the bell turned until it hit the clapper. The Russian bell ringer works in a bell tower **колоко́льня** and controls many bells at once via ropes connected to a number of clappers **языки́**. To ring a bell is **звони́ть, уда́рить в ко́локол**.

Going to church
Це́рковь

Let us assume your background does not include the Russian Orthodox Church **Ру́сская Правосла́вная Це́рковь**. What might you expect to see on some Sunday morning?

Visitors attending church should wear comfortable shoes because all but the infirm must stand for the entire service. (There are benches in the back for those who can't stand. It is also true that many arrive well after the service has started.) Clothing should be modest and restrained; in church men may not wear a head covering, and (in Russia) women must. Women must wear skirts. Other physical aspects to church conduct: crossing oneself is performed rather broadly and without hurry (right shoulder before left shoulder) and almost any time one feels like it, but especially when the Father, Son, and the Holy Ghost **Оте́ц, Сын, Свято́й Дух** are mentioned, when **Го́споди поми́луй** or **Пода́й Го́споди** is heard, or at the beginning and end of any prayer. The several kinds of bows include a slightly bowed head (during censing **кажде́ние**, when the priest **свяще́нник** or the deacon **дья́кон** swings the censer **кади́ло**); a low bow **ни́зкий покло́н**, with one hand reaching the floor; and a floor bow **земно́й покло́н**, with hands, forehead, and knees touching the floor. The latter is not recommended on Sundays or holidays for lack of room in the church.

True believers **ве́рующие** arrive before the service **Богослуже́ние**, which in this case would be the main service, **обе́дня, литурги́я**; often they bow and cross themselves three times before entering the church. Once inside they cross themselves again, bowing toward the altar; then they buy candles **све́чи** and consecrated church breads **просфо́ры** to accompany prayer lists **запи́ски** at a booth often to the right of the entrance. (The point is to ask the priest to include in his prayers those people named in the lists.) Males drift quietly off to stand generally on the right side of the church and females drift off to the left side. This is not a strict separation, but it does correspond to the gender differentiation on the iconostasis **иконоста́с**, where the Savior **Спаси́тель** is always pictured on the right side of the Royal doors **Ца́рские врата́** and the Virgin **Свята́я Де́ва, Бо́жья Ма́терь** on the left side. To the right of Jesus **Иису́с** is usually an icon depicting the saint **Свято́й** or holiday after which the church was named. The (sometimes unmarked) central aisle from the church entrance to these royal doors technically should be left unoccupied (translation—avoid standing on the red carpet traversing the center of the church). Those who have bought candles, often in memory of a loved one, go to the icon of their choice, cross themselves, light their candle, place it in the candle holder **подсве́чник**, and cross tehmselves again. If they have arrived late, in a crowded church, they hand their candle to the person in the direction of the icon, name it, and ask that the candle be passed on.

The music seems not to cease, the priest[8] sings or chants his prayers, joined by many of the parishioners **прихожа́не**, some volunteering harmony. But the choir **хор** supplies the

musical staples (they, too, are joined by those present): no musical instruments are used, rather the chant **распе́в** is used in such a way that anyone coming from somewhere else can know what to sing. (Those interested in Russian church singing should consult Johann von Gardner's *Russian Church Singing*, St. Vladimir's Seminary Press, Crestwood, New York, 1980.) The parishioners often cross themselves and bow many times during the service. The phrase "Lord, have mercy" **Го́споди поми́луй!** is heard so often that even the uninitiated can recognize it. The priest occasionally disappears behind the Royal doors, to pray or to prepare the Sacraments, and returns. (Those interested in the religious significance of the rituals should consult Timothy Ware, *The Orthodox Church*, Penguin Books, London, 1993).

Church services
Богослуже́ния

The philosophical beginning of the church day is, as in Judaism, the night before at vespers **вече́рня**: the service glorifies (1) creation, in Psalm 104, (2) the incarnation of Christ with O Gladsome Light **Све́тя Ти́хий**, (3) introduces the theme of the feast day, **Тро́парь**. (If the feast is major, then there is a blessing of loaves, wine, wheat and oil), and (4) it concludes with the singing of Hail Mary.

Hail Mary
Моли́тва Богоро́дице, Ангельское приве́тствие

Богоро́дице Де́во, ра́дуйся, Благода́тная Мари́е, Госпо́дь с Тобо́ю, благослове́нна Ты в жена́х, и благослове́н плод чре́ва Твоего́, я́ко Спаса роди́ла еси́ душ на́ших.[j]

Matins **Утреня** has two parts, developing both the themes of (1) the teaching of Christ as illuminator, and (2) the feast day. This is followed by the first of the canonical hours **Часы́**. Especially in the urban church (as opposed to

---

8. Pray that God hasn't sent you a tone-deaf priest.

the monasteries) where traveling distances must be considered, the vespers, matins, and the first canonical hour are combined into one night service **Всенощное Бдение.**

The Divine Liturgy
Литургия, обедня

This major church service is usually held once a week on Sundays in parish churches, and no more than once a day in monasteries. The limitation is one Liturgy for each sanctuary (chapel) and each priest per day. Some churches have several chapels **приделы.** In an urban setting

Divine Liturgy is preceded by the third and sixth canonical hours that are read, literally, by a reader **чтец.** During this time the priest begins the first part of the Liturgy: the Royal doors are closed and the priest is in the sanctuary **алтарь** at the Table of Oblation **жертвенник** preparing the sacramental breads **просфоры** and wine and reading the names of those for whom prayers are offered. The deacon emerges with his censer and reads two prayers.

The second part of the Liturgy, the Liturgy of the Word **Литургия оглашённых** is a description of the teachings of the church; it begins when the priest opens the Royal doors and proclaims, "Blessed is the kingdom of the Father,

Блажени нищии духом, яко тех есть царство небесное.[9]	Blessed are the poor in spirit: for theirs is the kingdom of heaven.
Блажени плачущии, яко тии утешатся.	Blessed are they that mourn: for they shall be comforted.
Блажени кротцыи, яко тии наследят землю.	Blessed are the meek: for they shall inherit the earth.
Блажени алчущии и жаждущии правды, яко тии насытятся.	Blessed are they which do hunger and thirst after righteousness: for they shall be filled.
Блажени милостивии, яко тии помиловани будут.	Blessed are the merciful: for they shall obtain mercy.
Блажени чистии сердцем, яко тии Бога узрят.	Blessed are the pure in heart: for they shall see God.
Блажени миротворцы, яко тии сынове Божии нарекутся.	Blessed are the peacemakers: for they shall be called the children of God.
Блажени изгнани правды ради, яко тех есть царство небесное.	Blessed are they which are persecuted for righteousness' sake: for theirs is the kingdom of heaven.
Блажени есте, егда поносят вам, и изждёнут, и рекут всяк зол глагол на вы лжуще, мене ради. Радуйтейся и веселитеся, яко мзда ваша многа на небесех.[1]	Blessed are ye when men shall revile you, and shall say all manner of evil against you falsely, for my sake. Rejoice and be exceeding glad: for great is your reward in heaven.

9. These are a modern transcription of Old Church Slavonic, which was never a spoken language. There are, nevertheless, rules for speaking it; for example, pronounce г as *g* regardless of whether it is part of the genitive case, and do not use ё.

the Son and the Holy Ghost" Благословéнно цáрство Отцá, Сы́на, Святóго Ду́ха. Psalms 102 and 143 are sung, and on non–high feast days the Beatitudes are sung, while on high feast days the hymns commemorating that particular holiday are sung.

The Beatitudes
Зáповеди Блажéнства

The Beatitudes are sung during the Liturgy as the Gospels are being carried into the sanctuary behind the iconostasis. This entrance is called **Мáлый вход.**

Then a reading from Acts or Epistles **Апóстол** is followed by **Аллилу́йя**, and a reading from the Gospel **Евáнгелие** is followed by censing. The sermon is the last event in this part of the liturgy, and, sometimes, it is the longest. (The entire service takes about 1 1/2 hours, or more if there is a special occasion.) According to ritual it is at this point that nonbelievers are asked to leave.

Finally, the third part is the Liturgy of the faithful **Литургúя вéрных**, where the expression of belief consummates in the Eucharist or communion. It begins with the Great entrance **Велúкий вход,** when the bread and wine (literally, Gifts) **Дары́** are brought around to the sanctuary. The deacon leads in the repetition of the Nicene Creed from the "amvon" (see the drawing of the church floor plan).

Credo, Nicene Creed
Сúмвол вéры, Вéрую

Вéрую во едúнаго Бóга Отцá, Вседержúтеля, Творцá нéбу и землú, вúдимым и невúдимым. . . .[k]

After hymns for the transubstantiation of the bread and wine, everyone joins in the Lord's Prayer.

The Lord's Prayer
Молúтва Госпóдня, Отче наш

Отче наш, Иже есú на небéсех! Да святúтся имя Твоé: да приúдет Цáрствие

Твое: да будет вóля Твоя, я́ко на небесú и на землú: хлеб наш насу́щный даждь нам днесь: и остáви нам дóлги наша, я́коже и мы оставля́ем должникóм нашим: и не введú нас во искушéние, но избáви нас от лукáваго. (Я́ко твоé есть цáрство, и сила, и слава, отца, и сы́на, и свя́таго ду́ха, ныне и прúсно и во веки векóв.) Амúнь[10]

Here is the King James version of the prayer so you can compare them.

Our Father, which art in Heaven. Hallowed be Thy name. Thy kingdom come, Thy will be done, on earth as it is in heaven. Give us this day our daily bread. And forgive us our debts, as we forgive our debtors. And lead us not into temptation, but deliver us from evil. For Thine is the kingdom, and the power, and the glory, forever. Amen.

Then those who are prepared take communion **причáстие**, first the celebrants, then the children, and finally the laity. (Those who do take communion must first go to confession **исповéдаться** except for children, who are not considered able to sin up to about age ten. The frequency of communion depends on the local priest: some recommend once a week, some once a year.) Then the priest gives thanks, blesses the people, and the service is over.

The clergy
Духовéнство

There are three degrees and two kinds of clergy.

The lowest degree of clergy is the deacon **дья́кон**, who is allowed to assist in the conferring of sacraments; the most common is the priest **свящéнник**, who can administer the sacraments; and the third is the bishop and above **епúскоп (архиерéй)**, who ordains the priests. The bishop can go on to become a metropolitan **митрополúт** or even a patriarch **патриáрх**, while the two lower orders cannot.

---

10. This last line is spoken by the priest rather than the parishioners.

The white clergy **бе́лое духове́нство** may marry before they become priests, but they cannot rise above the level of priest.[11] The black clergy **чёрное духовенство** go to the monastery **монасты́рь**, a life of celibacy, and the chance to become a patriarch.

To address them, a deacon or priest can be called "father" (Andrew), **Оте́ц (Андре́й)**, as can monks, **мона́хи**. Nuns, **мона́хини** (*fam.* **мона́шки**) answer to **ма́тушка**. Familiarly and commonly, the priest is simply **ба́тюшка** and his wife is **ма́тушка**, no names attached.

The Sacraments
Та́инства

In Russian Orthodoxy, the sacraments **та́инства** are baptism **креще́ние**; chrismation (or, anointing with holy chrism, similar to confirmation) **миропома́зание** (both of the preceding occur at the same service in the Russian church); penance **покая́ние** or confession **и́споведь**; communion or Eucharist **причаще́ние, Евхари́стия**; matrimony **брак** or marriage **венча́ние**; unction **соборова́ние, елеосвяще́ние**; and ordination **рукоположе́ние свяще́нств, свяще́нство**.

The Old Testament **Ве́тхий Заве́т** is recognized as foreshadowing New Testament **Но́вый Заве́т** events. (The prophets sometimes form one of the tiers of the iconostasis.) But the emphasis is on the New Testament, especially the gospels **Ева́нгелия от Матфе́я, от Ма́рка, от Луки́, от Иоа́нна.**

TRANSLATIONS

a. Kolyada, kolyada
    Open the gates,
    Snow[s] have fallen on the ground
    From time to time.
    Christmas has come

To the master's window.
Get up, master,
Wake up the mistress.
Be hospitable to us,
[Feed us with bread and salt],
Show us the road.
What sleek calves our mother has!
They jump over the garden beds,
Clicking their hoofs,
Not touching the ground.
Our mistress has
Thick cream,
Rich sour cream,
[And] yellow butter . . .
We will take not a ruble, nor fifty kopecks,
One twenty-five piece,
A pie and a tart,
A gold piece.

b. The household servants were dressed up as bears, Turks, innkeepers, and lords, both frightful and funny. They brought the cold and their gaiety in with them, at first huddling timidly in the entrance hall, then, hiding behind one another, they moved to the ballroom. Bashfully at first, and then more gaily and friendlier, they began to sing, dance, and play Christmas games. The countess recognized the faces, laughed at costumes, and went off to the drawing room. Count Ilya Andreyich sat in the ballroom with a radiant smile, approving the players. The young people vanished somewhere.

c. At Christmas and Carnival the mummers go from house to house and then have a party with the food and money they have collected. Thus, during the Christmas holidays in 1960 in Klimovo, women went around the village dressed up as fighters or a bear and his trainer, and the children dressed up as gypsies.

d. "Fortune-telling in the bathhouse, that was frightening!" said an old maid at the supper table who lived with the Melyukovs.

". . . Once a young lady took a rooster and two place settings and sat down, just as she was sup-

11. Actually, the rule is that they cannot get married after being ordained. The patriarch with children from two marriages achieved them all before ordination.

posed to. She sat for a while just listening. Suddenly, [something] is coming . . . with bells ringing. A sleigh arrives. She hears someone coming. Something in human form enters, very much like an officer. He sits down at one of the place settings."

"Oh!" screamed Natasha, her eyes staring in horror.

"Was he really talking?"

"Yes, he's like a man; everything is just the way it's supposed to be; he begins to persuade her. She should have tried to get him to talk until early morning, but she got scared and put her hands over her face. So he grabbed her. It's a good thing the girls came running in . . .

e. Once on Epiphany Eve
  The girls were telling fortunes;
  They took off a shoe and
  Threw it over the gate;
  Drew designs in the snow;
  Listened at the window;
  Fed counted grains to a chicken;
  Melted clean wax;
  Into a cup of pure water
  They put a gold ring
  [or] emerald earrings;
  They spread out a white kerchief,
  And over a cup
  Sang fortunetelling songs.

f. The Christmas holidays ended with Epiphany. On that day a "procession of the cross" would go "to Jordan," that is, a hole bro-

ken in the river ice. After the water had been blessed, some of the people swam in the river.

g. The Little Pussy Willows

  Boys and girls
  Took home their candles
      And their pussy willows

  The little candles are warm,
  Passers-by cross themselves,
      And it smells like spring.

  A frisky little wind
  Just a bit of rain,
      Don't blow out the candle!

  On Palm Sunday
  I'll be the first up tomorrow
      For the holy day.

h. Cherkutino used to be a large trading center; the peasants from the surrounding villages would come to attend the fairs on St. Peter's Day or during carnival week.

i. They used to work hard gathering hay between St. Peter's Day and Elijah's Day.

j. Hail Mary, full of grace. The Lord is with you. Blessed are you among women, and blessed is the fruit of your womb. For you have borne the Savior of our souls.

k. I believe in One God, the father, the Almighty, creator of heaven and earth, seen and unseen. . . . [The Creed continues at some length.]

17

Play
О́тдых

This chapter provides a view of the Russian's free time, how it's used, and especially the terminology applied to it. Because the scope of such a project is close to overwhelming, the space devoted to a topic does not necessarily reflect its importance or popularity. Rather, the activity's popularity is described, while space is given over to the accompanying language that is less familiar. The subject is divided into discussions of the following:

Free time
Annual vacations
Short trips
Leisure time
Official sports
Children's play
Traditional amusements

FREE TIME
Свобо́дное вре́мя

For children
У дете́й

Free time is naturally limited by certain fixed obligations. For children this means that some schools are in operation six days a week, even though most adult occupations are now on a five-day week. Therefore only one full free day per week remains. Except for those attending two-shift schools, children also have some of the afternoon off, attending school only during a rather long morning. For younger pupils this school day is shorter (four forty-five-minute classes a day) than for older pupils (who attend for six or more hours a day). It would be a mistake to say that the time away from classes is really "free time," however, because a major component of education is homework. Another major component of education is attendance at various organized activity groups (such as photography "circles" **кружки́**, chess clubs, and biology clubs) often connected with the schools.

Annual vacations from school include the fall holidays **осе́нние кани́кулы**, which slightly precede and include November 7 (the anniversary of the Revolution); the ten days after the New Year **нового́дние кани́кулы**; a spring vacation **весе́нние кани́кулы**, a week at the end of March; and a summer vacation **ле́тние кани́кулы**, which begins at the end of May (for upper school, the end of June after examinations and **пра́ктика**), and continues until September 1, when school resumes.

University students, however, have significantly less free time than U.S. students. Except for some very good students **отли́чники**, who can work out their own study schedule on approval, class attendance is generally compulsory, and many more subjects are required than in the United States; also, course reading lists are immense, and classes are often held six days a week. Some time is allowed to prepare for exams or to write dissertations, but, again, it would be a misnomer to call this free time. Annual vacations include two weeks at the end of January **зи́мние кани́кулы** and the summer vacation **ле́тние кани́кулы** for the months of July and August.

Universities can grant a year's reprieve **академи́ческий о́тпуск** from studies for those who are not doing well and need more time, or for those incapacitated by a baby, for example.

Rather than waiting tables in summer resorts, the popular summer work for the Russian student is to join a student construction brigade **студе́нческий строи́тельный отря́д** (**ССО**). This is paid work, often involving fairly distant but rudimentary construction projects, and frequently has the atmosphere of a work party. These work brigades are not the only possibility, of course. Some students do summer work in their own field of study—an anthropological field trip, an archaeological dig, and so on.

For adults
У взро́слых

The working adult, no less than the school child and the university student, is pressed for time. The eight-hour day is standard enough, but time is consumed in many other ways that subtract heavily from what might otherwise be free time. Many people, for instance, take evening and correspondence courses—a popular way to a better job. Though attendance at various meetings is less obligatory than it used to be, parents must go to PTA meetings, workers are urged to attend trade-union meetings, and so forth. To this must be added the time necessary to support life: buying things takes time.

A paid annual vacation **о́тпуск** for adults varies from eighteen days to a month and sometimes more, depending on place of work, position occupied, and length of service. Time off without pay is **администрати́вный о́тпуск**.

Annual vacations
Ежего́дные отпуска́

The summer vacation used to come in two varieties depending on whether one could get a **путёвка**, in this case, a reservation at one of the following: (1) a sanatorium **санато́рий**, (2) a "resort" **дом о́тдыха**, (3) a headquarters for hikers **турба́за**, or (4) a small hotel or boardinghouse **пансиона́т**. The **путёвка** gave the right to go to such places at varying rates, sometimes totally free but more often at a reduced rate, or sometimes at the full price. The **путёвка** was a way of distributing limited resort facilities to the deserving and was usually handled by a trade union or employer. In the general population it was easier for a production worker to get a **путёвка** than it was for a nonproduction worker (a teacher, for instance).

A sanatorium **санато́рий** is closest to what we would call a rest home. People go there for reasons of health rather than recreation, for mud baths, mineral waters, and the like. Those who literally require special medical care are also sent to a sanatorium, usually for no less than twenty-four days.

The дом о́тдыха (literally, *house of rest*) is not what we mean by a rest home nor is it really comparable to our resort. One goes there not for reasons of health but as a reward for having worked well. But it differs from a resort because of the considerable regulation of activities: morning exercises, meals at a certain time, and rest at a specified hour. A дом о́тдыха is usually attended for twelve or twenty-four days.

The дом о́тдыха or санато́рий is often located at a spa куро́рт—any region where the climate, beaches, mineral waters, or any physical aspect of the area is thought to be conducive to good health. The use of these places has been sharply curtailed in the recent past, partly because many of the spas were located in what are now war zones, or because new little countries hope to get world prices for their facilities.

It is fairly common for Russian couples to vacation separately by choice. This joke appeared in **Вече́рняя Москва́**:

—Я сказа́ла му́жу, что, е́сли не бу́ду от него́ ежедне́вно получа́ть по письму́, неме́дленно верну́сь с куро́рта домо́й.

—И что же он?

— Пи́шет два ра́за в день![a]

The турба́за (тури́стская ба́за) is a sort of hiking headquarters. Some are set up as a base for shorter hikes, and others are the starting points for much longer hikes. The length of stay at the турба́за varies.

The small hotel or boardinghouse **пансиона́т**, also available through a **путёвка**, has rooms and a dining hall or cooking facilities. The **пансиона́т** is attended by entire families and is in a location conducive to rest and recreation, often with equipment (such as rowboats) for rent **оборудование напрока́т**.

Even for those who do not have a **путёвка**, a number of vacation possibilities remain open. One is renting a room or two in a house in the country **да́ча**. The word **да́ча** describes more the use to which a house is put rather than what the house looks like. It can range from a peas-

ant hut **изба́** to a rather large affair, some even tinged with former elegance. It is always in the country, but it is usually not far from a large city. The advantages of peace and quiet, country air, and unhurried living must be balanced against the disadvantages inherent in the lack of "conveniences," including plumbing, stores, and supplies. Dacha living may be thought of as a kind of "covered" camping with the concomitant pleasures and displeasures; it used to be a vacation device of the urban middle classes; now it is where they live in the summer while they tend the vegetable garden.

Summer vacations can involve long trips, especially if grandparents or relations live in the country.

Another vacation possibility is renting a room in a resort area, but finding a room to rent is not easy. Such information is either passed from friend to friend, or reservations are arranged on a previous visit to the area. A local housing bureau **кварти́рное бюро́** at the destination may also be of help. To go on a long trip without a **путёвка** is ехать дикарём: «Мы е́здили дикаря́ми» (дика́рь, *savage*).

For those with cars, camping areas **ке́мпинги** with tents **пала́тки** or cabins **до́мики** and cooking and recreational equipment are available for rent. Many have restaurants.

Children often accompany their parents in the summer, and many also attend a summer camp **ле́тний ла́герь**. A wide network of free camps used to be available, operating on a schedule of three shifts **сме́ны** per summer, each lasting twenty-six days. They still exist, but you have to pay for them. The atmosphere is similar to our Boy and Girl Scout camps (taken together, for they are coeducational).

The new passion
Но́вая страсть

If we are not discussing the new business class who might make money hand over fist, and if we are not discussing the urban very poor, then the new national passion is one's garden plot **садо́вый уча́сток**, usually about 600 square meters **шесть со́ток**, little parcels of land not too far out of town. There one grows vegetable staples and as many fruit trees as room allows. Large cities are empty on summer weekends as residents go to tend their garden, building a summer house when they can. The plots are cheek by jowl and form a "garden community" **садо́дческое това́рищество**. After all, they are a community, because the allotments are normally distributed among workers of the same plant or enterprise.

Short trips
За́городные экску́рсии

This plot, with its dacha (if something has been built), forms a base from which the more usual pastimes of gathering can occur: berries **я́годы** and mushrooms **грибы́** in the summer and fall. (Mushrooms require some warmth and considerable water. One way of describing a light warm rain is "mushroom rain" **грибно́й дождь**.) This recreation is a major theme in Russian[1] life and lore. You will come across berry picking and mushroom hunting as a national tradition in fairy tales (**Ма́ша пошла́ в лес по грибы́**...) and in classic Russian literature; you will also find them a contemporary recreation for Russians high and low. You can properly doubt the "Russianness" of someone unable to distinguish a bolete from a gill mushroom.

In winter the short trip is not as frequent as in the summer, but at this time of year the point of the trip is skiing through winter forests. When Russians say they are going skiing, by the way, they mean cross-country skiing, unless downhill is specified. Skiing is a way to get somewhere, not a slide down a hill.

These short trips for skiing, berry and mushroom collecting, swimming, or simply picnicking must be considered the favorite basic delights of the Russians, perhaps approached only by chess and reading.

---

1. It is not, of course, confined to Russians. In the fall, our woods are combed by Italians, Poles, Chinese, and Japanese—all looking for their favorite mushrooms.

LEISURE TIME
Досу́г

Reading
Чте́ние

Russians are avid readers; what is written and by whom is of far greater concern there than in the United States. The awe and reverence that writers of literature command make them something of national monuments, and they are of much greater import than their corresponding (essentially) academic counterparts in the United States—imagine, if you can, a poetry reading that fills a football stadium.

The shift of the economic and political systems has left writers with fewer walls to rail against, and now androgynous music makers also fill stadiums. But an informal count has three to four out of ten people reading on the subway, with even a few reading on the escalators!

Libraries and their uses are discussed in the *Communications* section.

Theater, concerts, ballet, and circus
Теа́тр, конце́рт, бале́т, цирк

Attendance at any of a number of types of spectacles is also perhaps more commonly desired in Russia, if not more commonly achieved. The problem in almost all cases is paying for tickets. Theatergoers approaching the entrance to a popular event will often be asked, «**Нет ли у вас ли́шних биле́тов?**» (**ли́шний**, *extra*). To go to a movie in the large cities you must usually buy your tickets in advance.

Getting tickets is not a problem for the foreigner with dollars; see your kindly Service Bureau **Бюро́ обслу́живания** in the hotels. Ticket prices are much lower than ours for almost all spectacles, but the demand for them is large enough sometimes to turn a ticket into a prize; tickets to the theater or ballet serve, therefore, as a very nice gift.

Tickets are often bought at a centrally located ticket office **театра́льная ка́сса**. Not all productions are equally popular, however. If the ticket sales for one show are lagging, then the ticket seller **касси́рша** might insist that you buy a ticket to another less popular performance in addition to the one you want; in this case the latter is called «**Биле́т с нагру́зкой**» "a ticket with a load": devious, effective, common, and illegal.

Applause very frequently takes the form of clapping in rhythm, and Russian performers also have the delightful custom of clapping while their audiences are clapping for them. Foreigners should know that whistling at a ballet indicates disapproval (and is, in fact, quite rare), although whistling as approval is common at popular music events.

Tickets to Russian theatrical events look as if they have been torn out of a book because they have been.

Часть програ́ммы

МАРИИНСКИЙ ТЕАТР
и
ТЕАТР КОРОЛЕВСКОЙ ОПЕРЫ КОВЕНТ ГАРДЕН
представляют
в Санкт-Петербурге
совместную постановку
12-й спектакль со дня премьеры (29 декабря 1991 года)

Сергей ПРОКОФЬЕВ

ОГНЕННЫЙ АНГЕЛ

Опера в 5-ти действиях
(Спектакль в 2-х актах с одним антрактом)
Либретто композитора
по одноименному роману Валерия БРЮСОВА

Музыкальный руководитель и дирижер
Валерий ГЕРГИЕВ

Режиссер-постановщик
Дэвид ФРИМАН

Художник-постановщик
Дэвид РОДЖЕР

Главный хормейстер — заслуженный артист России
Валерий БОРИСОВ

Дирижеры-ассистенты —
дипломант Всероссийского конкурса Леонид КОРЧМАР,
лауреат Всесоюзного конкурса Александр ПОЛЯНИЧКО

Художники по свету —
Стив ХИТСОН, Владимир ЛУКАСЕВИЧ

Режиссеры-ассистенты —
Роберт ЧИВАРА, Юрий ЛАПТЕВ, Мария ВОНЧ-ОСМОЛОВСКАЯ

Хормейстеры —
заслуженный артист России Леонид ТЕПЛЯКОВ, Сергей ИНЬКОВ

Ассистент художника
Мотти ДУГЛАС

Ассистент художника по костюмам
Сьюзан ЗИГМУНД

ДЕЙСТВУЮЩИЕ ЛИЦА И ИСПОЛНИТЕЛИ:

Рупрехт, рыцарь	Народный артист России, лауреат Государственной премии СССР Сергей ЛЕЙФЕРКУС
Рената, его возлюбленная	Галина ГОРЧАКОВА
Хозяйка придорожной гостиницы	Заслуженная артистка России Евгения ПЕРЛАСОВА
Гадалка	Лауреат Всесоюзного конкурса Лариса ДЯДЬКОВА
Агриппа Неттесгеймский	Владимир ГАЛУЗИН
Иоганн Фауст, доктор философии и медицины	Заслуженный артист России Сергей АЛЕКСАШКИН
Мефистофель	Народный артист России Константин ПЛУЖНИКОВ
Настоятельница монастыря	Ольга МАРКОВА-МИХАЙЛЕНКО
Инквизитор	Заслуженный артист России Владимир ОГНОВЕНКО
Яков Глок, книготорговец	Заслуженный артист России Евгений БОЙЦОВ
Матвей Виссман, университетский товарищ Рупрехта	Юрий ЛАПТЕВ
Лекарь	Заслуженный артист России Валерий ЛЕБЕДЬ
Работник	Заслуженный артист России Михаил КИТ
Хозяин таверны	Заслуженный артист Бурятии Евгений ФЕДОТОВ
Мальчик	Артем МАЛКОВ
	Заслуженный артист России

Another special feature of any theater (ballet, circus, or the like) is the cloakroom **гардероб**. As a rule, if not actually a law, you must remove your overcoat, hat, and sometimes boots. (Exceptions are movies and sports events.) Upon entering, you will see racks of coats, usually behind a waist-high counter, and on the other side of the counter will be the coat checkers **гардеробщик, гардеробщица**, who will give you a coat check **номерок**. Coats are not hung on a hanger **плечики, вешалка**, but on hooks via a loop **вешалка** at the back of the neck of the coat. If you go, make sure yours is in good working order, or checkers will use a buttonhole. Checking does serve the useful function of limiting applause after a performance; the rush to be first in line to retrieve belongings can seem like a charge of the Light Brigade. Hint: to get ahead in the coat line without waiting, rent a pair of binoculars from the coat checkers before the performance. Those who have done so get their coats first. The checkers will say something like «**С биноклями вперёд**» or «**С биноклями без очереди**». Tips present a problem: officially, one does not tip, but tipping is regularly practiced to recognize a special service. ("I gave him a tip" is «**Я дал ему на чай**» or «**Я дал ему чаевые.**»)

Once you have rid yourself of your outer wear, proceed to your seat. Ushers **билетёры** are stationed at the entrances to concert or theater halls rather than in them. They may be asked which aisle **проход** or stairway **лестница** must be used, but you are expected to find the correct row **ряд** and seat **место** by yourself.

The theaters built in the old-fashioned opera house arrangement have seating areas designated as follows, starting at the bottom:

партер   the orchestra seats, in some theaters called **кресла**

бенуар   the seats around and behind the orchestra seats and on the same level

бельэтаж   the dress circle, the tier immediately above the **бенуар**

ярус   any of the tiers above the **бельэтаж**

галерея, галёрка   the topmost balcony

ложа   a box

A newer concert hall will still have the front, main floor seats labeled **партер**, but the section behind them is called **амфитеатр**, while the balcony above is **балкон**. A program **программа** is usually available for a nominal fee.

As you go from the aisle to your seat, face those who are already seated even if it seems awkward. If you pass them with your derriere in their direction, they will think you rude.

Hobbies
Хобби

Many other amusements can take up smaller packages of time. The word **хобби** has recently crept into the language. Collecting things is a fairly common hobby: «**Он коллекционирует солдатиков разных стран, а моё хобби—коллекционирование марок**» (**марка** stamp). The larger activities, those requiring considerable tools, equipment, or space, must usually be indulged in via a club, and many others are also considered a sport.

Song and dances
Пение и танцы

Both singing and dancing are normal concomitants of any party, especially when any type of celebration is involved. Russians seem to know countless songs, and many are able to sing in harmony. If the songs are accompanied, the instrument will most likely be a guitar **гитара**, not a balalaika **балалайка**. The latter is now restricted mostly to professional folk song troupes or to amateur folk song groups formed in, and associated with, the countryside. Dancing, however, takes many forms, from the traditional Russian folk dances to the relatively sedate ballroom varieties, from the Hebrew Havah Nagilah to versions of what is sometimes called dancing in this country, even including the Charleston **чарльстóн**. The term **рок-н-ро́лл** is part of Russian vocabulary as **джаз** has long been. Contemporary popular musicians are so hip as to out-startle their Western counterparts.

Homemade tapes are frequently made from Western records (blank recording tape makes a good gift), which are valuable on the black market that has grown to meet increasing demand.

The foregoing is city life. In the country, the dances are **пля́ски** and the songs include **частýшки**. The former are familiar to you from the many folk dancing troupes, and the latter are a contemporary art form that flourishes: competitions can be seen on television. The "chastushka" may be thought of as a limerick sung to a tune that everyone knows, with or without the accompaniment of an accordion **гармóнь**. They are four-line stories in rhyme and rhythm, and are often witty, funny, sharp, dirty, and expressive. Due to the nature of the contents, only recently published collections should be considered representative.

Among the more respectable are:

Подари́ла я плато́чек,
И сказа́ла: «Береги́!»
А он, чёртова зара́за,
Вытира́ет сапоги́.

Хорошо бы иметь тýфельки
На лёгоньком ходý,
Чтобы мама не услы́шала,
Когда домой идý.

Эх, ночь темна́,
Я бою́сь одна́.
Дайте провожа́того,
Только нежена́того.[b]

Н. Старшинов, *Я приду на посиделки.*
Молодая гвардия, Москва, 1991.

Russia is also the land of the singing poet **бард**, an art form carried to its ultimate by Vladimir Vysotskiy. The singers compose their own music and their own lyrics **áвторская пéсня** and then sing and play them on their own guitars. The songs can be heard around the campfire and at the dinner table; they express strong feeling and unalloyed views. Many of their songs are so popular that they are regarded as folk songs.

The museum
Музéй

Visiting a museum in Russia is more like paying tribute to a national heritage than attention to self-edification and "culture." (Art was not for art's sake in the USSR.) For one thing, the museum building itself is often a major part of the exhibit, if not the entire exhibit, for this is the way the major old churches, cathedrals, and palaces have generally been preserved or even rebuilt. As merely one example, the Winter Palace **Зи́мний Дворéц** is now an extension of the Hermitage **Эрмита́ж**, one of the most famous art museums in the world. Museum visitors are often asked to don slippers **та́почки** over their shoes to protect that part of the exhibit they will be walking on. Museums often require a small entrance fee from the natives and a large one from foreigners; as usual, you deposit your overcoat and hat at the cloakroom.

The "club"
Клуб

The club is the major official outlet for authorized and organized activities. It can range from an edifice as grand as a Palace of Culture **Дворéц Культýры** down to the **изба́-чита́льня** set aside in a small country house. Often it is neither of these, but a medium-sized building in which the most common facility is an auditorium **зри́тельный зал** and whatever smaller rooms are necessary or possible.

The club is most often attached to one's place of work and the building itself is often called **дом** or **клуб**: «Клуб железнодоро́ж-ников (желе́зная доро́га, railroad), Дом писа́телей, Дом А́рмии». The club can also be maintained by sports or scientific organizations, however.

For most people, and especially those in smaller communities in the countryside, the **клуб** is the center of social life. Dances are held there or movies shown. A rather frequent amusement is the amateur hour **ве́чер худо́жественной самоде́ятельности**, a function not confined to country life. The following are fragments from a passage of the book **Колле́ги** by **В. Аксёнов** that shows what went on in at least one such event (however fictional) that took place in a small club in the country. The hero, **Зеле́нин**, is talking to his bride, **И́нна Зеле́нина.**

В воскресе́нье Зеле́нин потащи́л Инну в клуб.

—А что там за де́йство сего́дня?

—Снача́ла бу́дет ле́кция об уме́нии краси́во одева́ться... Ле́кция интере́сная, чехослова́цкие мо́ды че́рез прое́ктор бу́дем пока́зывать... Мы и реши́ли вести́ войну́ за хоро́ший вкус.

—Кто это «мы»?

—Правле́ние клуба.

По́сле ле́кции начался́ концерт. Зеле́нин то и дело появля́лся на сце́не, уча́ствовал в конфера́нсе, прилепи́в бо́роду, игра́л в ске́тче роль профе́ссора, отца́ беспу́тного сы́на, со́льным но́мером чита́л стихи́...

Зеле́нин чита́л стихи́, Тимофе́й игра́л на бая́не заду́мчивые ва́льсы, Да́ша пе́ла часту́шки, Бори́с с како́й-то то́ненькой де́вочкой, о кото́рой сза́ди сказа́ли, что она́ бето́нщица, пока́зывали акробати́ческий этю́д. Вдруг Зеле́нин подошёл к кра́ю эстра́ды и гро́мко сказа́л:

—Сле́дующий но́мер—ноктю́рн Шопе́на... исполня́ет Инна Зеле́нина.[c]

Besides providing such social or cultural events, the club is also the place where any of a variety of special-interest groups can engage in their special interests. Thus a club might have a billiard or ping-pong table, maintain a supply of skis for lending, house an amateur radio station or reading room, or organize a wide range of sports, cultural, or interest groups. Some professional clubs exclude (unaccompanied) nonmembers.

Playing cards
Ка́рточные и́гры

No card games are of major national interest as bridge is in the United States. But cards are far from unheard of. Children do play equivalents of hearts, rummy, old maid, and the like: **Де́ти игра́ют в просто́го дурака́ (в подкидно́го дурака́, в аку́льку и т.д.)** The favorite gambling game **аза́ртная игра́** is twenty-one **два́дцать одно́;** (also see gambling in the *Money* section). Solitaire **пасья́нс** used to be looked upon as both old-fashioned and bourgeois. (To play solitaire is **раскла́дывать пасья́нс.) Префера́нс,** a relative of whist (and therefore, bridge), is played sometimes. In any case, everybody knows the names for cards.

A deck **коло́да** of cards has four suits **четы́ре ма́сти:** spades **пи́ки** (also **ви́ни**), clubs **тре́фы** (also **кре́сти**), diamonds **бу́бны,** and hearts **че́рви, че́рвы.** And each suit has **дво́йка, тро́йка, четвёрка, пятёрка, шестёрка, семёрка, восьмёрка, девя́тка, деся́тка, вале́т, да́ма, коро́ль,** and **туз.**

пи́ковая тро́йка, тро́йка пик three of spades

черво́нный вале́т, вале́т черве́й jack of hearts

бубно́вая деся́тка, деся́тка бу́бен ten of diamonds

трефо́вый туз, туз треф, туз кресте́й ace of clubs

Read the original version of "The Queen of Spades" (**Пи́ковая да́ма**) by Pushkin. The opera by Tchaikovsky, "The Queen of Spades," based on Pushkin's story, is perhaps even better known to Russians.

Dice
Ко́сти

For gambling purposes dice ко́сти (literally, *bones*) are used; gambling is not a respectable behavior and therefore is now flourishing.

However, the word *bones* ко́сти is also used to denote domino pieces, and the game of dominoes домино́ is both quite respectable and very popular. Backgammon на́рды is associated with the Caucasus.

OFFICIAL SPORTS
При́знанные ви́ды спо́рта

Following is a list of sixty-one sports officially recognized (in 1964) by the Presidium of the Central Council of the Union of Sport Societies and Organizations of the USSR.[2] The list also includes the titles of several other sports included in a listing of international competitions for 1989.

For each sport the various norms of achievement required to reach a certain level of proficiency are established. The following are titles bestowed upon those who fulfill the norms:

Спорти́вные зва́ния-разря́ды: (зва́ние title; **разря́д** rank, grade) **Ма́стер спо́рта СССР междунаро́дного кла́сса (междунаро́дный,** international), **Ма́стер спо́рта СССР**

Спорти́вные разря́ды:
Спортсме́н I (пе́рвого) разря́да
Спортсме́н II разря́да
Спортсме́н III разря́да
Спортсме́н I ю́ношеского разря́да
   (ю́ноша is a youth)
Спортсме́н II ю́ношеского разря́да
Спортсме́н III ю́ношеского разря́да

Not all sports use all the categories (for one reason, not all sports are played outside the former USSR). In chess the title **гроссме́йстер**

2. Еди́ная всесою́зная спорти́вная классифика́ция на 1965-1968 гг., 2е изд. (Москва́: «Физкульту́ра и спорт,» 1967).

replaces **Ма́стер спо́рта междунаро́дного кла́сса.**

Each of the ranks has a medal **значо́к,** which can be, and often is, worn by those who attain the requirements for that rank. This is just one of the ways of encouraging wide participation in these sports.

The list contains a large number of popular amusements (model airplane and car racing, for instance) and also a large number of paramilitary endeavors, including ham radio operation, parachuting, and even fire-fighting exercises. Many of the latter have norms established by the Armed Forces or their auxiliaries. Naturally, the list gives the whole range of official possibilities—popularity is something else again. Those sports that are especially popular in Russia for either participants or spectators are starred. Sports with two, three, five, or many aspects of the general sport under discussion or that are comparable to the collection of sports we call the pentathlon or decathlon are designated by a dagger. The basic minimum equipment for engaging in the sports has been noted in parentheses after each sport, with translations when necessary.

авиамоде́льный спорт model airplane racing

автомоби́льный спорт automobile racing

автомоде́льный спорт model car racing

акроба́тика acrobatics

альпини́зм mountain climbing, mostly practiced in the Caucasus and points south as the Urals are not very high (**рюкза́к,** knapsack; **спа́льный мешо́к,** sleeping bag; **пала́тка,** tent; **верёвка,** rope; **ледору́б,** ice axe; **ска́льный молото́к,** piton hammer; **топо́р,** axe)

бадминто́н badminton (**раке́тка; вола́н,** shuttlecock; **се́тка,** net)

баскетбо́л* basketball (**баскетбо́льный мяч; корзи́на,** basket)

биатло́н[†] biathlon (**лы́жи, ружьё**)

бокс boxing. You probably recognize **нокаути́ровать**, **хук**, **апперко́т**. (**Боксёрские перча́тки** gloves; **ринг**; **гонг**)

борьба́ во́льная, класси́ческая и са́мбо (самозащи́та без ору́жия) freestyle, Greco-Roman, and judolike wrestling (**мат**)

велосипе́дный спорт—го́нки на тре́ке, велоспо́рт bicycle racing on a track (**велосипе́д**)

велосипе́дный спорт—го́нки на шоссе́ и кросс, велого́нка bicycle racing on roads and cross-country

вертолётный спорт helicopter piloting (**вертолёт**)

во́дное по́ло water polo (**бассе́йн**; **мяч**; **воро́та с се́ткой**)

во́дно-лы́жный спорт water skiing (**во́дные лы́жи**; **мотоло́дка**)

во́дно-мото́рный спорт motorboat racing (**мотоло́дка**)

во́дно-прикладны́е ви́ды спо́рта и упражне́ния aspects of sports and exercises that have military applications

волейбо́л* volleyball (**волейбо́льный мяч**; **се́тка**)

гимна́стика спорти́вная* gymnastics (**бру́сья гимнасти́ческие**, parallel bars; **перекла́дина гимнасти́ческая, турни́к**, a horizontal bar; **кана́т**, a rope; **конь**, a side horse or a long horse; **козёл**, a (short) horse; **бату́т**, a trampoline; **ко́льца гимнасти́ческие**, rings; **шве́дская сте́нка** a stall ladder, **бревно́**, beam)

гимна́стика худо́жественная a combination of ballet and gymnastics for women only (**о́бруч**, a hoop; **скака́лка**, jumprope; **мяч**, a ball; **ле́нта**, a long ribbon)

горнолы́жный спорт downhill skiing which includes: **скоростно́й спуск, специа́льный сла́лом, гига́нтский слалом, супергига́нт, комбина́ция** (**лы́жи, лы́жные па́лки**)

городки́ "Gorodki," a Russian game described in some detail later (**бита́**; **городки́**)

гре́бля академи́ческая rowing, as we think of it (**ло́дка** boat; **вёсла** oars)

гре́бля на байда́рках и кано́э) kayak and canoe rowing (**байда́рка**; **кано́э**)

гре́бля на я́лах и наро́дных ло́дках Russian yawl and rowboat rowing (**ял** a *small boat*; **наро́дная ло́дка** Russian rowboat)

дзюдо́ judo

ко́нный спорт horseback riding (**ло́шадь**; **седло́** saddle)

конькобе́жный спорт, скоростно́й бег на конька́х* ice-skate racing (**коньки́**)

лёгкая атле́тика* track and field (**барье́р**, hurdle; **диск**, discus; **копьё**, javelin; **мо́лот**, hammer; **шест**, high jump pole; **ядро́**, shot)

лы́жный спорт—го́нки, совреме́нное зи́мнее двоебо́рье† и многобо́рье† шко́льников* cross-country ski racing (**лы́жи**; **лы́жные па́лки**)

лы́жный спорт—прыжки́ на лы́жах с трампли́на ski jumping (**лы́жи**; **трампли́н** ski jump)

морско́е многобо́рье† events including swimming, shooting, rowing, sailing, and cross-country running

мотобо́л soccer on a motorcycle (**мотоци́кл**; **мяч**)

мотоцикле́тный спорт motorcycle racing

ориенти́рование на ме́стности pathfinding, "orienteering" (**ка́рта**; **ко́мпас**)

парашю́тный спорт parachute jumping (**парашю́т**; **самолёт**)

па́русный и бу́ерный спорт sailing and iceboat sailing (**па́русная ло́дка**, sailboat; **бу́ер**, iceboat)

пла́вание swimming (**пла́вательный бассе́йн**, swimming pool)

планёрный спорт glider piloting (**планёр**)

подво́дный спорт underwater swimming (**ла́сты**, fins; **аквала́нг**)

пожа́рно-прикладно́й спорт aspects of sport applicable to fire-fighting

прыжки́ в во́ду   diving (бассе́йн; трам-пли́н)

радиоспо́рт   ham ràdio operating (переда́тчик transmitter; приёмник receiver)

ре́гби   rugby (мяч)

ручно́й мяч 7:7 (семь-семь)   team hand-ball, played like both soccer and basketball, and especially popular in the Ukraine. The "7" refers to the number of people on the team (**мяч; се́тка**)

самолётный спорт   airplane piloting (**самолёт**)

са́нный спорт   sled racing

совреме́нное пятибо́рье, троебо́рье и мно-гобо́рье[†]:

> **пятибо́рье**   horseback riding, fencing, shooting, swimming, running
>
> **троебо́рье**   shooting, swimming, running

многобо́рье   swimming, shooting, chin-ning oneself, grenade throwing, cross-coun-try bicycle racing, broad jumping, cross-country running

спорти́вное рыболо́вство   sport fishing (**у́дочка**, pole, hook, line, sinker)

сте́ндовая стрельба́   trap and skeet shooting (**винто́вка**, rifle; **мише́ни**, targets)

стрелко́вый спорт   rifle and target shooting (**винто́вка**, rifle; **пистоле́т**; **револьве́р**; **мише́нь**, target)

стрельба́ из лу́ка   archery (**лук**, bow; **стрела́**, arrow; **мише́нь**)

судомоде́льный спорт   model boat racing

те́ннис   tennis (**те́ннисный мяч; раке́тка; се́тка; корт**)

те́ннис насто́льный (пинг-понг)   table ten-nis (**мяч целлуло́идный; раке́тка; насто́льная се́тка; стол**)

тури́зм*   hiking, not tourism here (**рюкза́к**)

Evening Moscow sports

ФУТБОЛ

Участники чемпионата России до-играли вчера 12-й тур. Армейцы, про-демонстрировавшие вялую, безыни-циативную игру в Лужниках, доби-лись лишь ничьей в матче с со-чинской «Жемчужиной». 1:1 — та-ков итог встречи, прямо скажем, не доставившей двум тысячам зрите-лей удовольствие. Голы на счету Файзулина и Гогричиани.

Столичный «Локомотив» при яв-ном преимуществе на своем поле уступил владикавказскому «Спарта-ку». Две контратаки удались гостям, и обе завершились взятием ворот — 2:0.

«Океан» обыграл в родных сте-нах «КамАЗ» — 2:1. Обе команды действовали грубо, за что и удосто-ились множества «желтых карточек».

БОКС

В Финляндии подведены итоги чемпионата мира. Увы, для россий-ских спортсменов они оказались без-

радостными: лишь двенадцатыми чи-слятся они в таблице по числу за-воеванных медалей. В активе наших соотечественников всего четыре бронзовые награды. В то время, как у кубинцев, возглавляющих список, 8 золотых и 3 серебряные.

Возможно в скором времени в мире пройдет несколько представи-тельных турниров по боксу с уча-стием женщин. За это ратует руко-водитель Международной федера-ции Арвар Чоудри. Для слабого по-ла будут разработаны специальные правила, которые сделают поединки менее жесткими.

НАСТОЛЬНЫЙ ТЕННИС

Китайские спортсменки еще раз подтвердили высокий класс, выиграв на чемпионате мира в Швеции зо-лотые медали. В финале они взяли верх над сборной Гонконга — 3:0. Наши девушки обосновались лишь на пятом месте, что, конечно же,

не очень радует поклонников этого вида спорта.

ТЕННИС

Не так хороши дела у первой ра-кетки мира Моники Селеш. Репор-теры поспешили сообщить, что по-сле ножевого ранения спортсменка быстро пошла на поправку, однако последние сведения свидетельствуют о том, что состояние теннисистки более худшее, чем предполагалось. Есть опасения, что лезвие задело нервные окончания на спине, в ре-зультате чего Моника пока не спо-собна «даже тарелку придерживать левой рукой».

Подготовил Ю. ИВАНОВ.

РЕЗУЛЬТАТЫ 18-го ТИРАЖА «СПОРТПРОГНОЗ»
1—2, 2—1, 3—2, 4—Х, 5—2, 6—1, 7—Х, 8—2, 9—1, 10—2, 11—Х, 12—Х, 13—Х.
Результаты 7-й пары определе-ны жеребьевкой.

ИТОГИ 18-го ТИРАЖА «СПОРТЛОТО»
«6 из 45». Допущено 1 782 414 вариантов. 6 номеров — нет. 5 но-меров — 31 — по 29 852 руб. 4 но-мера — 1833 — по 1176 руб.
«5 из 36». Допущено 3 652 547 вариантов. 5 номеров — 12 — по 508 949 руб. 4 номера — 1401 — по 1756 руб. 3 номера — 47 984 — по 76 руб.

...И 18-го ТИРАЖА «СПОРТПРОГНОЗ»
Допущено 856 563 варианта. Уга-дано: 13 исходов — нет. 12 исхо-дов — 1 — 311 596 руб. 11 исхо-дов — 51 — по 34 619 руб.

тяжёлая атлётика weight lifting (**штáнга
с дúсками**, barbell; **гúря**, a weight;
гантéли, dumbbells)

фехтовáние fencing (**рапúра**, foil; **шпáга**,
еpее; **эспадрóн**, saber; **мáска фехто-
вáльная**)

фигýрное катáние на конькáх* figure
skating (**коньки́**)

фри́стайл skating, freestyle

футбóл* soccer (**футбóльный мяч**;
сéтка; **пóле**, field)

**хоккéй, хоккéй с шáйбой, канáдский
хоккéй*** ice hockey (**клю́шка**, hockey
stick; **шáйба**, puck; **коньки́**; **ворóта
хоккéйные**, goals; **катóк**, skating rink)

хоккéй с мячóм, рýсский хоккéй a kind
of ice hockey using a ball, not a puck
клю́шка; мяч; коньки́

шáхматы и шáхматная композúция*
chess and chess problems; so universally
played, it is described in detail separately
(**шáхматная доскá; фигýры; пéшки**)

шáшки и шáшечная композúция checkers
and checkers problems (**шáшечная доскá;
шáшки**)

шорт-трек any of many foot races inside a
stadium, including a relay race **эстафéта**,
which is named for the baton **эстафéта**

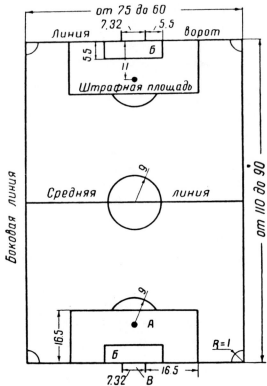

В - *ворота* (goal)
Б - *площадь ворот* (goal area)
А - *точка 11-метрового удара* (penalty spot)
Все размеры в метрах (all measurements are
in meters)

Площáдка для игры́ (пóле)

Soccer
Футбóл

Soccer is more important in Russia than baseball is in the United States. Huge stadiums are
regularly filled with eager fans **болéльщики**:
"I'm rooting for 'Spartak'"—«**Я болéю за
Спартáк**.» Moreover, almost every little boy
learns to play soccer. Soccer teams are at least
as famous as our baseball teams and a correla-
tion to the World Series can be found in play
for the Cup **Кýбок**, not to mention world,
European, and Russian championships—
**пéрвенство мúра, пéрвенство Еврóпы,
пéрвенство, чемпионáт Россúи**—and the
Olympic games **Олимпúйские úгры**. The

most commonly used team names are
Спартáк, Динáмо and **Торпéдо**, all of which
may be from any city or organization, although
the best known are the Moscow teams.
Sometimes the team name gives a clue to who
is represented: **Локомотúв** designates the railroad workers and **Кры́лья Совéтов** the airplane makers. Others simply announce who
they are: **ЦДСА** (**цэдэсá**) **Центрáльный
Дом Совéтской Áрмии, ВВС** (**вэвээ́с**)
Воéнно-воздýшные сúлы. The foreign
(namely, English) origin of the game is reflected
in some of the terminology that seems to leap
from a page of otherwise impenetrable prose: the
game is played in two halves, **пéрвый тайм**
and **вторóй тайм**, both of which last forty-five
minutes with a ten- or fifteen-minute break,

перерыв. The game is played by two teams команды of eleven members, who can have the following positions:

Футбо́льная кома́нда:

оди́н врата́рь (formerly голки́пер)

три полузащи́тника (formerly ха́вбек)

два защи́тника (formerly бек)

пять напада́ющих (formerly фо́рвард)

Actually, terminology using the Russian roots is used now, but the eradication of foreign roots is far from complete: ко́рнер is also углово́й уда́р, and а́ут is мяч вы́шел за боkovу́ю ли́нию; офса́йд and гол remain the same, except that "He made (kicked) a goal" can be either Он заби́л мяч or Он заби́л гол; a penalty kick is одиннадцатиметро́вый штрафно́й уда́р or пена́льти, a referee is судья́ or ре́фери; and помо́щник судьи́ is a linesman.

To express displeasure with a referee, or, for that matter, with the players, a common entreaty is **На мы́ло!** ("Make soap out of him!") To encourage a goal they yell **Ша́йбу!**

Chess
Ша́хматы

The name of the game is not without interest: **шах** in Persian means *king*, as in the Shah of Iran. This root as used in chess is also the origin of our word "check," both the financial and political kind. **Мат** in Arabic means *dead*: **шах + мат** yields *checkmate*—the king is dead.

Chess is the most popular table game in Russia. Apparently, it is played by everyone, and is one of the country's officially recognized "sports." Following is the major Russian terminology, including the Russian (European) notational system. For those to whom chess is a way of life, all rules and regulations appear in **Ша́хматный ко́декс.**

The chessboard **ша́хматная доска́** has black squares **чёрное по́ле** and white squares **бе́лое по́ле.** The European notational system is

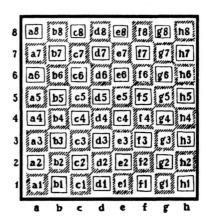

Ша́хматная доска́

used, as shown in the illustration. Notice that the letters are in Latin script. They are pronounced in Russian as **а, бэ, цэ, дэ, е, эф, же, аш.**

For Russians there are two kinds of chessmen, the pawn **пе́шка** and all the remaining pieces **фигу́ры.** There are names, both formal and colloquial, for the individual pieces and standard notation for them in Russian: a turn, move, or play **ход** may be specified further as Black's turn **ход чёрных, ход—чёрными;** or White's turn **ход бе́лых, ход—бе́лыми.** The ways of writing down what happened in a chess game vary.

In discussions and comments on games, the same notations are used, though perhaps the Russians use more of them, as shown here:

~ любо́й ход

! хоро́ший, си́льный ход

!! прекра́сный, блестя́щий ход

? плохо́й ход, оши́бка

?? гру́бая оши́бка

!? ход, приводя́щий к нея́сным осложне́ниям

= ша́нсы сторо́н приме́рно равны́

± положе́ние бе́лых лу́чше

± у бе́лых преиму́щество

∓ положе́ние чёрных лу́чше

∓ у чёрных преиму́щество

Ша́хматная доска́

English	Formal Russian	Conversational Russian	English abbreviation	Russian abbreviation
pawn	пе́шка	пе́шка	P	п[2]
rook or castle	ладья́	ту́ра	R	Л
knight	конь	конь	Kt	К
bishop[1]	слон	офице́р	B	С
queen[3]	ферзь	короле́ва	Q	Ф
king	коро́ль	коро́ль	K	Кр

1. One wonders how "elephant," "officer," and "bishop" all came to signify this piece.
2. In describing the plays the Russian abbreviation for pawn is usually not written at all.
3. Promotion or queening is **пе́шку прово́дят в ферзи́**.

Event		Notation	
English	Russian	English	Russian
check	шах	ch x †	+
checkmate	мат	xx ††	x
capture	взя́тие	x	:
double check	двойно́й шах	dbl ch	++
castling on the king's side	коро́ткая рокиро́вка	0 - 0	0 - 0
castling on the queen's side	дли́нная рокиро́вка	0 - 0 - 0	0 - 0 - 0

The progression of moves can be written in two different ways; the full notation **по́лная нота́ция** is used when games are officially being described, while the short notation **коро́ткая нота́ция** is often used in the commentator's notes.

The game is traditionally divided into three sections: the opening **дебю́т**, which might involve a gambit **гамби́т**; the midgame **ми́ттельшпиль**; and the end game **э́ндшпиль**. In the course of the game, various plays **комбина́ции** might be used. If no win is possible, then the game is a draw **ничья́**: «**Па́ртия зака́нчивается вничью́.**» A draw may result from a stalemate **пат**.

In describing the game, notice that the two sides, **чёрные** and **бе́лые**, are often referred to in the plural: **Бе́лые проведу́т одну́ из свои́х пе́шек в ферзи́ и даду́т мат.**

По́лная нота́ция	Кра́ткая нота́ция
Kg1-f3	Kf3 (1)
e2-e4	e4
Cc1-e3 Kg4:e3	Ce3 K:e3
d7-d8Ф	d8Ф
e2-e4 e7-e5	e4 e5
d2-d4 e5:d4	d4 ed (2)
Фd1:d4 Kb8-c6	Ф:d4 Kc6
Фd4-e3 Kg8-f6	Фe3 Kf6
Фd3-h7 + ?	Фh7 + ?

(1) ука́зывается то́лько по́ле, куда́ ста́вится фигу́ра и́ли пе́шка;
(2) при взя́тии пе́шкой пи́шется вертика́ль, на кото́рой она́ стоя́ла, и вертика́ль, на кото́рую она́ перешла́ в результа́те взя́тия.[d]

"Gorodki"
Городки́

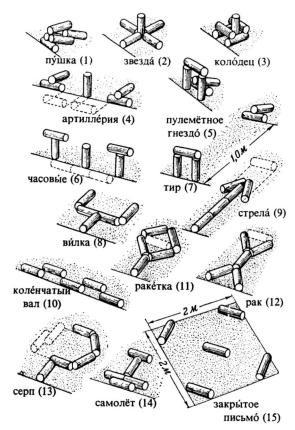

пу́шка (1) звезда́ (2) коло́дец (3)

артилле́рия (4) пулемётное гнездо́ (5)

часовы́е (6) тир (7)

стрела́ (9)

ви́лка (8)

коле́нчатый вал (10) ракётка (11)

рак (12)

серп (13) самолёт (14) закры́тое письмо́ (15)

Городо́шные фигу́ры. Only the first few figures should be thought of as generally familiar to Russians. The remaining ones are shown here to give some idea of the extent of the game.

(1) Cannon
(2) Star
(3) Well
(4) Artillery
(5) Machine gun nest
(6) Sentries
(7) Shooting range
(8) Fork
(9) Arrow
(10) Crankshaft
(11) Racket
(12) Crayfish
(13) Sickle
(14) Airplane
(15) Sealed (closed) letter

This game, like лапта́, which is described in the discussion on children's games, is a traditional Russian game both in origin and development, but unlike лапта́ it has gained the superior status of an officially recognized sport. As a result, the equipment for the game is now regularly manufactured and generally standardized. The game is relatively simple and anyone can play, regardless of age or size. It consists of throwing a long (one meter) stick бита́ at a set of small cylindrical (two by eight inch) sticks городки́, thereby removing the small set of sticks from the target area го́род. Though presumably any even number of people can play, an official team кома́нда consists of five players. (A player at городки́ is a городо́шник.) The target area measures two meters square, in the front line кон of which the городки́ are arranged.

Each team has its own target area го́род, and each player in turn has two throws of the бита́ to try to knock the five small sticks out of place. The first figure must be disarranged at a distance of thirteen meters броски́ с ко́на, but the remaining figures, except the last one, are thrown at from a distance of six and one-half meters броски́ с полуко́на.

The technique of the game involves throwing the бита́ sideways, not end over end, so that it hits the center of the stack of городки́ broadside лобово́й уда́р, (literally, *frontal attack*).

Because городки́ is an officially recognized sport, requirements must be met for official recognition as "Master of Sport" and other titles, which included, for the years 1965–1968, the following:

Ма́стер спо́рта—затра́тить не бо́лее 156 бит на 90 фигу́р и вы́полнить да́нную но́рму в тече́ниие го́да два́жды: оди́н раз на соревнова́ниях не ни́же городско́го масшта́ба при усло́вии уча́стия в них не ме́нее трёх спорти́вных организа́ций разли́чных ве́домств и ДСО; второ́й раз на пе́рвенстве СССР, пе́рвенствах и зона́льных соревнова́ниях сою́зных респу́блик, Москвы́ и Ленингра́да, всесою́зных пе́рвенствах ве́домств, пе́рвенствах центра́льных и республика́нских сове́тов ДСО.

Установи́ть реко́рд СССР в коли́честве затра́ченных бит на 15, 30, 45, 60, 90 фигу́р на ли́чных и́ли кома́ндных соревнова́ниях.

I разря́д—затра́тить не бо́лее 165 бит на 90 фигу́р.

II разря́д—затра́тить не бо́лее 140 бит на 60 фигу́р и́ли 216 бит на 90 фигу́р.

III разря́д—затра́тить не бо́лее 165 бит на 60 фигу́р и́ли 90 бит на 30 фигу́р.

I ю́ношеский разря́д (16-18 лет)—затра́тить не бо́лее 174 бит на 60 фигу́р и́ли 85 бит на 30 фигу́р с расстоя́ния 13 м. II ю́ношеский разря́д (до 16 лет)—затра́тить не бо́лее 105 бит на 30 фигу́р и́ли 50 бит на 15 фигу́р с расстоя́ния 10 м.ᵉ

The score
Счёт

Though both words have other uses, **счёт** is the score and **очко́** is a point. The sports fan uses the following terminology to keep track of who is winning:

Како́й счёт?   What is the score?

Семь пять.   (7:5) Seven to five.

Ско́лько очко́в он набра́л?   How many points did he make?

Три очка́.   Three points.

То́лько одно́.   Only one.

Сухо́й счёт.   No score (made by one side, literally dry score).

Они́ сыгра́ли всуху́ю.   They didn't score one.

Он размочи́л счёт.   He made the first score (for his team); literally, "He got the score wet."

(The last three of the terms above are used in soccer scores.)

сквита́ть счёт, сравня́ть счёт   to even the score

ничья́   a tie

Матч зако́нчился вничью́.   The game ended in a tie.

Two sets of words are commonly used for winning and losing:

вы́игрыш   a win

про́игрыш   a loss

Кто вы́играл?   Who won?

Кто проигра́л?   Who lost?

побе́да   a victory

пораже́ние   a defeat

Кто победи́л?   Who won (beat)?

CHILDREN'S PLAY
Де́тские и́гры

Toys
Игру́шки

There is a universality about toys. Babies start out with a rattle **погрему́шка** and from there graduate to various stuffed toys **мя́гкие игру́шки**, such as a doll **ку́кла** (**быва́ют и говоря́щие, и шага́ющие ку́клы**) or a teddy bear **ми́шка** (**медве́дь** is called **Ми́ша**). Later on, dolls become more sophisticated when they are often made to represent characters in children's fairy tales, both modern and ancient: **До́ктор Айболи́т** (from Chukovsky's rendition of Dr. Doolittle), or **Бурати́но** (Pinocchio), and many others that can be identified only through familiarity with the stories themselves. **Ку́кла** is used for puppets also. Puppetry is a commonly enjoyed recreation that has been elevated by the now world-famous puppet theater of V. Obraztsov: **Дава́й игра́ть в ку́кольный теа́тр** is "Let's play (with) puppets."

The classic figure in a puppet show remains **Петру́шка**. He is represented as a peasant and clown who by wile and wit is able to do in his adversaries, the latter often being those of considerably higher status in society than he.

(**Петру́шка** is also used to denote this puppetry as a whole, and, by association, has become pejorative slang for something or someone who is stupid, funny, awkward, or strange: **Вот кака́я петру́шка получи́лась!**)

Children must also have their blocks **ку́бики**. Blocks are often made specifically to form a traditional shape: the Savior's Tower **Спа́сская ба́шня**, the major entrance to the Kremlin from Red Square, is a favorite subject.

A cross between dolls and blocks is achieved with the ubiquitous **матрёшка**, a gaily painted and stylized figurine of a peasant woman. Many pull apart to reveal a smaller edition of the same figure inside, which also pulls apart, and so on.

Another fairly common Russian toy is a figurine or doll so constructed that it will always right itself. **Ва́нька-вста́нька** is one name for such a device, especially if the figure is a male; **неваля́шка** is another name applied to the female counterpart.

Other common and universal toys are:

мяч a ball (**Малыши́ игра́ют в мя́чик.**)

скака́лка a jump rope (less common, **пры́галка**)

возду́шный шар a balloon

юла́, волчо́к a top

свисту́лька a whistle (**свисте́ть**, *to whistle*)

змей a kite, also a snake

бараба́н a drum

калейдоско́п a kaleidoscope

ката́лка a pull toy

теле́жка a wagon

заводна́я игру́шка a windup toy

о́бруч a Hoola-Hoop (**Мари́на ка́ждое утро кру́тит обруч.**)

лоша́дка, конь на па́лочке a toy horse

Many toys are simply reductions of things children might have to deal with in the future: a small car **маши́нка**, a truck **грузови́к**, a crane **подъёмный кран**, a sailboat **кора́блик**—not to mention tools of all shapes and sizes. Organized play areas, those connected to nurseries or kindergartens, often have larger pieces of equipment. A sandbox **песо́чница** (from **песо́к**, *sand*) requires a small bucket **ведёрко**, a shovel **лопа́тка** or **сово́к**, perhaps a rake **гра́бли**, and a wheelbarrow **та́чка** for making mud pies **пирожки́, кули́чики**, or for building a fort **кре́пость** (not a castle, as in English). These play areas also might have a swing **каче́ли** and a seesaw, also called **каче́ли**. Russian swings, by the way, are likely to hold more than one person. Often, these swings are suspended from two to four long steel bars or pipes instead of the chains or ropes we generally use. (Originally they were long wooden poles suspended from the limb of a tree.) Another piece of playground equipment resembles a rocking chair, except that two seats face each other, both mounted on the same rockers. This is a **кача́лка**. The very well-equipped play area might even have a small rendition of a merry-goround **карусе́ль**. And in the winter a common sight is an "ice mountain" for sliding **ледяна́я гора́, ледяна́я доро́жка**.

Some children's toys also go under the heading of sports equipment. Summer entertainment can include skateboards **ске́йты**. Winter weekends are often spent skiing **ката́ться на лы́жах**, so that skis **лы́жи** are very commonly owned or easily accessible. Because Russians ski cross-country, their skis are narrower than ours. For children, the bindings are greatly simplified and are strapped onto regular boots; adults often use ski boots, reserving safety bindings for mountain skiing, a far less popular kind of skiing. Winter also requires skates **коньки́** and a myriad of sleds **са́нки** (**сала́зки**, a somewhat old-fashioned term); the latter are used both for grandmother's convenience (hauling grandchildren) and children's fun.

Toys and play equipment are also often homemade. For instance, stilts **ходу́ли** (**Он хо́дит на ходу́лях**), a kite **змей** (**Де́ти запуска́ли зме́я**), a whistle **свисту́лька**, a scooter самока́т, and the inevitable slingshot рога́тка are often of the homemade variety.

Russian toy collections tend to be relatively small, not from lack of parental regard or even money but because storage space is limited.

Games outside
Игры на у́лице

Winter and snow bring all sorts of possibilities for play. One can throw snowballs **игра́ть в снежки́**, build and use a fort **стро́ить сне́жную кре́пость**, slide down a hill on a sled **са́нки**, and build a snowman **лепи́ть сне́жную ба́бу**, (literally, *snowwoman*). Children almost always learn to ice skate **ката́ться на конька́х** and also to ski **ката́ться на лы́жах**.

In the summer, children, especially girls, play hopscotch **игра́ть в кла́ссы** according to the same principles that ours do. Boys play a game with pocketknives **игра́ть в но́жички** that requires them to gain a specified territory (**дава́й зе́млю дели́ть**), throwing a knife into the ground a certain way. Marbles are nonexistent.

Ку́ча-мала́ falls somewhat short of being a game. The setting requires a group of children playing outdoors (or sometimes indoors). For one reason or another, one of them falls. Suddenly one or several others yell «**Ку́ча-мала́!**» whereupon all the children race to pile on top of the one who fell. In some places the point is to avoid being the last one to join the pile, thereby becoming the fool **дура́к**.

Горе́лки is a traditional game still often played—in summer camps, for instance. The children line up in pairs with one child left over, who is "it," **горе́лка** in this case. The first pair, holding hands, starts running while the rest of the children chant

Гори́-гори́ я́сно,
Что́бы не пога́сло.
Глянь на не́бо,
Пти́чки летя́т,

Колоко́льчики звеня́т!
Раз, два, не воро́нь!
Беги́, как ого́нь![f]

The moment the chanting is finished, the **горе́лка** races to catch the pair that had started running; the one who is caught becomes the **горе́лка** for the next turn, and the other two are now partners.

Russians have many of the group chasing-games we do. A parallel to playing cowboys and Indians is **игра́ть в «казаки́-разбо́йники»**. Russian cops and robbers—**сы́щики и во́ры**—often consists of more than two groups of children chasing one another. Roles in the game are assigned by drawing lots **выбира́ют по жре́бию**. Depending on the number of children, the "characters" might include two detectives **два сы́щика**, two thieves **два во́ра**, one judge **оди́н судья́**, and two police officers **дво́е полице́йских**, for instance.

Playing hide-and-seek **игра́ть в пря́тки** is as common as it is here and uses the same ground rules: the person who is "it" refrains from "peeking" and counts up to any agreed upon number (**раз, два, три...**) while the other children run and hide; when done, the "it" yells, «**Я иду́ иска́ть!**» "Here I come, ready or not!" In the variation **па́лочки-стука́лочки**, a stick is left at home base and those who have hidden must return to base and bang with the stick before they are found (**Я тебя́ ви́жу**).

Playing tag is **игра́ть в догоня́лки** or **игра́ть в са́лки**. The person who is "it" is the **са́лка** (**са́ло**, fat or lard), who must run and tag another who then becomes the **са́лка**: «**Са́лка, са́лка, дай колба́ски!**» "Nyah, nyah, can't catch me!" Another form of tag is **пятна́шки**, in which **пятна́шка**, the one who is "it," tags another player either with a thrown ball or tagging the player by hand.

Perhaps leapfrog **игра́ть в чехарду́** falls short of being a game, yet children play it. Jump rope is **пры́гать через верёвочку**, and **рези́ночка** is a constantly rising level that must be jumped over. In **ручейки** the children line up in twos and hold hands so as to form a tunnel; the child who is "it" runs through the tunnel, chooses a partner on the way while the now partnerless partner becomes the new "it". And races are run everywhere:

На старт!   On your mark!

Внима́ние!   Get set!

Марш!   Go!

Раз, два, три. . . **Марш!**   One, two, three. . . Go!

Lapta
Лапта́

Totally unfamiliar to us, however, is a traditional Russian game called **лапта́**. The formal requirements of the game are minimal and vary according to what is locally available. A ball about the size of a tennis ball or perhaps smaller and a bat **лапта́**, which may be a stick, are required. The official bat is no more than 1.2 meters long with a diameter of no more than 5 centimeters. The playing field should be about seventy to eighty meters long and thirty to forty meters wide. (A scrub version, **кругова́я лапта́**, requires less space and is therefore popular in cities.) The players divide into two teams of five to fifteen players each. One team **бью́щая кома́нда, го́род** is at bat, and the other **водя́щая кома́нда, по́ле** is on defense in the field. Someone from the defense pitches **подаёт мяч** to an opponent at bat, who tries to hit the ball as hard and as far as possible. If a defensive player catches a fly ball, then the teams change places **го́род про́дан, горожа́не иду́т в по́ле**; otherwise the batter runs to the other end of the field (a line previously established among the players) and then back again. The runner must avoid being hit with the ball or being tagged by someone with the ball—either results in an "out" **го́род взят** and the teams change places. A run earns one point **одно́ очко́**. (You are much more likely to read about **лапта́** than to see it. Though Russians officially

are supposed to take pride in the game, contemporary children prefer to play soccer if they possibly can.)

Games inside
Игры в до́ме

The games **карава́й** and **ко́шки-мы́шки** are played by smaller children. For **карава́й** (literally, a large round loaf of bread) one child is chosen to be in the center of a circle formed by the other children holding hands. The game begins when the children circle to the left and sing (about the child in the center, here called **Алёша**), «**Как на Алёшины имени́ны, испекли́ мы карава́й**». Then the children in the circle raise their (joined) hands high and say, «**Вот тако́й вышины́**», lower their hands to the floor and sing, «**Вот тако́й нижины́**», spread out as far as possible while singing, «**Вот тако́й ширины́**», then rush to the center and sing, «**Вот тако́й ужины́**». Next they begin circling again, this time chanting, «**Карава́й, карава́й, кого́ лю́бишь, выбира́й**», until the child in the center has chosen the next one to stand in the center. The cat-and-mouse game, **игра́ в ко́шки-мы́шки**, requires one child as the mouse and one as the cat. The other children join hands in a circle and try to keep the cat from catching the mouse by letting the mouse in and out of the circle freely while making it difficult for the cat.

Blindman's buff is a common childhood game: **Де́ти игра́ют в жму́рки** (**жму́риться**, to squint or close the eyes). The principle is the same as always: the child who is "it" is blindfolded and spun around while the other children ask questions: «**Где стои́шь?—На мосту́**»; «**Что продаёшь?—Квас**». Then they issue the challenge: «**Ищи́ три го́да нас!**» Rules vary; sometimes the "blindman" has only to catch one of the other children, but sometimes must also identify the prey. In a variation the blindman is called the cat **кот,** and the other children give themselves bird names, **га́лка, сини́ца,** or **воробе́й,** for instance. The **кот** must identify the bird, who then becomes the blindman.

Horses and riders лошади и всадники is a more boisterous game, perhaps springing up while the teacher is absent from class. The children form pairs of "horses" carrying their riders piggyback; the point is to force the other riders to fall off or lose balance without doing so oneself.

Another game, играть в фантики, involves a carefully folded candy wrapper фантик. The object is to make one's фантик go farther when it is thrown in a certain way.

Russian children also play a version of "telephone," Играют в глухой телефон, испорченный телефон. The children line up, a leader thinks of a word, whispers it to the first one in line, who whispers it to the next, and so on. The last person says the word out loud. If the word has changed, a search ensues for the person who first misunderstood the word, who then becomes "it."

A relative of bingo is лото, requiring a leader to call numbers and players with cards to be filled, five in a row, or the like. It is frequently encountered as a teaching toy, with numbers replaced, for instance, by pictures of objects that the children must identify before they can fill out their cards.

You can also play tic-tac-toe in Russia: Дети играют в крестики-нолики. (X— крестик, O—нолик.)

Who is "it"?
Чья очередь?

Rather inconveniently, the Russians have no one word like "it" to denote the person playing the main role in children's games. Russian equivalents vary according to the game itself. Thus, if they are playing горелки then горелка is "it"; if салки, then салка; if пятнашки, then пятнашка; if жмурки, then кот; and so on. Another practice, though more formal, is to refer to "it" as водящий. A common solution to the problem is simply to ask "Whose turn is it?" «Чья очередь?» or «Кому водить?» or «Кто водит?»

Determining the first person to be "it" is commonly done in either of two ways, by using a counting rhyme считалка or by drawing lots выбирать по жребию, по жеребьёвке.

The counting rhymes referred to here (for many are used) are those used as we use "eenie, meenie ..."; moreover, parallel to the lack of a single "it" word, no generally recognized, equivalent rhyme exists for choosing who is to be "it." The following are examples of считалки.

Эники, беники,
Ели вареники,
Эники, беники
Клёц.

Аты, баты—Шли солдаты,
Аты, баты—На базар.
Аты, баты—Что купили?
Аты, баты—Самовар.

На златом крыльце сидели
Царь, царевич, король, королевич,
Сапожник, портной,
Кто ты будешь такой.[g]

Экета, пэкета, цукота мэ,
Абель, фабель, доминэ,
Ики, пики, грамматики,
Он-зос-пёс.

В этой маленькой корзинке
Есть помада и духи,
Ленты, кружево, ботинки,
Всё, что нужно для души.[h]

TRADITIONAL AMUSEMENTS
Традиционные развлечения

The amusements and delights of the former upper classes are not be considered here because they were often an attempt to do what was thought to be done in the "sophisticated"

West, and most of the forms are therefore familiar to us. For the Russian peasants, however, things were different. All of life was a do-it-yourself affair, including recreation. Unable to read, they told stories instead; singing and dancing were very popular; and toys were made from available materials.

Many of the country joys were connected with the holidays or with the various turning points of life—births, weddings, and funerals. Singing and dancing were major accompaniments to these celebrations, and their songs and dances **обря́довые пе́сни и хорово́ды** are the oldest; the songs we think of as Russian folk songs are of more recent origin. Traditional dancing most often took the form of a **хорово́д**, which was essentially any kind of group dance in a circle. (Even children holding hands and skipping around a Christmas tree is therefore a **хорово́д**.)

Children played a game called **ба́бки**, which required a set of cattle knucklebones. One piece, **свинча́тка**, was made heavier by stuffing it with lead **свине́ц**; the other pieces, **ба́бка, ба́бки**, were lined up in a row, and the object was to use the heavy piece to knock the others out of place. You could keep the ones you knocked out. (The closest American equivalent is surely marbles.)

Children were not the only ones who played on swings **каче́ли** suspended by two long poles hung from a tree. Traditionally, the **каче́ли** did not make their appearance until **ма́сленица**.

A kind of Russian baseball **лапта́**, though very traditional, is discussed under contemporary games children play because it is still popular. Another very Russian game is **городки́**, now an officially recognized sport and therefore described in that section.

The sewing bee?
Посиде́лки (*pl. only*)

The Russian stove **ру́сская печь** was a creditable solution to the problem of winter cold. The **посиде́лки** was the Russian peasant answer to long winter evenings. The (usually unmarried) girls of the village would congregate at a house **изба́**, often one rented for the purpose. They brought some handwork to do, spinning, sewing, and so on. The girls were joined at these affairs by the young men of the village. In some places it was customary for the men to supply the necessary food or libation, and in others the men were guests. The evening was spent mostly in singing, sometimes in dancing, and frequently in playing games; often singing games or contests were the vehicle for merriment. You might also assume that these evenings were enlivened by some flirtation.

The institution **посиде́лки** in its original form may still exist. We can be sure however that the word itself has not disappeared. It now refers to any group of people who might sit outside their building on a warm summer night both to talk and perhaps escape the heat.

TRANSLATIONS

a. "I told my husband that I would immediately come home from the resort if I didn't get a letter from him every day."

"What did he do?"

"He writes twice a day!"

b. I gave [him] a scarf
And told him, "Take care of it."
But the dirty son of a gun
Wipes his boots with it.

It would be nice to have some slippers,
With a light step,
So that mother wouldn't hear,
When I come home.

Oh, the night is dark,
I'm afraid [to go] alone.
Give me an escort,
But not a married one.

c. On Sunday, Zelenin took Inna to the club.

"What's going on there today?"

"First there's a lecture on how to be well dressed. The lecture is interesting, we're going to show slides of Czechoslovakian fashions. . . . We decided to wage a war for good taste."

"Who's 'we'? "

"The directors of the club."

A concert began after the lecture. Zelenin appeared on the stage from time to time. Sometimes he did some announcing; with a glued-on beard he played, in a skit, the role of a professor who was the father of a dissolute son; he also gave a poetry reading. . . .

Zelenin recited verses, Timofey played slow waltzes on the accordion, Dasha sang "chastushki" [sung doggerel, competitively composed], and Boris did an acrobatic etude with a thin little girl whom people in the back described as a cement worker. Then all of a sudden, Zelenin stepped to the edge of the stage and said loudly, "The next number will be a Chopin nocturne played by Inna Zelenin."

d.   (1) [We] only show the square that the piece is moved to. (2) If a pawn makes a capture, [we] note the vertical on which it stood and then the vertical that it went to as a result of the capture.

e.   Master of Sport: Use no more than 156 sticks on 90 "gorodki" figures and accomplish this in one year—once at contests not lower than the municipal level that are participated in by no less than three sports organizations of various departments and the Voluntary Sports Society; and the second time at USSR championship games, championships and regional competitions of the republics, Moscow and Leningrad, all-union championships of departments, and championships of the central and republic councils of the Voluntary Sports Society.

OR

Set a new USSR record in the number of sticks used on 15, 30, 45, 60 or 90 "gorodki" figures in single or team competitions.

First Class: Use no more than 165 sticks on 90 figures.

Second Class: Use no more than 140 sticks on 60 figures or 216 sticks on 90 figures.

Third Class: Use no more than 165 sticks on 60 figures or 90 sticks on 30 figures.

First Class Youth (16-18 years): Use no more than 175 sticks on 60 figures or 85 sticks on 30 figures from a distance of 13 meters.

Second Youth Class (up to 16 years): Use no more than 105 sticks on 30 figures or 50 sticks on 15 figures from a distance of 10 meters.

f.   Burn, burn brightly,
     So that it won't go out.
     Look at the sky.
     The birds are flying,
     The bells are ringing!
     One, two—don't gape [dawdle],
     Run like fire!

g.   On a golden porch there sat:
     A tsar, his son; a king, his son;
     A shoemaker; a dressmaker.
     Answer, which are you?

h.   This little basket
     Has cosmetics and perfume,
     Ribbons, lace, and shoes—
     Everything your heart desires
     [your soul requires].

Appendices

Suggestions for Those in Business

Abbreviations

The Table of Ranks

Reading Chemical Formulas

The Morse Code

The Braille Alphabet

An Index of Common Russian Birds

*Some References from the Beginning
to the End of Russian*

Maps

Appendices

SUGGESTIONS FOR THOSE IN BUSINESS

У стра́ха глаза́ велики́.
Fear has big eyes.

Russians are proud, and, as a people, seem to have an inferiority complex. These traits combine to make them touchy. They do not see theirs as a third world country, and they will not respond favorably if they think you do. Treat them as equals who merely do things differently. If gifts are in order, do not send what you no longer want or can no longer use. Acknowledge the progress or possibilities rather than the details of need. Curb any tendency to show off electronic equipment, or anything else—do not try to "wow" them. The desire to impress may work in our society, but not elsewhere. As a corollary, esteem is worth more to a Russian than practicality: thus, Russians tend to buy first class when second class would have achieved the same goal at a lower price.

Bad press and some bad deals have made many Russians suspect that U.S. businesspeople are interested only in ripping them off, or at least taking advantage of them. If your business is honest you can expect to spend some time and effort in dispelling the notion. But do not gush, and don't act friendly unless you intend, seriously, to be a friend.

Some mechanics

Don't deal with anybody you can't verify as legitimate. For example, to street people you are nothing but hard currency with legs.

Dress so as not to overwhelm with formality or insult with informality: a very dark suit with a very white shirt is formal, yet jeans are too informal. All women in business should wear skirts, as should older women.

If you are significantly younger than your Russian counterparts, either address them as Mr. or Ms. (in English) or learn and use first names and patronymics together. The latter will get you more points. (See Chapter 3.)

Expect that telephone messages might not be transmitted. Telephone manners are often abrupt and loud, partly due to murky connections.

Meals are not used for business. Business talk might include bottled water or tea and cookies. (Coffee is very expensive. Avoid asking for it.)

Handshakes are, desirably, firm and more frequent than is our custom.

Those interested in business Russian might be surprised at how much they already know. The following were obtained from one issue of the business weekly **Коммерса́нт**:

интерва́л	администра́ция	фи́рма	ликвида́ция
до́ллар	фа́ктор	пессими́ст	сертифика́т
курс	анало́г	контра́кт	регио́н
и́ндекс	персона́льный	су́мма	ко́пия
креди́т	индивидуа́льный	материализа́ция	профессиона́льный
банк	президе́нт	альтернати́вная	эколо́гия
облига́ция	ста́тус	компа́ния	эксперти́за
ва́учер	регистра́ция	рекомендова́ть	информи́ровать
тенде́нция	ма́ссовая	ли́ния	капита́л
фина́нсовый	семина́р	комфорта́бельный	квалификацио́нный
пози́ция	рефо́рма	такси́	пункт
сезо́н	ве́ктор	рэ́кет	контро́ль
пери́од	пре́сса	бандити́зм	бла́нки
спекуля́ция	ло́гика	мане́ра	инста́нция
прогно́з	аргумента́ция	фонд	арбитра́ж
экспортёр	аналити́ческий	ми́нимум	приватизи́ровать
и́мпорт	пробле́ма	синдика́т	конве́рсия
ситуа́ция	апоге́й	ассортиме́нт	коммерциализа́ция
центр	бюдже́т	опера́ция	монополи́ст
автомоби́ль	дефици́т	стати́стика	аукцио́н
ланч	результа́т	бри́финг	ме́неджер
систе́ма	и́ндекс	а́либи	опцио́н
экспе́рт	тренд	о́фис	оптима́льные
диску́ссия	лими́т	аппара́т	страте́гия
спи́кер	инциде́нт	корру́пция	инвестицио́нный
пре́ссинг	конце́рн	ки́ллер	пул
сканда́л	автома́т	тради́ция	портфе́ль
консервати́вный	пассажи́р	аспе́кт	диверсифика́ция
докуме́нты	тексти́ль	адапти́ровать	консервати́вный
но́рма	прести́ж	клие́нт	деномини́ровать
инстру́кция	экспа́нсия	консульта́ция	конце́пция
се́рвис	специали́ст	специали́ст	хеджи́рование
проду́кция	кри́зис	ситуа́ция	риск
пате́нт	кво́та	скорректи́ровать	транза́кция
реко́рдный	оффшо́рный	пате́нт	синдика́т
ата́ка	партнёр	регламента́ция	номина́льный
резе́рв	дистрибу́тор	максима́льная	традицио́нно
интерве́нция	перифери́я	су́мма	алгори́тм
мобилизова́ть	калькуля́тор	индекса́ция	инвести́ция
комме́рческий	се́рверы	атави́зм	эмпири́ческий

банк | конфигура́ция | конве́нция | ма́ркет-ме́йкер
коми́ссия | компоне́нты | процеду́ры | ма́ркетинг
рефинанси́рование | аудиокассе́та | ко́ды | дивиде́ндный
инве́стор | видеокассе́та | факс | потенциа́л
чек | фло́ппи диски | ла́зерный | инду́стрия
банки́р | колле́га | ксе́рокс | реинвести́рование
официа́льный | ли́дер | лице́нзия | коэффицие́нт
корреспонде́нтский | при́нтер | инфраструкту́ра | ликви́дность
компью́терный | приз | бро́керский | проце́нт
би́знес | лотере́я | экспеди́торский | стабилиза́ция
ди́лер | моде́ль | проце́сс | кри́зисный
популя́рный | техноло́гия | специа́льный | негати́вно
фи́рма | гара́нтия | функциони́рование | а́удит

ABBREVIATIONS

These are a few common abbreviations used in writing:

в. **век** century

В **восто́к** east

вкл. **включе́ние, включи́тельно, включа́я** inclusion or including

вм. **вме́сто** instead of

в т.ч. **в том числе́** including

гл. обр. **гла́вным о́бразом** mostly, mainly

Ж **Же́нская (убо́рная)** women's room

ж.д. **желе́зная доро́га** railroad

З **за́пад** west

зав. **заве́дующий** manager or chief

зам. **замести́тель** substitute or deputy

и др. **и други́е** and others

им. **и́мени** named after

и пр. **и про́чее** and so on

и т. д. **и так да́лее** and so forth

и т.п. **и тому́ подо́бное** and so on, et cetera

Л. **Ленингра́д** Leningrad

М. **метро́** subway (station)

Москва́ Moscow

Мужска́я (убо́рная) men's room

м.б. **мо́жет быть** perhaps

м.г. **мину́вшего го́да** last year

напр. **наприме́р** for example

н.э. **на́шей э́ры** Anno Domini (до н.э. Before Christ)

ок. **о́коло** near or about

пом. **помо́щник** assistant

приб. **приблизи́тельно** approximately

ред. **реда́кция, реда́ктор** editorial office or editor

С **се́вер** north

с.г. **сего́ го́да** this year

сл. обр. **сле́дующим о́бразом** as follows

см. **смотри́** see or refer to

СПб **Санкт-Петербу́рг** St. Petersburg

ср. **сравни́** compare

стр. **страни́ца** page

т.е. **то есть** that is

т.к. **так как** since

т. наз. **так называ́емый** so-called

т. обр. **таки́м о́бразом** in this way, thus

тов. **това́рищ** comrade

ул. **у́лица** street

Ю **юг** south

Initials of institutions

The following list introduces some common abbreviations, those one might encounter on the street or in newspapers that occur without further explanation. Also check the index for abbreviations that are explained in the text.

АО Акционе́рное о́бщество   joint stock company

АП Аре́ндное предприя́тие   an enterprise using rented space

АЭС Атомная электроста́нция   nuclear electric power plant

ВВС Вое́нно-возду́шные си́лы   Air Force

ВС Верхо́вный сове́т   Supreme Soviet

ГЭС Гидроэлектроста́нция   hydroelectric power plant

ГОСТ Госуда́рственный станда́рт   State standard (of quality or production)

ГУВД Гла́вное управле́ние вну́тренних дел   Main Internal Affairs Directorate (of MVD)

ИТА Информацио́нное телегра́фное аге́нтство   news agency

ИТАР Информационное телеграфное аге́нтство России   news agency of Russia

КП Контро́льный пункт   check point or checking point, **Коммунисти́ческая па́ртия**   Communist Party

МБ Мирово́й банк   World Bank

МВД Министерство вну́тренних дел   Ministry of Internal Affairs

МВС Министерство вне́шних сноше́ний,   Ministry of External Relations (**быв. Министерство внешних экономи́ческих связей,** *former* Ministry of External Economic Relations)

МВФ Междунаро́дный валю́тный фонд   International Monetary Fund

МИД Министерство иностра́нных дел   Ministry of Foreign Affairs

МП, мп Ма́лое предприя́тие   small business (with specific size limits and tax advantages)

МПС Министерство путей сообще́нийя   Ministry of Rail Communication

НЛО Неопо́знанный лета́ющий объе́кт   unidentified flying object

НПО Нау́чно-произво́дственное объедине́ние   Scientific Production Association

ОВИР Отде́л виз и регистра́ций   Department for Visas and Registration

ОМОН Отря́д мили́ции осо́бого назначе́ния   police special forces (SWAT team)

ООН Организа́ция объединённых на́ций   United Nations

ПО Произво́дственное объедине́ние   Production Association

РАН Росси́йская Акаде́мия нау́к   Russian Academy of Sciences

РАФ Ри́жская автомоби́льная фа́брика   Riga   Automobile Factory

РКП Росси́йская коммунисти́ческая па́ртия   Russian Communist Party

РТР Росси́йская теле-радио (компа́ния)   Russian Television and Radio

РФ Росси́йская Федера́ция   Russian Federation

СНГ Сою́з незави́симых госуда́рств   Confederation of Independent States (CIS)

СП Совме́стное предприя́тие   joint venture

США Соединённые шта́ты Аме́рики   United States of America

ТОО Това́рищество с ограни́ченной отве́тственностью   association with limited responsibility (i.e., incorporated)

ТЭС Теплоэлектроста́нция   steam power plant

УК Уголо́вный ко́декс   criminal code

ЦБР Центра́льный банк России   Central Bank of Russia

ЦСКА Центра́льный спорти́вный клуб а́рмии   Central Sports Club of the Army

ЦУМ Центральный универса́льный магази́н   Central Department Store

УВИР Управле́ние виз и регистра́ций Directorate for Visas and Registration of Foreign Citizens

The state is not the only one to resort to abbreviations. The following are not part of formal speech, but you will hear them: **ЧП (чэ-пэ), чрезвыча́йное происше́ствие** Emergency! (**У меня чп!** I need some help!) **ОБС (о-бэ-эс), одна́ ба́ба сказа́ла** is "some dame said" and means "I'm not at all sure of the information." **БСК (бэска́) бред си́вой кобы́лы (в лу́нную ночь)** is "the raving of a gray mare (on a moonlit night)" and means "Balderdash!"

THE TABLE OF RANKS
Та́бель о ра́нгах

You will hear many times, if you have not already, of Peter the Great's Table of Ranks. He established it in 1722 as a way to force both allegiance and work from the upper classes: one could not occupy a high position without a rank, each of which had obligations. One had to work to obtain these ranks, but the highest of them were hereditary. There were three sets of corresponding ranks, one civilian and one each for the army and navy. By the use of differing salutations **обраще́ния** for the various ranks, one's status was made clear on or before first acquaintance. *Your highness* is recognizably higher than *your lordship*, and so on. These ranks are applied to most of the educated people so that their use or reference come up all the time in literature. You can use this table to gauge the status of, let's say, someone addressed as **Ваше высокоблагоро́дие**. Only the civilian and army ranks have been included here.

Кла́ссы	Чи́ны гражда́нские	Чины вое́нные	Обраще́ния
1	Ка́нцлер	Генера́л-фельдма́ршал	Ва́ше высокопревосхо-ди́тельство
2	Действи́тельный сове́тник	Генера́л-от-кавале́рии Генерал-от-инфанте́рии Генерал-от-артилле́рии	"
3	Та́йный сове́тник	Генерал-лейтена́нт	Ваше превосходи́тельство
4	Действи́тельный , ста́тский советник Обер-прокуро́р, Герольдме́йстер	Генерал-майо́р	"
5	Ста́тский сове́тник		Ва́ше высокоро́дие
6	Колле́жский сове́тник, Вое́нный сове́тник	Полко́вник	Ваше высокоблагоро́дие
7	Надво́рный сове́тник	Подполко́вник	"
8	Колле́жский ассе́сор	Капита́н, Ро́тмистр	"
9	Титуля́рный советник	Штабс-капита́н, Штабс-ротмистр	Ваше благоро́дие
10	Коллежский секрета́рь	Пору́чик	"

Кла́ссы	Чи́ны гражда́нские	Чины вое́нные	Обраще́ния
11	Корабе́льный секрета́рь		Ваше благоро́дие
12	Губе́рнский секрета́рь	Подпору́чик, Корне́т	"
13	Провинциа́льный секрета́рь, Сена́тский регистра́тор, Кабине́тский регистра́тор	Пра́порщик	"
14	Колле́жский регистра́тор		"

READING CHEMICAL FORMULAS
Чте́ние хими́ческих фо́рмул

For most elements, the full name of the element is used when chemical formulas are read. Elements 103 through 109 have no universally accepted name; they want to say 103 is rutherfordium but it's lawrencium; they say 104 is kurchatovium and we say it's rutherfordium. A few Berkeley physicists have been unwilling to accept international judgments on who has the right to name what. (See "IUPAC/IUPAP Committee Mediates Custody Battle over Heavy Elements," *Physics Today,* November 1993, p. 20 .) The pronunciation of the chemical abbreviation is not used except in the following cases:

Element	Symbol	Pronunciation
водоро́д	H	аш
кислоро́д	O	о
фо́сфор	P	пэ
се́ра	S	эс
углеро́д	C	цэ
азо́т	N	эн
вана́дий	V	вэ

For some other elements, the Latin rather than the Russian name for the element is frequently used in reading:

фе́ррум	желе́зо
плю́мбум	свине́ц
ку́прум	медь
сили́ций	кре́мний
ци́нкум	цинк
арсе́никум	мышья́к
арге́нтум	серебро́
ста́ннум	о́лово
сти́биум	сурьма́
а́урум	зо́лото
хидра́ргирум	ртуть

Examples
Приме́ры

$2H_2 + O_2 \rightarrow 2H_2O$ два аш два плюс о два даёт два аш два о.

$H_2SO_4 + Ba(NO_3)_2 \rightarrow BaSO_4 + 2HNO_3$ аш два эс о четы́ре плюс ба́рий эн о три два́жды даёт ба́рий эс о четы́ре плюс два аш эн о три

$2HCl + Mg \rightarrow MgCl_2 + H_2$ два аш хлор плюс ма́гний даёт ма́гний хлор два плюс аш два

H_2O аш два о (вода́)

CO_2 цэ о два (углеки́слый газ)

$2HCl$ два аш хлор (соля́ная кислота́)

$Cu(OH)_2$ ку́прум о аш два́жды (гидра́т о́киси ме́ди)

$Fe(OH)_3$ фе́ррум о аш три́жды (гидра́т о́киси желе́за)

H_2SO_4 аш два эс о четы́ре (се́рная кислота́)

$Ba(NO_3)_2$ ба́рий эн о три два́жды (азо́тно-ки́слый ба́рий)

Периоди́ческая Систе́ма Хими́ческих Элеме́нтов Д. И. Менделе́ева

Г Р У П П Ы   Э Л Е М Е Н Т О В

Пе-рио-ды	Ря-ды	1	II	III	IV	V	VI	VII	VIII	0
1	I	**1 H** Водоро́д 1,00797								**2 He** Ге́лий 4,0026
2	II	**3 Li** Ли́тий 6,939	**4 Be** Бери́ллий 9,0122	**5 B** Бор 10,811	**6 C** Углеро́д 12,01115	**7 N** Азо́т 14,0067	**8 O** Кислоро́д 15,9994	**9 F** Фтор 18,9984		**10 Ne** Нео́н 20,183
3	III	**11 Na** На́трий 22,9898	**12 Mg** Ма́гний 24,312	**13 Al** Алюми́ний 26,9815	**14 Si** Кре́мний 28,086	**15 P** Фо́сфор 30,9738	**16 S** Се́ра 32,064	**17 Cl** Хлор 35,453		**18 Ar** Арго́н 39,948
4	IV	**19 K** Ка́лий 39,102	**20 Ca** Ка́льций 40,08	**21 Sc** Ска́ндий 44,956	**22 Ti** Тита́н 47,90	**23 V** Вана́дий 50,942	**24 Cr** Хром 51,996	**25 Mn** Ма́рганец 54,9381	**26 Fe** Желе́зо 55,847 **27 Co** Ко́бальт 58,9332 **28 Ni** Ни́кель 58,71	
4	V	**29 Cu** Медь 63,54	**30 Zn** Цинк 65,37	**31 Ga** Га́ллий 69,72	**32 Ge** Герма́ний 72,59	**33 As** Мышья́к 74,9216	**34 Se** Селе́н 78,96	**35 Br** Бром 79,909		**36 Kr** Крипто́н 83,80
5	VI	**37 Rb** Руби́дий 85,47	**38 Sr** Стро́нций 87,62	**39 Y** И́ттрий 88,905	**40 Zr** Цирко́ний 91,22	**41 Nb** Нио́бий 92,906	**42 Mo** Молибде́н 95,94	**43 Tc** Техне́ций [97]	**44 Ru** Руте́ний 101,07 **45 Rh** Ро́дий 102,905 **46 Pd** Палла́дий 106,4	
5	VII	**47 Ag** Серебро́ 107,870	**48 Cd** Ка́дмий 112,40	**49 In** И́ндий 114,82	**50 Sn** О́лово 118,69	**51 Sb** Сурьма́ 121,75	**52 Te** Теллу́р 127,60	**53 I** Иод 126,9044		**54 Xe** Ксено́н 131,30
6	VIII	**55 Cs** Це́зий 132,905	**56 Ba** Ба́рий 137,34	**57 La*** Ланта́н 138,91	**72 Hf** Га́фний 178,49	**73 Ta** Танта́л 180,948	**74 W** Вольфра́м 183,85	**75 Re** Ре́ний 186,2	**76 Os** О́смий 190,2 **77 Ir** Ири́дий 192,2 **78 Pt** Пла́тина 195,09	
6	IX	**79 Au** Зо́лото 196,967	**80 Hg** Ртуть 200,59	**81 Tl** Та́ллий 204,37	**82 Pb** Свине́ц 207,19	**83 Bi** Ви́смут 208,980	**84 Po** Полоний [210]	**85 At** Астат [210]		**86 Rn** Радо́н [222]
7	X	**87 Fr** Фра́нций [223]	**88 Ra** Ра́дий [226]	**89 Ac**** Акти́ний [227]	**104 Ku** Курча́товий [264]					

* ЛАНТАНИ́ДЫ

58 Ce Це́рий 140,12	59 Pr Празео-ди́м 140,907	60 Nd Неоди́м 144,24	61 Pm Проме́тий [145]	62 Sm Сама́рий 150,35	63 Eu Евро́пий 151,96	64 Gd Гадоли́-ний 157,25	65 Tb Те́рбий 158,924	66 Dy Диспро́зий 162,50	67 Ho Го́льмий 164,930	68 Er Э́рбий 167,26	69 Tm Ту́лий 168,934	70 Yb Итте́рбий 173,04	71 Lu Люте́ций 174,97

** АКТИНИ́ДЫ

90 Th То́рий 232,038	91 Pa Протак-ти́ний [231]	92 U Ура́н 238,03	93 Np Непту́ний [237]	94 Pu Плуто́ний [242]	95 Am Амери́ций [243]	96 Cm Кюри́й [247]	97 Bk Берке́лий [247]	98 Cf Калифо́р-ний [249]	99 Es Эйнштей-ний [254]	100 Fm Фе́рмий [253]	101 Md Менделе́е-вий [256]	102 No Нобе́лий [255]	103 Lw Лауре́нси [257]

Element 85 can be **Аста́т** or **Астати́н**. Element 97 can be **Берке́лий** or **Бе́рклий**. Element 103 can be **Лауре́нсий** or **Лоуре́нсий**.

THE MORSE CODE
Азбука Морзе

Знаки Морзе	Буквы		Цифры	Знаки препинания и сигналы телеграфной службы
	Рус-ские	Ла-тинск.		
·—	А	Aa	·———— 1	(,) запятая ·—·—·—
—···	Б	Bb	··——— 2	(.) точка ·· ·· ··
·——	В	Ww	···—— 3	(;) точка с запятой —·—·—
——·	Г	Gg	····— 4	с запятой —·—·—
—··	Д	Dd	····· 5	(:) двоеточие —····
·	Е	Ee	—···· 6	(?) вопросительный
···—	Ж	Vv	——··· 7	знак ··——··
——··	З	Zz	———·· 8	(№) —·—··—
··	И	Ii	————· 9	(+) он же конец
—·——	Й	Jj	————— 0	депеши ·—·—·
—·—	К	Kk		(„") кавычки ·—··—·
·—··	Л	Ll		() скобки —·—·—·
——	М	Mm		(!) восклицательный
—·	Н	Nn		знак ——··——
———	О	Oo		(—) минус —····—
·——·	П	Pp		Знак подчерки-
·—·	Р	Rr		вания ··——·—
···	С	Ss		(/) дробная
—	Т	Tt		черта —··—·
··—	У	Uu		Знак раздели ———···
··—·	Ф	Ff		Перебой (исправление
····	Х	Hh		ошибки) ········
—·—·	Ц	Cc		Знак. отделяющий целое
———·	Ч	Oo		число от дроби ·—·—·
————	Ш	Ch		Знак предложения
——·—	Щ	Qq		(начинаю
—·——	Ы	Yy		передавать) —·—·—
··——	Ю	Üü		Знак согласия
·—·—	Я	Ää		на приём ·—·
·——·—	Ь,Ъ	Xx		Начало
··—··	Э	Éé		действия ·—·—·

Radio amateurs (hams) exchange QSL cards, have a magazine **Радио** comparable to *QST*, and must learn the Morse code, too.

THE BRAILLE ALPHABET
Азбука Брайля

The following is the Braille alphabet both in Latin and Cyrillic letters:

аа	бb	цс	дd	ее	фf	гg	хh	иi	жj
кk	лl	мm	нn	оо	пр	чq	рr	сs	тt
уu	—v	щх	—y	зz	й—	ъ—	ь—	ь—	
е—			ш—	я—		о—	э—	вw	

AN INDEX OF COMMON RUSSIAN BIRDS
Указатель русских названий птиц

This list of common Russian birds is arranged in alphabetical order. Starred entries are discussed in Chapter 14. Information is presented in the following order:

1. When specified, the most common species follows the entry in parentheses: **синица (большая)**.
2. When a common word is used for the female, it follows without parentheses: **тетерев, тетёрка**.
3. The wing **крыло** length in millimeters is given merely to indicate relative size. The **синица (кр. 66-82 мм)** is a tiny bird, while the golden eagle (**беркут; кр. 595-725 мм**) is correspondingly huge.
4. The common name for the bird family follows if it seems necessary to the description.
5. The scientific genus and species name is given in italics.
6. The English translation is given if it appears in either of two books by Alexander Wetmore: *Song and Garden Birds of North America* (Washington, D.C.: National Geographic Society, 1964) and *Water, Prey and Game Birds of North America* (Washington, D.C.: National Geographic Society, 1965).
7. Description or comments follow this.
8. Finally, and in parentheses, the name for the bird is given as found in **Русско-английский словарь, ред. А.И. Смирницкий (Москва: ОГИЗ, 1949)**.

The major Russian source for names and descriptions has been **Б.К. Штегман и А.И. Иванов, Краткий определитель птиц СССР (Москва: Наука, 1964)**.

аист (белый), кр. 554–680 мм, *Ciconia ciconia*. Russian tradition holds that babies come from cabbage patches, but the Western notion of storks is beginning to take hold. The bird is common only in the southwest regions of Russia (stork).

бека́с кр. 122–36 мм, *Capella gallinago,* common snipe.

бе́ркут кр. 595–725 мм, *Aquila chrysaetus,* golden eagle.

буреве́стник кр. 217–53 мм, *Puffinus puffinus,* manx shearwater. Perhaps because of Gorky's «Пе́сня о буреве́стнике,» this bird has become the herald of the Revolution (storm petrel).

ва́льдшнеп кр. 177–98 мм, snipe family, *Scolopax rusticola.* This bird is commonly hunted (snipe, woodcock).

***воробе́й кр.** 69–83 мм, *Passer domesticus,* house or English sparrow.

во́рон кр. 385–530 мм, *Corvus corax,* common raven. The bird is completely black and very large.

воро́на (чёрная), кр. 310–75 мм, *Corvus corone corone.* It is more common in the south (crow).

***воро́на (се́рая), кр.** 292–340 мм, *Corvus corone cornix.* It is black with large gray patches; it is more common in central Russia (crow).

га́га (обыкнове́нная), кр. 258–328 мм, *Somateria mollissima,* common eider.

гага́ра (поля́рная), кр. 315–413 мм, *Gavia immer,* common loon.

га́лка кр. 209–48 мм, crow family, *Corvus monedula.* The bird is mixed in color, with black head, wings, and back, and the rest in various shades of gray. It flies in great flocks and is famous for making an awful noise (mainly because of its numbers): **Они́ ору́т (и́ли шумя́т), как га́лки** (jackdaw, daw).

***глуха́рь кр.** 268–390 мм, grouse family, *Tetrao urogallus.* It is iridescent black and very large (capercaillie, wood grouse).

го́голь кр. 187–231 мм, duck family, *Bucephala clangula,* common goldeneye: **ходи́ть го́голем—ходи́ть чи́нно и ва́жно.**

го́лубь (си́зый), кр. 184–240 мм, *Columba livia,* domestic pigeon. A children's name for a pigeon is **гу́ля. Гоня́ть голубе́й** is a game played by boys with pet pigeons. The pigeons are released and later signaled to return in the hope that other pigeons will join those originally released. The game was so popular that the expression **гоня́ть голубе́й** has become synonymous with wasting time (pigeon, dove).

***грач кр.** 287–350 мм, crow family, *Corvus frugilegus.* It is all black (rook).

гусь (се́рый), кр. 398–495 мм, *Anser anser.* According to popular theory, if the goose is white, it is domesticated; if it is gray, it is wild (goose).

дрозд (пе́вчий, пёстрый, чёрный), thrush family, *Turdidae.* Three or four species are very common, with the same build as our robin, *Turdus migratorius,* though the Russian varieties are usually colored a speckled brown and white (ouzel, thrush, blackbird).

дя́тел (большо́й пёстрый), кр. 119–50 мм, woodpecker family, *Dendrocopos major.* This is only one of many other woodpeckers easily recognized as such by us (woodpecker).

***жа́воронок (полево́й), кр.** 99–124 мм, *Alauda arvensis,* skylark. Also refers to a "morning" person (as opposed to an owl) (lark).

***жура́вль (се́рый), кр.** 520–620 мм, *Grus grus.* The bird is colored gray with some brown (crane).

заря́нка or **мали́новка кр.** 68–75 мм, *Erithacus rubecula.* This is the English robin redbreast. It is small with a brown back, red bib, and white underparts (robin).

зя́блик кр. 85–94 мм, finch family, *Fringilla coelebs.* The bird is distinctive by its coloration: gray head, orangish underparts, brown back (finch).

и́волга кр. 132–63 мм, oriole family, *Oriolus oriolus.* A long bird, almost all yellow except for brown wings, it is usually found near the water and is famous for its morning song. American meadowlarks, blackbirds, and orioles are in the family Icteridae, not Oriolidae, and live only in the Western Hemisphere (oriole).

коростéль or **дергáч, кр.** 124–44 мм, coot family, *Crex crex*. This is a wading bird with brown back, white throat, gray breast, and white side stripes (landrail).

кóршун (чёрный), кр. 428–545 мм, eagle and hawk family, *Milvus korschun*. Infamous for its inroads on the chicken population, this large bird is also a symbol of fast attack: **Что ты на меня налетáешь, как кóршун?** (kite, black kite).

крéчет кр. 355–425 мм, falcon family, *Falco gyrfalco*. This very large falcon has largely white underparts and brown or black top parts (gerfalcon).

кряква кр. 235–95 мм, *Anas platyrhynchos*, mallard. The bird is so common that the phrase **дикая ýтка** probably refers to it. It is well known for its greediness: **Онá прожóрлива, как ýтка.**

*кукýшка кр. 180–246 мм, cuckoo family, *Cuculus canorus*. The bird is mostly gray with some black and white stripes (cuckoo).

кулúк This term can apply to any of a large family of small, usually long-billed and long-legged wading or shore birds (the order Charadriiformes). If it seems obvious that the use of the word indicates a specific kind of bird, then the closest equivalent is probably the sandpiper (snipe).

куропáтка бéлая, *Lagopus lagopus,* willow ptarmigan.

куропáтка сéрая, кр. 139–58 мм, pheasant family, *Perdix perdix*, gray partridge (partridge).

лáсточка (деревéнская), кр. 117–30 мм, *Hirundo rustica*, barn swallow. There are, of course, many other swallows, but this is the one people see most often (swallow).

лéбедь (-кликýн), кр. 560–635 мм, *Cygnus cygnus*. Even swans accompany spring (swan).

Люди всегдá с волнéнием ждут лебедéй. И когдá они прилетáют, когдá на рассвéте поднимáются с разлúвов со своúм велúким весéнним клúчем «клинк-кланк!»—люди провожáют их глазáми, кровь начинáет звенéть у них в сéрдце, и онú знáют тогдá, что пришлá веснá.

Юрий Казакóв «Арктýр—гóнчий пёс».

лунь (полевóй), кр. 335–98 мм, *Circus cyaneus,* marsh hawk. A silver gray hawk, it flies low over fields looking for its prey: **Он как лунь седóй.**

овсянка кр. 80–99 мм, finch family, *Emberiza citrinella*. The bird is yellow with red brown spots (yellow bunting).

орёл (степнóй), кр. 520–638 мм, *Aquila rapax*. There, as here, the eagle is a symbol of power: **«орёл–царь-птúца.»**

перепéл, перепёлка, кр. 97–111 мм, pheasant family, *Coturnix coturnix* (quail).

рябчик кр. 150–64 мм, grouse family, *Tetrastes bonasia*. This quail is small, and mostly brown with white spots and a small black bib. It is traditionally considered to be the most elegant food (hazel hen, hazel grouse).

> Ешь ананáсы
> рябчиков жуй
> День твой послéдний
> прихóдит, буржýй.

Маякóвский

свиристéль кр. 107–19 мм, waxwing family, *Bombycilia garrulus*, Bohemian waxwing. This very pretty bird looks like a gray cedar waxwing and is famous for eating berries, especially those of the mountain ash.

*синúца (большáя), кр. 62–82 мм, titmouse family, *Parus major*. The bird has a mostly green and blue back with white and yellow underparts (tomtit, titmouse).

*скворе́ц кр. 118–35 мм, *Sturnus vulgaris*, starling.

*снеги́рь кр. 77–97 мм, finch family, *Pyrrhula pyrrhula*. This finch has orange-red underparts, a mostly gray back, black head, and wing stripe (bullfinch).

сова́ Owls are best known not for their wisdom but for their presumed (daytime) blindness and/or absent-mindedness: **Он сиди́т, как сова́ на забо́ре**—"He doesn't pay attention to anything." Their name also typifies a "night" person. Some common Russian owls:
уша́стая сова́ кр. 273–300 мм, *Asio otus*
со́вка кр. 138–60 мм, *Otus scops*
сыч (домо́вый) кр. 149–80 мм, *Athene noctua*
бе́лая сова́ кр. 395–470 мм, *Nyctea scandiaca*.

со́кол (-сапса́н), кр. 289–390 мм, *Falco peregrinus*, duck hawk or peregrine falcon. The falcon is a symbol of courage, speed, and daring (falcon).

*солове́й (восто́чный), кр. 82–92 мм, *Luscinia luscinia*. The bird is colored in gradations of gray (nightingale).

*соро́ка кр. 175–230 мм, *Pica pica*, black-billed magpie.

стриж (чёрный), кр. 165–79 мм, swift family, *Apus apus*. Resembling a large dark swallow, this bird is famous for its very fancy flying; its wings seem to alternate in flight (martlet, sand martin, stone martin, swift).

*те́терев, тетёрка, кр. 220–63 мм, grouse family, *Lyrurus tetrix*. The bird is colored black with red marking on top of its eyes and some white on its wings (heath cock, black cock, black grouse).

трясогу́зка кр. 73–99 мм, wagtail family, genus *Motacilla*. The two kinds are common, both gray on top, but one has yellow underparts, the other white. These rather long thin birds do wag their tails as they walk, whence their name in Russian as well as English (wagtail).

фи́лин кр. 420–550 мм, *Bubo bubo*. This bird is a very large and fierce hunter. It is in the same genus as our great horned owl (eagle owl).

ца́пля (се́рая), кр. 420–75 мм, *Ardea cinerea*. The common heron is smaller than the crane **жура́вль**; in flight the heron bends its neck back, while the crane will stretch out full length. The heron also has a few long feathers extending from the back of its head, while the crane has a smooth head.

ча́йка (обыкнове́нная), кр. 288–340 мм, *Larus ridibundus*, black-headed gull. Depending on the circumstances, the gull is either a scavenging nuisance or a rather romantic accompaniment to a sea voyage. Chekhov's Seagull probably had something to do with the latter (seagull, mewgull).

чиж кр. 65–75 мм, finch family, *Carduelis spinus*. Mostly yellow with brown and black accents, this small bird has been immortalized in a song known to every Russian child. There are many versions, both more and less vulgar, but the one given below seems to be standard (siskin).

> **Чи́жик-пы́жик,**
> **Где ты был?**
> **На Фонта́нке**
> **Во́дку пил.**
>
> **Вы́пил рю́мку,**
> **Вы́пил две.**
> **Зашуме́ло**
> **В голове́.**

щего́л кп. 70–88 мм, finch family, *Carduelis carduelis*, European goldfinch. This is a very brightly colored bird (white, black, red, yellow), often caught and kept in a cage as a pet.

я́стреб (-тетеревя́тник) кр. 299–395 мм, *Accipiter gentilis*, goshawk. This hawk was named after its prey, as was the smaller **перепеля́тник** (hawk).

фаза́н кр. 190–240 мм, *Phasianus colchicus*, ringnecked pheasant.

SOME REFERENCES FROM THE BEGINNING TO THE END OF RUSSIAN[1]

To start, one requires at least a dictionary and here we recommend the *Oxford Russian-English Dictionary* by Marcus Wheeler (Stephen Marder compiled *A Supplementary Russian-English Dictionary,* Slavica Publishers, Columbus, Ohio, 1992, which includes the words omitted in the preceding), and then next perhaps the *Oxford English-Russian Dictionary* edited by P. S. Falla; both were combined into one volume and updated in 1993. Then after a little while you might want some access to the rich world of Russian idioms in *A Book of Russian Idioms Illustrated* by M. I. Dubrovin, Russian Language Publishers, Moscow, 1980. The list is far from exhaustive but by this stage in your development you'll need the pictures used for illustration. (Leaf through the book once per annum beginning in second year.)

Intermediate students who want only a reading knowledge of Russian in a technical subject should know that their Russian task is easiest: after an initial flurry of looking up everything, they suddenly can read. Recommendations of references should come from those in the technical field.

Intermediate and advanced students should branch out. Those who enjoy pulling words apart might start out with Gribble's *Russian Root List with a Sketch of Russian Word Formation,* 2nd ed., Slavica, 1982. Thereafter, almost any etymological dictionary can be useful in the meanwhile but the deadly serious in graduate school will want **Макс Фа́смер, Этимологи́ческий словарь русского языка́, М. Прогресс, 1964–1973**. These four volumes are the place to find the origin of a Russian word; this Russian translation is even a bit more reliable than the original, although it removed the dirty words.

Intermediate and advanced students should get in the habit of spending an hour or so every two weeks just browsing at the library. For example, examine the nine-volume goods dictionary **Товарный словарь, ред. И. А. Пугачев, Москва 1956-1961**, any Russian medical encyclopedia, any Russian newspaper, or even Brokgaus and Efron cited below. For browsing around the house you could get a dictionary of locutions that Russians themselves have difficulty with in the thorough *Словарь трудностей русского языка* by Rozental, or you may actually need Denisov's *Учебный словарь сочетаемости* if you must do your own composing in Russian. The latter will remind you that translation is not a matter of just plugging in words.

Use an all-Russian dictionary early in your career. The one to acquire if at all possible is *Толко́вый словарь русского языка́,* редактор **Д. Н. Ушако́в, Государственное издательство иностранных и национальных словарей, Москва** 1935–1940. This four-volume dictionary consistently answers all but the naughty questions. And those who still can't find their words should go to the library and look them up in the seventeen-volume *Словарь современного русского литературного языка,* **Академия Наук СССР, Москва-Ленинград,** 1950–1965.

Those who have regular interactions with the contemporary press will require access to, or possession of, a dictionary of abbreviations. The following is enormous and has everything conceivably needed by the English-speaking inquirer, even including pronunciation. What it doesn't have is yesterday's date. Henry Zalucky, *Compressed Russian: Russian-English dictionary of acronyms, semiacronyms and other abbreviations used in contemporary standard Russian, with their pronunciation and explicit correlates in Russian, and equivalents in English* (Amsterdam; New York: Elsevier 1991).

Advanced students require a dictionary or other reference of Russian proverbs and sayings. (Avoid at all costs mere listings thereof.) The *Russian-English Dictionary of Proverbs*

---

1. I am very grateful indeed for helpful suggestions from Professors Wayles Browne of Cornell and Barry Scherr of Dartmouth.

and Sayings: 500 entries by Kuzmin and Shadrin, Russky Yazyk, Moscow, 1989, has a good selection and explanations but you will eventually find 500 to be too *few*. It has a very useful index.

For the insatiably curious:

Энциклопедический словарь, издатели **Ф.А. Брокгауз и И.А.Ефрон, в 41 томе С.-Петербург, 1890–1904.** This is a reference you may want access to rather than own because the forty-one volumes actually consist of two books *each*—and then don't forget the four supplements that carry matters up to 1907. Refer to it even if you have nothing to look up. If your Russian is missing, the pictures are good.

For graduate linguists:

В. В. Виногра́дов, *Русский язы́к: грамма́ти́ческое учение о слове.* **М.-Л., Учпедгиз, 1947 и позже.** An extensive summary of what earlier grammarians have said about the classes and categories of Russian words.

А. А. Зализняк, *Грамматический словарь русского языка.* **М. 1977.** This is a reverse dictionary—that is, arranged by final letters of the words, so that it is valuable for studying suffixes and word-formation. Each word is supplied with a code showing how to decline or conjugate it, and its accent pattern.

For historico-linguistic folklorists:

Владимир Даль, *Толко́вый словарь живого великорусскаго языка, 4-е изд.* 1912. This edition with many corrections and updates from the efforts of B. de Courtenay is the desirable one, reprinted within living memory by JUH. This is a four thick-volume production that is the happiest of hunting grounds for those interested in words and folklore.

For those who like the finer things in life:

Handbook of Russian Literature, ed. Victor Terras, New Haven, Yale University Press, 1985. This book is a necessity if you can think of any question to do with Russian literature. Consider it, rather, an encyclopedia of Russian literature.

Victor Terras, *History of Russian Literature*, New Haven, Yale University Press, 1992. This is the biggest, best, and most current history of literature. One wonders what the field would do without Professor Terras.

D. S. Mirskiy, *A History of Russian Literature,* New York, Knopf, 1949. Prince Mirskiy was so able at transmitting his joy in his subject that not to read Russian literature is impossible. He makes the reading rather a personal affair: he is your close but very knowledgable friend who can barely wait to describe yet another delight and who asks you to disagree with him.

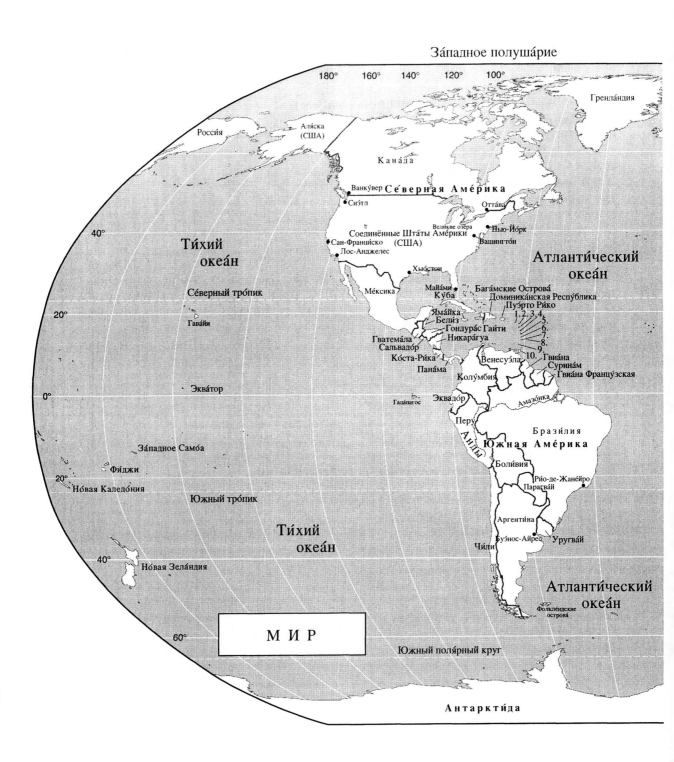

180°   160°   140°   120°   100°

Гренландия

Россия

Аля́ска
(США)

Кана́да

Ванку́вер **Се́верная Аме́рика**

Сиэтл

Оттава

Великие озёра

Нью-Йо́рк

Соединённые Шта́ты Аме́рики
(США)

Вашингто́н

Сан-Франци́ско

Лос-Анджелес

**Ти́хий
океа́н**

**Атланти́ческий
океа́н**

40°

Се́верный тро́пик

Хью́стон

Ме́ксика

Майа́ми

Куба

Бага́мские Острова́

Домини́канская Респу́блика

Пуэ́рто Ри́ко

20°

Гава́йи

Яма́йка

Бели́з

Гондура́с Гаи́ти

Никара́гуа

1. 2. 3. 4.
5.
6.
7.
8.
9.
10.

Гвиа́на

Гватема́ла
Сальвадо́р

Сурина́м

Ко́ста-Ри́ка

Гвиа́на Францу́зская

Пана́ма

Венесуэ́ла

Галапа́гос

Эква́дор

Колу́мбия

0°

Экватор

Амазо́нка

Перу́

Бразилия

Анды

Ю́жная Аме́рика

За́падное Само́а

Боли́вия

Ри́о-де-Жане́йро

Фи́джи

Парагва́й

20°

Но́вая Каледо́ния

Южный тро́пик

Аргенти́на

**Ти́хий
океа́н**

Чи́ли

Бу́энос-Айрес

Уругва́й

Но́вая Зела́ндия

40°

**Атланти́ческий
океа́н**

Фолкле́ндские
острова́

М И Р

60°

Южный поля́рный круг

Антаркти́да

The Former Soviet Union

During perestroika and especially after August 1991, local governments within Russia were allowed to rename their regions. These new names often reflected the linguistic inclinations of the native inhabitants, and could be required by law only within the borders of the area under discussion. As a result there are two or more differing names a Russian might use: one is the new (locally) official name that *must* be used within the region and *especially in writing in or to the region*, and the other is the unofficial traditional Russian name for the place, which will be the common one you hear. Sometimes Russians wishing to demonstrate sympathy with local state governments will use the new official title even though it sounds strange. The central Russian government has taken no stand. The Russian Language Institute of the Academy of Sciences is of the opinion that the standard literary language is not subject to local laws.

OFFICIALLY	UNOFFICIALLY	OFFICIALLY	UNOFFICIALLY
Респу́блика Башкортоста́н	Башки́рия	Респу́блика Се́верная Осе́тия	Се́верная Осе́тия
Респу́блика Буря́тия	Буря́тия	Респу́блика Татарста́н	Тата́рия
Респу́блика Дагеста́н	Дагеста́н	Респу́блика Тува́	Тува́
Респу́блика Кабарди́но-Балка́рия	Кабарда́, Балка́рия	Респу́блика Удму́ртия	Удму́ртия
Респу́блика Каре́лия	Каре́лия	Чече́нская Республика (Ичке́рия)	Чечня́
Респу́блика Ко́ми	Ко́ми	Респу́блика Ингуше́тия	Ингуше́тия
Респу́блика Мари Эл, (или Марийская республика)	—	Респу́блика Чува́шия	Чува́шия
Респу́блика Мордо́вия	Мордо́вия	Респу́блика Саха́—Яку́тия	Яку́тия

The names of autonomous oblasts and national okrugs remain as they were, except perhaps that officials in Khabarovsk Kray are reducing the Yevreyskaya autonomous oblast to a rayon. All names cited here reflect current, not future practice.

The names of countries that were formerly part of the Soviet Union have similar dual titles: Belarus' **Белару́сь,** Moldova **Молдо́ва,** and Kyrgyzstan **Кыргызста́н** if you live within those states, but Belorussiya, Moldaviya, and Kirgiziya if you are using Russian elsewhere. The map shows the Russian names.

Names of capital cities also have variations: not **Та́ллин,** but **Та́ллинн;** not **Алма́-Ата́,** but **Алматы́** (recently Kazakh leaders decided to move the capital to **Акмалу́,** the former **Акмо́линск/Целингра́д);** not **Ашхаба́д,** but **Ашгаба́т.**

Be very careful to note that use of place names can be a political statement: thus, Georgians wishing to return to their native village in Abkhaziya must pronounce the name of the capital as "Sukhum" (rather than the Georgian "Sukhumi"), or they are not allowed back. A rose might smell as sweet with another name, but government is no rose. Nor is lack of one.

August 1994

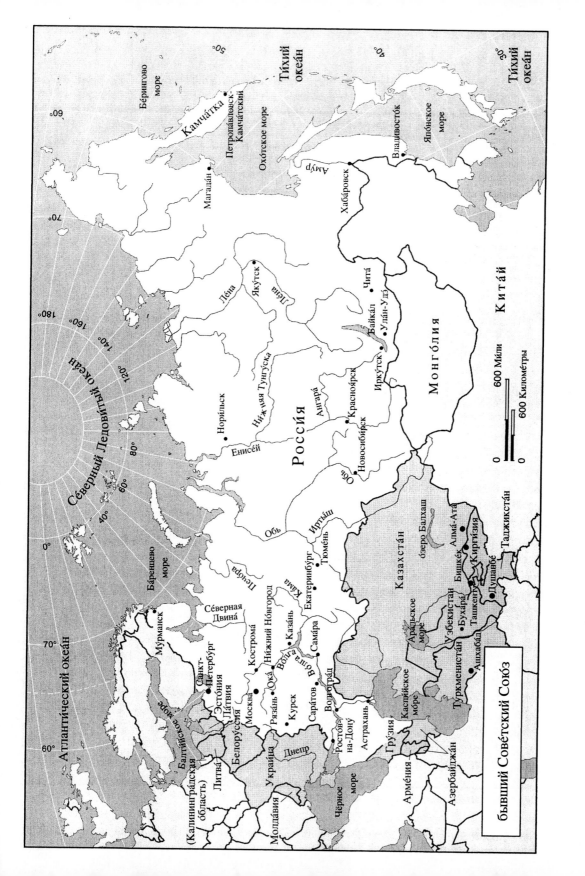

Европейская часть России

Печора

Архангельск

Северная Двина

Российская Федерация, Россия

Финляндия

Онежское озеро

Ладожское озеро

Хельсинки

Санкт-Петербург

Нева

Балтийское море

Таллинн

Эстония

Псков

Новгород

Вологда

Киров

Пермь

Кострома

Тверь

Ярославль

Рига

Латвия

Москва

Нижний Новгород

Волга

Казань

Кама

Литва

Вильнюс

Смоленск

Ока

(Калининградская область)

Минск

Белоруссия

Тула

Рязань

Самара

Орёл

Варшава

Польша

Курск

Саратов

Волга

Словакия

Львов

Украина

Киев

Харьков

Днепр

Дон

Волгоград

Казахстан

Будапешт

Молдавия

Кишинёв

Венгрия

Ростов-на-Дону

Астрахань

Румыния

Одесса

Азовское море

Крым

Бухарест

Севастополь

Ялта

Каспийское море

Босния

Сербия

Сараево

София

Болгария

Чёрное море

Сочи

Кавказские горы

Ставрополь

Македония

Грузия

Албания

Тбилиси

Греция

Армения

Баку

Афины

Ереван

Турция

Азербайджан

Средиземное море

20°

0   250 Мили

0   250 Километры

LIST OF ILLUSTRATION SOURCES

p. 9 Henri Cartier-Bresson / MAGNUM Photos

p. 20 *Московские новости*, 9 мая 1993

p. 27 (top) Sylvain Grandadam / Photo Researchers, Inc.

p. 65 *Отрывной календарь на 1960 годъ* (Париж:Изданые зарубежнаго Союза Русскихъ Военныхъ Инвалидовъ, без даты)

p. 72 (right) Феликс Лев *У самого Белого моря* (Москва: Малыш, 1970)

p. 80 *Домоводство*, 4-е изд. (Москва:Колос, 1965), стр. 438

p. 82–83 С. А. Токарев *Этнография народов СССР* (Москва: Изд. Московского университета, 1958) стр. 74, 79.
Народы европейской части СССР, том 1, ред. В. А. Александров и др. в серии Народы мира (Москва: Наука, 1964) стр. 375, 378

p. 89 (top) Игорь Е. Середюк *Культура вашей квартиры* (Киев:Будивельник, 1967) стр.17

p. 89 (bottom) Е. и М. Никольские *Книга о культуре быта* 2-е изд. (Москва: Профиздат, 1967) стр. 27

p. 91 Там же, стр. 96

p. 97 (top) *Русские народные сказки*, ред.А. Нечаев и Н. Рыбакова, 3-е изд. (Москва: Детская Литература, 1967) стр. 17

p. 97 (bottom) *Народы европейской части СССР*, стр. 299

p. 99 (top) Е. Э. Бломквист «Крестьянские постройки русских, украинцев и белорусов».
Восточнославянский этнографический сборник, ред. Токарев, Труды института этнографии им. Миклухо–Маклая, новая серия, том 31 (Москва: Академия наук СССР, 1956) стр. 215

p. 99 Там же, стр. 139

p. 101 Токарев *Этнография*, стр. 64

p. 102 *Народы европейской части СССР*, стр. 397

p. 104 Е. Э. Бломквист, *Восточнославянский этнографический сборник*, стр 273

p. 105 Анохина и Шмелева *Культура и быт колхозников Калининской области* (Москва: Наука, 1964) стр. 125

p. 106 *Товарный словарь*, ред. И. Ф. Пугачев, том 7 (Москва: Гос. изд. торговой литературы, 1956–1961) стр. 555

p. 110 *Родная речь III*, 1969. стр. 166–167

p. 112 Лев Ухоботов, Москва

p. 121 *Родная речь*, 1967, стр. 157

p. 124 Там же, стр. 150

p. 165 Там же, стр. 26

p. 184 *Родная речь*, 1967, стр. 69

p. 200 Лев Ухоботов, Москва

p. 214 *Товарный словарь*, том 7й, стр. 998

p. 214 Там же, стр. 999

p. 214 Там же, том 8, стр 717. том 2, стр. 710

p. 216 *Soviet Life*, from Sovfoto

p. 226 *Вечерняя Москва*, 19 мая 1993

p. 250 *Народы европейской части СССР*, стр. 149

p. 252 А. Е. Супрун, *Русский язык советской эпохи* (Ленинград: Просвещение, 1969) стр. 49

p. 256 Е. И. Никитина *Родное слово: книга для чтения в первом классе*, стр. 72–73

p. 265 *Родное слово 2*, стр. 72

p. 267–269 Лев Ухоботов, Москва

p. 274–280 *Родное слово 2*, стр. 336

p. 318 Перышкин и др. *Физика:Учебник для шестого класса*, стр. 44

p. 322 Там же, стр. 133

p. 323 Н. А. Максимов *Физическая география: Учебник для пятого класса* (Москва: Просвещение, 1967) стр. 96

p. 324 Там же, стр. 21

p. 327 Nikolai Malyshev / Sovfoto

p. 333 Белов, *Лад*

p. 338–9 Лев Ухоботов, Москва

p. 357 *Вечерняя Москва*, 19 мая 1993

p. 358 *Спортивные игры*, том I, ред. М. С. Козлов, 2-е изд. (Москва: Физкультура и спорт, 1955) стр. 60

p. 361 Там же, том II, стр. 336

Unlisted photographs were provided through the good graces of the author and those who were photographed.

A note on sources:

Major sources for pictures and information include: **Товарный словарь, Народы европейской части СССР,** and **Токарев, Этнография народов СССР,** cited above, plus a wide variety of school textbooks, and other mundane language carriers, not to mention a wide variety of informants themselves. All of the language was obtained from a Russian source directly even though I sometimes considered it a waste of time or merely imprudent to include a citation.

English Index

abacus, 308
abbreviations, common, 373–375
abortion, 23, 149, 154
academic council, 236
academic ranks, 237
academician, 228, 237
Academy of Sciences, 219
accent, 251
acceptance of invitation, 18
acquaintance, 17
A.D., 321
address, 184, 196
addressing someone, 15
advance, 168
advertisement, 195
age, 48, 196. *See also* name, growing
    up with
agreement, 18
agriculture, 265
AIDS, 23, 156
ailments, 155
airplane, 212
alarm, 258
alcoholic drink, 12
alcoholism, 14
alimony, 168
alleluia, 25
allowance, 169
alphabets, 255, 313, 314, 378
amateur hour, 353
ambulance, 153, 154
Americans, 7
amphibians, 288
anatomy, 36–39
animal husbandry, 283
animals
    domisticated, 281–285
    in nature, 286–301
    talking to, 285
    what do they say, 285
annual vacation, 348, 349
Annunciation, 336
answering an address, 15
answering machine, 189
Anti-Semitism, 6
apartment, 23, 88
    communal, 88, 96
    self-contained, 88
appetizer, 132, 133, 139, 145
April Fool's Day, 335
apron, 74
area, 315, 317
arithmetic operations, 308–312

arm, 39
Army and Navy Day, 329
army school, 242
The Art of Russian Cooking, Volokh,
    Anne, 109
Ascension, 336
aspic, 133
assignment booklet, 231
Assumption, 336
astrologers, 19
atmospheric pressure, 323
attention getting, 14
auditorium, 238
automobile, 203
    parts of, 203

baba au rhum, 140
baby, 48, 154
    bed, 93
    clothes, 74
    feeding, 154
    language, 254
    parts of the body, 36
    swaddling, 154
    wrapping, 154
babysitting, 4
baby-talk, 25
backgammon, 354
Back-to-school day, 219
baggage, 211
balcony, 89
ballet, 350
bank, 169
baptism, 25
bargaining, 179
Barkhudarov, L. S., *Twelve Names
    for Twelve Things*, 318
barometer, 323
barrel, 104, 113
bath, 44
bathhouse, 43–45
bathing suit, 74
bathroom, 22, 44, 45, 93, 96, 107
bathtub, 93
BBC, 193, 194
B.C., 321
beard, traditional Russian, 83
Beatitudes, 343
bed, 92, 99
    how to make a, 93
bedroom, 92
bees, 285

beekeeping, 284
beer, 143, 144
believers, 325, 341
bells, 213, 217, 340
belt, 73, 78, 81
belyashi, 139
bench, 99, 100, 103
berries, 125, 135, 139, 141
    picking, 350
bet, 169
bills, 167
binary system, 306
bingo, 366
bird market, 281
birds, 292, 294–295
    index of, 378
birth, 25
birth certificate, 25, 48, 163
birth control, 337
birthday, 30, 63–65
    anniversary, 31
Birthday of Our Lady, 336
bishop, 343
blacks, 7
blindman's buff, 365
blini, 132, 133, 139, 145
blood, 41
blouse, 72, 75
blue jeans, 76, 79
boarding house, 348, 349
boats, 212
body, parts of, 35–39
bonds, 169
bone, 40
A Book of Russian Idioms Illustrated,
    Dubrovin, M. I., 382
Book of Tasty and Healthful Food,
    109
books, 195
    trade, 197
borsch, 134
bowl, 102
boy, 48
Braille Alphabet, 378
brain, 41
branch (stores), 177, 179
brandy, 143
Bratus, B. V., *The Formation and
    Expressive Use of Diminutives*,
    254
bread, 111
breakfast, 131, 132, 139
brews, home, 144

bribe, 161, 163
bride, 25
broadcasting, 193
bucket, 104
buckwheat, 110, 137
bullheads in tomato sauce, 289, 291
bum, 162
burial, 28, 29
bus, 201
bush, 266
business, 4, 371–373
button, 78

cabins, 349
cable TV, 194
cafe, 145
cafeteria, 145
caftan, 83
cake, 139–141
calendar, 320
    church, 65
camcoder, 194
camp, 194
camping areas, 349
candidate degree, 227
candles, 31
caps, 76
card games. *See* games, card
Carnival, 331, 332
carp, 290
carriage, 215
casserole, 135
    cereal, 138
cat, 31, 283
cat–and–mouse (game), 365
Caucasians, 4, 6, 24, 43
caviar, 132, 133, 289, 290, 292
cavities, 159
celebrations, 30
Celsius, 321
cemetery, 30
census, 243
central Asians, 4, 7, 24
cereals, 110, 132, 137
ceremonies, 25
Černyšev, V., *Les Prènoms Russes,
    Formation et Vitalitè*, 64
champagne, 31
championship, 358
character, 3–7
charms, 21
"chastushka", 353
cheating, 7, 233
chebureki, 138
cheese, 113–115, 131, 134
    curd, 114
chemical formulas, 376
chemicals, 119
chess, 359
children, 4, 48
children's play, 362–366

chocolate, hot, 142
chops, 136
chrismation, 25
Christ is risen, 334
christening, 25
Christmas, 326, 329, 336
    day, 330
    eve, 330
    holidays, 329
    tree, 326, 330
chug-a-lug, 13
Chukovskiy, Kornei, *From Two to
    Five*, 62
church, 26, 338, 340. *See also*
    Orthodox Church
    calendar, 65
    cattle days, 283
    services, 341
circulatory system, 41
circus, 350
city code, 189
classes, 162
    intelligentsia, 162
    peasants, 162
    workers, 162
Classic Russian Cooking, Toomre,
    Joyce, 109
classroom, 237
    furniture, 238
    organization, 238
cleaner, 181
clergy, 343
climate, 263–264
clinics
    children's, 151, 155
    dental, 151, 158
    outpatient, 153
cloakroom, 352
clock, 319
closet, 90, 92
clothes, 71. *See also specific kinds of
    clothes*
    baby, 74
    contemporary, 72
    Russian folk, 81
    schools, 74
    sizes, 78
    styles, 79
    traditional peasant, 71
    work, 74
"club", 353
CNN, 194
coat, 75
    closet, 89
    fur, 75, 83
    rack, 89
    raincoat, 75
    sizes, 78
coathanger, 92
cocktail, 142
COD, 185, 197
cod, 290

coffee, 141, 142, 145
coffee cake, 111, 141
coffin, 28, 30
cognac, 143
coins, 47, 167
"cold pole", 263
college, 162, 222
    administration, 236
    grades in, 233
colloquial, 248
commercial courses, 225
communications, 183–197
communion, 25, 343
compass, 324
compote, 130, 141
Compressed Russian, Zalucky, Henry,
    382
computer, 192, 237
concert, 350
condolence, 30
condom, 22, 154
conduct, 3–31
    in school, 232
conductor, 201, 211
congratulations, 18
Conquest of Snow City, Surikov, 333
conservatory, 270
container, 94
contraception, 154
conversational Russian, texts for
    developing, 248
cookies, 140
cooking, 130, 131
cooperative, 145, 266
cordial, 144
corner, 87
corset, 74
cosmetics, 45. *See also* makeup
cosmetologist, 181
coulibiac, 139
coupons, 26
courses, 132
cow, 283–285
crab, 288
cracker, 140
cream, 114
Credo, 25, 343
cremation, 29
crepes, 141
cribsheet, 233
cross, 21, 340
crossing, 340
croutons, 112
crustaceans, 288
curriculum, 228
    in college, 231
    in grade schools and high schools,
        228
    in vocational schools, 230
Cyrillic, 254

dacha, 349, 350
Dal's dictionary, 23
dam, 211
dancing, 352, 367
date, 321
day-care center, 222
deacon, 343
death certificate, 28
decimal system, 306
deck, 353
decor, 91, 96
delicatessen, 178, 179
denial, 18
dentist, 159
dentistry, 148, 159
dentures, 159
department (in store), 175
    bulk food, 178
departments (of university), 237, 238
deposit, 169
dessert, 132
detergent, 94
devil, 19, 21
diagnosis, 155
diagnostic centers, 151
diaphragm, 22
dice, 354
*Dictionary of Russian Personal
    Names*, Morton, Benson, 53
diet, 178
digestive system, 41
diminutives, 254
dining car, 211
dinner, 131–134, 139, 241
diploma, 31, 163, 233
    high–school, 226
disability, 10, 153
disagreement, 18
discounted merchandise, 177
diseases, 155, 156
dishes, 95, 132–141
    main, 135
    washing, 93
dispensary, 153
dissertation, 228
"distribution", 163
distance, 317
Divine Liturgy, 342
divorce, 28, 87
doctor, 4, 148, 152–154, 156, 236
    assistant, 149, 153
    cosmetic, 181
    specialists, 148–149
Doctor Zhivago, Pasternak, Boris, 54
doctor's degree, 237
doctorate, 227
documents at university, 238
documents for work, 163
dog, 282–285
dominoes, 354
dough, 111, 139

doughnuts, 140, 145
dowry, 26
Dr. Doolittle, 362
draft card, 48
dress, 72, 78, 81
drinking at the table, 12
drinks, 141–144
driver, 201, 215
driver's license, 203
driving, 205
drying food, 129
Dubrovin, M. I., *A Book of Russian
    Idioms Illustrated*, 382
dumplings, 138
duty officer, 238

earrings, 46
Easter, 140, 332, 333–336
    bread, 111, 334
    dessert, 114, 141, 334
    eggs, 334
eating places, 144–145
editor, 194
education, 219–244, 254, 348
    levels in, 221
egg, 115, 131–134, 138, 140, 145
elective courses, 230
electricity, 324
Elevation of the Holy Cross, 336
elope, 26
e-mail, 192, 193
emergency, 153
Èmigrès, 6
emotions, 6
employment office, 164
endearment, 258, 260
engagement, 26
entrepreneurship, 163
entrance hall, 89
envelope, 184, 192
environment, 264
Epiphany, 330, 332, 336
    eve, 332
equinox, 321
Eucharist, 343
Eugene Onegin, Nabokov, V., 266
euphemism, 22, 24
evil eye, 21
evil force, 21, 28
evil spirit, 44
Exaltation of the Cross, 336
examination, 233
    entrance, 226
excuse, 18
exercise commands, 158
expletives, 260
extracurricular activities, 241
extrasensory practitioner, 158
eye, 37
    color of, 42

face, 36
facial, 181
Fahrenheit, 321
fair, 336
    street, 177
Falla, P. S., *Oxford English-Russian
    Dictionary*, 382
family, 5, 49, 174
family bonds, 4
family contract, 266
fan, 91
fang, 288
farmer, 265, 266
fast food, 145
fasteners, 78
fasts, 337
fat, 116, 132, 288
fatalism, 6
fax, 192
feelings, 6
felt boots, 77, 78, 82
field, 265
Fifty Russian Winters, Wettlin,
    Margaret, 5
filling, 139–141
fine, 196
first-aid, 153
fish, 134, 140, 288–292
    cooking terms, 135
flavorings, 144
flour, 110, 111, 131, 138
flower, parts of, 267
folk beliefs, 21
font, 25
food, 109–145
    canned, 130
    preservation, 129
    preserved commercially, 129
    raw materials, 110–129
    store, 116
footwear, 72, 77, 78
forest, 264–265
*The Formation and Expressive Use
    of Diminutives*, Bratus, B. V., 254
formulas, common, 314
    reading, 315
fortunetelling, 331
fraction, 307
franks, 118, 131, 135
free time, 347–348
Friederich, Paul, *Structural
    Implications of Russian
    Pronominal Usage*, 253
friendliness, 8
friends, 5, 174, 183
From Two to Five, Chukovskiy
    Kornei, 62
fruit, 123, 135, 139, 145
    dried, 130

funeral, 28
　procession, 30
　service, 28
fur, 79, 299
　coat, 75, 83
　hat, 76

galushki, 138
gambling, 169, 353
games
　card, 169, 353
　inside, 365
　outside, 364
　traditional, 366
garden, 270
garden plot, 106, 349
garnish, 132, 135
gas stations, 206, 207
gasoline, 206
geometric figures, 313
gestures, 8, 10
getting things, 173
A Gift to Young Housewives,
　Molokhovets, Elena, 109
gifts, 31, 161, 328, 353, 371
"Gifts of Nature" stores, 118, 178
Gingerbread Man, 100
gingivitis, 159
girdle, 73, 74
girl, 48
girls' party, 28
Glagolitic, 254
glasses, 47, 157
globe, 324
gloves, 79
goat, 283–285
godparents, 25
Gogol, *The Overcoat*, 65
gold medal, 233
goods, 176
　foods, 176
　manufactured, 175
"gorodki", 361
gown, 73
grades, 230
graduate work, 227
graduation, 31, 233, 240, 241
grains, 110
Grandfather Frost, 326
grass, 267
gratitude, 19
grave, 29
Greek alphabet, 313
greetings, 15, 16
Gribble, Charles, *Russian Root List
　with a Sketch of Russian Word
　Formation*, 382
groom, 25
guest, 90
gum, 126

gymnasium, 219, 237, 242

haberdashery, 176
Hail Mary, 341
hair, 37
　color of, 42
　and the married woman, 83
haircut, 181
　traditional Russian, 83
hairdo, 181
ham, 129, 133, 135
hand, 39
Handbook of Russian Literature,
　Terras, Victor, 383
handshake, 10
hard currency, 174
harvest, 264
Harvest Celebration, 335
head, 36
headwear, 74, 76, 79, 82
healer, 158
health insurance, 147
heart, 41
helmet, 77
hemp, 97
herbal medicine, 272
herbs, 266
　medicinal, 272
Hermitage, 353
herring, 133, 134, 292
hide–and–seek, 364
higher education, 226
hiking headquarters, 348, 349
A History of Russian Literature,
　Mirskiy, D. S., 383
History of Russian Literature, Terras,
　Victor, 383
hitchhiking, 206
HIV infection, 23
hobby, 352
hobo, 162
holidays, 325–348
　"altar", 335, 336
　"twelve", 335
　church, 335
　contemporary, 325
　folk, 329
holy unction, 25
Holy Week, 333
home remedies, 154
homeless, 88, 162
homeopathy, 158
homework, 240, 348
homosexuality, 9, 23
honey, 144
honeymoon, 26
hopscotch, 364
hors d'oeuvre, 132, 292
horse, 283–285
　transportation, 213

horses and riders, 366
hospital, 147, 152
　bed, 93
　children's, 155
hospitality, 11, 111
hot dog, 118, 131, 135
hothouse, 270
"house of rest", 349
house spirit, 19
housewarming, 31
housework, 6
housing, 87–107
　contemporary rural, 105–107
　space, 88, 317
hut, 87, 96–105, 349
　decor of the, 98
　design of the, 98
　icon in the, 103
　lighting in the, 103
　plumbing in the, 104
　rooms of the, 98, 99
hygiene, 148

ice cream, 141
ice (for drinks), 13
icon, 339
　in the peasant hut, 104
　shelf, 99
iconostasis, 339, 341
identification cards, 47
Ilya Muromets, 3
incantation, 158
independence, 5
Independence Day, 326
index (in book), 196
information, 192
infusion, 144
injection, 156
inoculation, 156
insects, 286
inspector, 201
institute, 222, 226
　of beauty, 181
　research, 163
intelligentsia, 162
interest (bank), 169
interjections, 257
internist, 148
internship, 148
intestines, 41
introduction, 17
invitation, 17
IUD, 22

jacket, 72, 74
jam, 141, 130
jelly, 130
jewelry, 46
Jewish names, 64

Jews, 4, 6
job, 4, 163
John the Baptist Day, 334
joint, 40
journalist, 194
juice, 142, 145
jumper, 73

Khrushchev, 87
kindergarten, 223
kisel', 141
Kiselyova, L. A. and others, *A Practical Handbook of Russian Style*, 248
kissing, 8
kitchen, 93, 96, 103
    cabinets, 93, 94
    sink, 93, 94, 106
    utensils, 94, 95
knitting, 79
kolkhoz, 265
kulich, 140, 334
kumiss, 114
kutya, 30
Kuzmin, Shadrin, *Russian-English Dictionary of Proverbs and Sayings*, 382
kvas, 134, 142, 144

labor agreement, 164
labor union, 164
lapta, 365
Latin alphabet, 313
latitude, 324
laundromat, 181
laundry, 93
lawn, 267
leapfrog, 364
leash, 282
leave–taking, 19
leeches, 286
left-handness, 10
length, 315
Lent, 332, 338
leotards, 74
lesbian, 23
letter, 184, 185, 192
library, 196
library card, 196
lice, 156
lighting fixtures, 92
linden tree, 81
line, 174
linoleum, 91
liqueurs, 144
"lisp", 253
list, 174
literacy, 219
locks, 211
Lomonosov, 219

long distance, 189
    arranging a call, 189, 192
    information, 189
longitude, 324
Lord's Prayer, 343
lottery, 170
luck, 19, 20
lunch, 132
lyceum, 242

macaroni, 138
magazine, 195
mail, 183–188
    carrier, 194
mailbox, 185
makeup, 45
mammals, 295–299
manners, 9
    addressing the Russian, 54, 62
    drawing attention to oneself, 4
    that express friendship, 5
    gifts for host and hostess, 11, 328
    suggestions for those in business, 371
    at the table, 11–14
    in the theater, 352
    using *you* or *thou*, 252
    waiting in line, 174
marbles, 364
Marder, Steven, *A Supplementary Russian-English Dictionary*, 382
Mardi Gras, 332
market, 115, 177, 179
    black, 178
    flea, 177
    pet, 178
    public book, 197
marriage, 28, 87
Marriage & Family Service, 154
marriage broker, 26
Marxism-Leninism, 219
massage, 181
materials, 79
mathematical expressions, 313
    reading, 316
mathematical terminology, 315
matins, 341
May Day, 326, 329
mayonnaise, 134
meals, 131–134
The Meaning of Icons, Ouspensky, L., Losskey, V., 340
measures, 315–324
    old units of, 317
meat, 115–118, 131–135, 139
    cooking terms, 135
    cuts of, 116, 133
    sauces used for, 136
medals, 46, 355
medical
    center, 152

chart, 150
check-up, 150, 154
commission, 153
education, 148, 149
institutions, 149
personnel, 148
record, 150
treatment, 151
medicine, 147–157
    herbal, 157
    home, 156
    preventive, 153
memorial service, 28, 30
men, 6
mending, 181
menstruation, 22
menu, 144
meringue, 141
merry-go-round, 336, 363
Michurin, 290
midwife, 149, 154
milk, 113, 137, 138, 132, 141, 142
    kitchen, 155
    product dishes, 138
minibus, 202
Ministry of Agriculture, 179
Ministry of Communications, 194
Ministry of Health, 151
Ministry of Higher and Secondary Education, 227, 237
mirror, 47
Mirskiy, D. S., *A History of Russian Literature*, 383
Miss World 1992, 303
molasses, 140
mollusks, 288
Molokhovets, Elena, *A Gift to Young Housewives*, 109
monastery, 344
money, 10, 19, 47, 161, 167–170, 219
    attitude towards, 4, 168
    and medicine, 147
money order, 185, 191, 192
Moped, 203
Morse code, 378
Morton, Benson, *Dictionary of Russian Personal Names*, 53
moss, 97
motor scooter, 203
motorcycle, 203
mouth, 38
mug (animal's face), 36
multiplication table, 310
mummery, 330
murder mystery, 197
muscles, 41
museum, 353
mushrooms, 121, 137, 140
    picking, 350
mustard, 94, 154
muzzle, 36, 282

Nabokov, V., *Eugene Onegin,* 266
name, 53. *See also* Table of Names
   after the Revolution, 63
   before the Revolution, 63
   choosing one for a child, 65
   day, 63, 64, 65
   formal given, 54
   forms of, 54
      pejorative, 55
      diminutive, 54, 56–61
      endearing, 55, 56–61
   maiden, 62
   men's, 62
   monks', 64
   nuns', 64
   pronunciation of, 66
   saints', 63, 64
   women's, 62
name-calling, 259
"naming" ceremony, 25
nationality, 47, 66
   and surname, 66
nature, 263–301
nervous system, 41
nettle, 120, 131
New Testament, 344
New Year's
   cards, 328
   children's party, 326
   Day, 326
   party, 328
news, 193
newspaper, 194, 235
   and magazines, subscription to, 192
Nicene Creed, 343
nickname, 70
nightgown, 74
nonbelievers, 325
noodles, 138
North pole, 263
numbers
   declining, 307
   reading and writing, 306
numerical nouns, 305
nurse, 149, 152, 153, 155, 236
nuts, 126, 139

obscenity, 23
October Revolution Day, 326
office supplies, 176
oilcloth, 93
Old Style, 329
Old Testament, 344
olives, 134
Olympic games, 358
oral surgery, 148
orchard, 270
order, 5
orthodox church, 63, 335. *See also* church

The Orthodox Church, Ware, Timothy, 341
orthodox cross, 340
Ouspensky, L., Losskey, V., *The Meaning of Icons,* 340
outhouse, 105
overalls, 74
The Overcoat, Gogol, 65
Oxford English-Russian Dictionary, Falla, P. S., 382
Oxford Russian-English Dictionary, Wheeler, Morris, 382

package, 188, 192
pajamas, 74
Palace of Culture, 353
Palm Sunday, 333, 336
pan, 94, 102
pancakes, 131, 332
pants, 72, 76, 81
parents' committee, 240
parishioners, 341
parking lot, 203
parties, 30
paskha, 114, 141
pass, 48, 201
passport, 47, 163, 196
pasta, 113
Pasternak, Boris, *Doctor Zhivago,* 54
patient, 150, 152
   care, 149
patriarch, 343
patronymics, 54
   pronunciation of, 66
peasant house. *See* hut
peasant household, 98
   cooking equipment, 101, 102
peasants, 162
pedestrians, 206
pediatrics, 148
pelmeni, 132, 138, 145
pen pal, 186
Pentecost, 334, 336
perch, 290, 291
periodicals, 194
perma-frost, 264
personal relationships, 7
pest control, 181
pesticides, 119
pet, 281
   market, 178
   name for, 68
   store, 281
Peter the Great, 219, 254, 27, 326, 375
pharmacist, 149
pharmacy, 148, 156
photocopy, 192
phrases, stock, 14
pickle, 120, 128, 129
pie, 31, 132, 139, 141, 145

pig, 283, 284, 285
"pig Latin", 257
pilav, 110
Pinocchio, 362
pirozhki, 123, 139
plant, 266–281
   house, 91, 271
   index of, 273–281
   kingdom, 266
   medicinal, 272
   parts of, 268–269
plate, 95
platform, 210
play, 347
playpen, 90
plumbing, 104
pocket, 80
pointing, 11
polite phrases, 14–19, 30
polyclinic, 149
poppyseed, 140
porch, 99, 100
pornography, 183, 197
Posner, Vladimir, 7
post office, 191, 194
   box, 185, 194
   main, 188, 190
postal zone, 184
postcards, 329
posture, 8, 9
pot, 94, 102
poultry, 118, 134, 136
A Practical Handbook of Russian Style, Kiselyova, L. A. and others, 248
precious stones, 46
pregnancy, 22, 154
pregnancy leave, 154
premium, 169
Les Prénoms Russes, Formation et Vitalité, Černyšev, V., 64
prescription, 156
Presentation of Christ in the Temple, 336
Presentation of the Virgin Mary, 336
preserves, 125, 126, 130, 141
president of the university, 236
press, 183
pressure, 323
pretzels, 140
priest, 25, 340, 341, 343
principal, 236
private sellers, 179
privatization, 266
privileges, 164
professor, 228, 237
proprieties, 11
prosthetic device, 10
prostitute, 22
protein, 115
"PTA" meeting, 240
public facilities, 22

public health, 153
Public Health Authorities, 153, 181
public telephone, 189
publisher, 194
pudding, 138, 139, 141
"pull", 173
purse, 47
Pushkin, A. S., *Thou and You*, 261
Pushkin Russian Language Institute, 248
pussy willows, 333, 344

quality, 175
"quality sign", 175
quarantine, 155
quarter, 232
quinary system, 306
quiz, 233

races, 42, 365
radio, 183, 193
  waves, 193
Radio Liberty, 193
railroad cars, kinds of, 211
ramp, 10
rationing, 173, 179
reading, 350
receipt, 174, 175, 185, 188
recommendations for work, 164
rector, 236
Red Book, 265
references, 382
refrigerator, 94
registry office, 25, 26, 28
regulations, 7
rejection, terms of, 258
relatives, 49–51
religious, 28, 29
renting, 181
repair, 180
repair facilities, 206
repeater (school), 232
reproductive organs, 41
reptiles, 288
request, 17
research institute, 237
research ranks, 237
restaurant, 144, 145
retirement, 31
reunion, 31
rickets, 114
ring, 26, 46, 190
river fleet, 211
road signs, 206, 208
roads, 206, 215
roll, 111, 135, 140
route, 201, 203
rug, 89, 91
rules, 7
rush–hour traffic, 201
Russia Day, 326, 329

Russian Academy of Sciences, 228
Russian alphabet, 254
  reform in 1918, 255
  reform of Peter the Great, 254
Russian Church Singing, von
  Gardner, Johann, 341
Russian dialects, 250
*Russian-English Dictionary of
  Proverbs and Sayings*, Kuzmin,
  Shadrin, 382
Russian letters, pronunciation of, 255
*Russian Root List with a Sketch of
  Russian Word Formation*,
  Gribble, Charles, 382
Russian Surnames, Unbegaun, B. O.,
  68

sacraments, 25, 344
Saint's Days, 337
salad, 119, 129, 132, 133
  dressings, 134
salary, 163
salmon, 133, 288, 290
salting food, 129
samovar, 102
sanatorium, 348
sandwich, 111, 134, 145
"sanitary stop", 22
sanitation, 22, 148, 153
Santa Claus, 326
sauce, 134
sauerkraut, 120, 129
sauna, 154
sausage, 117, 131, 145
Savings Bank, 169, 191, 192
scales, 318
scarf, Russian, 283
school, 219–243
  after the Revolution, 219
  atmosphere, 239
  before the Revolution, 219
  boarding, 241
  building, 237
  collective, 240
  council, 236
  discipline, 240
  elementary, 233
  evening and correspondence, 225
  grades, 222, 231
  graduate, 221
  high, 222
  junior high, 222
  language, 242
  nursery, 222, 223
  record, 163
  regulations, 236
  rooms, 237
  special, 242
  with a specialty, 242
  technical, 162
  time at, 241

trade, 162
  vocational, 224, 237
  year, 232
science, 237
score, 362
seasonings, 127–128
seasons, 132, 321, 264
section, 175
seedlings, 270
seeds, 126
self–assurance, 4
self–confidence, 4
self–service, 145
semolina, 141
seniority, 151, 164, 169
Service Bureau, 350
services, 180–181
  personal, 181
sewing, 79, 80
sewing bee, 367
sex, 22
shashlyk, 132, 136, 145
shaving, 46
sheep, 283–285
shelf, 89, 99, 100, 103, 145
shepherd, 283
ships, 211–212
shirt, 72, 75, 78, 81
shoelaces, 77, 78
shopping, 173–181, 199
shopping bag, 47
shortage, 197
shortbread, 140
sick–list, 151
signs, good and bad, 20
silverware, 95, 96
singing, 352, 367
sink, bathroom, 93
sink, kitchen, 93, 94, 106
skeleton, 40
skin, 39
  color of, 42
skirt, 72
slang, 248
sled, 363, 364
sleighs, 214
slip, 74
slippers, 77, 78, 90, 353
Slonim, Mark, *The Writer and His
  Creation*, 31
slum, 87
smell, 123, 125
smile, 7, 9, 181
snack, 131, 241
  bar, 211
snobbery in language, 249
Snow Maiden, 326
soap, 94
soccer, 358
social distance, 8
Social Security, 153
social worker (at school), 236

soda, 94
solstice, 321
sorcerer, 158
sore throat, 13
soup, 116, 119, 128, 129, 132, 134, 139
sour cream, 114
sovkhoz, 265
spa, 349
spare parts, 204
speaker, 193
speculation, 173
speech, 199, 247, 248
    and education, 248, 249
    styles of, 247
    use of the uvular (French) r, 254
speed, 323
spice cookie, 128
spiced apples, 130
spices, 127–128
spirit, 105
sport standards, 354
sports, official, 354–358
spring, 332
St. Cyrill, 254
St. Methodius, 254
Stalin, 87
steak, 135, 136
stew, 116, 119, 132, 135
stipend, 227
stockings, 72, 77, 79, 81
stocks, 169
stool, 100
stop, 201
stores
    agricultural cooperative, 179
    commercial, 175, 177
    department, 177
    food, 178
    grocery, 178
    hard currency, 174, 177
    kinds of, 176
    private 175
    second–hand/antique, 177
stove portable, 106
    Russian, 99, 101
streetcar, 201
stress, 249
strike, 164
Structural Implications of Russian Pronominal Usage, Friederich, Paul, 253
stump, 268
sturgeon, 133, 288, 289, 292
subscription, 192, 194, 195, 197
substitute teaching, 235
subway, 202
suit, 72
    bathing, 74
summer camp, 349
supermarket, 179

superstitions, 19–21, 44, 65, 83, 288
    house spirit, 105
    yard spirit, 105
supper, 131, 132
A Supplementary Russian-English Dictionary, Marder, Steven, 382
Surikov, *Conquest of Snow City*, 333
surname, 66
    pronunciation of, 66
suspenders, 78
swearing, 23
sweat, 52
sweater, 72, 75
sweet desserts, 140
swings, 333, 336, 363, 367
syrniki, 138

table, 90
    setting of the, 95
table of contents, 196
Table of Elements, 377
Table of Names, 53, 54, 56–61
table of ranks, 375
table songs, 14
tag, 175
tag (game), 364
taiga, 264
tardiness, 232
Tartar, 159
tattletale, 240
taxes, 7, 169
taxi, 202
    stand, 202
tea, 131, 132, 139, 141, 145
    mushroom, 141, 142
teacher, 223, 233, 242
    homeroom, 232, 235, 241
teacher's council, 236
teeth, 38
    bridge, 159
    crown, 159
    false, 159
    filling, 159
telegram, 190, 192
    kinds of, 190, 191
telephone, 188
    lines, 183
television, 183, 193
telex, 192
temperature, 321
term paper, 233
Terras, Victor, *Handbook of Russian Literature*, 383
Terras, Victor, *History of Russian Literature*, 383
tests, 230, 233
    grade, 228
theater, 350
thermometer, 322, 323
thesis, 227, 230

thou, 17, 62, 63, 252, 261
Thou and You, Pushkin, A. S., 261
threshold, 100
ticket, 201, 350
    office, 350
    punching the, 201
tic–tac–toe, 366
tie, 72
tiles, 99
time, 319
time zones, 319
tip, 352
toast, 112, 131
toastmaster, 13
toilet, 22, 93, 104, 106
toilet paper, 22, 93
token, 189, 202
Tolstoy, *War and Peace*, 331
tombstone, 29
tools, 164–167
Toomre, Joyce, *Classic Russian Cooking*, 109
torte, 31
towel, 100
toys, 362–364
trackless trolley, 201
tracks, 210
trade union, 48, 151, 174, 235, 237
trademark, 175
traffic jams, 199
traffic lights, 205
trains, 201, 210–211
    long–distance, 210
    schedule, 210
Transfiguration, 336
transportation, 199–217
    public, 199, 201
treatments, 156
tree, 264–265
Trinity, 336
Trinity Sunday, 334
troika, 214, 217
trolley, 201
trousers, 72, 76
trucks, 204
trunk, 38
tundra, 264
turnstile, 202
tutors, 226
TV, 193
tvorog, 138, 139, 140
Twelfth Day, 336
Twelve Names for Twelve Things, Barkhudarov, L. S., 318
twins, 306

Unbegaun, B. O., *Russian Surnames*, 68
underwear, 72, 73, 82
unemployment, 164, 170

uniforms, 74
university, 222, 226
urinary organs, 41

vaccination, 156
vareniki, 123, 138
VCR, 193
vegetables, 118, 139
  cooking, 136
  root, 131
vegetable oil, 134
vespers, 341
vest, 72
vice–principal, 235
Victory Day, 326, 329
vital statistics, 164
vitamins, 113
vodka, 143, 144
Voice of America, 193
Volokh, Anne, *The Art of Russian Cooking*, 109
volume, 315, 317
von Gardner, Johann, *Russian Church Singing*, 341
Vysotsky, Vladimir, 353

wages, 4, 164, 168
wagon, 214
wallet, 47
War and Peace, Tolstoy, 331

ward, 152
Ware, Timothy, *The Orthodox Church*, 341
warnings, 258
washing machine, 93
washing tub, 93
watch, 47, 319
water, 142, 145
weather, 322
wedding, 25, 26
  anniversary, 28
  meal, 26
  night, 28
  Palace, 26
weed, 271, 273
weight, 318
  gain, loss, 46
well, 104
Wettlin, Margaret, *Fifty Russian Winters*, 5
wheelchair, 10
Wheeler, Morris, *Oxford Russian-English Dictionary*, 382
whistle, 274
whistling, 19
Whitsunday, 334, 336
window, 91
wine, 143
winter, 91
Winter Palace, 353
witch, 21, 97
witnesses, 26

women, 6, 48
  in language, 6
Women's Consult, 154
Women's Day, 325, 329
woodcarving, 98
work, 161
  clothes, 74
  days off, 325
  record, 163
  time for, 164
  and women, 163
wreath, 30, 279
The Writer and His Creation, Slonim, Mark, 31

Xerox, 192
X–ray (room), 152

yarmulke, 76
yawning, 21
yeast, 111, 139
yoke, 104
you, 62, 63, 252

Zalucky, Henry, *Compressed Russian*, 382
zip code, 184, 185, 192
zipper, 78

Указатель

абитурие́нт, 233
абонеме́нтный я́щик, 185, 194
або́рт, 23, 154
абрико́с, 123
Аване́сов Р. И., *Ру́сское литерату́рное произноше́ние*, 66
ава́нс, 168
АВИА, 185
аво́ська, 47
авто́бус, 200, 201
автома́т, 210
автомоби́ль, 203–206
автомоби́льный спорт, 355
автомоде́льный спорт, 355
автоотве́тчик, 189
а́втор, 195
автосто́п, 206
Агропромы́шленный ко́мплекс, 265
Ада́мово я́блоко, 37
аджи́ка, 128
а́дрес, 184, 196
аза́ртные и́гры, *См.* и́гры аза́ртные
а́збука, 254. 313, 378
азиа́т, 43
азу́, 135
а́ист, 378
айва́, 123
Академгородо́к, 242
акаде́мик, 228, 237
академи́ческие до́лжности и зва́ния, 237
а́канье, 251
ака́ция, бе́лая, 265, 274
ака́ция, жёлтая, 274
Аки́шина А. А., Формано́вская Н. И., *Ру́сский речево́й этике́т*, 14
акроба́тика, 355
Аксёнов В., *Колле́ги*, 48, 353
а́ктовый зал, 237, 238
акуше́рка, 149, 154
а́кция, 169
Алекса́ндров, *Наро́ды европе́йской ча́сти СССР*, 83
алиме́нты, 168
аллерго́лог, 149
Аллилу́йя, 25, 29, 343
Алло́, 189
ало́э, 272
алта́рь, 338, 342
алфави́т, 254
    гре́ческий, 313
    лати́нский, 313

алыча́, 123, 274
альпини́зм, 355
амари́ллис, 272
амбро́зия, 271
амбулато́рия, 153
амво́н, 338
амфитеа́тр, 352
анало́й, 338
анана́с, 123
анато́мия, 36, *См. также* те́ло, строе́ние
анестезио́лог, 149
ани́с, 128, 274
анке́тные да́нные, 164
антреко́т, 136
анча́р, 274
аню́тины гла́зки, 274
АОН, 189
апельси́н, 123
АПК, 265
апо́стол, 343
апте́ка, 156, 158, 273
апте́чка дома́шняя, 156
ара́хис, 126
арбу́з, 125
Аргуме́нты и фа́кты, 266
арифмети́ческие де́йствия, 308
арихиере́й, 343
Аркту́р-гончий пёс, Казако́в Юрий, 380
арома́т, 125
артишо́ки, 119
арши́н, 317
аскари́да, 286
аспара́гус, 272
аспира́нт, 221, 227
аспиранту́ра, 221, 227
ассисте́нт, 237
асти́льба, 270
а́стра, 270, 274
АТС, 189
атмосфе́рное давле́ние, 323
аттеста́т зре́лости, 31, 222, 224, 226, 233
аудито́рия, 238
африка́нец, 43
ацидофили́н, 113
аэропо́рт, 212
Аэрофло́т, 212

ба́ба, 6
Ба́ба-яга́, 97
ба́бка морко́вная, 139

ба́бки, 366
ба́бочки, 286
ба́бушка, 49-51
ба́бьи спле́тни, 272
бага́ж, 211
багу́льник, 274
бадминто́н, 355
база́р, 179
базили́к, 128
байба́к, 297
байда́рка, 212
бакале́я, 178
баклажа́н, 120
баклажа́нная икра́, 133
бакте́рии, 266
балала́йка, 352
бале́т, 350
балко́н (в теа́тре), 352
балко́н (в кварти́ре), 89
балы́к, 292
бана́н, 123
бандеро́ль, 188, 192
банк, 169
ба́нка, 94
ба́нный, 44
ба́нщица, 45
ба́ня, 43, 44, 154
бара́н, 284
бара́нина, 116, 135, 138
бара́нка, 111, 112
барахо́лка, 177
барбари́с, 274
бард, 353
ба́ржа, 216
баро́метр, 323
барс, 297
барсу́к, 296
ба́рхатцы, 270, 274
баскетбо́л, 355
бассе́йн, 356
ба́ссет, 283
бати́ст, 79
бато́н, 112
бахча́, 270
бего́ния, 272
бедро́, 39
безгра́мотности ликвида́ция, 220
бездоро́жье, 214, 264
безе́, 141
безрабо́тица, 164
бека́с, 118, 293, 379
белена́, 274
бе́лка, 296
Белове́жская пу́ща, 298

белóк (в яйцé), 115
белóк (часть глáза), 37
белолóз, 276
белоры́бица, 290, 292
белýга, 133, 289
бéлый гриб, 122, 129
бельё, 82, 133
    для новорождённых, 74
    жéнское, 73
бельэтáж, 352
бензи́н, 206
бензоколóнка, 206
бенуáр, 352
берéменность, 22, 154
бересклéт, 274
берéт, 74, 76
берёза, 265, 274, 334
берёзка, 274
берёста, 274
бéркут, 379
бес, 19
бескозы́рка, 74
бесплóдие, 154
бессмéртник, 274
беф-стрóганов, 135
биатлóн, 355
библиотéка, 196
би́знес, 4
бизóн, 298
билéт, 210, 350
    проезднóй, 201
    читáтельский, 196
билетёр, 352
бинóкль, 352
би́ржа трудá, 164
бискви́т, 141
битá, 361
битóчки, 134, 136
бифштéкс, 135
бич, 162
Благовéщение, 336
блат, 173
бли́жнее зарубéжье, 188
близнецы́, 306
бли́нная, 145
бли́нчики, 138, 140
блины́, 131, 132, 139, 332, 334
Блок А., *Вéрбочки*, 333
блонди́н, 42
блохá, 286, 287
блýза, 75, 76
блýзка, 72, 75, 76, 79
блю́до, 95, 119, 132
блю́дце, 95
бобр, 297
Богослужéние, 341
Богоявлéние, 336
божни́ца, 99, 103
бóжья корóвка, 286
Бóжья мать, 339
бок, 38
бокáл, 96

бокс, 356
боксёр, 283
болéзни, 148
    дéтские, 155
болéльщик, 358
больни́ца, 147, 152
больни́чный лист, 151
больнóй, 152, 158
бомж, 88, 162
борзáя, 282
борови́к, 122, 131
бородá, 36
боронá, 167
борщ, 134
борьбá
    вóльная, 356
    класси́ческая, 356
ботви́нник, 120
ботви́нья, 134
боти́нки, 74 , 77
бóчка, 113, 317
боя́рышник, 274
брáга, 144
Брак и семья́, 154
брак, 28, 344
браконьéрство, 118
бракосочетáние, 26
брáнные обращéния, 258, 259
браслéт, 46
брат, 49-51
    молóчный, 154
брáчная ночь, 28
бриллиáнт, 46
бри́тва, 46
бритьё, 46
бровь, 37
Брокгáуз Ф. А., Ефрóн И. А.,
    Энциклопеди́ческий словáрь,
    383
брóкколи, 119
брудершáфт, вы́пить на, 253
брусни́ка, 125, 131, 274
брю́ки, 72, 74, 76
брюнéт, 42
брю́хо, 36
бýблик, 111, 112
бýбны, 354
буди́льник, 319
бýер, 212
бужени́на, 116, 133
бузинá, 275
бук, 275
букáшка, 286
булáвка, 80
бýлка, 111, 112
бýлочка, 140
бульвáр, 185
бульдóг, 283
бульóн, 131, 134
бультерьéр, 283
бумáжник, 47
Бурати́но, 362

буревéстник, 379
бурлáк, 216
Бурлаки́, Рéпин, 216
бурундýк, 297
бурья́н, 271
бýсы, 46
бутербрóд, 111, 134
бутербрóдная, 145
бутóн, 267
буты́лка, 317
буфéт (мéбель), 92, 94
буфéт (кафé), 145, 211, 237
бык, 284
бычóк, 291
бюллетéнь медици́нский, 151
бюрó обслýживания, 350
бюстгáлтер, 73

вагóн, 211
вагóн-ресторáн, 211
ВАК, 227
вакцинáция, 156
вáленки, 77, 78, 82
валерьáна, 272
вáльдшнеп, 118, 293, 379
валю́та, 174
валю́тный магази́н, 174, 177
вани́ль, 128
вáнна, 44, 93
вáнная, 22, 44, 89, 93, 96
Вáнька-встáнька, 363
вáнька-мóкрый, 272
варенéц, 113
варéники, 138
варéнье, 123, 126, 130, 141, 153
василёк, 271
вáта, 79
вáтник, 75
ватрýшка, 139
Введéние во храм, 336
вéдомость, 168
вёдра пусты́е, 20
ведрó, 95, 104, 167, 317
век, 319
Вели́кий посt, 338
велосипéдный спорт, 356
велосипéд, 356
венéц, 26, 27
вéник, 44, 45, 274
вéничек, 95
венки́, 30, 279
вентиля́тор, 91
венчáние, 26, 27, 344
вéрба, 275
Вéрбное воскресéнье, 333
Вéрбный базáр, 333
Вéрбочки, Блок А., 333
вéреск, 275
верстá, 317
вертолёт, 356
вертолётный спорт, 356

Ве́рую, 25, 343
ве́рующие, 29, 325, 341
вершо́к, 317
вес, 318
вёсла, 356
весна́, 36, 264
весну́шка, 36, 37
весы́, 318
ве́тка, 269
ветла́, 275, 276
Ве́тхий заве́т, 344
ветчина́, 116, 129, 133, 135
ве́чер, 319
   встре́чи выпускнико́в, 31
   самоде́ятельности, 353
вечери́нка, 30
вече́рнее отделе́ние, 225
вече́рня, 341
ве́чная мерзлота́, 264
Ве́чная па́мять, 29
ве́шалка, 89, 92, 352
Взя́тие сне́жного городка́,
   Су́риков, 333
взя́тка, 161, 163
вид, 266
видеока́мера, 194
видеомагнитофо́н, 193
видеопле́йер, 193
ви́дик, 193
ви́лка, 92, 96
ви́лы, 166
винегре́т, 133
вино́, 143
виногра́д, 125
Виногра́дов В. В., *Русский язы́к*
   граммати́ческое уче́ние о
   сло́ве, 383
винт, 165
винче́стер, 193
висо́к, 37
ви́шня, 123, 275
вклад, 169
внекла́ссные заня́тия, 241
внук, вну́чка, 49-51
во́бла, 143, 291, 292
   вя́леная, 129
вода́, 142
води́тель, 201, 205
води́тельские права́, 203
во́дка, 143
во́дное по́ло, 356
во́дно-лы́жный спорт, 356
во́дно-мото́рный спорт, 356
водолече́ние, 151
водопрово́д, 93
водопрово́дчик, 180
во́доросли, 266
водоснабже́ние, 104
во́жжи, 214
во́згласы, 260
возду́шный шар, 363
Вознесе́ние, 336

во́зраст, 48, 196, *См. также* и́мя и
   во́зраст
во́инский биле́т, 48
Война́ и мир, Толсто́й Л.Н., 331
вокза́л, 210
   речно́й, 211
вола́н, 355
волейбо́л, 356
волк, 297
во́лосы, 37
   цвет, 42
волчо́к, 363
во́лчьи я́годы, 276
воробе́й, 285, 294, 379
во́рон, 379
воро́на, 295, 379
воро́ний глаз, 275
воро́та, 99
восклица́ния, 257
воспита́тель, 223, 242
восто́к, 324
Восьмо́е ма́рта, 325, 329
вошь, 156, 286, 287
врата́рь, 359
врач, 148, 152, 154, 156
   де́тский, *См.* педиа́тр
   зубно́й, 159
   по вну́тренним боле́зням, *См.*
      терапе́вт
   у́хо-го́рло-нос, 149
   участко́вый, 150, 154
врач-космето́лог, 181
времена́ го́да, 264, 321
вре́мя, 319
   рабо́чее, *См.* рабо́чее вре́мя
   свобо́дное, 347
Все́нощное бде́ние, 342
Всеобу́ч, 220
Всео́бщее обяза́тельное нача́льное
   обуче́ние, 220
второго́дник, 232
второго́дничество, 240
ВТЭК, 153
вуз, 221, 222, 224, 226, 230, 233,
   236, 237
Вход Госпо́ден в Иерусали́м, 336
вы, 62, 63, 252, 253
вы́дра, 297
   морска́я, 298
вы́игрыш, 362
выключа́тель, 92
вы́кройка, 80, 81
вы́мя, 117
выпускни́к, 31, 221, 226
выпускно́й ве́чер, 31, 233, 240, 241
вы́резка, 116
вы́рубка, 265
высота́, 317
Вы́сшая Аттестацио́нная
   Коми́ссия, 227
вы́хухоль, 297
вычита́ние, 309

вьюно́к, 271, 275
вяз, 265, 275
вяза́ние, 79
вязи́га, 129, 140

га́га, 379
гага́ра, 379
гада́ние, 330, 331
гадю́ка, 288
газе́та, 192, 194, 235
газо́н, 267
га́йка, 165
галантере́я, 176
галере́я, 352
гале́та, 140
га́лка, 379
гало́ши, 78
га́лстук, 72
галу́шки, 138
гардеро́б, 92, 238, 352
гармо́нь, 353
гарни́р, 119, 132
гастроно́м, 178
гастроэнтеро́лог, 149
гвозди́ка, 128, 275
гвоздь, 165
гекта́р, 317
геометри́ческие фигу́ры, 313
геоме́трия, 313
георги́н, 270, 275
гера́нь, 91, 271, 275
геркуле́с, *См.* ка́ша геркуле́совая
геронто́лог, 149
гигие́на, 148
   ли́чная, 43
гигиени́ческие паке́ты, 22
гико́ри, 126
гимна́зия, 220
гимна́стика, 356
гингвити́т, 159
гинеко́лог, 154
гинеколо́гия, 148
гита́ра, 352
глаго́лица, 254
глаз, 37
   заболева́ния, 148
   цвет, 42
глазу́нья, 138
глина́, 101
гли́сты, 126, 273, 286
гло́бус, 324
глокси́ния, 272
глуха́рь, 118, 293, 295, 379
гни́да, 288
го́вор ме́стный, 251
говя́дина, 116, 135, 136
го́голь, 379
год, 319
   високо́сный, 319
годовщи́на сва́дьбы, 28
годовы́е ко́льца, 268

голбе́ц, 99
голе́ц, 290
голова́, 36
головно́й убо́р, 83
голо́дный, 109
Го́лос Аме́рики, 193
голосова́ниеж, 206
голоше́йка, 81
голуби́ка, 125, 275
голубо́й, 23
голубцы, 135, 137
го́лубь, 379
гомеопа́т, 272
гомеопа́тия, 158
гомосексуа́льность, 9, 23
го́нчая соба́ка, 282
горбу́ша, 290
горе́лки, 364
го́рло, 41
го́рница, 99
горнолы́жный спорт, 356
горноста́й, 297
го́род, 270
го́род (в и́грах), 361, 365
городки́, 361
горо́х, 121, 135, 136, 270
горо́шек души́стый, 275
горте́нзия, 271, 275
ГорУНО, 236
горчи́ца, 94, 127, 154, 275
горчи́чник, 127
горшо́к, 101, 102
Го́рько!, 26
горя́чее, 132
го́спиталь, 152
господа́, 14
господи́н, госпожа́, 14, 63
гости́ная, 90
Гости́ный Двор, 177
гость, 90
гра́бли, 166, 167
гра́дусник, 323
граждани́н, гражда́нка, 14, 63
гражда́нская панихи́да, 28
грамм, 318
*Граммати́ческий слова́рь ру́сского
    языка́*, Зализня́к А. А., 383
гра́мотность, 220
грана́т, 123, 275
грасси́ровать, 254
графи́н, 96
гра́ция, 74
грач, 295, 379
гре́бля, 356
грейпфру́т, 123
гре́нки, 112, 132
гречи́ха, 110, 275
грибно́й дождь, 350
грибы́, 121, 134, 137, 266, 350
Гри́нвичский меридиа́н, 324
гроб, 28
громкоговори́тель, 193

гроссме́йстер, 354
грош, 179
груди́нка, 116, 137
грудно́й ребёнок, 48
грудь, 36, 38
груздь, 122, 129
грузови́к, 204
гру́ппа продлённого дня, 241
гру́ша, 123
гря́дка, 270
губа́, 37, 38
гу́бка, 44
губна́я пома́да, 45, 47
гуля́ш, 135
ГУМ, 177
гу́сеница, 286
гуси́ный лук, 275
гусь, 284, 285, 379
    ди́кий, 293
ГЭС, 211

давле́ние, 323
да́льнее зарубе́жье, 188
дар, 25
Дары́, 338, 343
Дары́ приро́ды, 118, 178
да́та, 321
да́ча, 349
дво́йня, 306
двор, 98, 99, 105
Дворе́ц бракосочета́ний, 26
Дворе́ц культу́ры, 353
дворня́га, дворня́жка, 282
дворово́й, 105
двою́родная сестра́, 49-51
двою́родный брат, 49-51
деви́чник, 28
де́вичья фами́лия, 62
де́вочка, 48
де́вственница, 28
де́вушка, 48
Дед Моро́з, 326-328
дед, 49-51
дежу́рный, 238
дежу́рство, 239
декана́т, 238
деле́ние, 311
дели́мое, 311
дели́тель, 311
дельфи́ниум, 270
де́нежный перево́д, 185, 191, 192
Дени́сов, *Уче́бный слова́рь
    сочета́емости*, 382
День А́рмии и Фло́та, 329
День весны́, 325, 329
День Ива́на Купа́лы, 334
День октя́брьской револю́ции, 326,
    329
День Побе́ды, 326, 329
день рожде́ния, 30, 63, 64, 65
День Росси́и, 326, 329

день, 319
де́ньги, 19, 47, 161, 167
дерга́ч, 380
дере́вня, 97
де́рево, 264, 266
дерматоло́гия, 148
десна́, 38
десяти́на, 317
десяти́чная дробь, 306
детекти́в, 197
де́тские я́сли, 222, 223
Де́тский мир, 177
детский сад, 222, 223
дефици́т, 174, 188, 197
джаз, 353
дже́мпер, 72, 75
джем, 130
джи́нсы, 76
дзюдо́, 356
диа́гноз, 155
диа́конские врата́, 338
диафра́гма, 22
дива́н-крова́ть, 92, 93
дие́та, 178
ди́кая ряби́нка, 279
дикобра́з, 296
дипло́м, 222, 225, 226, 233
дипло́мная рабо́та, 231
дире́ктор, 236, 237
диске́та, 193
диспансе́р, 153
диссерта́ция, 227, 228
дичь, 118, 136
длина́, 315, 317
дневни́к, 231, 232
Дни святы́х, 337
до востре́бования, 192
доба́вочный, 188
доберма́н-пи́нчер, 283
дог, 283
догоня́лки, 364
дождеви́к, 122
Дожи́нки, 335
До́ктор Айболи́т, 362
До́ктор Жива́го, Пастерна́к Бори́с,
    54
до́ктор нау́к, 237
до́ктор, 148
докторáнт, 221, 228
до́кторская сте́пень, 221, 227, 237
докуме́нт об образова́нии, 163
докуме́нты, 47
долгота́, 324
долото́, 165
до́ля, 307
дом, 87, 97
    крестья́нский, *См.* изба́
    о́тдыха, 348, 349
дома́шние зада́ния, 240
дома́шняя пти́ца, 118
домино́, 354
домкра́т, 167

домово́й, 19, 105
до́нник, 275
доро́жка, 91
доро́жные зна́ки, 208
доска́, 238
досу́г, 350
доце́нт, 237
дочь, 49-51
дошко́льник, 222, 223
драгоце́нные ка́мни, 46
дрель, 165
дро́вни, 215
дро́жжи, 111, 139
дро́жки, 214, 215
дрозд, 379
друг по перепи́ске, 186
друг, 5
дуб, 275, 265
дублёнка, 75
луга́, 213
ду́пель, 293
дупло́, 269
дура́к, 364
дурно́й глаз, 21
дуршла́г, 95
духове́нство, 343, 344
духо́вка, 94, 323
душ, 45
души́ца, 128
ды́ня, 125
ды́шло, 214
дья́кон, 340, 343
дюйм, 317
дя́дя, 49-51
дя́тел, 379

Ева́нгелия, 338, 343
евре́й, евре́йка, 6
ёж, 296
ежеви́ка, 125, 275
еле́й, 25
елеосвяще́ние, 344
Елисе́евский магази́н, 179
ёлка, 275, 326, 327
  Рожде́ственская, 330
Ёлочка, Кудашо́ва Р., 326
ель, 264, 265, 275, 279
ено́т, 297, 299
ено́т-полоску́н, 297, 299
епи́скоп, 343
ермо́лка, 76
ёрш, 288, 290
ёршик, 95

жа́ба, 288
жа́бра, 288
жа́воронки, 295, 332, 379
жа́жда, 142
жаке́т, 72, 75
жарго́н, 248

жа́рить, 131
жарко́е, 135
жва́тельная рези́нка, 126
жва́чка, 126
желто́к, 115
желу́док, 41
жёлудь, 275
жёмчуг, 46
жена́, 49
жени́х, 20, 25, 87
же́нщина, 48
женьше́нь, 272, 275
жеребе́ц, 284
жеребёнок, 284
жеребо́к, 299
жеребьёвка, 366
же́ртвенник, 338, 342
же́сты, 10
жето́н, 189, 201 202
Живо́й как жизнь, Чуко́вский
  Корне́й, 248
живо́т, 38
животново́дство, 283
живо́тные
  в приро́де, 286
  дома́шние, 281
  ко́мнатные, 281
  обраще́ния к ним, 285
  что они́ говоря́т, 285
жид, 6
жила́я пло́щадь, 317
жиле́т, 72, 75
жили́ще, 87
  совреме́нное се́льское, 87
жи́молость, 275
жир, 116, 132
жму́рки, 365
жне́йка, 167
жре́бий, 364, 366
жук, 286
жук ма́йский, 287
Жуко́вский, *Светла́на*, 331
жура́вль (коло́дец), 104
жура́вль (пти́ца), 295, 381, 379
журна́л, 192, 195
журнали́ст, 194
ЖЭК, 180

забасто́вка, 164
заболева́ния, 155-156
зава́линка, 98
зави́вка, 181
завка́федрой, 237
за́втрак, 131, 241
за́вуч, 235
завхо́з, 236
за́говор, 158
загс, 25, 28
зада́ние, 241
зада́ча, 241, 308, 310, 311
заку́ска, 132, 133, 292, 328

заку́сочная, 145
заливно́й, 133
Зализня́к А. А., *Граммати́ческий*
  слова́рь ру́сского языка́, 383
зао́чное отделе́ние, 225
за́пад, 324
запасны́е ча́сти, 204
за́пах, 123
запека́нка, 135, 136, 138, 139
запи́ски, 338, 339, 341
За́пись а́ктов гражда́нского сос-
  тоя́ния, *См.* загс
За́поведи блаже́нства, 343
запра́вка (бензи́ном), 206
запра́вки (в кулина́рии), 134
запра́вочная ста́нция, 206
запята́я, 306
зарпла́та, 163, 168
зарубе́жье бли́жнее, 188
зарубе́жье да́льнее, 188
заря́нка, 379
застёжка, 78
засто́лье, 12
за́яц, 296
  в обще́ственном тра́нспорте,
    202
за́ячья капу́ста, 276
зверобо́й, 272, 276
звон, 340
звона́рь, 340
звоно́к, 190
здравпу́нкт, 153
зельц, 118
землеро́йка, 298
земляни́ка, 125, 276
земново́дные, 288
зе́мская шко́ла, 220
зе́ркало, 47, 89
  разби́тое, 20
зерно́, 110
зима́, 263
Зи́мнее у́тро, Пу́шкин А. С., 264
Зи́мний ве́чер, Пу́шкин А. С., 264
Зи́мний Дворе́ц, 353
Зи́мняя доро́га, Пу́шкин А. С., 215
злак, 264, 267
зла́я си́ла, 28
змея́, 288
Знак ка́чества, 175
зна́ки доро́жные, 208
зна́харь, зна́харка, 158
значо́к, 46, 354
золота́я меда́ль, 233
золото́й шар, 276
зоомагази́н, 281
зра́зы, 135
зрачо́к, 37
зри́тельный зал, 353
зуб, 38
зуби́ло, 165
зубна́я па́ста, 159
зубна́я щётка, 159

зубно́й ка́мень, 159
зубр, 144, 298
зубро́вка, 144, 276
зу́бы, 159
зя́блик, 379

и́ва, 265, 276
Ива́н-да-Ма́рья, 276
Ива́н-чай, 276
и́волга, 379
игла́ (швейная), 80
иго́лка (на ве́тке), 269
игру́шки, 362
и́гры
        аза́ртные, 169, 353
        ка́рточные, 354
Из исто́рии русских имён, о́тчеств
        и фами́лий, Чича́гов Б. К.,
        68
изба́, 31, 43, 96-105, 349, 367
изба́-чита́льня, 353
изво́зчик, 215
изда́тель, 194
изда́тельство, 195
изразцы́, 99
изю́бр, 298
ико́на, 103, 339
иконоста́с, 338, 341
икра́, 133, 289, 290
икра́ (часть те́ла), 39
Илья́ Му́ромец, 3
имби́рь, 128
имена́ числи́тельные, 305
имени́нник, имени́нница, 63
имени́ны, 63, 64, 65
и́мя, 53-55, *См. также таблица*
        имён
        де́вичье, 62
        до револю́ции, 63
        и во́зраст, 62
        ласка́тельные фо́рмы, 55, 56-61
        по́лное ли́чное, 54
        по́сле револю́ции, 65
        пренебрежи́тельные фо́рмы, 55
        произноше́ние, 66
        уменьши́тельные фо́рмы, 54, 56-
                61
имянарече́ние, 25
инвали́дность, 153
инде́ец, 43
и́ндекс подпи́ски, 195
и́ндекс почто́вый, 185
индю́шка, 284
инжи́р, 123
институ́т, 162, 163, 222, 226
институ́т красоты́, 181
Институ́т русского языка́ и́мени
        Пу́шкина, 248
инструме́нт, 164
интернату́ра, 148
интерье́р, 91

инфекциони́ст, 149
ирга́, 123, 276
и́рис, 270, 276
и́споведь, 344
ище́йка, 283

каба́н, 284, 298
кабачо́к, 137, 270
кади́ло, 340
кады́к, 37
кажде́ние, 340
казаки́-разбо́йники, 364
Казако́в Юрий, *Арктур-гончий пёс*,
        380
Казако́в Юрий, *Ти́хое у́тро*, 301
Как аукнется, так и откли́кнется,
        258
кака́о, 142
ка́ктус, 272
кала́н, 298
кала́ч, 111, 112
календа́рь, 320
        церко́вный, 283
кале́ндула, 270, 278
кали́на, 276
кало́ши, *См. гало́ши*
кальма́р, 288
кальсо́ны, 72
ка́мбала, 288, 291
Ка́менный о́стров, 275
ка́мера, 194
камы́ш, 276
канаре́йка, 282
кандида́т нау́к, 237
кандида́тская сте́пень, 221, 227, 237
кандида́тский ми́нимум, 227
кани́кулы, 348
кану́н, 338
канцтова́ры, 176
ка́персы, 128
ка́пли да́тского короля́, 274
капро́н, 79
капу́ста, 120, 134, 137
капу́стница, 287
капюшо́н, 76
карава́й, 111, 112, 365
кара́куль, 76, 299
каракульча́, 299
каранти́н, 155
кара́сь, 289, 291
кардамо́н, 128
кардиоло́гия, 148
каре́та, 215
ка́риес, 159
карма́н, 80
карп, 289, 291
ка́рта медици́нская, 150
карта́вость, 253
карто́фель, 119, 134, 135, 136, 137,
        270
ка́рточные и́гры, 353

карто́шка, 131
карусе́ль, 336, 363
каса́тик, 276
ка́ска, 77
ка́сса, 210
        театра́льная, 351
касси́рша, 174, 175, 192, 351
кастрю́ля, 94, 131
ка́тер, 212
кафе́, 145
ка́федра, 237
кафта́н, 83
каче́ли, 333, 336, 363, 367
ка́чество, 175
        знак, 175
ка́ша, 102, 110, 132, 137, 138
        геркуле́совая, 110
        гре́чневая, 110, 131, 137, 138
        гу́рьевская, 141
        ма́нная, 110
        моло́чная, 138
        пшённая, 110, 137
ка́шка, 276
кашта́н, 265, 276
Каще́й Бессме́ртный, 328
кварти́ра, 88, 89, 174
        в почто́вом а́дресе, 185
        коммуна́льная, 88, 96
        отде́льная, 88
кварти́рное бюро́, 349
квас, 127, 131, 142
ква́шеная капу́ста, 131
кваше́ние, 129
квита́нция, 185, 188
кедр, 264, 276
ке́ды, 78
кекс, 141
ке́мпинг, 349
ке́пка, 76
керога́з, 106
кероси́нка, 106
кета́, 133, 290
кефа́ль, 291
кефи́р, 113, 132
киби́тка, 215
ки́жуч, 290
кизи́л, 123
килогра́мм, 318
киломе́тр, 317
ки́лька, 292
киндза́, 276
кинза́, 128, 276
кипари́с, 265, 276
кипято́к, 141
кири́ллица, 254
кирпи́ч, 101
кисе́ль, 141
ки́тель, 74
ки́чка, 28
кишка́, 41
клавиату́ра, 193
кла́виша, 193

кла́дбище, 30
кладова́я, 99
кладо́вка, 90
класс (гру́ппа расте́ний), 266
класс (в шко́ле), 237
кла́ссный журна́л, 235
кла́ссный руководи́тель, 232, 235
кла́ссы (игра́), 364
кле́вер, 276
клеёнка, 93
клема́тис, 276
клён, 276
клеть, 99
клёцки, 138
клещ, 287
клещи́, 165
кли́зменная, 152
кли́мат, 263
кли́рос, 338
кли́чка, 68
клоп, 181, 286, 288
клуб, 353
клубни́ка, 125, 276
клык, 288
клю́ква, 126, 276
ключ, 95
Кни́га о вкусной и здоровой пище,
      95, 109
кни́га, 195
кни́жный магази́н, 197
кни́жный ры́нок, 197
кно́пка, 78
кобы́ла, 284
ковбо́йка, 76
ковёр, 91
коври́жка, 140
ко́вшик, 102
ковы́ль, 276
код го́рода, 189
ко́жа, 39
      цвет, 42
      боле́зни, 148
коза́, 283, 284, 298
козя́вка, 286
ко́йка, 93
коко́шник, 83
колбаса́, 117, 131, 133, 136
колго́тки, 72, 77
колду́н, колду́нья, 21, 158
коле́но, 39
коли́бри, 294
Колле́ги, Аксёнов В., 48, 353
коллекти́в, 233
коллекти́в шко́льный, 240
коллекти́вное хозя́йство, 265
ко́лли, 282
Колобо́к, 100, 178
коловоро́т, 165
коло́да, 354
коло́дец, 104
колокола́, 340
колоко́льня, 340

колоко́льчик, 213, 215, 276
колоно́к, 298
ко́лос, 110
колхо́з, 265
колье́, 46
кольцо́, 26, 46
коляда́, 330
коля́дка, 330
колядова́ние, 330
коля́ска, 10
кома́нда, 359, 365
кома́р, 287
комба́йн, 167
комбина́ция, 74
комбина́ция из трёх па́льцев, 10
комбинезо́н, 74
комиссио́нный магази́н, 177
комме́рческий магази́н, 175
ко́мната, 96
ко́мнатные расте́ния, 271
комо́д, 92
ко́мпас, 324
компости́ровать, 201
компо́т, 123, 130, 141
компью́тер, 192
кон, 361
конве́рт, 184, 192
конду́ктор, 201
ко́ник, 103
ко́нный спорт, 356
конопля́, 97, 277
консе́рвы, 130
конструктиви́зм, 87
консульта́ция
      де́тская, 155
      же́нская, 154
контраце́пция, 154
контролёр, 210
контро́льная, 233
конура́, 281
конце́рт, 350
коньки́, 363, 364
конькобе́жный спорт, 356
конья́к, 143
кооперати́в, 266
координа́ты, 324
копе́йка, 167
кора́, 269
кора́блик, 363
кора́бль, 212
коре́йка, 116
коренни́к, 214
ко́рень (в матема́тике), 314
ко́рень (расте́ния), 268
коре́нья, 131
ко́ржик, 140
корзи́ночка, 141
кориа́ндр, 129, 276
кори́ца, 128
коро́бка, 94
коро́ва, 283, 284, 285
коромы́сло, 104

коро́нка, 159
коросте́ль, 380
ко́рпус, 185
корреспонде́нция, 192
корса́к, 298
ко́ршун, 380
коры́то, 93
коса́, 166
косме́тика, 45
космети́чка, 45
космето́лог, 181
косоворо́тка, 81
костёр, 265
ко́сти, 353
кость, 40, 116
      деформа́ция, 148
костю́м, 72, 79
костяни́ка, 277
косу́ля, 298
кот чёрный, 20
котёл, 94
котёнок, 284
ко́тик, 298
      морско́й, 298
котле́та, 116, 136
котролёр, 201
котте́дж, 106
ко́фе, 94, 141, 142
ко́фта, 75
кочерга́, 101
коша́чья ла́пка, 277
кошелёк, 47
ко́шка ди́кая, 297
ко́шка, 283, 284, 285
ко́шки-мы́шки, 365
краб, 288
кра́н, 45
крапи́ва, 120, 131, 277
Кра́сная кни́га, 265
кра́сное де́рево, 277, 280
крем, 45
крема́ция, 29
кре́ндель, 140
крендельк
и́, 140
кре́пость, 363
кре́сло, 92
крест правосла́вный, 340
кре́стики и но́лики, 366
Крестный ход, 334
крестья́не, 162
кре́чет, 380
Креще́ние, 330, 332, 336
креще́ние, 25, 340
креще́нские моро́зы, 332
кри́нка, *См.* кры́нка
крова́тка, 93
крова́ть, 92, 99
кровено́сная систе́ма, 41
кровь, 41
кро́кус, 272
кро́лик, 284, 296
крольча́тина, 118

кроссо́вки, 78
крот, 298
кругова́я пору́ка, 240
кружо́к, 235, 241, 348
крупа́, 110
крупе́ник, 138
круши́на, 277
крыжо́вник, 126, 277
крыльцо́, 99, 100
кры́нка, 102
кры́са, 298
кры́ша, 98
кры́шка, 94
крючо́к, 78
кря́ква, 380
ксе́рокс, 192
ку́бики, 363
ку́бок, 358
кувши́н, 96, 102
кувши́нка, 277
Кудашо́ва Р., *Ёлочка*, 326
кузне́чик, 287
ку́киш, 10
ку́кла, 362
кукуру́за, 110, 121, 136
кукуру́зное ры́льце, 272
куку́шка, 285, 295, 380
куку́шкины слёзки, 277
кула́к, 39
кулебя́ка, 139
кули́к, 380
кулина́рия, 130
кули́ч, 111, 140, 334
кули́чики, 363
культтова́ры, 176
культу́ра ре́чи, 248
кум, кума́, 25
кумы́с, 114
кунжу́т, 129
куни́ца, 298
купа́льник, 74
купа́льница, 277
купа́льный костю́м, 74
купе́ль, 25
купю́ра, 167
ку́ра, 136, 284
курага́, 123, 140, 153
кура́нты, 328
ку́рица, 284, 285
куропа́тка, 118, 293, 285
куро́рт, 349
Курс совреме́нного ру́сского языка́,
    Фи́нкель А. М. и Баже́нов Н.
    М., 251
курсова́я ра́бота, 233
ку́ртка, 75
куст, куста́рник, 266
    ка́рликовый, 264
кутья́, 30, 330
куха́рка, 130
ку́хня, 89, 93, 96, 103, 130, 132
    ме́бель и посу́да, 94

гарниту́р, 93
ку́хонный комба́йн, 94
ку́ча-мала́, 364
ку́чер, 215

лабора́нт, 237
ла́вка, 43, 99, 100
лавр, 277
лавро́вый лист, 128, 131
ла́герь, 194, 349
ладо́нь, 39
ла́йка, 282
лак, 45
лампа́дка, 100
ланге́т, 136
ла́ндыш, 272, 277
лапта́, 361, 365, 367
ла́пти, 81, 82
лапша́, 113, 134, 138
ла́пы, 36
ларёк, 145
ла́ска, 298
ла́сковые обраще́ния, 258, 260
ла́сточка, 380
лебеда́, 271, 277
ле́бедь, 380
левко́й, 277
левша́, 10
лёгкая атле́тика, 356
ледяна́я гора́, 363
лежа́нка, 99
лезбия́нка, 23
ле́йка, 166
лека́рственные расте́ния, 272
лека́рство, 156
лён, 79, 277
Ле́нин, 65
лепесто́к, 267
лес, 264
    вечнозелёный, 264
    ли́ственный, 265
    сме́шанный, 265
    хво́йный, 264
леса́, 288
ле́стница, 167, 352
ле́то, 264
лётчик, 212
летя́га, 298
лече́бница, 152
лещ, 289
лещи́на, 126, 279
ликёр, 144
ли́лия, 270
лимо́н, 123
лимона́д, 13, 142
лино́леум, 91
ли́па, 82, 265, 272, 277
лиса́, лиси́ца, 297
лиси́чка, 122
лист больни́чный, *См.* больни́чный
    лист

лист, 268, 269
ли́ственница, 264, 278
листо́к нетрудоспосо́бности, 151
литр, 317
литурги́я, 341, 342
Литурги́я ве́рных, 343
Литурги́я оглаше́нных, 342
ли́фчик, 73
лице́й, 242
лицо́, 36
    цвет, 42
личи́нка, 286
лиша́йники, 266
лоб, 37
ло́джия, 89
ло́дка, 212, 215, 356
ло́жа, 352
ло́жка, 95, 96
ло́коть, 39
лом, 167
ломоно́с, 278
лопа́та, 101, 166
лопа́тка (игру́шка), 363
лопа́тка (часть те́ла), 95
лопу́х, 271, 278, 279
лоси́ны, 76
лососи́на, 133
лосо́сь, 290
    вя́леный, 129
лось, 297
лосьо́н, 45
лотере́я, 170
лото́, 366
ло́тос, 278
ло́шади и вса́дники, 366
ло́шадь, 283, 284, 285
    масть, 69
лужа́йка, 267
лук, 127, 131, 135, 137
лу́ковица, 267, 268
лунь, 380
лучи́на, 103, 104
лы́жи, 363, 364
лы́жный спорт, 356
лы́ко, 82
льви́ный зев, 278
льго́ты, 164
люпи́н, 270
лю́стра, 92
лю́тик, 278
люце́рна, 278
лягу́шка, 285, 288

магази́н, 116, 173
    валю́тный, 174, 177
    кни́жный, 197
    комиссио́нный, 177
    комме́рческий, 175
    продово́льственный, 178
магнитофо́н, 193
мазь, 156

ма́йка, 72, 75
майоне́з, 134
мак, 127, 278, 140
макаро́ны, 113, 138
макия́ж, 45, 181
ма́ковка, 140
макре́ль, 291
маку́шка, 269
мали́на, 126, 272, 278
мали́новка, 379
малы́ш, 48
ма́льва, 278
маля́р, 180
мандари́н, 123
мане́ж, 90
мара́л, 298
маргари́тка, 278
марина́д, 133
ма́рка, 192
маршру́т, 201
маршру́тка, 202
ма́сленица, 331, 332, 367
маслёнка, 95
маслёнок, 122
масли́ны, 127, 278
ма́сло, 131
масса́ж, 181
массажи́ст, 158
ма́ссовая информа́ция, 193
Ма́стер спо́рта, 354, 361
масть (ка́рточная), 353
масть (ло́шади), 69
мат, 23
математи́ческие выраже́ния, 313, 316
матио́ла, 277
матра́с, матра́ц, 93
Матрёнин двор, Солжени́цын, 337
матрёшка, 363
маттио́ла, 278
матч, 362
мать, 49-51
мать-и-ма́чеха, 272
маци́с, 129
маши́на, 203
маши́нка, 363
Мая́к, 193
ме́бель, 92
    шко́льная, 238
мёд, 144
меда́ль, 46
медбра́т, 149, 153
медве́дь, 297
мединститу́т, 148
медици́на, 147
    страхова́я, 147
медици́нские учрежде́ния, 149
медици́нский бюллете́нь, 151
медици́нский термо́метр, 323
медо́вый ме́сяц, 26
медосмо́тр, 150
медпу́нкт, 153, 237

медсанча́сть, 149
медсестра́, 149, 152, 236
медуни́ца, 278
междоме́тия, 257
междугоро́дняя, 189
ме́лочь, 167
менструа́ция, 22, 154
меню́, 144
ме́ра, 315
ме́рин, 284
ме́сто, 352
ме́сяц, 319
ме́сячные, 22, 154
метёлка, 101
метр, 315
ме́трика, См. свиде́тельство о рожде́нии
метро́, 202
меха́, 299
ми́дия, 288
микроавто́бус, 202
ми́ксер, 94
миксту́ра, 156
мили́ция, 188, 189
мимо́за, 272, 278
минда́ль, 141, 140, 278
Минздра́в, См. Министе́рство здравоохране́ния
Министе́рство Вы́сшего Образова́ния, 237
Министе́рство здравоохране́ния, 151
Министе́рство Свя́зи, 194
Министе́рство Се́льского Хозя́йства, 179
Министе́рство социа́льного обеспече́ния, 153
Минсвя́зь, См. Министе́рство Свя́зи
Минсельхо́з, См. Министе́рство Се́льского Хозя́йства
Минсобе́с, См. Министе́рство социа́льного обеспече́ния
минта́й, 291
ми́нус, 309
мину́та, 319
Мир пра́ху, 30
миро́, 25
миропома́зание, 25, 344
ми́ска, 94, 101
    супова́я, 95
митрополи́т, 343
Мичу́рин, 263
Ми́ша, 297
ми́шка, 362
млекопита́ющие, 295
многобо́рье, 357
мно́жимое, 311
мно́житель, 311
моги́ла, 29
моде́м, 192
можжеве́льник, 264

мозг, 41
мо́йка, 106
мокри́ца, 271, 287
моли́тва, 341, 343
моллю́ск, 288
мо́лния, 78
молодня́к, 265
молодо́й челове́к, 48
молоко́, 113, 141
    топлёное, 113, 132, 179
молото́к, 165
    деревя́нный, 95
Молохове́ц Еле́на, Пода́рок молоды́м хозя́йкам, 109
молоча́й, 278
моло́чная ку́хня, 155
моло́чная сестра́, См. сестра́ моло́чная
моло́чные блю́да, 138
моло́чный брат, См. брат моло́чный
моль, 286, 287
монасты́рь, 344
мона́х, 344
мона́хиня, 344
моне́та, 47, 167
монсте́ра, 272
монта́жка, 167
монтёр, 180
мопе́д, 203
мо́рда, 36
морко́вь, 120, 137, 270
моро́женое, 141
моро́шка, 278
морс, 13, 126, 142, 277
морско́е многобо́рье, 356
морщи́на, 37
мост (о зуба́х), 159
мотобо́л, 356
мото́роллер, 203
мотоци́кл, 203
мотоцикле́тный спорт, 356
моты́га, 167
мотылёк, 286
мох, 97, 266
мохови́к, 122
моча́лка, 44, 95
моча́ло, 44
мочевы́е о́рганы, 41
    заболева́ния, 148
мо́шка, 286
муж, 50
мужи́к, 6
музе́й, 353
мука́, 110, 131
мунди́р, 74
мураве́й, 286
муска́тный оре́х, 128, 278
муска́тный цвет, 129
му́скул, 42
муто́н, 299
му́ха, 285, 287

мухомо́р, 122
мучны́е изде́лия, 138
мы́ло, 44, 94
мы́льня, 45
мы́шца, 42
 заболева́ния, 148
мышь, 296, 298
мя́коть, 116
мясны́е консе́рвы, 118
мясны́е субпроду́кты, 117
мя́со, 115, 131, 133, 134, 139
мясору́бка, 94
мя́та, 127, 278
 пе́речная, 272
мяч, 363

н. э., 321
наба́т, 340
на́бережная, 185
нава́га, 291
наво́зник, 122
на́волочка, 93
нажда́чная бума́га, 165
наки́дка, 75
нали́вка, 144
нали́м, 291
нало́г, 169
нало́женным платежо́м, 185, 197
намо́рдник, 36, 282
наперстя́нка, 278
наперсто́к, 80
напёрсток, 80
напи́льник, 165
напи́тки, 141-143
наполео́н, 141
напряже́ние, 324
на́рды, 354
Наро́ды европе́йской ча́сти СССР,
 Алекса́ндров, 83
нарци́сс, 278
насеко́мые, 286
насле́дство, 28
насо́с, 167
насто́йка, 144
нау́ка, 237
нау́чный сотру́дник, 237
Нахи́мовское учи́лище, 242
национа́льность, 47, 66
нача́льная шко́ла, 222, 233
начи́нка, 140
нева́ляшка, 363
неве́рующие, 325
неве́ста, 20, 25
неврапатоло́гия, 148
негр, 7, 42
недотро́га, 278
незабу́дка, 278
нейло́н, 79
не́льма, 290, 292
неотло́жка, 153, 154
нерв, 41

не́рвная систе́ма, 41
не́рка, 290
не́рпа, 298
нечи́стый, 21
НИИ, 163, 237
ни́тка, 80
ничья́, 362
новосе́лье, 31
но́вости, 193
Но́вый год, 325, 326
Но́вый заве́т, 344
но́вый стиль, 320
нога́, 36, 39
ногтки́, 278
но́готь, 39
нож, 95
но́жички (игра́), 364
номенклату́ра, 161
номеро́к, 352
но́рка, 298
нос, 37
носи́лки, 167
носки́, 72, 77
нота́ция, 360
нототе́ния, 291
ночь, 319
ну́трия, 298, 299
ньюфа́ундленд, 283
ня́ня, 149

обе́д, 131, 132, 134, 241
 ко́мплексный, 145
обе́денный переры́в, 132
обе́дня, 341
Оби́да, Солоу́хин, 337
облепи́ха, 123, 272, 279
облига́ция, 169
обло́жка, 195
о́браз, 103, 339
образова́ние, 219, 248
 вы́сшее, 226
 ступе́ни, 221
обраще́ния, 62
обруча́льное кольцо́, 46
обруче́ние, 26
о́бувь, 77
общепи́т, 144
обще́ственное пита́ние, 144
обще́ственно-поле́зный труд, 232
о́бщество, 4
объём, 315, 317
овёс, 110, 279
овощере́зка, 94
о́вощи, 118, 136, 137
овсю́г, 271
овся́нка (пти́ца), 380
овся́нка (ка́ша), 110
овца́, 283, 284, 285, 299
овча́рка, 282
овчи́на, 299

огло́бли, 213, 215
огоро́д, 270
огуре́ц, 120, 270
оде́жда, 71
 ве́рхняя, 75
 наро́дная, 81
 ни́жняя, 72
 совреме́нная, 72
одея́ло, 93
одува́нчик, 271, 279
ожере́лье, 46
ози́мые, 111
ока́зия, 183
окла́д, 164, 339
окно́, 91
о́канье, 251
о́корок, 116
окро́шка, 134, 142
окружа́ющая среда́, 264
о́кунь, 290
 морско́й, 291
ола́дьи, 140
олеа́ндр, 272
оле́нь, 298
 се́верный, 297
Олимпи́йские и́гры, 358
ольха́, 265, 279
о́муль, 290, 292
онда́тра, 299
онколо́гия, 148
ону́чи, 81
опа́ра, 139
опёнок, 122
опе́к, 299
опозда́ние, 232
оранжере́я, 270
о́рден, 46
ордина́тура, 148
оренбу́ргский плато́к, 283
оре́х, 126, 153
 гре́цкий, 126, 279
 кедро́вый, 126
оре́шник, 126, 279
орёл (о моне́те), 20
орёл (пти́ца), 380
ОРЗ, 155
ориенти́рование на ме́стности, 356
ортопеди́я, 148
оса́, 287
освети́тельные прибо́ры, 92
освеще́ние, 103
Осень, Пу́шкин А. С., 264
о́сень, 264
осетри́на, 133
осётр, 289
оси́на, 265, 279
осмо́тр, 154
осо́ка, 279
осо́т, 271
Оста́нкино, 194
остано́вка, 201

оста́ток, 311, 313
остри́ца, 286
От двух до пяти́, Чуко́вский
    Корне́й, 62
отвёртка, 165
отде́л, 175, 197
отде́л ка́дров, 163
о́тдых, 347
оте́ц, 49-51
открыва́шка, 95
откры́тка, 185, 191, 192, 328
отли́чник, 348
отме́тка, 231
отоларинголо́гия, 149
отпева́ние, 28
о́тпуск, 348
    декре́тный, 154
Отче наш, 343
о́тчество, 53, 54
    произноше́ние, 66
официа́нт, 144
офтальмоло́гия, 148
охо́тничья во́дка, 144
о́чередь, 144, 151, 174, 188, 366
Очи чёрные, 42
очки́, 47, 157
очко́, 365

паёк, 179
пала́с, 91
пала́та, 152
пала́тка (магази́н), 145
пала́тка (тури́стская), 349
па́лец, 36, 39
па́лочки-стука́лочки (игра́), 364
па́лтус, 291
па́льма, 91, 271, 272, 279
пальто́, 75
    мехово́е, 299
па́мятник, 29
па́ндус, 10
панирова́ть, 131
панихи́да, 28, 30, 339
панихи́дный сто́лик, 338
пансиона́т, 348
панталóны, 76
пантокри́н, 158, 298
па́поротник, 266, 279, 335
парашю́тный спорт, 356
парикма́херская, 181
пари́лка, пари́льня, 45
парохо́д, 212
па́рта, 238
парте́р, 352
па́рус, 216
па́русный и бу́ерный спорт, 356
па́спорт, 47, 196, 163
пассажи́р, 212
пассерова́ть, 131
Пастерна́к Бори́с, *До́ктор Жива́го,*
    54

пасту́х, 283
пасту́шья су́мка, 271, 279
па́сха, 114, 141, 140, 333-336
пасья́нс, 354
па́тока, 140
патриа́рх, 343
патрона́жная сестра́, *См.* сестра́
    патрона́жная
пау́к, 286, 287
па́хта, 113
пацие́нт, 150
паши́на, 116
педера́ст, 23
педиа́тр, 155
педиатри́я, 148
пединститу́т, 235
педсове́т, 236
пека́н, 126
пеларго́ния, 272
пелена́ние, 74
пелёнка, 74
пельме́ни, 95, 132, 138
пельме́нная, 145
пе́ние, 352
пе́нсия, 192
пень, 268
пе́рвая по́мощь, 153
пе́рвенство, 358
пе́рвое апре́ля, 335
Пе́рвое мая, 325, 329
первоцве́т, 279
пере́дник, 74, 82
пере́дняя, 89
перезво́н, 340
перекати́-по́ле, 266
переме́нный ток, 324
пе́репел, 118, 293, 380
переплёт, 195
переры́в, 241, 359
переу́лок, 185
перехо́д, 206
пе́рец, 128, 131
пе́речница, 95
перио́дика, 194
перро́н, 210
пе́рсик, 124
пе́рстень, 46
перцо́вка, 144
пёс, 284
песе́ц, 264
песка́рь, 291
пе́сни
    а́вторские, 353
    обря́довые, 367
    репертуа́р, 14
песо́чница, 363
пе́стик, 267
пе́тля, 165
Петру́шка, 362
петру́шка, 127
пету́х, 284, 285
пе́чень, 41

заболева́ния, 148
пече́нье, 140
печёнка, 136
печь, 43, 99
    ру́сская, 100, 101
пешехо́д, 206
пе́шка, 359
пи́во, 143
пиджа́к, 72
пижа́ма, 74
пи́жма, 279
пика́п, 205
пи́ки, 354
пи́кша, 291
пила́, 165
пи́лка, 45
пило́тка, 74, 76
пио́н, 270
пиро́г, 31, 94, 132, 139, 140, 141
пирожки́, 139, 140, 363
пирожко́вая, 145
пиро́жное, 141
писа́тель, 196
Писа́тель и его́ тво́рчество, Слони́м
    Марк, 9
письмо́, 184-186, 192
пи́хта, 264, 279
пи́ща, 109
пищевари́тельная систе́ма, 41
пия́вка, 286
пла́вание, 356
пла́вки, 72
плавни́к, 288
планёрный спорт, 356
платфо́рма, 210
пла́тье, 72
плау́н, 279
пла́хта, 82
плащ, 75
племя́нник, племя́нница, 49-51
плéсени, 266
плетёнка, *См.* ха́ла
пле́чики, 92, 352
плечо́, 38
плита́, 94
плов, 110, 138
пло́мба, 159
плоскогу́бцы, 165
плоскодо́нка, 215
плотва́, 291
плоти́на, 211
пло́тник, 180
плóшка, 102
пло́щадь, 315, 317
плюс, 309
плю́шка, 140
плющ, 272
пля́ски, 330, 353
По щу́чьему веле́нию, 292
побе́г, 268
побе́да, 362
по́вар, 130

поведе́ние, 3-31, 232
    за столо́м, 11
пове́рья наро́дные, 21
пове́ть, 99
пови́дло, 130
поводо́к, 282
пово́зка, 214, 215
пога́нка, 122
пого́да, 322
по́греб, 129
погребе́ние, 29
пода́рки, 11, 31, 161, 328
Пода́рок молоды́м хозя́йкам,
        Молохове́ц Еле́на, 109
подберёзовик, 122, 129
подборо́док, 36, 37
подва́л, 98
подво́дный спорт, 356
подгу́зник, 74
поджа́рка, 116
подли́вка, 137
подно́с, 94
пододея́льник, 93
подоро́жник, 271, 279
подоси́новик, 122, 129
подпи́ска, 192, 194, 197
по́дпол, 98
подсве́чник, 338, 341
подсне́жник, 279
подсо́лнечник, 270, 279
подсо́лнечные се́мечки, 126
подста́вка, 94
подстака́нник, 131
подтя́жки, 78
поду́шка, 93
по́езд, 210
    да́льнего сле́дования, 210
    при́городный, 210
пожа́рно-прикладно́й спорт, 356
позвоно́чник, 40
По́знер Влади́мир, 7
по́йнтер, 282
покая́ние, 344
покло́н, 341
поко́йный, 28
покрыва́ло, 93
пола́ти, 99, 100
по́лдник, 131, 241
по́ле (спорт.), 358, 359
по́ле, 265, 365
полёвка, 296
ползунки́, 74
поликли́ника, 149
    де́тская, 151
    стоматологи́ческая, 151, 159
по́лка, 89, 100
полнолу́ние, 336
полови́к, 89
полови́на, 307
половы́е о́рганы, 41
    заболева́ния, 148
половы́е отноше́ния, 22

поло́к, 43, 45
полоте́нце, 44, 100
полуфабрика́т, 116, 118, 178
полу́чка, 168
полы́нь, 279
по́люс се́верный, 263
помидо́р, 120, 135, 270
поми́нки, 30, 330
помо́лвка, 26
по́мощь пе́рвая, 153
по́мощь ско́рая, 154
понёва, 28, 81, 82
по́нчик, 140, 145
поплаво́к, 288
попуга́й, 282
пораже́ние, 362
порногра́фия, 197
поро́г, 21, 100
поро́да соба́к, 282
поросёнок, 284
порошо́к, 94
    для мытья́ посу́ды, 94
    хозя́йственный, 94
портни́ха, 79
портфе́ль, 238
портя́нка, 77
поря́док, 266
посеща́емость, 227
посиде́лки, 353, 367
пост Вели́кий, 332
посте́ль, 92, 93, 99
посты́, 337
посу́да, 93, 94
посы́лка, 188, 192
пот, 39
похоро́нное бюро́, 28
по́хороны, 28
по-чёрному, 43, 44
по́чка, 268, 269
по́чта, 183, 190, 191
    электро́нная, 192
почтальо́н, 194
почта́мт, 188
    гла́вный, 190
    междунаро́дный, 192
почто́вая ка́рточка, 185
почто́вое отделе́ние, 192
почто́вый я́щик, 185
по́яс, 38, 73, 78
поясни́ца, 38
праба́бушка, 51
пра́вила прили́чия, 11
Правосла́вная це́рковь, *См.* це́рковь
    правосла́вная
пра́дед, 51
пра́здники, 25, 325-344
    двунадеся́тые, 335
    престо́льные, 335, 337
    совреме́нные, 325
    церко́вные, 335
пра́зднования, 30
пра́ктика, 148, 348

пра́чечная, 93, 181
предба́нник, 44
предостереже́ния, 258
презервати́в, 22, 154
пре́мии, 161
Преображе́ние, 336
преподава́тель, 237
престо́л, 338
префера́нс, 354
приватиза́ция, 266
приви́вка, 156
прида́ное, 26
приде́л, 342
приёмный поко́й, 152
приме́та, 19-21
при́мула, 270, 272, 279
при́мус, 106
припра́ва, 127
приро́да, 263
пристяжна́я, 214
Прися́дем на доро́жку, 9
притво́р, 338, 342
прихожа́не, 341
прихо́жая, 89
прича́стие, 343
причаще́ние, 25, 344
Прия́тного аппети́та!, 12
проводни́ца, 211
прогно́з, 322
програ́мма, 193, 352
продавщи́ца, 174
прода́жа по тало́нам, 173, *См.*
    также тало́н
продлёнка, 241
продма́г, 178
продтова́ры, 176
проду́кты, 110
    загото́вка, 129
про́звище, 62
про́игрыш, 362
произведе́ние, 311
проле́тка, 215
промтова́ры, 175, 176
про́пуск, 48, 238
про́сека, 265
про́со, 110
проспе́кт, 185
проститу́тка, 22
простоква́ша, 113
просторе́чие, 248
простре́л раскры́тый, 280
простыня́, 93
просфо́ры, 338, 341
проте́з, 10, 159
про́тивень, 94
профе́ссор, 228, 237
профилакто́рий, 153
про́филь, 163
профко́м, 151
профориента́ция, 162
профсою́з, 164, 174, 235, 237
профсою́зный биле́т, 48

проход, 352
процедура, 151
проценты, 169
прыжки в воду, 357
прыжки на лыжах с трамплина, 356
пряжка, 78
пряник, 127, 128, 140
пряность, 128
прятки, 364
психиатрия, 148
птицы, 292, 378
птичий базар, 281
птичий рынок, 178
ПТУ, 162, 222, 225, 231
Пугачёв И. А. и др., *Товарный словарь*, 382
пуговица, 78
пуд, 318
пудель, 283
пудинг, 94, 138, 141
пудра, 45, 47
пуловер, 75
пупок, 38
пустырник, 279
путёвка, 153, 348
путь, 210
пух, 283
пушица, 279
Пушкин А. С., *Зимнее утро*, 264
Пушкин А. С., *Зимний вечер*, 264
Пушкин А. С., *Зимняя дорога*, 215
Пушкин А. С., *Осень*, 264
Пушкин А. С., *Ты и Вы*, 253
пчела, 285, 287
пчеловодство, 284
пшеница, 110, 111
пыльник, 267
пырей, 271, 279
пышка, 140
пюре, 135
пятиборье, 357
Пятидесятница, 336
пятнашки, 364

работа, 161
    и женщины, 163
    устройство на, 163
рабочее время, 164
рабочие, 162
рабфак, 220
равно, 307
равноденствие, 321
рагу, 135
Радио России, 193
Радио Свобода, 193
радио, 193
радиовещательная станция, 193
радиоволны, 193
радиола, 193
радиоприёмник, 193
радиопроигрыватель, 193

радиоспорт, 357
радиоточка, 193
радиоузел, 193
разбитое сердце, 270, 279
развлечения традиционные, 367
развод, 28
раздевалка, 45, 237, 238
раздевалка, 45
размер (в одежде), 78
размер, 317
разность, 307
рак, 148, 288
ракетка, 355
ракита, 279
ракитник, 279
раковина, 93, 94, 106
РАН, 228
ранец, 238
раскладушка, 93
распашонка, 74
распев, 341
расписание, 210
распределение, 163
Распятие, 338
рассада, 270
рассольник, 134
расстояние, 317
растение, 266-281
    двухлетнее, 267
    комнатное, 271
    лекарственное, 158, 272
    многолетнее, 267
    однолетнее, 266
    садовое, 266
растительное масло, 134
растительное царство, 266
рахит, 114
реальное училище, 220
реаниматолог, 149
реанимация, 152
ребёнок, 48
ребро, 40
ревень, 121
ревматология, 148
регби, 357
регистратура, 150, 159
редактор, 194
редис, 120, 270
редька, 119, 270, 279
резеда, 279
резьба, 98
рейтузы, 76
ректор, 236
ремень, 74
ремонт, 180
рентген, 152
рентгенолог, 149
репа, 119, 120, 270
репей, 279
репейник, 271, 279
Репин, *Бурлаки*, 216
ресница, 37

ресторан, 144, 145
рецепт, 130, 156
речь, 247, 248
    и образование, 248
решето, 95
решка, 20
риза, 339
рис, 110
рогатка, 364
рогоз, 279
род, 266
роддом, 154
родители крёстные, 25
родительский комитет, 240
родительское собрание, 240
родословная, 282
родственник, 49, *См. также* семья
роды, 154
рождение, 25
Рождественская ёлка, 330
Рождество, 325, 326, 329, 336
Рождество Пресвятой Богородицы, 336
рожь, 110, 111
роза, 270
    китайская, 272
    чайная, 272
розвальни, 214, 215
розговенье, 334
Розенталь, *Толковый словарь русского языка*, 382
розетка, 92
розмарин, 129
рок-н-ролл, 353
ромашка, 272, 279
ромовая баба, 140
роспись, 98, 101
Российская Академия наук, 228
россомаха, 298
рост, 317
рот, 41, 38
рубанок, 165
рубаха, 74, 81, 82
рубашка, 72, 74, 75, 81
рубец, 117
рубль, 167
ругань, 23
рука, 36, 39
рукомойник, 99, 102, 104, 106
рукоположение, 344
рулет, 140, 141
румянец, 42
руссификатор, 193
Русский речевой этикет, Акишина А. А., Формановская Н. И., 14
Русский речевой этикет, Формановская Н. И., 63
Русский язык грамматическое учение о слове, Виноградов В. В., 383
Русский язык за рубежом, 248

Русское литературное произношение, Аванесов Р. И., 66
ручной мяч, 357
рыба, 133, 134, 288
   белая, 290
   вяленая, 292
   горячего копчения, 292
   копчёная, 292
   красная, 289, 290
   маринованная, 292
   солёная, 292
   сушёная, 292
   холодного копчения, 292
рыбак, 288
рыболовство спортивное, 357
рыжик, 122, 129
рыло, 36
рынок, 115, 177, 179
   книжный, 197
рысь, 298
РЭУ, 180
рюмка, 13, 96
рябина, 124, 265, 279
   на коньяке, 124, 144
   черноплодная, 124, 272, 281
рябиновка, 124
рябчик, 118, 293, 380
ряд, 352
ряженка, 113
ряженье, 327, 328, 330

С лёгким паром!, 45
сад, 270
сажень, 317
сазан, 289, 291, 292
сайка, 111, 112
салазки, 215, 363
салака, 288, 292
салат, 133, 270
салат зелёный, 120
салат оливье, 133
салатник, 95
салки, 364
сало, 116
самбо, 356
самовар, 102
самогон, 144
самокат, 364
самолёт, 212
самолётный спорт, 357
самонадеянность, 4
самообслуживание, 145, 179
самоуверенность, 4
самшит, 280
санаторий, 348, 349
сандалии, 78
сани, 214, 215
санитария, 148
санитарка, 149
санитарная остановка, 22

санки, 215, 363, 364
санный спорт, 357
сантиметр, 78, 317
санэпидемстанция, 153, 181
сапоги, 74, 77, 78
саранча, 287
сарафан, 73, 81, 82
сарделька, 118, 135
Сбербанк, 169, 191, 192
сбивалка, 95
свадебный марш, 26
свадебный ужин, 26
свадьба, 25
сват, 26
сваха, 26
свекольник, 120
свекровь, 50
сверло, 165
сверчок, 287
свет, 92
светильник, 92
Светлана, Жуковский, 331
светляк, 287
светофор, 205
свечи, 31, 338, 341
свёкла, 120, 133, 137, 270
свёкор, 50
свидетели, 26
свидетельство о рождении, 25, 48, 163
свидетельство об образовании, 222
свинина, 116
свинья, 283, 284, 285
свиристель, 380
свистулька, 274, 363
свитер, 72, 75
связь, 183
Святая дева, 341
Святки, 329, 332
святой, 341
святцы, 63, 64, 65
священник, 25, 340, 343
священство, 344
сглазить, 21
сговор, 26
сдача, 167
сдоба, 111, 139
сдобные изделия, 140
север, 324
севрюга, 133, 289
седина, 42
Седьмая вода на киселе, 51
секатор, 167
сексопатолог, 154
секундомер, 319
селезень, 284
селёдка, 292
селёдочница, 95
село, 97, 265
сельдерей, 127
сельдь, 129, 133, 288, 292
сельское хозяйство, 265

сёмга, 133, 290
семейный подряд, 266
семейство, 266
семечки, 126
семья, 49
сенбернар, 283
сени, 99, 100
сенная лихорадка, 274
сердце, 41
   болезни, 148
серёжки, 269, 279
серна, 298
серп, 166
серьги, 46
сестра, 49-51
   милосердия, 149
   молочная, 154
   патронажная, 155
сетка, 47
сеттер, 282
сечка, 95
сиг, 290
Символ веры, 343
синица, 294, 380
сирень, 270, 280
система счисления, 306
ситец, 79
сито, 95
скакалка, 363
скалка, 95
скамья, 99, 100
скатерть, 95
СКБ, 231
скворец, 293, 381
скворечник, 293
скейты, 363
скелет, 40
сковорода, 94, 102
сковородник, 101
скорая помощь, 154
скорая, 154
скорлупа, 115
скорость, 323
скумбрия, 291
слагаемое, 308
сладкое блюдо, 141
сладкое, 132
слесарь, 180
слива, 280
слива колючая, 280
сливки, 114, 141
слизняк, 288
сложение, 308
Слоним Марк, *Писатель и его творчество*, 9
служащие, 162
смалец, 116
смена, 349
сменное отделение, 225
сметана, 114, 131, 132, 134, 136, 141
смородина, 126, 131, 273, 280

сморчо́к, 122, 137
снеги́рь, 294, 381
Снегу́рочка, 326-328, 335
снежки́, 364
сне́жная ба́ба, 364
сне́жный городо́к, 333
СНО, 231
сноби́зм, 249
соба́ка, 282, 284, 285
   поро́дистая, 282
соба́чья бу́дка, 281
соболе́знование, 30
со́боль, 298
соборова́ние, 344
собра́ние сочине́ний, 197
сова́, 381
Сове́т шко́лы, 236
сове́тское хозя́йство, 265
со́вка, 381
совок, 167
совхо́з, 265
со́да, 94
содержа́ние, 196
сок, 142
соковыжима́лка, 94
со́кол, 381
сокраще́ния, 373-374
соле́ние, 129
солёный огуре́ц, 120, 129
Солжени́цын, *Матрёнин двор*, 283, 337
солитёр, 286
солнцестоя́ние, 321
соловей, 294, 381
солони́на, 118
соло́нка, 95
Солоу́хин, *Оби́да*, 337
соль рассы́панная, 20
соля́нка, 134, 135
сом, 292
сон-трава́, 280
сорня́к, 271
соро́ка, 295, 381
сороконо́жка, 286
сорочи́ны, 30
соро́чка, 72, 74, 75
сорт, 175
соси́ска, 118, 131, 135
соси́сочная, 145
сосна́, 264, 265
сосо́к, 38
со́ус, 134, 135, 136
со́усник, 95
соче́льник, 330
Союзпеча́ть, 194
спа́льня, 89, 92
спание́ль, 283
спа́ржа, 119, 280
Спаси́тель, 339, 341
Спа́сская ба́шня, 363
спекуля́ция, 173
спе́ция, 128

спецоде́жда, 74
спешко́ла, 228, 242
СПИД, 23, 156
спина́, 38
спира́ль, 22
спиртны́е напи́тки, 12
спи́сок, 174
спи́сывать на экза́мене, 233
спорт, 354
спортивные разряды, 354
спра́вка о сме́рти, 28
Спра́вки, 192
сре́дняя шко́ла, 222, 223, 224, 228, 233
сре́дства лече́бные, 156
Сре́тение, 336
ССО, 348
ста́вка, 169
стаж, 151, 164, 169
стака́н, 131
ста́линский дом, 87
стаме́ска, 165
ста́нция техни́ческого обслу́живания, 206
ста́нция, 210
стари́к, стару́ха, 48
ста́роста, 227
ста́рый стиль, 320
стациона́р, 152
ствол, 269
сте́бель, 268
сте́нка, 90, 92
сте́пень, 314
сте́рлядь, 289
сти́ли в оде́жде, 79
сти́ли ре́чи, 247
стили́стика, 248
стипе́ндия, 227
стира́льная маши́на, 93
стира́ть, 94
стол, 90, 95
   обе́денный, 91
   пи́сьменный, 92
столе́тие, 319
столе́тник, 272, 274
столо́вая, 89, 90, 145, 237
столя́р, 180
стоматоло́гия, 148, 159
стоя́нка, 203
страни́ца, 195
Страстна́я неде́ля, 333
стрекоза́, 287
стре́лка мину́тная, 319
стре́лка часова́я, 319
стрелко́вый спорт, 357
стрельба́ из лу́ка, 357
стрельба́ сте́ндовая, 357
стремя́нка, 165
стри́ж, 381
стри́жка, 181
строчо́к, 122
струбци́на, 165

стря́пать, 130
студе́нт, 163, 222
Студе́нческий строи́тельный отря́д, 348
Студе́нческое констру́кторское бюро́, 231
Студе́нческое нау́чное о́бщество, 231
сту́день, 116, 117, 133
стул, 92
сту́пка, 95
ступня́, 36, 39
стюарде́сса, 212
Суво́ровское учи́лище, 242
суда́к, 290
су́дно, 211, 212
судомоде́льный спорт, 357
судья́, 359
суеве́рие, 19
сук, 269
су́мка, 47
су́мма, 308
суп, 132, 134
суре́пка, 271
Су́риков, *Взя́тие сне́жного городка́*, 333
суро́к, 298
су́слик, 295, 296
суста́в, 40
   заболева́ния, 148
су́тки, 319
сухари́, 112, 140
сухожи́лия, 42
сухофру́кты, 123, 130
су́шка, 111, 112
счёт, 362
счёты, 308
счита́лка, 366
сы́воротка, 113
сын, 49-51, 68
сыр, 113-115, 131, 134
сы́рники, 114, 138
сырое́жка, 122
сыро́к, 114
сыч, 381
сы́щики и во́ры (игра́), 364

таба́к, 280
та́бель о ра́нгах, 375
табле́тка, 156
табли́ца имён, 55, 56-61
   же́нские имена́, 60-61
   му́жские имена́, 56-59
табли́ца элеме́нтов, 377
табуре́т, 89
табуре́тка, 100
та́волга, 280
таз, 45, 94, 95
Та́инства, 344
та́инство, 25
тайга́, 264, 299

тайм, 358
Та́йная вече́ря, 339
та́кса, 283
такси́, 202
   маршру́тное, 202
   стоя́нка, 202
таксофо́н, 189
та́лия, 38
тало́н, 26, 179, 201
   к зубно́му врачу́, 159
тамада́, 13, 26
тампо́ны, 22
та́нцы, 352
та́почки, 77, 78, 90, 353
тарака́н, 181, 286, 287
таранта́с, 215
тара́нь, 291, 292
таре́лка, 95
тахта́, 93
та́чка, 167
ТВ, 193
творо́г, 114, 131, 132, 138
творо́жники, 138
тво́рческий о́тпуск, 228
теа́тр, 350
телеви́дение, 193
теле́га, 214, 215
телегра́мма, 190, 192
теле́жка, 145
теле́кс, 192
телефо́н, 188
   глухо́й, 366
   -автома́т, 189
телефо́нная кни́га, 189
телефо́нный разгово́р
     междугоро́дный, 192
телёнок, 284
те́ло, строе́ние, 36-39
телогре́йка, 75
тельня́шка, 74
теля́тина, 116, 135
температу́ра, 321
те́ннис, 357
те́ннис насто́льный (пинг-понг), 357
те́нниска, 76
тень, 45
тепли́ца, 270
терапе́вт, 148, 154
терапи́я, 152
тёрка, 95
термо́метр, 322, 323
тёрн, 124, 280
те́сто, 111, 139
тестомеси́лка, 94
тесть, 49
те́терев, 118, 293, 295, 381
тётя, 49-51
тефте́ли, 136
те́хникум, 162, 163, 222, 225, 230
тёща, 49
тигр, 299
тимофе́евка, 280

тип, 266
тира́ж, 196
тиски́, 165
тисс, 280
ти́тульный лист, 195
Ти́хое у́тро, Казако́в Юрий, 301
тка́ни, 79
тля, 287
тмин, 128
това́р, 175, 176
това́рищ, 14, 62
Това́рный слова́рь, Пугачёв И. А. и
     др., 382
тойтерье́р, 283
То́карев, *Этногра́фия наро́дов
     СССР*, 83
*Толко́вый слова́рь живо́го велико-
     ру́сского языка́*, Даль
     Влади́мир, 383
Толко́вый слова́рь ру́сского языка́,
     Розента́ль, 382
Толко́вый слова́рь ру́сского языка́,
     Ушако́в Д. Н. и др., 382
толку́чка, 177
толокня́нка, 273, 280
Толсто́й А. К., 276
Толсто́й Л.Н., *Война́ и мир*, 331
тома́т, 120, 136
то́нна, 318
то́поль, 265, 280
топо́р, 165
торго́вая ма́рка, 175
торжества́, 25
торт, 31, 140
торше́р, 92
тост, 13
то́чка, 306
трава́, 266, 267
травмпу́нкт, 153
тра́вник, 272
тра́вы, 272, 264
   лека́рственные, 157, 158
традеска́нция, 272
трамва́й, 200, 201
тра́нспорт, 199
   вью́чный, 215
   гужево́й, 213
   обще́ственный, 201
трансформа́тор, 324
тра́урный ми́тинг, 28
требуха́, 117
трево́га, 258
треска́, 291
треть, 307
тре́фы, 354
трико́, 74
троеббо́рье, 357
Тро́ица, 334
тро́йка, 72, 214, 215, 306
тролле́йбус, 200, 201
тростни́к, 280
трудова́я кни́жка, 163, 164

трудоустро́йство, 164
трудя́щиеся, 162
трусы́, 72, 73, 76
трущо́ба, 87
трясогу́зка, 381
туале́т, 22, 89, 93, 96
   обще́ственный, 22
туале́тная бума́га, 22, 93
тужу́рка, 75
ту́ловище, 38
тулу́п, 83
ту́ндра, 264
тупи́к, 185
турба́за, 348
тури́зм, 357
ту́фли, 72, 77
ту́ша, 115
тушь, 45
ту́я, 280
ты, 62, 63, 252, 253
Ты и Вы, Пу́шкин А. С., 253
ты́ква, 120, 136, 270, 273
ты́квенные се́мечки, 126
Ты́сяча мелоче́й, 177
тысячели́стник, 280
тычи́нка, 267
тюле́нь, 299
тюльпа́н, 280
тяжёлая атле́тика, 358

убо́рная, 22, 89, 93, 96, 106
   нару́жная, 105
у́гол кра́сный, 100, 333, 335
у́гол пере́дний, 100, 333
у́гол, 87
угорь, 292
у́дочка, 288
уж, 288
у́жин, 131, 132
   сва́дебный, 26
указа́тель, 196
   расте́ний, 273
УКВ, 193
укло́н, 242
уко́л, 156
украше́ние, 326
укро́п, 127, 270
у́ксус, 127, 134
у́лей, 285
ули́тка, 288
у́лица, 185
улы́бка, 181
уменьши́тельные фо́рмы, 254
умноже́ние, 310
умноже́ния табли́ца, 310
умыва́льник, 93, 106
универма́г, 177
универса́м, 179
университе́т, 162, 222, 226
унита́з, 22
УПК, 162

упражне́ния, 158
упря́жка, 213, 214
уроло́гия, 148
урю́к, 123
услу́ги, 180
    бытовы́е, 180
усо́пший, 28
успева́емость, 227
Успе́ние, 336
Уста́в шко́лы, 236
у́стрица, 288
у́тка, 118, 284, 285
    ди́кая, 293
у́тренник, 326
у́треня, 341
у́тро, 319
уха́, 134
ухва́т, 101, 102
у́хо, 37
уховёртка, 287
ухо́д за больны́ми, 149
ухо́д на пе́нсию, 31
уча́сток, 150
    приуса́дебный, 265
    садо́вый, 106, 266, 270, 349
уча́щийся, 222, 225
уче́бный план, 228
Уче́бный слова́рь сочета́емости,
    Дени́сов, 382
учени́к, 222, 224
Учёный сове́т, 236
учи́лище, 222, 225, 230
    медици́нское, 149
    педагоги́ческое, 235
учи́тель, 233, 242
учи́тельская, 237
учи́тельский сове́т, 236
Ушако́в Д. Н. и др., *Толко́вый*
    слова́рь ру́сского языка́, 382
уша́нка, 76
у́ши горя́т, 20

фаза́н, 293, 381
факс, 192
факультати́вный курс, 231
факульте́т, 237, 238
фами́лия, 53, 66
    и национа́льность, 66
фа́нтики, 366
фармаколо́гия, 148
фармаце́вт, 149, 156
фарту́к, 74
Фа́смер Макс, *Этимологи́ческий*
    слова́рь ру́сского языка́, 382
фасо́ль, 121, 137, 270
фе́льдшер, 149, 153
фе́рма, 266
    животново́дческая, 266
Фет А, *Осень*, 292
фехтова́ние, 358
фиа́лка, 280

ночна́я, 277
    узумба́рская, 272
фигу́ра, 359
фигу́рное ката́ние на конька́х, 358
фиг, 10
физкульту́рный зал, 237
фи́кус, 271, 272, 280
филиа́л, 177, 179
фи́лин, 381
фи́ник, 124
Фи́нкель А. М. и Баже́нов Н. М.,
    Курс совреме́нного ру́сско-
    го языка́, 251
ФИО, 54, 196
фиста́шки, 126
фитотерапи́я, 158
фло́кс, 270
флот речно́й, 211
фокстерье́р, 283
форе́ль, 290, 289
фо́рма, 94
Форма́новская Н. И., *Русский рече-*
    вой этике́т, 63
фо́рмула, 315
форму́лы хими́ческие, 376
формуля́р, 196
фо́рточка, 91
фотоаппара́т, 194
фотоко́пия, 192
фраму́га, 91
фриста́йл, 358
фру́кты, 123, 135
фуже́р, 96
фу́ксия, 272
фунду́к, 126
фура́жка, 74, 76
фут, 317
футбо́л, 358
футбо́лка, 76
фуфа́йка, 71, 75
фуфа́йский язы́к, 257

ха́ла, 111, 112
хала́т, 72, 74
халту́ра, 163
характери́стика, 164
харче́вня, 145
харчо́, 134
ха́та, 87
хва́тка, 163
хво́рост, 140
хвощ, 266, 271, 280
хек, 291
химчи́стка, 181
хирурги́я, 148
хлеб, 111, 112
хлеба́, 110
хлебосо́льство, 111
хлеб-соль, 111
хло́пок, 79
хмель, 280

хо́бби, 352
ход, 359
хо́дики, 319
ходу́ли, 363
хозтова́ры, 177
хокке́й, 358
холоде́ц, 116, 117, 133
холоди́льник, 94
хому́т, 87, 213
хомя́к, 295, 296
хорово́д, 326, 330, 367
хорь, 299
храм, 338
хрен, 127, 135, 280
хризанте́ма, 270
Христо́с, воскре́с!, 334
хрущ, 287
Хрущёв, 67, 87
хурма́, 124

ца́пля, 381
Ца́рские Врата́, 338, 341
Ца́рство ему небе́сное, 30
цветна́я капу́ста, 120, 136
цветни́к, 270
цвето́к, 268
це́лая, 307
цели́тель, 158
цена́, 175
це́нтнер, 318
це́нтры диагности́ческие, 151
цепо́чка, 46
церко́вно-приходска́я школа, 220
це́рковь, 325, 338, 340
    правосла́вная, 63, 335, 341
циге́йка, 299
цикламе́н, 272
цирк, 350
цифербла́т, 319
цмин, 274
цыплёнок, 136, 284

чабре́ц, 129
чавыча́, 290
чаевы́е, 352
чай, 127, 131, 141
    пусто́й, 11
ча́йка, 381
ча́йная, 145
ча́йник, 94, 141
ча́йный гриб, 142
чан, 104
ча́ры, 21
час, 319
часово́й по́яс, 319
ча́стник, 179
ча́стное, 311
часту́шка, 353
часть, 307
часы́ пик, 201

часы́, 47, 319
ча́шка, 95
чебуре́ки, 138
чебуре́чная, 145
чек, 174, 175
чёлн, 212
чё́люсть, 37, 40
чё́пчик, 74
че́рви (ка́рточная масть), 354
червь, 286
череда́, 271, 280
черемша́, 280
че́реп, 40
черёшня, 124, 280
черёмуха, 124, 280, 265
черни́ка, 125, 126, 273
черносли́в, 124
чёрные, 4, 7, 43
чёрные си́лы, 21
чёрный ры́нок, 178
чертополо́х, 271, 281
чесно́к, 128, 272
че́тверть, 307
че́тверть, 232
чехарда́, 364
чечеви́ца, 121
чешуя́, 288
чиж, 282, 381
чиж, 282
чи́сла, 303, 321
чита́тель, 196
чита́тельный зал, 196
чита́тельский биле́т, 196
Чича́гов Б. К., Из исто́рии ру́сских
    имён, о́тчеств и фами́лий, 68
чте́ние, 350
чтец, 342
чугу́н, 102
чу́до-пе́чка, 94
Чуко́вский Корне́й, Живо́й как
    жизнь, 248
Чуко́вский Корне́й, От двух до
    пяти́, 62
чула́н, 99
чулки́, 72, 77, 79

ша́йба, 165
шака́л, 299
шалфе́й, 129, 273, 281
шампа́нское, 31
шампиньо́н, 122
ша́нежки, 140
ша́пка, 76
шате́н, 42
шафра́н, 128
ша́хматы, 358, 359
ша́шки, 358

шашлы́к, 132, 136, 145
шашлы́чная, 145
швейная маши́нка, 80
шёлк, 79
шерсть, 79
ше́ствие, 30
ше́я, 36
шине́ль, 74
шипо́вник, 273, 281
широта́, 324
шитьё, 79, 80
ши́шка, 269
шкала́ Фаренге́йта, 321
шкала́ Це́льсия, 321
шкаф, 90, 92, 94
шко́ла-интерна́т, 241
шко́лы ликбе́за, 220
шко́льник, 222, 224
шко́льный комите́т, 240
шлем, 77
шлёпанцы, 77, 90
шлюз, 211
шлю́пка, 212
шля́па, 76
шмель, 287
шни́цель, 136
шнур, 92
шнурки́, 77, 78
шорт-трек, 358
шо́рты, 76
шоссе́, 185
шофёр, 201
шпарга́лка, 233
шпиг, 116
шпина́т, 120, 131
шпро́ты, 129, 292
штаны́, 76, 81
што́пор, 95
штормо́вка, 75
штраф, 196
шу́ба, 75, 83, 299
шумо́вка, 95
шуру́п, 165

щаве́ль, 119
щего́л, 282, 381
щека́, 37
щёки горя́т, 20
щено́к, 284, 285
щётка, 95
щи, 110, 120, 134
    зелёные, 131, 134
щу́ка, 289, 292

эва́тор, 324
эвкали́пт, 273

эдельве́йс, 281
экза́мены, 230, 233
    переводны́е, 228
экипа́ж, 215
экле́р, 141
экра́н, 192
экстрасе́нс, 158
эле́ктрик, 180
электри́чка, 210
электро́нная по́чта, 192
электропли́тка, 94
эндокриноло́гия, 148
Энциклопеди́ческий слова́рь,
    Брокга́уз Ф. А., Ефро́н И.
    А., 383
эпидемиоло́гия, 148
эрдельтерье́р, 283
Эрмита́ж, 353
эстафе́та, 358
эстраго́н, 129
этике́тка, 175
Этимологи́ческий слова́рь ру́сского
    языка́, Фа́смер Макс, 382
Этногра́фия наро́дов СССР,
    То́карев, 83
эшело́н, 205

юбиле́йные да́ты, 31
ю́бка, 72
ювели́рные изде́лия, 46
юг, 324
юла́, 363

я́беда, 240
я́блоко, 141, 124
    в те́сте, 141
    мочёное, 130
    печёное, 141
ягнёнок, 284
я́годы, 125, 135, 141, 350
язы́к, 38
я́йца, 115, 131, 134, 138
    кра́шенные, 334
я́канье, 251
ял, 212
ямщи́к, 215
янта́рь, 46
я́рмарка, 177, 337
яровы́е, 111
я́рус, 339, 352
я́сень, 265, 281
я́стреб, 381
я́хта, 212
ячме́нь, 110

Мир тéсен.
It's a small world.

Transliteration Systems for Russian

Unfortunately, transliteration systems abound: institutions, editorial offices, and authors use their own systems, and the resultant proliferation confuses the uninitiated and promotes sloppiness among the professionals. The three major systems are given below. The U.S. Board on Geographic Names transliteration system is used by most U.S. government offices and publications and is preferred by the *Chicago Manual of Style* and the author. The Library of Congress system is used by the Library of Congress. Most other libraries and some scholarly journals in the social sciences and humanities (e.g., *Slavic Review*) use the L. C. system minus the ligatures and diacritical marks. The "linguistic" system is used by the *PMLA Bibliography*, *Slavic and East European Journal*, and the *Russian Language Journal*.

Russian		U.S. Board on Geographic Names	Library of Congress	"Linguistic" System
А	а	a	a	a
Б	б	b	b	b
В	в	v	v	v
Г	г	g	g	g
Д	д	d	d	d
Е	е	ye, e[1]	e	e
Ё	ё	yë, ë[2]	ë	e
Ж	ж	zh	zh	ž
З	з	z	z	z
И	и	i	i	i
Й	й	y	ĭ	j
К	к	k	k	k
Л	л	l	l	l
М	м	m	m	m
Н	н	n	n	n
О	о	o	o	o
П	п	p	p	p
Р	р	r	r	r
С	с	s	s	s
Т	т	t	t	t
У	у	u	u	u
Ф	ф	f	f	f
Х	х	kh	kh	x
Ц	ц	ts	t͡s	c
Ч	ч	ch	ch	č
Ш	ш	sh	sh	š
Щ	щ	shch	shch	šč
Ъ	ъ	"	″	″
Ы	ы	y	y	y
Ь	ь	'	′	′
Э	э	e	ė	è
Ю	ю	yu	i͡u	ju
Я	я	ya	i͡a	ja

1. Transliterated as *ye* at the beginning of a word, after vowels, and after ъ and ь; elsewhere as *e*.

2. In Russian, stressed *e* is sometimes pronounced as *yo*, in which case it sometimes is written as *ë*. When printed in Russian as *ë*, it is transliterated as *yë* at the beginning of a word, after vowels, and after ъ and ь; elsewhere as *ë*.